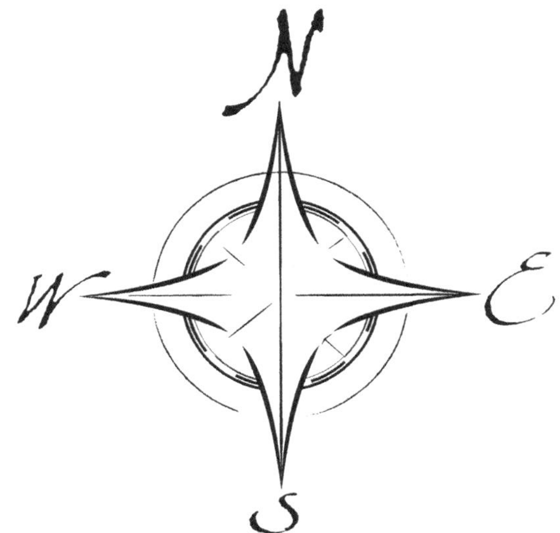
N
W
E
S

The Four Corners of Darkness

Visit Shine-A-Light Press on our website:
www.ShineALightPress.com
on Twitter: @SALPress
And on Facebook: www.facebook.com/SALPress

Visit The Four Corners of Darkness on our website:
www.TheFourCornersBooks.com
on Twitter: @4CornersTrilogy
And on Facebook: www.facebook.com/TheFourCornersBook

Visit C.S. Elston on his website:
www.cselston.com
on Twitter: @cselston
And on Facebook: www.facebook.com/cselston

Illustrations by Madison McClean

Author's Photo by Christie Bruno

ISBN 978-0-997-6722-6-8

Library of Congress Control Number: 2020936672

Printed in the U.S.A.
U.S.A. $15.99

For my sister, Jen. When I wrote the first book in this series, I set out to create a character who is the greatest sister in the world because that's what Kinsey needed. It turns out writing Tatum was easy because I had the honor of growing up with you. So, thanks for being awesome! I probably don't tell you often enough but, I tell other people all the time what an amazing sister I have. So, I thought I should make sure you knew I felt that way as well. Seems only fair. Also, I still miss those cinnamon tortilla roll-ups. Those were pretty awesome, too!

Acknowledgments

As always, I would like to extend my deepest gratitude to my original proofreaders: My parents, Doug and Judy; my nephew, Connor; my sister, Jennifer; and my wife, Andrea. They have all been supportive in numerous ways, not the least of which is having read drafts of the book before publication and offering valuable feedback.

I would like to further offer a sincere 'thank you' to my niece, Madison McClean, for once again providing her beautiful artwork for the interior of this book. It has been three years between trips to Kadosh for the Snyder family but five for the rest of us and Madison's artistic abilities have continued to grow in that time. That growth truly shows in the eight drawings the story inspired her to produce. I appreciate the hard work and feel grateful for the opportunity to share them with everyone who reads this book.

Table of Contents

Part Five *Another Journey*

Part Six *Overcoming Obstacles*

Part Seven *Sail Away*

Part Eight *Battle*

Reader's Guide

The Four Corners of Darkness

by C.S. Elston

The Four Corners of Darkness

by C.S. Elston

PART ONE
Normal

CHAPTER ONE
The Snyder Kids

"Maybe hurdles," Kinsey told his sister as they rounded the corner, taking a left from Crown Street onto Orchard Avenue, about three blocks down the road from where their journey used to begin at Ronald Reagan Elementary School. This next stretch of their walk had been part of the route they had taken home for years. The Crown Street leg, however, had been added last year when Kinsey made the transition to Lincoln Junior High School and Tatum had moved on to Roosevelt High School. She used to meet him at the elementary school when the final bell rang but, now he got out earlier than she did. So, Kinsey's after school routine began by saying goodbye to friends as he gathered up his stuff, walking to the high school, and meeting Tatum in the courtyard at the flagpole. From there, they resumed their tradition of walking home together.

"What makes you want to try hurdles?" she asked him.

"I don't know," he admitted as he took a couple of seconds to ponder the question. Then, finally, shrugging his shoulders, he added, "Just looks fun. Plus, I'm no distance runner and I'm not as fast as some of the other kids that I hear are going to try out for the sprints. But, I figure I just might be able to rule the hurdles."

"Sounds smart," Tatum acknowledged.

"Then I might also try a field event. Maybe pole vault or something. We'll see."

"Pole vault seems kind of scary."

"Nah. Most of the places you could fall are covered by a mat. Looks fun to me."

"When are try outs?" Tatum asked with a smile forming because of her little brother's ever-increasingly adventurous spirit. She had always been more naturally athletic than her little brother, and yet, here he was the one preparing to try out for a school sport.

"Two weeks from yesterday. I think I'm going to find some hurdler exercises online when we get home so I can start practicing."

"Good idea. Just get your homework done first." Even though the family dynamics had changed over the last three years, reducing the need for Tatum to perform many of the motherly duties, she hadn't lost the instinct to help keep her little brother in line and Kinsey kind of liked it that way.

"I know. I think Adam's going to come over and practice with me. I told him to wait a couple of hours though."

"Good. How'd that math test go, by the way?"

"I got a ninety-four," Kinsey said with a smile.

"Good job," Tatum said proudly as they exchanged a high-five. "Hey, change of subject . . . "

"Yeah?"

"I'll be getting my driver's permit next week."

"Oh, yeah . . . "

"Do you realize that means we're about six months away from me being able to drive us to and from school?"

"Yeah," Kinsey said but without the enthusiasm Tatum expected.

"You're not excited about that?"

"I am. It sounds cool. It's just that . . . "

"Just that, what?"

"I'll miss these walks."

"Not when it rains you won't."

"Even when it rains," Kinsey insisted as he looked up and noticed the mostly clear sky the Pacific Northwest was offering as winter began transitioning into spring.

"We'll still get to have our chats. They'll just happen inside a car."

"True. They'll be shorter though, too."

"Fair point. Maybe we'll have to find a longer route to take home. Or, we can stop at a coffee shop or something. In fact, maybe I'll try and get a weekend job at a place like Joe Flows so I can get us a discount."

"Deal," Kinsey said with a smile. "That sounds like fun."

"It does, doesn't it?"

"What kind of car are you going to get?"

"Unfortunately, I think that's more up to mom and dad than me."

"I guess that's true."

"I'm just hoping I get one. Might be borrowing one of theirs for a while."

"I'll help you start dropping hints."

"Teamwork," Tatum stated as she put her hand up and they exchanged another high five just before they rounded the corner and turned onto Strawberry Street.

"Homestretch," Kinsey announced.

"Homestretch," Tatum agreed as she quietly appreciated how much her brother had changed since they had returned from Kadosh. Sure, his physical appearance had changed some. He'd hit a growth spurt that stretched him out by several inches and slimmed him down. But, the biggest change was in Kinsey's general attitude toward his whole life. It wasn't just this new track and field endeavor. He was embracing his life at every turn. Tatum would go so far as to say he had even become gregarious which, a few years ago, is not a word that she thought she would ever use to describe her little brother.

Tatum's changes were far more subtle than Kinsey's had been. First of all, she had grown about another three quarters of an inch and then stopped. Plus, she had always been rather gregarious herself and that hadn't changed at all. But, where she would once take life's lemons and make lemonade, she was now receiving a lot fewer of those lemons and, therefore, was able to take the time to enjoy a much wider variety of fruit. For, that, she was truly thankful.

The terrifying expedition that the Snyder family had been forced to take to the foreign world of Kadosh had ended about three years earlier. Although it was the most trying experience of their young lives, both Tatum and Kinsey counted it as one of the best things that had ever happened to them. They came back changed. Although they had settled back into a routine, the change had stuck with them and the experience was far from a distant memory. Nothing would ever be the same because of their time in that awful place. Life was now better and they wouldn't trade that for anything that they could imagine.

Tatum and Kinsey continued to talk as they finished their walk home. Kinsey got the mail out of the mailbox as Tatum approached the front door and unlocked it. As the door opened, Kinsey hurried up the steps and they both walked inside. They were immediately greeted by the welcome smell, of a pot roast and its surrounding vegetables, that was filling the whole house as it cooked. Tatum shut the door behind them as Kinsey immediately exclaimed, "Oh! That smells awesome!"

"Yeah," Tatum agreed. "It does. Mom said she was throwing a roast, potatoes and veggies in the slow cooker with some onion soup mix this morning before heading out."

"Well, I was already looking forward to dinner. Now it can't come fast enough. That smell is going to make it hard to concentrate on homework."

"Want a snack to tide you over?"

"Cinnamon tortilla roll-up?"

"Sure."

"I'm always up for one of those."

"Get started on your homework and I'll bring it up to you."

"Deal. Thanks."

"You bet," Tatum said as she walked into the kitchen and Kinsey bounded up the stairs toward his bedroom.

Kinsey had always maintained a pretty well-organized space. But, as he had gained new interests and become more socially interactive with his family members over the last few years, he had been spending less time in the room and it had become a bit less picked up and clean than it used to be. He walked into the room and set his backpack on his bed before unzipping it. He pulled out his algebra, world geography, and Spanish textbooks as well as *To Kill a Mockingbird* by Harper Lee.

After a mental *Eeny, Meeny, Miny, Moe,* Kinsey selected his world geography textbook and took it with him as he sat on the floor with his back against his bed. He opened the book up to where he had dog-eared it and began to read about the seven country region known as North Africa. By the time Kinsey started the fourth paragraph, Tatum was walking through his open door with a tortilla rolled up with melted butter, cinnamon and sugar inside.

"Here you go," she told him as she handed him the plate.

"Thanks," Kinsey told his sister as he took the plate and set it down beside him.

"You bet. Now I'm going to go do my homework. Need anything else before I get started?"

"Nope. I'm good."

"Awesome. See ya."

"Bye," Kinsey said as he took a bite of his tortilla. He was immediately comforted by both the delicious flavor and the routine of this situation, and went right back to reading about the Atlas Mountains that are part of the fold mountain system running through much of Southern Europe and extending across a large portion of Morocco, Northern Algeria and Tunisia. His mind, however, was a bit distracted by the anticipation of both his workout with Adam and the arrival of his parents. Plus, no matter how good his sister's cinnamon tortilla roll-up tasted, and it was utterly delicious, the smell of slow cooking pot roast permeating his nostrils would have him fantasizing about dinner until the first bite had been taken. But, Kinsey wasn't the only hungry Snyder in the foursome . . .

CHAPTER TWO
Mr. & Mrs. Snyder

So much had changed in the Snyder family since they returned from Kadosh. Kinsey had more confidence. Tatum had more freedom to be the person she wanted to be and to do the things a teenage girl should be able to do. Grant and Jill were genuinely happy together. After years of quarrelling and strife, the Snyder home had finally become a relatively peaceful one.

It would be easy to say that the time the Snyders had spent in Kadosh had changed them. And, that experience was certainly the catalyst. But, the truth is rarely that simple. Especially when it comes to relationships. Many of the big changes happened for the Snyders after they returned home and most, if not all, of them could be traced directly back to Grant and Jill's marriage. Of course, it hadn't all happened at once. It had required some adjusting on both of their parts. But, they came back from Kadosh devoted to working it out. And, the work had truly paid off.

It started with a commitment to having all four of them around the dinner table six nights a week without a television on, no cell phones, tablets, computers, or digital devices of any kind. No distractions. Just conversation and the opportunity to enjoy each other. Not that it always went that way. At times there was some arguing. Especially in the beginning when Grant and Jill were still hanging on to some bitterness from their time before Kinsey's disappearance. Slowly but surely, the walls had come down and the bitterness had faded away. Replacing it was the new routine of a fun family dinner.

Grant and Jill began to like each other again. As the family became cohesive, the fire of the love Grant and Jill had for one another before they got married was rekindled and new habits formed. On Sundays, they even had game night after their dinner. Kinsey's favorite was the board game "Sequence," Tatum's was the board game "Life," Jill's was the card game "Oh Well," and Grant's was the board game "Monopoly." Saturday nights became movie night for Tatum and Kinsey and date night for Grant and Jill.

Occasionally, that date night meant a movie for Grant and Jill, too. It always included dinner out and they had gradually determined their favorite spots. Most of them were a bit of a drive from home. The closest was in Mukilteo which was about a twenty-five-minute drive in the evening on a Saturday. Once in a while, Jill could even talk Grant into driving south to Seattle and going to a more upscale restaurant. But, that didn't happen more than every other month because it took twice as long to get there, even longer if the Mariners were playing that night, and the meal always cost several times as much. Grant was a bit more frugal than Jill and heavy traffic drove him crazy.

But, instead of getting frustrated with one another, the couple had learned to accept their differences as quirks. This decision gave them the opportunity to love each other despite those differences and, in some cases, even because of them. For the first time in a long time, they were happy together. Where they used to avoid talking to one another, they had come to a point, much like a couple in a new relationship, where they could hardly wait until their next conversation. Sometimes, they even spoke multiple times during the work day and they always talked to one another on their way home even though they would be together by the time they hung up their phones. This had become another habit and the day before Kadosh came calling again was no exception.

"Isn't the conference in Chicago that same week?" Jill asked her husband through the software application that allowed her to use her phone through her car stereo as she eased her foot onto the brake pedal and slowed her approach to a line of cars stopped at a light.

"Yeah," Grant agreed as he walked across the parking lot and climbed into his car. "But, I've got Xavier covering that for me."

"Didn't he cover it for you last year, too?"

"He did."

"I thought you guys agreed to trade off."

"We did," Grant conceded as he started his truck and allowed the Bluetooth technology to connect his phone to the stereo system. "But, I don't really want to travel without my family anymore. So, I told him I was going to need him to take over most, if not all, of those duties from now on."

"How did he take that?"

"He seemed excited about the increased responsibilities."

"I hope they came with a raise," Jill said as the light turned green and she started to move forward.

"What?" Grant responded, playfully, as he finally set the phone down on the passenger seat now that his wife's voice was coming through the speakers. "Who's side are you on?"

"Yours," Jill flirted. "Always yours."

"Good. And, yes, Xavier got a ten percent pay increase."

"I'm sure that helped his enthusiasm."

"It seemed to. He's come a long way since he walked into the Lynnwood store looking like the modern incarnation of Vlad the Impaler."

"He just needed someone to give him a shot. That someone was you. I can understand why he's loyal."

"He should be loyal to Kinsey then because Kinsey was that someone, not me."

"Kinsey reminded you what the right thing to do was. You were the one who was in a position to actually do it and you did."

"You're right. I am pretty great."

"I didn't exactly say that."

"You were thinking it."

"Maybe," Jill said, still flirting. "You know the kids are old enough to stay home overnight by themselves now. If you do need to go on a business trip, at some point, I could go with you. Make it half work and half romantic getaway."

"That sounds a lot more appealing than two nights alone in a motel by the airport."

"Something to think about."

"Indeed. So, what's on the agenda tonight?"

"Pretty typical evening. Dinner's in the crockpot. Kids have homework, I'm sure."

"Huskies are playing the Beavers tonight."

"I might be willing to sit through a basketball game . . . now that the Huskies are finally good again."

"Careful, honey. Fair-weather fans aren't real fans."

"Your devotion is one of the many things I love about you but, that doesn't mean watching a team that hasn't made the Sweet 16 in over a decade any easier."

"Maybe this is the year."

"I've heard that before."

"You never know. March Madness starts right after the tournament. Let's see how they do."

"Uh-huh," Jill purposefully mumbled.

"I'm just impressed you know how long it's been. And, that you're willing to watch. I'll take it."

"As if you have a choice."

"Good point. Devotion and what not."

"Exactly."

"So, what's in the crockpot?"

"Chuck roast with potatoes, carrots, onions, celery and some onion soup mix."

"Oh, that sounds great. I'm starving."

"You're always starving. What'd you have for lunch?"

Grant was quiet.

"Your silence is speaking volumes."

"Just concentrating on the road. You wouldn't want me to get into an accident, would you?"

"What'd you have for lunch, Grant?"

"Salad."

"No, you didn't. What did you really have?"

"Fruit bowl."

"Grant?" Jill asked with a playful sternness in her voice.

"Burger."

"That's more like it. Keep going. What size was the burger?"

"Half a pound."

"Cheese?"

"Yeah."

"Bacon?"

"Yeah."

"Fries?"

"Yeah."

"Still hungry, huh?"

"Yeah."

"Of course you are."

"I wasn't when I ate the burger but that was four hours ago."

"You poor thing. You must be just famished."

"That's the support I was looking for."

Both Jill and Grant started laughing. They continued their playful conversation until both cars pulled into the driveway of their house. They gave each other a hug and a kiss on the lips before walking inside to greet their children and sit down for dinner with no idea the happy world they had finally managed to develop was on the verge of changing once again.

CHAPTER THREE
The Snyder Family

Just over three years earlier, the Snyder household had been in a state of impending collapse. Grant and Jill had reached a point in their relationship where they couldn't see past their own walls of resentment to experience any other feeling toward one another. As a result, anything resembling "family time" had essentially ceased to exist and the household was made up of four people who were dwelling together but living lives marked more by isolation than togetherness. Grant and Jill barely spoke to one another. When they did, it primarily consisted of angry yelling and screaming. So, Grant and Jill mostly kept to themselves.

Their oldest child, twelve-year-old Tatum, inherited the role of principal caregiver to both herself and her nine-year-old brother, Kinsey. The resulting relationship shouldn't have to exist between siblings but, under the circumstances, that relationship probably saved them both from even more emotional suffering than they were already experiencing.

The rage and bitterness that had been building between Grant and Jill for years had reached a pinnacle during a shouting match over a refrigerator door that had been left open for, what Jill had estimated, was at least the two hundredth time. Ultimately, the word "divorce" had finally been uttered and it appeared that both Grant and Jill were in favor of the idea. That was the moment when Kinsey, who had been bottling up all his frustrations, fears, and, most of all, sorrow, for years, finally let them come exploding out of him.

When the emotive time-bomb detonated, it was so extraordinary that it opened a portal to another world. After Kinsey physically disappeared through that portal, his family went searching for him. Their grief and anguish over his vanishing was so extraordinary, that they disappeared through the very same portal. The four of them each found themselves in a world where the emotional separation that they were experiencing back home had manifested itself physically and, it seemed, permanently. They had each awakened alone in separate parts of this strange place that they would later learn was called Kadosh. It was made up of a vast ocean and five islands created for the sole purpose of separating men, women, boys and girls by Raum, the demon-ruler of the world, who lived on the desolate island in the center of the other four.

The adage that absence makes the heart grow fonder proved to be true for the Snyders. Once in Kadosh, their self-imposed emotional walls began to crumble as they each realized how desperately they wanted to be with one another. This realization, however, meant they had to defy the odds and fight their way to a reunion with the rest of their family. Before their separate journey began, they convinced others on their respective islands to go with them. Unfortunately, some stayed behind and, among those who went, not all survived. Along the way, they had to battle with wild animals, terrifying creatures, and severe weather, all of which were under Raum's command. And, finally, they had to do battle with Raum himself.

The process showed them just how badly they wanted to be with one another. They were willing to fight for it through extreme danger in Kadosh. Therefore, they had to be willing to fight for it back home where the circumstances were far less severe. And, the three years since their return from the harrowing journey in Kadosh had given them the opportunity to work on creating strong relationships with each other, resulting in a healthy and happy home. All four of them would agree that they had never been better-off. As treacherous as their experience had been, each of them was surprisingly thankful for it. Put simply, life was better because of it.

This evening was no exception. It was a prime example of

what life had become for the Snyders. Getting up and ready in the morning, followed by breakfast together, school and work, then dinner together, talking, laughing, homework for the kids, a little time in front of the TV as a family and then it was off to bed so they could repeat it the following day.

Of course, the routine was not always an exact science. There were often exceptions. For example, on this evening, Kinsey's friend Adam had come over after dinner, as planned, to do some drills in the backyard in preparation for the upcoming track and field tryouts at school. The drill that they spent the most time doing was the closest they could get to practicing actual hurdles. They raided the garage and set up a couple of Grant's saw horses and practiced running and jumping over them for about an hour.

When they finished their workout and Adam went home, the routine quickly got back on track. There was still time for Kinsey to catch the second half of the Huskies and Beavers basketball game on TV with his sister and parents, who had watched the whole thing from the beginning. The Huskies won, which they had been doing a lot that season, and the family celebrated together with root beer floats.

Standing around the butcher-block styled island in the middle of the kitchen, all four of the Snyders spooned vanilla ice cream, in puddles of root beer, into their mouths and Kinsey decided that this was a good time to keep a promise he had made to his sister earlier that day.

"What kind of car are you going to get for Tatum?" Kinsey bluntly asked his parents.

Tatum shot her little brother a wide-eyed look as if to say *That's not the subtle kind of hint I had in mind.*

"None of your bee's wax," Jill shot back.

"So, you are getting her one."

"None," Jill said firmly.

"Car or bee's wax?"

"Tatum's birthday is six months away," Grant chimed in with a chuckle. "And, your input on her present has not been requested. So, let it go."

"We'll get her whatever we decide to get her and you'll find out what that is the same day she does," Jill stated emphatically. "On her birthday."

"Which is six months away," Grant added again.

"For the record," Kinsey started as he jumped back into the conversation, "I know when Tatum's birthday is. That's why I thought we should start planning now."

"We," Jill said with emphasis, "don't need to start doing anything. This is up to your father and I."

"She's going to be driving me to and from school," Kinsey argued. "Seems like I should have some kind of input."

"I drive you places," Jill told Kinsey. "Do you think you should have input on what kind of car I buy myself next time?"

"I hadn't thought of that," Kinsey said, ponderously. "Maybe I should. I need to be kept safe so, let's go big but practical."

"Now you're out of control," Jill said with a laugh.

"Big time," Grant agreed. "What part of 'let it go' wasn't clear enough for you?"

"All of it," Kinsey said, chuckling. "Doesn't compute."

"Obviously not," Grant agreed as he scooped up a spoonful of ice cream and plopped it on his son's nose.

"Hey!" Kinsey shouted as he started to try and get his dad back by scooping some ice cream up for retaliation.

"No, no . . . " Grant said, stopping Kinsey. "We're not starting a war here because I know who will have to clean it up."

"Yeah," Jill said, "me."

"Exactly," Grant agreed. "Your mom is innocent in this matter and we can't do that to her."

"Fine," Kinsey conceded, "even though you're the one who already started it."

"You're right," Grant said, also conceding. "I did."

"Why are you so quiet?" Jill asked her daughter. "Your birthday is what's driving this conversation."

"That's why I'm so quiet," Tatum insisted. "I'm staying

out of it because I don't want to discourage you from getting me a really nice present. Preferably in red."

"Smart girl," Jill said with a smile.

The playful conversation continued until Grant and Jill put the kids to bed and then went back downstairs to watch a little more TV before retiring for the night themselves. They were happy and planning for the future. But, unfortunately, the future they had planned would begin changing by morning.

PART TWO
Abnormal

CHAPTER FOUR
The Call

Kinsey went through his normal routine of getting ready for bed that night without any inclination that the night would turn out to be far from normal. He brushed his teeth while he picked out the clothes he would be too tired to decide on in the morning. He laid them over the back of his bedroom chair, went back to the bathroom and rinsed out his mouth before saying goodnight to his parents and sister. Finally, he flipped the switch to turn off the overhead light in his room and closed the door before switching on the bedside lamp to provide some reading light.

As he crawled into bed, Kinsey picked up his Bible from the nightstand and opened it to where he had left off that morning, before getting ready for school. Reading his Bible had become important to Kinsey since he returned from Kadosh. It had become important to the entire Snyder family.

Their conversations over the days that followed their return seemed to consistently circle back to the light they had experienced on Raum's island. The light that was so bright that they had to turn away from it. And, when they felt the warmth of the light vanish, they had opened their eyes to discover that they had been armed for battle against Raum. They needed to know where that light had come from and why it had aided them the way it had.

Driving past a church in Snohomish one Saturday, Grant had noticed the letter board sign out front that announced the sermon that would be preached the next day, "The Light of the World." Although the sign made it clear that the sermon would be taken from the eighth chapter of the Gospel of John in the New Testament, Grant's mind raced to the Old Testament. More specifically, he suddenly remembered a Sunday School class his grandparents used to take him to when he was a few years younger than Kinsey and the light reminded him of a lesson the teacher had taught, using an old felt board. The lesson was about Moses asking God, on Mount Sinai, to show his glory and God responding by saying that no one could look upon His face and live. But, finally God had allowed himself to be seen from the back and when Moses came down off the mountain afterward, he was so radiant that the people were afraid of him. The memory was not exactly the same type of event but, it was enough to cause

Grant to begin seeking answers in the Bible. Eventually, he read a passage in the book of Ezekiel that sounded a lot like what they had experienced on that island. This led to regular attendance at the very same community church where the sign had been and, where the Snyders hoped to find more answers. On the fourth Sunday, the pastor delivered a sermon on the Armor of God in Ephesians chapter six and everything started to truly click.

They continued to search but never found any specific reference to Kadosh in the Bible. However, they found plenty to convince them that what they had experienced was known to God and consistent with how He had chosen to reveal Himself in the Bible.

It was Kinsey who first told the family he had come to understand that they didn't have to find all of the answers. It was okay if they didn't understand everything because he knew that God did. He also knew that all the answers they did need could only be found by following Jesus. That's also when he told them that he intended to be baptized. At first, his family looked on with wide eyes but, by the time he was done talking, they had all agreed to be baptized together and found themselves in the middle of a family prayer time full of thanksgiving for the grace and mercy of God.

Their baptism was nearly a year ago and Kinsey had read at least a portion of the Bible every morning, usually before getting out of bed, except when he woke up needing badly to pee first, and then again every night before falling asleep. On this night, he found himself starting the book of First Peter and, perhaps because of the exercise he had undertaken with his friend Adam earlier, he was very tired and fell asleep after only one chapter and nine verses of the second chapter. So, the last thing he read was the second half of First Peter 2:9, which reads: ". . . that you may declare the praises of him who called you out of darkness into his wonderful light."

After that verse, he was sound asleep with the lamp still on. And, as he drifted into unconsciousness, the glowing ball from the lamp on the other side of his eyelids faded into nothingness. But, soon, another light appeared in the distance. Quickly growing closer, at a much faster pace than the previous one had disappeared. Kinsey realized that although he could have felt afraid of it, he was strangely drawn to it, and even comforted by it, instead.

The sphere of light charged forward as if it was going to bowl Kinsey over but, instead, stopped abruptly in front of him. Unlike the light on the island, Kinsey was able to look directly at this one. Of course, he was dreaming this time, too. The battle he had fought in Kadosh, and everything leading up to it, had been anything but a dream. It wasn't even a nightmare. It had been far too real.

Kinsey studied the light as he felt a heat emanating from it that was unlike anything he had felt since the massive light had briefly visited the island. This sphere wasn't quite as hot but it was the closest thing he'd experienced since. If the light on the island was like sitting at the perfect distance from a crackling fireplace, this was like being tucked into your own bed with a warm blanket. He considered reaching out to touch it but was stopped by the sound of a voice.

"You have been called out of the darkness," the voice boomed, "only to be called back. Not to remain in the darkness, or of the darkness, but to be the light of the Lord that leads others out of the darkness from which you first were called."

"I know," Kinsey replied as he quickly looked around before realizing the voice had come from within the light. And, know he did. Or, at the very least, he had strongly suspected from the moment they returned that they would be called back. He had no idea when or how. But, he was confident the call would come and, finally, it had.

"When?" Kinsey asked with a smile.

"Soon," the sphere replied. "You are being prepared."

Before Kinsey could ask how he was being prepared, how he would know it was time, or any of the other gazillion questions that were racing through his mind, the light sped away even faster than it had arrived.

"Wait!" Kinsey yelled as he sat straight up in bed, suddenly wide awake. He looked down at the Bible in his lap and re-read the verse he had fallen asleep reading: ". . . that you may declare the praises of him who called you out of darkness into his wonderful light."

By the time he was done reading it, his door was opening and Tatum stepped inside.

"You okay?"

"Yeah, he answered. "Just fell asleep reading. I think I was dreaming."

"Okay," she responded as Kinsey closed his Bible, set it on the nightstand, and turned off the lamp. "Goodnight."

"Goodnight."

Tatum closed the door and Kinsey laid back down. He turned onto his side, facing the lamp. He could still see his Bible in the glow of the alarm clock. He stared at it, wondering if a dream is all it was or if the call had finally come. His eyelids fluttered and finally closed as sleep drew closer.

Suddenly, he saw light again. He opened his eyes and the lightbulb in the lamp pulsed on and off three times before finally turning off for good.

Kinsey smiled. It wasn't just a dream. The call had finally come and the Snyders would be returning to Kadosh.

Kinsey studied the light as he felt a heat emanating from it that was unlike anything he had felt since the massive light had briefly visited the island. This sphere wasn't quite as hot but it was the closest thing he'd experienced since. If the light on the island was like sitting at the perfect distance from a crackling fireplace, this was like being tucked into your own bed with a warm blanket. He considered reaching out to touch it but was stopped by the sound of a voice.

"You have been called out of the darkness," the voice boomed, "only to be called back. Not to remain in the darkness, or of the darkness, but to be the light of the Lord that leads others out of the darkness from which you first were called."

"I know," Kinsey replied as he quickly looked around before realizing the voice had come from within the light. And, know he did. Or, at the very least, he had strongly suspected from the moment they returned that they would be called back. He had no idea when or how. But, he was confident the call would come and, finally, it had.

"When?" Kinsey asked with a smile.

"Soon," the sphere replied. "You are being prepared."

Before Kinsey could ask how he was being prepared, how he would know it was time, or any of the other gazillion questions that were racing through his mind, the light sped away even faster than it had arrived.

"Wait!" Kinsey yelled as he sat straight up in bed, suddenly wide awake. He looked down at the Bible in his lap and re-read the verse he had fallen asleep reading: ". . . that you may declare the praises of him who called you out of darkness into his wonderful light."

By the time he was done reading it, his door was opening and Tatum stepped inside.

"You okay?"

"Yeah, he answered. "Just fell asleep reading. I think I was dreaming."

"Okay," she responded as Kinsey closed his Bible, set it on the nightstand, and turned off the lamp. "Goodnight."

"Goodnight."

Tatum closed the door and Kinsey laid back down. He turned onto his side, facing the lamp. He could still see his Bible in the glow of the alarm clock. He stared at it, wondering if a dream is all it was or if the call had finally come. His eyelids fluttered and finally closed as sleep drew closer.

Suddenly, he saw light again. He opened his eyes and the lightbulb in the lamp pulsed on and off three times before finally turning off for good.

Kinsey smiled. It wasn't just a dream. The call had finally come and the Snyders would be returning to Kadosh.

CHAPTER FIVE
Bona Fide

It wasn't that Kinsey was excited to return to Kadosh. On the contrary. He dreaded the idea of being separated from his family again, which he could only assume would be the case. He also dreaded the idea of facing Raum and everything under the demon's command. But, he was excited to feel useful to God, whom he had come to know as a direct result of his first trip to Kadosh. He was excited and honored that God would choose him. And, he was excited to tell those who had stayed behind, when he led the exile from camp and the quest to find his family that there was indeed a way out. What it really came down to was, Kinsey wanted to finish what he had started.

His mind raced with considerations of what the second trip would be like and, as a result, it took him over two hours to fall back to sleep. Even after he did, he was restless for the remainder of the night. He must have awakened at least a dozen times and, each time, his attention was already on Kadosh. It was permeating his dreams and consuming his waking thoughts.

Finally, after reading the rest of First Peter, Kinsey decided to get out of bed and get ready for the day while everyone else in the house was still asleep. Typically, on a weekday such as this one, Kinsey would be the last one out of bed. But, on this Friday morning, Kinsey would be out of the shower and ready for school before his sister took over their bathroom. In fact, it was Grant who heard the water turn on, wondered who was already taking a shower, looked at the clock and, realizing that his alarm would be going off in less than twenty minutes anyway, decided to get up, too. Jill soon followed but Tatum was sound asleep until she heard Taylor Swift's voice coming from her alarm. She turned it off, rolled over, let out a yawn so big she briefly feared her jaw was going to break, stretched and flexed her muscles to wake them up, and ripped the covers off so she could roll herself out of bed.

While Tatum was getting ready, Kinsey, who had already dressed and packed his bag for school, was downstairs in the kitchen preparing breakfast for the family. As Grant, Jill and Tatum strolled into the kitchen, one-by-one, they discovered Kinsey sitting at the table. He had set out four bowls, four spoons, four glasses, four boxes of cereal, a carton of milk, a carton of orange juice, a roll of paper towels to be used as napkins, and a sugar bowl which had a fifth spoon sticking out of it. However, he hadn't poured anything.

"Good morning," Grant said to his son as he walked into the kitchen, closed the hatch on the single-serve coffee machine and hit the button to start brewing his coffee with the mug already in place below the dispenser.

"Good morning," Kinsey answered.

"You get my coffee ready to go for me?"

"Yep."

"And, breakfast too, huh?"

"Yep."

"What's the occasion?"

"I'll wait until mom and Tatum are down here."

"You got an announcement to make or something?"

"Yep."

"Well, now I'm really curious."

Kinsey didn't respond.

Grant's mind started working overtime to try and come up with possibilities but nothing seemed to satisfy him. He walked his coffee over to the table, spooned two scoops of sugar into his mug and stirred in silence as he watched his son who didn't flinch. Grant took a seat at the table and sipped his coffee as they both waited for Jill and Tatum.

"We should probably teach you to make bacon in case this ever happens again," Grant finally said.

"We?" came Jill's voice as she entered the kitchen. "Do you know how to make bacon, Grant?"

"I could probably figure it out," Grant answered with a sly grin.

"If you made bacon," Jill started, "it would be in the microwave. Not the same."

"Probably true," Grant agreed.

"Very true. It'd be all rubbery."

"Okay."

"In case what happens again?"

"What?" Grant asked.

"You said, we should probably teach Kinsey to make bacon in case this happens again. Clearly, he put out breakfast for us. So, what has happened?"

"He has an announcement to make."

"What announcement?"

"Ask him."

Jill looked at her son, expecting a response.

"I'm waiting for Tatum," Kinsey finally stated matter-of-factly.

Jill looked at her husband who simply shrugged his shoulders as if to tell her she knew as much as he did. She raised her eyebrows in concession and walked over to the coffee machine. After making her coffee, she walked back over to the table, scooped a spoonful of sugar, poured a couple of tablespoons worth of milk into her mug and stirred it with the spoon Kinsey had set out. Everyone sat in silence, glancing at one another, until Tatum finally walked down the stairs.

"Come on in here and sit down," Jill politely yelled.

"What's going on?" Tatum asked as she walked in to a familiar setting that, suddenly, felt anything but familiar.

"Your brother wants to tell us something."

"Okay . . . " Tatum said, skeptically, as she took the only remaining seat at the table and everyone's eyes shifted to Kinsey.

"We're being called back to Kadosh," Kinsey quickly blurted out.

"What?" Tatum and Grant both asked, almost in unison.

"How do you know?" Jill swiftly questioned.

Kinsey described his dream in great detail and Tatum remembered checking in on him afterwards. She asked why he didn't tell her then and he explained that he needed time to think the whole thing through. Everyone went silent for a moment until Grant finally broke in.

"I think, maybe, it was just a dream, buddy."

"It wasn't," Kinsey insisted.

"I have to agree with your dad on this one," Jill added.

"I wondered if that was true at first too," Kinsey admitted. But, then my light flickered on and off three times before turning off for good. It was a sign."

"Or," Grant suggested, "a bad light bulb."

"No," Kinsey stated emphatically. I had turned the light off before it even flickered back on.

"Are you sure?" Jill asked.

"Yes," Kinsey stated with increasing frustration. "I'm sure. Not that it seems to matter."

"Hey," Jill started, "we're just trying to understand."

"Understand this," Kinsey insisted as he stood up from the table, "it was more than a dream. We're being called back."

"If we're all being called back," Grant began to ask as Kinsey went to a kitchen drawer and pulled out two plastic bags, "why are you the only one who had that dream?"

Silence.

Tatum watched her brother fill the bags with dry cereal and knew immediately that, if nothing else, while she couldn't be sure whether or not it was anything more than a dream, Kinsey definitely believed what he was telling them to be true. She recalled watching her brother disappear three years ago and how she ran back to the house to get her parents' help but they didn't believe her at first. She didn't blame them. What she told them sounded outrageous and, even with what they had been through since that moment, her brother's story sounded pretty outrageous, too. Still, she knew how it felt to know what you were saying was true and have them not believe you.

Kinsey handed one of the bags to his sister and walked over to pick his backpack up.

"Faith like a child," Tatum exclaimed.

Everyone looked at her. Even Kinsey was a bit puzzled.

"What's that?" Jill asked.

"Maybe the first step was notifying Kinsey because he was the only one listening."

Grant and Jill exchanged looks that suggested they were ready to wrap this conversation up. Grant followed the exchange up with a glance at his watch.

"We should probably get you kids off to school," he announced.

"Yep," Kinsey said as if to say that their skepticism would not deter him. He got up from the table and grabbed his backpack.

Tatum silently followed her brother. Grant and Jill got up to walk their children to the door, feeling a little sheepish. As they did, they could see out the windows that the wind was picking up and the trees had begun to sway.

"Getting a little windy out there," Grant stated. "I don't remember that in the forecast."

Kinsey reached for the doorknob, turned it and opened the door.

The wind gust tore through the house and the howl quickly turned into the sound of specific whispered words, "Out of the darkness."

As quickly as the wind had burst into the house, it was gone and it pulled the door shut as it went.

Everyone stood in stunned silence until Grant broke it once again, "Everyone heard that, right?"

They looked outside and noticed that everything was eerily calm. No swaying trees. No floating leaves. Even the clouds looked still.

Kinsey looked everyone in the eyes, one by one to make sure he had their undivided attention before asking, "Do you believe me now?"

CHAPTER SIX
An Old Friend

The walk to school that morning was far quieter than normal. After hearing the wind whisper the exact words that Kinsey had heard in his dream, Tatum was now convinced that her little brother was right and they were being called back to Kadosh. Her silence was the result of being terrified by that fact. Tatum's mind had become flooded with memories of how difficult the journey was the first time, how she had become friends with girls who didn't make it back, and how close she knew she had come to not making it back either. She felt blessed to be among those who had returned home and was uncomfortable with the idea of tempting fate by making a second trip.

What if, she began to wonder, *one of us doesn't make it back this time? What if none of us do?*

Kinsey, on the other hand, had already begun to think of

things he would do differently on this second journey. Most of his thoughts were review because he had already played the scenarios through in his mind on multiple occasions over the past three years. The one that always remained consistent was the fact that he intended to start recruiting the moment he arrived and he hoped that he would be able to convince everyone to make the trek to Raum's island this time around.

With their minds on the same subject, but looking at it from completely different angles, Tatum and Kinsey hugged and said goodbye before departing for different schools and carrying with them very different attitudes. Tatum was perplexed and anxious. Suddenly, the always positive and even jubilant girl was worried and somber while the once quiet and demoralized young man who had become, as Tatum had thought the previous day, gregarious, was even more enthusiastic than either of them had been in a long time.

Kinsey started the day in his homeroom class, which lasted for the first three periods. When he walked through the door, he said good morning to his friend Adam as he took a seat at his desk. As he did, he was surprised to discover an adult he didn't immediately recognize sitting at Mrs. Larson's desk in the front left corner of the room. Typically, the overweight, forty-year-old Caucasian woman would be eating her yogurt as she prepared for the day. Instead, Kinsey was staring at a tall, thin, African-

American man, who looked closer to fifty. The man finished reading a note from Mrs. Larson through his black horn-rimmed glasses, took a sip of what Kinsey assumed was coffee from a travel mug that had a University of Southern California logo on the side of it, stood and walked to the front center of the classroom where he turned to face the white board and write his name on it with a blue marker. The bell rang just as the man finished and spun back around to face the students.

"Everybody get in your seats and get settled," he told the class. "I know you weren't expecting a sub today but, Mrs. Larson felt sick yesterday afternoon and decided to take the day at home. Hopefully, she'll be back after the weekend. I'm Mr. Ewing and I'll be filling in for her today. Let's start by taking roll."

Kinsey continued to watch as Mr. Ewing walked back over to the desk and picked up a spiral notebook that was already open. He lifted it in front of his face and began to read off the alphabetical list of names and wait for a hand to raise and someone to announce their presence so he could mark whether they were there or not before continuing to move down the list. With twenty-eight kids in the class and a last name of Snyder, Kinsey had to wait through twenty-three other names before it got to his. As he watched and listened, he thought about how Mr. Ewing had started to seem familiar. He tried to remember if he had ever had him as a substitute teacher before but didn't think he had. He couldn't figure out where he knew him from and it was starting to drive him a little crazy by the time his name was called.

"Kinsey Snyder," Mr. Ewing asked as his voice got higher toward the end of Kinsey's name. "Wait, Kinsey Snyder?"

"Yeah," Kinsey said as he rose his hand, a bit confused by the reaction to his name. "Here."

Mr. Ewing tipped his glasses down, blinked a few times, then pushed them back up his nose. "I knew a Kinsey Snyder once," he finally said as a smile formed on his face. "Cool kid."

That was all Mr. Ewing said before moving on to the last four names on the roll call. Then he taught the three periods like any other substitute teacher would. The one exception being the occasional glance and smile he gave Kinsey. It was like they knew each other but Kinsey couldn't figure out how or why. It seemed like Mr. Ewing had figured it out but Kinsey was still in the dark. Then it hit him.

Kadosh.

Mr. Ewing must have been one of the men who made it to Raum's island. By the time the bell rang to signal the end of the third period, Kinsey couldn't wait to approach Mr. Ewing in private. While everyone else funneled out of the back of the classroom, Kinsey told Adam he would see him later and raced to the front where his substitute teacher sat, smiling back at him.

"You figured it out, didn't you?"

"Kadosh," Kinsey blurted out.

"Kadosh," Mr. Ewing agreed as he leaned backwards in his chair.

"Are you . . . ?"

"Am I, what?"

"Not what, who."

"You haven't figured out who I am?"

Kinsey shook his head, glanced at the floor, then back up at Mr. Ewing. "Are you, Ray's dad?"

"Ray's dad? No, man. Close, but no. Kinsey, it's me. Ray."

"But," Kinsey hesitated, "you're old."

"Thank you. I'm aware of that fact. It's been forty years, man."

"It's been three years." Kinsey quickly corrected.

"For you, it's been three years. For me, it's been almost forty."

"How?"

"Did you notice when you got back that a single day hadn't passed while you were gone?"

"We did notice that. But, forty years?"

"I went back to my time. You went back to yours. I grew up. Got old. So will you."

"Have you been here this whole time?"

"Here?"

"Snohomish?"

"Snow-what?" Ray asked, knowing that was his exact reaction to the word when they first met in Kadosh, causing them both to laugh.

"It's really you," Kinsey said as he shook his head in elated surprise. He then lunged forward and gave Ray a hug. Letting go and standing back to look at his old friend who had aged forty years since he last saw him three years earlier, he asked his question again. "So, have you been here in Snohomish this whole time without coming to find me?"

"No. I was still in Long Beach until just a few weeks ago. Needed a change and I was looking at a map and saw this crazy word . . . Snohomish. I loaded up the car and started driving. Here I am."

Suddenly, another bell rang and Kinsey realized he was late for his next class. They traded phone numbers and promised to catch up over the weekend before Kinsey sprinted to the gym and Ray pulled his sack lunch out of his brief case. Neither of them could believe they had re-connected outside of Kadosh. And, neither of them would have believed what that connection would lead to before the end of the weekend that was mere hours away from getting started.

CHAPTER SEVEN
Gifts

At first, Kinsey couldn't wait to tell his family about Ray. But, as he thought about it throughout the rest of the school day, he decided he wanted to make it a surprise. So, at dinner that night, he asked if he could invite a new friend from school over for dinner on Saturday. Grant was quick to remind him that Saturday was movie night for the kids and date night for the adults. Kinsey asked if they could make an exception but his parents were unwilling to negotiate. Their only compromise was allowing him to invite his new friend over for dinner on Sunday instead.

Kinsey accepted their offer and made the arrangements with Ray over the phone immediately after helping his dad rinse the dishes and put them in the dishwasher. From there, it was a pretty normal weekend. The kids both did some homework on Saturday, Kinsey and Adam practiced their hurdles some more,

Grant mowed the lawn for the first time since early November, and Jill had an open house from 1-4p.m.

In the evening, Grant and Jill went to a long dinner at Ivar's, right next to the ferry in Mukilteo. The dinner was extended while they finished the bottle of Viognier they had ordered before the meal, then decided to share a chocolate hazelnut mousse and two cups of decaffeinated coffee as they talked the night away. A significant portion of the conversation was focused on Kadosh, their son's dream, and the mysterious wind that sounded as though it had howled the precise words Kinsey had said came to him in his dream.

Meanwhile, Tatum and Kinsey made popcorn and watched the two most recent *Star Wars* movies. The whole franchise had become a favorite of Kinsey's and he promised that Tatum she could choose the movies the following week. Although she liked *Star Wars*, she didn't care for it half as much as her brother did. So, she was already planning next week's agenda and knew it was going to include the 2017 live-action version of *Beauty and the Beast*. She smirked at the thought of watching her brother squirm when she made the announcement.

By the time Grant and Jill returned home, Kinsey was fast asleep on the couch and Tatum, through happy tears, was watching the end of their second movie alone. Grant carried Kinsey upstairs, briefly considering how much heavier his son had become over the years and that he might not be able to carry him up a flight of stairs much longer. He put Kinsey in bed while Tatum washed out the popcorn bowl and Jill folded the blanket her kids had been sharing. Tatum was in bed twenty minutes later and her parents were not far behind.

Sunday morning was all about church. Two different services were offered, one at 9:00a.m. and the other at 11:00a.m. Although the kids would have preferred to sleep in and go to the later service, Grant and Jill nearly always woke them up and made them get ready in time to attend the earlier one, usually offering brunch afterwards at The Nest, across the street from the church, as an enticement. This day was no exception.

Although the church the Snyders attended was at the edge of the downtown area of Snohomish, it looked like a quaint, country church. It was white, had a lot of angles, a black roof, a red door, a turret with a bell that rang five minutes before each service and a big, beautiful cross on top that was spotlighted every night. One of the many things the Snyders appreciated, as newer believers, was that the head pastor, Dr. Quinlan, took an expository approach to his sermons. This means that they selected one book of the Bible at a time and went through it, verse by verse. It was educational, applicable, and the preacher didn't shy away from topics that might be controversial. But, he didn't go looking for controversy either. He simply called a spade a spade, as Grant often said.

On this Sunday, they found themselves about three-quarters of their way through the book of First Corinthians. Other than a brief departure for the first eight verses of the twelfth chapter of Paul's letter to the Romans, the pastor remained in the twelfth chapter of First Corinthians and preached a sermon that compared the members of God's church, that is the entire Christian community, to a human body. He explained that a body is made up of many different parts with equally different purposes. In the same way, the church is made up of many diverse people, to whom God has given many distinct gifts and abilities, also for different purposes, but all to make the body, as a whole, function properly.

It was a sermon that connected with the Snyders. They had seen the truth of it play out in their own family since returning home from Kadosh. It was easy for them to take their own experience in their small family and apply it in broader strokes to the much larger church. But, the most interesting part of the church service happened after the sermon had concluded.

Grant had noticed an elderly gentleman, in the pew across the aisle, looking over at him and smiling during the service. At one point, he even asked Jill if she knew who he was. She said she had seen him before but she didn't know his name. So, when the congregation had been dismissed, Grant felt the need to go and introduce himself so that he could politely inquire about the unwarranted attention. But, before he could, he was stopped by one of the church administrators who was asking if Grant would consider joining the Sunday volunteer team to serve as an usher. Grant told the man he would consider it and then pointed out the elderly gentlemen who was slowly walking, alone, toward the exit and quickly explained why he wanted to talk to him. The administrator said that the man's name was Ulrich and told Grant that, referencing the sermon of the day, the man's gift was prophecy. Grant thanked him, told Jill he would meet the family outside, and hustled out of the building to catch up with the elderly gentleman.

"Ulrich," Grant shouted as he bounded down the steps.

Turning around, Ulrich looked at Grant with the same smile he had been sporting during the sermon.

"My name is Grant Snyder," Grant continued but then stopped, unsure of where to go next.

"Pleasure," Ulrich said as he extended a hand. "How can I help you?"

Grant stared blankly for a moment while he tried to figure out how to respond. "I'm not sure, actually. I just . . . I noticed you looking over at my family during the sermon."

Ulrich nodded in agreement.

"Was there a reason for that?" Grant finally asked. "It's just that . . . well . . . I was also just informed that you . . . "

"The Lord has seen it fit," Ulrich began, "from time to time, to use me to speak on truths not yet known."

"Right," Grant said even though he wasn't completely certain they were on the same page. "Is now one of those times? Might that be the reason you were looking at us during the service?"

"It is and it was."

"Okay." Grant waited for more information but Ulrich was not quick to give it up. "Do you have something you want to tell me?"

"Two things."

"Great. Go for it. Whenever you're ready. Tell me everything you think I should know."

"It's time for you to accept what your son is already aware of."

"The calling?"

"Yes."

"I thought that might be where this was heading. What's the other thing?"

"The calling is to a journey some would say has already been taken. But, much has changed and much more will still change. The journey will be different this time and you're all being prepared for it. God gives all of his children different gifts. Mine is the gift of prophecy. You will each find yours in the days to come. In fact, you'll know yours by the end of today. And, someone you don't know yet, but your son does, will be there to help you figure it out. God bless you and your family. God has great plans for all of you. Good day."

Ulrich walked away, leaving Grant nearly speechless. "Yeah. Thanks. You, too."

Seconds later, Jill approached with the kids and, Grant slowly turned around to greet them.

"Kinsey," Grant asked, "who exactly is it that you have coming over for dinner tonight?"

CHAPTER EIGHT
Reunion

Grant was behind the house, on the patio, grilling two big slabs of flank steak that combined for a total weight of almost three and a half pounds, while the other members of the Snyder family were in the kitchen preparing the side dishes and dessert. Jill was putting together a Caesar salad, Kinsey was roasting both corn on the cob and fingerling potatoes in the oven, and Tatum was placing her ramekins filled with a baked crème brulee mixture into the refrigerator where they would remain until after dinner when she and Kinsey would take turns blow-torching an added top layer of sugar. Everyone was focused on their individual tasks but, no one was so focused that they didn't hear the doorbell.

Everyone froze, albeit for just a nanosecond, before their eyes went wide and their heads swiveled toward the door. Kinsey tossed his oven gloves on the counter and ran to open it, leaving the other three to wait impatiently before they could find out who his mystery guest would turn out to be.

Grant, Jill and Tatum all watched and listened as Kinsey greeted his friend and invited him inside. They were surprised to see that it wasn't a boy Kinsey's age but a man who appeared to be older than Grant.

Kinsey led his friend inside and immediately introduced him, "This is Ray Ewing. He was my substitute teacher in homeroom on Friday."

Everyone looked on with faces that didn't hide their confusion very well as Jill extended a hand to greet the stranger. "Nice to meet you, Ray. I'm Jill."

"It's nice to meet you, as well."

"Forgive the surprised expressions," Jill continued as Grant came inside and also greeted Ray. "Kinsey didn't tell us who his guest was and this is the first time he's brought one of his teachers home."

"He was also with me in Kadosh," Kinsey finally added after a brief and uncomfortable moment of silence.

It was as if a shockwave rumbled through the kitchen. Other than Friday at school, also between Kinsey and Ray, this was the first time since they returned that the word Kadosh had been uttered by any of the Snyders in the presence of someone outside of the four of them. Kinsey ended the stunned quiet by beginning to explain what Ray had told him about how almost forty years had passed since he had left Kadosh. Ray picked up the pieces and occasionally filled in the blanks.

Grant almost burned the flank steak, listening to his son and this stranger instead of paying attention to the grill. Jill reached into the bag of croutons and started eating them like popcorn. Tatum, simply took a seat at the table. None of them spoke. They just listened.

Soon, it was time to gather around the table and pray before dinner. It was the first break from the topic, which had begun to include Ray and Kinsey talking about their time together in Kadosh. Of course, Kinsey's sister and parents had heard it all before but, this was their first opportunity to hear any of it from someone else's perspective. When Grant finished praying, however, he shifted the conversation slightly by asking Ray about his family both before and after his time under the rule of Raum.

"Two very different stories," Ray admitted. "When I ended up in Kadosh, there were six of us. My parents and three sisters. God had always been important to my mom. She had us in church every Sunday. She was always a sweet woman. Still is. Warm and kind. My dad was essentially her opposite. He was cold and mean. But, there he was, every Sunday, right there with us in that same pew. He believed in God but, I think he also blamed Him for everything that was hard in his life."

Grant and Jill exchanged a look of mutual empathy for the story they were hearing and the environment Ray had grown up in.

"So," Ray continued, "as kids, we didn't really understand how those two people sat in that same pew every Sunday and had completely different responses to what we were all hearing preached. My sisters and I figured God must not make a difference and our parents were who they would be, with or without Him. Or, at least three of us did. I was the third child. My oldest sister, Adrienne, was just like my mom. She had an unwavering faith that truly affected who she was. Sheila, she was older than me but younger than Adrienne, she was the one who took my dad's bitterness the hardest. She became quietly angry. Maybe even took on some of that bitterness herself. There were times I didn't hear her speak for multiple days in a row. So, when my other sisters decided to set out to find us, she refused to go."

"She's still there?" asked Tatum.

"Assuming she's still alive," Ray started to answer, "yeah. She's still there. Adrienne and Deanna, she's my little sister, both made it to Raum's island. Only Deanna made it home though. Adrienne died shielding Deanna from one of those crazy, leafy monsters with all the teeth."

"I remember them," Tatum stated, reflectively. "Your sisters, I mean."

"I'm so sorry," Jill added.

"Hey," Ray injected with his usual positive attitude, "four of us made it home. And, my dad was forever changed. The tragedy of losing two sisters was rough. But, life for those of us who made it back, in spite of that loss, was better than it had been before Kadosh. When my dad died, he was actually excited about meeting his Maker. That wouldn't have been true before our experience. You take the good with the bad and accept that God has a purpose for all of it."

"What about now?" Grant asked. "Any family of your own?"

"No," Ray stated mater-of-factly. "Not anymore. I was married to the love of my life for twenty-two years. She passed the day after this last Christmas."

"Again," Jill started, "I'm so sorry."

"I appreciate it," Ray responded. "But, honestly, don't be. I'm not. I had twenty-two years of partnership with my best friend. Too few people can say that. And, the best part is, I'll see her again."

The Snyders all stared at Ray but shared a collective smile with one another.

"That's wonderful," Jill stated.

"It is," Ray agreed. "It was. It will be again. Twenty-two years with only one regret. So, I squared everything away, sold everything that wouldn't fit in the car, said goodbye to my mom, my sister and her family, and hit the road about a month ago. I'd seen Snohomish on a map before I left and thought of Kinsey. I knew in that moment that I just had to come check it out. The first job I've had since my wife passed was subbing for Kinsey's class. I figure that had to be fate. So, here I am. I don't know what happens next but, I do know this is where I'm supposed to be."

"You said you only have one regret," Grant began, "do you mind if I ask you what that is?"

"Grant," Jill admonished, "that's private."

"No," Ray reassured everyone, "that's okay. Really. My only regret has nothing to do with my wife. It's that I couldn't go back to Kadosh and save Sheila."

The Snyders finally broke their trance with Ray and glanced around the room at one another.

"What?" Ray asked, noticing the change in the room. "What'd I say?"

"What if I told you," Kinsey started, "that chance might still be possible?"

CHAPTER NINE
The Answer

As everyone finally began to eat their dinners, Kinsey told Ray about the dream he'd had, the light that had been turned off but blinked at him three times, the voice in the wind the next morning that spoke the same words from his Bible reading and which had also been used in the dream, and the fact that Ray was his substitute teacher that very same day. While his parents and sister already knew everything he was explaining, Ray was in awe as he heard it all for the first time.

"It's even more amazing when you say it all together like that," Grant injected into the conversation before taking a bite of his steak. After chewing and swallowing, he continued while cutting another bite. "Plus, this morning, at church, I had a man, who is apparently known to be some kind of a prophet, tell me that Kinsey's calling is real and that we're all being prepared for it."

"That's why God brought me here," Ray finally said as tears formed in his eyes. "First, he brought me out of Kadosh. I was able to grow up and spend twenty-two years with an amazing woman who is now at home with Him. And now, He brought me here, so I can go back to Kadosh with you, and I can find Sheila. And, this time, I can bring her back with me."

"You have been called out of the darkness only to be called back," Kinsey said, repeating the words spoken to him in his dream verbatim as he stood up from his chair, pushed it out behind him and walked around the table with a beaming smile on his face. "Not to remain in the darkness, or of the darkness, but to be the light of the Lord that leads others out of the darkness from which you have been called," Kinsey finished as he threw his arms around his old friend and tears fell down both of their cheeks. They squeezed each other tightly as their breathing grew deeper and Ray's tears became heavier.

"I've waited so long," Ray said after about twenty seconds. He squeezed Kinsey even tighter and patted him on the back, silently thanking him for the friendly, compassionate hug.

"It won't be much longer," Kinsey said as he finally let go, still smiling, and returned to his seat.

"You all can't possibly know what a gift this is to me," Ray added as he used his napkin to wipe the tears from his face.

"I can only imagine," Tatum admitted as she considered how badly she would have wanted to return if Kinsey hadn't come back with them. She had to lift her own napkin and dab her eyes as tears welled up in the corners.

Ray was still for nearly a minute as he contemplated everything he had just been told. In that moment, he finally processed what Grant had said about the prophet and had to ask, "What did the man at your church mean when he said we're all being prepared?"

"Well," Grant started as he finished chewing his bite of potato and swallowed, "he said that God gives all of his children different gifts and that we would each find out what ours is in the days to come. Then he told me that I would know mine by the end of today. Which, to be fair, I was told this man is a prophet but that hasn't happened yet and the day is just about over. Actually, Ray, you'll appreciate this, he said that someone I don't know yet, but my son does, would be there to help me figure it out. Any idea what my spiritual gift is?"

"Can't say I have any insight to offer on that," Ray admitted. "Of course, I don't know my own, either. So, despite what that guy told you, I'm not sure I'm the best person to ask."

"Guess that about seals the deal on that then," Grant sighed just before his body suddenly stiffened. He swiftly sat up straight in his chair. His chest puffed out and his head tilted up. He was looking directly in front of him but at no one in particular. Without another warning, his eyes closed and he began to speak, but not in his native tongue.

"Unjala skiata mukiliata skiata makatia," he stated as if in a trance. "Don koraroo duesuekoo sawdinki karere doemoemoemoe soso. Shan vumoomoomoo sokose eepee kinomoton teekaron tekilabow leinkeikei seekeiralow."

As Grant's body slumped forward and his eyes opened, he immediately started looking around the table. Jill and the kids stared back at him in both puzzled disbelief and deep concern.

"What was that?" Jill finally asked.

"Yeah," Kinsey added, "at first it sounded like you thought you were at Starbucks, trying to order some kind of specialty macchiato. But, then . . . well, then you started making some weird cow noises and talking about a tiki torch or something. You really lost me, Dad."

Ray quietly watched the group, puzzled by what he was hearing.

"I'm not sure what I just said either," Grant admitted, a little nervous and shaken up by the incident. He wasn't scared though. It was a strange sensation and one that left him feeling totally without control over himself for a moment. But, the take-over wasn't a hostile one. If anything, it was comforting.

Ray continued to watch and listen, becoming even more

confused.

"Maybe we're just discovering dad speaks Parseltongue," Tatum quipped, just as skeptical as the rest of her family.

"First," Kinsey responded, "I don't see any snakes. And, second, probably more importantly, this is not the wizarding world of Harry Potter."

"Then what was that?" Tatum shot back.

"Are you guys serious right now?" Ray finally asked. "No one understood what he was saying?"

"It was complete gibberish," Jill asserted.

"No," Ray insisted, "it wasn't."

"Then do you speak whatever language that was?" Jill asked.

"You mean English?" Ray asked, getting more animated as he became even more perplexed.

Kinsey looked at his friend with a furrowed brow. "That was not English, Ray."

"Well," Ray began to shoot back as his words trailed off and his mind pondered the possible explanations, "it sounded like English to me."

"Then what'd he say?" Kinsey demanded.

"I'm not even sure it was him doing the talking," Ray admitted as he began to figure out what they had just witnessed.

Kinsey stared at Ray for a moment, then glanced at his dad before returning his gaze to his friend. "Who, exactly, do you think it was?"

"The Holy Spirit," Ray calmly stated.

"He's right," Grant said as he looked around the table. "I could feel it. Like the warmth of the light on Raum's island. But, instead of the heat being on the outside and touching my skin, it was moving from the inside out. Nothing else could do that."

"Considering what you all were just telling me," Ray commented, "that was pretty timely."

"Timely?" Grant asked.

"I think we just figured out what two of those gifts are," Ray told Grant. "You just spoke in tongues and I have the interpretation."

"What is it?" Kinsey asked.

"Yeah," Grant blurted out in agreement with his son, "what's the interpretation?"

"What did he say?" Kinsey asked again but, instead of being skeptical like he had been a moment ago, he was waiting in great anticipation for the answer. He wasn't the only one. All four members of the Snyder family stared at Ray with bated breath.

"In a nutshell?" Ray began. "He was praising God and telling Him that the preparation was complete and we would be leaving in the morning."

CHAPTER TEN
Departure

The moment everyone realized that they were heading back to Kadosh the very next morning changed the course of the rest of the evening. The Snyders all knew it was coming but, none of them had realized it would be coming so soon.

Ray called his little sister, Deanna, and talked to her whole family. He told everyone he loved and missed them. For him, it was goodbye without saying the word or sounding any alarms. For them, it was just a nice call from Uncle Ray.

The Snyders were blessed enough to be there to say goodbye to one another in person. Before their last trip to Kadosh, they were in utter turmoil. This time, the tears were from a place of love instead of sorrow. Sure, there was fear, but it wasn't the same kind of fear they were experiencing the last time. Before, they didn't know Kadosh existed, let alone the fact that they were about to be transported to it. Fear, the last time, was for the future of a family that was tearing itself apart. Now, it was for the future of a family that had decided, together, to take the upcoming adventure out of obedience to the One who was calling them. The One who was responsible for the love they felt toward one another. And, the One whom they were trusting to bring them back so that they could be together again.

That trust, however, didn't alleviate all of the fears. But, it did make them easier to deal with. They knew that, whether they survived Kadosh a second time or not, they would be together again eventually. In the meantime, they were fulfilling the purpose for which they had been called. It wasn't easy. But, it was worth every bit of the anxiety they felt.

Ray didn't go home to his new apartment that night. He stayed on the Snyders' couch. But, he didn't sleep. No one did. Rest would have been an appropriate course of action but, each of the five of them slowly realized that it wasn't up to them. With their minds racing, a single minute of sleep wasn't an option. Instead, each of them picked up a Bible and read it.

Kinsey was the first to realize he wouldn't have that book anymore when he got to Kadosh. But, he was also the first to realize that, while that was physically true, he actually would have it with him because he had spent the last couple of years hiding the book in his heart, just as he had learned to do from the

CHAPTER TEN
Departure

The moment everyone realized that they were heading back to Kadosh the very next morning changed the course of the rest of the evening. The Snyders all knew it was coming but, none of them had realized it would be coming so soon.

Ray called his little sister, Deanna, and talked to her whole family. He told everyone he loved and missed them. For him, it was goodbye without saying the word or sounding any alarms. For them, it was just a nice call from Uncle Ray.

The Snyders were blessed enough to be there to say goodbye to one another in person. Before their last trip to Kadosh, they were in utter turmoil. This time, the tears were from a place of love instead of sorrow. Sure, there was fear, but it wasn't the same kind of fear they were experiencing the last time. Before, they didn't know Kadosh existed, let alone the fact that they were about to be transported to it. Fear, the last time, was for the future of a family that was tearing itself apart. Now, it was for the future of a family that had decided, together, to take the upcoming adventure out of obedience to the One who was calling them. The One who was responsible for the love they felt toward one another. And, the One whom they were trusting to bring them back so that they could be together again.

That trust, however, didn't alleviate all of the fears. But, it did make them easier to deal with. They knew that, whether they survived Kadosh a second time or not, they would be together again eventually. In the meantime, they were fulfilling the purpose for which they had been called. It wasn't easy. But, it was worth every bit of the anxiety they felt.

Ray didn't go home to his new apartment that night. He stayed on the Snyders' couch. But, he didn't sleep. No one did. Rest would have been an appropriate course of action but, each of the five of them slowly realized that it wasn't up to them. With their minds racing, a single minute of sleep wasn't an option. Instead, each of them picked up a Bible and read it.

Kinsey was the first to realize he wouldn't have that book anymore when he got to Kadosh. But, he was also the first to realize that, while that was physically true, he actually would have it with him because he had spent the last couple of years hiding the book in his heart, just as he had learned to do from the eleventh verse of Psalm 119, by reading it before and after he slept each night. The thought gave him great comfort.

By 4:00a.m., the Snyders and Ray were all back at the table where they had been eating dinner the night before. This time, everyone but Kinsey was drinking coffee. Kinsey opted for chocolate milk instead as the group discussed the game plan for their time in Kadosh. By 4:45a.m., Grant had decided to prove he could make bacon – without a microwave. He did a good job, too. Jill was so impressed that she added some scrambled eggs and toast to the mix and everyone enjoyed a nice breakfast as they realized it would be their last good meal for a while. By 6:00a.m., they all agreed that it was time to lock the house up and walk out into the woods where the Snyders had vanished three years earlier.

It was still dark so, Grant brought a flashlight to help guide them. They were quiet as they took the same path through the yard, the cul-de-sac and into the woods as they had done previously. Instead of jogging like they had before, they found themselves walking quite slowly, as if trying to delay the inevitable separation they all knew was coming.

But, as they got deeper into the woods, the spot where all four of the Snyders had disappeared and, ultimately, reappeared came into view.

"There it is," Grant said as he pointed with the flashlight.

The group's collective heartrate increased significantly as they approached the spot and glanced around at one another without saying a word. Everyone felt the same nervousness but there was also a certain level of excitement.

Ray was particularly excited, after almost forty years of waiting, to go find his sister, Sheila. He had spent a significant amount of his quiet time, over the course of the night, thinking about what it would be like when he finally encountered her. He knew he would want to embrace her immediately but, assumed she wouldn't recognize him and didn't want to freak her out.

Grant interrupted the silence when he asked the group to grab hands so he could pray as the first light began to peek into the night sky. He turned the flashlight off and shoved it in his back pocket as he took his wife's hand in his. He squeezed it tightly, knowing it would be the last time for a while, before then grabbing Kinsey's hand and doing the same.

The group formed a small circle and Grant began to thank God for the opportunity that lay ahead of them. He thanked Him for choosing them and then asked for wisdom, guidance and protection on their journey. It was during the prayer when all five of them felt the same warmth billow up within them that they had felt on the outside when the light visited them on Raum's island. It was also the same warmth that Grant had felt the night before when he suddenly spoke in a language that only Ray had understood. Soon, it felt as though the warmth was gushing out of every pore on their skin and the volume was increasing until they felt like they might explode into a billion pieces. But, it wasn't scary, it felt so good they didn't want it to stop. Slowly, with their eyes still closed from praying, their hands released from one another and they felt themselves float off of the ground.

~

Suddenly, Kinsey became aware of a rushing sound as if someone had just opened the window in a car going a hundred miles per hour. But, he noticed that he didn't feel any wind pushing against him. It still felt as though what was inside of him was bursting out instead. He gradually opened his eyes and that's when he noticed the beauty that surrounded him. It was all light and represented every color he'd ever seen, and hundreds more that he was seeing for the first time.

~

The light seemed to have a movement to it. It wasn't just the fact that Tatum was traveling through it, although she was, the light also had a rhythmic, steady pulse to it. Like a heartbeat. The light was contracting and expanding ever so slightly.

~

Jill was disappointed to see the light begin to dissipate, and with it, the warm feeling that had been teeming out from within her. However, as the light was replaced by darkness, it dawned on her that darkness was what she had immediately seen the first time she had been transported to Kadosh. Then she woke up without a memory of the trip. She briefly wondered if she would forget this time, too. But, then she reasoned that this trip was different. Her family had been called to Kadosh by Raum before. This time, it was God calling them. That's why they were awake and that's why they both felt the warmth and saw the light.

~

As the feeling within Grant returned to what he would consider normal, he also noticed that the brilliant light was completely gone. All that was left was the pale glow of the moon above him. It was about the same time that he felt his feet gently touch the ground.

"We made it."

Ray's voice startled Grant, who didn't expect anyone to be with him, almost as much as the touch of Max's hand on his back had shortly after his arrival the first time. Grant stared at Ray who was looking at their surroundings.

"We're in Kadosh."

PART THREE
Kadosh

CHAPTER ELEVEN
In The Dark

"What are you doing here?" Grant asked, still puzzled by Ray's presence.

"What do you mean?" Ray asked, taken aback by Grant's confusion and quietly hoping Grant hadn't suffered a head injury, before insisting, "I came with you."

"I know that. I mean, what are you doing here with me instead of with Kinsey?"

"I'm older than you are, Grant."

"Oh," Grant sighed as he put the pieces together. "Right. I guess I just imagined us all going back to the islands we were on before. It never dawned on me that . . . Well, anyway, I guess that does make sense."

"You know what doesn't make sense?" Ray asked, changing the topic of conversation.

"What's that?"

"The fact that it's night," Ray said, pointing to the sky. "Never, in all the years I was here before, did anyone ever show up when it wasn't daylight. Doesn't look like there's anyone here to greet us either."

"Maybe nobody else is expecting new arrivals at night."

"Or, maybe it's something else."

"Something else?" Grant instinctively reached for his flashlight while he waited for a response but didn't get either. The flashlight obviously hadn't made it to Kadosh and Ray wasn't giving him an answer. Finally, he prodded, "Like what?"

"I don't know," Ray admitted. "Just feels off. Like something is different. Not with us. With Kadosh."

~

Tatum debated about staying right where she was until morning but, fairly quickly, decided it was too frightening to stay all alone and so exposed at night. She stood on a grassy patch of land, staring across the white sand at the dark water with the reflection of the eerie moon on its surface. She knew she could take cover in the jungle behind her but that seemed even scarier.

Deciding it would feel better to be on the move, she glanced up and down the beach in both directions, trying to remember which way Moirah had led her from that same spot. Unfortunately, three years had passed and the previous journey had taken place in the daylight. The view left felt correct, for some reason, so she turned and began to walk.

~

The moonlight was barely shining through the cracks of the thick canopy created by the towering trees around Jill. Therefore, she was forced to take baby steps through almost total darkness. Just a few feet from where she started, Jill stumbled as her foot hit a tree root that had grown above the ground but she kept her balance, placing a hand on the trunk of that same tree to feel her way past it.

She was far more aware of the sounds of the jungle this time then she had been when she arrived in Kadosh by surprise. The amazing volume of chirps, buzzes, trills and hums made her very aware of the fact that living creatures of all kinds were surrounding her. She just couldn't see any of them.

Stepping through a small stream and passing a massive mahogany tree, Jill suddenly spotted a clearing, where moonlight was shining in abundance. It was about five hundred feet away and her view of it was similar to seeing a light at the end of a tunnel.

Just after picking up the pace a bit, Jill was abruptly stopped in her tracks when she ran into a fallen tree. She banged her knee and it doubled her over, causing her to fall onto the trunk. While it hurt, she was so anxious to get to the light she saw ahead that she refused to let it slow her down. She quickly shook the minor injury off, climbed over the tree and continued to trek toward her goal.

~

Kinsey had come to the same log, that acted as a bridge from one side of the narrow river to the other, that he had crossed three years earlier with Ray. He wished Ray was with him now, too. But, by this time, Kinsey had realized that Ray must be with his dad on the island with all of the men.

Remembering how nervous he was to walk on the log the first time, Kinsey chuckled to himself as he quickly crossed over the river and jumped off of the log. He started making his way up the steep hill when the rain began to fall. Briefly looking back, Kinsey was thankful he had made it past the river before the rain caused the log to become wet and slippery. But, as both the steepness of the hill and the volume of the rainfall increased, he quickly realized that he would soon be trudging through mud.

~

Grant and Ray stopped under a large evergreen tree to get out of the noisily pouring rain as Grant yelled, "That came on quick!"

"Real quick," Ray agreed. "You think Raum has something to do with that? Maybe he already knows we're back."

"Wouldn't surprise me," Grant admitted. "We're in Kadosh. Nothing surprises me here."

~

Jill stood in the clearing and slowly turned in a circle, wondering both where to go from there and how she was going to muster up the courage to head back into the darkness. She had traded the inability to see for a heavy dose of rain that was drenching her but, she preferred the rain to the terrifying feeling of not knowing where she was going or what was lurking in the dark.

However, she knew she wouldn't be able to make any progress by standing still. So, she chose what she believed was the same direction she was going when she first saw the clearing and started to walk. She hoped, desperately, that the campsite she remembered was not very far away and, even more importantly, that the women hadn't moved on to another location.

~

The previously still water now had raindrops dancing all over the top of it. Tatum's slow walk had turned into a light jog, as if she could somehow outrun the rain, but it was getting easier as the sand developed into a harder surface the wetter it became. She considered taking cover under a tree but she wanted to keep moving and she was afraid of what could be waiting for her in the darkness if she left the safer feeling and more well-lit beach.

~

With his feet slipping and sliding on the muddy hillside, Kinsey was fighting his way toward the top. The rain was growing heavier by the minute and the ground beneath his feet was becoming increasingly unstable. His hands were muddy from catching himself while falling, but he was able to rinse them off in the downpour. *God's faucet,* he thought to himself. Kinsey had never experienced anything like it and it wasn't lost on him that this far rougher start to his time in Kadosh could be a sign of things to come.

Finally, both feet slipped simultaneously and he fell flat on the ground. Sliding backward several yards, Kinsey stopped and rolled over onto his back. He was completely caked in mud from head to toe. He laid there for about two minutes and let the rain rinse him off. *Make that God's shower,* he added in his head.

Kinsey stood and continued his march up the muddy hillside. As he finally reached the top, he squinted to see through the pouring rain because, in the distance, he was almost certain he was finally seeing another boy.

CHAPTER TWELVE
New Faces

"Hey!" Kinsey yelled as loud as he could, raising his arms in the air and waving his hands wildly, trying to be seen by the boy who was taking cover under a tree about half way down the other side of the hill. "Up here!" he continued.

He was so excited to see the other boy that his feet lifted off of the ground as he unintentionally jumped into the air. When he came back down, he slipped again. But, instead of landing on his front like he had each time he had slipped coming up the hill, he landed square on his back with his legs still up in the air. Before his legs even hit the ground, he had already begun the long slide toward the bottom of the hill.

Luckily, also different from his previous stumbles, he was sliding on the side of the hill he needed to go down rather than the side he had just come up. In fact, he soon passed the boy he had seen, who Kinsey was noticing for the first time was also with another boy, and they both watched him slide by with confused looks on their faces. The first boy even raised his right hand, tentatively waving back at Kinsey.

As his body finally came to a stop, Kinsey rolled over and looked behind him at the two unfamiliar boys. They were about a hundred feet away and walking toward him. He pushed himself up and out of the mud. Finally, he sat on the backs of his legs as some of the mud he was covered in oozed from his clothing and body, ultimately dumping back onto the ground from where it had originally come.

The second boy was the first to greet Kinsey, immediately extending a hand. "Let's get you up and out of the rain," he said.

Kinsey took his hand and accepted his help in getting to his feet before following them to a different tree that was only about fifteen feet away. He stood in the rain for a moment and rinsed his hands before raising them up to his face and using the rain like a shower to clean himself off. Finally, he joined the other two boys beneath the protective branches of the massive chestnut tree.

"I'm Pablo," the second boy said as he extended his hand again, silently thankful that the hand he would receive in return would be cleaner this time.

"Kinsey," came the reply as Kinsey shook his hand before

CHAPTER TWELVE
New Faces

"Hey!" Kinsey yelled as loud as he could, raising his arms in the air and waving his hands wildly, trying to be seen by the boy who was taking cover under a tree about half way down the other side of the hill. "Up here!" he continued.

He was so excited to see the other boy that his feet lifted off of the ground as he unintentionally jumped into the air. When he came back down, he slipped again. But, instead of landing on his front like he had each time he had slipped coming up the hill, he landed square on his back with his legs still up in the air. Before his legs even hit the ground, he had already begun the long slide toward the bottom of the hill.

Luckily, also different from his previous stumbles, he was sliding on the side of the hill he needed to go down rather than the side he had just come up. In fact, he soon passed the boy he had seen, who Kinsey was noticing for the first time was also with another boy, and they both watched him slide by with confused looks on their faces. The first boy even raised his right hand, tentatively waving back at Kinsey.

As his body finally came to a stop, Kinsey rolled over and looked behind him at the two unfamiliar boys. They were about a hundred feet away and walking toward him. He pushed himself up and out of the mud. Finally, he sat on the backs of his legs as some of the mud he was covered in oozed from his clothing and body, ultimately dumping back onto the ground from where it had originally come.

The second boy was the first to greet Kinsey, immediately extending a hand. “Let’s get you up and out of the rain,” he said.

Kinsey took his hand and accepted his help in getting to his feet before following them to a different tree that was only about fifteen feet away. He stood in the rain for a moment and rinsed his hands before raising them up to his face and using the rain like a shower to clean himself off. Finally, he joined the other two boys beneath the protective branches of the massive chestnut tree.

“I’m Pablo,” the second boy said as he extended his hand again, silently thankful that the hand he would receive in return would be cleaner this time.

“Kinsey,” came the reply as Kinsey shook his hand before

turning to the other boy and shaking his, too.

"Caleb," is all the boy said.

"How long have you been here?" Pablo asked, to Kinsey's surprise.

~

"I don't know," Tatum responded honestly. "A few hours?"

"Good," Tatum's new acquaintance, Ling, exclaimed. "You found us quickly then.

"I did?"

"We sometimes find people who have been out here on their own for weeks," the other girl, Fabia, added. "The truth is," she continued, "we don't know how many people we haven't been able to find at all. I would imagine there are a lot of girls out here we haven't found and they haven't found us. It would be horrible trying to survive out here on your own. Probably a lot of them don't last very long."

"Why is it so hard to find them?"

"I hear it used to be a lot easier but, everything changed when Kadosh went dark."

"Dark?" Tatum asked, sincerely puzzled. "What do you mean it went dark?"

"Look around," Fabia shot back, not realizing that Tatum

seemed to know what she meant by Kadosh.

"Isn't it just nighttime right now?"

Ling shrugged her shoulders.

"You don't know if it's nighttime?"

"It's been dark for a really long time," Fabia acknowledged. "Since before either of us got here."

"How long?" Tatum asked, quickly determining that she was being told there was no longer any daylight in Kadosh and beginning to wonder how the timing of the darkness lined up with her previous departure. "Years?"

Ling shrugged her shoulders again.

"We don't even know how long we've been here," Fabia admitted with a tone that expressed deep sadness. "It's impossible to tell time here."

"It didn't used to be," Tatum declared.

"That's what we've heard," Fabia agreed as both she and Ling recognized the implications of Tatum's statement.

Ling looked Tatum square in the eyes and asked, "How would you know that?"

~

"This isn't my first time in Kadosh," Jill said as her eyes darted back and forth between Hannah and Olivia, fully anticipating the expressions of shock that were coming her way.

"You've been here before?" Olivia asked, confused by the idea.

"That means you got out," Hannah stated in disbelief. "No one gets out."

"I did," Jill declared. "Three years ago."

"There's no way," Hannah stated as she shook her head. "It's impossible."

"It's not," Jill insisted. "I've done it. My whole family did. Others, too."

"I don't believe you," Hannah said as she looked away.

"How?" Olivia asked, softly.

~

"I'll be honest," Grant started as he looked directly into Ben's blue eyes, "it wasn't easy. People got hurt. Some died." Grant took a deep breath as his demeanor transitioned from pain to gratitude and his gaze moved to Ben's companion, Nicolai. "But, a lot of us made it home."

~

Minutes passed before anyone spoke again. The incessant

sound of the rain pummeling the earth was the only noise audible until Pablo broke the silence.

"We should get back to camp."

"You don't want to wait out the rain?" Caleb asked.

"Doesn't look like it's going to let up anytime soon," Pablo advocated. "I don't know about you but, I don't want to wait too much longer before I get a bite to eat."

"Speaking of eating, we were the ones who were supposed to come back with food."

"Well, we're going back with Kinsey instead."

"I'm not food though," Kinsey chimed in half serious and half joking but got no response. "Right?"

"It's not safe in the rain," Caleb insisted as quietly as he could while still being heard over the pounding rain drops and continuing to ignore Kinsey.

"It's not safe in the mud after the rain either," Pablo insisted. "Unless you want to wait around for everything to dry out. Meanwhile, we'll all starve to death. Does that sound fun to you? Or, even safe?"

While Caleb shook his head, Kinsey thought about what an odd but familiar pairing Pablo and Caleb were. It took him a bit but, Kinsey finally figured out what seemed so familiar. Pablo's inflated masculine qualities reminded him of his dad while Caleb's meekness reminded him more of himself before Kadosh.

Kinsey was already certain that he was going to like both of them and that gave him some comfort. But, he still had to ask one more time.

"I'm not food, right?"

"Of course you're not food," Caleb vowed.

"Unless we get REALLY hungry," Pablo added. "Or, you keep flapping your mouth about leaving Kadosh."

~

"I don't want to hear any more of that nonsense when we get back there," Nicolai directed at Grant. "No use giving anyone false hope."

"There is if it's not false," Ray fired back.

"Don't make me leave you two out here," Nicolai threatened.

"Wouldn't do you any good," Grant insisted. "We know our way back to camp because, like I said, we've been there before."

Nicolai just stared at Grant, searching for something to say but unable to find anything. Instead, he just grunted and stormed out from underneath the safety of the tree.

Ben shot Grant a quick smile before following Nicolai's lead. Grant sighed as he watched them go for a moment before finally gesturing to Ray and hustling to catch up. In that moment, he was quickly reminded of the fight he faced when he first announced to the men in camp that he was determined to set out and find his family. He also knew that the same fight was waiting for him when he returned but he was thankful that he had Ray as a partner this time because that return was just moments away.

CHAPTER THIRTEEN
Familiar Faces

Jill was right behind Olivia, whose soaking wet blonde hair was pasted to her neck and back, reflecting the moonlight. Olivia was directly behind Hannah as the three of them trekked through the exotic jungle in the torrential rainfall.

As Jill thought back on her last trip to camp, when she had first arrived in Kadosh, and how her mind was fixated on her family while she followed her new friend Elaine, she couldn't help but chuckle to herself about how different things were this time around. Of course, she was concerned about her family now as well. But, her experience having done this once already, gave her some knowledge and confidence that wasn't there before and it freed her mind up to consider her new acquaintances.

Physically, they appeared very different from one another. While they all stood under the tree, Jill had observed Olivia's pale skin, blue eyes, rounded lips, and high-boned but plump cheeks. She was now mentally contrasting those observations with Hannah's shorter and more dense black hair, dark skin and brown eyes. Hannah was also thinner and taller than Olivia.

So far, their personality traits were less distinguishable. Both seemed good-hearted, even nurturing. While Hannah was the one who had adamantly objected to the idea that leaving Kadosh was a possibility, she seemed a little calmer and more calculated than Olivia. For different reasons, she was looking forward to getting to know both of them in the days to come.

~

Like her mother, Tatum had two new traveling companions who were in fairly stark contrast to one another. And, while it showed physically, it had already become pretty obvious in their personality differences, too. Ling was from China but, she hadn't told Tatum that. Fabia had told her on Ling's behalf. That wasn't just because Ling spoke softly and quietly in spite of her impressive English vocabulary, it was also because Fabia did most of the talking. In fact, Tatum was estimating that, since they met, Fabia had spoken three or four times as many words as Tatum and Ling combined. And, she had begun to wonder if Fabia was ever going to shut up.

"Yeah," Fabia continued her discourse, "I got in all kinds of trouble as a kid. I was always running and jumping, knocking other kids over and breaking stuff."

Tatum had started to tune Fabia out as she decided Fabia was the kind of girl she could be friends with but might be best in small doses. Her grandiose energy was, after all, already a little overwhelming. Ling's shy and humble attitude, on the other hand, was far easier to handle but it would also make her more difficult to get to know.

However, getting to know Ling would have to wait anyway. At least, for a little while. Tatum suddenly spotted something very familiar to her. It was the rock formation she and Moirah climbed that separated two beautiful beaches and Tatum knew instantly that the girls' campsite was waiting on the other side.

~

Grant and Ray followed Ben and Nicolai into the valley and approached the familiar middle-age-like village that quickly reminded Grant of movies about Robin Hood just as it had the first time he laid eyes on it. Of course, it had been daylight then. But, the connection was the same, even though the darkness obscured a lot more of the details from Grant's line of vision.

It was clear that a fire had been blazing earlier, in the middle of the village, but the heavy rain had since reduced it to billowing smoke. That rain was also the reason that very few of the men were outside of their dwellings.

But, it didn't take long for those who were outside, coupled with the many peeking out from within their little huts, to begin noticing that Ben and Nicolai had returned with two other men. As a result, Grant and Ray quickly became the center of attention.

It was about that same time that the rain abruptly stopped as if someone had turned off the spigot and Grant briefly wondered if Raum had done exactly that. He ran his hand through his sopping wet hair and flung a fistful of water to the ground like he was just stepping out of the shower. Unfortunately, this shower was a cold one and he hadn't taken off his clothes before stepping into it. Weighed down, both physically and emotionally, Grant couldn't help but consider how miserable this return to Kadosh had already been. But, he knew Raum would want him to stay focused on the misery rather than the mission. Grant resolved, right then and there, that the mission would consume his thoughts and decision making until he was once again reunited with his family.

~

Kinsey scanned the faces of the boys who had come out to

greet him. He recognized quite a few of them. But, he was surprised by how many new faces there were, too.

As he was greeted by a number of the boys he remembered, and who remembered him as well, he could see the demeanor of both Pablo and Caleb begin to change. *They probably weren't sure whether or not to believe me*, he decided.

But, now they were seeing with their own eyes that he really had been to Kadosh before and they were wondering if they could get out, too. Kinsey Snyder had officially returned to a place of total despair but, with him, he had brought hope.

Unfortunately, Raum wasn't the only foe he would be facing. Emerging from the small crowd of both familiar and unfamiliar faces, was someone Kinsey had not looked forward to seeing again. Trevor stepped in front of him and stood firm, like a tall oak tree with shallow but widespread roots.

"What are you doing back here?" Trevor asked with a scowl that seemed even more severe than it had been three years earlier.

~

Tatum was so stunned by the question, coming from a pretty blonde girl named Yana that she remembered from before but had never really gotten to know, that she didn't immediately know how to answer it. It felt as though her heart rate had tripled and her mind had suddenly gone completely blank. *I know why I'm here,* she thought to herself. *Why aren't there any words coming out of my mouth?*

As her eyes scanned the faces of the girls that had gathered and she realized that more were coming, her nervousness only grew worse. This was a new sensation for Tatum, who was typically poised and composed, and she immediately hated it. *Why can't I think?* She silently wondered.

Then, out of nowhere, her eyes focused in on one girl who was slowly walking toward the group and she quickly recognized her as Ray's sister, Sheila. Her heartrate started to slow down and she grew calm with confidence. Of course she knew why she was there. Everything became clear again and a smile formed on her face for the first time since she had left home.

~

Grant patted Ray on the shoulder, signaling to his new friend that he would take the lead on this announcement. He walked in front of the crowd and looked the men in the eyes, like the commander of an army ready to fire up the troops before taking them into battle.

He got to the end of the line and turned to walk back toward Ray as he finally began to speak, "Many of you know we have been here before. You remember me. You remember that I led a group on a quest to find our families. What you don't know, is that we did find them. We did get home. But, we've returned. We came back for one purpose, and one purpose alone . . . "

CHAPTER FOURTEEN
The Mission

" . . . to take the rest of you," Tatum continued declaring, "each and every one of you, to find your families and send you home as well."

Silence.

Tatum glanced around, waiting for something to happen but nothing did. She didn't necessarily expect a round of applause, wild cheers or even a 'thank you.' In fact, she really didn't have expectations. But, if she had, silence would not have been among them. Mockery, laughter or a series of questions would all have made the list long before silence would have even been considered. But, silence is exactly what she found herself facing. After waiting for what felt like several minutes, she did the only think she could think of. She asked a question of them.

"Do you hear what I'm telling you? You can go ho - "

~

"We heard your sales pitch," came the voice of Diane, the woman who had been so difficult for Jill to deal with three years earlier, "we're just not buyin' it. We weren't before and we're still not. For all we know, you got everyone killed the first time and it just took you until now to find your way back here."

"If that were true," Jill responded, "why would I want to do it all over again?"

"You were crazy then and you're crazy now," Diane said as she stepped out of the crowd to approach Jill. "End of story."

"Maybe," Jill seemed to concede before taking a step forward to lock eyes with Diane. There were less than three feet between the two as Jill finished her thought, "Or, maybe I'm telling the truth."

~

"He is," Ray stepped between Grant and the man he was arguing with.

"And," the man quickly asked, "who are you?"

"Ray Ewing," Ray answered, introducing himself and extending a hand to shake, hoping to disarm the situation before it escalated any further.

"Victor," came the response, along with a handshake. "Were you here before, too?"

"Yeah, well, no, not exactly."

"Seems like a fairly simple question," Victor said, growing even more skeptical.

"I was in Kadosh before but, not on this island." Ray heard the murmurs in the crowd and quickly decided to try and answer the questions before they were asked. "It was about forty years ago. Well, forty years back home. I'm guessing it was more like three here. Maybe less. I still don't totally understand how time works here. But, I was friends with Grant's son, Kinsey. He helped me get home. I went back to my own time and he went back to his. Now we've both come back but, for he and Grant it's only been three years. For me, well, like I said before, it's been about forty years for me."

Victor could feel the crowd's desire for more information as the murmuring continued and he knew he needed to quash it so he said the only thing he could think of, "Only crazy people would come back to this place on purpose. You're lying."

~

"So," Kinsey quipped, "you're saying crazy is no longer an option?"

"I still think you're crazy," Trevor fired back, "but you're also a liar and I'm not going to let you give anyone else false hope. I'm not going to let you get anyone else killed."

Kinsey's gaze fell from Trevor's face and he stared at the dark ground for a moment. For the first time in three years, he realized that Trevor wasn't the problem. Sure, Trevor had been a thorn in Kinsey's side when he was in Kadosh before. But, Trevor believed he was doing the right thing. Kinsey remembered his mom once telling him that no one is ever wrong on purpose. So, it wasn't Trevor that was the problem. It was the false hopelessness that Trevor and so many others had bought into that was really to blame.

Kinsey was tempted to gloss over the fact that people had gotten hurt and even killed on the previous journey in order to keep hope alive in them but, he quickly reminded himself that the Bible had taught him it wasn't his job to protect people from the truth but to speak the truth, always, and let God take care of the rest. Besides, he had already told Caleb and Pablo as much so, he might as well come clean now.

"I'm not lying," he said as his head rose and he began to look the crowd of boys in the eyes, one by one. "I will never lie to you. People did get hurt. Some even died. But, the ones who made it got to go home. They got to go back and be with their families. They got to tell each other they were sorry and that they loved one another. They traded in anger and misery for love and joy. Sorrow and regret for hope and a future that I'm confident every single one of them would tell you was worth the effort they put in to get it."

~

"Who doesn't want that?" Tatum asked the whole group as she finished her short speech. She looked around and saw some heads nodding in agreement but when her gaze fixed back on Irisa, the large and aggressive woman right in front of her, all she got back was a look of hatred.

"Not everyone has somebody out there waiting for them," Irisa insisted.

"Even if that's true," Tatum began to earnestly ask, "don't you want to go home? Or, at the very least, get out of this place?"

"Home isn't any better than this place."

"That can't be true," Tatum sincerely stated.

"How would you know?" Irisa was getting even angrier.

"I don't know what home is like for you," Tatum admitted. "I couldn't possibly know that. But, I do know this place."

"You don't know anything."

"I know you sound hopeless. That's what Kadosh does to people. But, I also know you don't have to stay that way."

~

"So," Diane began as she stared into Jill's eyes, "that's it, huh? You came to save us?"

"I'm not here to save anyone," Jill asserted. "But, I am here to show you how you can be saved."

"I've seen that movie before. I didn't like the ending."

"That's because we saw two different endings," Jill fired back.

"You just admitted you got people killed."

"I also told you a lot of people got to go home. Or, are you only listening to the parts you want to hear?"

"Actually," Diane fumed before storming off, "I don't want to hear any of it."

~

"Some things never change," Ray quipped.

"Even when the people do," Grant agreed before turning to the crowd, some of whom had already began to disperse and follow Victor. "It doesn't have to stay this way. You don't have to be trapped in Kadosh."

"I told you not to do this," Niccolai shouted as he tapped Ben on the shoulder, signaling for him to follow, and began to back up in order to go with Victor, but continued to face Grant while finishing his thought first. "You're dividing us. And, you'll probably get some of us killed. You're not making anything better."

~

Kinsey silently watched most of the crowd turn and follow Trevor away from him, many of them returning to their various dwellings. But, instead of focusing on the facts that he didn't yet know where he was going to sleep that night or that he had trapped himself back in Kadosh, once again separated from the family he had nearly died to be reunited with, he simply smiled at the eight boys who remained in front of him.

"It's a start," he told them. "But, we have a lot of work to do."

PART FOUR
Recruiting

CHAPTER FIFTEEN
The More Things Change

Grant was thankful to have been offered shelter by two of the men who had stayed behind with him when most of the rest of the group had followed Victor back to their dwellings. Unfortunately, they weren't prepared for him so, while he appreciated the roof that would protect him from any additional rainfall, the hard ground he was lying on didn't exactly invite sleep. Having not slept at all the night before, he prayed that exhaustion would eventually overtake him and that his body would force him to get the rest he knew he desperately needed.

In the meantime, he began to appreciate the fact that he didn't hear any cars, airplanes or any other city sounds. He liked quiet and space. That's one of the things that had drawn him to move Jill and the kids out to Snohomish in the first place. But, what some people called progress had spread like a virus and was engulfing his beloved country lifestyle.

He remembered a business trip to Los Angeles two years earlier. It was the first time he had ever been there and, everyone warned him how much he was going to hate the traffic. He had a window seat when his plane landed at LAX and he saw first-hand what a sprawling city Los Angeles was. But, when he got into his rental car and began to experience the L.A. traffic for himself, he quickly decided it wasn't all that different from back home. Sure, there were more people, cars and more freeways with more lanes. But, still, it wasn't really any different. It was just more of the same thing. Traffic was still bumper to bumper and plaguing nearly every street on the map.

His trip to Los Angeles made him dislike so called progress even more than he had before he left. He went home and grew increasingly claustrophobic, even trying to convince Jill to move further out into the country to get away from it all. But, she wanted them both to stay closer to their work and for the kids to remain in their schools with their friends. She promised they could move to what she called "the sticks" when they finally retired. In fact, she insisted they would move as far out as he wanted to go. Until then, weekend fishing trips would have to suffice. And, apparently, a trip to Kadosh had been thrown in as a bonus.

The truth is, there had always been a little bit of cowboy in

Grant. He even grew up loving the old classic western movies, particularly the ones starring Clint Eastwood. He still appreciated them and even liked a lot of the more modern Hollywood attempts like the *Young Guns* movies, *The Assassination of Jessee James by the Coward Robert Ford,* and the remakes of *3:10 to Yuma* and *True Grit.* He had also enjoyed Eastwood's more modern attempt called *Unforgiven* as well as the films *Tombstone, The Revenant* and a number starring one of Grant's favorite actors, Kevin Costner, like *Silverado, Dances with Wolves, Wyatt Earp* and *Open Range.*

He had promised himself, however, while growing up, that he would never allow himself to like country music. Then Garth Brooks happened. Garth was followed up by a college roommate named Willie who introduced him to Alan Jackson and, suddenly, Grant found himself embracing all of the classics like Merle Haggard, Patsy Cline, Waylon Jennings, Loretta Lynn and Johnny Cash. By that point, the cowboy's hibernation was over and he would never return to his cave.

Finally, unlike the cowboy within, as Grant began to calculate the years until retirement, exhaustion indeed overtook him. Instead of panicking when the cost of a modern college education for two kids crossed his mind, the math overwhelmed him so much that he simply drifted off to sleep. Luckily, all the discomfort the ground was offering wasn't enough to wake him before the sun had risen. Good thing, too, because there would be no sunrise in Kadosh. In fact, there was no telling what time of day or night Grant was falling asleep or waking up, how long he slept, or any way of keeping any kind of schedule. Kadosh, after all, was in a perpetual state of darkness.

~

When Tatum woke up, her mind was not on movies or music. It wasn't on college, traffic, finances or even home. She did briefly consider how hard the ground was that she had been sleeping on as she slowly stood up and found it difficult to move. She also considered the fact that, while anxious and a bit nervous this time too, she had previously spent the first hours of her arrival at camp throwing up. And, she recalled learning later that her mom had done the very same thing. But, so far, Tatum was vomit free and had begun focusing on ideas for how to recruit more girls to join her on the journey home.

~

Walking around the familiar village of jungle huts, Jill began to notice the deterioration that had taken place in her absence. She reasoned that she hadn't looked as close when she first arrived and that everything is less noticeable in the dark. Of course, it was still dark, but she now found herself with a moment to truly take in her surroundings.

The first thing she spotted was a wall on the outside of a hut that appeared to have been damaged, possibly in a storm, and then patched with leaves similar to how she had seen, back home, broken windows on both cars and houses temporarily patched with sheets of plastic. Looking around the village, she realized this was a pattern and the presumably temporary patch jobs had developed into the permanent solution.

Her gaze suddenly switched from the buildings to the women themselves. Granted, gaining weight had always been next to impossible in Kadosh. But, Jill was noticing for the first time that the women looked unhealthy. They weren't quite emaciated but they were, at the very least, malnourished.

That's when she realized the women in the village were not working the way they had been in the past. She had been impressed, when she saw the village for the first time, with how it had become a functioning community. It now looked like the darkness had caused the community to steadily decline and Jill quickly realized that, if that pattern continued, it could soon be on the verge of collapsing altogether.

~

Kinsey decided that the deterioration of his surroundings was not the problem he was there to solve. In fact, if he played it right, rather than trying to fix anything, he could use that deterioration to his advantage in convincing the other boys that this place would not, and could not be their permanent home.

Raum had always been the oppressor in Kadosh. That fact was not new. But, this novel tactic of keeping the people in total darkness had obviously made it a lot harder to function. Their only light came from the ever-present night sky and the fires they built. This had made venturing into the woods to hunt for food or gather supplies, while still necessary, far more dangerous than it had been three years ago.

As if reading Kinsey's mind, the two boys who had given him a place to sleep, Mason and Zach, approached with a problem.

"He's not going to let any of us eat," Zach blurted out.

"Who?" Kinsey asked. "Trevor?"

"Yeah," Zach said as Mason took over.

"He says anyone who sides with you is on his own. He's going to starve us until we side with him. What are we going to do?"

"They're having trouble finding food anyway," Kinsey quickly responded. "I say we hunt."

CHAPTER SIXTEEN
The Hunt

Quietly leading two other girls into what she had discovered three years earlier was a weapons storage hut, Tatum was relieved to learn that this was one of the few things that hadn't changed in her absence. She looked around the hut, trying to determine what would be most useful for the girls on their mission to find food. She was certain that catching a fish or two wasn't going to feed everyone. After all, Jesus was the only one she knew who had managed to stretch a few fish and loaves of bread into a meal for the masses. She was going to have to try and find something more substantial. But, the truth was, she didn't have any way of knowing just yet what that would wind up being.

With a slight shrug of the shoulders, she reached forward and began acquiring three sets of her weapon of choice. She handed each of the girls a bow and a quiver full of arrows, then took the same for herself before signaling her new friends to silently slip back out of the hut and jog away from both the hut and the ocean waters into a part of the island she had never been before.

~

Slinking off into the dark forest with their spears in hand, Grant led Ray and their new friend, Qasim, who had given them a place to sleep earlier, toward what all three of them hoped would be their next meal. Unfortunately, they didn't yet know what that meal would be or where they would find it. But, Grant was calm and confident that God would provide something before they returned. He just hoped that return would be sooner than later.

~

Wendy and Brianna followed Jill, quietly creeping further into the dense jungle and hoping to come across something edible and at least somewhat appetizing. Nearly an hour and just over two miles from camp, they came across a fallen tree about ten feet outside of a small clearing. The moon-lit open space was similar to the one Jill had found shortly after arriving in Kadosh but significantly smaller. She signaled the women to kneel down behind the tree and then did so herself.

"Now what?" Brianna asked, growing impatient.

"Now we wait," Jill answered, telling Brianna exactly what she didn't want to hear.

"Wait for what?" Wendy injected.

"We wait for an animal to walk into that clearing," Jill said.

"That's the big plan?" Brianna asked, continuing to show her lack of patience. "What if it doesn't happen?"

"It will," Jill insisted. "Eventually."

"How eventual are we talking about here?" Brianna persisted.

"Do you honestly think I could possibly know the answer to that question?" Jill pushed back.

Brianna stared at Jill briefly before sheepishly averting her eyes and shaking her head.

"Do you have another idea?" Jill threw in as a bonus question. "Anything at all?"

Brianna shook her head again.

Jill looked at Wendy who also shook her head but added a shrug of her shoulders and a pair of wide eyes. Finally, Jill ended the conversation with two women who would not be arguing anymore, "Then let's wait it out."

~

Kinsey, Mason and Zach had been waiting for several hours. In fact, Zach fell sound asleep. Kinsey and Mason had both become a bit antsy by the time they heard the footsteps of four elk about fifty feet away. Kinsey's head swiveled back and forth until he focused in on where the sound was coming from but he couldn't see what it was that was making the noise yet. Mason reached over and shook Zach until he woke up and all three of them peered over the log.

Kinsey placed a rock in the pocket of his slingshot with his right hand, while gripping the handle with his left. Mason and Zach slowly lifted their spears above the log while all three of them waited for the noisemaker to become visible.

~

Suddenly, slowly breaking the surface of the river, Tatum spotted a full grown alligator. Without hesitating, she pulled the arrow back and took aim from behind the driftwood.

Following her lead, Amara and Emily lifted their bows and did the same.

~

Although the light from the moon didn't give Grant the best

possible look, he could tell it was a black bear by the broad skull and narrow muzzle. He quickly estimated the animal to be six to six and a half feet in length and figured it could weigh as much as five hundred pounds. Even if he was off by a little, he was certain it was plenty of meat to feed the entire camp. And, maybe provide himself with a nice rug to cushion his next night of sleep.

~

The bulky, wild boar abruptly stopped and began to sniff the air as Jill stood and started to swing her boleadora. As the three large, round stones whirred above her head, the boar heard the sound and began to turn toward her.

~

Kinsey had stretched the strips of his slingshot as far back as they would go, while taking aim at the head of the largest of the four elk now standing about a hundred feet in front of him. He knew, from watching videos online of elk butting heads, he didn't want to hit the animal on top of the forehead. Instead, he was hoping to go a little lower and on the side, where the temple would be on a human.

"Ready?" he quietly whispered without taking his eyes off of the prize.

"Ready," Zach and Mason whispered in unison.

Without any further warning, Kinsey released the pocket of his slingshot and the rock hurdled through the air.

~

The arrow struck the alligator in the top of the head, penetrating its dark, olive-brown, leathery skin. Immediately, the animal began to twitch and squirm as it submerged itself back into the water, taking additional arrows in the right side of its long body as it splashed about and ultimately disappeared.

~

Grant's spear was sticking straight out of the bear's chest and Ray's and Qasim's spears had each penetrated different shoulders but the beast was still charging forward and it was furious.

All three men started back peddling in fear for their lives. Qasim stumbled and Grant quickly lifted him up as they turned to start a full sprint.

~

While the other three elk had scurried off, the one hit just behind the left eye by Kinsey's rock seemed dazed and wobbly as it tried to keep its footing and both Mason and Zach were charging toward it, spears in hand, with Kinsey right behind them.

~

As soon as the alligator resurfaced, Amara hit it with a fourth arrow just behind its vast mouth. Brianna and Tatum both stuck additional arrows right next to the first one that Tatum had fired as the animal's thrashing finally began to wane.

~

With the boleadora wrapped firmly around the charging boar's legs, the animal face-planted in the dirt. Wendy quickly plunged her spear into the beast's side. A second later, Brianna thrust her spear into its neck as Jill looked on, no longer holding a weapon of her own.

~

Grant pulled one of the spears back out of the bear's

shoulder and then immediately plunged it right back into the animal. This time, he put it directly through the animals heart, quickly leaving it motionless.

~

As the elk's blood ran into the dirt, Kinsey stood over it and watched the animal breathe its last breath. He momentarily felt bad for taking a life but he knew it was necessary for survival and he was comforted by remembering in the book of Genesis how God had given humans dominion over the animals of the earth for this very reason.

"That thing must weigh a thousand pounds!" Zach exclaimed.

"Yeah," Mason agreed, "how in the world are we supposed to get something that size back to camp?"

CHAPTER SEVENTEEN
The Feast

Grant and Ray dragged, by hand, their makeshift travois, created from a mesh of tree branches and utilizing the spears that were no longer needed for hunting, with their future meal in the middle of it and Qasim brought up the rear. They had taken turns and had to rest several times which made the trek back to camp take at least three times as long as the trip out to the spot of their kill.

Finally stepping out of the mountain forest and into the valley, the village came into view and men immediately began to spot them approaching and took notice of the large cargo they were hauling. They looked on, chatting, whispering, and in many cases, offered the trio congratulations and praise, realizing that long-awaited food was finally being delivered.

Ben saw what was happening from behind the growing

crowd and left to inform Nicolai but, by the time the two of them returned, Victor was already advancing and the hunting party had set their prize down near what used to be the fire in the middle of the village. Victor's presence quickly hushed the murmurs as Grant, Ray and Qasim tried to catch their breath and revel in the pride of their accomplishment.

~

"Thanks for bringing us dinner," Diane stated with a cutting tone. "You can go now."

"Excuse me?" Jill asked, sincerely baffled by Diane's response to the sight of the reward Jill, Brianna and Wendy had brought back after all of their hard work.

"You and the people siding with you don't eat here," Diane stated, scornfully. "The food will stay. You can't."

"We went out there and found this boar," Jill insisted. "We killed it. You don't have any say in what we do with it."

"You took the weapons you used to kill that thing without permission and I have final say about everything that happens in this camp. Don't forget it."

~

"You don't have any say about this," Tatum fired back.

"About everything," Irisa seethed as she reached for the alligator, but was stopped short when Tatum stepped in front of her and cut off her access.

~

"No," Kinsey spoke authoritatively, surprising and enraging Trevor. "We did what you failed to do yourself. You have no right. No voice."

"I have every right and I have the only voice!" Trevor shouted venomously. "I'm in charge! Not you! Not anyone else. Me!"

"Not about this."

~

"We decide," Grant insisted as he glanced around at the men in the camp and noticed the concerned looks on their faces. He thought the looks suggested that Victor was losing ground with the other men. They didn't like that he was claiming to have sole authority because that meant their opinions didn't matter. Grant quickly decided to use the momentum to his advantage. "We decide," he repeated as he began again. "Ray, Qasim and myself.

And, we have decided that this food is for all of us."

~

"Even you, Trevor."

Kinsey's statement stunned the crowd, including Trevor. It had finally silenced the angry tyrant. The murmurs slowly began to return until, finally, Pablo stepped out of the crowd and grabbed the elk's hind legs.

"Caleb and I will skin and gut it," he announced. "Someone get that fire going again. The quicker we move, the sooner we eat."

~

Irisa was motionless as most of the other girls went swiftly to work.

~

Qasim's hut-mate, Doug, started the fire while Nicolai and Ben were skinning and gutting the bear. Grant convinced them to get the skin off in one piece so he could salt it and hang it to dry, eventually turning it into a rug.

~

Jill and Wendy set up a spit to roast the boar over the fire. Jill had seen this done at a luau in Hawaii when she and Grant took the kids to Kona two years earlier but, this would be the first time she had ever done it herself. Like everyone else, she was hungry, and knowing food was coming only made her feel it that much more. But, she knew there was a long wait ahead. A big animal like this was going to take hours upon hours to fully cook.

~

With the alligator now cooking, casual conversation was underway and almost all of the girls were in good spirits. Then there was Irisa. She stood, sulking, outside of her hut with a few other girls, watching the vast majority of the young ladies gathered around the fire. Soon, the smell of cooking meat wafted up her nostrils and her tummy began to get restless, growling like a wild animal. Unfortunately, this only made her grumpier and she finally went inside her hut to continue sulking alone. The girls who had been standing with her glanced at one another, shrugged their shoulders, and quietly joined their friends near the cooking food.

~

While it seemed like it took days to cook the elk, the general atmosphere remained positive because everyone was so excited to know that food was coming. Although they all wished they had a variety of seasoning to add to it, when the roasted elk was ready, it had been worth the wait. The boys talked and laughed as they enjoyed their meal. The mood was happier than it had been in a long time and everyone knew it.

Even Trevor realized it and it was driving him crazy. When he finally poked his head out of his tree-fort, Kinsey was waiting below.

"I was just about to yell up to you," Kinsey stated matter-of-factly.

"Yeah," Trevor started to respond, "why's that?"

"I think you should join us. Get some food."

"Why would you want me there?"

"I don't. Not really. But, it's only right."

"What difference does that make?"

"It makes all the difference. Come on," Kinsey said, gesturing with his head and then turning his body.

Trevor couldn't help it. He really wanted to eat. With only a couple seconds of hesitation, he finally started the climb down the tree ladder. He hopped down and, without another word, walked side-by-side with Kinsey to the fire where he would partake with the rest of the boys.

~

As Victor chowed down on his bear meat, Grant looked around the fire at the many faces of the men and felt good about the renewed feeling of togetherness and community. He thought about the diverse backgrounds represented by these men. They were from all over the world, used to a variety of different cultures and economic statuses but the force that had caused a literal division in their families had also brought them together for a different kind of family. It was the first time Grant had ever taken a moment to appreciate it.

He looked over at Ray and thought about how he and Kinsey had become friends here, three years ago for Kinsey but closer to forty for Ray, and that friendship had ultimately carried over into their lives back home. Grant couldn't help but feel hopeful that he and Ray were beginning to see signs of success and that they may actually be able to accomplish their mission of taking all of the men to be reunited with their families. Even men like Victor who had now set his stubborn disdain for Grant aside and joined them for a meal.

Unfortunately, this good feeling wasn't destined to last.

Tensions would be rising again and would catch Grant off guard. The pot full of resistance to the Snyders' and Ray's mission was still stirring and would soon boil over.

CHAPTER EIGHTEEN
Still Divided

Jill had managed to get much better sleep this time. Perhaps it was the full stomach. Or, maybe it was the feeling of peace among the women at that time and the satisfaction she was receiving by knowing she was a big part of attaining it. Of course, it could also have been the sheer exhaustion from the hunt and the amount of work that had gone into getting the boar from the clearing where they killed it all the way to the village for the feast.

Whatever made it happen, she was thankful for the improved rest. This was going to be a big day . . . or, night. It was impossible to know which. Either way, she knew in her heart that it was time to take the momentum of peace and try to use it for recruiting all of the women to make the journey and, at last, find their families.

~

Kinsey was surprised, when he poked his head out of Mason and Zach's tree fort, to see everyone who had already said they would be taking the journey to Raum's Island with him, plus more than two dozen other boys, standing below him, waiting for his appearance. He immediately climbed down the ladder, stepped off of it, and turned to face the small crowd.

"We're going with you," Caleb immediately spoke up.

"All of us," Pablo added as the other boys nodded affirmatively.

"Good," Kinsey said with a growing smile. "We need to convince everyone. There is strength in numbers but, more importantly, we don't want anyone left behind."

As the boys all began to nod again, and verbalize their agreement, a voice bellowed, seemingly out of nowhere.

"What is this?" Trevor asked, causing everyone to turn toward his voice just as he stepped out of the darkness and into view. "What've we got going on here?"

"We're talking about going to find our families," Pablo answered before Kinsey could.

"That's already been settled," Trevor stated with an angry tone brewing in his voice. "No one is going anywhere."

"You're the only one who has agreed to that," Kinsey finally interjected.

"Well," Trevor started as he approached Kinsey like he wanted to fight him, "I'm in charge so that does settle it."

Pablo stepped between Kinsey and Trevor, his nose and Trevor's separated by less than three inches, and spoke firmly. "You're not in charge of this, Trevor. And you don't speak for the rest of us anymore. Those days are officially over."

Trevor stared into Pablo's eyes for a moment before finally blinking and turning his head. He looked around and quickly noticed that the crowd had nearly doubled in size since his arrival and was continuing to rapidly increase. He searched his brain for an idea that would keep him out of a fist fight with Pablo but also help him to save face in front of what would soon be the entire population of their little village. Finally, he once again locked eyes with Pablo and said the only thing he could think of.

~

"Fine," Victor said directly to Nicolai before stepping to the side so he could also address Grant and Ray. "We'll have ourselves a line in the sand moment right here and now."

Victor spun around, searching the ground where he eventually spotted a large stick only a few feet away. He pushed Ben out of his path, stepped toward it, reached down and picked up the stick. Stabbing the ground with it, he started dragging it through the dirt to create a literal line, shoving men from the crowd out of his way as he walked. He stopped about fifty feet from where he had begun and turned to address the crowd.

"Simple," Victor started, "if you're going on this suicide mission, stand with them on this side of the line. If you're staying here where it's safe," Victor continued as he stepped across the line, "stand with me on this side."

~

Diane watched as the village slowly divided, pretty close to evenly, on either side of the line. Bitterly scanning the faces of those women who had dared to defy her, she made an announcement.

"For those of you standing on Jill's side of the line," she began with a hateful grin, "you're all cut off! No food, no shelter, and no weapons! No supplies of any kind! You made your choice, so get out, right now!"

~

Panic began to spread amongst the boys on Kinsey's side

of the line. But, not in Kinsey.

"That's not how this is going down, Trevor!" Kinsey shouted loud enough to silence all of the murmurs.

~

"You're once again forgetting who's in charge," Victor shouted back. "This is my village, no matter what anyone else says. Heck, this is my freaking island!"

"And you can keep it!" Ray yelled. "We're leaving anyway. But, we'll be taking what we need for the journey and you can't stop us."

~

"Then you'll have to go through us!" Irisa barked.

"Us being the key word," Yanna loudly stated from behind Irisa.

As everyone's eyes shifted to Yanna, she surprised them all, no one more than Irisa, as she stepped aside and gestured with her arm to let the girls on Tatum's side know they were welcome to do what they needed to. As Irisa turned red and went to scream at her, Yanna interrupted before she could even get started.

"If you persist in your attempt to start this little civil war of yours, you should know I'll be siding with them even though I have no intention of going on their trip. I know you think you're in charge, Irisa. But, right is right and wrong is wrong. You're wrong. So, consider yourself temporarily impeached."

Most of the girls on Irisa's side of the line were nodding in agreement and Irisa was forced to quickly face the fact that she had lost. She also realized there was more to lose if she continued. Instead, she threw her hands up in the air and marched off toward her bamboo hut.

"Thank you," Tatum said to Yanna before addressing her own group. "We have a lot of work to do. We'll pack up and gather supplies before we go but, the first thing that needs to be done is building a raft. Let's start gathering all the useable wood we can find. The bigger the better. And, bamboo should be our first choice."

As all of the girls from Tatum's side of the line scattered to go and find wood, the girls who remained from Irisa's side of the line began to scatter as well.

"I'm going to help them," Yanna suddenly announced. "Anyone want to join me?"

Some of the girls nodded in agreement and joined in gathering wood. Others quietly snuck away as Tatum and

Yanna shared a smile.

While Yanna started walking toward the beach to find driftwood, Tatum noticed that one of the girls who was calmly walking off toward her home was Sheila and decided it was time to approach her.

"Sheila," Tatum spoke loudly as she hurried to catch up.

Stopping, Sheila timidly turned around. "I'm not going," she said, matter-of-factly.

"I wish you'd change your mind," Tatum responded.

"I won't."

"Don't you miss your brother, Ray?"

Sheila's eyes went wide and her timid demeanor quickly disappeared. "How do you know about my brother?" she asked. "I haven't talked to anyone about my family since my sisters left."

"I don't just know about your brother, Sheila. He made it out of here when I did. And, now, he came back with my family and I."

"Why in the world would he come back?"

"Simple. He's here to take you home."

Yanna shared a smile.

While Yanna started walking toward the beach to find driftwood, Tatum noticed that one of the girls who was calmly walking off toward her home was Sheila and decided it was time to approach her.

"Sheila," Tatum spoke loudly as she hurried to catch up.

Stopping, Sheila timidly turned around. "I'm not going," she said, matter-of-factly.

"I wish you'd change your mind," Tatum responded.

"I won't."

"Don't you miss your brother, Ray?"

Sheila's eyes went wide and her timid demeanor quickly disappeared. "How do you know about my brother?" she asked. "I haven't talked to anyone about my family since my sisters left."

"I don't just know about your brother, Sheila. He made it out of here when I did. And, now, he came back with my family and I."

"Why in the world would he come back?"

"Simple. He's here to take you home."

CHAPTER NINETEEN
Bad Blood

Tatum had determined, from the wood that had been gathered, that they would be able to make the entire raft out of bamboo. With the number of girls that were going on the journey, and the hope that she would be able to recruit more before they left, she had split the group into eight smaller groups, instructed them to collect as much vine as possible for lashing and construct eight foot by twelve foot rafts. Then, they would be fastening the convoy into a more than seven hundred and fifty square-foot super raft, braced with additional bamboo at each section break, and reinforced on the bottom with securely joined bundled bamboo pontoons. When it was finished, they would roll it into the water on the bamboo trees lined up on the beach as rails and test its buoyancy and weight capacity.

While the eight groups were hard at work, she took Fabia and Ling to inventory the supplies they would need on their journey. Unable to shake the conversation she'd had with Sheila earlier, Tatum was noticeably distracted as she lamented the idea of leaving the island without her and the possibility of gravely disappointing Ray.

When Fabia called her on how distracted she seemed, Tatum explained the situation to her new friends and how it had surprised her when Sheila acted as if she didn't believe what Tatum was telling her. It had hurt Tatum's feelings a bit, to essentially be called a liar, but she was trying not to take it personally. It was truly a surprise, however, that Tatum was able to give her so many facts about her brother and yet Sheila still didn't believe her story. Fabia and Ling agreed that it sounded as if Sheila didn't want to believe because, if she did, she would have to face the decision of taking the journey with the other girls and, she was too afraid to do that.

"We need to convince her she's stronger than she thinks she is," Tatum decided out loud before grabbing the hands of her friends, looking up at the dark sky and starting to pray. "We need to convince them all, Father. But, we need You to show us how to do it."

~

Victor was walking in circles, inside his hut, frantically trying to figure out how to gain back control of "his" village. He wasn't about to let Grant, Ray or anyone else take it away from him. He was so angry, he grabbed a spear that was leaning up against the wall and swung it hard into a stack of clay pots, smashing them into dozens of pieces. He stared at the pieces for a moment as a devious plan began to formulate in his mind. Slowly, he set the spear down, reached for one of the two pots that hadn't been broken, picked it up, and walked stealthily out of his hut.

~

After stuffing the pot full of as much elk meat and bones as it could hold, Trevor slipped out of camp and jogged into the forest alone. Unbeknownst to him, however, Henry, one of his cronies, was quietly surveilling Trevor from a dark spot between huts and wondering what it was his fearless leader was up to.

~

Diane crept up to the mouth of the cave, having seen, numerous times in the past, evidence that this was a lair for the animal that she wanted to draw out. She reached inside of her pot and pulled out a bone, dripping with meat juices, and tossed it lightly inside the cave. She was careful not to throw it in too far, not wanting to hit the animal, but far enough and loud enough to draw attention.

~

With his left hand holding the pot against his torso, Trevor reached into the pot with his right hand and pulled out some elk meat and dropped it on the ground as he backed away from the cave. He took several steps before finally turning his body sideways so he could walk forward while still looking behind him.

~

Irisa suddenly heard a growl and knew, instantly, that she had the attention of the animal she was looking for. Her pace picked up a bit but, she knew she didn't want to run because she didn't want to be attacked. Right now, all she wanted to do was lure the animal. The attack would, hopefully, come a bit later.

~

The sound of careful footprints suddenly became audible in the distance, but Diane didn't see anything yet. Of course, it was dark, but she still anticipated seeing a pair of glowing eyes. However, she knew leopards stalked their prey and would, therefore, do their best not to be seen until the last possible second.

~

Victor dropped another piece of bear meat behind him and became concerned that he would run out before getting to the village. He knew it would soon be in view and decided to go a bit more sparingly. However, his nerves were kicking into high gear as the sound the wolf was making had increased which, either meant a pack had formed or the one animal had sped up. Neither was particularly good news at the moment but could be, for Victor's plan, by the time he reached the village.

~

Trevor's head looked like it was on a swivel and on one of its turns in the direction he was heading, he finally spotted the tree forts and the glow of the fire on the ground in the middle of them. As he picked his speed up, he could hear the pace of the bobcat follow suit. The only thing loud enough to drown out all of the movement may have been the sound of Trevor's own heartbeat.

~

Diane could see the leopard behind her as she entered the village. Her head continued to swivel but, now she was looking for Jill. She didn't see her anywhere and the leopard was getting closer by the second.

She didn't want to shout Jill's name because that would let everyone know that this event had been planned and, for this to work the way she wanted it to, she needed to keep that secret. Running past Wendy and Brianna's, the fire in the middle of the village, and the spot where their last confrontation had taken place, Diane could not find Jill and was beginning to think she had gone hunting again.

~

Suddenly, it dawned on him and he couldn't believe it hadn't hit him sooner. The entire reason for Victor's anger was the journey Grant was about to take all of these men on and the fact that Victor had been forced to consent to the depletion of their resources. He began to sprint for the weapons hut and, with the wolf rapidly gaining ground, he knew it was his last shot to make sure the wolf attacked Grant and not him.

~

The commotion around the village caught Tatum's attention. She could hear the yelling and screaming that had started less than a minute earlier and wondered what was causing it. Stepping out of the hut to hand Olivia an arm-load of bows, she suddenly spotted Irisa running toward her with a pot in her hand and then quickly noticed the feral dog hot on her tail.

As Irisa passed Tatum, she dropped the pot. The broken pot spilled the remaining contents of meat and juices right at Tatum's feet.

Luckily for all involved, Sheila was less than fifty feet away, watching the whole thing. She quickly bent down, picked up a handful of rocks and started pelting the feral dog until it stopped in its tracks, whimpered and ran away, presumably to where it had come from, and without harming anyone.

Not exactly what I had in mind, Tatum began to silently pray, *but thank you.*

~

"Oh," Trevor decried, "you just saved my life."

"What was your plan?" Henry asked.

"I don't even know," Trevor lied. "Maybe outrun it for as long as I could and then, who knows . . ."

"That's not what I mean and you know it. You brought that thing here on purpose. Why? To kill Kinsey?"

"No," Trevor continued to lie. "Of course not. I would never . . . I didn't . . .

"You're a liar," Henry insisted as the entire village gathered. "Worse. You tried to kill Kinsey and, in the process, you could have gotten us all killed. You're no better than a murderer."

CHAPTER TWENTY
Eleventh Hour

Diane could hardly believe she was being betrayed by one of her closest allies. Yet, it didn't dawn on her that perhaps she had taken things too far. Sins like hatred and jealousy have an inexplicable way of blinding people to what would otherwise be obvious truth. It wasn't just her closest allies that had turned on Diane, the entire village had. But, instead of looking within, her focus remained outward and, as a result, her hatred only grew stronger.

Jill stood back and silently watched as the women dragged Diane to her hut and used vines to tie her up until they could figure out what to do next. In Jill's heart, there was still hope that Diane would come around and join her and the other women on the quest to find their families. But, that hope was quickly fading. Not only because of Diane's actions but, also, because the beginning of that journey was mere hours away. Time, in this case, was not on her side.

~

The supplies had all been gathered but new men were approaching Grant and Ray, at a surprising rate, to inform them that they were joining the journey and that meant gathering more supplies. It was a tiring cycle but one that Grant and Ray both welcomed with open arms. In fact, Grant had even taken it upon himself to individually talk to each man, who had decided to stay behind, in order to give them one final chance to change their minds. It was a group that had shrunk significantly but it still consisted of more than a dozen members, including, of course, Victor. And, Grant didn't want anyone left behind. Not even the man who had just tried to have him killed. But, that was the person Grant was least looking forward to having any kind of conversation with so, he was putting him off to the end.

~

Tatum knocked on the bamboo outside of Sheila's hut as she poked her head inside the open door frame. "Hello?" she asked.

"I thought you'd be stopping by," Sheila answered.

"Yeah," Tatum started, "I had to give it one last shot."

"You're wasting your time."

"I don't think I am."

"You're wrong."

"It's not a waste of time, Sheila. Even if you do stick to your decision to stay."

"That doesn't make any sense. If I stay, then every minute you spent trying to convince me to go was a waste of time."

"No. Every minute I spend trying to convince you to go is the fulfillment of a promise I made to your brother. Keeping your promise is never a waste of time. No matter what the outcome is."

"Whatever."

"No. Not whatever.

"Yes. Whatever. I still don't believe you know my brother."

"Even after I told you the whole story he told me about your parents, church, you, him, your sisters . . . ?"

"It's just not possible."

"Before you arrived in Kadosh, would you have thought any of this was possible?"

Sheila didn't respond. She simply looked away. Tatum knew that was because the only honest response would be to admit things that she wasn't ready to admit. But, Tatum was running out of time. So was Sheila. Tatum was going to have to play hardball.

"Ray is here," Tatum firmly stated. "He's here to take you home. I'm on my way to find him. And, when I do, if you're not with me, it's going to break his heart. You, you are going to break his heart. Whatever it is you're afraid of, it isn't worth that. I'm heading out there to test the rafts and help tie them all together. Then we're going to load them up with our supplies and we're going to leave. Anyone not on those rafts, when we do, is stuck here with nothing but the few stubborn girls who stayed behind with them and a mountain of regret to chew on for the rest of their lives. Don't be stupid, Sheila. Be on that raft."

Tatum walked out as fast as she could carry herself, purposefully not giving Sheila a chance to respond. She wiped a tear from her face as the sorrow began to overwhelm her. It was hard to imagine that God brought Ray all the way to Snohomish, and then all the way back to Kadosh, only to have him go back empty handed. But, as she tried to let it go and psyche herself up to face Irisa, Tatum had resigned herself to accept that it was looking like that was exactly what was going to happen.

~

"I'll bet you're loving this," Trevor sneered as Kinsey climbed into his tree fort.

"Loving what?" Kinsey asked, sincerely. "Seeing you tied up? You're wrong. But, who cares? You did this to yourself and, somewhere in that thick skull of yours, you know it."

Trevor looked at Kinsey. He had changed between visits to Kadosh and Trevor recognized it. It was in that moment that he began to believe that there was a possibility Kinsey had been telling the truth. Unfortunately, even that glimmer of possibility wasn't enough to soften Trevor's hard heart. His gaze left Kinsey and he stared at the wall in anger.

"If I had it my way," Kinsey started back in with more sympathy and less frustration in his voice, "you'd be coming with us. I don't want to leave anyone here. Not even you. And, I really believe that if you would go, the last eight or nine guys out there who are still planning to stay, they'd come to. You're not just hurting yourself right now, Trevor. You're dragging them down with you. And, if you insist on staying, you're going to have to live with that."

"Just go," Trevor scoffed.

"Okay," Kinsey said but still waited for a few seconds to see if Trevor would have a last minute change of heart. Unfortunately, he didn't, and Kinsey quietly and somberly stepped out of the tree fort and slowly made his way down the ladder. Kinsey couldn't help but be surprised by how sad it made him to go without the boy who had never shown him anything but hatred. He could only assume that the grief inside of him wasn't his own but, instead, belonged to the Holy Spirit who dwelled within. Kinsey continued to listen as he stepped off of the ladder and walked away, hoping he would hear the sound of Trevor's voice crying out and begging Kinsey not to leave him there. But, Trevor never made a peep.

~

No one on any of the four islands was grieving any more deeply in that moment than Tatum. The rafts had all been launched, tested, secured and loaded. Only ten girls from the village were still on land. The rest were waiting on word from Tatum. It was formally time to depart but Tatum didn't feel ready. Leaving meant she had to face the fact that Sheila was, once again, choosing to stay behind and that was a tough pill to swallow.

"Ready?" came the sound of Fabia's voice from behind Tatum.

Tatum tightened her grip on the oar in her hands as tears fell from both eyes. Finally, she looked away from the shoreline and dropped the other end of the oar in the water.

"Ready," Tatum said so quietly she had to repeat herself after clearing her throat. "Ready."

As the other oars hit the water and the first set of strokes pulled the massive raft from shore, Tatum closed her eyes and began to silently pray. But, this wasn't a prayer in which she asked God for any favors. She was simply expressing both her disappointment in Sheila's decision and her lack of understanding in His plan for bringing Ray all this way. Suddenly, a Bible verse popped into her head. It was Romans 8:25 which reads, "But if we hope for what we do not yet have, we wait for it patiently." She opened her eyes as she and the other girls continued to stroke the water with their oars and wondered what God was trying to tell her with that verse. Certainly, she wasn't supposed to wait any longer before leaving. Or, was she?

"Wait!" Tatum heard in the distance but wondered if it was her imagination, until she heard it again. "Wait!"

Tatum, along with all of the other girls, turned toward the shoreline just in time to see Sheila dive into the water.

"Go back!" Tatum yelled.

The other girls turned back to see Tatum motioning to them.

"Not her," she yelled. "us! Go back! We have to get her!"

The girls did as instructed and started stroking the water in the opposite direction as Sheila swam hard, toward the raft. In less than a minute, she was throwing herself onto the raft, with the help of several girls who pulled her up. She quickly crawled across the crowded raft and over to Tatum. Neither of them could even speak. They simply hugged each other firmly and cried.

The first part of the mission was complete and the journey had officially begun.

PART FIVE
Another Journey

CHAPTER TWENTY-ONE
The Glow

With multiple sets of eyes glowing from the darkness, the boys were mindful that Raum, and those under his control, were aware of their departure and watching every step they took on their journey. Kinsey couldn't help but think back on the attacks, by bears and the odd boar and stegosaurus fusion beast that he and other boys had survived on their last expedition. The beast appeared to have been created from the terrain around them and was like nothing he had ever seen before or since that journey. Kinsey wanted the fact of their survival to comfort him and give him peace but, the memories of the attacks themselves were pretty terrifying and so was the fear of not knowing what Raum would send to destroy them this time. So, he did the only thing he could in that moment, he prayed.

~

Asking God for protection and peace, Jill's heart slowly began to calm down. She not only prayed for herself and the other women but, for her husband, son, and daughter, as well as everyone she hoped they were now traveling with. That, of course, included her new friend Ray and his sister Sheila, who Jill looked forward to meeting before going home.

Home.

The fondness of that word, compared with how she felt about it the last time she was in Kadosh, stirred her heart. There was no way to be sure how long she had been in this strange place but, she was very ready to leave. She found herself looking forward to watching, from the couch with her family, the Huskies play basketball again and suddenly found herself craving a bowl of popcorn. At the moment, it sounded a lot better than the root beer floats they'd had after the last game. In fact, she shivered a little as the thought of the heated bowl in her lap and a cup of hot cocoa in her hands made her realize how cool the air around her was without any clouds in the sky and no sun, likely going back for years, to warm things up.

~

With only the moonlight of the clear but dark sky to illuminate their path, Grant and Ray escorted the men toward the same shoreline the first group of men had journeyed to several years ago. Unfortunately, they had a long way to go before their trek would lead them to that shoreline. And, when they got there, they still had to build a boat or a raft in order to get from their island to Raum's.

Behind Grant and Ray, men pulled carts full of weapons, supplies for building the water vessel, oars they had recently fashioned to propel that vessel, and even a little bit of food. However, they knew their food supply would quickly run out. Grant had assured those concerned that Raum would eventually send something to attack them and, when he did, killing whatever it was would likely provide a new food source. The response offered one solution but, of course, added to other, perhaps even more obvious, concerns.

It was all part of a conversation that had taken place before they left the village that was now distantly behind them. By contrast, since their departure, the trip had been mostly silent. The exceptions being the sounds of the men's feet and the wooden wheels of the carts, as they made their way toward their goal, and the typical noises naturally coming from the forest itself.

The verbal silence finally came to an end when Ben came from behind and stepped in between Grant and Ray. "So, he began to ask, "what all did you guys say attacked you the last time you did this?"

After he and Grant exchanged a "Where do we begin?" look, Ray was the first to answer the question. "Well, for us, the first thing to attack was a Kodiak bear. Huge. Must've weighed fifteen hundred pounds."

"Fifteen hundred . . . ?" Ben trailed off as his trepidation mounted.

"I heard about that," Grant reflected. "For us, it was a cougar. Probably more like two hundred pounds but, man that thing was swift."

Ben glanced, nervously, back and forth between Ray and Grant, giving Ray a little pause before he finally decided to just lay it all out there. "And I heard the ladies had to face off with a big ol' Bengal Tiger."

Grant quickly realized what Ray was doing and decided that his friend was right. He had always been of the mind that ripping the band aid off quickly was better than a slow and painful process anyway. "Yeah," Grant began to add, "I don't think it was even half the size of that Kodiak but, from what I understand, it was several times the size of that cougar. And the girls had it the worst."

"How could it be worse?" Ben begged with terrified anticipation.

"They were attacked by a giant python," Ray injected.

"Fifty feet long," Grant corresponded. "Must've weighed a thousand pounds."

"You've got to be kidding me," Ben squirmed.

"No joke," Grant admitted.

"And people died?"

~

"Yeah," Tatum acknowledged, "just one in the first attack but, quite a few others as we went on. I've been very up front about that."

"What were the other attacks like?" Ling asked, not sure if she really wanted to hear the answer.

"Each one was worse than the one before it and no two were the same."

"Okay," Ling stated as she decided not to pry any further. Then she admitted just how deep her fear had become. "Maybe I should go back."

"It's way too late for that," Tatum stated, matter-of-factly. "The best thing we can do now is look out for one another. We've got each other's backs. Besides, someone a lot bigger and stronger than Raum has our backs, too."

Ling quickly shushed Tatum. "He might hear you."

"Let him."

"How can you say that after everything you've been through?" Ling countered, frankly.

"I can say it because of everything I've been through. I know exactly who has my back."

"Who are you talking about?"

"The light."

"What light? Look around."

"The light we encountered on Raum's island. I didn't know what it was then but, I do now. The Bible says that God is light. In Him there is no darkness at all. And, His Son, Jesus, declared Himself to be the Light of the World."

"God?" Ling asked with sincere skepticism and showing more assertiveness than Tatum expected from the naturally meek girl. "You're telling me you encountered God on that island and now He has our backs out here? All I see is darkness so, maybe you're wrong and, even if there is a God, Raum is more powerful."

"Darkness doesn't cover up light, Ling. Light exposes the darkness. You'll see."

As if God heard Tatum and wanted to prove her right, the moon suddenly seemed to shine a little brighter.

"What is that?" Tatum and Ling heard Amara ask from behind them. They looked to see what the commotion was over as the sounds of amazement intensified from the other girls. Right before their eyes, a divi-divi tree was standing on the beach just beyond the shoreline. It seemed to have grown in a manner that suggested its trunk was pointing to something out over the water but its leaves created a perfectly flat canopy for anyone or anything that sought shelter underneath. However, none of that was the amazing part. The girls had all seen trees like this before.

What made this divi-divi tree so unique was the fact that, right before their eyes, it had begun to glow. At first, they wondered if it was the reflection of moonlight. But, this was something else. This light was coming from somewhere else and it was growing more intense with each passing second.

It took a couple of minutes before Ling could break her stare. But, when she was finally able, she looked at Tatum and smiled a knowing, calm and peaceful smile. Suddenly, she too believed that God had their backs.

Unfortunately, Raum had plans of his own and he was about to make his presence known.

CHAPTER TWENTY-TWO
Warning

The women had stopped walking about an hour after seeing the glowing palm tree. They had taken their bathroom breaks and had a few bites of food while settling into their temporary campsite with a small fire in the middle. It was then time to rest, after the first long stretch of hiking and before the next one. But, most of them were too busy thinking about what they had just perceived to fall asleep.

Other than the night sky and fires they had started, most of these women hadn't seen a source of light in years. There were no street lamps, flashlights or ceiling lights in Kadosh and there hadn't been sunshine since the day the Snyders made it to Raum's island and went home. This made the glowing tree all the more beautiful and even more fascinating than it otherwise would have been.

Their collective faith in what Jill had told them, about the source of the light and its arming them for battle on Raum's island, was growing stronger. However, the glowing eyes from the dark shadows and the knowledge that Raum and his minions were watching, blanketed them with a heavy spirit of fear as well.

~

That fear spiked as the men suddenly heard footsteps of something approaching. Most of the men were lying down and using their arms for a pillow but, as the sound grew louder, heads began popping up like a labour of moles breaching the surface of the earth. Contrastingly, the men's bodies lifted slowly off of the ground as they leaned toward the noise to try and see what was causing it. Most of them gripped the weapons they had chosen to sleep next to. For Grant, that weapon was a spear. He lifted it up off of the ground, brought it close to him, pointed it toward the noise coming from the darkness, and leaned forward to try and see what he assumed was an approaching animal or one of Raum's monsters.

Instead, when the light from the night sky and the fire finally illuminated the noisemaker, Grant was stunned to see a man in front of him. The man was ten or fifteen years younger than Grant and strikingly handsome. His dark skin was flanked by long black hair and his smile showed off his white teeth, which nearly glowed in the dark. It was that darkness that next jumped out at Grant. The darkness seemed to surround the man. Not the same way that it did everyone else. They were all in the dark. But, this man had stepped out of the shadows and was approaching the same dimly lit area everyone else was in. Still, the darkness seemed to follow him. Grant suddenly thought about how angels had always been depicted with halos and surrounded by light and that's when it hit him, he was staring at a demon.

~

The demon they were staring at looked like a seventeen year old boy. But, Kinsey knew the truth. He felt it so strongly there was no doubt in his mind. After all, demons are fallen angels. So, it made sense to Kinsey that if angels are surrounded by light, demons would be surrounded by the absence of it. He briefly wondered why this demon was here but quickly remembered that there was a hierarchy in the heavenly realm and then decided that if this was true for the two-thirds of angels still serving their Creator, it was likely true for those who had chosen to follow Satan as well. That's when he decided that Raum was a servant of Satan's and this demon must be a servant of Raum's.

His heartbeat was pounding furiously as the demon stopped

near the fire and slowly turned in a circle to survey the boys. Kinsey was terrified but he knew he was the leader of this group and it was, therefore, up to him to take charge. Slowly, as he said a quick prayer, asking God to protect him and all of the other boys as well, he got to his feet and stood tall.

The demon fixed his eyes on Kinsey and smiled, showing off his impressive teeth again. But Kinsey focused in on his eyes which were filled with the same darkness that surrounded him. It looked as though that darkness was deep and, perhaps, had consumed the insides of a being that Kinsey knew was once created beautiful. All angels were. Suddenly, his fear turned into sadness and pity.

~

Tatum's eyes were still locked with those of the demon-girl who had risen from the depths of the waters and now stood on the front of the girls' raft. The floor of the vessel rolled a bit with the waves of the water beneath it and Tatum had to work to keep her balance on the bamboo under her feet as she stood mere inches from the face of Raum's soldier.

"It's nice to meet you, Tatum."

The fact that the demon knew her name startled Tatum but she knew she had to force herself to ignore it and speak with confidence.

"Why don't I believe that?" she asked.

"It's true," the demon answered. "The journey your family took several years ago is legendary in Kadosh. Everyone knows the tale. Well, not the humans. But, everyone else."

~

Grant couldn't help but think of all the depictions of demons he'd seen in his lifetime. They were always grotesque. But, he also knew that Satan was known as the ultimate deceiver so, he reasoned that this demon had been trained to take the form of an appealing being who would flatter and manipulate to get what he wanted.

"What do you say we cut to the chase?" Grant suggested. "You're not here to tell me how great I am. Or, my family is, for that matter. Raum must have sent you for a reason. What is it?"

"Smart man," the demon responded. "You don't disappoint. I can see why you have proven so formidable."

"The chase," Grant fired back. "Cut to it."

The demon was no longer smiling. "Raum knew you would return. He's far more prepared this time."

"So, what? You're here to warn me? Warn us?"

"Yes," the demon stated, a sly grin returning to his face.

~

"A second journey simply won't be successful," the demon continued. "You must turn back."

"That's not happening," Jill stated matter-of-factly. "I'm taking these women to be reunited with their families. They're going home."

"But, Raum-"

"No buts," Jill interrupted. "No one is going to stop us. Not you. Not Raum. No one."

"I'm trying to help you-"

"I know exactly what you're trying to do," Jill interrupted again. "And, it's not going to work."

~

"If you keep going," the demon insisted, now getting visibly angry, "you will all die."

"You're wrong," Tatum shot back. "The God that reigns over everything, including you and including Raum, is on our side. I think we both know how that story ends."

"Have it your way. But, remember, I tried to warn you."

The demon took a step backward and plunged into the water, disappearing the way she had arrived, almost like watching a video of that arrival in reverse, and, Tatum could only assume, rushing to report to Raum.

~

Kinsey turned to face the group of boys, hoping they could simply move on and move forward but also with the knowledge that it was pretty unlikely he would get his wish. And, he was about to find out just how right he was.

CHAPTER TWENTY-THREE
Second Thoughts

"Did you even hear what that dude just said to you?" asked Pablo.

"He wasn't a dude," Kinsey responded without thinking first, "he was a demon."

"A what now?" Caleb asked, his eyes bugging out.

"Oh," Pablo reacted, "this just keeps getting better. The only reason I agreed to go on this insane trip of yours was because you'd done it before and I thought you knew what you were getting us into. Now this hell-spawn tells us that it's going to be even harder than it was for you the last time? The truth is, you have no idea what you're getting us into, do you? All I know is, this is turning out to be way beyond what I signed up for."

"Of course it's going to be harder," Kinsey returned.

"What?" Caleb asked, sincerely freaking out.

"But that has nothing to do with the reason you wanted to come." Kinsey slowly turned, addressing everyone. "You wanted to do this for your families. You wanted to be reunited with them. To finally go home. I never said it was going to be easy. Just the opposite. But, the goal is worth the effort."

"Yeah but," Caleb started, "you know that part where he said we were all going to die? Yeah, I didn't much care for that part."

"I hate to say it Kinsey," Zach agreed, "but Caleb's right. Dead is not the goal. Dead doesn't get us home."

~

"You're right," Grant admitted. "In all likelihood, we won't all make it home. Some of us will probably die trying. Ray and I have never tried to hide that fact. But, we don't believe that'll happen to all of us. In fact, we believe most of us will find our families and we will make it home. That's why we felt it was worth it to come back here, at incredible personal risk, I might add, and show you the way out. The way for you to get to your home. Just like we're trying to get back to ours."

"Exactly," Ray agreed. "Besides, nothing's changed since we left-"

"Nothing's changed?" Doug interrupted in disbelief. "We just encountered a freaking demon!"

“Nothing’s changed since we left,” Ray tried again, “except that one of Raum’s minions has attempted to discourage us from continuing.”

“Did a bang-up job too,” Nicolai interjected.

“Which isn’t exactly something that should surprise us,” Grant added. “Raum wants us to stay put. We already knew that. We also knew he would send things our way to try and force us to turn back. He’s going to do whatever it takes to stop us from reaching his island. If we knew he was willing to attack us with animals, monsters, harsh weather . . . Why are we surprised that he would send someone to simply lie to us and trick us into turning around? It’d make things far easier on him if we just believed the lie.”

“How do you know he was lying?” Qasim asked.

“Because I’m familiar with the source of his lies,” Grant quickly answered, then paused a moment before attempting to explain what he meant. “This demon was one of Raum’s minions. But, Raum isn’t the ultimate source of evil in this place. He has a master, too.”

“Do you mean,” Ben started to ask but had some trouble getting the words out, “like, the devil? I mean, like the for real devil?”

“Yes,” Grant stated sincerely. “I mean the for real devil. Satan himself. And, he’s not some little chubby guy in red tights who carries around a pitchfork. He's the father of every lie ever told and the source of all enmity toward a holy and righteous God who loves each and every one of us. That's who Raum's working for. That's who wants us separated, not just from our families or from home, but from God Himself. The source of the light. The foundation of everything good. All love and all joy. That's what we're fighting for. That's where our journey is taking us. The past is the past. We can't change that. But, the future, all of it, tomorrow, the day after, and all the way on into eternity, it all depends on the choices we make right here and now."

~

"I for one," Sheila began as she reached up and took hold of Tatum's hand and they shared a smile, "can't turn back after a speech like that."

Tatum looked up and out at the rest of the girls on the giant raft. "Anyone still not sure they'd rather be back there with Irisa?"

There was no response. Not even a head swivel in the direction Tatum was pointing. The silence was the answer Tatum hoped for. She knew the girls were still committed.

"Good," Tatum acknowledged with a sly grin, "because this raft isn't turning around and that would be one heck of a swim."

~

Jill divided the camp in half. Her group kept each other company while standing guard and the other half slept. They planned to eventually switch places and, when everyone had rested up, ultimately start their journey again. Of course, the conversations the women had with Jill remained steeped in questions about the previous journey which, showed her there was still a heavy amount of fear of the unknown events that lay ahead. But, it also comforted her with proof that, in spite of the fear, there was an even heavier amount of resolve amongst the group. However, even though the somber mood continued, Jill was fairly relieved when the conversation between she and Olivia moved on to something besides their impending confrontations.

"I just hope I don't get all the way there only to find out my husband stayed behind," Olivia admitted, revealing the fear that was troubling her more than that of injury or even death.

Although the amount of light was insignificant, Jill could still see the tears begin to fall. She put an arm around her new friend and then wrapped her body up with the other arm. The tears grew heavier as Jill finally spoke.

"At least this way you'll know he didn't make the journey and find out that you stayed. Besides, either way, you'll get to go home."

She could feel her friend nodding in agreement but no more words were spoken.

~

Most of the girls slept as Tatum and a few others continued to row. This leg, however, was less about any kind of major progress and more about keeping the raft from floating off course. Many of those now sleeping would eventually take over and progress would be made soon enough. For now, rest was essential.

Tatum was ready for rest. She was tired. And, her rest wasn't far off. But, for now, she was content to revel in the progress that had already been made. Tatum felt a sense of pride but, not in any work that she had done herself. This pride was on behalf of all the girls on the raft with her and it was rooted in God. After all, He had orchestrated this whole thing. It was God who had provided them what they needed on Raum's island the first time around. He had then called them back to Kadosh. And, now He had most of the girls on this raft with Tatum. Including, sweet Sheila. She knew God would be with them the rest of the way as well. And, after the warning from the demon, she knew they were going to need Him more than ever before. But, what made that even more true was something Tatum didn't know. They would be encountering that same demon again very soon.

CHAPTER TWENTY-FOUR
Final Warning

They were guessing the break had lasted around six or seven hours but, the men had no way to know for sure. However long it had been, it certainly was not enough for two full shifts of sleep. Ray had commented to Grant on how tired their bodies were but that their minds were too active to sleep for very long. The journey they were taking was so immense and, for every one of the others, unprecedented, that it was occupying their thoughts whether or not they were awake. It wasn't by choice. It just was. When someone is in the middle of a life event of the magnitude these men were, it's only natural to remain on edge.

As a result, all of the men felt like they had barely taken long naps but, it would have to do for this stretch. The quest simply couldn't wait any longer. With adrenaline coursing through their veins, the men knew it was time to face whatever might lie ahead.

Of course, what that might be, was anyone's guess. But, no one was guessing that Raum would send another warning before any kind of attacks.

~

Tatum had noticed that there was no longer any shoreline anywhere in sight. They were adrift in the middle of the ocean with only the dimly lit sky to guide their way. It was strange to be surrounded by people and yet feel a sense of loneliness but, that's what feeling a bit lost did to her in that moment. As the oars in the water propelled them forward and the giant raft rolled over the waves, she had begun to pray for both peace in her heart and the hand of God in keeping them headed in the right direction.

Tatum's prayer was suddenly interrupted when, bursting from the depths of the waters, the same demon that had appeared to the girls mere hours earlier, surged upward and landed on the front of the raft, the same way it had done the first time. Water spurted everywhere as the girls stopped rowing and let out a collective gasp, looking on in deep fear.

The demon, who still looked like she could be one of them, was no longer feigning a friendly smile. "Turn back," she insisted as she spoke calmly but forcefully. "Now."

"We already told you," Tatum said as she defiantly stood up

to face the demon for a second time, "that isn't going to happen."

"This is your final warning," the demon shot back. "There will be no more."

"What does that mean?" Ling awkwardly asked. "What exactly?"

"It means," the demon said, as she only partially tried to hide the pleasure gained from knowing she was getting to someone, "that unless you turn back right now, you will soon encounter the wrath of Raum."

~

"Yeah," Caleb admitted, "um, guys, I don't like the sound of that at all."

"We've been through this," Kinsey asserted.

"But," Caleb started, "wrath is a really scary word."

"That's why he used it, Caleb."

"I used it," the demon interjected as he leaned in to Kinsey with a sly grin, but spoke loud enough for all the boys to hear, "because it's accurate. You of all people should know how true that is."

The demon was right. Kinsey knew what the wrath of Raum felt like. It was a scary thing and, rightfully so. It had, as he had witnessed firsthand, gotten people killed.

"Like I told them," Kinsey said directly to the demon, "I've been honest with everyone about what we're going to face."

"But," Caleb started back in, "remember how he said before that it's going to be worse this time?"

Kinsey watched the grin on the demon's face grow larger and it began to make him angry. For better or worse, Kinsey had stopped holding his frustrations in years ago. "We've been through that too, Caleb. How many times do we have to have the same conversation? I know exactly what we're getting ourselves into."

"In all fairness," Zach joined in, "if it's not going to be the same, you can't really know exactly what it is."

"I know more than anyone else here," Kinsey insisted. "Maybe not every detail but, I have a pretty good idea."

"True," Zach acknowledged.

"I," Caleb started in again, "I for one am thankful for the second chance to turn around."

"We're not turning around," Kinsey continued. "We made a decision and we're sticking with it. This is the entire reason I came back to this place. To get you home. Yes, the path to get there is going to be hard. It's going to be downright grueling. Some of us may even die. But, I promise you, it's going to be worth it."

"Yeah," Caleb started sheepishly, "that worth it part is what's hard for me. How can death be worth it? No offense and all but, you're starting to come off sounding a little crazy. I don't want to die because I followed some crazy guy right into the wrath of a demon. That would make me crazy and I'm not really the crazy type."

"We're not turning around," Kinsey repeated, all but ignoring Caleb's assertion that he sounded crazy. "None of us. It's too late for that."

"It's never too late," the demon claimed.

"Yeah," Caleb started, "all we have to do is start walking back the way we came. That's what turning around is."

"You should listen to your friend," the demon said to Kinsey before finally breaking the stare and speaking to the whole group. "You should all listen to Caleb. Smart one there."

"He's just scared," Kinsey insisted as he stepped close enough to the demon to feel his surprisingly cold breath. "They all are. But, I'm not. I'm not afraid of you and I'm not afraid of Raum."

"You should be," the demon said with a heightened tone.

"But I'm not. Not this time."

~

"None of us should be," Jill continued. "We have to remember the light and what that symbolized. The message that was being sent from that glowing tree. The source of that light is greater than the source of the darkness that surrounds us right now."

"What light?" the demon asked, visibly shaken for the first time. "You shouldn't be seeing any light. Raum has dominion here!"

"Raum doesn't have dominion over me," Jill maintained as the demon continued growing angrier. "He doesn't have to have dominion over any of us. Not if we choose the side of the light. When this is over, those who have chosen the light will never have to be surrounded by darkness again. You don't have to believe in me. But, I'm begging you all to believe in the source of that light."

"I'm all in," Hannah stated, almost immediately, replacing her own fear and apprehension with grit and fortitude.

Jill looked around as the women nodded their heads and voiced their agreement. Hannah's words were contagious. A smile slowly returned to Jill's face as she realized that the demon had lost this battle. "Good. From this moment on, we push through to the end." Finally, her eyes locked with the demon again. "Come what may."

"So be it," the demon stated before slapping her hands together and abruptly vanishing into thin air.

The women cheered victoriously and it warmed Jill's heart

even though she knew, deep down in that very same heart, that the first wave of Raum's attacks would be upon them very shortly.

PART SIX
Overcoming Obstacles

CHAPTER TWENTY-FIVE
Waiting

Other than the sounds of the ocean, the girls were sitting in complete silence. They all knew an attack was imminent, but had no idea where it was coming from or at exactly which moment it would strike. Tensions were high but, thankfully, so was resolve. The girls were determined to push forward despite the fact that they had every reason to be afraid as they traveled.

Tatum had instructed the girls to scoot themselves inward on the rafts as much as they could in order to get away from the water from which they thought the attack was likely to emerge. There were two things that made the instruction difficult to accommodate: the lack of room, and; the fact that they simply had to continue rowing in order to make progress on their journey. Still, the girls did the best they could.

They also found themselves peeking through the cracks in

the bamboo, wondering if the attack would, instead of coming from one of the raft's four sides, come from directly below them. Knowing an attack was coming but not knowing what would be attacking, where they would be attacked from, or how they would defend themselves had, understandably left the girls feeling completely vulnerable.

~

The boys were not feeling any less helpless than the girls were at that moment. They were deep in the forest, surrounded by darkness, and anticipating something unknown, or worse, multiple somethings unknown, to jump out and attack them at any moment. The main difference between the boys and the girls, other than land versus ocean, was that the boys were a lot more talkative about their predicament.

"How did you kill the Kodiak?" asked Caleb, obviously terrified that he, and the rest of the boys, were about to be attacked by a bear, the same way Kinsey's other group previously had been.

"We all fought hard," Kinsey recalled, hoping to reassure his new friend. "Just like we will this time. Several of us hit it with arrows but, ultimately, it was a spear through the heart from a kid named Will that did it. Made for a tasty meal, too."

Caleb chuckled which made Kinsey smile. He was glad he'd been able to calm Caleb down a little, even if it was likely to be short-lived.

"I'd never had bear meat before that," Kinsey continued. "Haven't since either. Maybe today's the day. Maybe it's a Kadosh thing."

"Yeah," Caleb agreed before pointing out what he considered an obvious flaw in Kinsey's previous sentence. "Hard to call anything a day around here though."

"All a matter of perspective, Caleb."

"Yeah, well, from my perspective, it's pretty clearly nighttime around here . . . always."

"I can see why you would say that," Kinsey acknowledged.

"Of course you can. Pretty noticeable. Dark everywhere," Caleb stated with his right index finger extended and moving in a twirling motion so he could point out all of the darkness they were surrounded by.

"True."

"So, what's your perspective?"

"Well, it's also true that, because it's dark all the time, we don't have a differentiator between night and day."

"Yeah, that's what I just said."

"Stick with me."

"Okay."

"I think that means it's up to us to decide when it's day and night. Typically, people sleep at night. We just slept not that long ago so, I'm choosing to think it's daytime right now. Just happens to be dark out."

"Yeah, dark like night."

"Exactly."

"What?" Caleb was bewildered by Kinsey agreeing with him so emphatically when they were so obviously opposed on the main topic.

"Dark *like* night. Not dark *is* night. Did you know there are places in Alaska where it goes dark for sixty-seven days in a row? I'll bet they still call it daytime when it's dark at noon."

"Okay, man. Whatever you say. I'm going to let this go and choose to steer the conversation back toward something that really matters. Like the looming danger of a bear attack."

"Fair enough. We don't know if it'll be a bear though."

"Right. But, it was last time so it's the best guess we have."

"Also fair."

~

"Unless," Hannah started in concession, "Raum decides to skip the animals altogether and go straight to that unnerving, centipede tree thing you mentioned. I'm not sure I can handle one of those. Sounds like it's right out of a Tim Burton movie based on a Doctor Seuss book. That'll just straight up creep me right out, something like that. Ugh. Makes me shiver all over."

"We got through it last time," Jill maintained, "we'll get through it this time, too."

"You got through it," Hannah insisted. "I haven't gotten through anything yet."

"Well," Jill argued, "you're going to get through this. We will be reunited with our families. Speaking of which, who's out there for you?"

Jill was hoping the distraction would be a good thing for Hannah. She couldn't help but wonder, however, if that would be the case as she watched a pensive look wash over her friend's face. It took a moment for Hannah to speak but, when she finally did, the look quickly made sense.

"My daughter. Maybe. Definitely no one else. Amara was the sweetest little girl but, by seventh grade, she had turned into someone I barely recognized. She never knew her daddy. Good thing, too. Oh, that man was mean. When I found out I was pregnant, I knew I had to get away from him. So, it was just the two of us. When she got mean, I got scared. How could she become her father when he wasn't even part of her life?"

As the tears, glistening in the moonlight, began to roll down Hannah's cheeks, Jill reached out and held her hand. Hannah continued to talk without ever missing a beat.

"Plus, I was working two jobs to make ends meet. I couldn't keep up anyway. I came home one night, after a ten hour stretch at the factory and another six on my feet doing retail. She wasn't there. I thought she was out with friends or, worse, a boy. All of which would be against the rules but, I never expected I'd find out she'd been arrested. Beat another girl up outside of a convenience store so she could take her jacket. I had worked so hard to give her everything she needed, I got her away from her daddy before he ever knew she existed so she wouldn't experience his cruelty, and then she became so mean and awful. It was bad enough that she had been that way but, then to learn that she had beaten a girl up and stole her jacket when there are five jackets hanging in her closet at home . . . I lost it. It was all I could do to keep myself from beating her senseless, just to show her how it feels, right there in the police station. Instead, I took her home and told her she wasn't coming out of her room until she was an adult. I told her she had a choice between prison at home or prison away from home. Of course, I never thought she'd choose prison away from home but, when I went back to her room a few hours later, after I'd cooled off a bit, she was gone. I lost it all over again. Then, somehow, I ended up here. If she did, too, I guess we both found prison away from home. I just pray it's changed her."

"How could it not?" Jill proposed, speaking her first words since Hannah had begun to tell her story.

"I figure, a place like this, will either return her to the sweet little girl she once was, or make her meaner than she ever would have become back home."

"Let's both pray it's the former."

~

The men were practically marching when they were suddenly forced to a stop by eight giant, glowing yellow eyes directly in front of them. In an instant, their hearts began to pound almost as loudly as their feet had been only a split second earlier. They immediately knew, the first attack was upon them.

CHAPTER TWENTY-SIX
Beasts

While the men remained frozen in anticipation, staring at the big yellow dots glowing from the eye-sockets on the unknown assailants in front of them, they watched the dots, almost in unison, quickly rise from about five feet off of the ground to about twelve. Suddenly, something happened that no one could have anticipated. Three massive, ferocious-looking dinosaurs slowly stepped out of the darkness.

Since there wasn't a paleontologist among them, no one knew that each of these beasts was called an acrocanthosaurus which, appropriately, means high-spined lizard. They each stood on two legs and had short arms like a tyrannosaurus but, a couple of things set them apart from their more famous cousins. The acrocanthosauruses stood with the length of their bodies more horizontal than the tyrannosaurus and they had a tall row of neural spines on top of the vertebrae of their necks, backs, hips and upper tails.

Grant was silently guessing they were thirty-five to forty feet in length and must have weighed between six and eight tons.

"I guess that answers the question of what Raum's going to attack us with first," Ray quietly whispered to Grant.

"Yeah," Grant agreed just as quietly, "welcome to Jurassic Park."

"Didn't they have like guns and Jeeps and stuff in that movie?"

"Sure did."

"Must be nice."

"Must be."

~

The beasts circling the girls on the giant raft were significantly smaller than those facing off with the men. But, they looked like they could have traveled through the same time portal and, to the girls, they didn't look small at all.

Eight saltwater crocodiles, each between eighteen and twenty-four feet in length and easily weighing over one thousand pounds, were swimming around the raft as if they were about to enjoy a cooperative feast. Suddenly, one of them dove under the raft and the girls let out a collective screech that echoed off of the lapping waters which trapped them while housing their vicious stalkers.

~

The boys were rapidly overtaken by hundreds of scorpions that pinched and stung them repeatedly. They waved their arms and tried to knock the arachnids away from them but they were clearly outnumbered.

~

In the midst of a swarm of their own, the women were trying to fight off thousands of large Tsetse flies that had descended upon them and were already biting their skin. The scene quickly escalated into chaos as the women ran in circles, bumping into each other and flailing their arms in the air while striking themselves in an attempt to remove the assaulting parasites that had already begun to attach themselves to the women's spines. Unfortunately, they quickly realized there was no escaping the throng of blood-sucking flies.

~

The men were scattered and terrified, feeling helpless as they watched the giant dinosaurs break through bushes and topple trees like they were snapping wooden skewers with their foreheads. Soon, there would be no place left to hide, even in the dark.

~

CHOMP! SNAP! CHOMP! CRACK! CHOMP!

The enormous crocodiles opened their jaws, one after the other, and tried to grab the girls with their sharp teeth to pull them into the water. They whipped their bodies, snapped their tails at the girls and headbutted the raft. Gasps and screams echoed off the water as panic overwhelmed the group.

~

It seemed as if the scorpions were everywhere. The crunching sounds of the arachnids being crushed under the boys' feet couldn't be heard over the screams of terror as they tried to get them off of their bodies but, the boys could feel them everywhere. If they weren't dying beneath them, they were crawling all over the boys and pinching their skin with grasping pedipalps.

~

Jill heard the splashing of water as Olivia accidentally fell into a nearby river and that's when the solution to their infestation finally hit her. "Water! Everyone get in the water!"

~

"The rock monster," Grant exclaimed in revelation.

"What?" asked Ray as he looked around for another attacker.

"The bigger they are, the harder they fall. Just like the rock monster.

"What are you saying?"

"We passed a cliff about a couple of hundred feet back. We need to roll or carry all of the logs from these trees they're knocking down back by the cliff."

"Then what?" Ray asked, sincerely bewildered by Grant's murky plan.

"Just get everyone to do it and then follow my lead."

~

"Everyone group back together," Kinsey yelled as loud as he could. "Bunch up and use the torches to start a fire! Let's cook these things!"

~

Tatum stood up and drew her arrow in the bow to take aim, firing quickly and striking one of the massive crocodiles in the head.

As Emily and Fabia followed her lead, Amara decided to go in a direction all her own. She plunged a spear directly into the head of a crocodile, right as it went to snap its jaw, and Yanna had the unfortunate privilege of seeing the wood enter the back of the predator's throat just before the tail of another one swept her. Yanna heard the sound of her ankle breaking as she collapsed onto the bamboo raft and hit her head, leaving her unconscious.

~

Qasim and Doug led groups of men who were in charge of distracting the dinosaurs by getting them to chase them away from the men who were moving as many of the fallen trees as they could to a patch of open field near a cliff. Ray and Grant were in charge of the rest of the men, who were quickly running out of steam from carrying and rolling the heavy logs into place. Luckily, adrenaline has a way of making it possible for human beings to take their bodies beyond known limitations and the encounter with gargantuan, prehistoric lizards that were trying to eat them, was sending their adrenaline into overdrive.

~

The Tsetse flies had no choice but to release their hosts as the women, one right after the other, submerged themselves in the river's water. Unfortunately, the flies continued to hover, in a giant swarm, just a few feet above the water, as if they were waiting for their next opportunity to strike.

~

Kinsey had all of the boys gathered close together and pulling scorpions off of one another. They were tossing them in the fire lit only a few feet away and encircling three quarters of the pack. They stomped their feet in place to kill any scorpions that were still on the ground as they made headway to rid the crowd of the ones that had managed to climb up their bodies. Moans and grunts were still emanating from the boys as they continued to feel the pinches and stings of the arachnids but, the screaming had subsided as fear slowly quieted down.

~

Grant began to wave and yell, signaling all the men to join him on the other side of the logs, back in the direction they had come from, and then watched as the dinosaurs chased after them. Qasim slipped and fell, rendering him helpless as one of the dinosaurs stepped over him. Thankfully, he was left unharmed, watching from behind the three dinosaurs as they pursued the others.

The men being chased ran along both sides of the logs to join those waiting on the other side who were praying the plan would work. As the dinosaurs hit the logs, they began to spin beneath their feet, quickly turning the scene into something out of an old-fashioned slapstick comedy. The ferocious beasts suddenly looked silly as they tried to recapture their balance but, instead, came crashing to the ground and, with the logs still beneath them, rolled right off the cliff.

Cheering and laughing filled the sudden void left by the disappearing sounds made by twenty tons of moving mass.

~

Without warning, the women watched the swarm of flies quickly disappear into the darkness. They were silent at first, unsure if they would return. But, as their confidence that the event had reached a conclusion grew, they began to cheer just as loudly as the men were doing a small ocean away.

~

With the last of the giant saltwater crocodiles now floating, lifeless, just feet away from the raft, Tatum rushed to Yanna's side. She had started praying out loud before arriving and, after realizing that Yanna was breathing but not conscious, she closed her eyes and continued.

"You, God, are the ultimate physician. Please, heal Yanna right now and wake her from her slumber. Bring her back to us so she can finish the journey she started with us in obedience to your calling."

Unexpectedly, everyone heard a cracking sound as Yanna's ankle seemed to reset itself. All eyes, including Tatum's, because she couldn't help but open them to look, were on that ankle when a voice caused them all to shift back to Yanna's face.

"Are they gone?"

"What?" Tatum asked, as an automatic reaction to hearing the voice of her previously unconscious friend.

"The crocodiles. Are they gone?"

"Yep," Tatum stated as the whispers of amazement among

the other girls quickly started. That's when it abruptly struck her. The man at church, Ulrich, had told her dad that they would all be discovering the gifts God was equipping them with in the days to come. Before they left for Kadosh, her dad had spoken in a language that seemed unintelligible to the rest of the family. Ray was the only one who understood it and he had interpreted it for them. Now, God had answered her prayer and healed a girl. She couldn't help but wonder what gifts God was giving to her mom and her little brother. And, she looked forward to finding them and discovering what those gifts were.

CHAPTER TWENTY-SEVEN
Lost and Found

Seeking rest, Hannah and Olivia built a fire as Jill and the other women both gathered wood to keep the fire burning and searched for food. Everyone was still shaken up from the attack of Tsetse flies and it showed physically. Some were still rubbing their hands on their bodies and spitting as if the flies were still on their arms, faces and in their hair.

Brianna was reaching toward a vine to pick some passion fruit when a hand crossed in front of hers and snatched the yellow fruit from right in front of her. Startled, she jumped back and let out a small yelp. Suddenly, her eyes caught the stare of another set of eyes. It was a short, frail woman, and the scariest part was, it was not anyone she recognized.

~

"Who are you?" Doug asked, aggressively, as he stared, skeptically, at the thin man who towered over him by almost a whole foot.

"Devonte," the stranger answered. "Who are you?"

"Doug."

"And them?" Devonte asked, pointing to the other men behind Doug.

"They're with me. Where'd you come from?"

"You mean to tell me," Devonte began to ask, ignoring Doug's question, "this whole time…there were others?"

"What whole time? How long have you been out here?"

"I've lost track."

"Kadosh will do that to you."

"Kadosh?" Devonte asked.

"That's what we call this place."

"How many?"

"How many what?"

"People."

"With me? I don't have an exact head count but-"

"There are more?"

"Besides us? Yeah, a few. Are you by yourself?"

Devonte nodded affirmatively.

"The whole time?"

Devonte nodded again.

You want to join us?"

~

Zach led Kai to the fire Caleb and Pablo had just gotten started. Boys began to greet Kai and introduce themselves to him. Kai was timid at first. After all, it appeared that he had been alone for quite a while. Now, suddenly, he was surrounded by strangers wanting to know all about him.

~

Jen's raft had seemingly come out of nowhere. The girls couldn't tell what it was at first. There was no sail and Jen had been asleep. It just looked like a flat mass floating in the water. But, now, there they were, talking like they met at the mall rather than the middle of a vast ocean.

Having walked from one side of the island to the other before realizing she was even on an island, Jen had spent the last, what she could only guess was several months, completely confused. One minute she was fighting with her dad in the city of Prescott, which happened to be in the northern half of the landlocked state of Arizona, and the next she was waking up, all alone, in this weird place where dawn never came. Ultimately, she decided she had nothing left to lose, built the raft, pushed off into the ocean, and hoped the current would guide her to civilization.

It was shocking to suddenly finally find other girls. Even more to find them out in the middle of the water. Especially after the amount of time she had been on the raft without seeing an ocean liner or even hearing the sound of any kind of aircraft. But, the most shocking revelation of all, was to learn that her dad might actually be on one of the other islands. When she found out the girls were in search of their families, Jen couldn't tie her raft to the back of theirs fast enough and join them on their quest.

~

Wendy was the first to raise some skepticism. She wanted to know how they could be sure Marissa wasn't another one of Raum's demons, sent to sabotage them.

The shocked look on Marissa's face when the question was raised was so sincere, it could have ended the conversation right there. But, in light of where they were and with what had recently taken place, the question was a fair one and the murmurs in the crowd demanded some more discussion.

Jill was quick to point out that she had recognized the demon Raum sent before. She informed the group that the Bible calls that discernment. Further, she knew in her spirit that Marissa was just another scared woman who wanted to be reunited with her family. She reminded everyone that they had trusted her this far and asked them to continue to do so.

~

Kai's story resonated with the other boys. His confusion was something they could relate to and his loneliness reminded them of how blessed they had been to find one another. They knew there had to be other boys out there who had never made it to camp once the lights went out, and stayed out, so everything about Kai's story made sense to them. Sympathy and compassion began to overtake the group and they wondered how many others were out there like Kai. Alone and frightened. It helped, too, that Kai was such a likeable kid. Still, not everyone was immediately ready to accept that this wasn't just another one of Raum's tactics. But, majority ruled and Kai was eventually welcomed as a part of the group.

When Kai asked about the other boys back at camp, he briefly thought going in search of what sounded like a possible safe haven seemed like an intriguing idea. But, as he heard everyone talk about finding their families, he considered how good it would be to go home, get out of this crazy place, and see his mom again.

Of course, leaving this horrible place was easy to get excited about. Until just moments earlier, he had been completely alone and utterly terrified in an unfamiliar place with none of the comforts of home. He had no bed to sleep in, no shower to hop into and clean off, no TV to watch, no change of clothes, no video games, no friends or family . . . no people at all. Just the animals in the forest – which were causing a significant portion of his fear. Maybe worse, food was scarce. What he really wanted at that moment was some cheese pizza. In fact, if he could get his hands on a large pizza from his favorite restaurant, Tony's, he knew he could eat the whole thing by himself. But, truth be told, that still sounded lonely.

He had told his mom that he hated her and she was the worst parent in the world, just before he woke up in what he now knew was Kadosh. He'd had a lot of time since then to let the regret he felt over that moment overwhelm him. What he wanted more than to eat a whole pizza by himself was to go to Tony's, share a slice of that cheese pizza with his mom, and tell her how sorry he was. He would tell her she was an awesome parent and that he loved her. Heck, if given the chance, he'd even let her ruin her half of the pizza with the Canadian bacon and pineapple she, for some odd reason, seemed to love so much.

His own thoughts caused his guard to come down and the group's enthusiasm quickly became contagious. Before he even knew it, he had decided he would stay with the group and make the rest of their journey with them. It was a decision he would need to be resolute about in the moments to follow because, the whole group was about to face a challenge none of them had ever encountered before.

CHAPTER TWENTY-EIGHT
Monsters

Tatum suddenly noticed that the water about seventy or eighty feet in front of the girls was an entirely different color from both the water closer by and anything they'd seen up to that point. As they got closer to it, she realized that color was red. She immediately thought about the fact that she had never seen red water before and quickly wondered if blood was causing the effect. Perhaps sharks had recently fed on a big whale or something.

But, after a few more strokes with their oars, the girls reached the edge of the red water and she realized algae was the actual cause. However, the truly disturbing realization that made them stop rowing was that the algae was moving and it appeared to be collecting itself into one giant mass.

~

The sudden burst of rain was turning the ground beneath the men into mud as they sought shelter under trees. Ray was the first to notice that the mud was grouping itself.

"What's it doing?" he asked Grant.

"Oh, great." Grant responded. "I've seen this before. Only, last time it wasn't mud. It was huge boulders."

~

The contents of the fire had formed into a winged animal that closely resembled an enormous dragon. Its body was made of black, brown and gray wood that was still on fire. Both eyes were made of red hot embers that were still burning and smoke was emitting from its nostrils. Jill and the other women slowly backed away in fear as they watched the monster come to life and begin to breathe fire.

~

Having molded out of large, fallen pine cones, the boys stared at the rodent-like beings which seemed to have their flattened heads permanently turned sideways as they scurried across the ground like they were vacuuming up food with the downturned corners of their distorted mouths. Kinsey was astonished by the sheer, sudden volume of the disgusting little creatures and feared they were about to be overtaken due simply to the quantity of them.

~

The red monster in front of the girls had risen up and now appeared to be standing on top of the water as if it were blocking them from continuing their journey. Tatum remembered the *Lord of the Rings* movies she'd watched on movie nights with Kinsey and couldn't help but think of Gandalf's "You shall not pass" moment. Only, in this case, the one delivering the line wouldn't be Gandalf, it would be Kadosh's version of the Balrog.

~

Just as Grant had suspected, the monster in front of the men looked similar to the rock monster he had faced his first time in Kadosh. It was just as massive but it was dripping mud and therefore appeared far less solid yet somehow felt even more menacing. The only good news he could think of at that moment was that the rain had stopped as soon as the monster had materialized.

~

As the intensity of the squeaking noise the rodents were making increased, Kinsey found himself wishing he could fashion a recorder out of a tree branch and turn into the Pied Piper of Hamelin so he could lure the vermin away. Since that was impossible, he needed another idea and he needed it quickly.

~

Jill scanned the area for anything that would trigger a brainstorm. Nothing was clicking in her mind and she feared that they were running out of time until, suddenly, her ears picked up on the sound of rustling water. She quickly turned to Marissa.

"Do you know if there's a river or a stream nearby?"

"Yeah," Marissa stated with a hint of confusion. "Why?"

"Because that thing's made of fire and we need to put it out."

~

As the mud-monster began slinging mud at the men, Grant shouted his orders. "We have to rebuild the fire! And, make it a scorcher!"

~

"Start paddling," Tatum yelled.

"What are we going to do," Jen began to ask. "are we going through it?"

"Not through it," Tatum responded. "Under it."

~

While the number of the bizarre-looking rodents was overwhelming, Kinsey watched the other boys kill them with big rocks and spears and it dawned on him that there was no better way. They were the larger and more dangerous predator regardless of the fact that they were outnumbered so, Kinsey joined the fight.

~

Marissa ran toward the river with Jill and the other women close behind her. Unfortunately, the volant creature chasing all of them was gaining ground as it set the path ablaze. If the fiery trail behind them didn't do enough to announce the creature's presence, the rumbling sound in its throat and the loud flapping of its wings would have done the trick. The combination of all three had the women running for their lives.

~

The fire built by the men was growing in size and those not working on it were attacking the mud monster by throwing rocks and hitting it with sticks. They were attempting to separate it but the effort seemed futile at first because the mud that came off continually slinked its way back to the monster and reattached itself.

~

"Dive!" Tatum yelled.

The girls immediately dropped their oars to their sides on the raft and dove in the water just before the raft crashed through the massive wall of algae. They swam, as Tatum had instructed them, at least ten feet below the surface before continuing ahead to chase their raft.

Looking above her as she swam, Tatum could see the roughly six-foot thick algae monster standing on the surface of the water. She pulled with her arms and kicked her feet until she was well beyond it and then finally started to ascend.

~

The women splashed as much water as they could toward the fire-breathing monster and it seemed that each drop wounded it. They used every resource they had, from their hands to pieces of wood. The more water they could send toward the monster, the better.

They were all forced to submerge themselves, however, when fire shot down at them from the dragon's mouth. But, they quickly got back on their feet and resumed their attack. It was a process that would repeat itself many times. And, every time it did, more smoke sprung from the body of the monster.

~

The men who built the fire were using branches to wave the dry heat from the fire at the monster while others were surrounding it with torches and some continued to pummel it with sticks and rocks. The monster fought back, covering the men with mud and, in many cases, knocking them clean off their feet as the mud hurled at them connected.

~

With the boys on the attack and dead rodents increasing in number, the rodents that were still alive finally began to disperse.

~

As girls' heads started popping up around the raft, Tatum instructed them to get their oars and use them to splash water on the raft in order to clean the potentially toxic algae off of it before climbing back on board.

~

The monster's motion was becoming noticeably less fluid. Grant looked closer and could tell that their efforts were starting to pay off. The mud was beginning to dry and even crack in some cases.

~

Smoke was now billowing out of the dragon-like creature and, with it, it appeared any sign of life. No fire was spewing from its mouth anymore and Jill decided to deliver what she hoped would be the death blow. She reached back and hurled a sopping wet piece of wood at it and, when it connected, the monster screeched as it fell straight to the ground and shattered into pieces of ash and charcoal.

Cheers immediately went up as the women began to celebrate. Unfortunately, they couldn't possibly have realized that, while the monster in front of them was certainly dead, the attack was far from over.

would be the death blow. She reached back and hurled a sopping wet piece of wood at it and, when it connected, the monster screeched as it fell straight to the ground and shattered into pieces of ash and charcoal.

Cheers immediately went up as the women began to celebrate. Unfortunately, they couldn't possibly have realized that, while the monster in front of them was certainly dead, the attack was far from over.

CHAPTER TWENTY-NINE
Slither

Kinsey and the boys were still high-fiving each other and celebrating their victory over the pinecones turned bizarre rodents when he announced that he thought they were nearing the other side of the island and encouraged everyone to keep pushing on. Still excited, the boys started calming down and began to gather their things. Suddenly, Kinsey's head spun to look behind him at the sound of one of the boys shrieking.

~

Olivia was staring at the back of her hand where the pollen string had landed when it fell out of the tree above her. She tried to shake it off but it wouldn't detach itself from her skin and she watched as it seemed to come to life and began to wiggle like a sticky worm.

~

The long kelp, stretching anywhere from one hundred to almost three hundred feet, seemed to be rising to the surface in surprising volume and, when it arrived on top of the water, it immediately began to slither around the girls' raft.

~

Dandelion snakes appeared to be coming from every direction and, while their heads spun in all directions, the men didn't know where to turn or where to go. The snakes were small, and most were on the ground, but some of them were using their petals like propellers to launch themselves through the air.

~

The pine needle worms were crawling all over both each other and the boys' feet. Kinsey and the others were kicking their legs in an attempt to shake the worms off and get away from them. Unfortunately, they were defying the boys and getting into their shoes, socks, and had even begun to crawl up their legs on both the outside and inside of their pants.

~

Jill led the women back into the water, which had just helped them defeat the fire-breathing dragon-like creature only moments earlier. They dove in and swam, trying to drown the worms, but it wasn't working. The pollen strings, which continued to drop from the trees, had turned into something akin to slinking leeches that refused to let go of the women's skin.

~

"Row through them," Tatum shouted.

The girls did as they were told and started rowing harder than they had, other than perhaps when they launched their raft through the algae monster, since leaving shore. And, indeed, the raft pushed through much of the kelp but, the snake-like creatures refused to go away that easily and began trying to make their way onto the raft from each of the two sides.

~

The men had gone back to their fire and were now waving

torches at the dandelion snakes, which seemed to keep them at bay but didn't cause a full retreat.

~

The women had discovered, the hard way, that trying to peel the parasites off of their skin hurt like crazy and essentially got them nowhere. As if they somehow knew to take note from what the men were doing, they focused in on building a fire of their own.

~

"Run for the shoreline," Kinsey shouted as he led the way.

~

Amara smacked a kelp snake on its bulbous head and then gave it another whack to knock it off the raft. She quickly reached forward and thumped another attacking piece of kelp to save Sheila, who was sitting in front of her and didn't even see the snake-like creature coming.

While some of the girls were screaming and trying to scoot away from the giant, slithering serpentines, most of the girls were playing solid defense. They knew the best way to stay safe was to remain in the raft and keep the assailants in the water. And, that's exactly what they were doing.

~

The snakes had begun lunging through the air at the men. Grant used his torch to knock the first one away like a bat to a baseball. Sparks flew as he connected and the snake drifted away.

"Nice," Ray stated with a nod toward Grant before taking his torch and doing the same with the second snake.

Soon, the men were smiling as they stood in a circle and, while the snakes sprang at them in mounting numbers, it began to look like they were taking batting practice and sparklers were igniting around the group like it was the Fourth of July.

~

Jill pulled a stick out of the fire and blew the flame out so she had the closest things she could get to a red hot poker. She then placed the hot end on one of the pollen strings and it immediately let go of her skin and curled up. She shook her arm and watched the worm-like organism fall to the ground and briefly glanced at the red mark left behind from the creature's grip on her skin before moving on to the next one. "It's working," she announced. "Burn 'em off!"

~

Kinsey led the boys, with trees whipping by and needle-worms falling and crawling all over them, toward what they hoped was the water but couldn't be sure. As he pumped his arms and legs, taking deep breaths while trying not to open his mouth too wide for fear of swallowing one of these disgusting little creatures that Raum had sent, Kinsey could think of nothing else to do but pray. And pray, he did.

Father, we're obeying you. I wouldn't even be here otherwise. We're risking our lives to get to our families. Rescue us, please. Deliver us to our families. And, deliver our families to us.

~

In the midst of all the commotion, Jen was the first to spot something in the distance. "Is that land?" she wondered, excitedly, out loud and at a high volume.

Everyone who wasn't in the middle of a battle with a kelp snake turned to see what Jen was looking at. Sure enough, it was a ways off, but everyone could see a landmass in the darkness.

"Row!" Tatum shouted as loud as she could. "Fight and row! Go, go, go!"

~

Grant had just given the command for the opposite half of the circle from where he stood to take a couple of steps forward while his half backed around to the other side. This movement allowed the remaining dandelion snakes on Grant's side to inch closer to the flames while the men on the other side continued to play flaming batting practice with the serpentine-like creatures on their side.

Finally, as the men steadied themselves with their backs to the men still swinging torches, Grant's half of the men faced the same dandelion snakes they had previously. But, now, the fire separated them and Grant lined up to take another big swing. When he did, he connected with the wood on top of the fire and sent it spiraling through the air at the snakes on his side, causing them to slither away in a hurry. He then commanded the men to start walking in a circle, clock-wise, while he did it again in the other three directions.

~

Now clean of pollen strings, Jill and Olivia were burning them off of the other women. Starting with Hannah and Marissa, the number of women free of the leech-like worm creatures quickly escalated.

~

There was no cheering when the water came into view. All the boys could do was sprint into it as fast as they had ever run before. They had singular focus as they dove headfirst and stayed submerged as long as their breath would allow.

Kinsey let himself sink to the ocean floor as he rubbed his hands all over his body like he was trying to set a new world record for fastest bath. He opened his eyes under the water and the light from the sky was enough for him to watch the needles fall from his skin and collapse lifeless on the ground.

Just as a smile began to emerge on Kinsey's face, he watched what he first thought was a giant eel swim in front of him. But, as it circled back around him, he quickly identified it as kelp. Then it began to wrap around him like a boa constrictor.

Kinsey used his feet to burst through the surface of the water and gasp for air. Thankfully, he was able to stand with the upper half of his body out of the water. But, he could barely find any breath. He tried to shout for help but no words would come out.

In that moment, he thought he may have breathed his last. He thought he may be about to see the gates of heaven. That was, until he heard the most comforting sound he ever had before. Not that it was the first time he had ever heard it. It was the same sound that had comforted him for as long as he could remember, even in the worst times he had ever endured. It was the sweet sound of his sister's reassuring voice.

"Kinsey!"

CHAPTER THIRTY
Islands' Edge

"Kinsey," Tatum yelled again. She was in the water, sprinting toward her brother, a split second after Kinsey had come into view.

Yanna, Amara and Emily pulled the raft onto the shore as Ling led the rest of the girls to help the boys who were being attacked by the kelp snakes.

As soon as she reached Kinsey, Tatum grabbed the kelp snake that was wrapped around her brother and started to unwind it like a rope around a tree trunk. Only, this rope was slimy and, worse, it didn't want to be unwound so it fought her at every pull, tug and yank.

Thankfully, Fabia and Jen immediately joined the struggle. Jen quickly grabbed the head of the snake from Tatum and pulled it to shore. With the kelp stretched from the sand to Kinsey, it must have been over eighty feet, with another hundred and fifty or more still wrapped around his body. Jen put the head on the ground, held it down with one foot and started stomping on it with the other.

Tatum continued pulling on the body of the snake as Fabia helped Kinsey to spin, unwinding the snake against its will. Soon, it looked like, from Kinsey to Tatum, and from Tatum to Jen, they were holding a giant sling shot. But, then Kinsey came fully unwound and collapsed into Fabia's arms from dizziness. By that point, Jen had smashed the bulbous head into a squishy, soupy mess and all four of them were exhausted.

Unfortunately, Kinsey wasn't the only one who had been attacked by the kelp snakes. The effort felt like it took hours but, eventually, all the boys and girls were on dry land and safe with no permanent injuries but a lot of tired people who were excited to see one another.

~

Grant immediately began instructing the other men on which materials needed to be located to build a vessel they could use to make it across the water to Raum's island. Clearly, they didn't have the time it would take to make a boat like the one he had traveled in the last time. That had been a smaller version of an early nineteenth century slave ship, made entirely out of wood, but without any of the elaborate trimmings or carvings seen in renderings of the old, comparable ships. This would have to be a more hastily assembled craft, which was scary considering the weather and other obstacles Grant and Ray had encountered on the last voyage.

~

The women were gathering materials as well and Jill had just decided to use giant taro leaves for the sails when she first noticed that the weather was eerily calm. The last time she'd made this journey, she and her traveling companions had arrived at the shoreline in the middle of a torrential downpour and a heavy thunder and lightning storm. Plus, they were being pursued by several of those trees turned giant centipedes. For now, it seemed the attacks were in the middle of a lull. But, she couldn't help but wonder how long the peace would last.

~

While the boys and girls had powered through their exhaustion to experience a jubilant reunion, they had also kept it short and begun expanding the girls' raft to accommodate the boys as well as adding makeshift sails created out of a variety of clothing items. Kinsey hoped they wouldn't encounter the cold weather he had previously experienced, as he instructed the boys to strip down to their skivvies.

Taking his shirt off to reveal a less than fit physique, Pablo sighed and commented, "Alright, but when I get home, I'm hitting the gym."

Reluctantly removing his pants to reveal his classic white briefs, Zach added, "And, I'm switching to boxers."

~

As most of the men either assembled the base of the raft out of logs or searched for wood they could turn into oars, Ray was busy connecting the few blankets they had together in order to create a sail of their own.

~

Hannah wondered out loud why the sails were so important when there didn't seem to be any wind to which Jill simply replied, "There will be."

"How could you possibly know that?" Hannah asked.

"Call it a combination of experience and discernment."

~

"When Raum gets angry. . ." Kinsey started to respond before being cut off.

"When?" Zach interjected out of complete panic, as everyone within earshot stopped what they were doing to listen in. "When Raum gets angry? Are you saying we haven't seen his anger yet?"

"No," Kinsey tried to explain. "I'm not saying that at all. We've definitely seen the result of Raum getting angry. But, he's only going to get more upset once we jump on these rafts and head for his island. The angrier he gets, the more of his wrath we're going to experience. That means everything we've already seen, plus storms and who knows what else."

~

"You," Devonte jumped in, calling out both Grant and Ray as the group began to circle around. "You two said you knew what we were facing. So, tell us. How much worse is this going to get?"

~

"A lot worse," Jill stated honestly.

"What does that mean?" Marissa asked, clearly terrified.

~

"It means," Tatum stepped in, "we're about to experience severe weather, sea monsters, even ghosts."

"Ghosts?" Yanna trembled.

"I don't like the sound of that at all," Caleb sighed deeply.

"The ghosts of the people who have tried to make it to Raum's island and failed," Kinsey stated matter-of-factly.

"I think I'm going to throw up," Caleb said as he sat down and put his head between his legs.

"How do you think I feel?" Zach asked Caleb, sincerely. "From what Kinsey's tellin' us, I get to greet these ghosts in the middle of a blizzard with nothin' on but my tighty-whities."

~

"Look at what you've already accomplished," Grant tried to reassure the group. "Look at how far you've already come. Don't give in to fear now."

"Giving in and accepting reality aren't necessarily the same thing," Ben stated with some sadness in his voice.

"Reality is," Ray joined the conversation to back Grant up, "it's time to finish what you started and go home."

"Or," Nicolai quantified, "become one of those ghosts."

"That's a possibility," Grant admitted. "But so is getting out of here. We've already done it once."

~

"Exactly," Olivia interjected. "We have no reason not to trust Jill. What are we standing around debating this for? We already made our decision when we left the camp. Let's finish this. Let's go home."

~

A lot of head nodding showed that the mood had begun to swing back toward the upbeat end of the temperament pendulum and the kids began to look like an athletic team getting pumped up before a big game. Everyone was fully aware of the consequences of what they were doing. The potential negative consequences could be as severe as loss of life. But, the potential positive consequences meant going home and being with family for good. And, with everyone in agreement that the positive consequences were worth the risk, they went back to building their rafts with renewed vigor.

The optimistic attitude was important, too. Although they knew great danger was just around the corner, no one knew how great that danger was going to get. But, that knowledge was coming and it was coming fast. After all, they were about to face a series of obstacles greater than any of them had even begun to imagine.

PART SEVEN
Sail Away

CHAPTER THIRTY-ONE
Peril

As the women inched closer to pushing their raft out into deeper waters and setting sail for Raum's island, Jill watched a massive lightning bolt crack through the sky. A few seconds later, thunder roared through the group and Raum quickly had the attention of every woman on the beach. That's when a raindrop hit Hannah square on her forehead. As she reached up to wipe it off, several more hit her on the nose and cheeks. The pace of the falling rain rapidly increased to a downpour and Jill exchanged a look with Hannah that suggested they both knew in that moment that they needed to prepare themselves for the fact that the wrath of Raum was in full swing.

~

"Let's pick up the pace," Grant shouted as the storm continued and the time elapsing between seeing the lightning and both hearing and feeling the booming thunder grew shorter. He was certain the onslaught would continue to get worse, he just didn't know how or in what way.

~

The kids were hustling as fast as they could to finish preparing for departure when Caleb let out a big gasp and shouted, "What the heck are those things?"

Everyone turned to see, crawling out of the water and onto the beach, hundreds of lobsters. But, these weren't the little one or two pound lobsters Kinsey had seen alive with rubber bands around their pincers in the tank at a nice seafood restaurant. The smallest among them had to weigh fifteen pounds and Tatum was guessing that several of the crustaceans may have been over fifty pounds. The body alone, on the bigger ones, had to be around three feet in length before adding the size of those vicious-looking pincers that were snapping away as if the monstrous sea-creatures were there to attack.

~

"Get on the raft!" Jill shouted as hundreds of white-faced capuchin monkeys were pouring out of the forest and onto the beach. If it weren't for the white fur on their heads, they would have been difficult to see in the dark because, at about a foot and a half tall and less than ten pounds, their small bodies were covered in black fur. However, the women were staring at hundreds of tiny, white monkey heads, swinging out of trees and onto the sand and then scurrying directly toward them.

~

The men ducked low, as they boarded the raft, to avoid the swooping eagle owls. The birds of prey were massive in size, with wing spans longer than five feet. As Ben stepped onto the raft, he reached for the sail pole to stabilize himself and one of the owls' talons caught his hand, cutting it badly.

~

Rain continued to pour down on the kids who were almost all on the raft. Kinsey squinted his eyes to see, through the darkness and rain, movement in the not-too-distant forest. As he wiped rain from his face and focused his eyes, he realized that the rodents were back and heading right for them.

"Ow!" he shouted as he suddenly felt severe pain in his lower left leg. He looked down and saw a giant lobster clinching him just above his left ankle. Kinsey quickly reached down and gripped each pincer with a hand. He pried them open until he heard them break, then stood back up and kicked the lobster away. Having cut his hands while gripping the pincers, he now had blood running in the rain and dripping from both his hands and his leg. Ignoring it, he kicked two more giant lobsters away from him before beginning to push the raft. With help from Tatum, Pablo and Jen, the raft launched into the water and the remaining few of the kids climbed safely on board.

~

Ray was abruptly hit in the back and faceplanted into the floor of the raft. As he turned over, he discovered that he'd been hit with a whopping ball of mud. Looking up from the floor and then out at the beach he was floating away from, he saw the owls had begun circling another mud monster like the one they had dried out and destroyed earlier. He continued to watch as several more dinosaurs stepped out of the forest and onto the beach having just missed their chance to join in the attack on the men.

Immediately, he quietly thanked God that they were finally on the raft, away from the dangers of the island, and on their way to hopefully reunite with family. Specifically, he hoped to see his sister, Sheila, for the first time in almost forty years. The thought brought tears to his eyes but they were interrupted before falling at the thought of what still lay ahead. After all, he knew as well as anyone, and better than most, that there was a lot more danger to face between where he was and where he hoped that reunion would take place.

~

Jill and Olivia watched the dragon flap its wings next to a swarm of Tsetsie flies and above the white-faced capuchin monkeys. They appreciated the brief moment of peace, a reprieve between the chaos that had been and the chaos they all knew was coming.

~

Tatum quietly and gently put her brothers hands together, then left one of hers to cover them as she reached down with her other hand and placed it on the leg that had just been attacked by the lobster. She closed her eyes and began to pray out loud as the rain slowed down.

"Heavenly Father, please, heal Kinsey the same way you did

Yanna earlier. We've all come so far and we know there is still more of this journey to be taken, more to be overcome. Kinsey needs to be healthy as we finish what we started in obedience to your calling. Thank you, Father, for choosing us to help these people. May we bring honor and glory to your name in the process. Your Kingdom come, Your will be done, on earth as it is in heaven."

Just as quietly and gently as she had started, Tatum removed her hands from Kinsey's body and the rain finally came to a complete stop. He looked down and saw that the rain had washed away all of his blood and his wounds were completely healed. He looked up at his sister, shocked.

"How did you do that?"

"I didn't," she responded. "All I did was pray."

"Woah," Kinsey exclaimed. "So dad speaks in tongues, Ray interprets, you heal. . .I wonder what mom does?"

"She's the smartest lady I know," Tatum quipped. "Maybe God just expanded on that and gave her the gift of wisdom or discernment."

"Makes sense."

"What about you?"

"Nada," Kinsey said with a heavy layer of disappointment.

"It just hasn't been revealed to you yet," Tatum reassured her brother. "I promise, it will be."

"Eeeeeek!" Amara screamed. "The kelp snakes are back!"

Everyone looked over the sides of the raft to see kelp moving but, it didn't appear to be moving toward them. In fact, it seemed to be swimming in a circle. But, as they looked closer, they noticed that the water itself was moving in a motion something like a whirlpool. Then they spotted something else. Something deep in the water. It was a milky-looking substance and it was quickly rising toward the surface. The higher the substance rose, the bigger it was growing. Whatever it was, it was ascending rapidly and amassing the span of its reach with equal speed.

"What is it?" Ling asked as she peered over the side of the raft in the center of the girls' boat as the substance grew to a size wide enough to reach at least ten feet beyond the raft in every direction and began to lose shape.

"Looks like a giant jellyfish," commented Sheila, warily.

"That's no jellyfish," Tatum gravely stated. "We've seen that before."

CHAPTER THIRTY-TWO
Ghosts

"What is it?" Olivia asked as she watched the pearl-colored, free-flowing substance move close to the surface, becoming increasingly clear that it wasn't a single creature but thousands of creatures traveling together. They appeared to be both white and translucent and their shape actually looked humanoid.

"Not what," Jill began to respond with deep sadness, "but who."

The spirits broke the surface on all sides of the raft, just like they had done on the Snyder family's first journey to Raum's island. They surrounded it like thousands of crazed soldiers attempting to break down the walls of an enemy's fort. However, just like before, the cruelest part of watching the spirits break through the surface of the water was the sound that came with them. They were making a wailing sound that could only come from the deepest felt grief imaginable. Worse, it caused an infectious burden of sadness that filled the hearts of everyone who heard it.

"These are the ghosts I warned you about," Jill announced. "They're not here to stop us, they actually want to go with us."

The women looked on and quickly realized that Jill was right. The spirits weren't trying to capsize the raft, they were trying to board it.

~

"But," Grant continued, "there are too many of them so, if we let them on, stop us is exactly what they'll do. We either keep them from getting on or we join them for eternity."

~

"They just want to finish their journey," Caleb stated. "Same as us."

"I know it's hard to accept," Kinsey responded as he looked into the eyes of Brett, a boy he had known on his first journey. Brett couldn't swim and when he was pulled into the water by the spirit of another boy, Brett had disappeared into the deep, never to be seen again, until now.

"Take me with you," Brett pleaded as he looked at Kinsey with profound sorrow.

Tears welled up in Kinsey's eyes and began to stream down his cheeks as he pushed Brett back into the water. "It's too late for them. Their journey is over and they didn't make it. But, we still can."

The heaviness of this moment was severe. Staring at the ghostly forms in the water, the kids couldn't help but fear that they were looking directly at their own destiny. Both Kinsey and Tatum knew this feeling from before but, somehow, it seemed even more difficult the second time around.

"Take me with you," another one of the spirits said, this one staring into Emily's eyes. Other spirits quickly followed, all of them begging in utter desperation.

Compassion ran rampant among the whole group and it nearly cost them their own journey but it eventually gave way as the panic that first arrived at the sight of the milky white substance in the water returned swiftly and more fierce than ever.

"Do you want to end up like them?" Tatum, with tears in her eyes, proposed to the group in a rhetorical question as she too pushed one of the spirits back into the water. "We have to press on. We have to survive. We have to get home."

No one thought the spirits wanted to capsize the raft. Of course, they not only wanted the raft to reach the others but, it was their strongest desire to be on it when it did. Unfortunately, Kinsey was right. They were no longer in body form because their journey had ended and they were now stuck. Worse yet, there were too many of them and trying to allow them to board the raft would be both useless and only serve to ensure that the living would experience the same fate as they had.

Emily was the next kid to reach forward and push one of the spirits back into the water. Fabia followed, then Mason and Jen. The action felt cruel but the entire group had finally accepted the fact that it was necessary.

The voices were getting louder and more jumbled together as the spirits tried to pull themselves onto the raft, fighting harder and harder for a second chance to finish their own journey that had previously ended in their death.

The kids had no choice but to push the spirits off of the raft. It was an effort that nearly seemed futile, however, because the spirits so grossly outnumbered the living and they seemed to be arriving in an endless stream. They clearly had no intention of stopping. Likely, many among them had been struggling with this same intention for hundreds of years. Possibly more.

~

Grant pushed spirit after spirit off of the boat and back into the water. His face was wet from his own tears. In fact, many of the men were having a similarly emotional response to the situation. How could they help it? They knew in their hearts that they could potentially reach the same end and, if another group someday passed through those waters, the group would be wise not to let them board either. It was all simply too much for anyone with even the smallest amount of compassion in their heart to keep inside.

On top of the guilt and empathy, they were now being forced to finally acknowledge the fact that there was clearly no returning from death in Kadosh. These spirits showed the severe truth that if the men or their families failed on this journey, the results would be eternal. That was an emotionally difficult thing to accept. And, now, they were facing it, and all that came with it, head on.

While it was already determined that the spirits would never see their families again, it was not yet too late for the living. So, the men fought hard to make sure they wouldn't be cursed into the same eternity as the spirits had.

~

Jill and the other women continued to fight hard but felt like they were losing the battle. There was no hesitation now as they pushed the spirits off the raft and back into the water. But, as soon as they pushed one into the depths, another would crawl over it and the cycle would continue as the one who had been pushed down would resurface to try again. There were simply too many of them and they were just too persistent.

The women were becoming exhausted and the fight had begun to feel useless. But, suddenly, the wind caught their makeshift sail and the raft began to pick up pace, moving away through the crowd of spirits in front of it and away from those on the sides and behind it. The women in the front of the raft began working their way toward the back, helping the others to push as many spirits off of it as they could.

Soon, the spirits were fading into the distance. Fear dwindled and guilt revisited. They stared behind them and watched as the milky white substance grew smaller and ultimately disappeared, taking with it that awful bemoaning, grief-drenched sound. The women sat still and in silence, forced to drink a bitter cocktail mixed of both liberation and gloom.

Slowly, the wind began to pick up. At first, the wind brought with it, a glimmer of hope. They were, after all, moving further away from the danger they had faced and closer to their goal. However, the upsurge in speed continued to rapidly increase and hope was soon replaced with that old, dreaded companion, fear. It began to feel out of control and they suddenly realized that pushed the spirits off the raft and back into the water. But, as soon as they pushed one into the depths, another would crawl over it and the cycle would continue as the one who had been pushed down would resurface to try again. There were simply too many of them and they were just too persistent.

The women were becoming exhausted and the fight had begun to feel useless. But, suddenly, the wind caught their makeshift sail and the raft began to pick up pace, moving away through the crowd of spirits in front of it and away from those on the sides and behind it. The women in the front of the raft began working their way toward the back, helping the others to push as many spirits off of it as they could.

Soon, the spirits were fading into the distance. Fear dwindled and guilt revisited. They stared behind them and watched as the milky white substance grew smaller and ultimately disappeared, taking with it that awful bemoaning, grief-drenched sound. The women sat still and in silence, forced to drink a bitter cocktail mixed of both liberation and gloom.

Slowly, the wind began to pick up. At first, the wind brought with it, a glimmer of hope. They were, after all, moving further away from the danger they had faced and closer to their goal. However, the upsurge in speed continued to rapidly increase and hope was soon replaced with that old, dreaded companion, fear. It began to feel out of control and they suddenly realized that the water. His face was wet from his own tears. In fact, many of the men were having a similarly emotional response to the situation. How could they help it? They knew in their hearts that they could potentially reach the same end and, if another group someday passed through those waters, the group would be wise not to let them board either. It was all simply too much for anyone with even the smallest amount of compassion in their heart to keep inside.

On top of the guilt and empathy, they were now being forced to finally acknowledge the fact that there was clearly no returning from death in Kadosh. These spirits showed the severe truth that if the men or their families failed on this journey, the results would be eternal. That was an emotionally difficult thing to accept. And, now, they were facing it, and all that came with it, head on.

While it was already determined that the spirits would never see their families again, it was not yet too late for the living. So, the men fought hard to make sure they wouldn't be cursed into the same eternity as the spirits had.

~

Jill and the other women continued to fight hard but felt like they were losing the battle. There was no hesitation now as they

Raum was the one who had sent the wind, which meant that he was now in control of where they were going.

CHAPTER THIRTY-THREE
Shipwrecked

Grant estimated that they were now traveling at a speed somewhere between ten and fifteen miles per hour. To most people that wouldn't sound terribly fast but it is actually faster than a standard sailboat is meant to travel, let alone an improvised raft with a couple of blankets barely being held together for a sail. So, regardless of what it may sound like, it felt incredibly fast. All the men could do was to hold on tight and ride it out until Raum took them wherever he had pre-determined that he wanted them to end up.

~

The raft was catching a few inches of air off of the top of the waves as it soared up and over them before crashing back down to the bottom. The women were all soaking wet as they gripped the bamboo raft with every bit of strength they could muster. Most of them had their eyes closed, including Jill, who was praying both, that the raft would hold together until they reached dry land and, that everyone would stay safely on board until the wind slowed down and they came to a stop.

~

Kinsey unexpectedly spotted something ahead of the raft but he couldn't tell what it was. In fact, it had barely registered that there was even something there before he realized it was headed right for them – more accurately, they were headed right for it.

In a split second, it felt as though the raft hit a concrete wall. The back of it rapidly lifted straight up until the raft was suddenly perpendicular with the ground below it. Every one of the kids was sent flying forward onto the shoreline and the raft crumbled into pieces that scattered all over them as they tumbled to a stop.

Tatum scrunched her nose and reached up to hold the part of the back of her head that had just been hit by a piece of bamboo. She slowly exhaled and let her eyes open but it took a few seconds for them to focus.

She knew the soreness would last a while but, she didn't have time to dwell on it. Instead she looked around as others began to dust themselves off and get to their feet – including Kinsey. That's when it dawned on her, the landscape was familiar. She had been here before. They had done it. They had made it to Raum's island.

~

Grant looked down the shoreline. So far, everything was just as he remembered it. Raum's island was small and shaped like a square. The only sign of life was the men who had just arrived. It was mountainous terrain but the boulders were jagged black lava rock and the bushes and trees had died a long time ago. Grant remembered that, in the daylight, he had first thought they looked like they had been burned in a fire. It was a dark, desolate place that would hold no hope if it weren't for the possibility of a family reunion being just moments away.

"Everyone okay?" Grant finally wondered out loud.

"Yeah," Ben responded. "At least, I think so. Sore but, alive. I think that'll have to do for now."

Ray got to his feet and started walking around to check on people. For a brief moment, he took notice of the sand beneath his feet. He had forgotten that it always seemed to sink a little deeper than any other sand he had ever walked on. *Is it just in my mind,* he wondered. He felt heavier and like the island was pulling him down. There was no doubt that it was a bleak, grim place. But, could it really be that the weight of it all was manifesting itself physically? He didn't know the answer. What he did know was that he was there to find Sheila. And, the last time he reunited with most of his family, it had happened after climbing the embankment. So, now that he could see everyone was up and moving, that was his next move.

"Let's get up there and see if anyone else is here," he suggested loudly as he pointed to where he had already started walking.

~

Leading the kids up the embankment, Kinsey hoped it would be just like the last time when he stood at the top and saw his dad. Simultaneously, he worried it would be nothing like that. They hadn't seen the other boats like they had before. What if his sister was the only one he was going to find this time? What if he crawled to the top of the embankment and no one was there? What if now, instead of seeing his dad, he crawled up there and was immediately greeted by more of Raum's monsters? What if Raum had grown tired of waiting and that's why he directed their raft to the island? This time, he could be there to greet them himself. Maybe he directed them there so he could quickly kill them and get it all over with. Kinsey's mind was racing and his hands had begun to shake. Of course, he was cold and wet so his teeth had begun to chatter, too. He was scared, uncomfortable and beginning to lose hope. But, he continued to climb, determined to face whatever fate awaited him at the top.

~

As Ray reached the top of the bank and stepped out onto more level ground, he immediately noticed that the landscape had changed. At first, it looked like the ground was glowing white instead of the black lava rock he remembered. It used to look like nature's gothic castle. It was still sinister but, not at all in the same way it had been the first time he was there.

He stepped out into the white stuff and noticed that it moved, when he walked on it, like a bunch of sticks. They racked together and made a clacking sound. He bent down and picked one up. It was smooth and dry. Dense but not terribly heavy.

Suddenly, he let go and jumped back. He looked out at the environment in front of him. What he was staring at, the substance that was reflecting the moonlight to create the illusion of a glow, was a ground covered in human bones.

~

Are these the bones of the people who died the last time we were here? Jill wondered to herself before trying to inject some logic. *They can't be. Or, at least, not all of them. There wouldn't be this many. Maybe Raum spit the bones out of his pit. Maybe these are the bones of everyone who has ever died here. Either way, yuck!*

That's when it happened. It was harder to see this time, because of the darkness, but Jill finally noticed movement on two of the other sides of the island. Hope began to well up inside of her as she tried to focus her eyes on what or who it was. Finally, she could tell, it was people.

"Why are there only people on two of the other sides and not all three?" she wondered, this time out loud.

"I think those are the kids over there," Olivia stated, matter-of-factly.

Jill quickly looked in the direction Olivia was pointing. "My babies are together?" She squinted, trying so hard to see, and then her eyes widened and filled with tears of gladness. A smile formed on her face as she realized her kids, as long as they were alive, were on one side of the island and the group on the other side should include her husband. A family reunion may very well be, finally, just moments away.

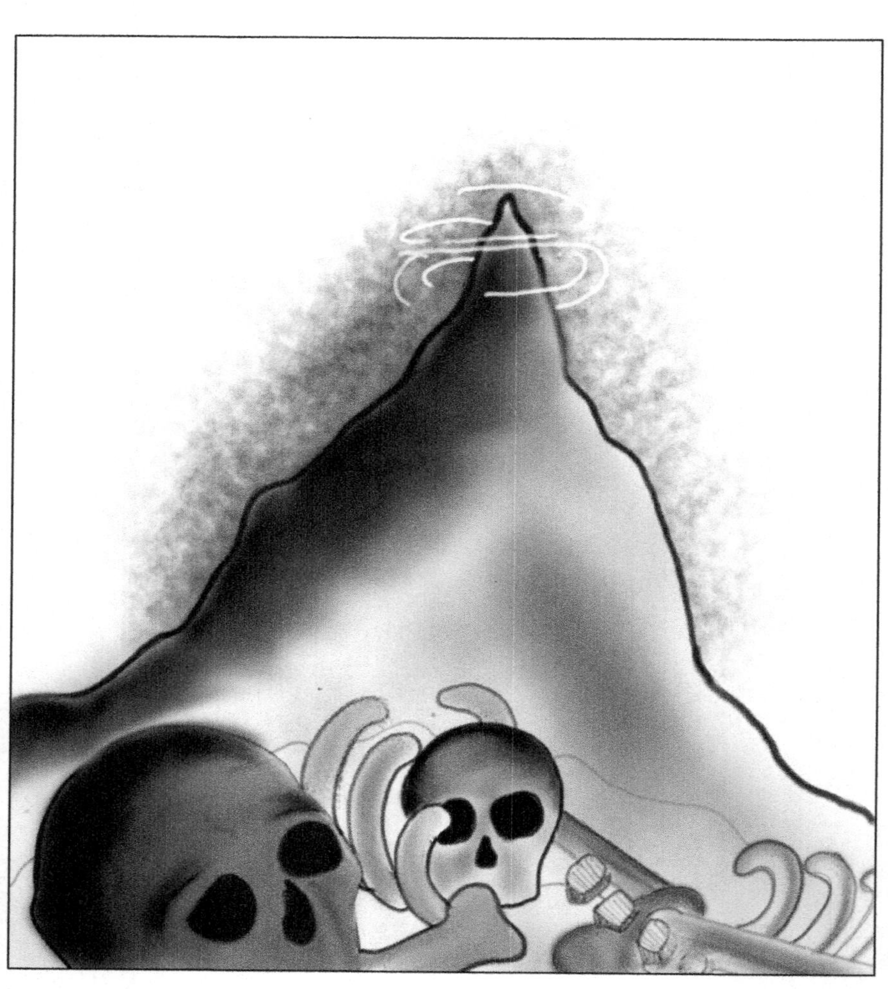

PART EIGHT
Battle

CHAPTER THIRTY-FOUR
Raum Remembers

Anxiety and dread had given way to anticipation and hope as people were running toward one another from three of the four sides of the small island. Kinsey couldn't help but wonder if Raum would interrupt them the way he had the first time they arrived in this same place but, he kept running anyway. His euphoria, like that of everyone there, particularly the people who had never been to the island before, appeared to be unbreakable. But, suddenly, the moment took a turn.

Before anyone was able to reach the other groups, they were all forced to halt when the ground began to shake like they were having a small, localized earthquake. Everyone practically skidded to a stop as they all tried to keep their balance. All four of the Snyders and Ray each knew exactly what was coming next.

"Here comes Raum," Tatum announced.

That's when the hideous smell saturated the island and seemed to punch everyone in their nose. It was like the most foul, rotten garbage any of them had ever smelled. Even the Snyders and Ray thought it was worse than what they remembered from their first encounter with Raum. Unfortunately, as the ground continued to shake, the smell intensified, just as it had before. No one thought it could get any worse. . .until it did. The process repeated itself like a downward spiral until people finally began to throw up.

In the very center of the island, separating everyone once again, the bones and the black lava rock beneath them burst into pieces and Raum shot out of the opening. The bones and the rocky terrain he landed on crumbled all around him, creating a loud thud and the clinkity-clack sound of all the pieces of bones and rock bouncing off of one another, as the ground shook again from the weight of this monstrous demon.

He was every bit as revolting as Jill remembered him being. Black like the lava rock that was hidden beneath all of the bones littering the island. He was large and powerful but oozing like the mud monsters. His body appeared to be primarily made up of slithering serpents like black versions of the dandelion and kelp snakes as well as the pollen string and needle worms that had attacked the various groups on their journey. The black puss that oozed from various parts of his body fell to the ground and then slithered back to him before disappearing back into his grotesque body.

Although Raum didn't look exactly the same as Grant remembered him, his essence hadn't changed at all. And, Grant did take notice of the fact that he was still sporting that same circular mouth with thousands of long, pointed teeth. A mouth that still spewed the most violent noise that Grant had ever heard in his entire life.

Raum also still had a pair of wings but they now looked exactly like the wings on the dragon-like creature that the women had previously faced. Only, these wings were bigger and, just like the rest of his body, Raum's wings were crawling with black worms and snakes and they dripped seeping black puss. Similarly, his eyes appeared to be made out of red hot, burning embers and there were cracks in his body like veins. But, instead of flowing blood, the cracks displayed flickering fire.

It was clear that either Raum represented all of the nastiest parts of everything he had thrown at the men, women, boys and girls to try and stop their journey or each of those monsters represented a different part of his revolting being. Either way, he had sent different monsters this time around and those same changes existed in the form he was now taking.

But, there were also attributes that were uniquely his own which hadn't changed at all. The most distinguishable of these were five pointed horns growing out of his head. The one above his forehead was the largest and most prominent. It stuck straight out and was flanked on either side by smaller horns that went in the opposite direction. The other two were on the side of his head. They were the smallest and they also projected frontward.

Every person on the island had at least one hand covering their noses to try and filter the horrendous stench and some also tried to cover an ear at the same time because of the horrible sound Raum was making. But, no one could keep their eyes off of the hideous monster who was still separating them from their families. The presence of this massive demon, and everything that came with it, had understandably put fear into the hearts of everyone on the island, particularly those who had never seen him before this.

It was clear to everyone that Raum had been trying to stop the people in their quest to reunite with one another. Now, they had arrived at his island and were close to accomplishing their goal. But, Raum was determined to keep that from happening and he was an intimidating force that seemed like he would be the obvious pick to win any battle. What wasn't clear, however, was that Raum remembered Ray and the Snyders and he was distracted by the fact that he was particularly incensed by the audacity they had shown by returning.

Standing in the middle of the three groups, Raum suddenly

turned toward the women and looked directly at Jill. He sneered and growled as the other women took a step away from the woman who had led them there.

Raum abruptly turned and stepped toward the men. He looked at Ray, then at Grant. Again, he sneered and growled.

Finally, Raum turned and stepped toward the kids. He looked at Tatum, then bent forward for his closest look yet. Kinsey met his gaze as the demon stared down at him with uncontainable agony and rage pouring out from within him.

"The light will come," Kinsey shouted, with pure confidence, loud enough for everyone on the island to hear. "The light will arm us for battle and rescue us all!"

With a cry of wrath, Raum raised his arms and wings in unison. He then tilted his head back and opened his mouth. As he flexed his arms and wings and puffed out his chest in fury, he didn't make the noise he'd been making before. Instead, fire shot out and went straight up in the air like it had been fired out of a flamethrower.

Fear began to swiftly overwhelm the seemingly helpless crowd of people as they shrunk back, intentionally stepping away from Raum but also unintentionally from the family members they had already fought so hard to reunite with.

That's when Ray finally spotted Sheila. She wasn't looking at him and most likely wouldn't have recognized him if she was.

But, Ray knew it was her and tears welled up in his eyes from the gratefulness that filled his heart. Tatum had done it. She had brought his sister this far, now they needed to make sure she got home.

"Kinsey," Caleb shouted. "He's coming after you! Run!"

As most of the boys and girls backed away from Kinsey in a hurry, Tatum stepped forward and took her brother by the hand.

"The light will come," Kinsey stated matter-of-factly as he looked down at his hand in his sister's and then up at her face before returning his gaze to the dinosaur-sized demon in front of him. "I promise."

"I know it will," Tatum agreed. "But, maybe we should step back and wait."

The fire finally stopped flowing from Raum's mouth. He flapped his wings and lowered his arms as his head tilted back down to look Kinsey in the eyes again. But, while the fire and the growl had quieted, it was clear that his rage had not.

"Go ahead." Kinsey told his sister. "I'm not moving."

CHAPTER THIRTY-FIVE
As Promised

"Then I'm not either," Tatum vowed in spite of Raum's death-stare and the fresh display of his hostile supremacy in this ghastly place.

Before Kinsey could even respond, the almost black sky was abruptly torn open by the brightest sunshine any of them had ever seen. The dazzling light shocked everyone but Ray and the Snyder family. Even Raum, who, like Ray and the Snyders, had been through this at least once before, appeared to be caught by surprise, as he shielded his eyes from the blinding light that, Kinsey and his family had promised the others would come. And, there was no denying, it had finally arrived.

The same rustling wind that Kinsey remembered from before, swooshed out over the island like a storm had touched down. It felt calming to the people but it infuriated Raum. He bellowed intensely but, the light was so brilliant that no one, not even the demon roaring, could open their eyes to look.

Even Kinsey, who had managed to look on the first time, couldn't adjust his eyes to the light. What he could do, was to picture, in his mind's eye, what he vividly remembered from the first time he encountered the light on Raum's island.

A great cloud surrounded by intense illumination descended rapidly out of the glaring sunlight. Hovering about fifty feet above the ground they were all standing on, the cloud constantly had fire flashing out from it and there was glimmering metal in the midst of the flames. Kinsey had later put it all together and realized that there was a supernatural blacksmith he couldn't see, who was forging armor inside the abundant fires.

The light remained so intense that no one could look upon it. For Raum, it was not just his eyes needing to adjust from the darkness that made the light unbearable. It was also fear. Raum knew, just as well as Ray and the Snyders did, exactly where and what the source of that amazing light was. That knowledge appropriately left him trembling in dread.

For everyone else, the warmth that the light brought with it was soothing and glorious. It was both regal and inviting. It instilled in everyone on that island, except for Raum, a sense of joy and liberation that hadn't been felt in Kadosh since Ray and the Snyders had last stood on that very same ground.

Of course, that ground wasn't covered in bones the last time. But, the bones beneath their feet were the furthest things from their minds in that moment. Nothing could distract them from the magnificence of that light and everything that came with it.

Still unable to open his eyes, Kinsey imagined that what was taking place was just as it had been previously. And, he was right. He next remembered seeing four hooved creatures appear from inside of the cloud. They had a mostly humanoid shape but each of them also had four faces and four wings. Centered above their shoulders, each creature had both a human face and the face of an eagle. On the right of those faces, was the face of a lion, and on the left, the face of an ox. The two wings that were spread out on each creature touched the wings of another. The creatures also had wings down at their side, covering both their bodies and their barely visible human hands.

Their legs were straight with no knees and they stood on their hooves. Kinsey recalled briefly wondering how they moved without joints in their legs and it caused him to wonder once again. They had moved as he watched before. In fact, they darted back and forth like lightning bolts. It reminded him of a character named The Flash from comic books his friend Adam collected. Kinsey recalled seeing the creatures reach into the flames of the fires burning in the cloud with their human hands to pull something out. Once again, Kinsey had later put it all together and decided that they were retrieving the very items they had come to deliver to the people who needed their help in defeating Raum.

He recognized, in that moment, that how the creatures moved was one of the many questions that he likely would not find an answer to on this side of heaven. He was not only fine with that realization, the thought of it made him smile. *God loves a mystery,* he thought. *He also loves revealing mysteries. The things I'll learn when I get to heaven are going to be awesome. Everything in God's time.* All he needed to know at that moment was that, for whatever reason, these incredible beings didn't need joints in their legs. That fact was one of many that made what they were and how they did everything absolutely extraordinary.

Also extraordinary, Kinsey recalled just how beautiful the skin of the creatures was. It shimmered and shined like freshly polished bronze. They were like nothing Kinsey had ever seen before and something he would certainly never forget.

At this point, everyone was enjoying both the comforting warmth that enveloped them and the quickly vanishing odor of Raum's hideous island. The foul stench was being replaced by a pleasing scent that could only be coming from the light itself. The fragrance was like a perfect combination of delightfully exotic spices.

Although everyone's eyes were still closed and, therefore,

they couldn't see it, a watermelon-sized sphere made up entirely of light hovered in front of each person. Just like the first time Ray and the Snyders had been to Raum's island, these lights had traveled together, like a flock of birds, creating one formation and the appearance of one massive light. But, now, having been delivered by the creatures in the cloud of fire, they were there for a group purpose and that purpose was a series of singular assignments.

Slowly extending from each light, appeared arms made entirely of that same light. The arms reached forward and touched the individual people, instantly filling everyone with confidence and peace on a level that would seem preposterous to anyone who knew the seemingly insurmountable situation that they were facing. But, as the light touched each person, they also stealthily armed them for the impending battle.

Although Ray and the Snyder family knew the peace and coziness wouldn't last, they were still saddened when every bit of the lights, the cloud and both its fire and the four beautiful creatures within it, disappeared and were gone without any trace of their ever having been there at all. They also took with them the pleasant aroma that had camouflaged the horrible smell that otherwise covered the island.

As everyone observed the sudden change in the air on their skin, the immediate lack of bright light through their eyelids, and the abruptly unfortunate conversion of aroma in their noses, they also perceived an alteration in the weight on their bodies. Opening their eyes, they slowly discovered they had been outfitted with armor – just as Kinsey and the others had promised they would be.

Everyone suddenly had dense breastplates on their chests, snug belts around their waists, new rugged shoes on their feet, hard helmets on their heads, impenetrable shields in one hand and pierce-ready swords in the other. The light had vanished, but what it left behind gave everyone certainty that victory was in their near future.

They looked themselves over, then looked at one another, and finally, they looked up at Raum. The revolting demon was looking right back down at them, scanning their faces. It would have pleased him that the light had once again chosen not to stay for the battle but, Raum had been in this position before and it hadn't turned out the way he hoped or expected. Instead of pleasure, what he felt in that moment was determination. And, it showed in every repugnant morsel of his appearance. He was resolute in making sure that history didn't repeat itself. It was clear that he had a second chance with Ray and the Snyders and he was ready to take it. He was going to do everything in his power to make sure that the end result was different this time around.

And, let's face it, Raum had already displayed a lot of power. When this battle ended, if he had any control over it at all, he would be the only survivor.

CHAPTER THIRTY-SIX
Doing Battle

Raum's slithering, black arms folded inward. He reached his massive hands into his own torso and pulled out a big, dripping ball of mud. But, because he was black, the mud looked more like tar. He raised the ball up in the air as he opened his vile mouth, showing off the thousands of long, pointed teeth that walled the inside, and let loose with his intense roar.

Although he didn't surprise anyone with the throw, Raum hurled his ball of black mud directly at Kinsey and Tatum. Fortunately, they both dove out of the way just in time for the mud to splatter on bones in between them. Landing on bones themselves, fragments went everywhere. It hurt as they hit the hard skeletal remains and other pieces flew up and landed on them.

They watched as the mud slithered its way back to Raum and

disappeared into the foot of his body. Raum was angry that he had missed. He bent down and picked up a pile of bones, then spewed fire straight up into the air above his head. About five seconds later, he started hurling the various pieces of human skeletal remains in every direction. The men, women, boys and girls all quickly took cover, crouched down behind their new shields, as some of the bones bounced off while others broke when they hit.

Realizing he needed something bigger than the shields that were protecting the people from the onslaught of bones, Raum kicked a bunch of the remains out of his way and dug up some new ammunition: boulders. He lifted them up and began hurling them at the crowd. The size and weight of the boulders made this attack completely different from the previous one.

Although the large rocks were being tossed in every direction, just like the bones had been, these weapons were hitting with explosive force and knocking people tumbling backwards like soccer balls that had just been kicked downfield by a striker. They each bounced their way through the skeletal remains, getting cut up and bruised along the way. As bones shattered from the impact of the massive stones, they exploded like hand grenades and threw shrapnel everywhere. It was impossible to defend attacks from both directions so, everyone was forced to protect themselves from Raum's boulder attack and risk getting hit by bone fragments from behind them.

Grant looked around and was immediately reminded of the last time Raum hurled boulders at them. He had seen a man's lifeless body, only four or five yards away from him, just after it had been struck by one of these large rocks. There were many others that didn't survive either. They had lost some along the way but, Raum's island is where the majority of the deaths had occurred. He began to pray that this time would be different. That all those who had died would find peace in the afterlife and that their deaths would not be in vain because they had paved the way for others to make it home.

The Snyders started reminding everyone of the game plan they had previously laid out for them. It was the same thing that had worked the last time he and his family had faced this massive demon. Obviously, Raum was more powerful than any one of them. But, they significantly outnumbered him and needed to amplify their strength in order to take advantage of his only known weakness. They needed to get off of defense and start playing offense instead. So, still hidden behind their shields, everyone started moving closer to Raum. The closer everyone got, the angrier the demon became. He was breathing fire through his nostrils as he continued to throw the rocks and bellow that same brutal roar.

But, while the men, women, boys and girls were getting close the way they had been told, and the way the Snyders and Ray had in their last confrontation, Raum wasn't splitting into all of his gross parts that he was made up of. It had worked before but, perhaps Raum had learned his lesson and was determined to stay whole. Maybe he had decided that was how he would keep from being defeated this time.

Still, everyone pressed on and continued to get closer. Ray was ultimately able to get close enough to use his sword to stab Raum in his left foot. When he did, he could hear the creature that made up that part of Raum's body let out a scream. Ray pulled his sword out and looked up at Raum just as he dropped the boulders from his hands. He leapt out of the way as the boulders crashed to the ground and shattered dozens of bones.

Everyone looked on as Raum once again spewed fire into the air from the back of his throat, flapped his wings and soared off of the ground about twenty feet before crashing back down. The ground shook like they were at the epicenter of another seismic event. Pieces of bone shot everywhere and people were forced to hide behind their shields like they were under attack from a Medieval army's onslaught of arrows.

Raum continued to breath fire into the air as the bones settled back to the ground. He then lowered his head and shot fire directly out at the people, slowly turning in a circle to make sure he hit everyone. The people remained behind their shields, mostly protected but there was no escaping the intense heat. When Raum finally stopped, practically in unison, everyone jumped to their feet and charged him, repeatedly stabbing him in his feet and legs. The screams from the creatures within Raum were piercing everyone's ears. It was almost enough to make people feel bad for the creatures. . .almost.

Raum growled as he resorted to kicking people away from him, like someone who was more annoyed than injured. After all, it wasn't him that was getting hurt, and he certainly wasn't dying, that curse belonged to the creatures he had imprisoned in this bodily form.

But, the men, women, boys and girls all knew that if they could kill the creatures that gave this demon his ability to manifest himself physically, there would be no one left to stop them from going home. The main problem that Ray and the Snyders recognized was that Raum had increased in size from their last encounter. There were more creatures making up his body. And, worse, there were fewer people there to kill the creatures this time. The odds were not in their favor.

No matter how hard Raum fought them off, however, the people were so determined that they continually bounced back to stab Raum again, killing the creatures one by one. Finally, Raum decided he had no choice but to spread his enormous, foreboding wings as he breathed fire into the air one last time. He followed the fire up by bellowing the most violent noise yet. He flapped his wings and rose into the air about forty feet and then retracted, balled himself up, and fell back to the ground where he landed with another giant thud. The ground shook once again, even more than it had previously, but this time, Raum purposely broke apart.

Raum had finally disassembled. Every one of the menacing creatures that were making up his body, were now separated on the ground and springing into action. The people had gotten their wish. However, now, instead of facing Raum as one ferocious giant, they had to face the fact that they were significantly outnumbered by swarming hordes of monsters. Even Ray and the Snyders knew in an instant that, unless they somehow got more help, none of them were going to make it off this island alive.

CHAPTER THIRTY-SEVEN
Reinforcements

Without warning, everything seemed to freeze. It was as if time itself was standing still. That is, for everyone but Kinsey. He stood in the middle of the chaos and stared at the people fighting the ferocious beasts. Even the drool that dangled from the mouths of the creatures was frozen. He wasn't sure what to think until, far in the darkness, a small ball of light appeared. It was just like the one in his dream back home. The same dream that announced the family's calling. And, just like it had in that dream, it was traveling toward Kinsey at a rapid speed. Also, just like it had before, the sphere of light stopped abruptly in front of Kinsey. Unlike the light that had cracked open the sky, he was able to look directly at this one as it spoke.

"You, son of man, have been gifted in the areas of prophecy and miracles."

"I have?" Kinsey asked because he was sincerely surprised.

"Indeed," the voice coming from the light quickly responded. "Look around you at the great many bones on the floor of this island. Dry as they may be, I ask you, can these bones live?"

"Live?" Kinsey asked in confusion. But, as he thought about it, the word miracle had just been used. He knew he couldn't do anything to make those bones come to life, but that didn't mean it was impossible. He now understood that in the spiritual realm, nothing was impossible. So, he answered the only way he knew how. "You alone know."

"Prophesy to these bones and say to them, 'Dry bones, hear the word of the Lord! This is what the Sovereign LORD says to these bones: I will make breath enter you, and you will come to life. I will attach tendons to you and make flesh come upon you and cover you with skin; I will put breath in you, and you will come to life. Then you will know that I am the LORD.'"

Without hesitating, Kinsey did exactly as instructed. He prophesied verbatim. As he did, a rattling sound began all around him. He watched as every fragment of every bone on that island came together, bone to bone, in forms of all sizes. Tendons and flesh appeared on them, lifeless organs appeared behind the rib cages and within the skull, and then skin covered them. They were people of both genders and all ages.

"Prophesy to the breath;" the voice from the sphere spoke again, "prophesy, son of man, and say to it, 'This is what the Sovereign LORD says: Come breath, from the four winds and breathe into these slain, that they may live."

Once again, Kinsey did exactly as instructed and wind began to swirl all around him. Breath entered the newly formed bodies and they stood up on their feet. It was in that moment that Kinsey realized he was staring at a vast army. He, his family and his new friends were no longer outnumbered.

"Son of man," the light said one last time, "these bones are the people who have died on this island under the rule of the demon you fight today. They say, 'Our bones are dried up and our hope is gone; our lives are over and we are cut off for eternity.' Therefore prophesy and say to them: 'This is what the Sovereign LORD says: My people, I am going to open your graves and bring you up from them; I will bring you victory. Then you, my people, will know that I am the LORD. You have called on me and I have heard your cry. I will put my Spirit in you and you will live. Then you will know that I the LORD have spoken, and I have done it, declares the LORD."

For the final time, Kinsey prophesied exactly as he had been told to. As he did, everyone around him suddenly became armed for battle the same way everyone else had after the light had opened up the sky. Suddenly, they all had breastplates, belts, shoes, helmets, shields and swords. The moment that Kinsey finished prophesying, the light sped away and everything unfroze. However, when the people and the creatures realized that this vast army had suddenly appeared, they all stopped and stared in amazement. No one but Kinsey understood what had just happened.

"Fight!" Kinsey shouted.

There would be time to contemplate the unfathomable later. For now, the people needed to be thankful for the help and finish what they had set out to do. So, everyone quickly turned their attention back to the unearthly creatures that stood between them and one another. Suddenly, they found themselves in a position where they could actually double-team the beasts and they quickly captured the momentum as they killed the creatures right and left.

Tatum decapitated a dragon that was beginning to take flight as her mom sliced a dandelion snake in half. Kinsey used his shield to deflect the fire coming from another dragon and directed it to burn a horde of those crazy rodents they had fought off on the other island earlier as Grant put his sword through the body of a giant lobster like he was making a massive seafood shish kabob.

Just as they had in Ray and the Snyder's last encounter with Raum, the creatures all turned into a black mist that swiftly glided away toward the giant hole that Raum had exploded out of when they died. The mist was the various pieces of Raum's spirit that had been divided up among the many creatures that were now fighting his battle. Once the creatures were killed, the pieces of Raum's spirit were recollecting themselves into one whole spirit back in Raum's dwelling. Thanks to the resurrection of the dead on this island, they were beating Raum one beast at a time, the same way they had done before Kadosh went dark.

When they finally watched the last piece of Raum's spirit slither away and go back into the ground, they cheered in jubilant triumph. Men, women, boys and girls, including those who had been dead just minutes earlier, all high-fived and hugged one another for a few seconds and then quickly realized they could finally reunite with their families. One by one, they all began a boisterous dash toward one another just as the sun began to dawn on Kadosh for the first time since Ray and the Snyders' last departure from the strange world.

Tatum quickly found Sheila and then started searching for Ray. Finally, she spotted him standing next to her dad. "Come on," she instructed Sheila as she hurried toward them.

Reunions were happening all around them as they rushed toward Grant and Ray. Tatum even spotted Kinsey and Jill embracing but she was so excited to introduce young Sheila to old Ray that she didn't even slow down.

Jill watched as her new friend Hannah and, who Jill correctly assumed was her daughter, Amara, held each other and cried. She could see Amara telling her mother how sorry she was and Jill knew that Hannah had received what she had been hoping for. This terrible place had taken her angry, mean daughter and returned the sweet girl she had been missing so much.

Finally, the moment Tatum had been waiting for arrived. "Sheila," she said as she stopped in front of Grant and Ray, "this is your brother all grown up."

"Ray?" was all Sheila could get out as she fell into his arms. Ray embraced her and the tears began to flow down both of their faces and he bent his head down and kissed the top of hers.

"Sheila?" another voice came from a few feet away.

As everyone looked over, Ray's jaw just about hit the ground. "Adrienne?"

It was his sister who had died in Kadosh, what had been nearly forty years ago for Ray. She had been among the resurrected. The joy felt in that moment was too immense for words. Ray set out to get one of his sister's back but, now he was returning with both of them. It was more than he ever dreamed possible and he wished he could hold them both in his arms forever.

As Ray explained his age to his sisters, Jill and Kinsey approached and all four Snyders hugged one another. Their love for each other had grown beyond even what they felt the last time they had reunited on that island. And, just like that last reunion, they suddenly felt a warm breeze begin to flow through the island like it was hugging everyone there. A providential energy simultaneously began to bubble around each individual family reunion just as the sun had begun to paint the sky in gorgeous shades of orange and pink.

Once again, the pleasant breeze turned into a strong but comforting wind as the Ewing and Snyder family circle was the first to experience the sensation of the warmth entering their bodies. Gradually, the heat increased and began to surge back out again. Suddenly, they all knew they were on their way back home.

CHAPTER THIRTY-EIGHT
Victory's Reward

Slowly, the embrace ended and the Ewings and the Snyders all started to float off of the ground. The rushing sound they had heard, as they departed the woods back home, returned. They looked around and, once again, took in the beauty of the pulsating light and color that surrounded them. It was so gorgeous that they couldn't help but feel a hint of disappointment when it began to disperse but that disappointment quickly faded as they realized that meant they were almost home.

Moments later, their feet gently touched the ground. Everyone embraced again, sharing their joy. But, then Tatum noticed someone was missing.

"Where's Sheila?" she asked the group in a brief moment of panic. "Where's Adrienne?"

"Home," Ray answered as everyone quickly realized that

meant they had gone back to their time the same way Ray previously had. "It's weird. I remember it both ways. Growing up with them and without them. They're both married now. Sheila's got two kids. Adrienne has three. Happy. They're both happy."

Everyone's eyes filled with tears as they appreciated the weight of what had been accomplished. As Grant looked down to wipe his eyes, he spotted his flashlight laying on the ground. He picked it up and turned it on.

"Ready to go home?" he asked the group.

"Very," Kinsey was the first to answer.

Everyone agreed with Kinsey's response as they started walking.

"Who's hungry?" Grant asked.

"You're always hungry," Jill responded. "But, right now, so am I."

"The last thing we ate here was breakfast," Kinsey chimed in, "but I could go for another round of that bacon Dad made."

Jill, Tatum and Ray all quickly agreed.

"What do you know?" Grant exclaimed. "Everyone likes my bacon. I'm not such a bad cook after all."

"No offense," Tatum sheepishly added, "but it's the bacon, not your cooking. Everyone likes bacon."

"Oh," Grant reacted, feigning disappointment.

"He's got you there," Ray told Grant.

"I don't mean to kill the whole bacon conversation," Tatum jumped in, "because I'm really looking forward to it, starving by the way, but does anyone know how Adrienne made it this time? She wasn't on my island at all."

"I do," Ray and Kinsey said in unison.

"She told me about it like forty years ago," Ray added. "Kinsey should tell it though. From what I hear, he was heavily involved."

"I'll tell you over bacon," Kinsey stated matter-of-factly. "It's a pretty big story. Better not do it on an empty stomach."

"That's my boy," Grant said as he tussled his son's hair before unlocking their front door. He opened the door and everyone started piling inside. Grant stopped Kinsey with a hand on his shoulder. "You know, this is about the point where, last time, you told us we would be going back."

"Right," Kinsey responded as everyone turned to listen to what he had to say.

"You're not going to do that again, are you?" Grant asked.

"No," Kinsey stated to everyone's relief. But that relief wouldn't last long. He continued, "I mean, last time I said we might have to go back. This time, I know we're going back."

"Excuse me?" Jill asked in complete perplexity.

"We were able to get a lot of people out this time. Even the ones who had died on Raum's island. But, that's not everyone.

We'll be going back. But, this next trip will be the last one."

As they stepped inside and Grant closed the door behind him, a yellow tulip in the garden widened its petals and nodded approvingly.

Meanwhile, Ray, Tatum, Grant and Jill all looked at each other apprehensively, knowing full well that Kinsey was, once again, absolutely and terrifyingly right. While God was still clearly watching them, so was the enemy.

About ten feet away from the tulip, one of the rodents Kinsey and the boys fought on their island was also paying attention. It growled in disgust, blew snot out of its smooshed nose and burrowed its way under the ground, off to warn Raum of the Snyder's looming return.

N
W
E
S

The Four Corners of Darkness

by C.S. Elston

The Four Corners of Darkness

Reader's Guide

1. The Snyders are described as being happier and "better off" because of their first experience in Kadosh. Can you think of a time in your own life where a struggle turned out to be the catalyst for improvement in your life?

2. Like Tatum in "The Four Corners" and Kinsey when he has his prophetic dream in chapter four, have you ever experienced an event where you knew something was true but no one seemed to believe you?

3. Were you as surprised as Kinsey that Ray went back to his own time and, from Kinsey's perspective, had aged so much in such a short period?

4. Grant and Ray are the first to discover their spiritual gifts. Have you discovered your own? Do you know anyone who has? Suggested reading from the Bible about spiritual gifts: Romans 12, 1 Corinthians 12-14, and Ephesians 4.

5. What differences did you notice between how the Snyders traveled to Kadosh in "The Four Corners" and how they and Ray traveled there in chapter ten?

6. Kinsey recognized that it is not his job to make truth sound more appealing. How does this differ from the way society often handles truth?

7. The Snyders are given a second chance to go back to Kadosh and try to show more people the way out. Is there any event in your past that you wish you could be given a chance to improve from your first attempt?

8. When the Snyders return to their respective camps with food in chapter seventeen, they are greeted by opposition. Their response is to diffuse the situation with kindness. Have you ever been on either side, or even just a witness to a similarly surprising reaction?

9. Grant states that they would make things easier on Raum if they just believed Raum's lies and stopped their journey. What lies does Satan use to keep us from fulfilling our own purposes?

10. In chapter 25, everyone is anticipating an attack from Raum. They don't know how, when or what is coming. Only that something is and it's going to be bad. Have you ever experienced dreadful anticipation in the real world? What was that like for you?

11. In chapter 27, new people join the quest. Was that a surprise to you? Or, did you suspect that others were out there and that the groups may encounter them? Knowing your individual personality, had you been there, what would your reaction have been to this discovery? Would you welcome them? Or, would you feel skeptical about their intentions?

12. The expression "When it rains, it pours" could easily be applied to the back-to-back attacks experienced by all four groups as they were trying to escape Kadosh. Have you ever had a time in your life where it felt like the daily onslaught of obstacles just wouldn't quit compiling?

13. Because Ray and the Snyders had been through this journey before and shared their experiences with their companions, it would be fair to assume that everyone is aware that the other groups are probably experiencing something similar to what they are going through. With that in mind, the old adage that "misery loves company" seems appropriate. When you face trials, does it help to know that you're not the only one to face them?

14. When groups encounter the spirits of the dead who want to continue their journey, they are forced to make a decision that could be perceived as heartless. Have you ever had to make a difficult decision you knew was right even though it could be taken as just the opposite?

15. Clearly, the Snyders will return to Kadosh one last time. The title of the third book is *The Four Corners of Winter.* What are your predictions for their final journey to the world seemingly controlled by Raum?

Also by C.S. Elston

Now Available:

"The Four Corners"

"The Gift of Tyler"

"The Gift of Rio"

Coming Soon:

"The Four Corners of Winter"

"The Gift of Matias"

"The Gift of Amanda"

After award-winning stage work in the nineties, Chris Elston moved to Los Angeles where he wrote more than two dozen feature film and television screenplays. He has been invited to participate in screenwriting events for Cinema Seattle and Angel Citi Film Festival. In 2013, Chris left Los Angeles for the suburbs of his hometown, Seattle, Washington, to get married and start a new chapter in his own story. Five and a half years later, the journey of the chapter that followed landed he and his wife in Prescott, Arizona where they now reside.

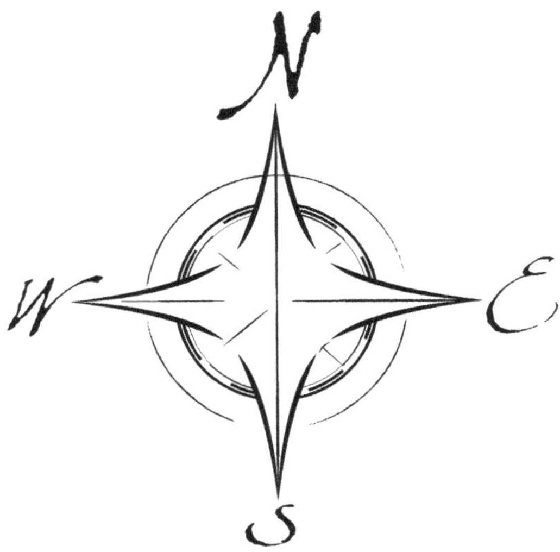
N
W
E
S

Made in the USA
Middletown, DE
28 August 2020

Customer-Oriented Global Supply Chains:

Concepts for Effective Management

Ephrem Eyob
Virginia State University, USA

Edem G. Tetteh
Paine College, USA

Managing Director:	Lindsay Johnston
Senior Editorial Director:	Heather Probst
Book Production Manager:	Sean Woznicki
Development Manager:	Joel Gamon
Development Editor:	Myla Harty
Acquisitions Editor:	Erika Gallagher
Typesetter:	Nicole Sparano
Cover Design:	Nick Newcomer, Lisandro Gonzalez

Published in the United States of America by
Information Science Reference (an imprint of IGI Global)
701 E. Chocolate Avenue
Hershey PA 17033
Tel: 717-533-8845
Fax: 717-533-8661
E-mail: cust@igi-global.com
Web site: http://www.igi-global.com

Library of Congress Cataloging-in-Publication Data

Customer-oriented global supply chains : concepts for effective management / by Ephrem Eyob and Edem Tetteh, editors.
p. cm.
Includes bibliographical references and index.
Summary: "This book provides insights and supports executives, middle managers and practitioners concerned with the management of supply chain with expertise, knowledge, information and organizational management development in different types of industries"--Provided by publisher.
ISBN 978-1-4666-0246-5 (hardcover) -- ISBN 978-1-4666-0247-2 (ebook) -- ISBN 978-1-4666-0248-9 (print & perpetual access) 1. Business logistics--Management. I. Eyob, Ephrem, 1954- II. Tetteh, Edem, 1972-
HD38.5.C87 2012
658.7--dc23

2011044974

British Cataloguing in Publication Data
A Cataloguing in Publication record for this book is available from the British Library.

Editorial Advisory Board

List of Reviewers

Table of Contents

Detailed Table of Contents

Preface

Global supply chain has continued to gain great attention in recent decades due to globalization and economic policies by companies striving to gain bigger market share and countries that make every effort for freer trade. The concept of supply chain has evolved progressively over time, from simple supplier systems with one or two suppliers to global chains with complex networks of suppliers, vendors, warehouses, manufacturers, shippers, wholesalers, and/or retailers. This evolution has driven firms to be more agile, flexible, adaptive, and cost effective, providing services and products that fulfill their customers' requirements. For example, the constant increase in energy costs and the rapid economic growth causing a boost in the demand for products and services in new emerging economic power countries such as Brazil, India, and China. This has contributed to increase costs in transportation systems, which are highly dependent on fossil fuels. Managing the supply chain has become more challenging and requires innovative thinking to reduce the total cost of the chain. The dynamic environment of extreme global competitiveness presents firms, small and large, with domestic or international novel challenges and issues to consider. This implies identifying and focusing on the most important issues in typical supply chain systems to face and find effective solutions for. Accordingly, what does the future hold for domestic supply chains as it is moving from primarily regional and national to the global focus? To answer this question, the book covered concepts, theories of industry, and industry's cases of global supply chain through implications of trends and opportunities, as well as their impacts on the global economy. This edited book, entitled "Customer-Oriented Global Supply Chains: Concepts for Effective Management," brings a collection of chapters that analyze concepts related to competing goals such as increase flexibility, adaptability, and effectiveness of the global supply chain, the need to reduce total costs, improve services, and ultimately, satisfy the customers. The book adopted an interdisciplinary approach through a careful selection of chapters developed by leading researchers and practitioners from different countries and continents.

The objectives of the book are to cover state-of-the-art research trends in the area of global supply management networks and analysis. It's a useful reference book for academicians and practitioners seeking to conceptualize this emerging area. Currently, there are few good books addressing a vast array of global supply chain theories and practices. In order to provide the best balanced coverage of concepts and issues related to the selected topics of this book, researchers from around the world were asked to submit proposals describing their proposed coverage and the contribution of such coverage to the book. All proposals were carefully reviewed by the editors in light of their suitability, researcher's records of similar work in the area of the proposed topics, and the best proposal for topics with multiple proposals. The goal was to assemble the best minds in supply chain, information science, and technology fields from all over the world to contribute entries to the book. Upon the receipt of full entry submissions, each submission was forwarded to at least three expert external reviewers on a double-blind, peer review basis. Only submissions with strong and favorable reviews were chosen as entries for this book. In many cases, submissions were sent back for several revisions prior to final acceptance.

Therefore, the editors believe that making this publication available will be a valuable contribution to students, researchers, and practitioners in the logistics and supply chain communities.

The following paragraphs provide a brief synopsis on the chapters covered.

Chapter 1, by Veronique Nabelsi, covers the application of supply chain tools such as lean management, agile systems in healthcare industry in order to cut costs and improve quality of healthcare services. She argues for improvements that require more integrated supply chain management practices, efficient processes, and systems to develop a strategic framework for customer-oriented or patient-driven supply chain management.

Knowledge Sharing in Supply Chain by Zhu, Ngoro, Ajmal, and Kristianto, borrows from the physical sciences principles of thermodynamics concepts for knowledge sharing in supply chains. The authors found that distance and the knowledge capacity of the supplier are important to reduce knowledge sharing uncertainty. Furthermore, higher contact frequency between the supplier and the buyer without considering supplier capacity is proven to be insignificant to reduce knowledge sharing uncertainty. The thermodynamics analogy, according to the authors, which is the topic of chapter 2, provides a new approach to explain knowledge sharing in supply chains.

Authors Paolo Renna and Rocco Padalino propose a development of a multi-agent scheduling approach to support manufacturing systems in different dynamic conditions in supply chains in chapter 3. The negotiation protocol is based on financial assets mapped with the process of the manufacturing system. A fuzzy method is used to assign each component based on the objectives pursued. Simulation was used to test the proposed approach and to compare it with classical dynamical scheduling approaches. Their approach showed better results compared to the classical dynamic scheduling approaches.

Ron Meier and Dan Brown's chapter 4 introduces project managers' perceptions on the importance of developing relationships with preferred suppliers. The relationship between the project manager and suppliers, according to them, has the potential to impact planning, project costs, time management, quality management, technical expertise, and product availability. They identify key characteristics and attributes of supplier-oriented purchasing behaviors in project-oriented environments and show that the most strongly valued attributes are clustered with quality, communication, attentiveness, and professionalism.

The topic of coopetition in supply chain is covered in chapter 5 by Lincoln Wood. Coopetition is the mixing of competitive and cooperative relationships in a supply chain. Using a case study in the agriculture sector of New Zealand companies in the horticulture industry, various elements of the supply chain are examined from both strategic and operational perspectives. The connections to the customer are shown to be enhanced through careful implementation, as the group of companies act to adjust their supply chains to make them increasingly customer-orientated. The author argues that significant benefits are shown to accrue in the supply chain including improved information flow, increased ability to supply, and flexibility to meet customer requirements.

Alavizadeh, Djavanshir, Tarokh, and Mohammed, in chapter 6, cover agile value creation and co-evolution in global supply chains covered the concept of co- contribution to creating value for customers. According to the authors, co-evolution and agility are ongoing processes. They argue that as technology changes and market varies, new challenges appear constantly, and companies should strive to address them by changing their strategies.

The chapter by Addo-Tenkorang and Eyob introduces a best practice concurrent approach for reducing the lead-time at an engineer-to-order product design/development stage by seeking to integrate business Information Technology systems such as ERP in the design and operational phases to improve supply chain, which is covered in chapter 7.

Chapter 8, by Janet Sanders, provides an overview of the importance of total quality management in supply chain management. It provides a summary of the evolution of quality and how supply chain management fit into the evolution. It then discusses the importance of quality for each entity of the value chain and how the reduction of variability along the entire supply chain is critical to optimum delivery performance. Furthermore, discussion on how quality and continuous improvement tools and methodologies can be mapped with supply chain management strategies to optimize the performance of the entire supply chain is included

Kaninika Bhatnagar examines the role of women in supply chain management, in chapter 9, in the context of management practices, education, and HR issues. The role of a diverse workforce, particularly women, is reexamined from the perspective of maximizing the bottom-line and profit sharing in the logistics industry.

Norizan Mohd Kassim investigates how image, perceived service quality, and satisfaction determine customer retention in the banking industry in Malaysia, and by extension, competition with international financial institutions. Data was obtained using a sample of retail banking customers in Malaysia and showed that image is both directly and indirectly related to retention through satisfaction, while perceived service quality is indirectly related to retention through satisfaction, all of which is found in chapter 10.

The objective of cloud computing was covered by Daim, Britton, Subramanian, Brenden, and Intarodeon in chapter 11, to predict the adoption rate of Cloud Computing in the future with a soft timeline using a scenario-based forecasting model. The authors conclude with recommendations and predictions in the near future, which could serve as tools businesses could use to determine if cloud computing is the right step in meeting their technology and business needs, especially in supply chains where small suppliers are laggards in adopting integrating software.

The topic of radio frequency identification (RFID) was covered by Albert Lozano Nieto in chapter 12. The chapter covers a relatively new technology for automated identification; RFID is based on the exchange of information using radio frequency signals between the reader queries and special tag. Among the different uses of RFID in the supply chain, this chapter focuses on those related to inventory control and the detection of counterfeited products.

Chapter 13, by Saban and Mawhinney, discusses the importance of human collaboration in supply chain management. The authors argue supply chain performance is often tied with acquiring the best technology or process to be marginally useful. The authors promote supply chain performance and human collaboration for better results. To change conventional thinking, this chapter proposes a holistic approach to achieving human collaboration among distributed partners, clarifies the forces that facilitate human collaboration, and identifies the steps management can take to create more collaborative team members.

Tetteh, Eyob, and Amewokunu use a Multivariate Analysis of Variance (MANOVA) approach to evaluate the performance of work cell, shift, worker's experience, and *kaizen* event participation level during a lean enterprise deployment effort at a multinational firm in its supply chain, all covered in chapter 14. Furthermore, the significance of the effects of these variables were assessed based on various lean supply chain tools such as first in first out, setup wheel system, standard operating procedures (SOP), clip system, and key performances indicators (KPI). The results support the criticality of the use of metrics and their impacts in implementing a lean manufacturing in a global supply chain environment.

The purpose of chapter 15 is to chronicle and analyze existing challenges and theoretical issues in the domain of product, system, and the emerging area of global supply chain sustainment. These challenges encompass the provision of reliable, efficient, cost-effective, and quality services by key players and major stakeholders in product and global supply chain. The author argues that sustainment concept serves as a vehicle for elevating the rate of product and system utilization. This will have a tremendous impact at reducing the burden of product or system's operational issues thereby allowing for the leveraging of the enormous potentials of sustainment. Both contemporary as well as classical journal papers and publications are included in this study to trace and describe the development, state of sustainment perspectives, available tools, and methodologies in product and global supply chain system sustainment.

Chapter 16 highlights the importance of contracts for coordination between companies in a supply chain. It considers a dyadic situation, with a supplier and a retailer. Coordination is achieved by two types of decisions: economic, concerning prices established and stated over a contract, and physical exchange of products, concerning the inventory that is going to be held by the retailer. First, one contract with a simple pricing scheme is considered, and then, two contracts with inventory holding cost shared among the companies of the supply chain. The former is presented to explain the general situation, and the two latter ones are used to explain different schemes of inventory cost share. A numerical example is also shown. The objective is to illustrate that a supply chain may be efficiently coordinated if the companies establish contracts with inventory holding cost share.

Overall, the sixteen chapters provide strength and quality to this book for supply chain professionals, information science and technology researchers, and also decision makers in the quest of obtaining greater understanding of the concepts, issues, problems, trends, challenges, and opportunities related to this field of supply chain. It is the sincere hope of the editors of this book that this publication and its vast amount of information will assist researchers, teachers, students, and practitioners in enhancing their understanding of global supply chain management and solutions applied. The editors anticipate their audience will enjoy reading this book.

Ephrem Eyob
Virginia State University, USA

Edem G. Tetteh
Paine College, USA

Acknowledgment

We are indebted to many people among them chapter contributors, referees, and members of the advisory board, IGI Global staff, and other individuals with whom we had contact who helped in many ways to put this edited book together. Particularly, we are deeply appreciative of the assistance of a number of people at IGI Global. Without their dedicated guidance and feedback, this book would not have been completed successfully. First and foremost, Myla Harty, Assistant Development Editor at IGI Global, helped us stay on track and gave much positive feedback during the development stage. She was instrumental in finding answers for our day-to-day problems related to the book project.

We extend our appreciation to the editorial advisory board team who gave their valuable time, effort, and counsel to improve the final product, and gave meaningful input.

The reviewers are thanked for their hard work, dedication, and for their meticulous reviews and comments to the authors. Without their constructive suggestions, the overall quality of the book would not have reached its potential for contribution in this field.

Ephrem would like to thank his wife Zaid and their children, Simon and Estelle, who were patient with his late nights at the computer, and he wants to thank them for their love and faithful support while preparing this book. Edem would like to dedicate this book to his wife, Momo, and their daughter, Shania, and sons, Kyle and Evan. Without their love, support, patience, and encouragement, he could not have edited this book.

Finally, to all that we have missed to list, we would like to express our heartfelt gratitude for your efforts and assistance.

Ephrem Eyob
Virginia State University, USA

Edem G. Tetteh
Paine College, USA

Chapter 1
Towards Patient-Driven Agile Supply Chains in Healthcare

Véronique Nabelsi
Université du Québec en Outaouais, Canada

ABSTRACT

Healthcare organizations in many countries are compelled to pursue drastic supply cost reductions, while continuing to improve patient health outcomes, as they must meet ever increasing economic and performance pressures brought on by changes in national health policies. As demonstrated in many other industries, these improvements require more integrated Supply Chain Management (SCM) practices, processes, and systems. The author develops a strategic framework for Customer-Oriented or Patient-Driven SCM, integrating the evolving economics of the healthcare industry and the emerging dynamics of global supply chains. The chapter focuses on modern SCM approaches such as agile and lean supply chains, in order to efficiently realign hospitals and their Material Management Systems (MMS) on patient health outcomes.

INTRODUCTION

The healthcare industry is inherently global as most high-end medical products, drugs, and equipment are manufactured by multinational suppliers. Healthcare product development, manufacturing, distribution, and group purchasing organizations (GPOs) are increasingly integrated through Inter-Organizational Systems (IOS) in order to optimize made-to-stock replenishment processes. This global context is creating unprecedented opportunities for hospitals in many countries, as they are compelled to pursue drastic supply cost reductions.

Yet healthcare organizations, whether private or public, must accomplish this transformation while improving patient health outcomes. They are submitted to increasing economic and

DOI: 10.4018/978-1-4666-0246-5.ch001

performance pressures brought by changes in national health policies, entailing major strategic redirections.

As demonstrated in many other industries, these improvements require that healthcare organizations adopt integrated Supply Chain Management (SCM) practices, processes, and systems, especially concerning internal operations and their interface with external partners. A Customer-Oriented or Patient-Driven value perspective can serve as an anchor to reengineering hospital supply chains toward a lean and agile model, and help ensure regulatory compliance.

We develop a strategic framework for Patient-Driven SCM, integrating the evolving economics of the healthcare industry, the emerging dynamics of global supply chains, and the broad SCM approaches required to realign on patients key hospital Material Management Systems (MMS).

We first discuss the emerging efforts to refocus healthcare supply chains onto a customer-oriented or patient-driven perspective. We then address key challenges in implementing these principles for hospital materials management. We conclude with an outline of future research opportunities and challenges in hospital SCM, and some strategic implications for healthcare senior management.

REFOCUSING HEALTHCARE SUPPLY CHAINS

Evolution of Customer-Oriented Principles

Integrating Supply and Demand Chains

Customer-orientation in Supply Chain Management (SCM) refers to a company's responsiveness to end-user requirements. The concept has been closely linked to Demand Chain Management (DCM) practices, seeking to optimize supply practices around customer value drivers. It is defined as: "*a supply chain that emphasizes market mediation to a greater degree than its role of ensuring efficient physical supply of the product*" (de Treville, Shapiro, & Hameri, 2004, p.617).

A key issue in DCM is to integrate customer value drivers with responsive SCM decisions (Walters, 2008). It provides a framework to ensure supply decisions are linked directly to market-oriented Key Performance Indicators (KPIs), and specifies potential responses and initiatives to optimize the demand chain. This approach is therefore centered on final outcomes from the customer viewpoint as opposed to business performance traditionally defined from an internal or corporate perspective.

In order to systematically integrate KPI and decision criteria, and jointly manage marketing and operations, customer-oriented SCM requires a tighter integration of customer and supply processes (Jüttner, Christopher, & Baker, 2007). DCM implies that SCM processes are fully integrated along with Customer Relationship Management (CRM) functions. This helps facilitate back-end and front-end value chain integrity, enabling the organization to cross boundaries seamlessly. This is typically accomplished through the implementation of an Enterprise Resource Planning (ERP), which must be configured to ensure that KPI, decisions, and processes are built around customer-driven value criteria.

Towards Agile Supply Chains

A more advanced form or customer-oriented supply chain is an evolution from DCM toward Agile SCM. Ensuring responsiveness requires integrated decisions and processes, dependent in turn onto collaborative information and planning between supply partners. Key drivers of business agility emphasize the coherence between customer-oriented information sharing enabled by IOS, leading to information-driven optimization (Agarwal, Shankar, & Tiwari, 2007). A key technology to enable agile SCM integration is Radio-Frequency Identification (RFID), with significant reductions in key traditional KPIs, such as inventory inaccuracy, bullwhip effects, and replenishment cycle time (Sarac, Absi, & Dauzère-Pérès, 2010). Its integration with artificial intelligence promises major breakthroughs in supply agility in various industries, and enabling fast and flexible adaptation for customer value (Lee, Ho, Ho, & Lau, 2011).

Agile SCM also integrates more traditional lean principles throughout core processes. These typically include key drivers of DCM, such as Strategic Supplier Partnership, Customer Relationship, Information Sharing, Information Quality (Li, Rao, Ragu-Nathan, & Ragu-Nathan, 2005). As opposed to optimizing traditional operational KPIs, an agile and lean supply chain will focus first on market-oriented and second on financial performance (Khan, Bakkappa, Metri, & Sahay, 2009). This type of SCM refocuses well-established lean practices onto flexibility and therefore supports end-customer value drivers.

Enhancing Agility with Collaboration

A core tenet of agile and lean SCM is collaboration between value chain partners in order to fulfill coordinated and synchronized decisions and processes. Efficient and effective integration can only be achieved to the extent information is voluntarily shared between parties for joint goals and win-win opportunities. Information flows must be managed to fully leverage collaboration potential, but with relative and changing directionality, permanence, horizon, frequency, and accuracy (Holweg & Pil, 2008).

As such, collaboration in SCM must be viewed from the theoretical perspectives of inter-firm relationships, where demand unpredictability at various nodes of the chain is moderated by industry transactional challenges (Germain, Claycomb, & Dröge, 2008). These factors determine the relative applicability of agile and lean principles to any industry context based on its contractual challenges.

Towards Patient-Driven Practices

Global Supply Chain in Hospitals

The hospital supply chain is a multi-tiered system of organizations and processes with multiple intermediaries (Figure 1). The concept of healthcare supply chain is defined as "the information, supplies, and finances involved with the acquisition and movement of goods and services from the supplier to the end user in order to enhance clinical outcomes while controlling costs" (Schneller & Smeltzer, 2006, p. 30 as cited in Sinha & Kohnke, 2009). The supply chain is characterized by a multitude of distribution channels (Rivard-Royer & Beaulieu, 2003) and a wide variety of products to be managed (Kumar et al. 2008). Another specific property is that supply chain activities are fragmented among several actors, including both clinical and non-clinical, functioning in separate silos. Some activities that could be carried out by the Materials Management Service are performed by medical staff (Nabelsi, 2007).

Each year, hospitals spend billions of dollars to purchase medical supplies and equipment needed to provide quality of health care. These assets are an important and growing part of hospital budgets representing as much as 30% and the labor costs related to operating the supply chain are close to 20% (Nabelsi, 2007; Bourgeon et al., 2001). The hospitals staff devoted directly or indirectly in the supply chain activities are the Medical Community accounted for 4% and the Materials Management Service for 15% of the labor costs (Nabelsi, 2007). A recent study suggests that by 2011 the overall supply chain expenses could exceed 50% of a hospital's total annual spending (Kowalski, 2009).

Refocusing Supply Chains on Patients

The delivery of patient care represents a complex supply chain that is often wrought with expensive, time-consuming, and unnecessary waste. Waste-

Figure 1. Hospital supply chain

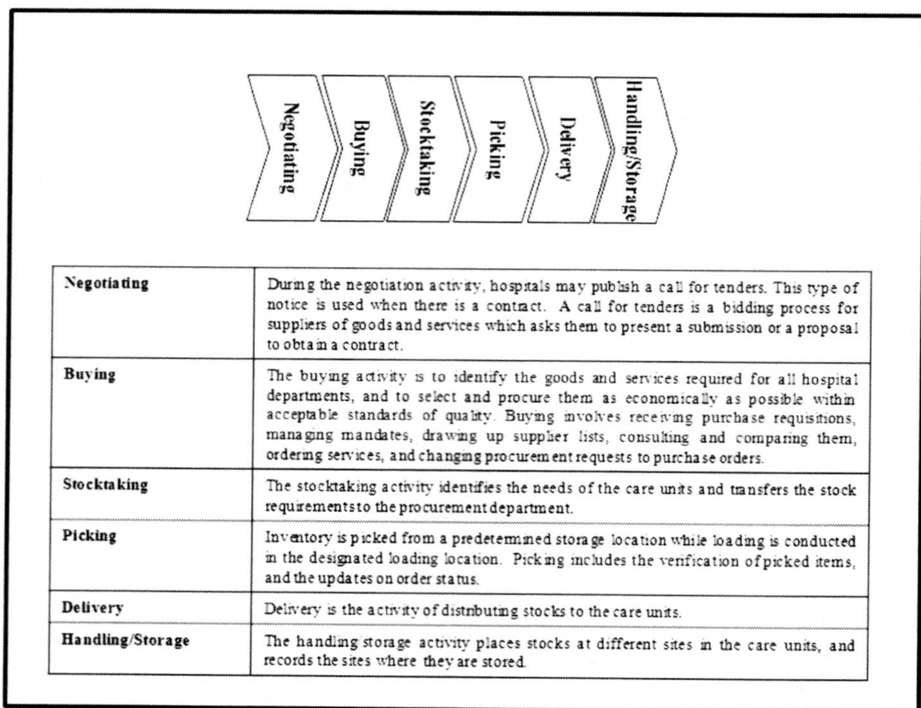

Negotiating	During the negotiation activity, hospitals may publish a call for tenders. This type of notice is used when there is a contract. A call for tenders is a bidding process for suppliers of goods and services which asks them to present a submission or a proposal to obtain a contract.
Buying	The buying activity is to identify the goods and services required for all hospital departments, and to select and procure them as economically as possible within acceptable standards of quality. Buying involves receiving purchase requisitions, managing mandates, drawing up supplier lists, consulting and comparing them, ordering services, and changing procurement requests to purchase orders.
Stocktaking	The stocktaking activity identifies the needs of the care units and transfers the stock requirements to the procurement department.
Picking	Inventory is picked from a predetermined storage location while loading is conducted in the designated loading location. Picking includes the verification of picked items, and the updates on order status.
Delivery	Delivery is the activity of distributing stocks to the care units.
Handling/Storage	The handling/storage activity places stocks at different sites in the care units, and records the sites where they are stored.

ful processes contribute to long waiting times, inefficient processes, expensive inventories, overutilization, and inappropriate use of staff. Patients, nurses, physicians and other health care professionals interact constantly throughout the supply chain. This interaction requires a significant amount of communication across a multitude of people, processes, and systems.

The supply chain must be aligned with patient care, requiring multiple dynamic processes where each patient's unique situation triggers new inputs from various medical professions. In order to improve the efficiency of this complex process, patient information and needs must be properly communicated and disseminated throughout the supply chain. Figure 2 illustrates how patient needs are drawn to attention and fulfilled by all actors throughout the supply chain management process. Materials management activities are properly aligned with patient needs, as diagnosed and prescribed by healthcare professionals, and communicated in a timely fashion to suppliers and dispenser.

Patient safety is improved when the supply chain provides the right product at the right place, right time, and right price (Taunton & Feinbaum, 2006). Supply chain management in hospitals must be patient-centric and based on actual demand of the point of care to better delivery of health care services (Nabelsi 2011).

Optimizing Medical Supplies and Equipment

In several hospitals, supplies are the second leading costs after physician salaries in providing patient care. These assets cover a wide range of supplies supporting the clinical chain activities from prevention to recovery (Rivard-Royer, Beaulieu, & Friel, 2003). Many hospitals lose

Figure 2. Patient-driven supply chain

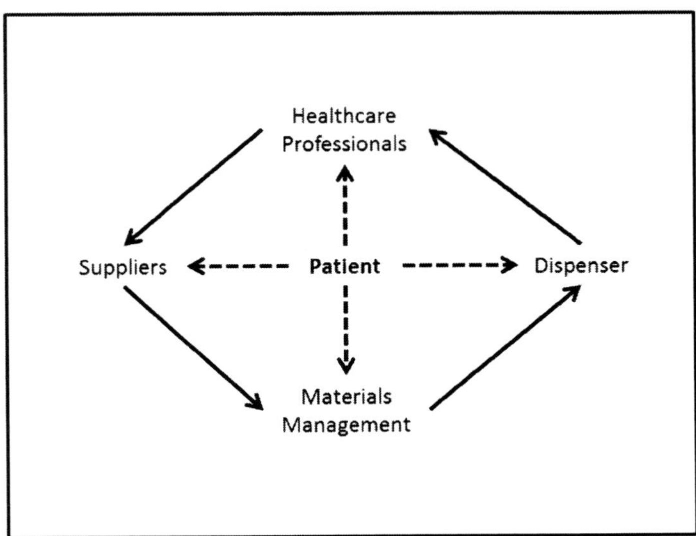

hundred thousands of dollars of medical devices such as wheelchairs, infusion pumps, portable X-ray machines and other mobile assets (Tzeng, Chen, & Pai, 2008). Studies have demonstrated that hospitals over-procure 20-30% of their moveable assets. It has been estimated that an average 200-bed hospital will lose between $400,000 and $600,000 in equipment annually. Furthermore, nurses spend up 30% of their working time to search for misplaced, stolen or lost mobile assets for the specific equipment they need for patient care delivery (Aguado et al., 2007). Hospitals currently lose up to 15% of its assets due to inappropriate and inefficient monitoring procedures (Nabelsi, 2007).

Integrating Hospital Supply Chains

Most of the research on supply chain is from the manufacturing sector but there have been several attempts to examine its applicability in the healthcare sector (Kumar et al., 2008; Sengupta, Heiser, & Cook, 2006). Based in the Toyota production system, lean principles has been explored in health care sector by different authors to reduce wasted and increase the quality of care for patients (Tutuncu & Kucukusta, 2008; Shah et al., 2008; Jimmerson, Weber, & Sobek, 2005; Breyfogle & Salveker, 2004; Young et al., 2004; Spear & Bowen, 1999). This concept involves identifying the tasks associated with organizational processes to determine how to improve quality and processes by eliminating non-value added activities.

A study realised by Shah et al. (2008) suggests that integration of lean production principles improve the supply chain performance. Young et al. (2004), see many applications of lean thinking in eliminating delay, repeated encounters, errors and inappropriate procedures. Similarly, Breyfogle and Salveker (2004) demonstrated that lean management principles can be applied to health care processes through the use of the six sigma methodology. Other researchers have adapted tools and principles from lean manufacturing to health care sector, and demonstrated their effectiveness in improving hospital operations (Jimmerson, Weber, & Sobek, 2005). For Spear and Bowen (1999), the lean production integration consists of four principles, as summarized in Table 1.

Some studies have recognized the value of the adoption of lean principles in hospitals to improve quality, enhance their focus on patient-centred care, create new service capacity, and reduce costs. According to Tutuncu & Kucukusta (2008), the health care supply chain integration counts three factors of integration: the organization's internal integration, integration with suppliers and customer integration. Due to the nature of the service that care provide in hospitals, internal customer and external customer (the patient) have a significant influence on the integration of the quality management system. Awad and Nassar (2010) defined the term integration as, "the quality of the state of collaboration that exists among departments that are required to achieve unity of effort by the demands of the environment" (p. 2).

In order to achieve a dynamic balance between supply and demand, integrated supply chain processes leverage operational flexibility by deploying one integrated value chain that serves the entire business (Stank, Brzica, & Ficenec, 2009). Stank, Brzica and Ficenec (2009) have identified five key elements of supply chain process integration: (i) a focal point for interface, (ii) greater process and component standardization, (iii) improved business intelligence and integrated information systems, (iv) an integrated demand forecasting and planning process, and (v) a centralized decision-making process to identify strategic initiatives. The benefits of supply chain integration may be realised by an effective linkage among the supply chain activities.

CHALLENGES OF AGILE SUPPLY CHAINS IN HEALTHCARE

Evolving National Health Policies

Industry Evolution in the United States

The challenges in developing agile hospital supply chains are numerous. Initiatives are required at all levels and stages of the chain, along with coordinated efforts through complex partnerships between organizations. Implementation lifecycles often span several years, and major obstacles persist in developing the necessary organizational and professional capabilities within the healthcare community.

Several countries have attempted to initiate change from the top, by passing new healthcare legislations that transform traditional (bureaucrat-

Table 1. Lean production principles

Principle 1 ***Standardized Work***	Defines how people perform their work and ensures that all work is highly specified to its content, sequence, timing, and outcome. Processes must be designed such that deviations from this specification are readily apparent. Standardized work reduces or eliminates decision making related to how work should be performed.
Principle 2 ***Seamless Linkages***	Establishes that people performing the work must be connected to one another with direct and unambiguous links. There is complete certainty about exactly who has performed what work at each process handoff. Seamless linkages reduce or eliminate the need for information transfer and the errors (defects and delays) such transfers introduce.
Principle 3 ***Direct Pathways***	Designates that the process must be designed so that production flows are simple and direct and do not change from one production run to another. Such predictable flows ensure that the exact appropriate resources are devoted to production. Simple and direct pathways reduce or eliminate decision making related to where work should be directed as it flows through the process.
Principle 4 ***Process Improvements***	Outlines the scientific method of hypothesis testing that employees must use to improve the process and discourages them from learning from personal experience alone. Such methods reduce or eliminate decision making based on intuition while promoting decision making based on scientifically derived evidence.

Source: Summary of Spear & Bowen (1999)

ic) modes of SCM in hospitals. The most notable effort has been the recent health reform passed by the United States Congress, where several policies and guidelines touch upon indirectly to materials management, looking beyond the underlying information technology and focusing more specifically on organizational capabilities (Epstein, Fiscella, Lesser, & Stange, 2010). Several issues remain, as found by a recent survey led by the Center for Innovation in Healthcare Logistics at the University of Arkansas in conjunction with the Association for Healthcare Resource & Materials Management (AHRMM). Among other challenges, a vast majority of the 1381 professionals surveyed emphasized the following, in order of importance (Nachtmann & Pohl, 2009):

1. Lack of data standards
2. Lack of trust
3. Quality of information
4. Quantity of data
5. Loss of competitive edge

There is significant consensus on the 2 first issues among all 4 categories of organizations surveyed, namely manufacturers, Group Purchasing Organizations (GPOs), distributors, and healthcare providers. This finding confirms that competitiveness of the overall supply chain depends on integration, based on improvements in both information technology and organizational capabilities to enhance trust and collaboration (Hsu, Su, & Liao, 2010; Rutledge, Huber, & Mathews, 2010; VanVactor, 2011). It is a more specific situation supporting the renewed focus on creating more competitive behaviour throughout the healthcare industry, in order to stimulate innovation and overcome bureaucratic practices (Porter & Teisberg, 2004; Teisberg, Porter, & Brown, 1994).

Towards a Hybrid Model in Canada

While most North American industries benefit from tightly integrated supply chains, it has not been the case for all Canadian hospitals, where many have been slower to realizing performance improvements. Due to the predominance of the public healthcare sector, along with nascent private sector involvement, the competitiveness culture has only recently taken roots in some regions (Trerise, 2010).

In addition, improvements in patient safety have been prioritized after several years of evidence collection, leading many public healthcare regulatory bodies to reconsider the way supply chains are properly aligned to reducing medical errors (Baker et al., 2004). Canadian hospitals are progressively changing with the emergence of new approaches to clinical governance, based on more collaboration among value chain partners, but especially between management and medical operations (Mintzberg, 2002).

National Health Reforms in Europe

In Europe, several countries have experienced similar efforts, with efforts focused on bringing a renewed sense quality improvement in healthcare, with collaboration at the core of most national approaches.

1. In the UK, the National Health Service (NHS) has adopted lean thinking as a key tenet of its transformation strategy, positioned within the broader debate of process standardization in hospitals (Waring & Bishop, 2010).
2. In Germany, value chain collaboration has been often a sub-component of successive health policy reforms, with a lack of integration among efforts leading to lesser improvement than expected in operational performance (Pannowitsch, 2009).
3. In France, the healthcare system has been allowed to develop progressively through

a blended public-private system, where distinctive lean capabilities have emerged allowing a diversity of small and large hospitals to improve performance (Ballé & Régnier, 2007a; Steffen, 2010).

4. In Spain, long term efforts to reengineer medical supply chains around patient needs have proven to yield significant results, leading to further policy improvements (Dacosta-Claro, 2002; Dacosta-Claro & Lapierre, 2003).
5. In Switzerland, the diversity of medical prescription systems among cantons has led to the emergence of significant differences in healthcare demand and supply chain performance, with treatment costs per patient increasing with higher practice size (Busato, Matter, Künzi, & Goodman, 2010).
6. In Sweden, bottom-up improvements efforts have proven to be more conducive to developing patient-centric operations, supported by more proactive collaboration on the part of healthcare professionals along the supply chain (Elg, Stenberg, Kammerlind, Tullberg, & Olsson, 2011).
7. In the Netherlands, several efforts to implement lean thinking have relied on the Focused Factory concept, where primary care units are reengineered to optimize patient flow, revealing several limitations in fully realizing patient-centric care (Blank & Merkies, 2004; Pieters, Oirschot, & Akkermans, 2010)

Emerging Reforms in Developing Countries

Finally, while national policies have been more difficult to emerge in developing countries, significant progress has been recorded in Asia. For example, some Indian hospitals have accomplished major improvements in supply chain efficiency, especially by reducing the bullwhip effect through more effective collaboration (Narang, 2011; Samuel, Gonapa, Chaudhary, & Mishra, 2010; Singh Gaur, Xu, Quazi, & Nandi, 2011). Chinese hospital supply chains have also benefited from various changes such as deregulation, leading to major policy proposals such as Vendor Managed Inventory (VMI) that lead to win-win collaboration between medical supply organizations (Chen, 2010; Shi, 2010).

Overall, the past 10 years have demonstrated that national health policies have been linked closely with the emergence of patient-driven supply chain practices. The co-occurrence of top-down and bottom-up initiatives have led to a diversity of performance improvements, with some variance depending on hospital size, ownership, and mission. National culture has not been explored as a key issue in implementation lifecycles, although a more comparative approach could lead to new findings in healthcare reform and its impact on supply chains and cost reductions (Simonet, 2010).

Developing Patient-Driven Supply Chains

Integrated Evidence-Based Supply Management

National health reforms have been a driving factor in creating incentives towards lean principles across the healthcare industry. Global convergence in approaches is providing renewed opportunities for supply chain partners to collaborate more widely, and ensure that efficiency benefits are passed directly to patients in the form of more value-added medical operations.

In the United States, one key implication of national health reforms has been the focus on Value-Based Purchasing (VBP) in health services, with ensuing SCM practices refocused on reducing costs while improving patient health outcomes (Ferman, 2009; Haywood, 2010). This has been linked closely to a more focused concept, Evidence-Based Purchasing (EBP), where patient-related KPI are driving hospital supply chains more directly (Fatholahi, 2009; Frith, 1999). As such, patient-driven supply chains are viewed not in isolation, but instead as a fully integrated system, linking the patient's needs, their health insurance purchasing capabilities, and hospital medical and materials planning processes.

This integrated approach is an extension of the fundamental shift towards Evidence-Based Medicine (EBM), which has taken roots over the years as a bottom-up approach to the standardization of clinical processes and guidelines (Rauen, Makic, & Bridges, 2009; Umscheid, Williams, & Brennan, 2010). Many healthcare professional groups have been concerned with the challenge of developing new practices that optimize clinical interventions in an integrated fashion (Broekhuis & Donk, 2011; Ferenc, 2010). With the rise of EBM as a standard discipline across healthcare professions, it offers renewed opportunities to allow lean and agile principles to take roots in hospital operations, and help align medical and materials management to emphasize more accurate patient information communication and decision-making (Anthony & Hudson-Barr, 2004; Zikmund-Fisher et al., 2010).

Lean and Agile Process Configurations

The development of patient-driven supply chains remains mostly an implementation challenge. However, the potential for performance improvement are important, with more research required to improve and optimize hospitals in every parts of their operations.

Recent studies of various clinical units have shown the significant impact on patient health outcomes from a tighter alignment between patient needs and materials management (Flowers, Tomlinson, Levy, Deponio, & Rosenbaum, 2009). Results are coherent across all process foci in medical operations.

1. Job-Shop Process: While orthopaedics and operating rooms operate much like a job-shop, with multiple medical, device, and surgical professionals involved in resolving each case, there is significant improvement in post-treatment recovery from the application of value-stream modeling to eliminate waste in routing patients and analyze costs according to optimize medical interventions (Chung et al., 2010; Yousri, Khan, Chakrabarti, Fernandes, & Wahab, 2011).
2. Batch Process: In highly commoditized batch operations, such as laboratory and blood services, integration across the supply chain has proven most valuable, but directly driven by properly processing patient-related information (Bakar, Hakim, Chong, & Lin, 2009; Grant, 2010).
3. Assembly Process: With time-sensitive units such as emergency and trauma, requiring the rapid combination of several medical disciplines along with necessary equipment, similar efforts in synchronizing personnel and materials around patient needs have proven crucial in reducing wait time and increasing recovery rates (Dickson, Anguelov, Vetterick, Eller, & Singh, 2009; Setijono, Naraghi, & Ravipati, 2010; Stratton & Knight, 2010; Willoughby, Chan, & Strenger, 2010).
4. Continuous Process: In the case of high-value operations such as radiology and oncology, where diagnosis and treatment are much like a continuous process, new models of value-driven intervention decisions can help improve service timeliness and effectiveness (Feeley, Fly, Albright, Walters, & Burke, 2010; Lodge & Bamford, 2007; Teichgräber & de Bucourt, 2011; Van de Castle & Szymanski, 2008).

Overall the simultaneous implementation of quality and productivity initiatives has led to the progressive emergence of patient-driven supply chains. Patient needs and information are becoming the driving factor in hospital materials management, with ensuing effects on supply requirements planning and supply chain management. Evidence-based and value-based principles are slowly bringing renewed efficiency in hospitals, with supply activities representing one of the key areas for performance improvement.

Critical Factors in Creating Lean and Agile Healthcare Supply Chains

Cultural Change

Hospitals are undergoing complex top-down and bottom-up change processes, requiring renewed collaboration across the value chain (Ahgren, 2010). Lean principles are progressively making their way through management and medical operations, and materials and supply chain management are adjusting consequently. These advancements have been closely linked with emerging changes in clinical governance, allowing systematic policy deployment within healthcare organizations, and facilitating joint decision-making to implement change initiatives (Travaglia, Debono, Spigelman, & Braithwaite, 2011).

Yet a certain number of organizational constraints persist, and make it difficult for lean and agile supply chains to take roots in most healthcare operations. Most of the challenges relate to the difficulty to transpose efficiency criteria from the manufacturing world to hospitals (Brandao de Souza, 2009). A recent survey of lean implementation initiatives in a national health service has identified 6 key constraints that need to be overcome before lean and agile principles can bear results (Grove, Meredith, MacIntyre, Angelis, & Neailey, 2010):

1. High process variability
2. A lack of understanding of lean
3. Poor communication and leadership
4. Target focused
5. Problems defining waste
6. Difficulty in determining who the customer is and what they value

On the other hand, there is hope that lean and agile principles could be properly blended with healthcare culture. This would be especially useful to create focus and empowerment in context of high-pressure and time-sensitive teams, such as emergency and trauma (Fillingham, 2007). The same process would also extend to learning processes in the context of more routine care, such as nursing wards (Ballé & Régnier, 2007b). In the context of highly specialized healthcare units, some may be able to reengineer processes to a point of emulating focused factories found in the manufacturing world (Kumar, 2010).

Some studies have also found that empowerment and learning are not so much driven by management pressure, but instead by the particular needs of local patient population (Rahimnia & Moghadasian, 2010). Hence, becoming a lean and agile hospital would be most dependent on the cultural co-adaptation of medical staff and patients in the front-line (Tucker, Singer, Hayes, & Falwell, 2008). This is why most efforts to implement quality and productivity initiatives should rely on process reengineering methods that are most adapted to the realities of healthcare provisioning (Towill, 2009).

Managerial Change

While bottom-up cultural change is most promising, top-down managerial change is equally important to ensure lasting results, undisrupted by undue restructuring. In fact, it has been noted for several years that hospital management remains a key issue in allowing healthcare operations to evolve, with several issues common to most professional bureaucracies (Mintzberg, 1997):

1. Fragmentation of efforts
2. Confusion in mission and in mission statements

3. Problems of bundling research with clinical work
4. Selectivity in informing board members
5. Dangers of professional management
6. Difficulties of combining external advocacy with internal roles in the senior manager's job

As such, transformation of healthcare processes is required at all levels, including throughout the administrative hierarchy, attempting to realign perspectives among diverse management styles (Sladek, Bond, & Phillips, 2010). Yet one challenge that is often overlooked is the scarcity of management expertise, as medical professionals are highly specialized and rarely have the opportunity to migrate through hierarchical structures (Dwyer, 2010).

Solutions to this issue can be found in a more strategic career management of medical professionals, ensuring they develop and rely upon a rich network of experts to coach new leaders (Pappas, Flaherty, & Wooldridge, 2004). Physician executives are generally more likely to enter management careers if they can properly assess career opportunities in terms of life-long learning goals and motivations (Fabius, 2007). It would require, as some authors have argued, that hospitals and physicians between align their mutual interests and develop a partnership culture (Carlson & Greeley, 2010; Trybou, Gemmel, & Annemans, 2011).

Technological Change

In conjunction with cultural and managerial change, hospitals are challenged to implement new information technologies that enhance operational performance. Lean and agile supply chains interact at various levels throughout healthcare processes, and require integration of diverse systems, to create a properly configured Health Information System (HIS). A key component of an HIS is an integration of supply chain and e-procurement systems, which in turn depends on a stronger partnership with suppliers to overcome both technology and business-related obstacles to collaboration (Lilley, 2008).

One of the most important component of an HIS, touching upon the whole healthcare industry, is the introduction of Electronic Medical Records (EMR). This technology has been amply demonstrated to increase productivity and ensure quality medical services. Yet key challenges remain to increasing adoption rates at hospital, regional, and national levels (Kumar & Aldrich, 2010). Among other issues for EMR adoption, complex clinical governance structures, lack of integration capabilities, as well as lack of systematic process reengineering and implementation practices are among the most important.

In addition to optimizing traditional healthcare management systems, there is a need to integrate front-line information and propagate it throughout the hospital. This primary information collection and processing would require more reliance on Clinical Decision Systems (CDS), which apply advanced artificial intelligence technologies to implement complex medical protocols and guidelines and optimize physician decision-making (Anton et al., 2009). It has been demonstrated to improve health and achieve cost savings in most healthcare operations, especially where high-pressure and time-sensitive decisions are required (Hughes, 2009). They have also been found to be most effective when combined with other quality and safety initiatives, and are therefore a catalyst factor in ensuring effective transition towards lean and agile hospitals (Scott, 2009). A proper functioning of CDS applications would also require renewed Knowledge Management (KM) practices in hospitals, with significant improvements in linking clinical and materials processes (Maruster & Jorna, 2005).

Along with HIS, EMR, and CDS, Radiofrequency Identification (RFID) has been proposed to help optimize hospital supplies and assets. Once properly integrated with other enterprise systems, this technology provides timely information on patients, processes, and equipment, while saving time and reducing costs, along with improving quality and patient safety (Revere, Black, & Zalila, 2010). Among other applications, the integration of location-based mobile applications throughout clinical units may allow patients to receive more timely services and supplies, thereby reducing product shortages and overloads in diverse clinical units (Fenies, Gourgand, & Rodier, 2006; Mahendrawathi, Pranantha, & Johansyah Dwi, 2010; Wen, Liu, & Liu, 2010). This integration capability would allow healthcare providers at all stages of medical operations to streamline personnel and materials requirements planning, which would be planned from end-to-end, from admissions to discharge (Jiao, Li, & Jiao, 2008). An RFID implementation may also greatly improve waste management and improve safety and productivity through the automation of several logistical tasks (Hoffmann & Schubert, 2009; Ozkil et al., 2009).

CONCLUSION

We have reviewed key issues in the emergence of lean and agile supply chains throughout the healthcare industry. We first defined the concept of customer-oriented supply chains, and then transposed the concept to develop a patient-driven vision of SCM in hospitals. We then proceeded to studying the main changes occurring around and inside hospitals, whether in their national health policy environments, and in the progressive transformation of their medical operations. We completed our review with a discussion of the critical success factors for developing patient-driven lean and agile supply chains, namely cultural, managerial, and technological change.

One key conclusion we can draw is that the application of lean and agile principles in hospitals is still in infancy. Many changes are still necessary at all levels of healthcare organizations in order to properly align supply chains with the rest of the organizations. As well, the diverse medical professions concerned with this integration are still evolving slowly towards more modern approaches to operations and information management. As such, it is likely that further research shall focus primarily on technology implementation and its co-reconfiguration along with organizational restructuring.

Finally, it is important to note that while lean and agile SCM have been most successful in the manufacturing world, healthcare management must keep in mind that its impact in hospital performance will be very progressive, and certainly less significant than that found in industry. Recent research on reengineering various clinical units has demonstrated that productivity and quality improvements are difficult to come about, and that the spread of necessary best practices takes time. However, our review also confirms the emergence of significant enablers, among others changes in clinical governance practices that help support operational and administrative change at all levels.

Overall, it is clear that hospitals are emerging to become some of the most important players in global customer-oriented supply chains, and to be profoundly transformed through a patient-driven approach to lean and agile SCM.

REFERENCES

Agarwal, A., Shankar, R., & Tiwari, M. K. (2007). Modeling agility of supply chain. *Industrial Marketing Management*, *36*(4), 443–457. doi:10.1016/j.indmarman.2005.12.004

Ahgren, B. (2010). Mutualism and antagonism within organisations of integrated health care. *Journal of Health Organization and Management*, *24*(4), 396–411.

Anthony, M. K., & Hudson-Barr, D. (2004). A patient-centered model of care for hospital discharge. *Clinical Nursing Research*, *13*(2), 117–136. doi:10.1177/1054773804263165

Anton, B. B., Schafer, J. J., Micenko, A., Wolf, D. M., DiNucci, S., & Donovan, P. (2009). Clinical decision support. How CDS tools impact patient care outcomes. *Journal of Healthcare Information Management*, *23*(1), 39–45.

Bakar, A. H. A., Hakim, I. L., Chong, S. C., & Lin, B. (2009). Measuring supply chain performance among public hospital laboratories. *International Journal of Productivity and Performance Management*, *59*(1), 75–97. doi:10.1108/17410401011006121

Baker, G. R., Norton, P. G., Flintoft, V., Blais, R., Brown, A., & Cox, J. (2004). The Canadian adverse events study: The incidence of adverse events among hospital patients in Canada. *Canadian Medical Association Journal*, *170*(11), 1678–1686. doi:10.1503/cmaj.1040498

Ballé, M., & Régnier, A. (2007a). From cars to catheters: Adapting lean principles within a healthcare environment. *Development and Learning in Organizations*, *21*(4), 28–30. doi:10.1108/14777280710758871

Ballé, M., & Régnier, A. (2007b). Lean as a learning system in a hospital ward. *Leadership in Health Services*, *20*(1), 33–41. doi:10.1108/17511870710721471

Blank, J. L. T., & Merkies, A. H. Q. M. (2004). Empirical assessment of the economic behaviour of Dutch general hospitals. *Health Economics*, *13*(3), 265–280. doi:10.1002/hec.824

Brandao de Souza, L. (2009). Trends and approaches in lean healthcare. *Leadership in Health Services*, *22*(2), 121–139. doi:10.1108/17511870910953788

Broekhuis, M., & Donk, D. P. v. (2011). Coordination of physicians' operational activities: a contingency perspective. *International Journal of Operations & Production Management*, *31*(3), 251–273. doi:10.1108/01443571111111919

Busato, A., Matter, P., Künzi, B., & Goodman, D. C. (2010). Supply sensitive services in Swiss ambulatory care: An analysis of basic health insurance records for 2003-2007. *BMC Health Services Research*, *10*, 315–315. doi:10.1186/1472-6963-10-315

Carlson, G., & Greeley, H. (2010). Is the relationship between your hospital and your medical staff sustainable? *Journal of Healthcare Management / American College of Healthcare Executives*, *55*(3), 158-173.

Chen, G. S. (2010). *On the supply chain management of public hospital materials.* Paper presented at the 2010 International Conference on E-Product E-Service and E-Entertainment, ICEEE2010, Henan.

Chung, W.-C., Fan, P.-L., Chiu, H.-C., Yang, C.-Y., Huang, K.-L., & Tzeng, D.-S. (2010). Operating room cost for coronary artery bypass graft procedures: does experience or severity of illness matter? *Journal of Evaluation in Clinical Practice*, *16*(6), 1063–1070. doi:10.1111/j.1365-2753.2009.01251.x

Dacosta-Claro, I. (2002). The performance of material management in health care organizations. *The International Journal of Health Planning and Management*, *17*(1), 69–85. doi:10.1002/hpm.653

Dacosta-Claro, I., & Lapierre, S. D. (2003). Benchmarking as a tool for the improvement of health services' supply departments. *Health Services Management Research*, *16*(4), 211–223. doi:10.1258/095148403322488919

de Treville, S., Shapiro, R. D., & Hameri, A.-P. (2004). From supply chain to demand chain: The role of lead time reduction in improving demand chain performance. *Journal of Operations Management*, *21*(6), 613–627. doi:10.1016/j.jom.2003.10.001

Dickson, E. W., Anguelov, Z., Vetterick, D., Eller, A., & Singh, S. (2009). Use of lean in the emergency department: A case series of 4 hospitals. *Annals of Emergency Medicine*, *54*(4), 504–510. doi:10.1016/j.annemergmed.2009.03.024

Dwyer, A. J. (2010). Medical managers in contemporary healthcare organisations: A consideration of the literature. *Australian Health Review*, *34*(4), 514–522. doi:10.1071/AH09736

Elg, M., Stenberg, J., Kammerlind, P., Tullberg, S., & Olsson, J. (2011). Swedish healthcare management practices and quality improvement work: Development trends. *International Journal of Health Care Quality Assurance*, *24*(2), 101–123. doi:10.1108/09526861111105077

Epstein, R. M., Fiscella, K., Lesser, C. S., & Stange, K. C. (2010). Why the nation needs a policy push on patient-centered health care. *Health Affairs (Project Hope)*, *29*(8), 1489–1495. doi:10.1377/hlthaff.2009.0888

Fabius, R. J. (2007). The broadening horizon for physician executives: The six constituencies of health care. *Physician Executive*, (May-June): 72–74.

Fatholahi, A. (2009). A scientific approach to buying decisions: Value-based purchasing takes hints from evidence-based processes. *Hospital Materials Management*, *34*(4), 5–7.

Feeley, T. W., Fly, H. S., Albright, H., Walters, R., & Burke, T. W. (2010). A method for defining value in healthcare using cancer care as a model. *Journal of Healthcare Management*, *55*(6), 399–411.

Fenies, P., Gourgand, M., & Rodier, S. (2006, Oct. 2006). *A decisional model for the performance evaluation of the logistic process: Application to the hospital supply chain.* Paper presented at the 2006 International Conference on Service Systems and Service Management.

Ferenc, J. (2010). Time well spent? Assessing nursing-supply chain activities. *Materials Management in Health Care*, *19*(2), 12–16.

Ferman, J. H. (2009). Healthcare reform and a VBP program. Value-based purchasing concepts continue to evolve through the legislative process. *Healthcare Executive*, *24*(2), 56–59.

Fillingham, D. (2007). Can lean save lives? *Leadership in Health Services*, *20*(4), 231–241. doi:10.1108/17511870710829346

Flowers, W. P., Tomlinson, D., Levy, E., Deponio, M., & Rosenbaum, M. (2009). Optimizing hospital supply chain processes for savings. *Healthcare Financial Management: Journal of the Healthcare Financial Management Association*, *63*(2), 1–4.

Frith, L. (1999). Priority setting and evidence based purchasing. *Health Care Analysis*, *7*(2), 139–151. doi:10.1023/A:1009497307073

Germain, R., Claycomb, C., & Dröge, C. (2008). Supply chain variability, organizational structure, and performance: The moderating effect of demand unpredictability. *Journal of Operations Management*, *26*(5), 557–570. doi:10.1016/j.jom.2007.10.002

Grant, D. B. (2010). Integration of supply and marketing for a blood service. *Management Research Review*, *33*(2), 123–133. doi:10.1108/01409171011015810

Grove, A. L., Meredith, J. O., MacIntyre, M., Angelis, J., & Neailey, K. (2010). UK health visiting: Challenges faced during lean implementation. *Leadership in Health Services*, *23*(3), 204–218. doi:10.1108/17511871011061037

Haywood, T. (2010). The cost of confusion: healthcare reform and value-based purchasing. *Healthcare Financial Management: Journal of the Healthcare Financial Management Association*, *64*(10), 44–48.

Hoffmann, M., & Schubert, K. (2009). Material flow management at the university hospital in Jena. *Stoffstrommanagement am Universitätsklinikum Jena, 11*(10), 38-41.

Holweg, M., & Pil, F. K. (2008). Theoretical perspectives on the coordination of supply chains. *Journal of Operations Management, 26*(3), 389–406. doi:10.1016/j.jom.2007.08.003

Hsu, T.-H., Su, H.-Y., & Liao, P.-P. (2010). Enhancing value creation of device vendors in the medical service industry: A relationship perspective. *The Service Industries Journal, 30*(11), 1787–1801. doi:10.1080/02642060802624316

Hughes, C. (2009). *Using clinical decision support to improve health and achieve cost savings.* San Diego, CA: Anvita Health Inc.

Jiao, Y. Y., Li, K., & Jiao, R. J. (2008, 21-24 Sept. 2008). *A case study of hospital patient discharge process re-engineering using RFID.* Paper presented at the Management of Innovation and Technology, 2008. ICMIT 2008. 4th IEEE International Conference on.

Jüttner, U., Christopher, M., & Baker, S. (2007). Demand chain management-integrating marketing and supply chain management. *Industrial Marketing Management, 36*(3), 377–392. doi:10.1016/j.indmarman.2005.10.003

Khan, A., Bakkappa, B., Metri, B. A., & Sahay, B. S. (2009). Impact of agile supply chains' delivery practices on firms' performance: Cluster analysis and validation. *Supply Chain Management: An International Journal, 14*(1), 41–48. doi:10.1108/13598540910927296

Kumar, S. (2010). Specialty hospitals emulating focused factories: A case study. *International Journal of Health Care Quality Assurance, 23*(1), 94–109. doi:10.1108/09526861011010703

Kumar, S., & Aldrich, K. (2010). Overcoming barriers to electronic medical record (EMR) implementation in the US healthcare system: A comparative study. *Health Informatics Journal, 16*(4), 306–318. doi:10.1177/1460458210380523

Lee, C. K. M., Ho, W., Ho, G. T. S., & Lau, H. C. W. (2011). Design and development of logistics workflow systems for demand management with RFID. *Expert Systems with Applications, 38*(5), 5428–5437. doi:10.1016/j.eswa.2010.10.012

Li, S., Rao, S. S., Ragu-Nathan, T. S., & Ragu-Nathan, B. (2005). Development and validation of a measurement instrument for studying supply chain management practices. *Journal of Operations Management, 23*(6), 618–641. doi:10.1016/j.jom.2005.01.002

Lilley, K. (2008). An integrated strategy for e-procurement: The case for Leeds teaching hospitalsIn Hübner, U., & Elmhorst, M. A. (Eds.), *E-business in healthcare* (pp. 177–195). London, UK: Springer.

Lodge, A., & Bamford, D. (2007). Health service improvement through diagnostic waiting list management. *Leadership in Health Services, 20*(4), 254–265. doi:10.1108/17511870710829364

Mahendrawathi, E. R., Pranantha, D., & Johansyah Dwi, U. (2010, 5-7 Dec. 2010). *Development of dashboard for hospital logistics management.* Paper presented at the Open Systems (ICOS), 2010 IEEE Conference on.

Maruster, L., & Jorna, R. J. (2005). From data to knowledge: A method for modeling hospital logistic processes. *IEEE Transactions on Information Technology in Biomedicine, 9*(2), 248–255. doi:10.1109/TITB.2005.847194

Mintzberg, H. (1997). Toward healthier hospitals. *Health Care Management Review, 22*(4), 9–18.

Mintzberg, H. (2002). Managing care and cure - Up and down, in and out. *Health Services Management Research*, *15*(3), 193–206. doi:10.1258/0951484023201 76639

Nachtmann, H., & Pohl, E. A. (2009). *The state of healthcare logistics: Cost and quality improvement opportunities*. Fayetteville, AR: Center for Innovation in Healthcare Logistics, University of Arkansas.

Narang, R. (2011). Determining quality of public health care services in rural India. *Clinical Governance: An International Journal*, *16*(1), 35–49. doi:10.1108/14777271111104574

Ozkil, A. G., Zhun, F., Dawids, S., Aanes, H., Kristensen, J. K., & Christensen, K. H. (2009, 5-7 Aug. 2009). *Service robots for hospitals: A case study of transportation tasks in a hospital.* Paper presented at the IEEE International Conference on Automation and Logistics, ICAL '09.

Pannowitsch, S. (2009). Institutionalized healthcare reform in Germany? Error correction or political strategy? *German Policy Studies*, *5*(1), 141–168.

Pappas, J. M., Flaherty, K. E., & Wooldridge, B. (2004). Tapping into hospital champions-strategic middle managers. *Health Care Management Review*, *29*(1), 8–16.

Pieters, A., Oirschot, C. v., & Akkermans, H. (2010). No cure for all evils: Dutch obstetric care and limits to the applicability of the focused factory concept in health care. *International Journal of Operations & Production Management*, *30*(11), 1112–1139. doi:10.1108/01443571011087350

Porter, M. E., & Teisberg, E. O. (2004). Redefining competition in health care. *Harvard Business Review*, *82*(6), 64–76.

Rahimnia, F., & Moghadasian, M. (2010). Supply chain leagility in professional services: How to apply decoupling point concept in healthcare delivery system. *Supply Chain Management: An International Journal*, *15*(1), 80–91. doi:10.1108/13598541011018148

Rauen, C. A., Makic, M. B. F., & Bridges, E. (2009). Evidence-based practice habits: Transforming research into bedside practice. *Critical Care Nurse*, *29*(2), 46–59. doi:10.4037/ccn2009287

Revere, L., Black, K., & Zalila, F. (2010). RFIDs can improve the patient care supply chain. *Hospital Topics*, *88*(1), 26–31. doi:10.1080/00185860903534315

Rutledge, V., Huber, D., & Mathews, J. (2010). Progression of strategies used by a healthcare system preparing for healthcare reform: past and present. *Frontiers of Health Services Management*, *27*(1), 13–27.

Samuel, C., Gonapa, K., Chaudhary, P. K., & Mishra, A. (2010). Supply chain dynamics in healthcare services. *International Journal of Health Care Quality Assurance*, *23*(7), 631–642. doi:10.1108/09526861011071562

Sarac, A., Absi, N., & Dauzère-Pérès, S. (2010). A literature review on the impact of RFID technologies on supply chain management. *International Journal of Production Economics*, *128*(1), 77–95. doi:10.1016/j.ijpe.2010.07.039

Scott, I. (2009). What are the most effective strategies for improving quality and safety of health care? *Internal Medicine Journal*, *39*(6), 389–400. doi:10.1111/j.1445-5994.2008.01798.x

Setijono, D., Naraghi, A. M., & Ravipati, U. P. (2010). Decision support system and the adoption of lean in a Swedish emergency ward: Balancing supply and demand towards improved value stream. *International Journal of Lean Six Sigma*, *1*(3), 234–248. doi:10.1108/20401461011075026

Shi, H. (2010). *Research on supply management in hospital based on VMI.* Paper presented at the 17th International Conference on Industrial Engineering and Engineering Management, IE and EM2010, Xiamen.

Simonet, D. (2010). Healthcare reforms and cost reduction strategies in Europe: The cases of Germany, UK, Switzerland, Italy and France. *International Journal of Health Care Quality Assurance, 23*(5), 470–488. doi:10.1108/09526861011050510

Singh Gaur, S., Xu, Y., Quazi, A., & Nandi, S. (2011). Relational impact of service providers' interaction behavior in healthcare. *Managing Service Quality, 21*(1), 67–87. doi:10.1108/09604521111100252

Sladek, R. M., Bond, M. J., & Phillips, P. A. (2010). Do doctors, nurses and managers have different thinking styles? *Australian Health Review: A Publication of the Australian Hospital Association, 34*(3), 375-380.

Stank, T., Brzica, M., & Ficenec, J. (2009). The benefits of supply chain integration using a third-party integrator. *Transfusion, 49*(11 Pt 2), 2536–2538. doi:10.1111/j.1537-2995.2009.02472.x

Steffen, M. (2010). The french health care system: Liberal universalism. *Journal of Health Politics, Policy and Law, 35*(3), 353–387. doi:10.1215/03616878-2010-003

Stratton, R., & Knight, A. (2010). Managing patient flow using time buffers. *Journal of Manufacturing Technology Management, 21*(4), 484–498. doi:10.1108/17410381011046599

Teichgräber, U. K., & de Bucourt, M. (2011). Applying value stream mapping techniques to eliminate non-value-added waste for the procurement of endovascular stents. *European Journal of Radiology*.

Teisberg, E. O., Porter, M. E., & Brown, G. B. (1994). Making competition in health care work. *Harvard Business Review, 72*(4), 131–141.

Towill, D. R. (2009). Frank Gilbreth and health care delivery method study driven learning. *International Journal of Health Care Quality Assurance, 22*(4), 417–440. doi:10.1108/09526860910964861

Travaglia, J. F., Debono, D., Spigelman, A. D., & Braithwaite, J. (2011). Clinical governance: A review of key concepts in the literature. *Clinical Governance: An International Journal, 16*(1), 62–77. doi:10.1108/14777271111104592

Trerise, B. (2010). Establishing an organizational culture to enable quality improvement. *Leadership in Health Services, 23*(2), 130–140. doi:10.1108/17511871011040715

Trybou, J., Gemmel, P., & Annemans, L. (2011). The ties that bind: An integrative framework of physician-hospital alignment. *BMC Health Services Research, 11*(1), 36. doi:10.1186/1472-6963-11-36

Tucker, A. L., Singer, S. J., Hayes, J. E., & Falwell, A. (2008). Front-line staff perspectives on opportunities for improving the safety and efficiency of hospital work systems. *Health Services Research, 43*(5), 1807–1829. doi:10.1111/j.1475-6773.2008.00868.x

Umscheid, C., Williams, K., & Brennan, P. (2010). Hospital-based comparative effectiveness centers: Translating research into practice to improve the quality, safety and value of patient care. *Journal of General Internal Medicine, 25*(12), 1352–1355. doi:10.1007/s11606-010-1476-9

Van de Castle, B., & Szymanski, G. (2008). Supply chain management on clinical unitsIn Hübner, U., & Elmhorst, M. A. (Eds.), *E-business in healthcare* (pp. 197–217). London, UK: Springer.

VanVactor, J. D. (2011). A case study of collaborative communications within healthcare logistics. *Leadership in Health Services*, *24*(1), 51–63. doi:10.1108/17511871111102526

Walters, D. (2008). Demand chain management+response management=increased customer satisfaction. *International Journal of Physical Distribution and Logistics Management*, *38*(9), 699–725. doi:10.1108/09600030810925980

Waring, J. J., & Bishop, S. (2010). Lean healthcare: Rhetoric, ritual and resistance. *Social Science & Medicine*, *71*(7), 1332–1340. doi:10.1016/j.socscimed.2010.06.028

Wen, Y., Liu, Z., & Liu, J. (2010, 9-10 January). *Logistics mode reengineering of hospital materials based on JIT theory.* Paper presented at the Logistics Systems and Intelligent Management, 2010 International Conference on.

Willoughby, K. A., Chan, B. T. B., & Strenger, M. (2010). Achieving wait time reduction in the emergency department. *Leadership in Health Services*, *23*(4), 304–319. doi:10.1108/17511871011079010

Yousri, T. A., Khan, Z., Chakrabarti, D., Fernandes, R., & Wahab, K. (2011). Lean thinking: Can it improve the outcome of fracture neck of femur patients in a district general hospital? *Injury*, *42*(11). doi:10.1016/j.injury.2010.11.024

Zikmund-Fisher, B. J., Couper, M. P., Singer, E., Ubel, P. A., Ziniel, S., & Fowler, F. J. (2010). Deficits and variations in patients' experience with making 9 common medical decisions: The DECISIONS survzey. *Medical Decision Making*, *30*(5), 85S–95S. doi:10.1177/0272989X10380466

ADDITIONAL READING

American College of Medical Quality. (2010). *Medical quality management: Theory and practice* (Rev. ed.). Sudbury, MA: Jones and Bartlett Publishers.

Androwich, I. American Medical Informatics Association, & American Nurses Association. (2003). *Clinical Information Systems: A framework for reaching the vision*. Washington, DC: American Nurses Pub.

Chen, H. (2005). *Medical informatics: Knowledge management and data mining in biomedicine*. New York, NY: Springer.

Duquenoy, P., George, C., & Kimppa, K. (2008). *Ethical, legal, and social issues in medical informatics*. Hershey, PA: Medical Information Science Reference. doi:10.4018/978-1-59904-780-5

Elhauge, E. (2010). *The fragmentation of U.S. health care: Causes and solutions*. New York, NY: Oxford University Press. doi:10.1093/acprof:oso/9780195390131.001.0001

Holdford, D. A., Brown, T. R., & American Society of Health-System Pharmacists. (2010). *Introduction to hospital & health-system pharmacy practice*. Bethesda, MD: American Society of Health-System Pharmacists.

Husmeier, D., Dybowski, R., & Roberts, S. (2005). *Probabilistic modeling in bioinformatics and medical informatics*. London, UK: Springer. doi:10.1007/b138794

Kelemen, Á., Abraham, A., & Liang, Y. (2008). *Computational intelligence in medical informatics*. New York, NY: Springer.

Kowalski-Dickow Associates, & American Society for Healthcare Materials Management. (1994). *Managing hospital materials management*. Chicago, IL: American Hospital Pub.

Langabeer, J. R. (2008). *Health care operations management: A quantitative approach to business and logistics*. Sudbury, MA: Jones and Bartlett Publishers.

Lazakidou, A. A., & Siassiakos, K. M. (2009). *Handbook of research on distributed medical informatics and e-health*. Hershey, PA: Medical Information Science Reference.

Moumtzoglou, A., & Kastania, A. (2011). *E-health systems quality and reliability: Models and standards*. Hershey, PA: Medical Information Science Reference.

Nowicki, M. (2011). *Introduction to the financial management of healthcare organizations* (5th ed.). Chicago, IL: Health Administration Press.

Reilly, M. J., & Markenson, D. S. (2011). *Health care emergency management: Principles and practice*. Sudbury, MA: Jones and Bartlett Learning.

Schneller, E. S., & Smeltzer, L. R. (2006). *Strategic management of the health care supply chain* (1st ed.). San Francisco, CA: Jossey-Bass.

Shiver, J. M., & Eitel, D. (2010). *Optimizing emergency department throughput: Operations management solutions for health care decision makers*. Boca Raton, FL: CRC Press.

Shortliffe, E. H., & Cimino, J. J. (2006). *Biomedical informatics: Computer applications in health care and biomedicine* (3rd ed.). New York, NY: Springer.

Srinivasan, A. V. (2008). *Managing a modern hospital* (2nd ed.). New Delhi, India: SAGE Publications.

Stegwee, R. A., & Spil, T. A. M. (2001). *Strategies for healthcare Information Systems*. Hershey, PA: Idea Group Pub.

Tan, J. K. H. (2009). *Medical informatics: Concepts, methodologies, tools, and applications*. Hershey, PA: Medical Information Science Reference.

Vian, T., Savedoff, W. D., & Mathisen, H. (2010). *Anticorruption in the health sector: Strategies for transparency and accountability*. Sterling, VA: Kumarian Press.

Whewell, R. (2010). *Supply chain in the pharmaceutical industry: Strategic influences and supply chain responses*. Farnham, UK: Gower.

KEY TERMS AND DEFINITIONS

Agile Supply Chains: An approach to SCM centered on customer value and emphasizing responsiveness and flexibility across the value chain.

Evidence-Based Hospital Performance: An integrated approach to managing hospital performance with KPIs centered on patient health outcomes.

Healthcare Information Systems: Applications of enterprise information systems principles to integrating and managing healthcare organizations.

Materials Management Systems: Integrated SCM information system for hospital materials lifecycle, where key phases include negotiating, paying, stockholding, picking, delivery, and handling.

Medical Informatics: An interdisciplinary research area, blending Medical Sciences, Information Systems, and Computer Science, focused on developing computer applications for healthcare.

Patient-Driven Supply Chains: An approach to healthcare SCM based on agile and lean principles whereas hospital materials demand is directly linked to patient needs and health outcomes.

Supply Chain Integration: Collaborative effort between firms to implementation inter-organizational systems in order to integrate supply processes and synchronize information flows and decisions.

Chapter 2
Knowledge Sharing in Supply Chain

Liandong Zhu
University of Vaasa, Finland

Robertus Wahyu Nayan Nugroho
Technical University of Liberec, Czech Republic

Mian M. Ajmal
Abu Dhabi University, UAE

Yohanes Kristianto
University of Vaasa, Finland

ABSTRACT

This chapter introduces the thermodynamics analogy as a means of studying knowledge sharing in supply chain. The study finds that distance and the knowledge capacity of the supplier are important to reduce knowledge sharing uncertainty. Furthermore, higher contact frequency between the supplier and the buyer without considering supplier capacity is proven to be insignificant to reduce knowledge sharing uncertainty. For intellectuals, the mechanism provides a new approach to explicate knowledge sharing in supply networks. Besides, it provides deep-rooted opening point for supplementary empirical assessment. The mechanism facilitates managers to expand their understanding of composite circumstances embedded into global supply networks to share their knowledge. With that enhanced understanding, the managers can spotlight their actions, which help further to perk up their firms' competitiveness provoked by the knowledge sharing activities.

INTRODUCTION

In recent years, scholars have paid escalating concentration to the role of knowledge in gaining competitive advantage leading to the emergence and development of the knowledge-based view of organizations (Eisenhardt and Santos, 2002). The debate on knowledge sharing arises from a growing recognition of the importance of knowledge in the 'new knowledge economy' and its impact on organizational competitiveness. Since, the role of knowledge becomes more important in knowledge based organization where it competes

DOI: 10.4018/978-1-4666-0246-5.ch002

based on knowledge intensive products/services rapidly (Chase, 1997). Recently, an increasing number of organizations are entering into relationships with other organizations to create value through continuous knowledge management (Hagedoorn, 1993; Robertson and Yu, 2001). Such inter-organizational knowledge management has been proposed as a fundamental strategic process and an important means by which organizations may achieve sustainable competitive advantage in the future (Contractor and Lorange, 2002; Podolny and Page, 1998; Powell and Brantley, 1992; Powell et al., 1996). However, in broader perspective of inter-organization, the complexity of knowledge becomes larger. It encourages codifiable and explicable knowledge by developing common language and ontology (Chen et al., 2000). The definition of ontology used here is that it consists of a representational vocabulary with precise definitions of the meanings of the terms of this vocabulary plus a set of formal axioms that constrain interpretation and well-formed use of these terms. Ontology use here then is analogous to use of business forms with standard operating procedures, since informational structure is represented as terminology (Kim, 2002).

A difficulty of knowledge ontology development is that some of valuable knowledge is stored in individuals that many of them are fuzzy and not possible to formalize (Polanyi, 1966). Indeed, knowledge sharing is important in inter-firms relationship since it is as social capital that support business agility and has been somewhat neglected in previous studies (Howells, 2002; Madhavan and Grover, 1998). With the result that supply chains more concentrated to maximize the benefit of information sharing by creating business architecture (Meyr et al., 2002; Disney, 2003).

In global and agile supply chains, furthermore, knowledge sharing is very important to create flexible manufacturing and product development. Effective sharing of knowledge enables supply chains for reducing time to market and developing process modularity. Communication amongst engineers in supply chains reduces product development time and enables them to develop modular manufacturing process by sharing their product interface development. This interface development will reduce incoming material inspection time and make participants more freely to maximize their innovations. Therefore, our research question is "How to maximize knowledge sharing benefits in supply chain networks?"

Paper is developed as follow; Section 2 reviews some literature from knowledge sharing in supply chain perspective to give insight to readers about the challenges for knowledge sharing in supply chain. Section 3 describes the critical success factors of knowledge sharing by considering the previous challenges. Then Section 4 discussed the managerial implications for the proposed methodology. Finally, section 5 makes conclusion and discussion of how knowledge sharing must be applied in terms of global supply chains networks.

KNOWLEDGE SHARING IN SUPPLY CHAIN

Knowledge is recognized to be a 'justified true belief' (Nonaka, 1994). Knowledge sharing between individuals is the process by which knowledge held by an individual is converted into a form that can be understood, absorbed, and used by other individuals (Ipe, 2003). Still if the perspective in this article is on the supply chain setting, we believe that the collaborative nature of these exchange relations stresses interpersonal collaboration and sharing of knowledge. Knowledge sharing is also vital because it provides a link between the individual and the organization by moving knowledge that resides with individuals to the organizational level, where it is converted into economic and competitive value for the organization (Hendriks, 1999). Network forms of organizing economic activities have rapidly increased in number since 1990. Globalisation, increased technological complexity and the reduction of inter-organizational transaction costs through the use of the internet are some of the factors behind this development (Ford, 2002).

Various benefits of knowledge sharing in network settings have been discussed in the literature. Without the capacity for sharing knowledge, companies can't access and utilize the specialized resources and capabilities of the various partners involved in the network (Foss et al. 2010). This capacity to share knowledge is also a necessary condition for the creation of new knowledge (Nonaka and Takeuchi, 1995), and it has been argued that networks with superior knowledge transfer mechanisms will be able to 'out-innovate' networks with less effective knowledge-sharing routines (Von Hippel, 1966). As knowledge sharing refers to sharing of not just codified knowledge but also beliefs, experiences, and contextualized practices (Davenport and Prusak, 1998), it is only through knowledge sharing that a base of jointly held knowledge, necessary for mutual understanding, can be created (Nonaka and Takeuchi, 1995). This jointly held knowledge base is also vital for the development of trust between partners, necessary for deeper collaborative relations (Dyer and Nobeoka, 2000).

There are, however, numerous dilemmas associated with knowledge sharing in network settings. Previously as individuals in companies have always shared knowledge, knowledge sharing was considered to be a natural function of workplaces, an activity that took place automatically. Now it has been acknowledged that even under the best circumstances, knowledge sharing is a complex process (Hendriks, 1999; Lessard and Zaheer, 1996). Previous research suggests that there are a number of challenges associated with knowledge sharing in network settings. On one hand, Dyer and Nobeoka (2000) suggest that these problems are related to three principal reasons: lack of motivation of participants to participate and openly share valuable knowledge in the network, the problem of free riders, and the costs associated in finding the opportunities to share knowledge. On the other hand, knowledge sharing between different organizations can also be inhibited due to fear of losing competitive edge by sharing valuable knowledge, fear that can be further increased by top management directives that do not support inter-company knowledge sharing (Sun and Scott, 2005). Existing differences between organizational cultures and practices can also create situations that hamper knowledge sharing (Ajmal et al., 2010): there can be clashes due to personal differences of conflicting values, people might not be open to new ideas or ways of doing things, or organizational processes might be inflexible and hard to change (Sun and Scott, 2005). Finally, also the existing relationship between two or more companies and how it is managed affects knowledge sharing, for example if there is no common objective set for the collaboration or if experiences of past behavior create mistrust and discourage knowledge sharing (Larsson et al., 1998).

While all these cases suggest, many different challenges relate to the settings of knowledge sharing. However, several challenges exist also related to knowledge and the knowledge sharing process itself. For example the tacit and sticky nature of knowledge can create problems related to how the knowledge can be shared, and at the other end, the limitations related to absorptive capacity can create problems in receiving and understanding the shared knowledge (Polanyi, 1966; von Hippel, 1994). So, even if explicit and codified *knowledge* is easily shared, the tacit, sticky and complex *know-how* is hard to codify and imitate, and thus difficult to share (Kogut and Zander, 1992; Szulanski, 1996). Also the limitations related to absorptive capacity can create problems in understanding the knowledge that is being shared (Cohen and Levinthal, 1990). Finally, the embedded nature of knowledge makes it context dependent, narrowly applicable, and personalized (Weiss, 1999). Therefore, even information that is very context-dependent, i.e. embedded, is not likely to be shared among individuals.

Due to above mentioned nature, the relationships between partners in supply chain networks tend to be more complex than the traditional business networks. Traditional business relationships consider only the exchange of tangible value, and do not see intangibles as objects of exchange between business partners. On the contrary, in supply chain networks this intangible value exchange is considered to be the real foundation for value creation (Allee, 2002). This variance in the nature and the level of collaboration between the different actors of a supply chain network poses new challenges to inter-organizational knowledge sharing. A growing body of empirical evidence indicates that organizations that are able to share knowledge effectively from one unit to another are more productive and more likely to survive than organizations that are less adept at knowledge sharing (e.g. Baum and Ingram, 1998; Darr et al., 1995).

However, even if knowledge sharing is essential for the functioning of any business network, it is especially important in supply chain networks as it directly influences the co-creation of value between the different actors participating in the network. Without the capacity for sharing knowledge, companies can not access and utilize the specialized resources and capabilities of other companies in order to create new knowledge (Nonaka and Takeuchi, 1995). Knowledge sharing is a complex process (Lessard and Zaheer, 1996) as it refers not only to information but also beliefs, experiences, and contextualized practices that are difficult to convey (Davenport and Prusak, 1998). Following section discusses the critical factors of knowledge sharing in supply chain networks.

SOME CRITICAL FACTORS OF KNOWLEDGE SHARING IN NETWORKS

Supply chain itself can be understood as a network of autonomous (or semi-autonomous) business entities involved in various business activities that produce and deliver, through upstream and downstream links, goods and/or services to customers. Lin and Shaw (1998) emphasized the notion of value in seeing a supply chain as a series of activities that delivers value to its customers, in the form of a product or a service (or a combination of both), whereas many other authors emphasized the notion of core flows in describing a supply chain in terms of flows (of information, cash, and materials) through a series of processes, beginning with suppliers of raw materials and finishing with the end customers.

Small Geographical Difference Supports Knowledge Sharing

One issue in knowledge sharing that needs to be extended in terms of its application is interoperability issue as a result of collective learning (Lawson and Lorenz, 1999). It is believed that higher geographical difference makes knowledge miss-interpretation stronger (Haldin-Herrgard, 2000). The author discussed further that sectoral difference also a main factor for determining pattern of knowledge sharing. There must be one important missing element, perhaps, generating trust by clustering knowledge sharing networks instead of imparting of knowledge in different geography (Howell, 2002).

On the basis of the above discussion we conclude that the clustered networks according to the same geography may enhance the knowledge sharing. Knowledge sharing and creation in business networks is profoundly influenced by the underlying value systems. In other words, the challenges of 'knowledge management' are remarkably different across the continuum.

Competence-Based Trust Supports Knowledge Sharing by Reducing Information Loss from Sender to Receiver

Competence-based trust describes a relationship in which an individual believes that another person is knowledgeable about a given subject area. Furthermore, competence-based trust had a major impact on knowledge transfers involving highly tacit knowledge. This is a significant finding, because much value added knowledge found in organizations is often experiential and difficult to codify.

Developing performance measurement for competence based trust has also been applied into supplier network knowledge sharing in Toyota (Dyer and Nobeako, 2000). Toyota used three innovations of the suppliers association, the knowledge transfer consultants and small group learning teams. Suppliers association is applied for sharing explicit knowledge amongst suppliers, and knowledge transfer consultant and small group learning teams are used for sharing tacit knowledge. Since trust can be embodied in some way to social rewards such as approval, status, and respect (McLure and Faraj, 2005) then higher competence based trust productivity has also additional benefit as a shape of conflict resolution by minimizing risks that stem from exposure to opportunistic behavior by partners, uncertainty, ambiguity and incomplete information, which typify inter-organizational arrangements (Panteli and Sockalingam, 2005).

On the basis of the above discussion we conclude that the ability for grouping a similar expertise in terms of its subject and level could be a factor for minimizing the knowledge sharing uncertainty.

MODELING KNOWLEDGE SHARING IN SUPPLY CHAINS

This section models knowledge sharing in supply chains by considering the previously mentioned critical success factors in knowledge sharing. We use some approaches from natural sciences to represent knowledge sharing activities. In defense of this application, most of knowledge sharing activities use human as main actor. Thus, human as a part of nature also follow the nature behavior. For instance if people do repeatedly the same task then he or she will getting faster and faster in terms of their speed of the task completion. This situation analog to fly wheel phenomena that always used in cars and industrial engines to generate inertia. The following sections detail the models briefly.

Thermodynamics Properties of Knowledge Sharing

Since knowledge is assumed power for individuals, thus it is a fundamental property of social structures. There is much less agreement about what power is, and how we can describe and analyze its causes and consequences. Since power is defined as the degree of occupation of the knowledge sender to its receiver, then we refer our discussion to computer generated information.

Higher transferred knowledge needs more bit of information because the network needs more memory. Higher computer memory increases power consumption of the IT system that automatically creates higher processing temperature. Thus, it is reasonable if we analyze the knowledge sharing as a thermodynamics system.

First, we can refer to Figure 1. Each arc in Figure 1 represents in-degree or out-degree of knowledge transfer in or out of objects 1, 2, 3, and 4. These arcs deliver some amounts of information bits from one sender to one receiver at certain level of absolute temperature T .

In considering thermodynamic properties of the knowledge sharing, we will find the entropy to represent the knowledge uncertainty. Since computer uses binary number to represent bit of memory, then we start our entropy calculation by using coin as an example of binary number of memory.

Suppose we have 1 coin that represents binary combination 0 (tail) and 1 (head). The probability to get head is $\frac{1}{2}$ and so as probability for

Figure 1. Graph example of knowledge sharing in supply chains

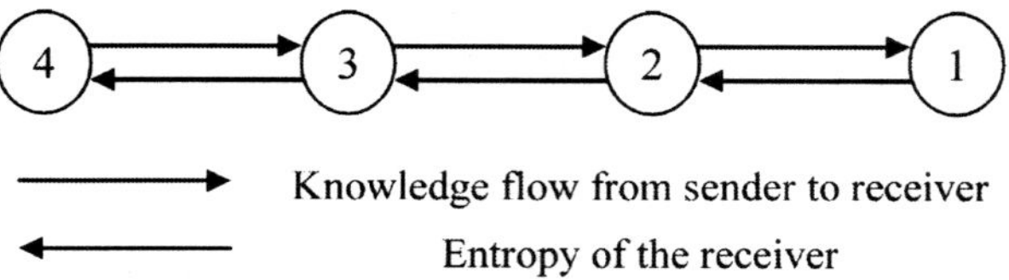

Knowledge flow from sender to receiver

Entropy of the receiver

tail. Thus if we have only one coin then the entropy of the system is that:

$$S = \log\left(\frac{1}{2}\right)$$

or

$$S = -\log\left(2\right)$$

This is the minimum entropy for one bit since the decimal number of binary number 10 is equal to 2. Thus for K bits of memory we have the entropy as follows:

$$S = -\log\left(K\right) \tag{1}$$

The energy given is then formulated as:

$$G_{Sender} = -T_{Sender}.\log\left(K\right) \tag{2}$$

Minus sign in (1) and (2) signifies that the system generates energy to share its knowledge but it will be eliminated from the section calculation to make easier understanding. Since we consider knowledge sharing by using communication tools then we might also use energy given to the system according to Planck equation as:

$$G_{Sender} = \frac{h.c}{\lambda} \tag{3}$$

Combining (2) and (3) for obtaining sender temperature for K bits then we have

$$T_{Sender} = \frac{hc}{\lambda \log\left(K\right)} \tag{4}$$

Equation 4 shows that if we share K bit of the knowledge at wavelength λ_0 then our system will have temperature T at entropy level $\log\left(2\right)$. Obviously, when the knowledge sender shares its knowledge to the receiver object, it will not free of miss-interpretation. It is shown that higher knowledge sharing frequency $\frac{c}{\lambda}$ positively reduces the effect of knowledge sharing uncertainty $\log\left(K\right)$.

If we assume the following that the sender and the receiver of the knowledge both radiate as spherical black bodies, and that the receiver is in thermal equilibrium, then we can derive a formula for the relationship between the receiver's temperature and the sender's surface temperature. To begin, we use the Stefan–Boltzmann law to find the total power (energy/second) the sender is emitting:

The receiver has an absorbing area equal to a two dimensional circle, rather than the surface of a sphere.

$$G_{Sender} = \left(\sigma T^4_{Sender}\right)\left(4\pi R^2_{Sender}\right) \tag{5}$$

where

σ is the Stefan–Boltzmann constant, T_{sender} is the surface temperature of the sender, and R_{Sender} is the radius of the sender transmitter to the central data processing of the receiver. For instance for satellite communication, then distance between satellite and its earth station. Distance between data processing unit and radio transmitter.

The sender emits that power equally in all directions. Because of this, the receiver is hit with only a tiny fraction of it. This is the power from the Sun that the Earth absorbs:

$$P_{Receiver} = P_{Sender}\left(1-\alpha\right)\left(\frac{\pi R_{Receiver}^2}{4\pi D^2}\right) \quad (6)$$

where

$R_{Receiver}$ is the distance of the receiver antenna to the central data processing of the receiver.

D is the distance between the sender and the receiver.

α is the albedo of receiver that represent the information loss as a function of the receiver entropy.

We examine whether the memory capacity of the sender influences information loss or not. Thus we create maximum sender temperature at

$$T_{Sender} = \frac{hc}{\lambda \log\left(2\right)}$$

Conversely, maximum information loss appears at the maximum usage of sender memory capacity at C bit or,

$$T_{Sender} = \frac{hc}{\lambda \log\left(C\right)}$$

Thus α can be reformulated as:

$$\alpha = \frac{\frac{hc}{\lambda \log\left(K\right)}}{\frac{hc}{\lambda \log\left(2\right)} - \frac{hc}{\lambda \log\left(C\right)}} = \frac{\log\left(2\right)\log\left(C\right)}{\log\left(K\right)\left(\log\left(C\right)-\log\left(2\right)\right)} \quad (7)$$

Equation 7 shows us that using less memory for sending knowledge reduces information loss, Figure 2 shows $2 \le K \le C$ at different memory capacity that is started at the lowest capacity (8-inch - IBM 23Floopy Disc) to 7, 97 G-Bytes memory. It shows that developing high speed and capacity of memory is important for knowledge sharing since it increases knowledge sharing efficiency by reducing information loss at different stage of memory capacity usage (Figure 2).

Furthermore, the importance of using higher memory speed and capacity can be exhibited as Figure 3 to show that the increasing of at higher capacity memory and speed gives lesser impact to information uncertainty magnification, regardless the distance between the sender transmitter to the receiver. Figure 3 informs us that the sender capacity to share its knowledge is an important factor for minimizing knowledge sharing uncertainty. Capacity here can be computer memory chips capacity, people expertise, or organization capability to codify its knowledge to be more explicit.

Furthermore, we need to examine whether the increasing of distance between the sender knowledge transmitter to the receiver influences knowledge sharing uncertainty magnification or not. Thus we use an analogy of Sun radiation to Earth surface to describe this kind of knowledge sharing at different distance. We suppose that the receiver is circular form to receive equally signals from the sender at the same probability at:

$$\frac{\log\left(K\right)_{Receiver}}{\log\left(K\right)_{Sender}}$$

Figure 2. Information loss as a function of memory capacity usage at different storage capacity (byte)

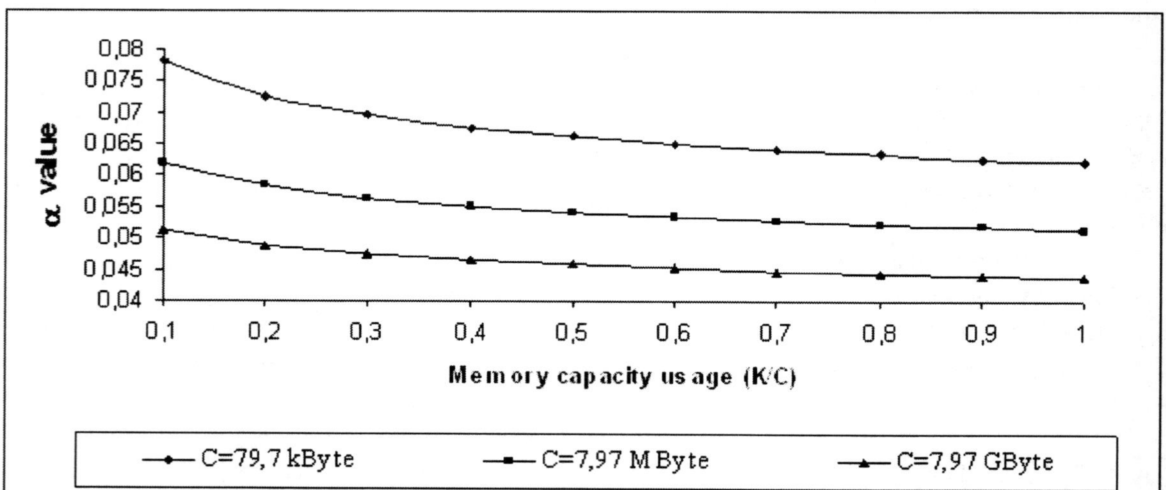

Figure 3. Effect of information loss growth α to uncertainty growth α_n / α_1 from a sender to a receiver

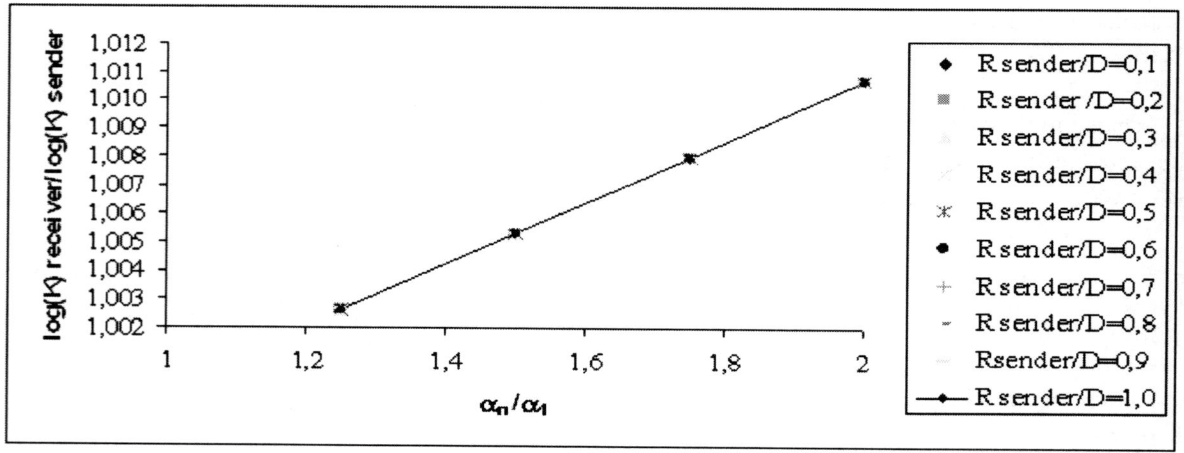

the sender, however, is a sphere by considering that the knowledge are emitted to all directions. Thus we have the received power of the receiver as:

$$\pi.R^2_{Receiver} \tag{8}$$

where

$$P_{Receiver} = \left(\sigma T^4_{Receiver}\right)\left(4\pi R^2_{Receiver}\right)$$

is the black body temperature of the receiver.

Now, our second assumption was that the receiver is in equilibrium with the sender, so the power absorbed must equal the power emitted:

$$T_{Receiver} \tag{9}$$

So plug in Equations 6, 8, and 9 into this and we get

$$G_{Sender} = G_{Receiver} \tag{10}$$

After canceling of factors, the final result is

$$\left(\sigma T^2_{Sender}\right)\left(4\pi R^2_{Sender}\right)\left(1-\alpha\right)\left(\frac{\pi R^2_{Receiver}}{4\pi D^2}\right) = \left(\sigma T^2_{Receiver}\right)\left(4\pi R^2_{Receiver}\right) \tag{11}$$

If we compare Eq.11 and Eq.5 and we fix the wavelength, then we can see that longer distance between the knowledge sender and receiver makes

$$T_{Receiver} = T_{Sender}\sqrt{\frac{\sqrt{1-\alpha}R_{Sender}}{2D}}$$

higher. This signifies that longer distance makes information uncertainty is magnified at level

$$\log\left(K\right) \tag{12}$$

Equation 11 expresses the quantitative measure of knowledge sharing uncertainty magnification as functions of distance between the sender transmitter and the receiver, and information loss. We can see that either longer distance between the sender transmitter and central information processing to the receiver exponentially increases the received knowledge by the receiver. This conclusion supports the use of more sophisticated communication tools such as satellite might increase the power of the sender over the receiver (see Figure 4).

Furthermore, Equation 11 can be used to show the effect of distance to information uncertainty at computer memory. By using minimum

$$\frac{T_{Sender}}{T_{Receiver}} = \frac{\log\left(K\right)_{Receiver}}{\log\left(K\right)_{Sender}} = \frac{1}{\sqrt{\frac{\sqrt{1-\alpha}R_{Sender}}{2D}}}$$

and maximum $\alpha = 0,04$ to represent the available memory storage capacity in the market, then we can exhibit the uncertainty magnification as a function of information loss in Figure 3.

Figure 5 shows that at higher distance ratio $\alpha = 0,08$ the uncertainty magnification is weaken at the same rate of different level of information loss $\frac{R_{Sender}}{D}$. This signifies that information loss does not influence information uncertainty magnification.

In conclusion, we suggest general knowledge ontology by preparing well structured and less complicated of knowledge, and competent people and organization in sharing their knowledge in order to get maximize the sender capacity so as to minimize knowledge sharing uncertainty. Secondly, we suggest close distance in sharing knowledge at any size of memory capacity. This because of lower distance minimizes knowledge sharing uncertainty magnification. Finally, the frequency of knowledge sharing gives effect to knowledge sharing uncertainty level but without

Figure 4. Knowledge sharing from several senders (local station, private broadcasting network etc) to several receivers (transmitting tower, home antenna etc)

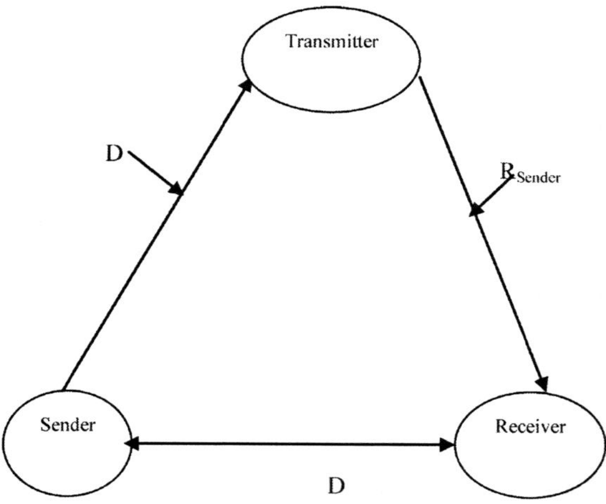

Figure 5. Effect of distance ratio $\frac{\log(K)_{Receiver}}{\log(K)_{Sender}}$ *to uncertainty growth* $\frac{R_{Sender}}{D}$ *from a sender to a receiver*

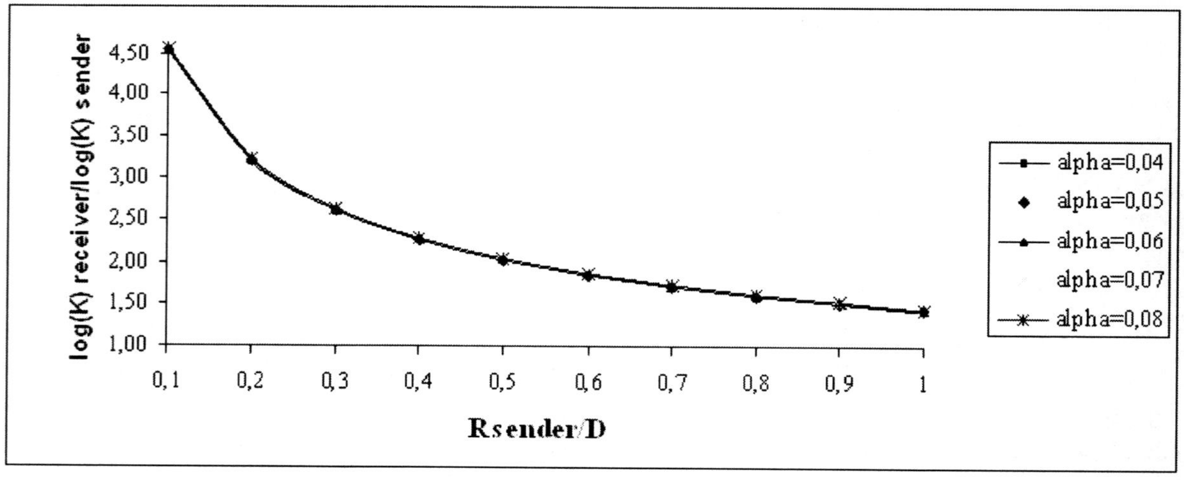

considering the sender capacity the same frequency cannot reduce the knowledge sharing uncertainty.

CONCLUSION

Managerial Implications

From this discussion, the supply chain networks can take advantage of the proposed model by presenting the maximum knowledge sharing amongst participants. In this section, we outline the main implications regarding the impacts of sharing strategy on the both of sender and the receiver.

First, minimizing knowledge sharing entropy benefits the increasing of knowledge loss in network. A trustable knowledge sender is important to minimize loss of knowledge that reduces knowledge sharing uncertainty. For practitioners in supply chain integration, it is important to share complete knowledge to their receiver, for instance it is important to share demand information and also its variation to supplier since the supplier can get more credible knowledge in terms of how to deliver the knowledge sender without putting some delivery delays.

Second, it is important to setup distance between transmitter and knowledge receiver at the initial stage of knowledge sharing process. For practitioners it can be illustrated as follows. For instance a sender would like to share its knowledge by putting transmitter in city A to send knowledge to receiver in city B, transmitter can be an communication tools or a third party for instance consultant or transporter. If after certain time of the sender would like to install a sophisticated tool of Radio Frequency Identification (RFID) by guiding the receiver with e-book, professional consultants from the sender service provider is useless. The reason is that the distance between the sender and the receiver is not ideal. Indeed, making closer communication, for instance, by using local third party logistics or local mediator is more effective to reduce knowledge sharing uncertainty to a better area. Thus, closer distance is useful to attract the receiver to join the knowledge sharing.

Third, the frequency of communication between the sender and the receiver does not give any influence to the success level of knowledge sharing. The reason is that the supply chain needs higher quality of communication instead of the quantity of communication to share their knowledge. Thus, more frequently contact is proven to be an insignificant factor for the success of knowledge sharing.

In conclusion, the proposed knowledge sharing model here focused on global supply chain network that possibly to be conducted by using Information Technology (IT) or human. There are two suggestions for practitioners that need to be considered in sharing their knowledge that are developing trustable knowledge to reduce information loss and act locally according to the receiver mind in order to reduce distance between the sender and the receiver.

REFERENCES

Ajmal, M. M., Helo, P., & Kekäle, T. (2010). Critical factors for KM in project business. *Journal of Knowledge Management*, *14*(1), 156–168. doi:10.1108/13673271011015633

Allee, V. (2002). *The future of knowledge: Increasing prosperity through value networks*. Boston, MA: Butterworth-Heinemann.

Baum, J. A. C., & Ingram, P. (1998). Survival-enhancing learning in the Manhattan hotel industry, 1898-1980. *Management Science*, *44*(7), 996–1016. doi:10.1287/mnsc.44.7.996

Chase, R. L. (1997). A knowledge based organization: An international survey. *Journal of Knowledge Management*, *1*(1), 38–49. doi:10.1108/EUM0000000004578

Chen, F., Drezner, Z., Ryan, J. K., & Simchi-Levy, D. (2000). Quantifying the bullwhip effect in a simple supply chain: The impact of forecasting, lead times, and information. *Management Science*, *46*(3), 436–443. doi:10.1287/mnsc.46.3.436.12069

Cohen, W. M., & Levinthal, D. A. (1990). Absorptive capacity: A new perspective on learning and innovation. *Administrative Science Quarterly*, *35*(1), 128–152. doi:10.2307/2393553

Contractor, F. J., & Lorange, P. (2002). The growth of alliances in the knowledge-based economyIn Contractor, F. J., & Lorange, P. (Eds.), *Cooperative strategies and alliances* (pp. 3–24). Oxford, UK: Pergamon. doi:10.1016/S0969-5931(02)00021-5

Darr, E., Argote, L., & Epple, D. (1995). The acquisition, transfer, and depreciation of knowledge in service organizations: Productivity in franchises. *Management Science*, *41*(11), 1750–1762. doi:10.1287/mnsc.41.11.1750

Davenport, T. H., & Prusak, L. (1998). *Working knowledge: How organizations manage what they know*. Boston, MA: Harvard Business School Press.

Disney, S. M. (2003). The effect of vendor managed inventory (VMI) dynamics on the bullwhip effect in supply chains. *International Journal of Production Economics*, *85*, 199–215. doi:10.1016/S0925-5273(03)00110-5

Dyer, J. F., & Nobeako, K. (2000). Creating and managing a high performance knowledge-sharing network: The Toyota case. *Strategic Management Journal*, *21*, 345–367. doi:10.1002/(SICI)1097-0266(200003)21:3<345::AID-SMJ96>3.0.CO;2-N

Eisenhardt, K. M., & Santos, F. M. (2002). Knowledge-based view: A new theory of strategy? In Pettigrew, A., Thomas, H., & Whittington, R. (Eds.), *Handbook of strategy and management*. Thousand Oaks, CA: Sage Publications.

Ford, C. M. (2002). The futurity of decisions as a facilitator of organizational creativity and change. *Journal of Organizational Change Management*, *15*(6), 635–646. doi:10.1108/09534810210449541

Foss, N. J., Husted, K., & Michailova, S. (2010). Governing knowledge sharing in organizations: Levels of analysis, governance mechanisms, and research directions. *Journal of Management Studies*, *47*(3), 455–482. doi:10.1111/j.1467-6486.2009.00870.x

Hagedoorn, J. (1993). Understanding the rationale of strategic technology partnering: Interorganizational modes of cooperation and sectoral differences. *Strategic Management Journal*, *14*, 371–385. doi:10.1002/smj.4250140505

Haldin-Herrgard, T. (2000). Difficulties of diffusion of tacit knowledge in organizations. *Journal of Intellectual Capital*, *1*(4), 357–365. doi:10.1108/14691930010359252

Hendriks, P. (1999). Why share knowledge? The influence of ICT on the motivation of knowledge sharing. *Knowledge and Process Management*, *6*(2), 91–100. doi:10.1002/(SICI)1099-1441(199906)6:2<91::AID-KPM54>3.0.CO;2-M

Howells, J. R. L. (2002). Tacit knowledge, innovation and economic geography. *Urban Studies (Edinburgh, Scotland)*, *39*(5/6), 871–884. doi:10.1080/00420980220128354

Ipe, M. (2003). Knowledge sharing on organizations: A conceptual framework. *Human Resource Development Review*, *2*(4), 337–359. doi:10.1177/1534484303257985

Kim, H. (2002). Predicting how ontologies for the semantic web will evolve. *Communications of the ACM*, *45*(2), 48–54. doi:10.1145/503124.503148

Kogut, B., & Zander, U. (1992). Knowledge of the firm, combinative capabilities, and the replication of technology. *Organization Science*, *3*(3), 383–397. doi:10.1287/orsc.3.3.383

Larsson, R., Bentsson, L., Henriksson, K., & Sparks, J. (1998). The inter-organizational learning dilemma: Collective knowledge development in strategic alliances. *Organization Science*, *9*(3), 285–305. doi:10.1287/orsc.9.3.285

Lawson, C., & Lorenz, E. (1999). Collective learning, tacit knowledge and regional innovative capacity. *Regional Studies*, *33*(4), 305–317. doi:10.1080/713693555

Lessard, D. R., & Zaheer, S. (1996). Breaking the silos: Distributed knowledge and strategic responses to volatile exchange rates. *Strategic Management Journal*, *17*(7), 513–543. doi:10.1002/(SICI)1097-0266(199607)17:7<513::AID-SMJ832>3.0.CO;2-P

Lin, F., & Shaw, M. J. (1998). Reengineering the order fulfillment process in supply chain networks. *International Journal of Flexible Manufacturing Systems*, *10*(3), 197–229. doi:10.1023/A:1008069816606

Madhavan, R., & Grover, R. (1998). From embedded knowledge to embodied knowledge: New product development as knowledge management. *Journal of Marketing*, *62*(4), 1–12. doi:10.2307/1252283

Mcclure, W. M., & Faraj, S. (2005). Why should I share? Examining social capital and knowledge contribution in electronic networks of practice. *Management Information Systems Quarterly*, *29*(1), 35–57.

Meyr, H., Rohde, J., & Stadtler, H. (2002). Basic for modelingIn Stadtler, H., & Kilger, C. (Eds.), *Supply chain management and advanced planning: Concepts, models, software and case studies* (2nd ed., pp. 45–70). Berlin, Germany: Springer – Verlag.

Nonaka, I. (1994). A dynamic theory of organizational knowledge creation. *Organization Science*, *5*(1), 14–37. doi:10.1287/orsc.5.1.14

Nonaka, I., & Takeuchi, H. (1995). *The knowledge-creating company: How Japanese companies create the dynamics of innovation*. New York, NY: Oxford University Press.

Panteli, N., & Sockalingam, S. (2005). Trust and conflict within virtual inter-organizational alliances: A framework for facilitating knowledge sharing. *Decision Support Systems*, *39*, 599–617. doi:10.1016/j.dss.2004.03.003

Podolny, J. M., & Page, K. L. (1998). Network forms of organization. *Annual Review of Sociology*, *24*, 57–76. doi:10.1146/annurev.soc.24.1.57

Polanyi, G. (1966). *Tacit dimension*. London, UK: Routledge & Kegan Paul.

Powell, W. W., & Brantley, P. (1992). Competitive cooperation in biotechnology: Learning through networksIn Nohria, N., & Eccles, R. G. (Eds.), *Networks and organizations*. Boston, MA: Harvard Business School Press.

Powell, W. W., Koput, K. W., & Smith-Doerr, L. (1996). Interorganizational collaboration and the locus of innovation: Networks of learning in biotechnology. *Administrative Science Quarterly*, *41*(1), 116–145. doi:10.2307/2393988

Robertson, P. L., & Yu, T., F. (2001). Firm strategy, innovation and consumer demand: A market process approach. *Managerial and Decision Economics*, *22*, 183–199. doi:10.1002/mde.1016

Sun, P. Y.-T., & Scott, J. L. (2005). An investigation of barriers to knowledge transfer. *Journal of Knowledge Management*, *9*(2), 75–90. doi:10.1108/13673270510590236

Szulanski, G. (1996). Exploring internal stickiness: Impediments to the transfer of best practice within the firm. *Strategic Management Journal, 17*(Winter Special Issue), 27-43.

Von Hippel, E. (1966). *The sources of innovation*. New York, NY: Oxford University Press.

Von Hippel, E. (1994). Sticky information and the locus of problem solving: Implications for innovation. *Management Science*, *40*(4), 429–439. doi:10.1287/mnsc.40.4.429

Chapter 3
Negotiation Protocol Based on Budget Approach for Adaptive Manufacturing Scheduling

Paolo Renna
University of Basilicata, Italy

Rocco Padalino
University of Basilicata, Italy

ABSTRACT

The research proposed concerns the development of a multi-agent scheduling approach able to support manufacturing systems in different dynamic conditions. The negotiation protocol defined budget approach is based on a financial asset that each part obtains when it is released into the manufacturing system for processing. The part spends the budget to perform the manufacturing operations by the workstations; the virtual market in which part agent and workstation agents coordinate the decentralized system. A fuzzy tool is proposed to assign the budget to each part based on the objectives pursued. A simulation environment based on Rockwell ARENA® platform has been developed in order to test the proposed approach. The simulations are used to compare the proposed approach with classical dynamical scheduling approaches proposed in literature. The results show how the proposed approach leads to better results, and it can be selective among the different priority of the parts.

INTRODUCTION AND MOTIVATION

Nowadays, the competition is played in a market environment characterized by demand fluctuations, new product introduction, reduction of the products life cycle and random disturbances. Some disturbances can be: the failures of manufacturing machines or technological equipment; the importance of the parts can be modified; the objectives of the manufacturing system can change; etc. In this environment, a static scheduling approach leads to reduce drastically the performance of the manufacturing system when

DOI: 10.4018/978-1-4666-0246-5.ch003

exceptions occur. Therefore, the manufacturing systems need to dynamic scheduling to keep a high level of the performance when the conditions change. The dynamic scheduling concerns the possibility to take all decisions based on the current state of the manufacturing system. Ouelhadj and Petrovic (2009) classified the dynamic scheduling in three categories: completely reactive scheduling, predictive–reactive scheduling, and robust pro-active scheduling. (Mehta and Uzsoy 1999; Vieira et al. 2000, 2003; Aytug et al. 2005; Herroelen and Leus 2005). In briefly, the completely reactive scheduling is obtained taking the decisions in real time without a global scheduling in advance. The robust pro-active scheduling is performed building the scheduling in advance trying to capture the exceptions in advance. The predictive-reactive scheduling is a compromise between the two above opposite approaches.

The architecture to support the scheduling approaches in manufacturing systems can be classified in centralized and decentralized systems.

The centralized architectures are not flexible enough to adapt themselves to the dynamism and complexity needed in dynamic manufacturing system conditions.

The main requirements of a dynamic scheduling approach are the following:

- Agility: it is the ability to adapt quickly the scheduling to the dynamic conditions of the manufacturing system;
- Scalability: it is the possibility to add resources into the architecture and the expansion is possible without disrupting the entire architecture established
- Fault tolerance: the architecture can reduce the impact of failures occurred to any parts of the architecture.
- Computational efficiency; the problem of scheduling can be more complex to resolve in a single step.

The above requirements can be obtained by a decentralized architecture (Shen et al., 2001). The Multi Agent Systems are able to support the development of decentralized architecture. A MAS is an artificial system composed of a population of autonomous agents, which cooperate with each other to reach common objectives, while simultaneously each agent pursues individual objectives (Ferber, 1999). Among the several definitions agent, Woodbridge and Jennings (1995): "*an agent is a computer system that is situated in some environment, and that is capable of flexible and autonomous action in this environment in order to meet its design objectives. By flexible we mean that the system must be responsive, proactive, and social*". Multi-agent systems (MAS) have already demonstrated their potential in meeting such complex requirements (Monostori et al., 2006). In manufacturing, such as systems have demonstrated their ability to build up agile and reactive behaviour in various settings like enterprise integration and supply chain management (Swaminathan et al., 1996), dynamic system reconfiguration (Shen et al., 1998), learning manufacturing systems (Monostori et al., 1996), distributed dynamic scheduling (Chiuc and Yih, 1995; Váncza and Márkus, 2000), as well as factory control (Brennan, 1997).

A MAS to pursue a global objective needs to implement a coordination mechanism among the autonomous agents. The most common coordination mechanisms used are the Contract net protocol (Smith 1980), market based, auction based (Siwamogsatham and Saygin, 2004) and game theory (Zhou et al., 2009b).

In this chapter, a coordination mechanism based on market-like approach is proposed. The market like approach works like a classical marketplace where the increase of the demand for a product causes its price to rise, and vice versa, to fall. In the case of the manufacturing systems, the resources become the products and parts are buyers asking for these products.

The parts have a budget to spend to perform the manufacturing operations buying a resource. The amount of budget allows the generic part to buy the resource that asks a price lower or equal the budget of the part. Therefore, the level of the budget defines what resources the generic part can buy and the related level of services of the resources (working time, efficiency, quality, etc.). The crucial activities of this coordination approach are the following: how the resources define its price and the budget assigned to the parts when they enter to the manufacturing system. The price of the resources outlines the mechanism of real time scheduling and control of the manufacturing system. The budget assignment to the parts interprets the objectives to pursue in terms of priority of the parts typology, due date, throughput, throughput time, etc.

The aim of this approach is to capture the dynamic conditions of the manufacturing system keeping a high level of performance and able to modify easily the objectives changing only one parameter: the budget assigned to the parts. A fuzzy tool is developed to assign the budget to each part based on the objectives of the manufacturing system. A simulation environment based on Rockwell ARENA® platform has been developed in order to test the proposed approach. In particular, the proposed approach is compared with a classical market like approach proposed in literature in order to highlight the behaviour in very dynamic conditions.

The chapter is organised as it follows. In Section 2 the discussion of the literature review is reported. In Section 3 describes the manufacturing environment and the main principles of our proposed distributed control method in Section 4. In section 5, the experimental environment is outlined. Finally, in section 6 the simulation test results are detailed while conclusions are drawn in section 7.

LITERATURE REVIEW

Many authors have addressed the problem of adaptive scheduling related to job shop with most of the approaches proposed based on heuristics and use dispatching rules.

Jeong and Kim (2005) have used simulation to evaluate the manufacturing system performance and selected an appropriate dispatching rule for scheduling the subsequent period. Chryssolouris and Subramaniam (2001) have proposed a dynamic scheduling approach based on a genetic algorithm (GA). At each event of the manufacturing system (machine breakdown, job arrival, mix change, etc.), the GA was run to select a new scheduling method. Trentesaux et al. (2000) proposed a distributed management system that selected the dispatching rule for an FMS based on the state of the manufacturing system. This research was rather focused on the design of a scheduling system. Maione et al. (2003) presented a MAS with a negotiation protocol using also fuzzy logic. As they found, this soft computing technique led to better performance but required more computational time in order to obtain acceptable results.

Cowling et al. (2001, 2003, 2004) and Ouelhadj et al. (2003a, 2003b) proposed a novel multi-agent architecture for integrated and dynamic scheduling in steel production. Each steel production process is represented by an agent, including the continuous caster agents, the hot strip mill agent, the slab yard agent, and the user agent. The hot strip mill and continuous caster agents perform the robust predictive–reactive scheduling of the hot strip mill and the continuous caster, respectively. Robust predictive–reactive scheduling generates robust predictive–reactive schedules in the presence of real-time events using utility, stability, and robustness measures and a variety of rescheduling heuristics.

Aydin and Fogarty (2004) proposed a parallel implementation of the modular simulated annealing algorithm for classical job-shop scheduling.

A multi agent-system based on Java technology is proposed. The empirical results obtained show that the method proposed is scalable and decreases the CPU time compared with other approaches proposed in the literature.

Wonga et al. (2006) proposed an agent-based approach for the dynamic integration of the process planning and scheduling functions. The simulations show that the hybrid-based MAS, with the introduction of supervisory control, is able to provide integrated process plan and job shop scheduling solutions with a better global performance.

Zhou et al. (2009a) proposed an agent-based Decision Support System (DSS) for the effective dynamic scheduling of a Flexible Manufacturing System (FMS). The proposed DSS mainly includes six components: User Interface Agent (UIA), Criteria And Rules Selection Agent (CRSA), Performance Evaluation Agent (PEA), Scheduling Decision Selection Agent (SDSA), FMS database and Scheduling Knowledge Base (SKB). The functions of each component are discussed and a corresponding prototype system is developed. Finally, some examples are used to illustrate the decision process and to study the performance of the FMS under different dynamic disturbances.

Recently, some authors have developed coordination approaches inspired by the behavior of social insects like ants, bees, termites and wasp to. Valckenaers and Van Brussel (2005) presented the design of a holonic manufacturing execution system, that is an instantiation of the PROSA architecture (1998). The control and coordination mechanism is inspired by the ant colony foraging behaviour.

Zhou et al. (2008) proposed an algorithm based on Ant Colony Optimization in a shop floor scenario with three levels of machine utilization, three different processing time distributions, and three different performance measures for intermediate scheduling problems. The experimental results show that ACO outperforms other approaches when the machine utilization or the variation of processing times is not high. The procedure proposed is a centralized approach.

Renna (2009) developed two pheromone approaches for the job shop scheduling problem in a Multi Agent System environment. One is based on the past information of a part (throughput time of the manufacturing cell); and the other on the queue of the manufacturing cell. The proposed approaches are tested in a dynamic environment; the simulation results show how the approach based on the queue of the manufacturing cell performs better when the environment conditions are very dynamic.

Renna (2011) proposed a coordination approach for the multi-agent architecture based on the computation of internal and external indexes of the generic manufacturing cell. Several scenarios were considered: from static to very dynamic conditions for internal and external exceptions of the manufacturing system. The simulation results highlighted that the performance of the proposed approach outperforms the performance of a classical workload approach (benchmark) in all conditions. In the related FMS literature there are quite a few publications that deal with an extremely dynamic environment, where also the manufacturing system itself changes frequently. Most of the researches take a centralized approach and propose decision models that require intensive computations, hence are inadequate to control the job shop in real time. In this chapter, an adaptive scheduling approach is proposed that is capable to operate in a very dynamic environment. The proposed method is based on a budget that each job can spend on purchasing the service of manufacturing resources. The price computation of the cell is based on the evaluation of its local state as well as of the global state of the manufacturing system. The main motivations of our investigations are the following:

- Developing a simple methodology where only one parameter has to be set in order to keep a proper performance level of the manufacturing system

- Reducing the information communication among the agents of the architecture in order to obtain an approach to implement in real case applications
- Evaluates the performance of the proposed approach in a very dynamic environment where internal and external exceptions occur
- Integrating our model into a supply chain or extended enterprise. In fact, the only typology of information exchanged between the shop floor and the upper management levels is the importance of each job type that determines the budget assigned to the job

The principal advantage of our method is the possibility to adapt the scheduling approach to the change of the objective of the production planning level by setting only the parameter of the budget.

MANUFACTURING SYSTEM CONTEXT

The testbed for the proposed negotiation approach will be a production system consisting of a given number of cells. Each cell can perform any kind of manufacturing operations so that the resulting system is generic. The manufacturing system processes jobs, each consisting of operations to be executed sequentially. Jobs belong to various job types.

Scheduling decides about the assignment of a manufacturing cell to the next operations of running jobs, therefore it is a pure dispatching problem. If such decisions are made in a distributed way, the dispatching problem is to be solved through a negotiation between autonomous agents representing cells and jobs in a real time fashion.

A cell agent is associated to each workstation; it is an intelligent entity aimed at scheduling the cell's work with as high efficiency as possible. Moreover, when a new job arrives to the manufacturing system the corresponding job agent is created; it analyses the job's status locating the following operation to be scheduled. Dispatching problems for a given job are handled by negotiation between job and cell agents using a version of the well-proven contract net protocol (Smith, 1980). Accordingly, the negotiation process consists of the following steps:

1. Job agent analyses the job status and determines the job's next technological operation to be executed
2. Job agent sends a message to the cell agents informing them that an operation is pending for processing; afterwards, it remains waiting for the cell agents' answers
3. Each cell agent evaluates the workstation status at negotiation time t, calculates and provides a price
4. Job agent receives evaluations coming from all the cells and builds up an index for evaluating each cell's offer
5. Finally, the job is assigned to the cell that provides the best offer at the time t.

As the reader can notice, the above procedure is a simple auction based negotiation protocol. It defines the environmental relations of the autonomous agents involved in the work, but makes no assumption towards the agents' decision-making mechanisms. This means that the above protocol can be adapted to different objectives and decision mechanisms of the autonomous cell and job agents.

The assumptions of the Job-shop scheduling problem researched in this chapter are the following:

- There are n tasks, and each task consists of m operations.

- Each typology part has been given processing order, processing time and due date.
- Orders for production of different parts arrive randomly.
- Operations cannot be pre-empted.
- Each machine can process only one task at once.
- Each machine performs the manufacturing operation with an efficiency, which sets the speed of the operation.
- The queues are managed by the First In First Out policy in order to investigate only the proposed strategy.
- Each machine can breakdown randomly.

In this research, the material handling time is included in the machining time, and the handling resources are always available.

BUDGET APPROACH

Our proposed approach is based on a budget level assigned to each job. The budget is an amount of fictitious money that the job can spend to acquire the manufacturing services. The financial aspects are not considered because we handle problems on the shop floor level where no real transfer of money is made. Essentially, the budget is used to coordinate the multi-agent system. The activity UML diagram in Figure 1 shows the process, with the following activities:

1. *Budget assigned to the part.* When a part enters to the manufacturing system, the amount of the budget is assigned to the part. In the following sub-sections is described the fuzzy tool proposed to define the amount of the budget.
2. *Determines the following technological operation.* The part agent determines the technological operation to perform based on the process plan of the part.
3. *Sends request.* The part agent sends a request to all manufacturing resources agent with the information related to the technological operation requested. The part agent waits for the answers by the resources' agent.
4. *Evaluates the resource state.* The resource agent evaluates the processing time of the technological operation requested, the queues of the parts, the failure state, etc.
5. *Computes and transmits the resource price.* The resource agent computes the price to submit to the part agent evaluating the resource state. As described in the following, a high price means high performance of the resource. Then, the resource agent submits the price to the part agent and waits for the part agent answer.
6. *Evaluates the price of the resource and selects the resource.* The part agent collects the price of the resources' agent and selects the price that the part agent can spend (based on the amount of the budget). In particular, the part agent selects the higher price that can spend in order to buy the better resource. In order to avoid a deadlock, if the budget is not enough to buy any resources, the part is assigned to the worst resource (the resource with the lower price).
7. *Transmits the resource selected.* The part agent transmits the assignation of the part to the resource to the resources' agent.
8. *Updates the resource state.* The resource agent updates the state of the resource in terms of queues and technological operation to perform.
9. *Updates the part state.* The part agent updates the information of the parts and verifies if other technological operations are required.
   If the part needs another technological operation, the above process is repeated when the part ends the technological operation assigned.

Figure 1. UML activity diagram

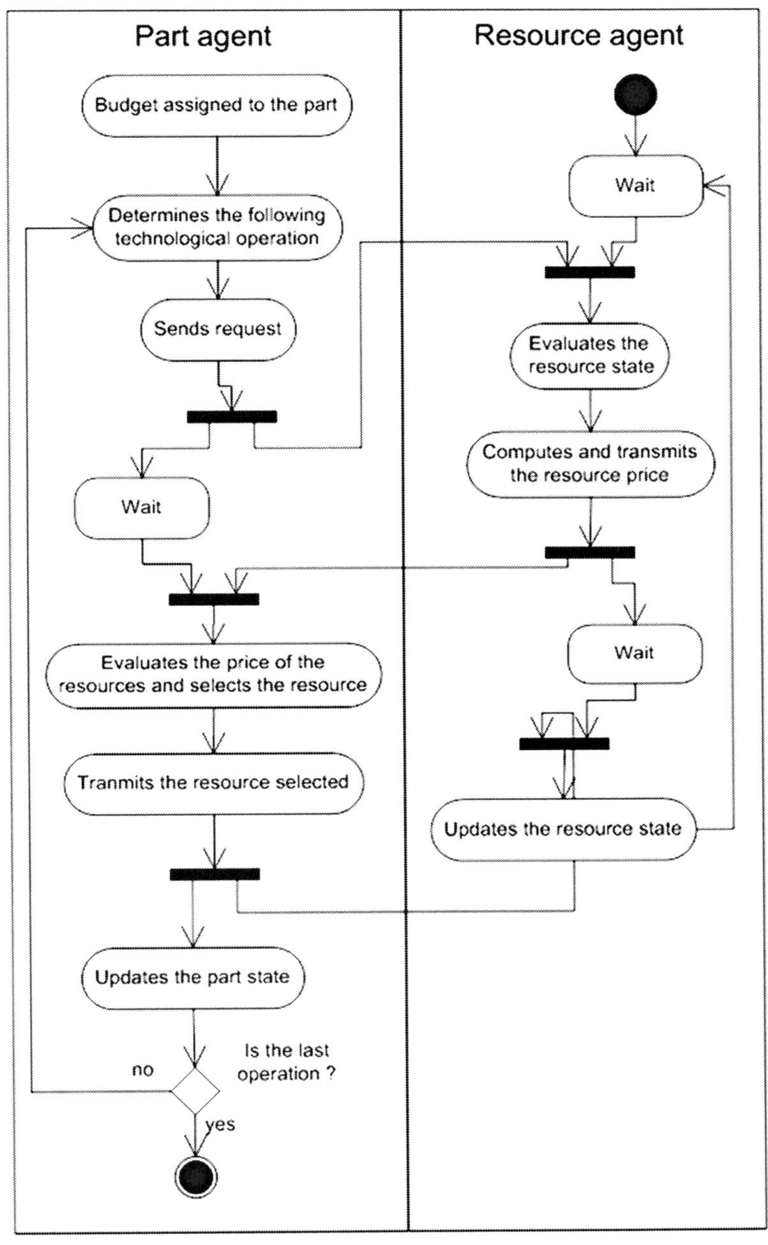

PERFORMANCE INDICES AND PRICE COMPUTATION

The price computed by the resource agent is based on the state of the manufacturing resource.

Details of the price computation are given by the following expressions. The first expression computes a performance about the flow time of the parts, that is between 0 (worst performance) and 1 (better performance, no parts are in the queue).

$$NorFlowTime_m(t) = \frac{Max\,ProcTime_{Type_{j,k}}}{FlowTime_m(t) + Max\,ProcTime_{Type_{j,k}}} \quad (1)$$

where m is the index of the resource, $Max\,ProcTime_{Type_{j,k}}$ is the maximum processing time for the technological operation k of the part of type j.

The effective service time ($EWT_j^k(t)$) is obtained by multiplying this value with the resource's efficiency CTC_m, that is minor of one. A greater value of CTC_m, means that the generic resource is able to process the part with higher speed.

$FlowTime_m(t)$ is the expected throughput time of resource m computed by summing up the processing times of the parts waiting in the resource's queue plus the residual service time of the part being just worked in the cell at the negotiation time t. This index is the measure of workload of the manufacturing cell. The index value is one if no parts are in the queue and the resource is in the idle state, and decreases with the increase of parts in the queue.

Then, a Cell Failure Index, *RFI*, is computed as follows:

$$RFI_m(t) = 1 - \frac{FT_m(t)}{t} \quad (2)$$

where $FT_m(t)$ is the total time of failure status of resource until negotiation time period t. *RFI* above is the index of reliability of the manufacturing resource. This index value is one if no failure happens and decreases with the increase of the failure time.

A Resource Processing Time Index, *RPTI*, is computed as

$$RPTI_m(t) = 1 - CTC_m(t) \quad (3)$$

where $CTC_m(t) > 0$ is the efficiency of resource m at time t. The value of $CTC_m(t)$ multiplied by $TaskT_{Type_{j,k}}$ produces the expected working time of the resource. In particular, a lower value of $CTC_m(t)$ leads to lower expected time to manufacturing a generic part.

Then, an Internal Resource Index, *IRI* is computed by the following expression as a combination of the two above indices:

$$IRI_m(t) = \beta \cdot RFI_m(t) + (1-\beta) \cdot RPTI_m(t) \quad (4)$$

Finally, the External Resource Index, *ERI* is determined as follows:

$$ERI_m(t) = NorFlowTime_m(t) \quad (5)$$

The *IRI* is the average of the indices related to the cell, while the *ERI* is the index related to the manufacturing system status.

The so-called Resource Efficiency Index of the manufacturing resource is the following *REI*:

$$REI_m(t) = \alpha \cdot ERI_m(t) + (1-\alpha) \cdot IRI_m(t) \quad (6)$$

where α is a weight between the internal and external efficiencies. Note that the value of *REI* can assume the values in the interval [0,1].

The resource agent computes the price as follows:

$$Price_m(t) = K \cdot REI_m(t), \quad (7)$$

where the constant K is the maximum price of the cell.

Therefore, if the value of the *REI* index is one (the state of the resource is the better possible: no parts in the queue, no failures occur and higher speed of processing time), the resource agent asks

Figure 2. Inputs and output data of the fuzzy tool

the higher price K; otherwise the price reduces proportionally to the reduction of the *REI* index.

The job agent selects the resource with the highest price required, because high price involves a high level of performance of the manufacturing resource. If the job does not have the sufficient budget to pay the resource, it has to select a resource that requests a price compatible with the budget of the job. If all resources request such a price that the part cannot pay, the part is dispatched to the resource that requests the lowest price (deadlock avoidance). Finally, the part and resource agents update their budget for processing the subsequent operations.

Budget Allocation

A fuzzy approach has been proposed to assign the value of budget to each part type. Figure 2 shows this fuzzy engine whose inputs data are the following:

- Technological operations: the number of operations that the parts have to get processed by the manufacturing system. The increase of this number leads to increase the level of the budget (more resources to buy).
- Profit margin: the level of profit margin related to the product type. The increase of the profit leads to increase the level of the budget (greater importance of the product type).
- Due date: a closer due date leads to increase the budget assigned to the part, so that the part can have a chance to get better manufacturing resources in order to minimize the delivery delay.
- Other: other inputs can be easily added to the fuzzy engine to include other characteristics of the part.

The only output of the system is the level of budget allocated to the job.

For each input there is defined the following fuzzy set (see Figure 3):

Table 1 shows the value of the inputs of the fuzzy systems for the test case where, as the reader can notice, the technological operations can assume values like 2, 3, 4 and 5. The profit margin of products is classified in three categories: 1 stands for low, 2 for medium, and 3 for high. Finally, the due date input depends on the value of the multiplier of the technological operation time.

The fuzzy inference rules applied are:

no.	rule		budget
1	IF due date is High	THEN	High
2	IF due date is Medium	THEN	Medium
3	IF due date is Low	THEN	Low
4	IF number of technological operations is High	THEN	High
5	IF number of technological operations is Medium T	THEN	Medium
6	IF number of technological operations is Low	THEN	Low
7	IF profit product is High	THEN	High
8	IF product profit is Medium	THEN	Medium
9	IF product profit is Low	THEN	Low

The budget assigned to the part is obtained by activating the above fuzzy rules; among the rules with the same consequent is adopted the rule with

Figure 3. Fuzzy sets

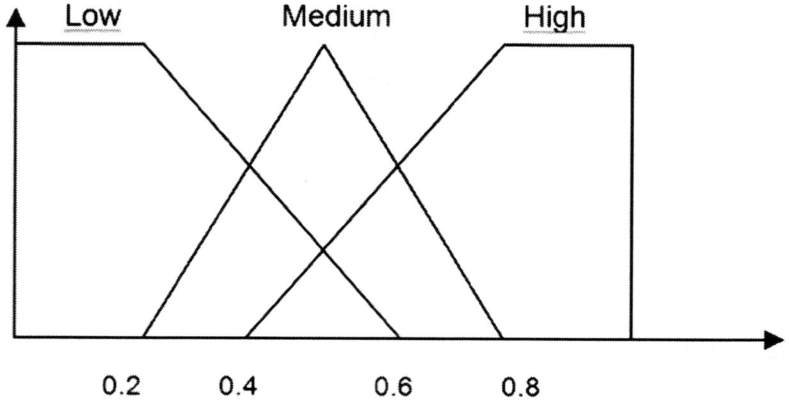

Table 1. Fuzzy inputs value

	low	medium	high
Technological operations	2	3 - 4	5
Profit margin	1	2	3
Due date	[3-4]	[2-3)	[1.5-2)

higher membership. The rules are arranged by the "maximum" method and the de-fuzzification is done by the centre gravity method. The crisp value *z_out* leads to assign the budget to the jobs by the following expression:

$$Budget = \begin{cases} High & 0.625 \leq z\_out \leq 1; \\ Medium & 0.325 \leq z\_out < 0.625; \\ Low & 0 \leq z\_out < 0.325; \end{cases} \quad (8)$$

Alternative Solution Methods

In order to validate the operation of the proposed approach, it has been compared with other on-line scheduling methods; some of them taken from the literature (Jeong and Kim, 1998; Smith, 1980). For all these solvers, the negotiation protocol is the same as presented in Section 3. Where they differ is the offer formulation and how the resource's choice is made. The following six methods have been experimented with:

- Budget: The Budget Approach, as described above.
- Budget+DIS: The Budget Approach is combined with the heuristic dispatching rule LowValueFirst: DueDate.
- Slack1: Each cell evaluates Service Time End (STE), the estimated finish time of the task subject to negotiation. STE is calculated in the following way:

$$STE_m(t) := \sum_{i}^{NQ} EWT_j^k(t) + Res_m(t) \quad \forall j \in Queue_m \quad (9)$$

where *NQ* is the number of jobs in the cell's queue, while Res_m is the estimated remaining operational time of the actual running job. The job agent calculates *SlackOp* in the following way:

$$SlackOp := \frac{DueDate}{\sum_{k=k^*}^{Ntask} Max\,ProcTime_k} \quad (10)$$

where k is the task under decision. Job agent choices the cell which has the following minimum difference:

If $SlackOp > 0$, $\min_m(SlackOp - STE_m)$

If $SlackOp < 0$, $\min_m(STE_m)$ (11)

Slack2: As the previous one, but *SlackOP* is divided by 2, to compensate for system delays. Several values are tested and value 2 leads to better performance measures for the test case investigated.

Slack3: *SlackOp* is calculated in a different way:

$$SlackOp := \frac{DueDate}{\sum_{k=k^*}^{Ntask} TaskTime_k} - NQ \cdot MTD - AvTTR \quad (12)$$

where *MTD* is the maximal possible delay in each task execution and k is the task under decision; in this model $MTD = 5$. *AvTTR* is the mean failure length.

MinSTE: Each cell evaluates the *STE* (Service Time End), the estimated finish time of the request task as in *Slack1*. The job agent chooses cell m corresponding to $\min_m(STE_m)$.

Table 2. Routings

Type	Tasks				
Type 1	2	1	3	4	
Type 2	3	2	1		
Type 3	1	4			
Type 4	4	3	1	3	2

SIMULATION ENVIRONMENT

The manufacturing system processes various parts that arrive according to an exponential distribution. A part type is specified by a sequence of tasks (so-called routing, see Table 2) to be processed and the maximum processing times (*MaxProcTime,* see Table 3) of the tasks. Tasks belong to various task types, each having a fixed routing.

Each *part* $Type_i$ has its $InterArrivalTime_i$, (exponential distribution is used) which can be easily set. Hence, the mix of jobs is determined stochastically by the *InterArrivalTimes* setting. An example is reported in Table 4. Each part has a *DueDate* that is set when the job arrives at the system. Each *DueDate* is calculated according to the following rule:

$$DueDate_i := CoeffDD_{Type_j} \cdot TPT_{Type_j} \quad (13)$$

The coefficient *CoeffDD* is characteristic to the job type (see Table 5); its actual value is

Table 3. Maximum process times

Type	$MaxProcTime_{Type_j,k}$					TPT
Type 1	20	25	15	18		78
Type 2	30	25	19			74
Type 3	15	27				42
Type 4	20	25	30	15	20	100

TotalProcessTime(TPT) is the sum of the *MaxProcTime* for each job type.

Table 4. Inter-arrival times

Type	Type 1	Type 2	Type 3	Type 4
Inter-Arrival Time	15	10	12	18

Table 5. CDDmin and CDDmax

Type	Type 1	Type 2	Type 3	Type 4
$CDDmin_i$	1.5	2	3	2
$CDDmax_i$	2	3	4	4

taken from uniform distribution, according to the following rule:

$$CoeffDD_i = unif(CDDmin_i, CDDmax_i).$$

The resources are able to process various task types; in the following table the resource - task type assignment is marked. The system is reconfigurable, so these assignments can be changed. Value 1 indicates that the cell can execute a particular type of task, and 0 otherwise (see Table 6).

We assume a real dynamic environment, so we consider a production stage: in each production stage the characteristics of the manufacturing resource CTC_m (see Table 7) and the time between failures TBF_m are modified. So the Expected Working Time EWT depends on CTC_m and it is:

$$EWT_j^k(t) = CTC_m(t) \cdot Max\Pr ocTime_{Type_j,k} \quad (14)$$

The *TaskDelay* is calculated according to the following rule:

$$TaskDelay := \begin{cases} 0 & P(p < \gamma) \\ unif(1,5) & P(p > \gamma) \quad where\ \gamma = 0.5 \end{cases} \quad (15)$$

p is a random number between 0 and 1 that emulates the probability that an unforeseen event causes a delay of the part during a manufacturing operation. The value γ=0.5 means that the probability of this event is the 50%. The cells may break down, and this failure model is also included in the model. Failure is a stochastic event (see Table 8): each failure happens according to an exponential rate that is $30 \cdot TBF_m$.

Failure Length (*FL*) is a stochastic variable taken from an exponential distribution: $FL := exp(C)$ where C is a constant. Finally, there are no setup times and transport times, while buffers and the queues can be infinite.

Experimental Plants and Streams

This section describes how a simulation test-bed, model, and case study have been developed in the Arena® simulation environment in order to test the behaviour of the presented approach. All the solvers have been compared with different streams of jobs and experimental plans. The experimental plan is a particular configuration of the manufacturing system. The stream is a sequence of parts arriving into the system. The idea is to compare results in all possible configurations of the manufacturing systems, under different workload and/or production mix conditions. In this section, there are presented 5 different streams of part arrivals and 5 different experimental plants. Hence, there are 25 experiments for each solution method. Each experiment is a combination of a stream and a plant with 50 replications.

- Experimental Plan 1: Plant is deterministic; absence of failure; Number of cells is 10; CTC_m as in Table 7; Cell – Task Type assignment as in Table 6.
- Experimental Plan 2: Number of cells is 10; *CTCm* as in Table 7; Cell – Task Type

Table 6. Resource - task type assignment

Resource	1-6	2-7	3-8	4-9	5-10
Task 1	0	1	0	1	1
Task 2	1	1	1	0	0
Task 3	1	0	1	1	0
Task 4	0	1	1	0	1

Table 7. CTCm

Resource	1-6	2-7	3-8	4-9	5-10
Stage 1	0.30	0.60	0.40	0.50	0.40
Stage 2	0.33	0.66	0.44	0.55	0.44
Stage 3	0.36	0.72	0.45	0.60	0.52
Stage 4	0.40	0.80	0.48	0.65	0.58
Stage 5	0.45	0.88	0.52	0.70	0.65

Table 8. TBFm in the stages

Cell	1-6	2-7	3-8	4-9	5-10
Stage 1	12.00	8.00	10.10	9.00	10.00
Stage 2	10.60	6.40	8.40	8.50	9.00
Stage 3	9.30	5.12	6.10	7.40	8.00
Stage 4	7.70	4.10	4.90	6.30	7.00
Stage 5	6.30	3.27	3.40	5.20	6.00

assignment as in Table 6; TBF_m as in Table 8; $FL := exp(30)$.

- Experimental Plan 3: Number of cells is 10; CTC_m as in Table 7; Cell – Task Type assignment as in Table 6; TBF_m as in Table 9; $FL := exp(15)$.
- Experimental Plan 4: Number of cells is 7; CTC_m as in Table 10; Cell – Task Type assignment as in Table 6; TBF_m as in Table 8; $FL := exp(30)$.
- Experimental Plan 5: Number of cells is 6; CTC_m as in Table 7; Cell – Task Type assignment as in Table 6; TBF_m as in Table 8; $FL := exp(30)$.

In Table 11 there are demonstrated the steam features.

SIMULATION RESULTS

The criteria used to evaluate the solvers are the Flow Time of the parts, percentage of parts in Delayed, Tardiness, Maximum value of Tardiness, Work-in-Process (WIP), and Throughput (see Table 12).

Initially, it has been conducted a sensitivity analysis of the parameters α and β together. The analysis of the simulation results highlight that the range of α and β that assures the better performance is [0.7-0.85];

Table 9. TBFm in the stages of Plan 3

Cell	1-6	2-7	3-8	4	5
Stage 1	25	30	20	25	25
Stage 2	24	28	19	23	24
Stage 3	21	25	17	20	21
Stage 4	18	22	15	18	18
Stage 5	15	18	13	16	15

Table 10. CTCm in Plan 4

Cell	1-6	2-7	3	4	5
Stage 1	0.25	0.40	0.30	0.35	0.27
Stage 2	0.26	0.42	0.32	0.36	0.28
Stage 3	0.27	0.45	0.33	0.36	0.29
Stage 4	0.28	0.48	0.34	0.37	0.30
Stage 5	0.29	0.52	0.36	0.38	0.32

Table 11. Streams

Type	CDD_{min}	CDD_{max}	IAT	Task	TPT
Stream1					
1	1.5	2	40	4	78
2	2	3	40	3	74
3	3	4	40	2	42
4	2	4	40	5	100
Stream2					
1	1.3	1.8	30	4	78
2	1.5	1.9	30	3	74
3	1.3	1.7	30	2	42
4	1.6	1.9	30	5	100
Stream3					
1	1.3	1.8	10	4	78
4	1.6	1.9	15	5	100
Stream4					
1	3	5	25	4	78
2	4	6	15	3	74
3	3	4	20	2	42
4	2.5	5	20	5	100
Stream5					
2	4	6	10	3	110
3	3	4	15	2	70

Table 12. Solver comparison results

Cell	Min STE	Slack 1	Slack 2	Slack 3	Budget + EDD
% Delay Jobs	**6.04**	**1987**	**211**	**365**	**-10.6**
Flow Time	**1.33**	**171**	**87.2**	**132**	**-7.72**
WIP	**0.68**	**164**	**84.2**	**127**	**-8.39**
Throughput	**0.38**	**-2.91**	**-1.04**	**-1.72**	**4.13**
Tardiness	**4.96**	**64.2**	**29.3**	**30.7**	**-14.9**
Max Tardiness	**3.15**	**143**	**55.3**	**65.5**	**-17.5**

In this range, the performance measures don't change significantly. Therefore, the parameters are set to the same value of 0.85 for the simulation experiments conducted.

In particular, it can be observed that the best two solvers are *MinSTE* and *Budget*. To improve these solvers it is necessary to combine them with a dispatching rule Earliest Due Date (EDD). In fact, *Budget+EDD* has the best performance crossing both plants and streams. In the following table, there are summarized the performances of all solvers compared to the *Budget* solver. The value is the percentage (%) difference between the solver written in the head cell and *Budget* solver. Except for the throughput, *Budget* approach improves all performance measures of *MinSTE*. The best improvement is in the percentage of delayed of jobs, while as regards throughput *MinSTE* is better than *Budget*. It is important to underline the *Budget* and *MinSTE* seem to work in the same way, independently from Streams or Plants instances. In fact, while *MinSTE* tries to find the faster cell to perform the subsequent task, *Budget* looks for the most efficient cell.

In most of the cases, the fastest cell and the most efficient one coincide; the different performances of these two solvers are thus due to only a small percentage of choices during one simulation. Performances of other solvers are very far from the aforementioned. This is because they are not able to predict the failure or delay of the system. In fact, their performances are acceptable only in the deterministic plant, even if always worse than *MinSTE* and *Budget*. The worst solver is *Slack1* because it makes no attempt to forecast delays or failures. However, the forecast of delays or failures is not always so useful, which is demonstrated by the case of *Slack2*. It happens that *Slack2*, where the forecast is made by a heuristic division of the *SlackOp* index, is better than *Slack3*, in which delays and failure forecasts are explicit.

The above simulations have been conducted with the same level of budget assigned to each job, in order to match up to other approaches in the same environment. Moreover, the value of budget is enough high (defined infinity) to avoid the case in which the part doesn't have a sufficient budget to acquire the best cell. The motivation is to compare the proposed approach with the other methodologies in same operational conditions and evaluate the difference of performance measures due only to budget approach.

Further simulations have been conducted in order to test the fuzzy tool that allocates budget to the jobs.

Therefore, three job types have been hypothesized, with three different levels of budget (low, medium and high). The price of each manufacturing cell is computed as in (7) where k=100.

The low value is always 20, while medium and high values change between 20 and 100 with a step of 10. Moreover, the simulations have been conducted with three values of inter-arrival time and two dimensions of the manufacturing

Table 13. Budget values combination

Exp. No	Budget – medium level value	Budget- high level value
1	20	20
2	20	40
3	20	60
4	20	80
5	20	100
6	40	20
7	40	40
8	40	60
9	40	80
10	40	100
11	60	20
12	60	40
13	60	60
14	60	80
15	60	100
16	80	20
17	80	40
18	80	60
19	80	80
20	80	100
21	100	20
22	100	40
23	100	60
24	100	80
25	100	100

Table 14. Inter-arrival and manufacturing cell classes

Exp. No	Inter-arrival time	Manufacturing cells
1	13	4
2	16	4
3	19	4
4	5	8
5	7.5	8
6	10	8

Figure 4. Parts with high importance

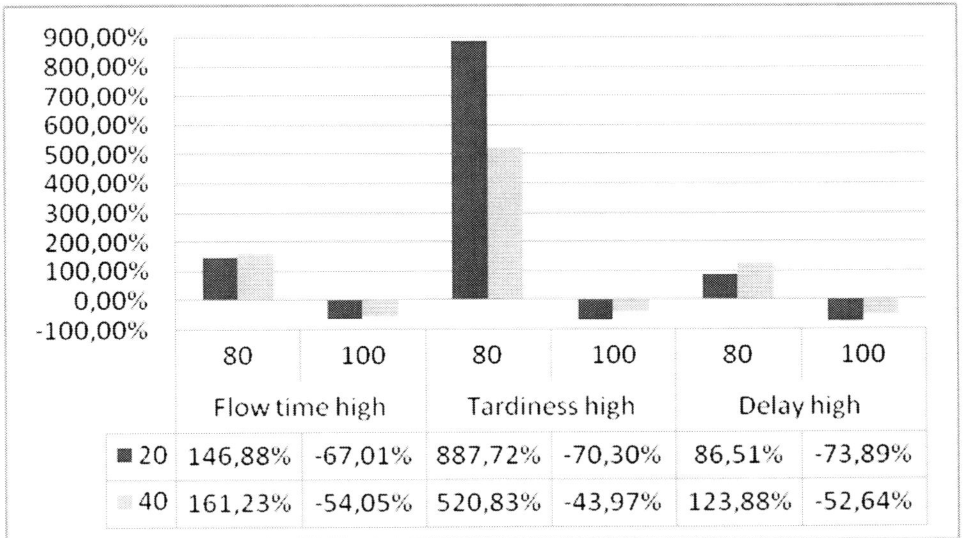

	80	100	80	100	80	100
	Flow time high		Tardiness high		Delay high	
20	146,88%	-67,01%	887,72%	-70,30%	86,51%	-73,89%
40	161,23%	-54,05%	520,83%	-43,97%	123,88%	-52,64%

systems. The experimental classes are reported in Table 13.

The 25 experimental classes of budget values are simulated for the values of inter-arrival time and number of manufacturing cell reported in Table 14.

The total number of experimental classes simulated is 150.

The simulation results are compared (basis of comparison) with the case of infinity budget assigned to each part typology (parts with same importance). The performance measures investigated are:

- flow time is the average throughput time of the parts.
- tardiness is the sum of the time in delay of the parts.
- number of jobs manufactured in delay is the total parts that are in delay.

Parts with three different importance level enter the manufacturing system, the performance are collected and reported for each importance level. The Figures 4, 5 and 6 report the performance measures for each product importance computing the average values over the inter-arrival time and number of manufacturing cells. There are reported the more significant results.

From the analysis of the aforementioned figures, the following issues can be drawn:

- The products with a high level can gain advantages only if the level of the budget assigned can be the maximum value possible: 100. Moreover, the improvement is better when the weight of medium importance product is the minimum value possible: 20. The advantages are the same for all three performance measures.
- In case of weight of 100 for high importance products, the products with a medium importance level have a very low difference between the weight of 20 and 40. The performance measure of parts in delay is the performance with minor deterioration. Also, the products with low importance have the same trend of the medium importance products.

Figure 5. Parts with medium importance

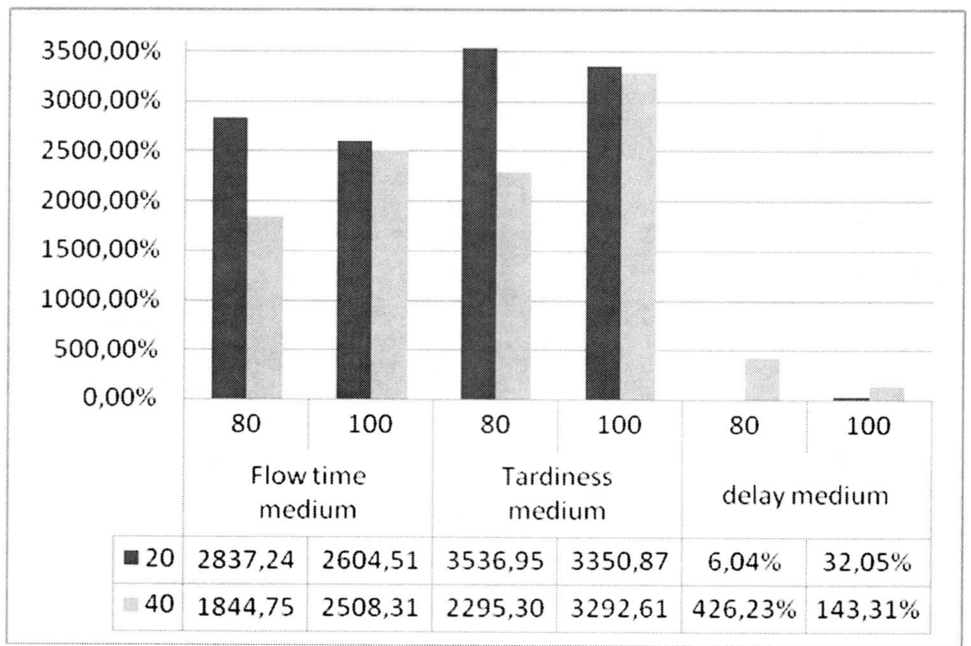

	Flow time medium		Tardiness medium		delay medium	
	80	100	80	100	80	100
20	2837,24	2604,51	3536,95	3350,87	6,04%	32,05%
40	1844,75	2508,31	2295,30	3292,61	426,23%	143,31%

Figure 6. Parts with low importance

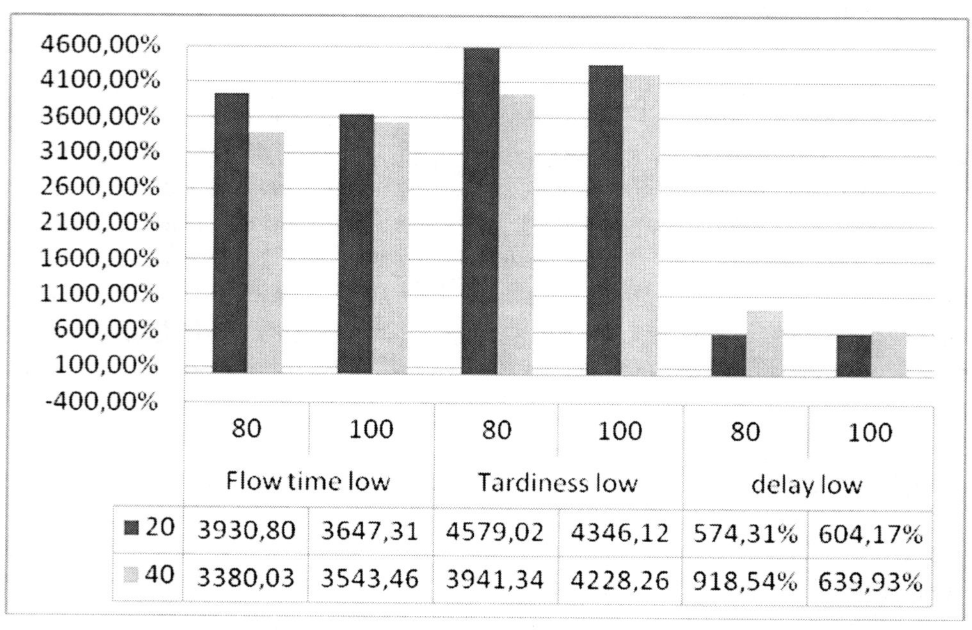

	Flow time low		Tardiness low		delay low	
	80	100	80	100	80	100
20	3930,80	3647,31	4579,02	4346,12	574,31%	604,17%
40	3380,03	3543,46	3941,34	4228,26	918,54%	639,93%

Figure 7. Parts with high importance

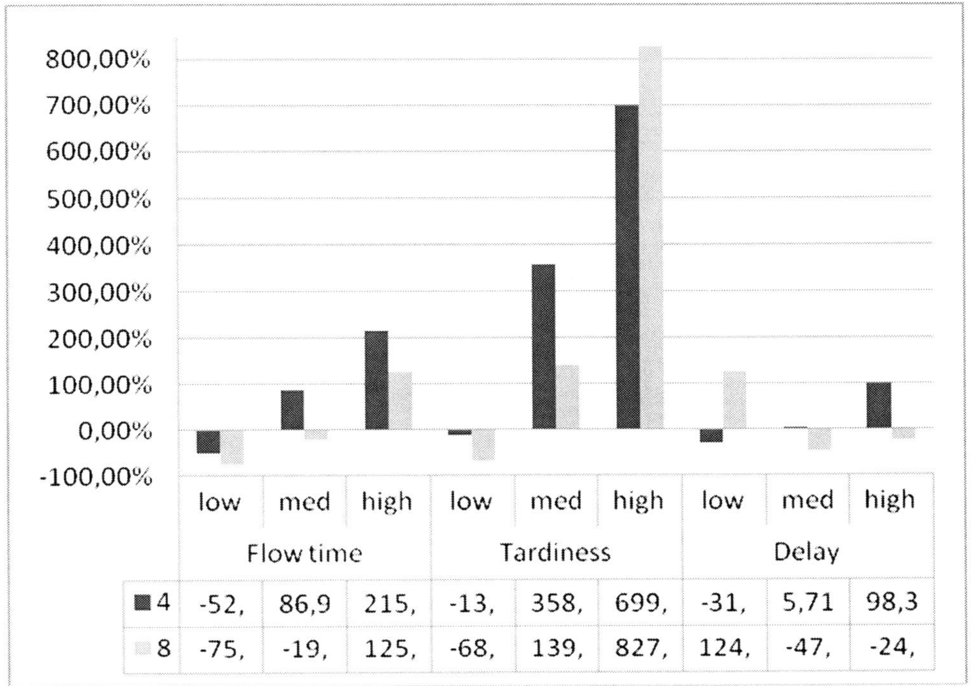

	Flow time low	Flow time med	Flow time high	Tardiness low	Tardiness med	Tardiness high	Delay low	Delay med	Delay high
4	-52,	86,9	215,	-13,	358,	699,	-31,	5,71	98,3
8	-75,	-19,	125,	-68,	139,	827,	124,	-47,	-24,

The drastically reduction of flow time of the high important products is obtained with an increment of the flow time of the medium important products about 25 times, while for the low importance products the increment is about 36 times.

Moreover, the products with medium and low importance have a trend of increment of the number of jobs in delay minor than the tardiness performance.

The Figures 7, 8, and 9 report the performance measures for each product importance computing the average value highlighting the manufacturing system dimension (4 an 8) and the inter-arrival time (low, medium and high).

From the analysis of the figures, the following issues can be drawn:

- The performance measures improve when the manufacturing dimension increases from four manufacturing cells to eight.
- From the point of view of manufacturing congestion, the performance measures are better when the inter-arrival is low, therefore with a high congestion level.

Though, the performance of the jobs with medium and low importance gets worse. The fuzzy inference enables assigning a budget to each job correlating to the importance of the job. It can be adapted to the change of the importance of the jobs in real time and this leads to a selective and adaptable. Therefore, the fuzzy reasoning leads to a selective approach

From the analysis of the simulation results, the following issues can be drawn:

- The budget approach proposed allows to discriminate the performance level by setting the importance of the jobs. The importance of the jobs is set by a fuzzy tool, therefore, defining qualitative parameters.

Figure 8. Parts with medium importance

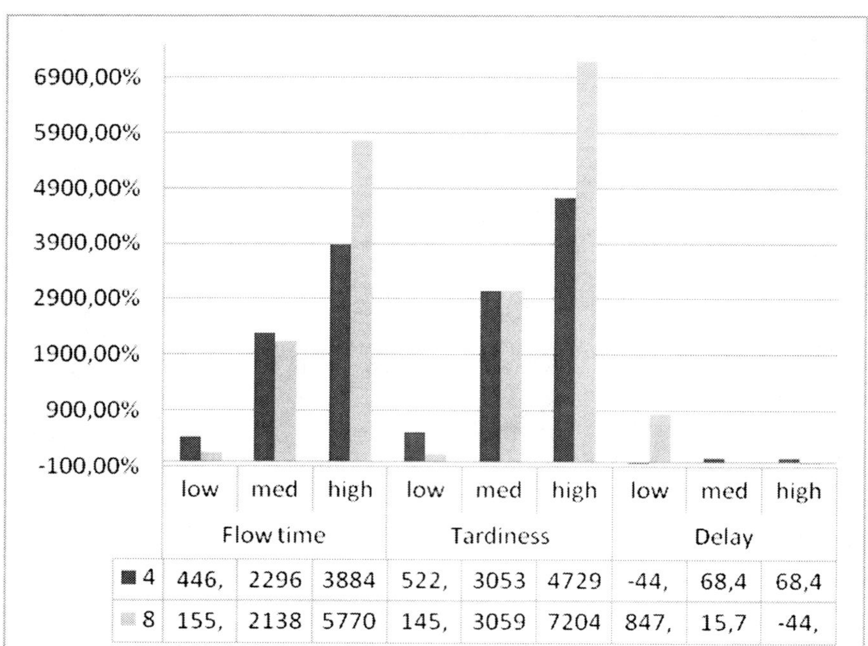

	Flow time low	Flow time med	Flow time high	Tardiness low	Tardiness med	Tardiness high	Delay low	Delay med	Delay high
4	446,	2296	3884	522,	3053	4729	-44,	68,4	68,4
8	155,	2138	5770	145,	3059	7204	847,	15,7	-44,

Figure 9. Parts with low importance

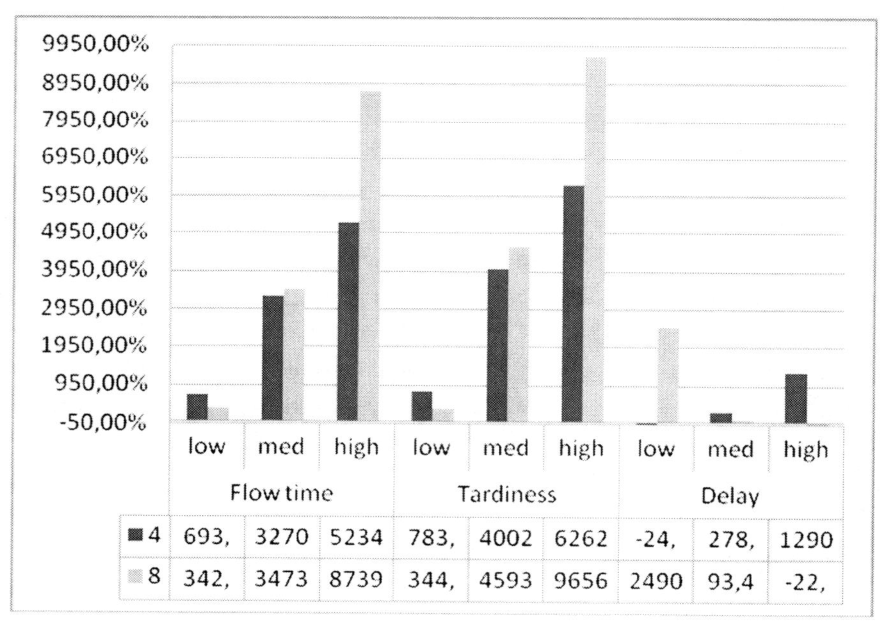

	Flow time low	Flow time med	Flow time high	Tardiness low	Tardiness med	Tardiness high	Delay low	Delay med	Delay high
4	693,	3270	5234	783,	4002	6262	-24,	278,	1290
8	342,	3473	8739	344,	4593	9656	2490	93,4	-22,

- The better performance for the high importance jobs is obtained when the configuration of the budget assigned to the part types is the following: HIGH=100, MEDIUM=20 and LOW=20. Then, the fuzzy tool works better when the classes are two.
- The performance measures are better when the congestion level is high (low inter-arrival) and the number of the manufacturing cells increases from four to eight.
- Finally, the extremely worst performance for medium and low importance performance have to be understood as a reduction compared to the case when all the parts have the same importance.

The fuzzy tool proposed allows to modify the performance level of different classes of job importance by setting only one parameter: budget assigned to the parts.

Moreover, the simulation results can be used to learn the opportune level of budget to assign at each typology part when the manufacturing conditions change.

The development of a hybrid approach, in which the proposed approach is activated when the congestion level is high and the selection of the products' importance, is necessary.

CONCLUSION

This chapter proposed an innovative scheduling approach for flexible manufacturing systems working in dynamic environments. Performance measures based on internal and external indices of efficiency have been elaborated. The negotiation protocol has been tested under different conditions of manufacturing system workload, with various numbers of cells and dynamic cell characteristics. The results show how the *Budget* approach leads to better performance, especially if it is combined with appropriate dispatching rules. Merits of the novel method are more characteristic when the manufacturing system is more dynamic. The *Budget* approach was also compared to other dynamic scheduling methods proposed in the literature. In particular, the *Budget* solver has performance much better than other solvers that try to estimate the next task slack because it considers also the possible failure state of cells; on the other hand, *Budget* is better than the *MinSTE* solver just because it is able to select dynamically the more efficient cell, not simply the fastest one. All in all, it has a high level of adaptivity without deteriorating performance. Overall system performance depends only on one intuitive parameter, the budget of the jobs. Several characteristics that define the priority of a part typology are combined by a fuzzy tool in an only parameter: the budget value of the part. The coordination approach is very simple, because the only parameter to set is the budget of the part. Moreover, if a new characteristic has to be added or modified to define the priority of the part, the coordination approach doesn't change, only the fuzzy tool needs to be modified to change the priority of the parts.

Hence, the overall system is well controllable and the approach can be extended towards production networks where the key to common competitiveness and efficiency is just the sharing financial risks and benefits. Future developments concern the application of the proposed approach in a real case study in order o validates the results obtained by the simulation experiments. Moreover, artificial intelligence approaches can be developed to learn the opportune level of budget. In particular, generic algorithms and neural networks can be integrated to learn and select the level of appropriate budget.

REFERENCES

Aydin, M. E., & Fogarty, T. C. (2004). A simulated annealing algorithm for multi-agent systems: A job shop scheduling application. *Journal of Intelligent Manufacturing*, *15*(6), 805–814. doi:10.1023/B:JIMS.0000042665.10086.cf

Aytug, H., Lawley, M. A., McKay, K., Mohan, S., & Uzsoy, R. (2005). Executing production schedules in the face of uncertainties: A review and some future directions. *European Journal of Operational Research*, *161*(1), 86–110. doi:10.1016/j.ejor.2003.08.027

Brennan, R. W., Balasubramanian, S., & Norrie, D. H. (1997). *Dynamic control architecture for advanced manufacturing system.* International Conference on Intelligent Systems for Advanced Manufacturing, Pittsburgh, PA, USA.

Chiuc, C., & Yih, Y. (1995). A learning based methodology for dynamic scheduling in distributed manufacturing systems. *International Journal of Production Research*, *33*(11), 3217–3232. doi:10.1080/00207549508904870

Chryssolouris, G., & Subramaniam, V. (2001). Dynamic scheduling of manufacturing job shops using genetic algorithms. *Journal of Intelligent Manufacturing*, *12*, 281–293. doi:10.1023/A:1011253011638

Cowling, P. I., & Johansson, M. (2002). Using real time information for effective dynamic scheduling. *European Journal of Operational Research*, *139*(2), 230–244. doi:10.1016/S0377-2217(01)00355-1

Cowling, P. I., Ouelhadj, D., & Petrovic, S. (2001). A multi agent architecture for dynamic scheduling of steel hot rolling. In *Proceedings of the third international ICSC world manufacturing congress*, (pp. 104–111). Rochester, NY, USA.

Cowling, P. I., Ouelhadj, D., & Petrovic, S. (2003). A multi-agent architecture for dynamic scheduling of steel hot rolling. *Journal of Intelligent Manufacturing*, *14*, 457–470. doi:10.1023/A:1025701325275

Ferber, J. (1999). *Multi-agent systems: An introduction to distributed artificial intelligence*. London, UK: Addison-Wesley.

Guanghui, Z., Jiang, P., & Huang, G. Q. (2009b). A game-theory approach for job scheduling in networked manufacturing. *International Journal of Advanced Manufacturing Technology*, *41*(9-10), 972–985. doi:10.1007/s00170-008-1539-9

Herroelen, W., & Leus, R. (2005). Project scheduling under uncertainty: Survey and research potentials. *European Journal of Operational Research*, *165*(2), 289–306. doi:10.1016/j.ejor.2004.04.002

Jeong, K.-C., & Kim, Y.-D. (1998). A real-time scheduling mechanism for a flexible manufacturing system: Using simulation and dispatching rules. *International Journal of Production Research*, *36*(9), 2609–2626. doi:10.1080/002075498192733

Jeong, S. J., Lim, S. J., & Kim, K. S. (2005). Hybrid approach to production scheduling using genetic algorithm and simulation. *International Journal of Advanced Manufacturing Technology*, *28*(1-2), 126–136.

Maione, G., & Naso, D. (2003). A soft computing approach for task contracting in multi agent manufacturing control. *Computers in Industry*, *52*, 199–219. doi:10.1016/S0166-3615(03)00127-1

Mehta, S. V., & Uzsoy, R. (1999). Predictable scheduling of a single machine subject to breakdowns. *International Journal of Computer Integrated Manufacturing*, *12*(1), 15–38. doi:10.1080/095119299130443

Monostori, L., Márkus, A., Van Brussel, H., & Westkämper, E. (1996). Machine learning approaches to manufacturing. *Annals of the CIRP*, *45*(2), 675–712.

Monostori, L., Váncza, J., & Kumara, S. R. T. (2006). Agent-based systems for manufacturing. *CIRP Annals - Manufacturing Technology*, *55*(2), 697-720.

Ouelhadj, D., Cowling, P. I., & Petrovic, S. (2003a). Contract net protocol for cooperative optimisation and dynamic scheduling of steel productionIn Ibraham, A., Franke, K., & Koppen, M. (Eds.), *Intelligent systems design and applications* (pp. 457–470). Berlin, Germany: Springer.

Ouelhadj, D., Cowling, P. I., & Petrovic, S. (2003b). Utility and stability measures for agent-based dynamic scheduling of steel continuous casting. In *Proceedings of the IEEE International Conference on Robotics and Automation* (175–180). Taipei, Taiwan.

Ouelhadj, D., & Petrovic, S. (2009). A survey of dynamic scheduling in manufacturing systems. *Journal ofScheduling*, *12*, 417–431. doi:10.1007/s10951-008-0090-8

Renna, P. (2009). A performance comparison between efficiency and pheromone approaches in dynamic manufacturing schedulingIn Chiong, R. (Ed.), *Intelligent systems for automated learning and adaptation* (pp. 273–298). Hershey, PA: Information Science Reference. doi:10.4018/978-1-60566-798-0.ch012

Renna, P. (2011). Multi-agent based scheduling in manufacturing cells in a dynamic environment. *International Journal of Production Research*, *49*(5), 1285–1301. doi:10.1080/00207543.2010.518736

Shaw, M. J. (1988). Dynamic scheduling in cellular manufacturing systems: A framework for network decision making. *Journal of Manufacturing Systems*, *13*, 13–94.

Shen, W., Norrie, D. H., & Barthes, J. P. A. (2001). *Multi-agent systems for concurrent intelligent design and manufacturing*. London, UK: Taylor & Francis.

Shen, W., Norrie, D. H., & Xue, D. (1998). *An agent-based manufacturing enterprise infrastructure for distributed integrated intelligent manufacturing system.* In PAAM'98.

Siwamogsatham, V., & Saygin, C. (2004). Auction-based distributed scheduling and control scheme for flexible manufacturing systems. *International Journal of Production Research*, *42*, 547–572. doi:10.1080/00207540310001613683

Smith, R. G. (1980). The contract net protocol: High-level communication and control in distributed problem solving. *IEEE Transactions on Computers C*, *29*(12), 1104–1113. doi:10.1109/TC.1980.1675516

Swaminathan, J. M., Smith, S. F., & Sahed, N. M. (1996). *A multi-agent framework for supply chain dynamics*. NSF Research Planning Workshop on AI & Manufacturing.

Trentesaux, D., Pesin, P., & Tahon, C. (2000). Distributed artificial intelligence for FMS scheduling control and design support. *Journal of Intelligent Manufacturing*, *11*, 573–589. doi:10.1023/A:1026556507109

Valckenaers, P., & Van Brussel, H. (2005). Holonic manufacturing execution systems. *CIRP Annals - Manufacturing Technology*, *54*(1), 427-432.

Van Brussel, H., Wyns, J., Valckenaers, P., Bongaerts, L., & Peeters, P. (1998). Reference architecture for holonic manufacturing systems: PROSA. *Computers in Industry*, *37*, 255–274. doi:10.1016/S0166-3615(98)00102-X

Váncza, J., & Márkus, A. (2000). An agent model for incentive-based production scheduling. *Computers in Industry*, *43*, 173–187. doi:10.1016/S0166-3615(00)00066-X

Vieira, G. E., Hermann, J. W., & Lin, E. (2003). Rescheduling manufacturing systems: A framework of strategies, policies and methods. *Journal of Scheduling*, *6*(1), 36–92. doi:10.1023/A:1022235519958

Vieira, G. E., Hermann, J. W., & Lin, E. (2000). Analytical models to predict the performance of a single machine system under periodic and event-driven rescheduling strategies. *International Journal of Production Research*, *38*(8), 1899–1915. doi:10.1080/002075400188654

Wonga, T. N., Leunga, C. W., Maka, K. L., & Fungb, R. Y. K. (2006). Dynamic shopfloor scheduling in multi-agent manufacturing systems*Expert Systems with Applications*, *31*(3), 486–494. doi:10.1016/j.eswa.2005.09.073

Wooldridge, M., & Jennings, N. R. (1995). Intelligent agents: Theory and practice. *The Knowledge Engineering Review*, *10*(2), 115–152. doi:10.1017/S0269888900008122

Zhou, B., Wang, S., & Xi, L. (2008). Agent-based decision support system for dynamic scheduling of a flexible manufacturing system. *International Journal of Computer Applications in Technology*, *32*(1), 47–62. doi:10.1504/IJCAT.2008.019489

Zhou, R., Nee, A. Y. C., & Lee, H. P. (2009a). Performance of an ant colony optimisation algorithm in dynamic job shop scheduling problems. *International Journal of Production Research*, *47*(11), 2903–2920. doi:10.1080/00207540701644219

KEY TERMS AND DEFINITIONS

Agile Manufacturing System: it is a manufacturing system in which is the organization that has created the processes, tools, and training to enable it to respond quickly to customer needs and market changes while still controlling costs and quality.

Coordination: it is the mechanism how the agent exchange information and cooperate to purse a common objective.

Discrete Event Simulation: it emulates a real system by a chronological sequence of events. Each event occurs at an instant in time and marks a change of state in the system.

Distributed Approach: it is a system where independent cooperate to pursue an objective without centralized information.

Fuzzy Logic: it is a logic derived from fuzzy set theory to deal with reasoning that is fluid or approximate rather than fixed and exact.

Multi-Agent System: it is a system composed of multiple interacting intelligent agents.

Scheduling: It is a decision making process to allocate resources to tasks over a given time periods optimizing one or more objectives.

Chapter 4
Supplier-Oriented Purchasing Behaviors in Projects

Ron Meier
Illinois State University, USA

Dan Brown
Illinois State University, USA

ABSTRACT

This chapter introduces project manager's perceptions of the importance of developing relationships with preferred suppliers as this has the potential to impact elements of cost, planning, time management, quality management, technical expertise, and product availability. This study identified key characteristics and attributes of supplier-oriented purchasing behaviors in project-oriented environments. The review of recent literature indicated that very little research exists that examines project procurement experts' perceptions of key aspects of supplier-oriented purchasing behavior. This research utilized a two round, modified Delphi methodology to capture the perceptions of 19 experienced project management procurement specialists. Results showed that the most strongly valued attributes could be clustered under the headings of quality, communications, attentiveness, and professionalism. Even though projects were typically characterized as short term endeavors, the characteristics found most important to project procurement managers were similar to those previously reported by procurement professionals in long-term functional environments.

INTRODUCTION

In the functional procurement environment scholars have noted a growing shift in procurement practices from transactional approaches toward long-term oriented relationship-based approaches (Brennan & Turnbull, 1999). Enhanced or modified forms of communication, coordination, collaboration and adaptation of product and processes to strengthen levels of commitment and trust were identified as important aspects of relationship-based procurement (Brennan & Turnbull, 1999; Hoffman, 2003; Jap, 1999; O'Toole & Donald-

DOI: 10.4018/978-1-4666-0246-5.ch004

son, 2000). Relatively little previous research has explored the importance of supplier-oriented purchasing behaviors in functional procurement environments and even less has been conducted in the context of project management.

By their nature, projects often attempt to do something new and of critical importance to the organization. In the project-oriented environment, a successful project is defined by the completion of the project objectives, to the satisfaction of customers and other key stakeholders, on time and within budget. Procurement management is one of the many aspects of project management which demands the attention of project managers if they are to successfully manage the time, cost, and customer satisfaction oriented constraints that are an essential element of successful projects (PMI, 2008).

Yeo (2006) suggested that better procurement management may have important implications for management in projects. Further, anecdotal conversations with project managers indicated that they often are very aware of the importance of developing relationships with preferred suppliers as this has the potential to impact elements of cost, planning, time management, quality management, technical expertise and product availability. Each of these relationship elements may substantially impact the probability of project success.

Meier, Humphreys & Williams (1998) defined supplier-oriented purchasing behaviors (SOPB) as purchasing strategies intended to create a position as a preferred customer when contrasted to targeted suppliers. When implementing SOPB strategies, the focal point of purchasing developed into understanding the requirements of targeted suppliers and the development of mutually favorable buyer-seller relationships. The domain of SOPB included activities such as: (1) the attainment and use of technical knowledge to improve collaborative supplier communications, (2) buying across an expansive variety of goods and services, and (3) strategic planning.

SOPB was found to focus on defining and identifying the rewards deemed important to key suppliers. Thus, SOPB targeted the often neglected concept of reward and holds considerable implications for purchasing managers. Past perspectives on the buyer's role as reported by Bertrand (1986) depicted organizations maintaining large numbers of supply sources in order to negotiate the best deals. This created adversarial relationships and fostered intense competition among suppliers. In the short term, this was an effective approach to lower prices and was viewed as an effective approach to buying since it created value for the buying firm and its subsequent customers.

However, in today's competitive environment this approach no longer works. In response organizations are focused on gaining efficiencies, reducing cycle times, and bringing innovative customer defined products to market as quickly as possible. To achieve these goals, buyers now recognize the need to compete for and collaborate with carefully chosen suppliers. In fact, businesses and purchasing managers recognize that in many industries contemporary purchasing is defined as the fight for good suppliers. Buyers are cutting their vendor lists and treating the remaining vendors as strategic partners. Buyers understand that they must satisfy the needs of targeted suppliers and position their respective organizations as preferred customers.

Previous research focused on the buyer-seller relationship from the customer-oriented seller behavior perspective. Further, discussions of the importance of buyer-seller relationships historically emphasized the importance of developing long-term buyer-seller relationships. This discussion had limited utility in the project context due to the limited and even short duration of projects. The objective of this study was to gain insight into project procurement experts' perceptions of key aspects or characteristics of supply-oriented purchasing behavior.

BACKGROUND

Research into buyer-seller relationships has resulted in the identification of a number of elements deemed important to successful relationship-based procurement. Noordewier, John, & Nevin (1990) identified five governance elements of procurement relationships: supplier flexibility, supplier assistances, information provided to supplier, monitoring of supplier and expectation of continuity. Heide & John (1990) proposed a model of procurement relationship that evolved around three dimensions: joint action, expected continuity and verification efforts. In their study, continuity expectations and verification efforts were shown to have significant positive effects on the levels of joint action as did the historical length of the relationship. In related research, Morgan & Hunt (1994) identified five precursors to relationship marketing: relationship termination costs, relationship benefits, shared values, communication and opportunistic behavior. They also found significant positive relationships between: commitment and cooperation, trust and commitment, trust and cooperation, and trust and functional conflict (amicably resolved disputes) and a negative relationship between trust and uncertainty.

In a Delphi study, designed to identify the key characteristics of supplier-oriented purchasing behavior, Pelletier (1996) identified the following categories of behaviors or activities important for attracting targeted suppliers to procurement relationships: a) communication openness between buyers and sellers, b) payment/credit, c) professionalism (i.e. reputation, trust, ethics, integrity, and honesty), d) knowledge of markets, technology, products and services, e) buying process/decision making, and f) relationship development (i.e. interaction and long-term orientation). Meier, Humphreys & Williams (1998) extended the work of Pelletier (1996) and further identified the behaviors comprising supplier-oriented purchasing behavior. These behaviors were segmented into organizational level policies and procedures and behaviors related to individual activities and relationships. Elements of procurement relationships identified in this review of literature included quality, communication, attentiveness, power, reputation/trust, adaptation, and cooperation/loyalty/commitment. Various studies have found many of these elements of procurement relationships are interrelated.

Quality

A previous study by Humphreys, Williams & Meier (1996) investigated the effects of technical product quality and interpersonal process quality and how each affected overall customer satisfaction. These terms were used in reference to the two basic sources of value delivered by the market offering (See Figure 1). Technical product quality addressed several dimensions of the market offering with conformance to specification and reliability (Garvin, 1987). The findings of Humphreys, Williams & Meier (1996) research indicated a nine item set dealing with product quality and interpersonal process quality. Results from a confirmatory factor analysis of technical product quality were concerned with (a) an organization's product operating trouble free, (b) products meeting customer standards, (c) products performing as expected, and (d) a products uniformity. Five items of interpersonal process quality, regarding customer contact persons were found to be significant. These included (a) overall consideration for the customer, (b) ability or willingness to be innovative in responding to customer needs, (c) ability to respond quickly and efficiently to requests, (d) eagerness to satisfy the customer, and (e) ability to do the job right the first time. The researchers' two dimension product quality and interpersonal process quality model produced the following results: chi-square statistic of 37.32 (df= 26; p = .070); a goodness-of-fit (GFI) of 0.92 and a root-mean-squared-residual (RMSR) of 0.058.

Figure 1. Components of the total market offering

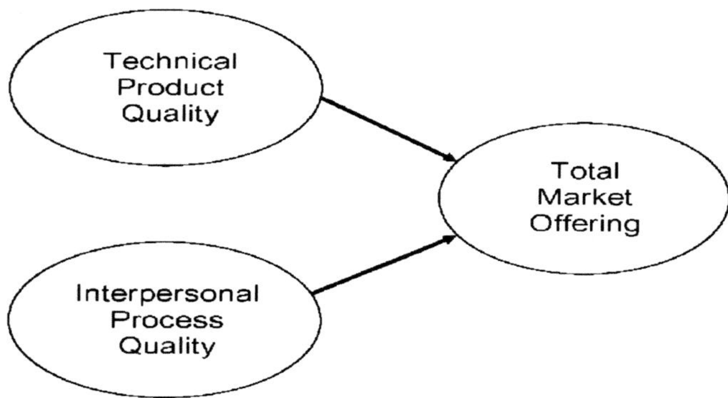

Communication

Communication and trust are iterative processes when building and sustaining buyer-seller partnerships. Communication is a necessary antecedent of trust but as the relationship matures, trust enhances communication (Anderson & Narus, 1990). Johnston, McCutcheon, Stuart & Kerwood, (2004) found that flexibility and willingness to share strategic plans and scheduling information were strongly linked to enhanced perceptions of relationship performance. Chow & Holden (1997) reported that buyers communicate more openly with salespeople they trust, however communication's impact on loyal purchasing behavior was not significant. Procurement partners co-operate for mutual advantage characterized by openness in communication and strategic collaboration (O'Toole & Donaldson, 2000). The need for more open information flow must be accompanied by attention to security issues including access controls (Hoffman, 2003).

Attentiveness

Bonner & Calantone, 2004 observed that while not all buyers desire long-term relationships with sellers, buyer attentiveness had a stronger positive influence on favorable buyer behavior than buyer dependence or length of relationship. They described buyer attentiveness as a reflection of the degree of attention focused on a particular buyer. Buyer attentiveness was described as arising from buyer beliefs about the supplier that were formed during repeated interactions and resulted in favorable purchase behaviors. They surveyed purchasing managers from 119 firms. Results: positive relationship between buyer attentiveness and favorable purchase behavior, seller reputation was positively related to attentiveness. Research conducted by Bonner and Calatine (2004) also found a positive relationship between buyer attentiveness and favorable purchase behavior.

It was not only attentiveness to the needs of buyers that may be important to project purchasing managers. Literature has documented a move toward buyers maintaining smaller vendor lists often with the intention of creating closer alliances between buyers and sellers as strategic partners. Research literature suggested that to achieve mutually beneficial, strategic supply chain partnerships, it may also be important for buyers to be attentive to and respond to the needs of targeted suppliers in order to become positioned as preferred customers (Meier, Humphreys and Williams, 1998). Crosby, Evans & Cowles (1990) found that attention to behaviors such as cooperative intentions, mutual disclosure and intensive contact follow-up produced stronger buyer-seller relationships.

Power

"Power is the ability of one partner to have an advantage over the other and it can allow one partner to coerce the other into doing something they otherwise may not do (Wilson as cited in Powers and Reagan, 2007, p. 1236)." It was suggested that managing power is an important element impacting creation of stronger buyer-seller relationships which in turn may enhance the strength of supply chain performance (Maloni & Benton, 2000; Benton & Maloni, 2005). Benton & Maloni (2005) stated that mediated power, which included reward, coercive and legal power can provide immediate advantage for the power source but may have negative impact on long term relationships between buyer and seller. They also found that the positive effect of non-mediated power sources (i.e. expert, referent and legitimate power) fostered perceptions of enhanced performance by both buyers and sellers with higher levels of satisfaction.

Adaptation to policies and procedures and targeted investments may be made by sellers as a consequence of imbalance in the power relationship, but when seeking long-term supply network relationships, adaptation and investment by both parties may also be seen in part as reciprocal demonstrations of commitment and trust in the relationship (Hallen, Johanson & Seyed-Mohamed, 1991; Brennan & Turnbull, 1999). Behavior which suggested cooperative rather than competitive attitudes enhanced the long term supply chain relationship (Wagner, Coley and Lindemann, 2011). Similarly, Janda and Seshadri, (2001) found that managing power relationships through cooperative negotiation was perceived to have a positive effect on purchasing efficiency and collaborative interaction had positive effects on purchasing effectiveness.

Reputation and Trust

"Reputation is important to a relationship as it represents a firm's perception of the capabilities of another organization (Powers and Reagan, 2006, p. 1235)." It was observed that perceptions of fair dealings lead to closer procurement alignment but commitment may not be significantly linked to reputation (Anderson & Weitz, 1992). Perceived flexibility led to enhanced reputation (Johnston, McCutcheon, Stuart & Kerwood, 2004). In a Delphi study conducted with sixteen Supply Chain experts, Meier, Humphreys and Williams (1998) found that maintaining a good reputation with suppliers was perceived to be among the most important individual level elements of supplier-oriented purchasing behaviors. Ganesan (1994) reported survey results that indicated reputation for vendor fairness was perceived to create an impression of vendor credibility but that vendors did not value buyer reputation.

In a survey of 300 purchasing managers, Powers and Reagan (2007), found trust to be of great importance to creating relationship value. Trust was identified as a critical element in achieving procurement effectiveness (Johnston, McCutcheon, Stuart & Kerwood, 2004). Trust was of increasing importance because of its ability to moderate risk in the buying process as buyer-seller relationships are sustained through repeat transactions (Chow and Holden, 1997). Trusts was reported as a valuable economic asset because it is believed to lower transaction costs and enhance information sharing thus facilitating coordination and increasing efficiency (Dyer & Chu, 2003).

Organizations generally do not trust one another. Trust is a micro level phenomenon wherein individuals or a group of individuals may develop trust-based relationships and transfer that trust orientation to an organization (Dyer & Chu, 2003; Chow & Holden, 1997). Trust has been defined as the non-contractual ability for individuals to rely on one another to demonstrate reliability, fairness and benevolence in their dealings (Dyer & Chu,

2003). They also observed that trust promoted negotiating efficiency by allowing individuals flexibility in granting concessions due to reasonable expectation that equity will be reciprocated in good faith over time (Dyer & Chu, 2003).

Trust has been described as both antecedent and outcome of positive relationships (Chow & Holden, 1997). Johnston, McCutcheon, Stuart & Kerwood, (2004) found that perceptions of buyer dependability and benevolence (the belief that one would act in the best interest of the partner even if there was no way of checking) were key to supplier's trust levels. Future transaction opportunities have been found to depend on perceptions of relationship qualities such as trust and satisfaction (Crosby, Evans, & Cowles, 1990).

Perceptions of trust impact relationships among all other elements of supplier-oriented purchasing behaviors. Chow & Holden (1997) found that individual trust in an organization had a strong positive relationship with loyalty and intentions just as trust in the individual sales person had a strong positive relationship to open communication. Jap (1999) noted in the results of a longitudinal survey of more than 220 buyers and suppliers that goal congruence and interpersonal trust facilitated the coordination effort.

Cooperation was found to be antecedent to trust. This appeared as an iterative process whereby cooperation leads to trust which leads to greater cooperation and so on (Anderson & Narus, 1990). In a study of 1365 respondents representing 504 sets of manufacturer/distributor relationship, (Anderson & Narus(1990) found cooperation to be an antecedent rather than a consequence of trust. Trust and information sharing were found to be mutually causal: trust may lead to information sharing and information sharing may lead to trust (Dyer & Chu, 2003).

Adaptation

Adaptation of product specification, product design, manufacturing processes, planning, delivery procedures, stockholding, administrative procedures or financial procedures occurred to assist in building sustained relationships between buyers and sellers. These were intended to strengthen levels of commitment and trust between parties but also have limited development of alternative relationships (Brennan & Turnbull, 1999). In their case study analysis, Brennan & Turnbull (1999) observed that when trust and commitment grow there is a greater likelihood of mutually advantageous adaptive behavior but there is a limit to the relationship development process beyond which the costs begin to outweigh the benefits.

Cooperation, Loyalty, Commitment

Cooperation has been defined as complementary actions taken in interdependent relationships to achieve mutually advantageous outcomes or singularly beneficial outcomes with expected reciprocity over time. (Anderson & Narus, 1999). Cooperation in this context included such activities as sharing of schedules and deadlines and joint problem solving. Perceptions of cooperation were based on both the supplier's and buyer's beliefs and actions (Johnston, McCutcheon, Stuart & Kerwood, 2004).

Loyalty had two components: loyalty intentions and loyalty behavior (Chow & Holden, 1997). Growing levels of competition have increased perceptions of the importance of loyalty in business. "Loyalty is about building and sustaining a relationship" (Chow & Holden, 1997, p. 275). In a Delphi study conducted with sixteen Supply Chain experts, Meier, Humphreys and Williams (1998) found that loyalty to suppliers was rated as an important individual level element of relationship development as a supplier-oriented purchasing behavior.

Commitment and trust were identified as key mediating variables in marketing relationships (Morgan & Hunt, 1994). Based on desire for stability in the relationship, (that is a willingness to make short term sacrifices to achieve long term stability) each party's level of commitment was based on perceptions of the other party's level of commitment (Anderson & Weitz, 1992). It is believed that commitment increases when the procurement relationship was characterized by open communication (Anderson & Weitz, 1992).

ISSUES

Two-way communication and information flow was found to minimize supply chain interruptions and enhance relationships in project environments (Hoffman, 2003). Effectively managed procurement is often a critical element in successful projects. It has been stated that unless project managers have expertise in the procurement process and manage the procurement process effectively the project will fail (Tipman, 2005). However, there has been little research on the extent to which project managers do not recognize the value of supplier-oriented purchasing behaviors related to procurement transactions, nor on which aspects of relationship-based procurement transactions are perceived to be most important in the time-bound project arena.

RESEARCH METHODOLOGY

Consistent with modified Delphi methodology; the researchers first conducted an extensive review of literature for the purpose of constructing an initial item pool reflecting the concept of supplier-oriented purchasing behaviors. This study employed a previously developed instrument designed to define key characteristics of supplier-oriented purchasing behavior (Pelletier, 1996). This instrument was contrasted against previous research literature and the content judged valid by a panel of experts.

In order to assure adequate coverage of the subject within the instrument, the panel then clustered the items on the selected instrument in groups reflective of factors identified in previous research. Pelletier's (1996) Delphi study did not address buyer – seller relationships in the project context. The literature addressed the importance of these interactions in the context of long term relationships. Projects by definition have predetermined lengths and anticipated end dates. It therefore seemed essential that the panel be asked to consider these factors as they were reworded to reflect the project realities, therefore statements were modified as needed to place items in a project management context for Delphi participants. This instrument was a two-part paper and pencil Delphi questionnaire. In the first part, Likert-type scales were used to gather perceptions regarding the degree of importance for each item. The second part consisted of open-ended questions where written response space was provided for the purpose of soliciting the respondents' suggested item revisions and comments or clarifications related to their Likert scale scores.

Once the initial instrument was finalized, the researchers assembled a panel of nineteen expert participants who had been identified based upon their expertise as project management practitioners, scholars, and consultants with experience in purchasing for projects. The 19 experts were members of the Project Management Institutes construction procurement special interest group. Panel participants were asked to anonymously rate each item on Likert-type scales to gather perceptions regarding the degree of importance for each item. Additional space was provided for panel participants to add any important item(s) they felt had been omitted.

In order to obtain critical information to revise and reduce the initial item pool, the mean and variance of Likert scale rankings for each item was calculated. When the mean degree of importance for each component was below the midpoint (2.5) of the Likert scale, (1 = strongly agree, 4 = strongly disagree) the component was confirmed as a key characteristic and retained in the pool of items. Conversely, items above the midpoint

Table 1. Quality characteristics

Statements: To attract targeted suppliers it is important for the Project Team to... (1 = strongly agree, 4 = strongly disagree)	*Mean*	*Variance*
Focus on customer requirements	1.00	0.00
Consider things other than price when evaluating products and services	1.37	0.25
Consider all aspects of the supplier's product offering before making a purchase decision	1.37	0.25
Practice continuous improvement in the purchasing area	2.37	0.25

Activities grouped mean = 1.52

were deleted from the item pool. The responses from the open-ended questions were analyzed and consensus opinions from the experts were used to further augment and revise the item pool.

RESULTS OF EACH DELPHI ROUND

Two rounds of surveys were completed in the Delphi study before consensus was achieved. The following sections discuss specific results from each round of the Delphi.

Delphi Round One

Round one of the Delphi study utilized a modified 37 item survey adapted from Pelletier (1996). The first part of the Delphi instrument required assessment of each item's importance for achieving supplier-oriented purchasing relationships. Part two was open-ended and solicited input regarding phrasing revisions, item deletions, and new items to be added. As a result of round one, the initial item pool was clarified and six new statements were added. Round one yielded 100% participation.

Delphi Round Two

The revised 43 item instrument was again distributed to the panel. The questionnaire format was similar to round one in which panelists used Likert scales to assess the item importance and part two solicited open-ended feedback. Panelists also received mean and variance information for each item. Armed with this additional information, they were asked to again rank each item on a Likert scale, (1 = strongly agree, 4 = strongly disagree) and using the stem "To attract targeted suppliers it is important for the Project Team to." When the mean degree of importance for each component was below 2.5, the midpoint of the Likert scale, the component was confirmed as a key characteristic and retained in the pool of items. As a result of this round all 43 items were retained in their original form. One hundred percent panel participation was achieved.

RESULTS

Tables 1, 2, 3, 4, 5, 6, 7 are presented in ranked order of importance based on the feedback from the Delphi panel. Based on grouped mean scores, the cluster of items in Table 1 were ranked as the most important group of characteristics and the cluster of items in Table 7 were ranked as the least important group of characteristics. Grouped item means ranged from 1.52 – 2.05. All items were ranked higher than 2.05 in importance (1 = strongly agree, 4 = strongly disagree).

Table 1 represents the Quality related characteristics ranked as most important by the panel of experts. It is interesting to note that while Quality issues would certainly seem important in ongoing supplier relationships, Quality as an element important to building successful supplier relationships seldom appeared in the review of previous research. However, given the high level

Table 2. Communications characteristics

Statements: To attract targeted suppliers it is important for the Project Team to... (1 = strongly agree, 4 = strongly disagree)	*Mean*	*Variance*
Communicate expectations about deliverable quality to suppliers	1.00	0.00
Establish open communications	1.37	0.25
Provide suppliers with feedback about their performance	1.47	0.26
Communicate with suppliers on an ongoing basis	1.68	0.23
Notify suppliers promptly when the project team will be unable to meet with them	1.74	0.20
Assist supplier representatives in contacting appropriat people within the project management team	2.05	0.39
Inform Suppliers about the project teams purchasing procedures	2.16	0.25

Activities grouped mean = 1.69

Table 3. Attentiveness characteristics

Statements: To attract targeted suppliers it is important for the Project Team to... (1 = strongly agree, 4 = strongly disagree)	*Mean*	*Variance*
Ask the supplier questions during their presentations	1.05	0.05
Take into account the supplier's customer service/support policies when making purchasing decisions	1.26	0.20
Be willing to establish relationships with suppliers	1.42	0.26
Provide ample time for suppliers to present their products	1.84	0.25
Maintain up-to-date knowledge about its industry	1.95	0.50
Share ideas, concepts, and processes	2.11	0.10
Have a good knowledge of the supplier's products	2.26	0.20

Activities grouped mean = 1.70

Table 4. Power and professionalism characteristics

Statements: To attract targeted suppliers it is important for the Project Team to... (1 = strongly agree, 4 = strongly disagree)	*Mean*	*Variance*
Keep suppliers informed of what is expected of them	1.00	0.00
Interact with suppliers in a professional manner	1.26	0.20
Be prepared for scheduled meetings with supplier representatives	1.26	0.20
Treat suppliers and their products with respect	1.47	0.26
Give undivided attention to supplier representatives during their sales presentations	1.63	0.25
Be consistent in the purchasing policies and procedures used with suppliers.	1.89	0.54
Be responsive to the needs of individual suppliers	2.26	0.20
Be reasonable when unexpected supplier problems arise	2.32	0.23
Keep purchasing policies simple for suppliers	2.37	0.25

Activities grouped mean = 1.72

Table 5. Reputation and trust characteristics

Statements: To attract targeted suppliers it is important for the Project Team to... (1 = strongly agree, 4 = strongly disagree)	*Mean*	*Variance*
Follow through on promises made to the supplier	1.26	0.20
Maintain a good working relationship with suppliers	1.42	0.26
Maintain a good reputation with suppliers	1.42	0.26
Establish a consistent record of business performance	2.11	0.54
Maintain a good credit rating with suppliers	2.21	0.18
Maintain a strong competitive position within their industry	2.32	0.23
Pay suppliers promptly	2.42	0.26

Activities grouped mean = 1.88

Table 6. Adaptation characteristics

Statements: To attract targeted suppliers it is important for the Project Team to... (1 = strongly agree, 4 = strongly disagree)	*Mean*	*Variance*
Display creativity and imagination in relation to solving buying needs	1.53	0.26
Be aware of new technology	1.58	0.26
Be receptive to supplier's ideas	2.00	0.00
Be willing to change in response to supplier's ideas	2.11	0.10
Develop purchasing procedures in cooperation with suppliers	2.37	0.25

Activities grouped mean = 1.92

Table 7. Cooperation, loyalty, & commitment characteristics

Statements: To attract targeted suppliers it is important for the Project Team to... (1 = strongly agree, 4 = strongly disagree)	*Mean*	*Variance*
Maintain good working relations with relevant departments within the supplier's firm	1.53	0.26
Be willing to support supplier's ideas with other members of my project team	2.00	0.56
Consistently purchase from selected suppliers	2.26	0.20
Help supplier's sell their ideas to other members of the project management team	2.42	0.26

Activities grouped mean = 2.05

of importance placed on issues related to Quality in project management, it was not surprising that Quality related items were included.

Table 2 presents the Communications characteristics as ranked by the Delphi panel experts. These items ranked as important are reminiscent of the Communications element descriptions found in the literature. Working to facilitate ongoing, open communication as well as sharing timely feedback were identified by the Delphi panel as important characteristics. Anderson & Narus (1990) described communication as an antecedent of trust that over time also enhanced communication. Flexibility and willingness to share information as well as planning communication to facilitate mutual advantage for buyers and sellers as characterized by openness in communication and collaboration were all highlighted as characteristics of buyer-seller relationships in previous research (Johnston, McCutcheon, Stuart & Kerwood, 2004; O & Donaldson, 2000).

Table 3 presents the important characteristics related to Attentiveness for project managers to attract targeted suppliers. Showing interest in and facilitating the suppliers presentations, developing knowledge of suppliers' industry and products and developing open relationships with select buyers were all identified as important to buyer-seller relationship attentiveness. Bonner & Calantone, (2004) described buyer attentiveness as arising from buyer beliefs about the supplier formed during repeated interactions and resulting in favorable purchase behaviors. They also described seller reputation as positively related to attentiveness.

Table 4 presents the important characteristics related to Power and Professionalism. Openly conveying expectations, showing respect, being responsive and professional all were identified as important characteristics related to Power. Giving undivided attention, being mutually responsive to needs and reasonable while problems are resolved were identified as important Professionalism related characteristics. The buyer – seller relationship has the potential for abuse of power. Displaying characteristics of professionalism may help offset imbalance in the power relationship when reciprocal demonstrations of commitment and trust in the relationship are practiced (Hallen, Johanson & Seyed-Mohamed, 1991).

Table 5 presents the important characteristics related to Reputation and Trust for project managers to attract targeted suppliers. Following through on promises, and working to maintain a good reputation were rated as important. Trust and reputation also related to business fundamentals such as maintaining a good performance record, good credit ratings, and history of prompt payment as well as sustaining a strong competitive position were also identified as important buyer seller relationships.

Trust and information sharing were previously found to be mutually causal: where trust may lead to information sharing and information sharing may lead to trust (Dyer & Chu, 2003). Trust was important because of its ability to moderate risk in the buying process (Chow and Holden, 1997) as well as potentially lower transaction costs and enhance information sharing thus facilitating coordination and efficiency (Dyer & Chu, 2003).

Johnston, McCutcheon, Stuart & Kerwood, (2004) found that perceptions of buyer dependability and benevolence (the belief that one would act in the best interest of the partner even if there was no way of checking) were key to supplier's trust levels. Individuals who developed trust-based relationships transferred that trust to an organization (Dyer & Chu, 2003; Chow & Holden, 1997). Perceptions of fair dealings (Anderson & Weitz, 1992) and flexibility (Johnston, McCutcheon, Stuart & Kerwood, 2004) led to enhanced reputation for both buyers and sellers.

Table 6 presents the important characteristics related to Adaptation for project managers to attract targeted suppliers. Creativity, knowledge, and willingness to work together to develop procedures all emerged as important. Adaptation of specifications, design, processes, and procedures occurred to assist in building sustained relationships between buyers and sellers (Brennan & Turnbull, 1999). They further observed that when trust and commitment grow there is a greater likelihood of mutually advantageous adaptive behavior.

Table 7 presents important characteristics related to Cooperation, Loyalty, and Commitment for project managers to attract targeted suppliers. Working to sustain good relationships, supporting supplier ideas and being a consistent customer were highlighted as important or somewhat important. In the literature loyalty had two components: loyalty intentions and loyalty behavior (Chow & Holden, 1997). It is interesting to note that the emphasis here was on behavior.

Cooperation was defined by Anderson & Narus (1999) as complementary actions taken in interdependent relationships to achieve mutually advantageous outcomes or singularly beneficial outcomes with expected reciprocity over time. The perception of cooperation was linked to both the supplier's and buyer's beliefs and actions (Johnston, McCutcheon, Stuart & Kerwood, 2004). It has been described as an iterative process whereby each party's level of commitment may be based on perceptions of other party's level of commitment and the degree of open communication (Anderson & Weitz, 1992).

SOLUTIONS AND RECOMMENDATIONS

This study offers an important contribution to project managers as they begin to ascertain and nurture their relationships with key strategic vendors/suppliers. Explicitly, this study begins to delineate the realm of supplier-oriented purchasing strategies as they relate to the elements of trust, reward, and loyalty as discussed by Johnston, McCutcheon, Stuart, & Kerwood (2004), Jap (1999), and Chow & Holden (1997). As reported previously in this manuscript, this is a topic typified by limited information and understanding and great potential for enhancing a firm's competitiveness. Thus, implications exist for both the practitioner/project manager and researchers.

Practitioner or Project Manager Implications

Information gathered from this study will be useful to project procurement specialists as they attempt to identify prospective business partners and for use as a general assessment tool for pre-qualifying vendors/suppliers. This information may assist project managers in augmenting the comprehension of their communication styles as well as providing ideas on how to adapt their behaviors to increase communication effectiveness with vendors/suppliers. By increasing communication effectiveness project managers can engage in more meaningful, efficient, and profitable relationships with their strategic vendors/suppliers. Project managers will also be able to utilize this information as a tool for the development and establishment of true Supplier-Oriented Purchasing Behaviors.

There is a need for managerial professionals to consider the implementation and application of Supplier-Oriented Purchasing Behaviors within buyer-seller relationships. Project managers implementing supplier-oriented practices can benefit by attracting desired vendors/suppliers with which to engage in meaningful business relationships. Panelists responded strongly in favor of business relationships based on quality, communications, attentiveness, power/professionalism, reputation/trust, adaptation, and cooperation/loyalty/commitment. These aspects were viewed by panelists as being key characteristics of Supplier-Oriented Purchasing Behaviors, and the foundation for strong buyer/seller relationships. Information assembled from this study may enable project managers to practice pre-qualified partnering through the use of Supplier-Oriented Purchasing Behaviors.

The concept of Supplier-Oriented Purchasing Behaviors presents organizations with new challenges within the area of human capital management. Organizations desiring to successfully implement Supplier-Oriented Purchasing Behaviors need to train their project procurement managers and support personnel on how to be supplier-oriented. Training will not only be required for project procurement managers, but also for those other project team members who have various types of contact with suppliers. Supplier-Oriented Purchasing Behaviors will require commitment from management in order for organization-wide implementation to be successful and beneficial.

The results of this study fill a void in research concerning Supplier-Oriented Purchasing Behavior. Previously there was very little information available regarding the domain and key characteristics of Supplier-Oriented Purchasing Behaviors from the perspective of project management. This research defines the relationship gap between supplier-oriented practices (buyer viewpoint) and customer-oriented selling behavior (seller viewpoint) which exists between project-oriented buyers and sellers. Previous research focused on customer-oriented selling behavior where the supplier becomes customer-oriented in an attempt to attract preferential buyers. When examining the relationship between customer-oriented selling behaviors, buyer trust in the seller, buyer commitment, and buyer cooperation may be seen as interrelated and dependent. This relationship leads to Supplier-Oriented Purchasing Behaviors, which in turn results in sellers placing trust in the buyer. Supplier-Oriented Purchasing Behaviors provides the "missing-link" within bilateral relationships between buyers and sellers.

FUTURE RESEARCH IMPLICATIONS

Utilizing the categories developed in this study and statements that achieved consensus, a scale needs to be developed to measure Supplier-Oriented Purchasing Behaviors. Statements on which the panelists reached consensus could be used by project managers to measure, assess, and strengthen their own Supplier-Oriented Purchasing Behaviors. Prior research was limited to what salespeople do to attract buyers. Very little research had been reported regarding what buyers can do to attract suppliers. Since previous studies have ignored project management specialists (buyer's viewpoint) this study asked project management professionals to state what was important.

In summary, the rationale for developing long-term buyer-seller relationships discussed in the literature lies in the expectation of potential benefits from sustained relationships with buyers. In conceptualizing this study it was considered that by definition projects are limited or short term endeavors. Therefore, it was expected that project procurement managers would have very different ideas about the importance of long term relationships with buyers. One of the most surprising findings was that project procurement managers rated factors previously identified as supporting the long-term relationship as important. This was similar to findings in previous research conducted in functional business environments. It is speculated that this may have occurred in part because the experts invited to participate in this Delphi study were career project management team members employed in projectized environments. Perhaps even though the project is typically a relatively short term endeavor, these experts see positive buyer-seller relationships as not only benefiting current projects but also enhancing the probability of success in future projects.

REFERENCES

Anderson, E., & Weitz, B. (1992). The use of pledges to build and sustain commitment in distribution channels. *JMR, Journal of Marketing Research*, *29*(1), 18–35. doi:10.2307/3172490

Anderson, J., & Narus, J. (1990). A model of distributor firm and manufacturer firm working partnerships. *Journal of Marketing*, *54*(1), 42–58. doi:10.2307/1252172

Atkinson, W. (2008). 12 steps to more effective supplier relationships. *Purchasing*, *137*(5), 17.

Benton, W. C., & Maloni, M. (2005). The influence of power driven buyer/seller relationships on supply chain satisfaction. *Journal of Operations Management*, *23*, 1–22. doi:10.1016/j.jom.2004.09.002

Bertrand, K. (1986). Crafting "win-win" situations in buyer-supplier relationships. *Business Marketing*, (June), 24-30.

Bonner, J., & Calantone, R. (2004). Buyer attentiveness in buyer-supplier relationships. *Industrial Marketing Management*, *34*, 53–61.

Bradley, A. (2005). The ups and downs of relationships. *Supply Management, 10*(21), 15.

Brandon-Jones, A., Ramsay, J., & Wagner, B. (2010). Trading interactions: Supplier empathy, consensus and bias. *International Journal of Operations & Production Management, 30*(5), 453–487. doi:10.1108/01443571011039588

Brennan, P., & Turnbull, P. (1999). Adaptive behavior in buyer-seller relationships. *Industrial Marketing Management, 28*, 481–495. doi:10.1016/S0019-8501(99)00057-7

Carr, A. S., & Pearson, J. N. (1999). Strategically managed buyer-supplier relationships and performance outcomes. *Journal of Operations Management, 17*(5), 497–519. doi:10.1016/S0272-6963(99)00007-8

Chow, S., & Holden, R. (1997). Toward an understanding of loyalty: The moderating role of trust. *Journal of Managerial Issues, 9*(3), 275–298.

Claro, D. P., Claro, P. B., & Hagelaar, G. (2006). Coordinating collaborative joint efforts with suppliers: The effects of trust, transaction specific investment and information network in the Dutch flower industry. *Supply Chain Management, 11*(3), 216–224. doi:10.1108/13598540610662112

Crosby, L., Evans, K., & Cowles, D. (1990). Relationship quality in services selling: An interpersonal influence perspective. *Journal of Marketing, 54*(3), 68–81. doi:10.2307/1251817

Day, A. (2009). Supplier relationship management. *Supply Management, 14*(16), 25–27.

Dubinsky, A. J., & Ingram, T. N. (1982). Salespeople view buyer behavior. *Journal of Purchasing and Materials Management, 18*(3), 6–11.

Dyer, J., & Chu, W. (2003). The Role of trustworthiness in reducing transaction costs and improving performance: Empirical evidence from the United States, Japan and Korea. *Organization Science, 14*(1), 57–68. doi:10.1287/orsc.14.1.57.12806

Elinor, R. (2005). Study shows SRM leaders. *Supply Management, 10*(25), 10.

Emiliana, M. L. (2010). Historical lessons in purchasing and supplier relationship management. *Journal of Management History, 16*(1), 116–136. doi:10.1108/17511341011008340

Ganesan, S. (1994). Determinants of long-term orientation in buyer-seller relationships. *Journal of Marketing, 58*(2), 1–19. doi:10.2307/1252265

Garvin, D. (1987). Competing on eight dimensions of quality. *Harvard Business Review, 6*, 101–109.

Gorelick, D. (1998). New rationale in buyer/seller relations. *Graphic Arts Monthly, 70*(8), 81.

Hallen, L., Johanson, J., & Seyed-Mohamed, N. (1991). Interfirm adaptation in business relationships. *Journal of Marketing, 55*(2), 29–37. doi:10.2307/1252235

Hannon, D. (2005). Supplier relationships key to future success. *Purchasing, 134*(10), 21–25.

Harris, C., & Streeter, C. (2010). A new purchasing philosophy. *Industrial Engineer, 42*(9), 42–46.

Heide, J., & John, G. (1990). Alliances in industrial purchasing: The determinants of joint action in buyer-supplier relationships. *JMR, Journal of Marketing Research, 27*(1), 24–37. doi:10.2307/3172548

Hoffman, W. (2003). Missing links. *PM Network, 17*(6), 50–54.

Humphreys, M., Williams, M., & Meier, R. (1996). Product quality, interpersonal process quality and their relationships to overall customer satisfaction. *Proceedings of the 1996 NAIT Convention*, Los Angeles, CA.

Humphreys, M., Williams, M., & Meier, R. (1997). Leveraging the total market offering in the agile enterprise. *Quality Management Journal, 97*(5), 60–74.

Humphreys, M., Williams, M. R., & Goebel, D. J. (2008). Toward an enhanced definition and measurement of purchasing's strategic role in buy-supplier relationships. *Journal of Business-To-Business Marketing, 15*(3), 323–353. doi:10.1080/15470620802059307

Humphreys, M., Williams, M. R., & Goebel, D. J. (2009). The mediating effect of supplier oriented purchasing on conflict in inter-firm relationships. *Journal of Business and Industrial Marketing, 24*(3/4), 198–206. doi:10.1108/08858620910939741

Janda, S., & Seshadri, S. (2001). The influence of purchasing strategies on performance. *Journal of Business and Industrial Marketing, 16*(4), 294–308. doi:10.1108/EUM0000000005502

Jap, S. (1999). Pie-expansion efforts: Collaboration processes in buyer-supplier relationships. *JMR, Journal of Marketing Research, 36*(4), 461–475. doi:10.2307/3152000

Johnston, D., McCutcheon, D., Stuart, F., & Kerwood, H. (2004). Effects of supplier trust on performance of cooperative supplier relationships. *Journal of Operations Management, 22*(5), 23–38. doi:10.1016/j.jom.2003.12.001

Kannan, V. R., & Tan, K. C. (2006). Buyer-supplier relationships: The impact of supplier selection and buyer-supplier engagement on relationship and firm performance. *International Journal of Physical Distribution & Logistics Management, 36*(10), 755–775. doi:10.1108/09600030610714580

Maloni, M., & Benton, W. C. (2000). Power influences in supply chain. *Journal of Business Logistics, 21*(1), 49–73.

Martin, N. (2004). Supplier relationship management. *Interactive Marketing, 6*(1), 34–43. doi:10.1057/palgrave.im.4340266

McGinnis, M. A., & Vallopra, R. M. (1999). Purchasing and supplier involvement in process improvement: A source of competitive advantage. *Journal of Supply Chain Management, 35*(4), 42–50. doi:10.1111/j.1745-493X.1999.tb00243.x

Meier, R., Humphreys, M., & Williams, M. (1998). The role of purchasing in the agile enterprise. *International Journal of Purchasing & Materials Management, 34*(4), 39–45.

Modi, S., & Mabert, V. A. (2007). Supplier development: improving supplier performance through knowledge transfer. *Journal of Operations Management, 25*(1), 42–64. doi:10.1016/j.jom.2006.02.001

Moeller, S., Faassnacht, M., & Klose, S. (2006). A framework for supplier relationship management. *Journal of Business-To-Business Marketing, 13*(4), 69–94. doi:10.1300/J033v13n04_03

Morgan, R., & Hunt, S. (1994). The commitment-trust theory of relationship marketing. *Journal of Marketing, 58*(3), 20–39. doi:10.2307/1252308

Neuman, K., O'Connor, C., & Myles, L. (2000). Communication key to supply chain efficiency. *Hospital Materials Management, 25*(4), 11–13.

Noordewier, T., John, G., & Nevin, J. (1990). Performance outcomes of purchasing arrangements in industrial buyer-vendor relationships. *Journal of Marketing, 54*(4), 80–94. doi:10.2307/1251761

O'Toole, T., & Donaldson, B. (2000). Managing buyer-supplier relationship archetypes. *Irish Marketing Review, 13*(1), 12–20.

Park, J., Shin, K., Chang, T., & Park, J. (2010). An integrative framework for supplier relationship management. *Industrial Management + Data Systems, 110*(4), 495-515.

Pelletier, J. (1996). *A Delphi study to define the domain and identify the key characteristics of supplier-oriented purchasing behavior*. Unpublished Master's thesis, Illinois State University, Normal.

Powers, T. L., & Reagan, W. R. (2007). Factors influencing successful buyer-seller relationships. *Journal of Business Research, 60*, 1234–1242. doi:10.1016/j.jbusres.2007.04.008

Project Management Institute (PMI). (2008). *A guide to the project management body of knowledge* (4th ed.). Newtown Square, PA: Project Management Institute.

Sharma, A., & Sheth, J. N. (1997). Supplier relationships: Emerging issues and challenges. *Industrial Marketing Management, 26*(2), 91–100. doi:10.1016/S0019-8501(96)00153-8

Smeltzer, L. R. (1997). The meaning and origin of trust in buyer-supplier relationships. *International Journal of Purchasing and Materials Management, 33*(1), 40–48.

Smith, P. (2005). More than a beautiful friendship. *Supply Management, 10*(3), 22–25.

Snell, P. (2008). Tackle aggression toward suppliers. *Supply Management, 13*(23), 10.

Tangpong, C., Michalisin, M. D., & Melcher, A. J. (2008). Toward a typology of buyer-supplier relationships: A study of the computer industry. *Decision Sciences, 39*(3), 571–593. doi:10.1111/j.1540-5915.2008.00203.x

Tipman, M. (2005, January/February). Projects and procurement. *Summit, 8*, 20–21.

van der Valk, W. (2009). Effective buyer-supplier interaction patterns in ongoing service exchange. *International Journal of Operations & Production Management, 29*(8), 807–833. doi:10.1108/01443570910977706

Wagner, S. M., Coley, L. S., & Lindemann, E. (2011). Effects of suppliers' reputation on the future of buyer-supplier relationships: The mediating roles of outcome fairness and trust. *Journal of Supply Chain Management, 47*(2), 29–47. doi:10.1111/j.1745-493X.2011.03225.x

Yeo, K. (2006). Managing uncertainty in major equipment procurement in engineering projects. *European Journal of Operational Research, 171*(1), 123–134. doi:10.1016/j.ejor.2004.06.036

KEY TERMS AND DEFINITIONS

Buying Behaviors: the decision processes and acts of people involved in buying and using products or services.

Delphi Study: The Delphi approach is a technique for gathering data that is similar to focus groups. Its value is that unlike focus groups, Delphi participants do not have to physically meet. The Delphi technique is a method of generating ideas and facilitating consensus among individuals who have special knowledge to share, but who are not always in contact with each other.

Interpersonal Process Quality: corresponds to the organizations attitudes/behaviors and the reliability/trustworthy aspects including empathy. Specifically includes; overall consideration for the customer, being innovative in responding to customer needs, ability to respond quickly and efficiently to requests, eagerness to satisfy me as a customer, and ability to do the job right the first time.

Procurement Management: the procurement requirements for a project and the description of how these requirements will be managed from developing procurement documentation through contract closure.

Project Management: the discipline of planning, organizing, securing and managing resources to deliver the successful completion of project goals and objectives.

Supplier-Oriented Purchasing Behaviors: purchasing strategies intended to create a position as a preferred customer when contrasted to targeted suppliers.

Technical Product Quality: regarding the subject organizations conformance to product specifications and reliability. Specifically; products that operate trouble-free, products meeting customer standards, products performing as expected and product uniformity.

Total Market Offering: The term used in reference to the two basic sources of value delivered by the market offering to achieve overall customer satisfaction. See technical product quality and interpersonal process quality.

Chapter 5
Coopetition in Supply Chains:
A Case Study of a Coopetitive Structure in the Horticulture Industry

Lincoln C. Wood
Curtin University, Australia

ABSTRACT

Supply chain management has been increasingly seen as a strategic tool to improve the competitiveness of companies. Coopetition, the mingling of competitive and cooperative relationships, has been utilised by New Zealand companies in the horticulture industry to help break into and develop new markets. Using a case study various elements of the supply chain are examined from both strategic and operational perspectives for this group of companies and their customers and suppliers. The connections to the customer are shown to be enhanced through careful implementation, as the group of companies act to adjust their entire supply chains to make them increasingly customer-orientated. Significant benefits that are shown to accrue include improved information flow, increased ability to supply, and flexibility to meet customer requirements.

INTRODUCTION

Primary sector commodity chains are very important in many developing countries and are still critical to several developed countries like Canada, Australia, and New Zealand. Price competition is rampant with many of these products being impacted by 'commoditisation' and 'perfect competition' due to the homogenous nature of the products. Under these circumstances price is a key consideration for buyers; suppliers are 'price-takers' as "they have no control over the price they receive for their products" (Burt, Petcavage, & Pinkerton, 2010, p. 323). The ability to supply

DOI: 10.4018/978-1-4666-0246-5.ch005

while controlling costs and developing appropriate supply chain structures to support customers can lead to significant advantages for producers. This chapter focuses on a case of New Zealand horticulture exporters and the development of a 'coopetitive' (Brandenburger & Nalebuff, 1996) structure within the supply chain, where the members simultaneously compete and cooperate with each other. A review of strategic supply chain management positions this case, which is followed closely by supporting lessons and an examination of how the firms involved have implemented a strategic supply chain management approach in their activities. The use of coopetitive structures to improve customer orientation is outlined, along with some important considerations for managers who seek to operationalise the concept. The thesis of this chapter is that coopetitive structures, carefully used both operationally as well as strategically, enable individual firms to more effective in their customer-orientation and improve their profitability and competitive positioning.

LITERATURE REVIEW

When understanding the management of the supply chain from the perspective of a group of firms it helps to understand *what* is being managed and *how* it is managed. Supply chain management has its roots in logistics management and the terms have come to mean similar things today (Jonsson, 2008). Both logistics and supply chain management have frequently been relegated to tactical level and charged with cost-efficiency in providing adequate customer service (Bovet & Martha, 2000), yet the discipline of supply chain management has increasingly been given significance and recognition at the boardroom level (Boubekri, 2001; Dath, Rajendran, & Narashiman, 2010).

One of the first scholars to recognise the significant implications of the supply chain on the competitive positioning of firms was Fine (1998, 2000), who investigated the dynamic changes in both the horizontal and vertical dimensions of various supply chains and concluded that "the ultimate core competency of an organization is 'supply chain design,' which [can be defined] as choosing what capabilities along the value chain to invest in and develop " (Fine, 2000, p. 213) to enhance success. The design of the supply chain therefore becomes a *strategic* concern to firms. But what does 'strategic supply chain management' mean? Hult, Ketchen, and Arrfelt (2007) assert that " 'strategic supply chain management' – [is] the use of a supply chain not merely as a means to get products where they need to be, but also as *a tool to enhance key outcomes*" (Hult et al., 2007, p. 1036; emphasis added); a supply chain is for getting goods to where they need to be but may also be of importance to a firm to enable attainment of other, *strategic*, outcomes. Paraphrasing Hill and Hill (2009, p. 25), the strategic role of supply chain managers will be to support competitive drivers in their company's market, for which the supply chain team is responsible.

Fisher (1997) also sees that supply chains are associated with product flow as well as providing a means for market mediation to ensure the right mix of products reach the market. Such traditional product flows require firms "to synchronise the requirements of the customer with the flow of material from suppliers in order to effect a balance between what are often seen as the conflicting goals of high customer service, low inventory investment and low unit cost" (Stevens, 1989, p. 3). These synchronised and integrated flows of material are similar to vertical integration where there is coordination over successive phases of production so there is operation as a unified process (Frank, 1925); however, supply chain management is not integration and sits on a continuum between integration and separate firms (Ellram, 1991). Overall, in the supply chain this synchronisation of flow should limit wastes in excess or obsolete inventories and should improve profits. In this way the supply chain may be used to 'enhance key outcomes', which will usually involve the marketing positioning of the supply chain (Bowersox, Closs, & Cooper, 2002), through improving the customer-orientation of the chain to create greater value for the customer.

Supply chains involve a complex web of interrelations surrounding various elements that may be leveraged to affect outcomes. Many of these components relate to the flow of materials and logistics networks but there are others as:

Strategic supply chain management deals with a wide spectrum of issues and includes several types of decision-making problems that affect the long-term development and operations of a firm, namely the determination of number, location and capacity of warehouses and manufacturing plants and the flow of material through the logistics network, inventory management policies, supply contracts, distribution strategies, supply chain integration, outsourcing and procurement strategies, product design, decision support systems and information technology. (Georgiadis, Vlachos, & Iakovou, 2005, p. 352)

Many additional outcomes envisaged through supply chain management relate to the utilisation of resources and capabilities throughout the supply chain. In their leading text book Stock and Lambert (2001, p. 703) perceive that the objective of logistics is to "[m]inimize total costs given the customer service objective"; where costs are contributed by transportation, warehousing, order processing and information costs, inventory carrying costs, and lot quantity costs (2001, p. 688).

One common and critical element of the supply chain are the locations of facilities such as warehouses and manufacturing sites (Bowersox et al., 2002; Chopra & Meindl, 2010; Georgiadis et al., 2005; Oakden & Leonaite, 2011; Stock & Lambert, 2001; Webster, 2008). The integration and locations over the network become important to support an effective flow of materials through the network, particularly with ensuring suitable lead times are observed in the chain (Webster, 2008).

Locating suitable facilities must be balanced with simultaneous consideration of available capacities (Webster, 2008), establishment of various types of inventories, and implementation of suitable inventory management policies and controls (Bowersox et al., 2002; Chopra & Meindl, 2010; Fine, 2000; Georgiadis et al., 2005; Oakden & Leonaite, 2011; Stock & Lambert, 2001; Webster, 2008). The physical flow of materials through the network and between facilities is undertaken through the use of various modes of transport, where appropriate decisions may impact on the competitiveness of the overall supply chain (Bowersox et al., 2002; Chopra & Meindl, 2010; Fine, 2000; Oakden & Leonaite, 2011; Stock & Lambert, 2001).

Between the firms in the supply chain there should be commonality and development of a process architecture, end-to-end along the chain (Cohen & Roussel, 2005). This represents a level of integration, and collaborative models must be carefully selected to generate appropriate integration along the chain (Georgiadis et al., 2005). Where less integration is required the decision may be made to outsource the product or process, raising the importance of the procurement function which manages these links in the supply chain (Chopra & Meindl, 2010; Fine, 2000; Georgiadis et al., 2005; Webster, 2008).

Attention to the processes and levels of integration along the chain, coupled with the logistics network design, help chains to manage trade-offs in managing order processing costs (Bowersox et al., 2002; Chopra & Meindl, 2010; Oakden & Leonaite, 2011; Stock & Lambert, 2001). Many other elements impact on these decisions and these interrelationships require careful consideration.

Product design becomes critical to the competitiveness of the supply chain as it enables chains to meet customer requirements while balancing other elements, such as the lead times of development or supply (Fine, 2000; Georgiadis et al., 2005;

Webster, 2008). Suitable components must be able to be sourced consistently while time-based competition becomes faster and more intense (Fine, 2000; Horvath, 2001), increasing the pressures on the chain. Similarly, quality concerns are becoming increasingly important and are changing the shape of the supply chains and operations within the supply chain (Lu & Wood, 2006; Webster, 2008).

The use of decision support systems confer advantages to firms that seek to make trade-offs and they point to new ways of sharing and using information in the supply chain. IT systems may support demand planning and scheduling and other operations relating to material flow, in addition to distribution and procurement (Chopra & Meindl, 2010; Georgiadis et al., 2005; Monczka, Handfield, Giunipero, & Patterson, 2009).

Designing suitable organisational structures to support the competitive drivers, may encourage centralisation of supply teams or executive responsibilities, stimulate the development of further cross-functionality, or the development of councils to work with suppliers (Cohen & Roussel, 2005; Monczka et al., 2009; Stock & Lambert, 2001). Based on various competitive priorities, suitable metrics or measurement criteria must be developed and applied internal and along the supply chain (Cohen & Roussel, 2005; Fawcett, Magnan, & McCarter, 2008; Monczka et al., 2009).

Ultimately, supply chain managers are concerned with providing the appropriate level of customer service through developing appropriate supply chain configurations and designs to enable desired levels of customer-orientation over time in a dynamic process (Fine, 2000). This is accomplished through viewing and utilising the supply chain as a strategic asset and frequently focuses either on efficient or responsive configurations (Fisher, 1997), although agile and flexible configurations are also possible (Gattorna, 2006). Various configurations of the supply chain therefore deliver different outcomes (in addition to the flow of products to customers) and may support alternate competitive positions for the company.

Competition Versus Coordination

Some scholars have postulated that changing economic circumstances have meant that "individual businesses no longer compete as stand-alone entities but rather as supply chains" (Christopher & Towill, 2000, p. 209). This requires a focus on the horizontal dimension of a supply chain, which has received less attention than the traditional vertical focus.

In the case where the supply chains of several competitors 'intersect' at the same tier, a case of coopetition may occur where firms are both cooperating to pursue congruent goals, while engaging in a limited form of competition. Cooperation occurs through coordination of activities, where coordination may be seen as a harmonious alignment of different units to achieve common goals (Min, 2001). Such coordination may be possible through controls and careful arrangements, with cooperation (and associated mutuality of the relationship and goodwill between parties) being absent entirely (Day & Klein, 1987). Day-to-day activities engaged in by employees shape the coordination that may have been influenced by contractual coordination (Hamel, Doz, & Prahalad, 1989), to create a procedural coordination in the partnership (Sobrero & Schrader, 1998). On the other hand, opportunistic behaviour, where a firm seeks to improve on their individual position at the expense of the group interests, is a form of competitive behaviour that must be discouraged (Park & Ungson, 2001).

Coopetitive situations, with dual tensions between cooperation and competition, may be formed as firms seek to secure access to resources or capabilities that they do not possess, without resorting to developing these themselves which is a possibly expensive or lengthy exercise (Porter, 1998, 2003). To make coopetition work the firms must overcome a barrier of inter-firm rivalry with their competitors (Fawcett et al., 2008) and ensure that surplus value created can be shared amongst participants (Jain, Nagar, & Srivastava,

Figure 1. Supply chains with both vertical and horizontal dimensions (Adapted from Figure 1.1 in Wood [2010a])

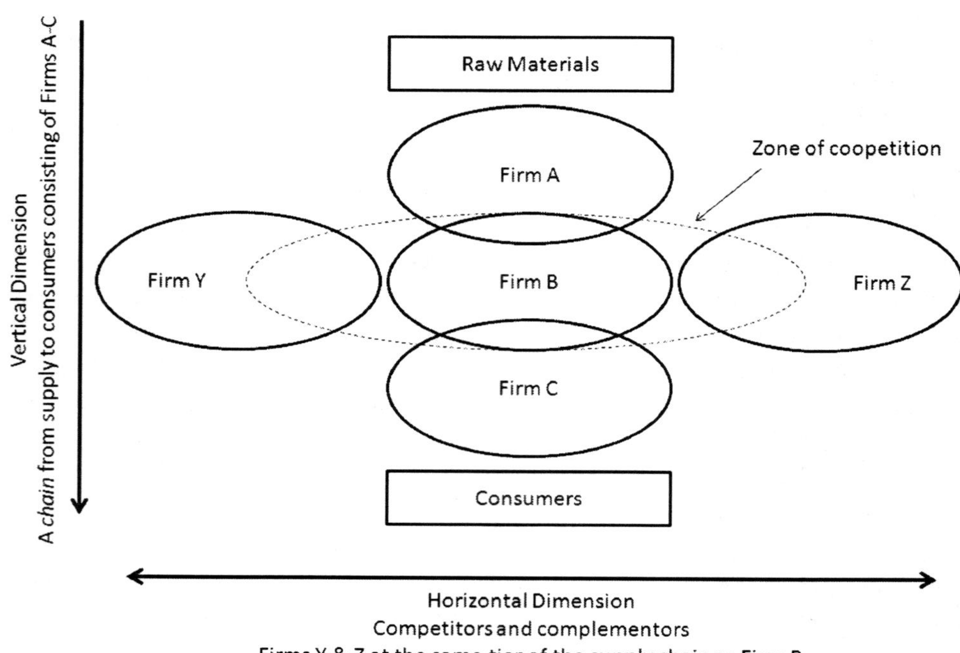

2006). Operational controls need to be instituted to ensure that there are mechanisms developed to encourage coordination of activities while discouraging potentially damaging opportunistic behaviours (Wood, 2010a).

Structure of the Supply Chain

A simple supply chain consists of sourcing processes, manufacturing or transformational processes, and distribution processes (Ballou, Gilbert, & Mukherjee, 2000, p. 9). At any level of this supply chain there may be incidences where firms involved in complementary or competing products work together to achieve congruent objectives, allowing coopetitive structures to form along the horizontal dimension of the supply chain (Figure 1). Such structures may aid the operations of the chain along the vertical dimension.

CASE STUDY: THE FRUITCOM SUPPLY CHAIN

New Zealand was once referred to as "Britain's Farm" due to the role played by the colony during WWII in supplying Britain with foodstuffs. The nation of New Zealand is a small and geographically isolated island nation in the South Pacific Ocean. Now, in the 21st century, the economy remains heavily reliant on agriculture, horticulture, and primary production, much of which must be exported as it is beyond the capacity of the domestic market to consume the full output. The economic landscape is characterised by strong growth and employment within small- and medium-sized enterprises (SMEs).

One of the key sectors in the horticulture industry is fruit. The fruit discussed[1] has been grown in New Zealand for several decades but only in commercial volumes since for around thirty years after a period of rapid and large-scale planting.

Only one variety is grown in commercial quantities. Under the Closer Economic Relations (CER) agreement with Australia, the Australian market can be considered an extension of the domestic market. Despite this broadening of the demand base, much of the fruit must still be exported.

There are many producers of the fruit in Australia, yet the growing seasons are similar to those in New Zealand, with some overlap in the seasons. There is still opportunity for New Zealand firms to export to Australia, where the supply of New Zealand fruit can extend the period of time when fresh fruit is available to Australian consumers. Effectively this means that the source of supply will be extended for Australian supermarkets.

Customers in the northern hemisphere import fruit from suppliers in the southern hemisphere to supplement their local supply during the off-season from their domestic producers. This means that importers in the USA or Europe may seek supply from New Zealand as well as Australia, Central American, and South American countries. As it is difficult to differentiate between sources of fruit the nature of the product becomes commoditised, forcing the price of the fruit down. The vast bulk of international demand is for a limited number of varieties, with a very demand-driven focus making it difficult to develop varieties unavailable elsewhere, which is a strategy followed by other New Zealand fruit producers (McKenna & Murray, 2002).

Structure of the FruitCom Supply Chain

Generally within a fruit supply chain there are growers, packers, exporters, importers, and retail chains (Figure 2), but the exact configuration and levels of integration along the supply chain may change in each instance depending on the historic arrangements.

Growers are responsible for the growth and future supply of fruit. They acquire land, plant trees, care for the orchard, and eventually arrange for harvest of the fruit. The application of sprays in modern horticulture is important to prevent bugs or insects from impacting on the crop. The decisions made by the growers, such as which types of sprays and when to apply them, as well as when and how to expand their crop through new planting, may have a significant impact on downstream availability.

Following harvest the fruit must be sorted, stored, and readied for export; these jobs are the responsibility of the packhouses and the packers. Several growers may work together with a single packhouse. Sometimes growers and the packhouse may be vertically integrated in a single organisation. Fruit may be differentiated by size, weight, dry-matter or other aspects of the fruit such as visual blemishes. Through the grading a variety of stock-keeping-units (SKUs) are created, corresponding to various combinations of physical characteristics and spray residues. While a consumer may only be exposed to several combinations, the packers may work with many hundreds, or even thousands, of SKUs for each type of fruit.

The role of the exporter is to mediate and match the supply with demand. This function is performed through their communication both up and down the supply chain, and the arrangement of transport for the produce from New Zealand. Each exporter will work with a range of packers, frequently concentrated in a single geographic region, allowing the FruitCom[2] coopetitive venture to therefore work with packers from all regions.

In the export markets the importers locate suitable source of supply for supermarkets or retail chains in their domestic market. They frequently coordinate marketing campaigns with retail chains and act as a conduit for marketing expertise and ideas to flow through the chain.

The FruitCom group consists of New Zealand-based exporters of the fruit. Their management structures relating to revenue and costs are beneficial to the constituent organisations as well as the supply chains they are embedded within. The FruitCom organisation was established around

Figure 2. Structure of the supply chain

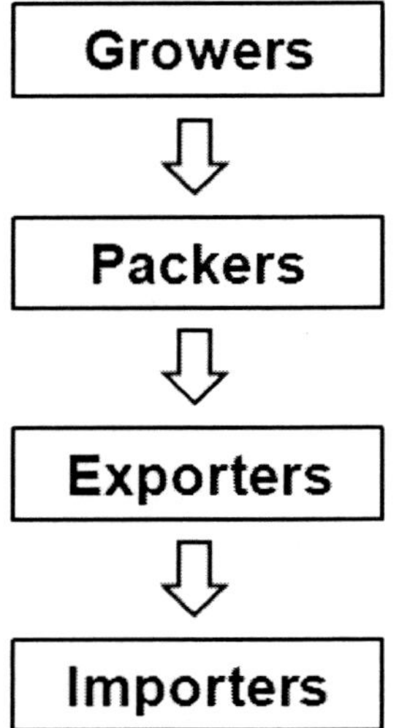

the start of the 21st century to enter new markets effectively and benefit the members who would coordinate their activities to supply these markets, while also continuing to compete with one another in other international markets and New Zealand and Australia. This coopetitive behaviour requires flexibility to act individually while there are also high-levels of participation in the coordinated group operations.

Each of the exporters works with a single client in Japan, each with separate pricing structures (Figure 3). This means that the exporters receive a varying range of revenue depending on the customer supplied. The total revenue over a single season is totalled and then split pro-rata amongst the exporters, on the basis of proportion of supply. If the exporter is supplying the customer in Japan that pays the least per unit of fruit, they still receive the same revenue as the others in FruitCom at the end of the season. A key element of this arrangement that provides flexibility to FruitCom is the way in which the firms are able to assist one another in the supply of fruit for the other customers, without disadvantaging themselves. They receive the same revenues for their supply, whether they are supplying their own customer or the customer of another member of the coopetitive cluster. There is no gain or loss from assisting other members with supply-related issues, allowing members to more easily adapt to an environment characterised by high levels of cooperation and coordination in their processes and activities. In much the same way the costs for the season are split on a pro rata basis, allowing each member proportionate shares of revenues and costs in a transparent and equitable fashion.

In the USA market the FruitCom coopetitive cluster works with a single importer that is the only source of the New Zealand fruit in the USA market. The importer is operationally sophisticated and manages flows, inventory, and development of markets and products very effectively. A different brand is used in this market, yet the FruitCom companies act in a similar fashion; the key difference is that instead of the costs and revenues being split on a seasonal basis as in Japan, in the USA the costs and revenues are split on a shipment basis. The proportion of supply for each shipment to the USA is divided in terms of revenue and costs between the contributing members. The rationale is that while the season in Japan is stable, in the USA benefits accrue on the basis of time-based competition; the exporters must be able to load ships effectively and quickly for a short period of time. Not all members are able to operationally support this process effectively, making it a better choice to aggregate revenues and costs over the shipment as opposed to the season.

Benefits from the Coopetitive Arrangements

The most significant strength gained from the coopetitive arrangement is the broadening of the supply base to all growing regions of New Zealand. Rather than a single exporter being tied to few regions, with limited exposure to supply from other regions, the entire output from all regions can be aggregated in order to meet demand from

Figure 3. Supply to separate customers through a single jointly coordinated supply chain

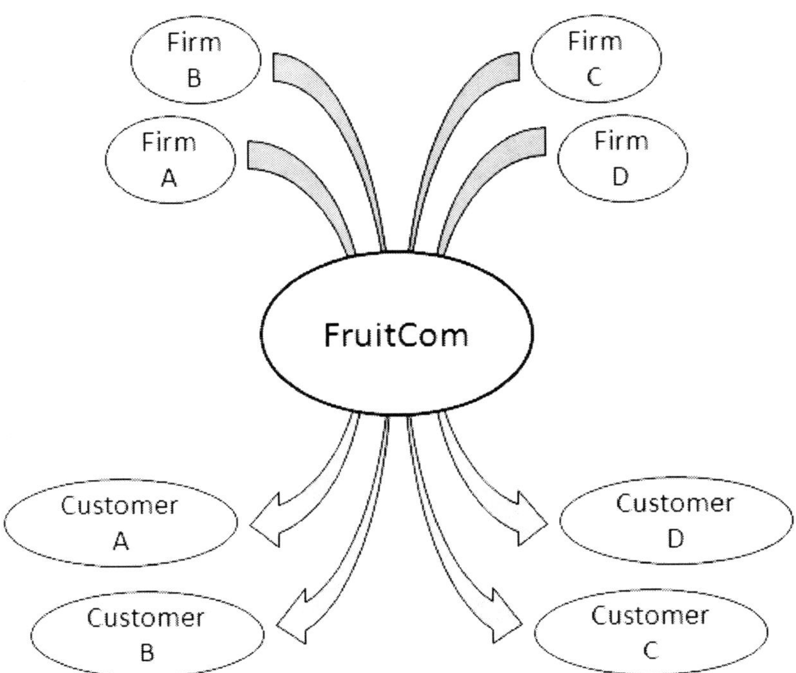

Japanese and US importers. In manufacturing this concept may help overcome issues surrounding variability of supply or disasters striking a supplier; in the horticulture industry the benefits may be more pronounced. Different climates and weather in alternate regions of supply mean that harvests occur at different times around New Zealand, leading to an overlap but with earlier supply from some regions and later supply from others presenting a profile of supply for New Zealand as a whole that is superior to that which may be gained by any single exporter (Figure 4).

This aggregation of supply leads to the overall volume of fruit being balanced and available over a greater period. Such balance reduces the pressure on the operations of the packers, who would otherwise scramble to find supply to meet the requirements of the exporters. All members in the industry respect this natural variability in the supply of the fruit and accept that things sometimes 'simply go wrong'. When the profile of the volumes harvested is adversely affected by weather the members coordinate their activities to supply key importers in Japan and the USA as best they can; they recognise that 'fruit is what it is' and they must respond to the challenges inherent in the natural variation of supply.

FruitCom's strategic coordination of supply in this manner is a form of 'risk pooling' (Simchi-Levi, Kaminsky, & Simchi-Levi, 2008, p. 48), which may be more commonly applied to demand so that "demand variability is reduced if one aggregates demand across locations" (Simchi-Levi et al., 2008, p. 48). However, in FruitCom's case the same risk pooling concept can be applied to supply, where the group reduces supply variability due to the aggregation of supply over several different areas. While the benefits of aggregation are greatest when there is low positive correlation between the sources of supply (Chopra & Meindl, 2010, p. 322), some positive correlation is present in FruitCom's case as large climate changes or weather patterns can impact on all regions of supply simultaneously.

Figure 4. Increased duration of harvest using coopetition

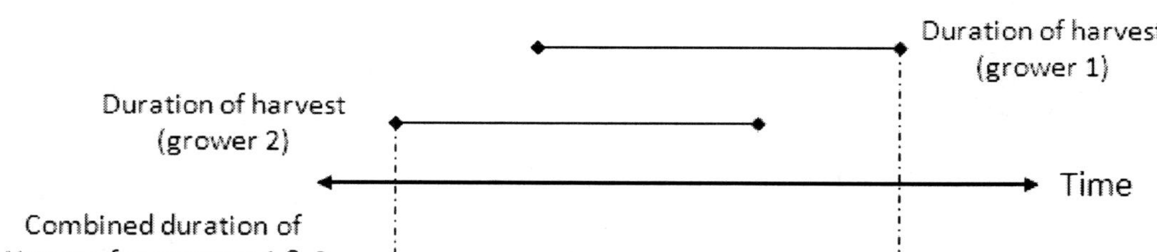

Despite the best efforts of the managers involved sometimes one of the FruitCom exporters faces challenges in their supply or operations whereby they are unable to supply their customer in Japan. Under these circumstances, where they 'come up short' and need assistance, the structure of FruitCom and the sharing of revenue means that the fruit may be sourced from other members. With the same brand and sourced from the same country, this activity is 'invisible' to the customer, but means that each member is much more able to meet their customer requirements (Figure 5).

After several years of operation the firms in the supply chain at many levels perceived significant benefits, not all of which had been foreseen. One of the key perceived benefits has been the higher returns flowing through the supply chain, yet it has also been noted that the returns have become much more stable from one season to the next (barring disasters such as significant weather impact on crops).

There had previously been competition between the packhouses for the business of local growers. Success in one season would allow a high pay out to growers, making the packhouse more attractive to other growers in forthcoming seasons. Such behaviours created significant churn, characterised by growers frequently changing of allegiance to new packers following significant swings in returns. With the stabilised returns offered through the FruitCom arrangements, flowing through each of the packhouses, the returns offered by the packhouses have become homogenised to the point where there is considerably lower levels of churn as growers see similar returns with reduced variation. Growers perceive greater stability in the industry and the returns received, allowing more effective planning for future seasons.

Challenges in the Operationalisation of Coopetitive Structures

The setup and operation of FruitCom has not been without challenge. Coordinating activities with competitors was initially worrying due to the possibility of opportunistic behaviours.

Planning and coordination within the FruitCom companies advances through the season in a joint effort, resulting in a 'flow plan' which indicates how they will match supply and demand. This is based on forecasts of both demand (provided by the various importers) and supply (provided by growers and packers). In both cases the forecasts may be more volatile than in manufacturing organisations; weather and climatic conditions can significantly impact on the crop and output in New Zealand, leading to variability in supply and frequent inability to meet expected levels of supply to importers.

Difficulties also ensue as each FruitCom member has many options for fruit placement–whether domestically or in Australia, the USA, Japan, or other markets. As prices change and the season develops the members may struggle to 'stick to

Figure 5. Drawing supply from the supply chain of other members of the coopetitive structure

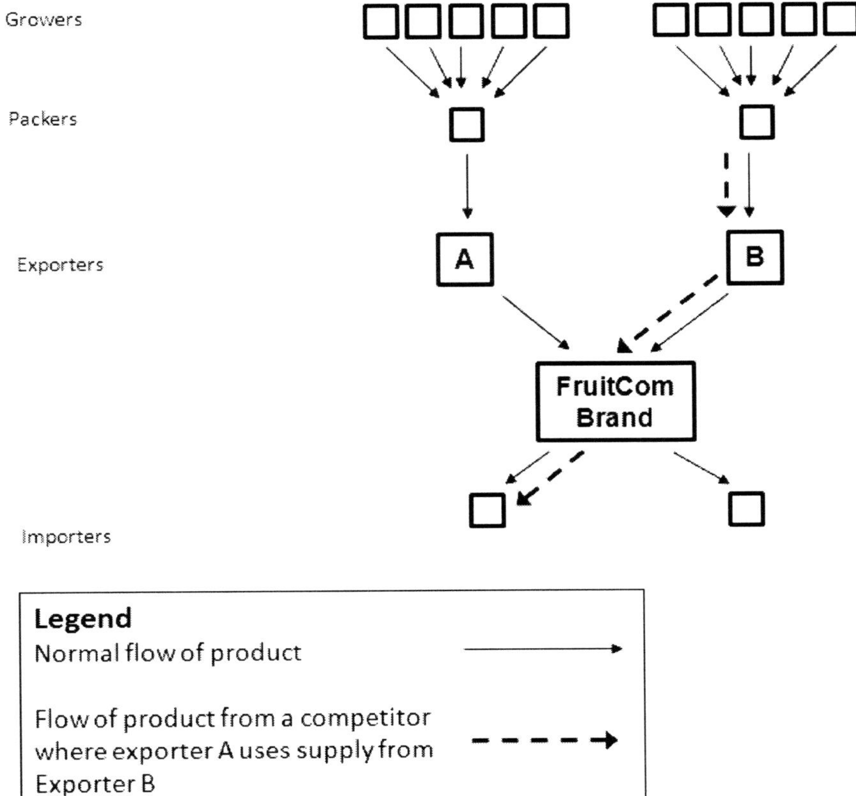

the plan' as other markets perform better than expected. If the market in Japan performs better than the original flow plans had arranged for, some FruitCom members must 'pull through' and find additional supply, while others may not be able to do so. When this occurs there is always some 'argy-bargy'[3] as the members jostle and change their internal plans. It is not considered to be 'good form' if a member has allocated fruit elsewhere, in a market where they compete with the other FruitCom exporters, and then comes up short to supply their customer in Japan, where they are coordinating activities with the FruitCom exporters. Such behaviours can damage the reputation of the brand needlessly where a member has supplied another market for more immediate and perceived higher-returns and then become unable to 'pull their own weight' regarding the FruitCom obligations, disadvantaging other members. Where such behaviours occur they may be easily traced and tracked, due to the small size of the market and the ability for key members in the industry to figure out what is happening regarding different shipping lines and ports; members frequently 'hear things' about the activities in the market.

Not all of the members are equally professional in their approaches to the business. Some are large organisations that operate with many types of fruits and vegetables; others may be small and specialise in few types of fruits or vegetables. Operational difficulties faced by some members have, in the past, reduced their ability to meet obligations to the supply according to the FruitCom flow plan. Such occurrences lead to the more sophisticated members 'carrying' the weaker members over this period.

Operational Issues

Working in the coopetitive structure has introduced new challenges and pressures into the supply chain. Most importantly, there is a significantly increased level of horizontal activity in the supply chain. While before there was some information sharing and networking between the exporters, now there is structured horizontal coordination of activities and intertwining of business processes. Initially, there were some minor issues with implementation. Frequent meetings coupled with pre- and post-season meetings helped members to articulate their firms' objectives and ensure ongoing congruence of goals.

While the coordination occurs primarily at the level of the exporters, the impacts flow throughout the supply chain. While the packers needed to incorporate a new brand, most individuals could see that the change required relatively insignificant adaptations of the existing processes; the new brand was not perceived as being an onerous problem.

There are challenges surrounding the sharing of information and plans with the competitors; the reluctance felt by individuals took time to overcome, creating a significant barrier to the coordination of activities. One manager pointed out that if you want to keep something secret you may be doing something that you shouldn't be doing. In the cooperative atmosphere, this coordination forms a check and balance on the activities of members. Additionally, the members must agree unanimously on a course of action. Under these circumstances there is one vote per firm; the larger firms that account for a greater proportion of the overall volumes get no greater say, despite the acknowledgement that their greater share of supply could give them greater 'power' in negotiations. Indeed, these larger firms are aware of potential power balances and actively seek to include the other firms in decisions and activities so there is a joint sense of ownership and contribution from the group.

At the strategic level there have also been challenges as the group seeks to bind their activities together. Coopetition is seen to reduce the flexibility of a member to take advantage of other opportunities in markets, or to pursue other opportunities as they arise.

Each of the members has a unique history with some firms considerably larger and more sophisticated than others. Due to different backgrounds there are various resources that have been accumulated amongst the different members, leading to different capabilities flourishing in different firms. Each firm has unique resources or capabilities that they contribute to FruitCom operations. When the customer requires marketing support, one of the FruitCom members with the greatest capabilities and marketing resources provides the support on behalf of FruitCom. Another member has a team that is well versed in working with shipping lines and they coordinate the shipping for FruitCom, maintaining economies of scale and leveraging their capabilities fully. As a result, each member of FruitCom benefits from the capabilities and resources possessed by other members. This allows improved responsiveness and reductions in costs, benefiting the customers.

Pressure

When the coopetitive venture was launched there was intense pressure between the key individuals, who were of good standing in the industry, to 'make it work'. Over time there has been recognition of the success of the venture both up and downstream, resulting in other parties in the supply chain emphasising that the FruitCom coordination should continue. This has occurred from the suppliers, where the buyers and packers have been buoyed by greater stability in returns and successes. If the coopetitive venture were to be discontinued the packers and growers would be 'furious' that this had been allowed to happen as the present arrangements are very beneficial to them. Similarly, the importers are able to effectively plan for the New Zealand fruit over a season and gain greater support from FruitCom for their operations.

This shows two forms of pressure on the members of FruitCom. The first is the horizontal pressure, between the members. This is based on the reputation and the close-knit structure of the industry. It is difficult for one of the key individuals from a member firm to go back on their word as they must have on-going relationships in the small industry with other individuals. Such an on-going relationship requires consideration of each action, and members are happy to cajole one another and apply pressure on the others if someone breaks their word or reneges on an agreement. Such social control is a form of 'network governance' (Jones, Hesterly, & Borgatti, 1997) and is a form of pressure that can be quickly developed at the initiation of the coopetitive venture based on past history between members. The second form of pressure is developed over time as the benefits have become apparent to customers and to suppliers; pressure is exerted by these parties in the supply chain to maintain the FruitCom relationships and coordination of activities, forming vertical pressure applied on FruitCom. Soon after formation there were early commercial successes that provided proof that the concept worked, as the firms "got some early runs on the board."[4] This was supplemented over several seasons, as the successes of the coopetitive venture became apparent to the members in the supply chain and appeared to be stable.

These sources of pressure help the members to overcome their otherwise natural urge towards competitive behaviours which would cause them to act in isolation. If one of the members were to create problems significant enough to disrupt normal FruitCom operations, this may damage the value of the brand in Japan and the long-term prospects for the group. The strong pressure, both horizontally and vertically, helps the group to cooperate rather than compete with one another.

STRATEGIC COOPETITION IN SUPPLY CHAIN MANAGEMENT

Within FruitCom there were several important benefits that were gained by their use of coopetition as a strategic supply chain management tool. As a concept, it allowed the members to better meet higher customer service levels while gaining greater revenues for themselves. This was accomplished through changes in the way in which they used inventory, arranged for transportation, engaged in sourcing, used pricing, and shared the flow of information along the supply chain. Appropriate metrics and measures were developed to aid them in coordinating their efforts. Overall, the coopetitive arrangement has enabled the firms to move ahead successfully.

Customer service levels have been increased so that any one of the customers is now more likely to be able to receive the bundle of fruit, based on their specifications, than they were before FruitCom was formed. For the members of FruitCom, costs have been lowered while revenues and customer service levels have been increased. At the strategic level the FruitCom coopetitive structure can be considered a success.

While the industry was well-disciplined prior to FruitCom formation, allowing the exporters to form FruitCom easily, the new organisation has also increased the flow of information upstream and downstream along the supply chain. This has enabled other members in the supply chain to better understand the requirements of customers and how trends in the industry are taking shape. New ventures are being trialled with the intention of rolling out the approach over all the suppliers for FruitCom, whereby there may be enhanced flexibility regarding the application and use of sprays. This would further improve the capability of FruitCom members to meet specific customer orders in the future.

Some elements of the supply chain have remained unchanged through the FruitCom implementation and growth; the general flow of materials, distribution strategies, and transportation modes, remain similar under both the prior competitive model and FruitCom's coopetitive model. Similar packing and warehousing processes are still used with minor changes to accommodate a new brand. Information technology use has remained relatively constant, with a reliance on spreadsheets, emails, and telephone calls as supplements to face-to-face meetings to coordinate activities. Yet differences emerge in the types of collaborative models employed and levels of integration through the supply chain. Different measurements have also been employed and internal changes to organisations and management of relations along the chain have been required to manage new types of joint flow plans (concerning inventory movement) and control of actions and behaviours of employees and other coopetitive members. Improvements from the perspective of a customer may be seen in the inventory management, lead times, and capacity exhibited by FruitCom.

Operationalising Coopetitive Structures

Key elements that have driven the success of FruitCom in their venture have been the presence of group pressure (both horizontal and vertical), congruence of objectives, and rules and procedures to enable members to work with partner behaviours.

Strong arrangements between the members and the presence existing industry networks can be used to exert pressure on other coopetitive members to help develop horizontal group pressure. Discovering the ability to secure 'early runs', leading to sustained and more tangible benefits, leads to benefits along the supply chain which foster the creation of vertical group pressure. These pressures to cooperate can overcome the substantial pull of competitive and opportunistic behaviour, which is at the core of an unwillingness to share information between members.

Structured discussions that occur both pre- and post-season allow the opportunity to identify gaps in the alignment of objectives and allows for explorations to reconverge goals in the group. Through the creation of the flow plan for the season the members are bound together with a set of congruent objectives. It is also critical for members to ensure that those individual employees that work and coordinate with other member firms are apprised of all changes and developments within the organisation. When one part of the firm takes a series of actions, individuals with coordinating and boundary-spanning roles, must be aware of this and able to communicate with their counterpart in other member firms in such a way so that there are no concerns about competitive or opportunistic behaviours.

The use of the group's volumes to gain economies of scale is a simple way to lower costs for the group and requires little effort to implement. Such efforts may represent a way to rapidly gain benefits from the coopetitive supply chain venture so that there is proven and tangible benefit to the individual organisation. Working together to ensure greater stability of supply may be a more multi-faceted element of the engagement but one which may bring more pronounced long-term benefits to the group, through creating additional value for their customers. The decision concerning which elements of the supply chain should be focused on first becomes strategic, but it is necessary to get some 'early runs' while working to build a foundation for long-term success and benefits to members.

When the coopetitive venture is formed it is also useful to conceptualise the various ways in which member firms may react, or the different types of behaviours that may be engaged in. Policies or structured approaches for communicating and dealing with member firms that fail to meet obligations, or even flout the agreed behaviours or objectives of the coopetitive venture, should be put in place at the start of the arrangement as it becomes increasingly difficult to implement such measures later when the venture is in operation.

Coopetitive Structures in the Greater Supply Chain

Within the FruitCom supply chain the coopetitive structure has helped foster a tighter vertical relationship and changed the dynamics of the constituent supply chains. It has been utilised in a manner that enhances the outcomes for the customers through the creation of additional value, while reducing costs for the coopetitive members, presenting a significant benefit to the members and their supply chains. In this manner the venture has been very strategic in the use the supply chain as a tool. The case study has examined several implications of this coopetitive tool in order to understand and illustrate how it may be used at an operational level to support strategic objectives.

It is important for firms engaging in coopetitive ventures to be wary of barriers to coordination and cooperation (Fawcett et al., 2008; Park & Ungson, 2001). While many traditional barriers to supply chain coordination apply, those relating to interfirm rivalry are more pronounced. Managers need to carefully consider how information is shared, how distrust and unwillingness to work together may be overcome, how potential power or capability imbalances between members may be mitigated, how cooperative pressures can be enhanced, how goal congruence can be achieved, and how the group may expand their competitive focus to be more encompassing of value-creation than merely seeking to reduce costs (Wood, 2010a, 2010b).

The positioning of coopetitive structures may be nearer to consumers or sources of supply; however, there is evidence that this approach may be suitable for firms involved in aggregating supply over various sources. Similar evidence is provided by Wu, Yue, and Sim (2006), who convincingly argue that similar 'supply clusters' in China provide a foundation for the cost benefits in Chinese manufacturing. Where competitors can align interests and coordinate their activities they can make a positive impact on the operation of the supply chain in the vertical dimension, not just in terms of cost (Wu et al., 2006) but through improved orientation of the chain towards the customer, providing closer alignment with customer requirements driven through enhanced information sharing and improved planning and control of the flow of materials.

CONCLUSION

In an environment where individual SMEs may struggle to improve their customer orientation a coopetitive approach may provide significant benefits. Through structured coordination of activities with their competitors the firms comprising FruitCom have been able to ensure more effective supply into new and developing markets for their fruit. It has enabled them to increase their ability to meet customer requirements while also improving returns for themselves, through the creation of increased value in the supply chain.

Coopetitive structures in the supply chain represent a new strategic approach to achieve supply chain outcomes other than the flow of products, and represent a shift away from the dominant vertical dimension of supply chain management that is frequently the only consideration in the literature and practice. Such structures require careful strategic consideration and forethought as to the operational implications and measures that will need to be implemented in order to ensure a greater chance of success. Considerations during operationalisation must include the nature and structure of communications (allowing goal congruence), the development of group pressure (both vertical and horizontal), and the implementation of policies and procedures to manage different types of behaviour of members of the coopetitive venture. It is important to note one significant limitation – the coopetitive structures discussed in this chapter are present in the horticulture industry and the results may not be generalisable to other industries.

FUTURE RESEARCH

A key area for future research lies in the operationalisation of coopetitive structures intra-firm, recently called for (Bonel & Rocco, 2007), but not yet addressed adequately within the literature. The research may require in-depth case studies within individual firms, yet it is doubtful whether investigations that restrict attention to the boundaries of a single firm will be adequate to address coopetitive issues without considering boundary spanning processes involved in supply chain management. Multiple case studies may be required to understand the subtle duality of competitive and cooperative pressures within a coopetitive group. Investigating the changes in processes that occur before and after coopetition ensues would provide significant insight into successful operationalisation of coopetitive structures.

REFERENCES

Ballou, R. H., Gilbert, S. M., & Mukherjee, A. (2000). New managerial challenges from supply chain opportunities. *Industrial Marketing Management*, *29*(1), 7–18. doi:10.1016/S0019-8501(99)00107-8

Bonel, E., & Rocco, E. (2007). Coopeting to survive: Surviving coopetition. *International Studies of Management & Organization*, *37*(2), 70–96. doi:10.2753/IMO0020-8825370204

Boubekri, N. (2001). Technology enablers for supply chain management. *Integrated Manufacturing Systems*, *12*(6), 394–399. doi:10.1108/EUM0000000006104

Bovet, D., & Martha, J. (2000). *Value nets: Breaking the supply chain to unlock hidden profits*. New York, NY: Wiley.

Bowersox, D. J., Closs, D. J., & Cooper, M. B. (2002). *Supply chain logistics management*. Boston, MA: McGraw-Hill/Irwin.

Brandenburger, A., & Nalebuff, B. J. (1996). *Coopetition*. New York, NY: Doubleday.

Burt, D. N., Petcavage, S. D., & Pinkerton, R. L. (2010). *Supply management* (8th ed.). Boston, MA: McGraw-Hill/Irwin.

Chopra, S., & Meindl, P. (2010). *Supply chain management: Strategy, planning, and operation* (4th ed.). Boston, MA: Pearson.

Christopher, M., & Towill, D. R. (2000). Supply chain migration from lean and functional to agile and customised. *Supply Chain Management: An International Journal*, *5*(4), 206–213. doi:10.1108/13598540010347334

Cohen, S., & Roussel, J. (2005). *Strategic supply chain management: The five disciplines for top performance*. New York, NY: McGraw-Hill.

Dath, T. N. S., Rajendran, C., & Narashiman, K. (2010). An empirical study on supply chain management: The perspective of logistics service providers. *International Journal of Logistics Systems and Management*, *6*(1), 1–22. doi:10.1504/IJLSM.2010.029718

Day, G. S., & Klein, S. (1987). Cooperative behaviour in vertical markets: The influence of transaction costs and competitive strategiesIn Houston, M. I. (Ed.), *Review of marketing* (pp. 39–66).

Ellram, L. M. (1991). Supply chain management: The industrial organisation perspective. *International Journal of Physical Distribution & Logistics Management*, *21*(1), 13–22. doi:10.1108/09600039110137082

Fawcett, S. E., Magnan, G. M., & McCarter, M. W. (2008). Benefits, barriers, and bridges to effective supply chain management. *Supply Chain Management: An International Journal, 13*(1), 35–48. doi:10.1108/13598540810850300

Fine, C. H. (1998). *Clockspeed: Winning industry control in the age of temporary advantage*. Reading, MA: Perseus Books.

Fine, C. H. (2000). Clockspeed-based strategies for supply chain design. *Production and Operations Management, 9*(3), 213–221. doi:10.1111/j.1937-5956.2000.tb00134.x

Fisher, M. L. (1997). What is the right supply chain for your product? *Harvard Business Review, 75*(2), 105–116.

Frank, L. K. (1925). The significance of industrial integration. *The Journal of Political Economy, 33*(2), 179–195. doi:10.1086/253662

Gattorna, J. (2006). *Living supply chains: How to mobilize the enterprise around delivering what your customers want*. Harlow, UK: Financial Times-Prentice Hall.

Georgiadis, P., Vlachos, D., & Iakovou, E. (2005). A system dynamics modeling framework for the strategic supply chain management of food chains. *Journal of Food Engineering, 70*(3), 351–364. doi:10.1016/j.jfoodeng.2004.06.030

Hamel, G., Doz, Y. L., & Prahalad, C. K. (1989). Collaborate with your competitors-and win. *Harvard Business Review, 67*(1), 133–139.

Hill, A., & Hill, T. (2009). *Manufacturing operations strategy* (3rd ed.). Basingstoke, UK: Palgrave Macmillan.

Horvath, L. (2001). Collaboration: The key to value creation in supply chain management. *Supply Chain Management: An International Journal, 6*(5), 205–207. doi:10.1108/EUM0000000006039

Hult, G. T. M., Ketchen, D. J., & Arrfelt, M. (2007). Strategic supply chain management: Improving performance through a culture of competitiveness and knowledge development. *Strategic Management Journal, 28*(10), 1035–1052. doi:10.1002/smj.627

Jain, K., Nagar, L., & Srivastava, V. (2006). Benefit sharing in inter-organizational coordination. *Supply Chain Management: An International Journal, 11*(5), 400–406. doi:10.1108/13598540610682417

Jones, C., Hesterly, W. S., & Borgatti, S. P. (1997). A general theory of network governance: Exchange conditions and social mechanisms. *Academy of Management Review, 22*(4), 911–945.

Jonsson, P. (2008). *Logistics and supply chain management*. London, UK: McGraw-Hill.

Lu, Q., & Wood, L. (2006). The refinement of DFM: Inclusion of process design. *International Journal of Operations & Production Management, 26*(10), 1123–1145. doi:10.1108/01443570610691102

McKenna, M. K. L., & Murray, W. E. (2002). Jungle law in the orchard: Comparing globalization in the New Zealand and Chilean apple industries. *Economic Geography, 78*(4), 494–514. doi:10.1111/j.1944-8287.2002.tb00197.x

Min, S. (2001). Inter-functional coordination in supply chain managementIn Mentzer, J. T. (Ed.), *Supply chain management* (pp. 371–390). Thousand Oaks, CA: Sage Publications.

Monczka, R. M., Handfield, R. B., Giunipero, L., & Patterson, J. (2009). *Purchasing and supply chain management*. Mason, OH: South-Western Cengage Learning.

Oakden, R., & Leonaite, K. (2011). *A framework for supply chains: Logistics operations in the Asia-Pacific region*. North Ryde, Australia: McGraw-Hill Australia.

Park, S. H., & Ungson, G. R. (2001). Interfirm rivalry and managerial complexity: A conceptual framework of alliance failure. *Organization Science*, *12*(1), 37–53. doi:10.1287/orsc.12.1.37.10118

Porter, M. (1998). Clusters and the new economics of competition. *Harvard Business Review*, *76*(6), 77–90.

Porter, M. (2003). The economic performance of regions. *Regional Studies*, *37*(6 & 7), 549–578.

Simchi-Levi, D., Kaminsky, P., & Simchi-Levi, E. (2008). *Designing and managing the supply chain: Concepts, strategies, and case studies* (3rd ed.). Boston, MA: McGraw-Hill/Irwin.

Sobrero, M., & Schrader, S. (1998). Structuring inter-firm relationships: A meta-analytic approach. *Organization Studies*, *19*(4), 585–615. doi:10.1177/017084069801900403

Stevens, G. C. (1989). Integrating the supply chain. *International Journal of Physical Distribution & Logistics Management*, *19*(8), 3–8. doi:10.1108/EUM0000000000329

Stock, J. R., & Lambert, D. M. (2001). *Strategic logistics management* (4th ed.). Boston, MA: McGraw-Hill/Irwin.

Webster, S. (2008). *Principles and tools for supply chain management*. Boston, MA: McGraw-Hill/Irwin.

Wood, L. C. (2010a). *Effective horizontal coordination in clusters: Bridging the barriers to effective supply chain management*. Doctoral Thesis, The University of Auckland, Auckland.

Wood, L. C. (2010b). *The role of clusters in creating value in supply chains: Evidence from the examination of clusters with RBV.* Paper presented at the ANZAM 2010: The 24th Australian and New Zealand Academy of Management, Adelaide, South Australia.

Wu, L., Yue, X., & Sim, T. (2006). Supply clusters: A key to China's cost advantage. *Supply Chain Management Review*, *10*(2), 46–51.

ADDITIONAL READING

Bengtsson, M., & Kock, S. (2000). "Coopetition" in business networks: To cooperate and compete simultaneously. *Industrial Marketing Management*, *29*(5), 411–426. doi:10.1016/S0019-8501(99)00067-X

Brandenburger, A., & Nalebuff, B. J. (1996). *Co-opetition*. New York, NY: Doubleday.

Chin, K.-S., Chan, B. L., & Lam, P.-K. (2008). Identifying and prioritizing critical success factors for coopetition strategy. *Industrial Management & Data Systems*, *108*(4), 437–454. doi:10.1108/02635570810868326

Dowling, M. J., Roering, W. D., Carlin, B. A., & Wisnieski, J. (1996). Multifaceted relationships under coopetition: Description and theory. *Journal of Management Inquiry*, *5*(2), 155–167. doi:10.1177/105649269652008

Luo, Y. (2004). *Coopetition in international business*. Copenhagen Business School Press.

Mariani, M. M. (2007). Coopetition as an emergent strategy. *International Studies of Management & Organization*, *37*(2), 97–126. doi:10.2753/IMO0020-8825370205

Meyer, H. (1998). My enemy, my friend. *The Journal of Business Strategy*, *19*(5), 42–46. doi:10.1108/eb039962

Min, Z., Feiqi, D., & Sai, W. (2008). Coordination game model of co-opetition relationship on cluster supply chains. *Journal of Systems Engineering and Electronics*, *19*(3), 499–506. doi:10.1016/S1004-4132(08)60113-9

Morris, M. H., Koçak, A., & Özer, A. (2007). Coopetition as a small business strategy: Implications for performance. *Journal of Small Business Strategy*, *18*(1), 35–55.

Padula, G., & Dagnino, G. B. (2007). Untangling the rise of coopetition. *International Studies of Management & Organization*, *37*(2), 32–52. doi:10.2753/IMO0020-8825370202

Soubeyran, A., & Weber, S. (2002). District formation and local social capital: A (tacit) co-opetition approach. *Journal of Urban Economics*, *52*(1), 65–92. doi:10.1016/S0094-1190(02)00005-0

von Friedrichs Grangsjo, Y. (2003). Destination networking: Co-opetition in peripheral surroundings. *International Journal of Physical Distribution & Logistics Management*, *33*(5), 427–448. doi:10.1108/09600030310481997

Walley, K. (2007). Coopetition. *International Studies of Management & Organization*, *37*(2), 11–31. doi:10.2753/IMO0020-8825370201

Zineldin, M. (2004). Co-opetition: The organisation of the future. *Marketing Intelligence & Planning*, *22*(7), 780–790. doi:10.1108/02634500410568600

KEY TERMS AND DEFINITIONS

Case Study: An in-depth investigation of a particular phenomenon or entity in management.

Clusters: Geographically close groups of firms in a similar field or industry that share many interconnections.

Coopetition: In a group of entities the simultaneous presence of competition and cooperation between the entities.

Group Pressure: Exertion of a form of control based not on rules or regulations but on social power resting on social relationships.

Horticulture: The industry associated with commercial cultivation and production of crops such as fruits and vegetables.

Information Sharing: In a group of entities the ability and willingness to collate and provide information and data to each other.

Strategic Supply Chain Management: The use of supply chains as a tool to achieve competitive outcomes.

ENDNOTES

1 The specific type of fruit discussed in this chapter has been disguised to provide anonymity to research participants.

2 FruitCom is a pseudonym that is used to provide anonymity to research participants.

3 ‘Argy-bargy’ is a colloquial phrase that refers to a verbal dispute or argument. Certainly in FruitCom the communications relating to this type of event are primarily verbal as opposed to written messages.

4 This is an idiomatic New Zealand phrase that refers to cricket where ‘runs’ are the points; to get “early runs on the board” means to gain some early successes.

Chapter 6
Agile Value Creation and Co-Evolution in Global Supply Chains

Ali Alavizadeh
Indiana University-Purdue University Fort Wayne, USA

Reza Djavanshir
The Johns Hopkins Carey Business School, USA

Mohammad J. Tarokh
K.N. Toosi University of Technology, Iran

Jaby Mohammed
The Petroleum Institute, UAE

ABSTRACT

Today's global economy requires that companies and their supply chains become more agile and lean to address the changing customers' requirements and market. A global customer-oriented supply chain network cannot be successful without agility and co-evolution. The literature on design, operation, evolution, and agile management of supply chains for such an economy is growing rapidly. However, existing research does not seem to reflect the co-evolutions of different segments of supply chains. This chapter sheds light on the concept of co-evolution and its application in supply chain management, as well as how it can contribute to creating value for all customers. It is worth mentioning that co-evolution and agility are ongoing processes. As technology changes and market varies, new challenges in terms of agility appear and companies should address them and modify their approach accordingly.

DOI: 10.4018/978-1-4666-0246-5.ch006

INTRODUCTION

Global disaggregation of production processes along with the development of information systems has had tremendous influence in the way supply chains function. These factors influence the strategies, designs, and operations of supply chains. Today, after years of streamlining internal operations, boosting plant productivity, improving value creation processes, and reducing costs, companies are focusing on agile supply chain strategies as the next frontier in organizational excellence (Akkermans, Bogerd, Yucesan, & van Wassenhove, 2003). Furthermore, as markets are becoming more transparent, customer demands are being met in a different and agile manner (Pepper & Rogers, 1999; Jensen, 1999) and, in general, the rate of change in the business world keeps increasing (Brown & Eisenhardt, 1998; Gleick, 1999). All these developments are having a profound impact on the ways in which supply chains of (extended) enterprises are to be managed (Akkerman et al, 2003). However, the global extensions of supply chains have created a complexity that makes it hard to envision any organization not using some form of a systemic approach to monitor, coordinate, or manage the evolutionary processes among the different and disaggregated segments of a supply chain in an agile manner. The rapid globalization of supply chain networks has put pressure on management to take into account risks, costs, and benefits design, operation, and management supply chains in agile manners. In today's competitive environment, to create value, a systemic and comprehensive approach is needed to avoid the risks of uneven evolutions among the different segments of supply chain networks. Uneven evolutionary processes are partly arising from integrating mixing traditional (legacy) and new technologies.

The literature on design, operation, evolution, and agile management of supply chain models for the Internet age is growing rapidly (e.g., Li, 2009, Tarokh, & Mehryar,2006, Gunaserkaran, Ngai, & McGaughey, 2006; Chesborough & Teece, 2002; Downes & Mui, 1998; Malone & Laubacher, 1998; Porter, 1998; Hagel & Singer, 1999). In particular, Li (2009) is emphasizing that, as the business environment evolves, agility in supply chains is becoming a core issue in the value creation process. However, existing models for designing and managing supply chains typically do not reflect the co-evolutions of different segments of supply chains, while considering the co-evolutionary processes captures valuable cost savings and benefits that accrue to organizations from the use supply chain network (Eisenhard & Galunic, 2000).

The key issue that makes agile value-creation and co-evolution in supply chains important to consider is that, although from a technical and a managerial decision making perspective agile value creation and co-evolutionary processes in improving the performance of organizations are recognized, they seem to be studied and considered independently as separate factors in industry. The literature review does not reveal a comprehensive study of agile value-creation and co-evolution of global supply chains. This may suggest that by some reason, academia appears to be less interested in studying the value created by co-evolutionary processes in supply chains than it is interested in agility of supply chains.

The objective of the current chapter is to discuss how co-evolution and agile value-creation can benefit a supply chain network. This chapter is organized as follows. After reviewing current literatures' definitions of supply chains and customer-oriented supply chain management, the concepts of agility and value-creation will be discussed, followed by a discussion on co-evolution in supply chain networks, conclusion remarks, and future suggestions for research in this area.

BACKGROUND

Supply Chain Management (SCM) has been defined by various scholars and organizations. Stock, Boyer, and Harmon (2010) have analyzed 166 unique definitions of SCM found in the literature and identified three major themes among the definitions. The themes include:

- Activities: flows of materials and information and internal and external relationships within companies, functions, and/or processes
- Benefits: value-adding processes, efficient and efficiency, and customer satisfaction
- Constituents: organizations, functions, and processes that comprise the supply chain (Stock, Boyer, & Harmon, 2010)

For the purpose of this discussion, the definition of the Council of Supply Chain Management Professionals (CSCMP) is used. According to this definition, supply chain management "encompasses the planning and management of all activities involved in sourcing and procurement, conversion, and all logistics management activities. Importantly, it also includes coordination and collaboration with channel partners, which can be suppliers, intermediaries, third-party service providers, and customers." (Supply Chain Management Terms and Glossary, 2010). In other words, SCM includes the management and activities of procurement, logistics, and collaboration among various constituents to deliver a product and/or service to the customer.

As seen in the definition, there are several important keys such as planning, management, and coordination. The latter will be discussed in the context of co-evolution in supply chain networks in this chapter. Another important key is linkage, which is implicitly contained in the above definition. In a research conducted by Lambert (2008), the participants, who held executive positions, mentioned that profitability and competitiveness could increase if all business processes and key internal activities are linked and managed across all involving companies in a chain. The businesses processes, as shown in Figure 1, include:

- Customer relationship management
- Customer service management
- Supplier relationship management
- Demand management
- Order fulfillment
- Manufacturing flow management
- Return management
- Product development and commercialization (Lambert, 2008)

In today's global economy with disperse manufacturers, suppliers, assembly factories, and customers, one can still identify these business processes, though with more complexity in terms of management and collaboration. In such a global economy, it has become more vital for the collaborating companies to be synchronized in order to increase efficiency and decrease error, and waste in general.

As a supply chain network expands, due to global competition or increase in demand, the complexity in terms of planning, management, and as such increases. This increase impacts the network reversely, meaning that when the manufacturer faces an increase in product/service demand, features, and so on, ideally it can adjust its resources to address the new needs. This adjustment is conveyed to the manufacturer's suppliers and now it is their turn to adjust their performance appropriately.

Customer-Oriented SCM

A supply chain consists of several linked organizations through which information, materials, financial assets, and other assets are flown. Any organization in this chain serves upstream companies while receiving assets from downstream organizations. All of these organizations coop-

Figure 1. The business processes within a supply chain (Source: Lambert, D. M. (Ed.). (2008). An executive summary of supply chain management: Processes, partnerships, performance (3rd ed.). Sarasota, FL: Supply Chain Management Institute. Used with permission. All rights reserved)

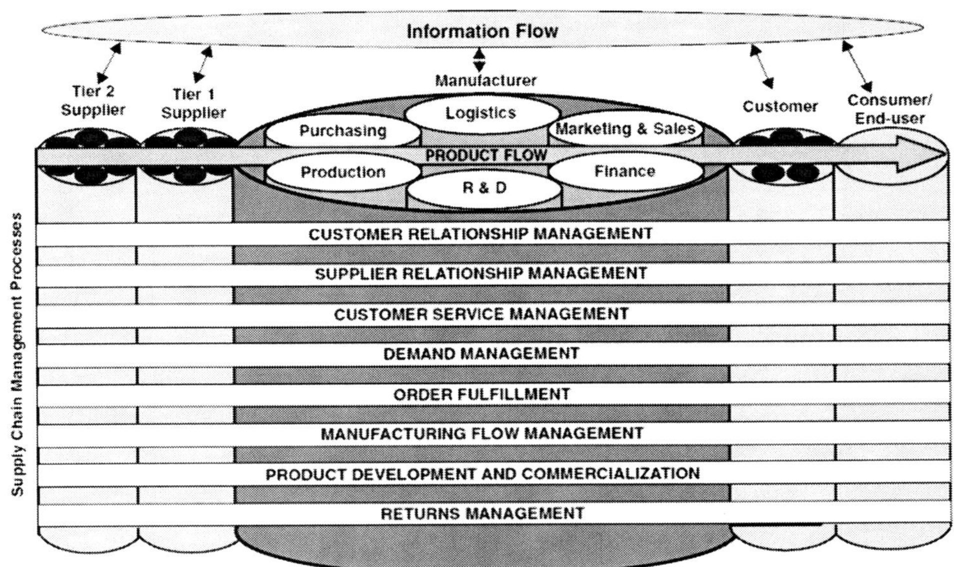

erate to address the ultimate customers' needs and demands, which can be individuals, or other organizations, as shown in Figure 2. In addition, one can identify two types of customers, namely internal and external.

It is important to note that customers' expectations and requirements change over time and therefore, it is critical that manufactures can response to these changes accordingly and on time. Although it may seem trivial to adopt change within a manufacturer's internal processes, it is not often the case. Depending on the complexity of the product/service's existing and new requirements, marketing requirements, cost, and as such, change implementation may take weeks to be fully implemented and integrated. However, such implementation cannot be completed without including vendors. For example, a seemingly simple change in the body of an automobile would require a certain die in the press to be changed, which means that the die manufacturer should design and manufacture it, which may require using different tools and materials that the die manufacturer needs to receive from its own suppliers. As seen, this chain of change and adjustment may continue backward to include third, fourth, and even more tiers of suppliers.

The ability to respond adequately to the changes in marketplace and in customers' requirement should be a common characteristic among all the constituents in a supply chain. Thus, it is relevant to discuss the concept of agile supply networks.

Agile Supply Chains

Agile Supply Chain Management has been defined by numerous authors in various papers. Hofman and Cecere (2005) first quote the dictionary for the definition of the word agile as, "moving quickly and easily; characterized by quickness, lightness, and ease of movement; nimble" (Hofman & Cecere, 2005, p. 18). They further go on to state that there are four dimensions that make a supply chain agile: speed, ease, predictability,

Figure 2. The relationship between a supply chain's internal organizations and the external customers

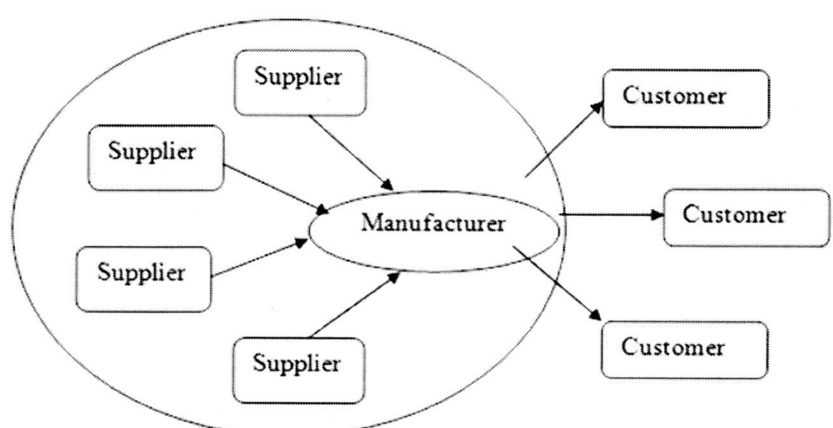

and quality. With respect to speed, Hofman and Cecere (2005) refer to an organization's ability to quickly identify changes in demand in an effort to correctly predict an appropriate and accurate supply chain response. With this in mind however, i.e., being capable of accurately predicting, an intelligent response does not necessarily mean that an organization has the ability to address the need. This is where ease comes into play. While an organization may be savvy enough to identify a correct action, it is not truly agile unless it can easily and efficiently contort itself into the supply chain predicated by the change in demand (or supply).

The company that is forward thinking enough to identify the need to realign, and then displays the ease of making that realignment, is a desirable one. However, it must be able to do so every time. A company that is aligned to produce reliably in three days is often more desirable than the one that can produce in two days 40% of the time and in six days the other 60%. Predictable results are paramount. Last, but certainly not least, is quality. This characteristic is obvious and requires very little explanation. An organization that can realign quickly and predictably is not an agile organization if the outputs are not of the highest quality.

Incorporating the three separate meanings, we define Agile Supply Chain Management as: the processes in managing and maintaining the supply chain with the ability to adjust quickly, accurately and predictably to the demands of clients and customers in an effort to produce a high-quality product and/or service. A supply chain that displays these characteristics is undoubtedly most resilient and best postured for success in an ever-changing global market.

While the characteristics of the agile supply chain were stated at a simplistic level, we would be remiss if we did not give credence to the following key characteristics: 1. Market sensitivity, equating to the "speed" mentioned above in that the chain should be able to quickly adjust to market demands, 2. Virtual, meaning that the various players in the supply chain should be easily linked via information systems, 3. Process Integration, indicating that an agile supply chain cannot achieve its full potential if all players in the chain do not coordinate together and 4. Network based, implying that the entire team must coordinate together in competition in order for the chain to compete in the current markets.

Becoming agile, an enterprise has to be agile in every part of its components and activities such as supply chain, organization, manufacturing and distribution. Agile supply chain can be considered to be structured under the goals of satisfying customers and employees within whom every organization can design its own business strategies, organizations, processes and information systems. The main emphasis of agile supply chain is on downstream collaboration with customers and collaboration with competitors and suppliers as a mean of integrating the total value creation process and building a virtual network of enterprises that behave like one great enterprise and try to satisfy the customer real needs as soon as possible (Fox, Chionglo, & Barbuceanu, 1993).

This emphasis leads to move from forecast driven supply chain to demand. Forecast driven supply chain is based on information sharing and integration between different organizations. The use of information technology to share data between buyers and suppliers and other related organizations is, in effect, creating a virtual supply chain. Virtual supply chains are information- based rather than inventory-based (Fox, Chionglo, & Barbuceanu, 1993). Information and, importantly, agile information systems are recognized as being a critical factor in achieving agility in the supply chain in a similar way as the flexible manufacturing systems made in the past, to agile manufacturing (Ching-Torng, Hero, & Yi-Hong, 2005). Agility-enabled attributes are supposed to be the aspects of agility content and to determine the entire supply chain behavior, so that agility enabled attributes enable the measuring of supply chain agility.

Integration in Agile SCM

To stay competitive, companies strive to achieve greater coordination and collaboration among supply chain partners in an approach called supply chain integration (Lee & Whang, 2001). Towill (1997) defines an integrated supply chain as a "seamless supply chain" where territorial boundaries between trading partners are eliminated allowing them to operate effectively as if they were part of one organization. And so Sohal (2003) claims that the basic components of integration typically include cooperation, collaboration, information sharing, trust, partnership, and shared technology. It is noticeable that integration can be applied to almost anything and at any level of the organization (Chan & Kumar, 2005). Christopher (1998) and Lambert, Stock, & Ellram (1998) define supply chain integration as following: "Supply chain integration is process integration upstream and downstream in the supply chain". According to Lambert, Stock, & Ellram (1998) there are seven key business processes that could be integrated across the supply chain: customer relationship management, customer service management, demand management, order fulfillment, manufacturing flow management, procurement and product development, and commercialization. The number of processes that should be integrated, or would be advantageous to be integrated, varies. In some cases linking just one key process is enough and in others linking multiple or all business processes is required. Thus, it should be carefully analyzed which business processes should be integrated in a supply chain. Supply chain integration is difficult for two main reasons (Ping, Zhou, & Chen, 2005): First, different companies in the supply chain may have different, conflicting objectives. Second, the supply chain is a dynamic system that evolves over time. Customer demand, supplier capabilities, and relationships in the supply chain evolve over time. According to Lee and Whang (2001), supply chain integration has four different perspectives, as shown in Table 1: information integration, planning synchronization, workflow coordination, and new business model.

The information integration is placed at the top of the supply chain integration. The integration cannot be complete without organizational integration, that is, tight linkage of the organizational relationships between companies in the supply chain. The critical questions of the supply chain integration are the choice of actors, with

Table 1. IT supply chain integration dimensions

Dimension	Elements	Benefits
Information integration	- Information sharing &transparency - Direct & real-time Accessibility	- Reduced bullwhip effect - Early problem detection - Faster response - Trust building
Synchronized Planning	- Collaborative planning, forecasting & replenishment - Joint design	- Reduced bullwhip effect - Lower cost - Optimized capacity - Utilization - Improved service
Workflow Coordination	- Coordinated production planning & operations, procurement, order processing, engineering change & design - Integrated, automated business processes	- Efficiency & accuracy gains - Fast response - Improved service - Earlier time to market - Expanded network
New Business Models	- Virtual resources - Logistics restructuring - Mass customization - New services - Click-and-mortar models	- Better asset utilization - Higher efficiency - Penetrate new markets - Create new products

whom it is critical to link, the choices of processes, which need to be linked with each of these actors, and the level of integration to each process link (Lambert, Stock, & Ellram, 1998). Organizational integration is achieved when a unified supply chain - where ideas, skills and culture are shared - is formed. The decision makers in multiple chain organizations are committed to collaborate in order to achieve common goals set for the supply chain (Christopher, 1998). Managing coordination among supply chain members, therefore, assumes significant importance. Cooper, Lambert, & Pagh (1997) argue that organizational integration can also be a catalyst for information integration (Christopher, 1998). The flatter organizations work better than cumbersome hierarchical ones and they are easier to link together electronically by information and communication technology (ICT) applications. In addition, ICT also provides an impetus for organizational structures. Information integration encompasses the sharing of relevant knowledge and information among members of a supply chain.

VALUE CREATION IN SUPPLY CHAINS

The value of a product/service is not limited to a single aspect. Rather, it is a package that includes all aspects such as performance, liability, service, and as such. Goetsch and Davis (2010) observe that the value of a product/service is the sum of the customer's perception on different factors including:

- Product/service quality
- The organization's personnel
- The organization's image
- Service provided by the organization
- The product/service price
- The product/service's overall cost

It is important to note that value is created as a sum by all the collaborating companies in a supply chain. Ironically, if the customer is unsatisfied with the product/service quality, more likely the manufacturer will be criticized. For example, a late delivery of a laptop may be due to a late delivery of a component caused by a supplier to the laptop manufacturer but the ultimate customer would more likely consider the manufacturer responsible for the late delivery. Womack and Jones (1996) mention that one reason companies find it difficult to obtain the right value in their final product is that each supplier along the supply chain tends to define value in its own needs. They suggest that the value must be jointly defined by all the participating companies in the supply chain.

Another important factor is the production cost. Traditionally, once a product is defined, the target cost will be determined based on the available resources and effort necessary to produce the product/service. Plus, the companies set the selling price based on what they think the market will bear (Womack & Jones, 1996). In terms of lean systems, i.e., a "waste-free" production system, the new approach is to take steps further to determine how a company can produce the product/service with least amount of waste (Womack & Jones, 1996). The waste is a general term that can be referred to anything, i.e., material, time, activity, etc., that does not add any value to the overall product/service total value. The impact of this new approach on a supply chain is tremendous. It requires all the companies to look at their internal processes to identify sources of waste and remove them. In addition, some non-value-adding processes, such as defective components, may be as a result of some common issues. In this case, the communication is the key factor to resolve the issue. It is needless to mention that all the communications, solutions, and as such must be documented and shared with the involved companies.

To create strategic value in today's fast changing and high velocity environment, the supply chain network of a company should enable the firm to continuously assess, alter and update its capabilities by adding, eliminating, reconfiguring, leveraging and synthesizing its resources. In general, developing and sustaining dynamic capabilities include interdependent processes such as new product development, making strategic decisions, and building new alliances to create strategic value for the company through reconfiguring resources into new value creating strategies (Eisnehardt & Martin, 2000). High velocity industries use dynamic business models with shifting actors that rely mostly on uniquely creating solutions by using successive approximations approach (iterative step-by-step solutions and analysis and improvements). However, high velocity industries lack stable structural boundaries that cause unpredictable emergent outcomes. The high velocity of the customers and other changes in the environment demand that the dynamic capabilities provided by the company's supply chain network not only should be aligned with the dynamics of the firm's internal/external environments, it should also be synchronized with the demand of its customers' evolving values, desires, and expectations, and its strategy and industry.

One could argue that the only way to compete and win in today's manufacturing or service industry is to adopt a methodology that will increase productivity, reduce cost, and resource needs and at the same time to eliminate wasteful inefficiencies through the entire supply chain network. Successful companies around the world have embraced lean concepts and have applied it in the entire supply chain to achieve the above objective.

Lean Value Stream and SCM

A relevant concept in SCM is Lean Value Stream (LVS). The value stream approach would be used to quickly identify and eliminate wastes that may well exist in the supply chain, starting from the resources such as water consumption, energy consumption, landfill avoidance, chemical consumption to logistics, manufacturing, and as such. The LVS approach focuses on finding quick hit projects that can be taken with very little time, effort, and investment which produce immediate savings and benefits. The LVS approach consists of seven steps which include financial assessment, initial education, benchmarking, supply chain sustainability strategy, action plan, team launch, and continuous improvement.

The core idea of lean concept is to maximize customer value while minimizing all types of waste. Simply, lean means creating more value for customers, both internal and external with fewer resources. A true lean organization understands what customer value is and focuses its processes to continuously increase it. Ideally, the ultimate goal is to provide perfect value to the customer through a perfect value creation process that has zero waste in the entire supply chain.

Lean organization always eliminates waste along the entire value streams, instead of at isolated points. This creates processes that need less human effort, less space, less capital, and less time to make products and services at far less costs and with much fewer defects, compared to traditional business systems. Lean organizations are able to respond to changing customer desires with high variety, high quality, low cost, and takes less time to adapt to a newer supply chain.

Lean applies to every business and every process. It is not a short term cost reduction program, but a way of thinking for the entire organization. All types of businesses, i.e., governmental and private, are using lean methodology as the way of doing business. Lean transformation is often used to characterize a company moving from a traditional old way of thinking, to lean thinking. This requires a complete transformation on how an organization conducts business. Value stream is a process for planning and linking lean initiatives through systematic data capture and analysis. Value stream process supports the transformation into a lean enterprise by providing a structure to ensure that the lean implementation team functions effectively. Any proven process can fail to achieve results if the people don't apply it properly or if they lack fundamental understanding of the nature of the process.

Another concept that is also widely talked about is sustainability which focuses on making the values created by the supply chain sustainable in terms of economics and environment. Sustainable development of a supply chain would meet the needs of the present without compromising the ability of the future generations to meet their own needs. Sustainability relates with economics, society, and environment. These three are considered the three legged stool model (Dawe & Ryan, 2003), as shown in Figure 3. The increase or decrease in the size of the length creates an unbalanced system. The commonality of all three is the generation of waste.

Lean value stream manufacturing would be considered a life cycle based effort on improving the life cycle of the product by having a better awareness of the product, improving the efficiency, environmental concerns, and sustainable innovations.

The lean value stream supply chain is a strategy for an organization to manage by fact and data. This approach is based on the financial data in order to identify where lean value stream concept could be applied. Unlike the quality control initiatives such as Six Sigma, Total Quality Management, sustainable lean value stream supply chain has the business objectives based on profitability from the business, as well as the environmental responsibility. Sustainable lean value stream supply chain looks at the complete life cycle of the product and assesses based on the product based on its design, process, and end of life of the product. It basically includes the forward supply chain and the reversible supply chain. The LVS approach to supply chain consists of seven steps (Mohammed & Sadique, 2010), which are shown in Figure 4.

The first and foremost step to apply lean value stream supply chain approach is the financial assessment. Understanding the big picture is very important to accurately identify and eliminate waste in the system. Financial analysis will help to understand the entire system better and also help to quantify the amount of waste in the system. First step in financial analysis is to identify all the processes one may want to study and to draw

Figure 3. Lean value stream supply chain concept application to sustainability

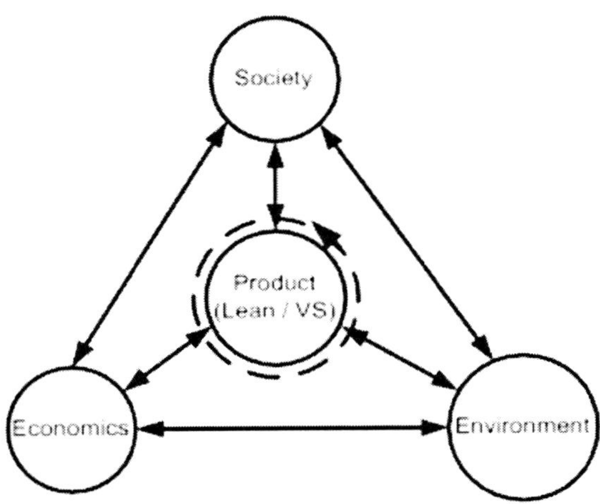

an initial process diagram for the entire organization with all the inputs and outputs (Figure 5).

Other steps to apply lean value stream supply chain include benchmarking and Value Stream Mapping. Benchmarking is used as a performance indicator, either in terms of cost, productivity, defects, or can be any form of measured parameter. In benchmarking, processes are compared to the best practices in the industry for improvement and unwanted actions identification. The Value Stream Mapping (VSM) method is a visualization tool used in lean manufacturing. Primarily it is used as a strategic planning tool and a change management tool. The goal of VSM is to identify, expose and decrease waste in the process. In lean manufacturing waste is any activity that does not add value to the final product. VSM method visually maps the flow of materials and information from the time products come in the back door as raw material, through all manufacturing process steps, and off the loading dock as finished products.

Mapping out the activities in the processes including all the inputs goes into each step of the process like, energy usage, water usage, and other data like cycle times, down times, in-process inventory, material moves, helps to visualize the current state of the process activities and guides towards the future desired state. Here are the five steps for developing a value stream map for the sustainability strategy:

1. Identify similar target product, product family, or service.
2. Draw a current state value stream map, which shows all the inputs like, water usage, electricity usage, delays, etc
3. Assess the current state value stream map in terms eliminating waste by reducing the amount of environmental waste
4. Draw a future state value stream map.
5. Develop an action plan to work toward the future state condition

Life Cycle Assessment

Life Cycle Assessment (LCA) is a technique that is used to assess the environmental aspects and potential impacts associated with a product, process, or service by compiling an inventory of relevant energy and material inputs and environmental releases, evaluating the potential impacts associated with identified inputs and releases; and interpreting the results to make a more informed decision. The functional unit is the central concept in the Life Cycle Assessment of the supply chain. The goal and scope definition is designed to obtain the required specification based on the product and process for the life cycle assessment study. Several Life cycle Assessment methodologies are used currently for developing the sustainability strategy (Bieda, 2007; Munier, 2005). For example, potential impacts due to green house gases (GHG) could be considered as one of the sustainability strategy. Selecting a strategy would depend upon where the type of product or process under consideration.

The International Organization for Standardization (ISO) has incorporated series of standards focusing on environmental management. Most

Figure 4. Steps in lean value stream supply chain

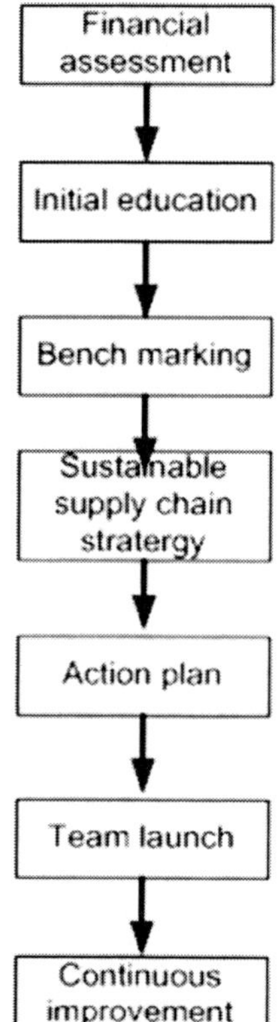

of the standards are included on the ISO 14040 series. The standards on the Life Cycle Assessment are as follows:

- ISO 14040: life cycle assessment, principles and framework
- ISO 14041: life cycle assessment, Goal and scope definition and life cycle inventory analysis
- ISO 14042: life cycle assessment, life cycle impact assessment

Figure 5. Organisational flow

- ISO 14043: life cycle assessment, life cycle interpretation

The International Standard Organization has been developing standards for LCA as a part of its 14000 series standards on environmental management. These standards address both technical and conceptual organization of the LCA.

CO-EVOLUTION IN GLOBAL SUPPLY CHAINS

The term co-evolution is a metaphor borrowed from biological sciences. In the context of supply chain networks, it means that as the interdependent elements of a supply chain network adapt to the successive changes in the environment (i.e., customers' changing values, desires and expectations), they also adapt to one another as well (Eisenhardt & Galunic, 2000). In order to create strategic value, supply chain networks may periodically make upgrades and changes in themselves. Successful creation of value that co-evolves with the customers' unique values, desires, and expectations along with other unpredictable changes defines the distinction between success and failure for supply chain networks.

In today's business environment, one may view supply chains as a network composed of suppliers, product developers, designers, product developers, distributors and customers. To enhance the strategic value creation processes of a company, a company's supply chain management should focus on four fundamental issues: 1. delivery of various flows, 2. product and service development, 3. operational efficiency, and 4. strategic coordination co-evolution.

1. Delivery of various flows: Effective delivery includes three types of flows (Akkermans, Bogerd, Yucesan, & van Wassenhove, 2003): information and knowledge, products and services, and financial and capital transactions. Information and knowledge flows include not only the intra-organizational flows of information and knowledge within the company, but also the flows of customer support, order coordination and tracing. Financial and capital flows include transmission of currencies, credits, order processing, billing information, sales, accounting, and legal documents. Products and materials flows include the delivery of products and materials between a company, its suppliers, and its customers.
2. Product and service development: Supply chain networks provide the resources needed to increase the overall capability of a company, particularly in products and services area. To create strategic value, the product and services should meet customers' changing values, desires and expectations. A company's supply chain network should enhance its capabilities to develop and offer unique products and services that its customers desire and value.
3. Operational efficiency: The operational efficiency is a critical element of a company's revenue margins. Providing the products and services in a cost effective way with minimum cycle-time are keys to managing a viable business (Gobeli, Koeing, & Mishra, 2002, p7). Therefore, supply chain network's operation is at the heart of a company's value creation efforts. Today, the increased automation and use of information systems has improved the efficiency and effectiveness of supply chain networks in terms of reducing costs, minimizing time and deviations. Therefore, increasing companies' operational efficiency.
4. The Process of Co-evolutions: In today's competitive business environment, strategic value is created by offering unique products and services that customers desire and value. This requires that companies and their supply chain networks should be capable of directly fulfilling their end-users' unique evolving values, desires and expectations. Adapting to those demands poses dynamic challenges in design, operation, and management of supply chain networks requiring solutions that co-evolve with the customers' unique values and expectations. Meeting these dynamic challenges require evolving collaboration and synergy among all the elements of a supply chain network. Therefore, an effective response to these challenges demands the supply chain network have the capacity to co-evolve with its customers' changing values, desires, and expectations. It also, requires that the supply chain network has the capacity to rapidly upgrade, reconfigure, leverage, and synthesize its resources to create unique strategic values that its customers value and desire. In today's high velocity and complex business environment, the capacity of companies' supply chain network to meet a variety of demands defines its success or failure.

The design, operation, and management of supply chain networks which are to be built to co-evolve, easily scale up and down, reconfigure dynamically, and create strategic value efficiently, require enormous consideration and analysis. The challenge is how a company should transform from a company-centric traditional supply chain to a modern complex supply chain customer-centric networks that co-evolves with its customers' unique values, desires and expectations. A critical factor in responding to this dynamic challenge is to build flexible architecture using information technology throughout the entire supply chain network (Prahalad & Ramaswamy, 2004, p.218; Prahalad & Krishnan, 2008, p.148).

Another challenge is to build a supply chain network with modular supply chain architecture. A modular architecture in supply chain networks supports both the capacity to change and reduce complexity. Building a supply chain network with modular architecture that reduces the complexity and using flexible information technology also make its operations, management, and governance easier. According to Prahalad and Ramaswamy (2004), management of governance of supply chain networks can encounter the following problems: the increasing complexity of managing networked relationships, managing different levels of collaboration, adapting to high velocity environment, the demand for decentralization, quest for zero latency, and the need to balance flexibility and control.

Agent-Based SCM

Globalization and global marketplace necessitate distant transaction and interaction among various constituents. Supply chain networks are not an exception. In this regard, the role of information technology and web-based transactions are vital. It is also, important to note that there must be a harmony among a company's information system, business processes, and organization's structure. At the supply chain level, however, it is equivalently important that such a harmony exits among various constituent companies in terms of the information system. Brown and Venkatesh (2003) discuss that how FedEx Corporation, as the biggest express transportation company in the world with approximately 30% of the market share has aligned its information systems with its organization structure and business processes to do business on the Internet. As they discussed, FedEx's information systems and networks were initially developed for improving internal operations but later on, FedEx established the hub-and-spokes concept and combined it with its centralized information systems. The system, called the Customer, Operations, Service, Master Online System (COSMOS) was the first centralized system in the industry implemented to track packages (Brown & Venkatesh, 2003).

The Internet enables the use of other supporting technologies, which not only transmit information but also share information based on the intended meaning and the semantics of the data. One of these technologies is agent software technology, which has been considered as an important approach for developing industrial distributed systems. Agent technology enables a flexible and dynamic coordination of distributed entities in business networks. It changes the metaphor for human-computer interaction from direct manipulation by the user to indirect management of background agent processes because intelligent agents can autonomously perform a lot of coordination and everyday tasks on behalf of their users (Fischer, Muller, Heimig, & Scheer, 1996). There is no unique and universally-used definition for the term "agent". The definition depends on the environment and the use of agents. The concept of agent is usually defined as follows (Wooldridge, 1999):"An agent is a computer system that is situated in some environment, and that is capable of autonomous action in that environment in order to meet its design objectives." The two important aspects of agents are their ability to operate asynchronously, act independently on behalf of the user, and that they co-operate and communicate with each other as needed using a specific language. They are dedicated to a specific purpose and carry out some set of operations in order to accomplish task. In order to be flexible, the agents in the software system must have the following properties (Wooldridge, & Jennings, 1995):

- Autonomy: agents operate without the direct intervention of humans and have some kind of control over their actions and internal state.

- Social: agents interact when appropriate, with other artificial agents and humans via some kind of agent communication language in order to address their own problems and to help others with their activities.
- Responsive: agents perceive their environment (which may be the physical world, a user, a collection of agents, the Internet, etc.) and respond in a timely fashion to changes that occur in it.
- Proactive: agents do not simply act in response to their environment; they are rather able to exhibit opportunistic, goal-directed behavior by taking the initiative where appropriate (Wooldridge, 1999).

Agent-based supply chain coordination has been proved to be an effective mechanism to improve the performance of SCM (Kwon, & Lee, 2002). It is a generic and common way of implementation integrated SCM. In this method, SCM will be divided into a set of different activities and each one will be managed with special intelligent software agents (Fox, Chionglo, & Barbuceanu, 1993). The supply chain is managed by a set of intelligent agents, each responsible for one or more activities in the supply chain, and each interacting with other agents in the planning and execution of their responsibilities (Kaihara, 2003).

As Christopher (1998) mentioned, to be agile, an enterprise should be: market sensitive, virtual, network-based, and integrated. Furthermore, a multi agent-based framework for agile SCM emphasize on these properties for becoming agile:

- High collaboration and integration between related firms involve supply chain based on information and communication technology and information sharing between their information systems such as databases, to build an integrated virtual enterprise (Network based, Virtual).
- Vast and accurate vision of the market, customers needs and interests and being aware of the competitors status, public interest, market tendency, current and future orientation, being able to forecast the real future demand, and being ready before the orders arrive (market sensitive).
- Having agile organization, selecting agile alliances, agile partners, and agile suppliers (Tarokh, &Mehryar, 2006).

An enterprise needs to continuously evaluate and assess their own organization's agility, partners' and suppliers' agility, and analyze the situation in order to identify barriers to agility. When an enterprise forecasts the future demand, it should define the minimum agility level to each required part of the product which has to be prepared by suppliers based on the inventory level, accuracy of the forecast, the market orientation, business operation environments, and as such. The organization can select suitable suppliers from current or potential ones having agile criteria for each raw material, which satisfy the required level of agility. Forecasting the future demand accurately and in details is not possible but one can predict the real demand as accurate as possible using intelligent agents (Lambert, Stock, & Ellram, 1998).

The integrated agile SCM is composed of a set of cooperating agents, where each agent performs one or more supply chain management functions, and coordinates its decisions with other relevant agents. These are two types of agents: *functional agents* and *information agents*. Functional agent's plan and/or control activities in the supply chain. Information agents support other agents by providing information and communication services (Fox, Chionglo, & Barbuceanu, 1993). The merging of these two functions and the inclusion of some activities found in Inventory Management and Activity Planning is possible with the availability of more sophisticated planning and scheduling algorithms.

The dynamics of the environment make cooperative behavior as an important factor in integrating supply chain agents. In order to optimize supply chain decisions, an agent cannot make a locally optimal decision, but must determine the affect its decisions will have on other agents. Then choose an optimum agent that is responsible for a set of functions or activities in the agile supply chain (Fox, Chionglo, & Barbuceanu, 1993). Each agent stores information and knowledge locally and it may access information and knowledge throughout the network. It has assumed that the agents are in a heterogeneous environment; hence, their interactions are made through message-based transactions (Fox, Chionglo, & Barbuceanu, 1993). Supply chain agents exist within an Enterprise Information Architecture (EIA). The EIA provides a distributed information environment where information may be stored anywhere in the network. The EIA manages the consistency of information. Other information, in which copies are stored locally by agents, may develop inconsistencies and are of no concern to the EIA. The EIA provides each agent with automated information acquisition and distribution. When an agent requests information, the EIA will find it. When an agent creates information of interest to others, the EIA will distribute it to those agents that wish to know. The EIA provides the "right information in the right way" to the decision makers (Fox, Chionglo, & Barbuceanu, 1993). At the core of the EIA and the supply chain management system lies a generic reusable enterprise model. For integration of supply chain agents should minimizes ambiguity and maximizes understanding and precision in communication. The enterprise model will also support "deductive query processing". Many of the terms in the generic model will be defined using Prolog axioms. These axioms will automate the answering of a significant number of questions raised by the system's users, thereby reducing software development costs (Fox, Chionglo, & Barbuceanu, 1993).

CONCLUSION AND FUTURE RESEARCH DIRECTIONS

This chapter reviewed the concept of co-evolution and agility in supply chain networks and how other concepts such as value creation and customer satisfaction are related to co-evolution. Several management and academic writers have recently asserted the importance of agility in the value creation processes in supply chains' designs, operations, management, or value creation processes. However, we believe that the relevant factor for supply chains' success is not agility alone. Rather, there is additional critical factor such as the co-evolutionary processes within supply chain. That is, in addition to agility, the co-evolution of the various disaggregated parts of supplying is also necessary to improve its value creation process. Therefore, we introduced the important role of co-evolutionary processes that can contribute to successful agile value creation processes and survival of supply chains in our dynamic business environment.

The following recommendations for future research flows logically from our study and represents what we believe to be knowledge gaps in design, operation, management, or value creation processes of supply chains that should be bridged. Our Future research recommendation list can be summarized as follows:

- Develop a comprehensive methodology for agile value creation in supply chains that is systemic in nature. Such a methodology would draw relevant knowledge from various disciplines to produce a complete, efficient and effective methodology for better design, operation, and management of global supply chain networks.
- Develop a systemic and integrated approach for assessing the importance of co-evolutionary processes in large scale and globally disaggregated supply chain networks.

- Examine the concept of "successful value creation" within global supply chain networks and its relationship to factors such as co-evolution of different segments of supply chains to see how global supply chain networks arrive at the conclusion that an undertaking is successful or unsuccessful in their value creations efforts

ACKNOWLEDGMENT

The authors would like to thank Ms. Missy Dubbs for her contributions in editing and reviewing the book chapter.

REFERENCES

Akkermans, H. A., Bogerd, P., Yucesan, E., & van Wassenhove, L. N. (2003). The impact of ERP on supply chain management: Exploratory findings from European Delphi study. *European Journal of Operational Research, 146*, 284–301. doi:10.1016/S0377-2217(02)00550-7

Besterfield, D. H., Besterfield-Michna, C., Besterfield, G., & Besterfield-Sacre, M. (2002). *Total quality management* (3rd ed.). Prentice Hall.

Bieda, B. (2007). *The use of life cycle assessment (LCA) conception of Mittal steel Poland SA energy generation – Krakow plant case study*. First International Conference on Energy and sustainability. Wessex Institute of Technology Press.

Brown, S. A., & Venkatesh, V. (2003). Building a successful business: The FedEx story. *Communications of the ACM, 46*(4), 84–89. doi:10.1145/641205.641210

Chan, F. T. S., & Kumar, N. (2005). Global supplier development considering risk factors using fuzzy extended AHP based approach. *Omega: The International Journal of Management Science, 37*(4), 417–431.

Ching-Torng, L., Hero, C., & Yi-Hong, T. (2005). Agility evaluation using fuzzy logic. *International Journal of Production Economics, 101*(2), 353–368.

Christopher, M. (1998). *Logistics and supply chain management: Strategies for reducing cost and improving service*. Prentice-Hall.

Cooper, M. C., Lambert, D. M., & Pagh, J. D. (1997). Supply chain management: More than a new name for logistics. *The International Journal of Logistics Management, 8*(1), 1–14. doi:10.1108/09574099710805556

Dawe, N., & Ryan, K. (2003). The faulty three legged stool model of sustainable development. *Conservation Biology, 17*(5), 1458–1460. doi:10.1046/j.1523-1739.2003.02471.x

Eisenhardt, K., & Galunic, D. C. (2000). Coevolving at last, a way to make synergies work. *Harvard Business Review*, 91–101.

Eisnehardt, K., & Martin, J. A. (2000). Dynamic capabilities: What are they? *Strategic Management Journal, 21*, 1105–1121. doi:10.1002/1097-0266(200010/11)21:10/11<1105::AID-SMJ133>3.0.CO;2-E

Fischer, K., Muller, J. P., Heimig, I., & Scheer, A. W. (1996). Intelligent agents in virtual enterprises. *First International Conference on Practical Applications of Intelligent Agents and Multi-Agent Technology (PAAM)*, London, (pp. 205–223).

Fox, M. S., Chionglo, J. F., & Barbuceanu, M. (1993). *The integrated supply chain management system. Internal Report*. Dept. of Industrial Engineering, University of Toronto.

Gobeli, D. H., Koeing, H. F., & Mishra, C. S. (2002). Strategic value creationIn Phan, P. (Ed.), *Technology entrepreneurship* (pp. 3–16). Greenwich, CT: Information Age Publishing.

Goetsch, D. L., & Davis, S. B. (2010). *Quality management for organizational excellence: Introduction to total quality* (6th ed.). Upper Saddle River, NJ: Prentice Hall.

Hofman, D., & Cecere, L. (2005). The agile supply chain. *The Supply Chain Management Review, November,* 18-19.

Kaihara, T. (2003). Multi-agent based supply chain modeling with dynamic environment. *International Journal of Production Economics, 85,* 263–269. doi:10.1016/S0925-5273(03)00114-2

Kwon, O. B., & Lee, K. C. (2002). MACE: Multi-agents coordination engine to resolve conflicts among functional units in an enterprise. *Expert Systems with Applications, 23,* 9–21. doi:10.1016/S0957-4174(02)00023-4

Lambert, D. J., Stock, J. R., & Ellram, L. M. (1998). *Fundamentals of logistics management.* McGraw-Hill.

Lambert, D. M. (Ed.). (2008). *An executive summary of supply chain management: Processes, partnerships, performance* (3rd ed.). Sarasota, FL: Supply Chain Management Institute.

Lee, H., & Whang, S (2001). *E-business and supply chain integration.* Stanford Global Supply Chain Management Forum.

Li, C. (2009). Agile supply chain: Coming in volatile markets. *Management Science and Engineering, 3*(2).

Mohammed, J., & Sadique, A. (2010). *Lean value stream manufacturing for sustainability.* 8th Global Conference for Sustainable Manufacturing, Abu Dhabi, UAE.

Munier, N. (2005). *Introduction to sustainability: Road to a better future.* Springer Publications.

Ping, L., Zhou, Z., & Chen, Y. (2005). Study on coordination in multi-agent-based agile supply chain management. *The Fourth International Conference on Machine Learning and Cybernetics,* Guangzhou, (pp. 18-21).

Prahalad, C. K., & Ramaswamy, V. (2004). *The future of competition.* Harvard Business Press.

Sohal, A. S., Power, D. J., & Terziovski, M. (2003). Integrated supply chain management from the wholesaler's perspective: Two Australian case studies. *International Journal of Physical Distribution & Logistics Management, 32*(2), 96–109. doi:10.1108/09600030210421714

Stock, J. R., Boyer, S. L., & Harmon, T. (2010). Research opportunities in supply chain management. *Journal of the Academy of Marketing Science, 38,* 32–41. doi:10.1007/s11747-009-0136-2

Supply Chain Management Terms and Glossary. (2010). Retrieved on December, 3, 2010, from http://cscmp.org/digital/glossary/glossary.asp

Tapping, D., Luyster, T., & Shuker, T. (2002). *Value stream management.* New York, NY: Productivity Press.

Tarokh, M. J., & Mehryar, M. (2006). Multi-agent based framework for agile supply chain management. *Proceedings of the 2006 IEEE International Conference on System of Systems Engineering,* Los Angeles, CA, USA.

Towill, D. R. (1997). The seamless supply chain – The predator's strategic advantage. *International Journal of the Techniques of Manufacturing, 13*(1), 37–56.

Womack, J. P., & Jones, D. T. (1996). *Lean thinking.* New York, NY: Simon & Schuster.

Wooldridge, M. (1999). Intelligent agentsIn Weiss, G. (Ed.), *Multiagent systems.* Cambridge, MA: MIT Press.

Wooldridge, M., & Jennings, N. R. (1995). Intelligent agents: Theory and practice. *The Knowledge Engineering Review*, *10*(2), 115–152. doi:10.1017/S0269888900008122

KEY TERMS AND DEFINITIONS

Agile: "Moving quickly and easily; characterized by quickness, lightness, and ease of movement; nimble" (Hofman & Cecere, 2005, p. 18).

Agile Supply Chain Management: The processes in managing and maintaining the supply chain with the ability to adjust quickly, accurately and predictably to the demands of clients and customers in an effort to produce a high-quality product and/or service.

Co-Evolution: In the context of supply chain networks, it means that as the interdependent elements of a supply chain network adapt to the successive changes in the environment (i.e., customers' changing values, desires and expectations), they also adapt to one another as well (Eisenhardt & Galunic, 2000).

Integrated Supply Chain: Towill (1997) defines it as a "seamless supply chain" where territorial boundaries between trading partners are eliminated allowing them to operate effectively as if they were part of one organization.

Supply Chain Management: "Encompasses the planning and management of all activities involved in sourcing and procurement, conversion, and all logistics management activities. Importantly, it also includes coordination and collaboration with channel partners, which can be suppliers, intermediaries, third-party service providers, and customers." (Supply Chain Management Terms and Glossary, 2010).

Chapter 7
Engineer-to-Order:
A Maturity Concurrent Engineering Best Practice in Improving Supply Chains

Richard Addo-Tenkorang
University of Vaasa, Finland

Ephrem Eyob
Virginia State University, USA

ABSTRACT

General Engineer-to-Order (ETO) design of product capacity projects among many others, includes design for large electric machine, huge centrifugal pumps, diesel/natural fuel power plant engines, steam turbine, boiler, ship power, et cetera. ETO is basically a product development process, which starts with a product specification and finishes with an engineering design as its deliverable. It rarely includes manufacturing processes. The main drawback is with issues concerning its long lead-time. Research shows that an excessive lead-time is more often than not caused directly or indirectly by factors related to the design phase. This chapter thus, endeavours to introduce a best practice concurrent approach for reducing the lead-time at an engineer-to-order product design/development stage by seeking to integrate business information technology systems in the design and operational phases. It also introduces a new concurrent best practice approach by way of seeking to integrate other related business systems, e.g., (Enterprise Resource Planning (ERP)) such as (Enterprise Service Architecture (ESA) application processes with Service-Oriented Architecture (SOA)) as a platform for applications and processes for effective communication. Furthermore, the chapter presents and discusses a model of classical concurrent engineering (CE) ETO operational process. ETO key elements, ETO success factors, and series of state of the art ETO classical ERP engineering design tools, as well as the "best practice" product life cycle are all discussed.

DOI: 10.4018/978-1-4666-0246-5.ch007

INTRODUCTION TO ETO FROM A CONCURRENT ENGINEERING PERSPECTIVE

Industrial manufacturing companies producing engineered products on an engineer to order (ETO) in a concurrent engineering approach (i.e. partners from various divisions in the organizations) have traditionally found business opportunities. Through the design and product development expertise and an ability to respond to demands for customisation with improved product performance, customers are increasingly seeking for more affordable prices and a much reduced lead-times, which also require improved manufacturing efficiency. These companies are thus being driven to improve the integration of the design, manufacturing and procurement functions (Cameron, and Braiden, 2004). In order to facilitate this improvement in the integration of the various partners involved, and to improve the overall product time to enhance and better define the product as well as properly document the design process, a concurrent engineering process needs to be adopted in the supply chain management (SCM). Concurrent engineering process which very much operates in the same vain as a collaborative engineering process, is a process in which the appropriate partner organizations are committed to integrating their system processes to work interactively. Thus, to visualize, develop and implement engineered products and programs that correspond with their pre-determined objectives. Concurrent engineering in this sense is moderate collaborative engineering approach that is much more focused on the engineering product design process of concurrent cross-functional partner organizations together in order to create products that are much better, much affordable and with a much reduced lead-time.

Engineer to order products may require a specific set of item numbers, bills of material (BOM), and routings; these are usually complex with long lead times. Customers are also normally heavily involved throughout the entire design process and manufacturing process for an engineer to order a product. It is usually limited to an engineering design process which involves the tasks of engineering analysis, concept design, architectural design, detailed design and manufacturing process design. It does not include the manufacturing phase of materials acquisition, fabrication and assembly. In a traditional ETO operation, product functionality is the major design focus (Chen, 2006).

The product design process phase takes enormous time of the entire process lead-time. Thus, the new and improved ETO – CE process flow model approach proposed in this chapter seeks to reduce the long lead-time by its CE approach of all the partners as well as communicating and exchanging product design information on a common platform. This new improved approach as compared with the classic ETO process flow approach will bring all partners in the design supply chains together both locally and globally by using a system oriented architecture (SOA) – extensible mark-up language (XML) communications on a common platform across the world-wide-web. Thus, providing an opportunity for even different design teams in different organizations, with different SCM information systems (IS) to link-in easily and faster to resolve any design issues. Thereby, reducing any delay in design processes, which is the cause of long lead-times in classical ETO processes. ETO – CE approach in improving product design supply chains enhances an industrial manufacturing organization's ability to gain effective and efficient control of the upstream through to the downstream of their ETO product design processes and assume a dynamic concurrent approach to supply chain rather than a reflexive to lead-time threats. The follow section gives more elaboration of how ETO – CE integration into supply chains could improve the chain.

Supply Chain: ETO-CE Process Integration

ETO's successful integration into manufacturing supply chain is by efficiently and effectively incorporating the various engineer-to-order activities and processes from the upstream in the supply chain (suppliers) through to the downstream (end customers). Considering the current global competitive pressures, manufacturing industries have followed through with series of business strategies and different approaches in their bid to enhance the value for the end customer (Kim, 2005; Chopra and Meindl, 2001). Industrial manufacturers who succeed globally continue to adapt, develop and improve their supply chain network value as the market condition becomes more progressive (Kumar et al., 2006; Reichhart, and Holweg, 2007).

The significance of speed in product development activities and processes, lean manufacturing practices, quality, cost and flexibility in the supply chain should be well supported and managed by advanced infrastructures in supplier sourcing, logistic management, information systems and technologies as well as very good customer relations management (Gunasekaran et al., 2008). Thus, value in ETO products is realised in product development of the supply chain, mostly in a concurrent approach through collaborative partnerships and integrations that recognize contributions from the product development process, procedure, information, finance, management of knowledge, innovation and relationship management (Barber, 2009). Therefore, the approach of successfully integrating ETO methodologies enhances supply chain flexibility and value. This reflects the current state of embedding process improvement into the supply chain operations of product development a as being proactive in managing supply-demand fulfillment concurrently (Lee, 2004; Ketchen et al., 2008; O'Marah and Hofman, 2010; Porter, 1990).

Integration strategy programs, applications and processes involving all stakeholders in product development (i.e. customers, suppliers, marketers, accountants, design engineers, production engineers, manufacturing engineers, etc.) during the capacity management, enhances the ETO supply chain to a shorter delivery lead-time on customer specification and orders (Swafford et al., 2006). Customer relationship effect in ETO methodology integration in the supply chain increases understanding in customer demand, managing complaints and improving customer satisfaction which critical responsive element through the ETO value chain (Li et al., 2006; Holweg, 2005). According to Zhou and Benton (2007) quality information sharing on a common and assessable platform among stakeholders enhances ETO supply chain practices such as just-in-time (JIT) and lean lead-time delivery. Thus, the capability to collect, disseminate various data, information from customers across ETO supply chain nodes concurrently will enable internal manufacturing strategies to respond effectively to the needs of customers. This paper presents a maturity concurrent engineering "best practice" approach in ETO methodology in product development. An improved CE- ETO model proposed in the subsequent sections in a concurrent approach is expected to reduce the lead-time making ETO methodology leaner by also successfully integrating enterprise resource processes and applications in the ETO supply chain.

Thus, new trends reunite technical and non-technical disciplines such as product engineering partners, marketing/brokers and accounting/ financial controllers. This collaboration aims at satisfying the customer. Therefore, the product design partners in industrial organizations must also collaborate in defining and analysing the product specification aimed at satisfying the end customer. Hence, the approach to ETO process, concurrently in a collaborative approach, mainly dwells with the product design aspect. ETO product and the engineering process lead-time is well managed and compensated for in the product design stage which turns to take a chunk of the process time. Engineer to order is a manufacturing process whereby finished products are built to unique customer specifications. These engineering product design processes are elaborated in detail in the following sections from engineering analysis to manufacturing process design.

Engineering Analysis

Engineering analysis is the aspect of engineering product design, which involves technical investigative processes and theories to reveal the properties and circumstances of an engineering system, product or concept design/structure. Engineering analysis also involves the tool and methods required in the technical investigative processes or theories. This when successfully investigated could lead to an engineering design or ironically to a simply failed process that could always be re-analysed to find out where the failures lay in the process? Therefore, this analysis must always be carried through before proceeding to produce a concept design of an ETO product to rectify the huge cost which comes with failures in the engineering systems and process design.

Concept Design

Concept design is the very first stage of an engineering design work where all the engineering drawings are mainly centered. These concept designs consist of very basic engineering 2D drawings and sectional views. The 2D engineering draws and sectional views are later developed along the process line to a more detailed 3D engineering draws with their sectional views as well. Concept design in an engineering design process has certain specific stages of conceptual design work stages that are required to transfer information into the needed requirements for the detailed engineering design of a specific engineering product. These stages include a description of the general concept, definition of the requirements or specifications of the concept plan and description of what the concept is aimed at realizing at the end as well as lists of activities for the concept. A good conceptual design comprises of the creation of a proposal or an initiative, the investigation of that proposal, or an initiative into a representation of the proposal. On this note, conceptual design can range from basic blueprint line diagrams to structural 2D engineering drawings. Thus, if the concepts are not clearly drawn, the proposal will not be completely understood, and the result potentially will be compromised.

Architectural Design

Architectural design means often the same as engineering design. It is the application of engineering design standards to engineering product design works and bill of materials (BOM) of the detailed design. Architectural design is the state in engineering product design where the conceptual design is further developed, modified or processed in a more detailed design capable of being sent to the next stage of product design.

Detailed Design

This stage in the engineering product design stage is where the detail engineering design is achieved by the design team. By using both the requirement specification (conceptual design), and the architectural specification (architectural design), provided in the previous stages of the design process. The outcome at this stage of the process will be a detailed design which will be featured in detail, describing the interfaces and functions provided by the engineering design product. This detailed design will then serve as the basis for the manufacturing process stage.

Manufacturing Process Design

This is the stage of the engineering product design where the detail design is processed for manufacturing. Material request and acquisitions are determined at this stage for fabrication and product assembly. Thus, the process and technology analysis, assembly process planning and component process planning in the detail design stages are all implemented at this stage.

The following section introduces some of the benefits for CE approach in ETO to improve the design chain and reduce the lead-times. It discusses existing research on these industrial manufacturing approaches and also their collaboration and integration successes as well as the various stages of a product life cycle (PLC).

BACKGROUND REVIEW

Over the past decade industries in almost all markets have been facing a boosting level of competitiveness. There are many reasons for this, but most of them can be followed to some of the following principal trends: shortening product life cycles, globalization of the market, rapid technological changes, environmental issues, and higher complexity of products, customers demanding products with more features, higher quality, lower cost, and demand for more and more customized products. Concurrent Engineering (CE) is an integrated product development approach that emphasises the response to customer expectations by producing better, cost effective and much faster product development process. It also supports multidisciplinary team values of co-operation and trust; thus, sharing and exchanging required knowledge and information in a manner that will enhance decision making processes and also emphasis on simultaneous consideration during the design stage and all the other Product Life Cycle (PLC) aspects of the product development. PLC is the progress of a product from its concept through to its development and introduction to the market and then its withdrawal from the market or final disposal. One of the most salient means to reduce development time is through the use of "concurrent engineering." Concurrent engineering is defined by the Institute for Defence Analysis (IDA) as "the systematic approach to the integrated concurrent design of products and related processes, including manufacture and support".

Thus, PLC management confronts the need to balance fast response to changing consumer demands with competitive pressure to seek cost reductions in sourcing, manufacturing and distribution. It needs to be based on a close alignment between customer-facing functions (e.g. marketing, sales, customer service) and supply functions (e.g., purchasing, manufacturing, and logistics) (Combs, 2004; Conner, 2004; O'Marah, 2003). Hence, Product life cycle (PLC) management has become a strategic priority in many company's boardrooms (Teresko, 2004). According to Yassine, and Braha, (2003); Concurrent engineering (CE) is an engineering management philosophy and a set of operating principles that guide a product development process through to an accelerated successful completion. In general, CE values rely on a single, but powerful, principle that encourages the incorporation of the later stages of production concerns into the upstream phases of a development process chain such as during the engineering-to-order (ETO) phase of a product development, etc. This would lead to shorter development times, thus, improving product quality, and lowering development–production costs.

Concurrent engineering is hereby aimed at the timely availability of critical design information to all the design development participants. For most intricate engineering tasks all significant information required by a specific design development team cannot be completely available at the start of that task. Therefore, CE requires the most of such information and the ability to share and communicate useful information on a timely basis with the right design experts. The concept of concurrent engineering (CE) has been known for quite a while now, and it has been widely recognized as a major enabler of fast and efficient product development. This chapter examines the extent to which CE "best practices", as obtained from a broad literature review, are being used effectively in companies globally. Some of the positive impact of formal CE programs is proven by previous research (Portioli-Staudacher, *et al.*, 2003). Figure 1 illustrates the stages of a product life cycle (PLC) highlighting the inputs and deliverables in one completed flow process with intermittent decision loop at each milestone stage of the flow process.

As the product development stage is wiry in market size but there is a growth supply chain, it is imperative that substantial research and development costs be incurred in getting the product to this stage. In addition, marketing costs may be too high to just test the market or undergo commencement promotion and set up distribution outlets. Therefore, it is highly unlikely that industries will make profits on products at the development stage when rigorous work has not been duly than to fulfil all the required customer requirements. Products at this stage have to be carefully monitored to ensure that they start to grow and pick in the market. Otherwise, the best option may be to withdraw or end the product. The need for immediate profit is not a pressure as the lack of it is an expectation at this stage. The product is promoted to create awareness of the market as well as satisfying customer requirements. Thus, if the product is not competitive, an initial pricing strategy is employed to build pricing momentum to maximise profits. Limited numbers of product will be available in few outlets of a distribution chain. Therefore, development stage should encompass a number of activities that will include:

Figure 1. Introduction stage (input and deliverables) - Product life cycle (PLC) - Input and deliverables (BizAgi process modeller)

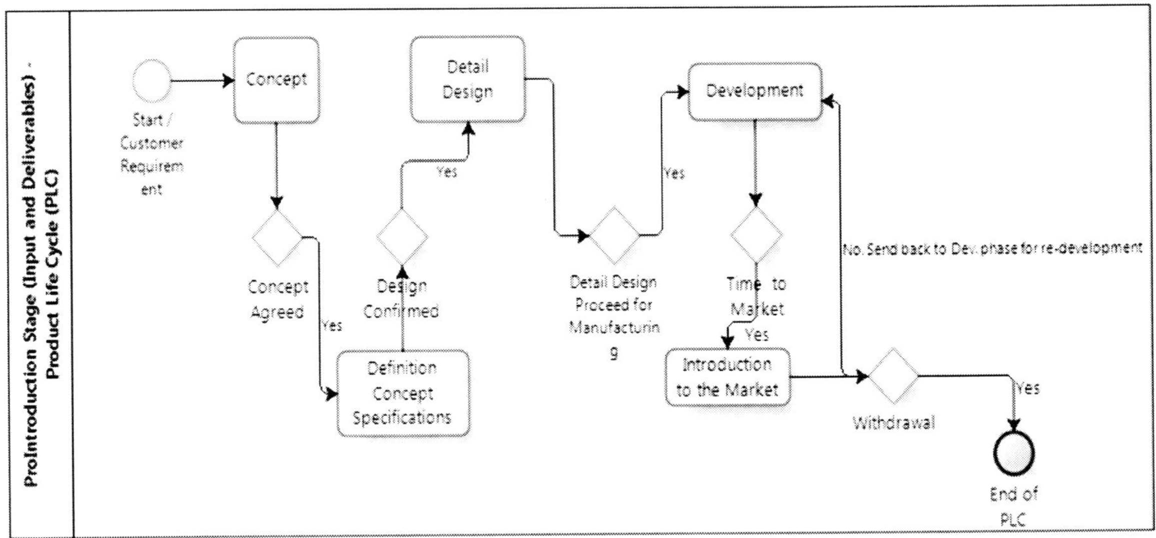

- Concept: Overview of the customer requirement that an opportunity seeks to address, supported by evidence of market need.
- Definition: High-level definition of customer requirements and analysis of a business opportunity.
- Design: Analysis of customer requirements creating project plan and detailed product specification.
- Development: Data and software (CAD/CAM) development.
- Development Testing: Testing of the product against pre-defined test schedules to ensure satisfactory performance against customer requirements.
- Development of pricing.
- Development of user guide
- Introduction of the product to the market (Time to Market). etc.

Product lifecycle management and the efficiency of information reuse relies on the definition and management of corresponding information and communication between various product design teams in various manufacturing organizations. Collaborating and sharing information concurrently in the ETO supply chains ensures the consistency and traceability of product information throughout the product lifecycle. The sales-delivery process of engineer-to-order (ETO) products presents a great potential for design reuse, i.e. the reuse of previously validated design solutions in the design of new product variants according to customer-specific requirements (Brie`re-Co^te´, *et al,* 2010). Much as lean manufacturing (LM) in manufacturing organizations is currently enjoying its second prime, manufacturers in several industries are implementing lean practices to keep pace with the competition and achieve better results by reducing product design lead-times significantly Demeter, and Mateusz (2011).

The principles of concurrent engineering (CE) in the same vein as that of lean production has enabled manufacturing organisations to significantly improve their competitiveness. The application of CE principles has enabled many organisations to simultaneously improve productivity, quality and customer service (Riezebos, *et al,* 2009). Similar benefits have been achieved through the integration of information technology (IT) in ETO processes. Thus, integrating IT and ETO – CE principles are seen to be interdependent and complimentary by some; whilst others have seen that as the approaches as being mutually exclusive. This section thus, presents reviews of the use of some ERP systems could collaborate within the ETO processes to concurrently improve the supply chain. The following section elaborates further on the trends and perspective in ETO new product introduction and development (NPI/D). In order to meet the ever increasing customer demand and preferences is well documented. Therefore, customisation has been stimulated as a source of competitive advantage for ETO industrial manufactures. Despite these factors, most of the researched work in operations and supply chain management has side-lined the need for improvement of the 'engineer- to-order' (ETO) supply chain sector (Gosling, and Naim, 2009). Hence the following section will highlight a few of the essence of the global trends and perspectives in ETO new product introduction and development supply chains.

CE Global Trends and Perspectives in ETO

According to Tennant, and Roberts, (2000), an effective New Product Introduction and Development (NPI/D) process, which is a concurrent process, can enhance an organisation's competitiveness. This can be done by compressing product development lead-times, and enabling the upstream and downstream processes in a supply chain to be considered when taking decisions at the product concept design phase. The application of Concurrent Engineering (CE) (or Integrated Product Development [IPD]) is gradually becoming the norm for developing and introducing new products to the market place (Ainscough and Yazdani, 2000). However, the degree to which companies have implemented it and the amount of success varies (Ainscough and Yazdani, 2000; Balbontin *et al.*, 2000). Many of the companies competing today in international markets consider new product introduction and development (NPI/D) as an important factor for achieving sustainable competitive advantages. Both academics and industrial managers alike are constantly searching for methods and practices that will allow them to improve the organization and management of their NPI/D processes and boost their effectiveness. The average success rate of NPI/D projects today is approximately 60% (Cooper, and Edgett, 2003). The aim of this research is to 1. shorten new product development times, 2. achieve more efficient developments, and 3. superior products.

Manufacturing companies have re-systematized their NPI/D processes and have moved from a sequential path, in which there is a negligible interaction among the departments involved and the activities required to develop the product which is carried out sequentially, towards an integrated path, known as concurrent engineering (CE) in which the activities overlap and all the departments collaborate from the beginning. This new organizational design has helped companies to improve their performance by leading to lower costs, higher quality, major knowledge creation and shorter product development times (Barba, 2001; Umemoto, *et al.*, 2004). All of this has raised competitive skills of companies. Hence, the aim is to avoid continuous setbacks and the other problems that arise with the traditional approach, improving NPI/D performance. This new practice tries to speed up the process, increasing flexibility, adopting a more strategic perspective with more sensitivity to change in the environment, solving problems through teamwork, developing diverse skills, and improving internal communication (Barba, 2001). To achieve the above mentioned objectives, CE is based on three basic elements (Koufteros, *et al.*, 2001):

1. Concurrent work-flow
2. Early involvement of all participants and groups contributing to product development
3. Team work. In other words, CE is the early involvement of a cross-functional team to simultaneously plan product, process and manufacturing activities and mentioned earlier in the previous paragraphs.

Many studies demonstrate that CE can successfully solve the typical problems of traditional. NPD, leading to clear improvements in quality and marked reductions in development time and costs (Calantone and Di Benedetto, 2000; Herder and Weijnen, 2000; Barba, 2001; Koufteros, *et al.*, 2001). On the other hand, further recent research also has also revealed that, the use of CE on its own does not always lead to positive results and that success in improving innovation capabilities depends on the context, in which CE is applied. That is, on the prevailing competitive and technological circumstances (Valle, and Va´zquez-Bustelo, 2009). Therefore, a conclusion is reached that the scale of a vagueness and intricacy present in the process of innovation may moderate the effectiveness of concurrent NPI/D characteristics on performance. Hence, the matter to be considered is not, whether CE is a mechanism for improving performance in the introduction of new products but, rather, under what circumstances such as improvement can be accomplished. It seems, however, that, in spite of many research efforts; a consensus is still lacking and that there are many empirical disagreements. This lack of agreement is the reason for this review of the global trends and perspective of CE.

According to Campbell, and Mohun, (2007), industrial manufacturing company endeavour to create an advanced core-system analytical solution that integration processes across their manufacturing industry. Thus, this will enhance the efforts by industrial processes by reducing lead-time variability and minimizing the transition times to achieve performance consistency. Therefore, to achieve this kind of core-system integrated product design and manufacturing collaboration, service-oriented architecture (SOA) turns out to be the most preferred systems' application platform. SOA is the most suitable systems' application platform for the recommended Enterprise Service Architecture to enhance this integration process effectively and efficiently. Further to this analytical leverage of CE system applications and processes; this collaboration has also been accordingly confirmed by Valle, *et at.*, (2009) research on 'Concurrent engineering performance: Incremental versus radical innovation'. They reveal that the use of CE on its own does not always lead to positive results and that success in improving innovation capabilities depends on the context, in which CE is applied. Gao, *et al.,* (2000), argues that the extensive applications of computer aided engineering (CAE) technologies are necessary so that the maximum design efficiency and effectiveness can be accomplished prior to initial sample production. The main characteristic of such an approach is depended on the system integration in accordance with the design process.

ETO KEY SEGMENTS

Most of those difficulties are caused by inefficient information; however, the most significant ETO problem is long lead-time. The ETO product delivery lead-time greatly influences the duration of any project. However, the completion of a product is dependent on the timely availability of ETO, Elfving, (2003). Extensive research has been carried out on solutions for reducing the lead-time and implementing time compression in supply chains Tsinopoulos, and Bell, (2008). Lead-time reduction is considered as fundamental for overall business improvement (Womack and Jones, 2003) and a cornerstone for lean thinking. One or a combination of three main strategies - elimination, combination and reduction can be used to reduce the lead-time. Research has identified two types of lead-time reduction in supply chains, reducing the mean lead-time and reducing lead-time variation (Hendericks, *et al. at.*, 2007). According to a study, long lead-time has more than half of its causes associated directly or indirectly with the design phase (Elfving, 2003).

Some of the typical examples are:

- Tiresome compilation and poor consistency of design input
- Modifications due to early commitment and lack of understanding
- Modifications due to design errors
- Primitive practice of supplementary design and endorsements
- Complications requiring a large number of design experts

Although there may be many other factors, the causes have their roots partially in poor coordination and poor communication due to the fragmented design environment and the involvement of a large number of various specialists. Therefore, providing a more effective computer-mediated collaborative environment seems to be conducive for resolving the problem.

AN IMPROVED ETO-CE OPERATION PROCESS AND MODEL FOR SCM

ETO is a product development process that starts with a product specification and finishes with an engineering design. In a classical ETO operation, product functionality is the major design focus. Various design testing may be carried out in the design process to verify the product design in progress. The design and standardization of a manufacturing process may be a development focus as well, when intended for serial/volume production.

Figure 2 illustrates a typical Engineer-To-Order (ETO) concurrent engineering approach process model. As already emphasised in the sections above, the whole process always begins with the interest of the customer. The customer's intension or need about a product is passed or received by a broker (Marketer). The confirmed specification in question is then passed on to the product engineering team or partners with the first contact being the architect or the estimator, who then, processes the data to produce a bill of materials (BOM). The BOM is then passed on to the product engineer design department. On receiving the product specification which has come to them the design engineer proceeds to perform their engineering analysis as per the product specification to develop the concept design of the product. With the concept design and cost details from the accounts and financial controller's department, a detailed design is then arrived at.

The detailed product design is then sent to a central product engineering database where the

Figure 2. An improved ETO concurrent engineering (CE) approach - Process model diagram - A typical ETO process model marked in the dotted area: Facilitated by BizAgi process modeller software

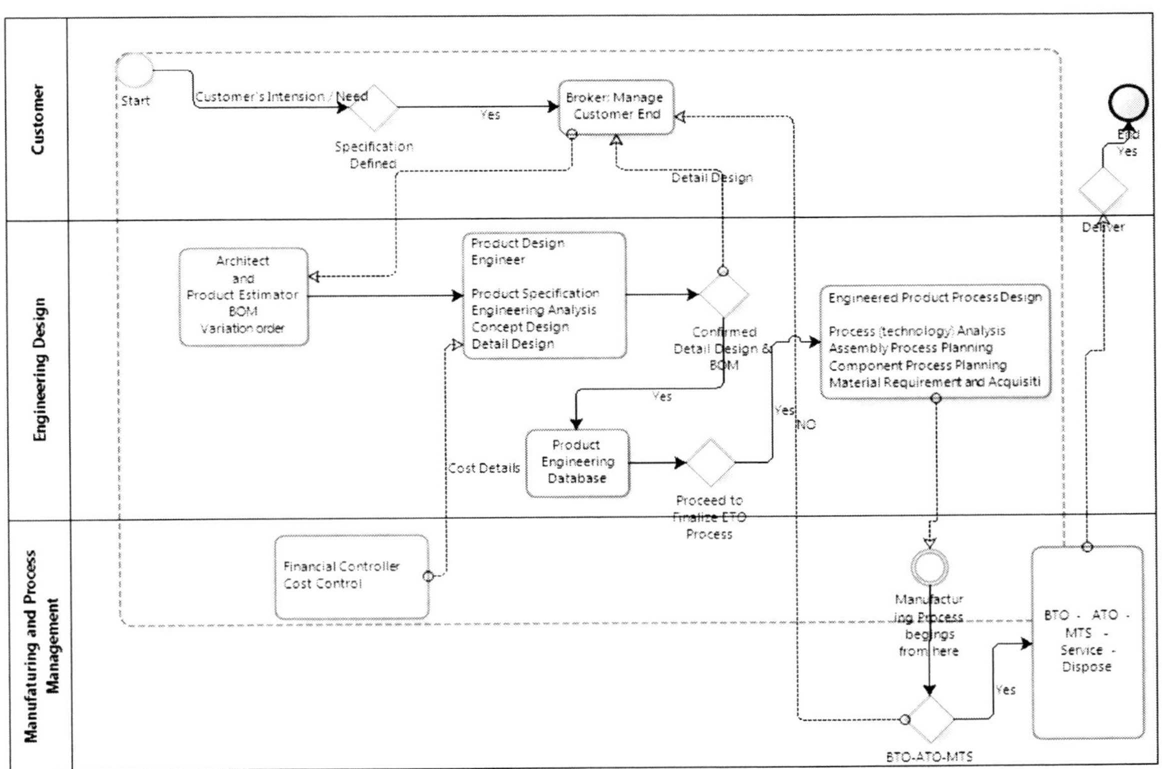

engineered process design department accesses it for engineering process analysis (technologies required for production), assembly process planning, and component process planning and finally tested for material requirement and acquisition, then passed on for manufacturing. This is the stage where the Engineer-To-Order process actually finishes and then prepares to enter the manufacturing stages - (Build-To-Order [BTO], Assemble-To-Order [ATO], and Make-To-Stock [MTS]) upon the customer's satisfaction of the ETO product via the broker or marketer. ATO – this is a manufacturing or production approach where all the basic components of the product are already available but not yet assembled, but this is done and sent quickly to the customer once the order for production is received. BTO – this is sometimes also referred to as "Make-To-Order" (MTO). It's a manufacturing or production approach where products are built or made once a confirmed order is received from a customer. This is the current approached employed for highly customized or low quantity production, and it is also the oldest method of order fulfilment in existence. MTO - this is sometimes also referred to as build to stock (BTS). This is an already manufactured and assembled production approach, which depends or is based upon the history or anticipation of supply and demand of the product in question. Thus, large quantity of the product is manufactured, assembled and stocked in warehouses and are supplied when the demand order is received.

These processes flow through from the final delivery of engineered-to-order product that is, if there are no arising faults over time during the ETO process. Finally, disposing off entire if the product exhausts through its life cycle. Thus, ETO is the operation mode that engages in product and process designs. It may include manufacture of the product design if it is one of a kind, but the two (design and manufacture) processes typically occur in sequence. An ETO concurrent engineering approach is an operation in which both design and manufacture processes occur in parallel, in order to optimally minimize the product development time that spans a product specification and delivery of the final product. ETO starts usually working closely with the customers at the stage of specifying a customer need or defining a product specification because when an ETO product is not well defined and confirmed a huge lose will be incurred when the product design progresses. The following section introduces and elaborates on ETO "best practice" as a focal point for this chapter.

ETO BEST PRACTICE

Engineer-to-Order (ETO) is an important production approach in concurrent engineered design and manufacturing; this plays an important role in economies by way of the industrial organizations optimal outputs. Typical ETO products include large electric machine, huge centrifugal pumps, diesel/natural fuel power plant engines, steam turbine, boiler, ship, etc., (Li, 2002). The collaborative design for ETO products has some special engineering design requirements relative to other products, see Box 1:

SUPPLY CHAIN MANAGEMENT TO CRITICAL SUCCESS FACTORS

ETO, a state of the art system tool with collaborative engineering Enterprise Resource Planning (ERP) systems, such as Enterprise Service Architecture (ESA) application processes. Service-Oriented Architecture (SOA) as a platform for this system application and processes provides effective communication for this collaborative engineering system approach, which proves that it is possible to have it all. Thus, clear cost notability and much competence and control among the various partners with a state of the art engineer-to-order ERP software system tools

Box 1. ETO product design

Multiple objectives: Besides the product structure and its production operation procedures (e.g., routings and routes), ETO product design should also evaluate the feasibility of production planning, services, quality, procurement, etc. That is to say, ETO product design must face to a whole supply chain instead of the independent design activities.
Multiple functions: This is to support the realization of multiple objectives. It is necessary for the department of sales and the ETO enterprise together with its key suppliers and customers; to participate in a collaborative design process instead of only the research and development (R&D) department.
Integrated design: Product design system should not be considered as isolated software but must be closely integrated with other related business systems, e.g., Enterprise Resource Planning (ERP) such as Enterprise Service Architecture (ESA) application processes with Service-Oriented Architecture (SOA) as a platform for applications and processes effective communication, to realize data, functions and process integration (Valle, and Va´zquez-Bustelo, 2009; Campbell, and Mohun, 2007).

which suits or easily links the design methods of each partner in the design team. The engineering design software industry is saturated with series of efficient engineering design units that have had to make unnecessary major changes to their software operation processes just to accommodate the reporting requirements of these ERP design software systems. Thus, if the finance and accounting management partners and team's reporting do not adequately reflect the real status of the engineer-to-order design product and their engineering operation process, their final value must be in some doubt.

In an engineer-to-order design environment, estimating the bill of materials (BOM), design process engineering, scheduling and cost are particularly difficult due to time constrains. Hence, identifying the right partners with the requisite capabilities at the right time is very essential for a successful engineer-to-order design process. Since a longer lead-time always incurs extra cost and penalties, engineering product design partner in an engineer-to-order process team need the capabilities to monitor the actual progress against the plan scheduled for the engineer-to-order process basis. These capabilities of the individual engineering product design partners coupled with the collaboration of their various state of the art Enterprise Resource Planning (ERP) engineering design software systems will always achieve a successful engineer-to-order design product for the collaborating partners.

A case example of ETO – CE approach in improving supply chains is the case of an Australian furnishing industry which was subjected to severe competition from global suppliers in the last decade. Supported by the government's Action Agenda, the Furnishing Industry Association of Australia developed the "Production Efficiency Program" to improve efficiency of the industry. This "Production Efficiency Program" as attributes and approach similar to that of the ETO – CE approach. Thus, the core of the program was three showcase projects demonstrating how return on investment can be achieved with the application of advanced manufacturing technologies to significantly reduce the design lead-time. Instead of committing large capital expenditure in IT based manufacturing systems, the showcases started by applying concurrent engineering principles by bringing all the design team and organizational partners together on a common platform. Hence, transformed the business practices to adopting latest IT systems for the designing, planning and control of manufacturing supply chain processes. The outcome as reported in the case study of the small furniture company achieved 30% increase in productivity by implementing a new scheduling system that assisted implementation of lean manufacturing and other manufacturing principles and best practices (Mo, 2009).

ETO CLASSIC TOOLS

Classical engineer-to-order state of the art tools for a collaborative engineering design product includes the following illustrated in Table 1.

CONCLUSION AND RESEARCH GAPS

ETO in its classical perspective is covered in the previous paragraphs above in a predominantly concurrent or collaborative design engineering process. Due to the need for effective control and reduction of lead-time in the entire ETO supply chain process, it is quite obvious that the design stage is responsible for a chunk of the frequent extended lead-time. Therefore, efficiency in reducing this as well as improving the integration and communication applications and processes in an ETO supply chain is very much an imperative. Thus, for future research, engineering enterprise system tool for engineering Enterprise Resource Planning (ERP) systems such as Enterprise Service Architecture (ESA) application processes with Service-Oriented Architecture (SOA) as a platform for applications and processes will enhance the efficiency required when effectively and efficiently integrated within the ETO supply chain. This approach will also go a long way to reduce the design lead-time and also improving effective communication in the design engineering chain for industrial competitive advantage. As a concluding remark, ETO supply chain managers in manufacturing industries should start to link their operational processes to create responsiveness by advancing product development processes. Employing manufacturing flexibility in a concurrent fashion within ETO supply chain management information systems and information technology systems as well as customer relationship integration earlier in a product development process chain will enhance a competitive advantage for the user.

Table 1. New and classic ETO tools

New ETO Design Software Tools	Classic ETO Design Software Tools
Team Centre	Solid Works
Siemens NX	Iron CAD
PTC Pro. Engineer	Mechanical CAD
Catia V6	AutoCAD

REFERENCES

Ainscough, M., & Yazdani, B. (2000). Concurrent engineering within British industry. *Concurrent Engineering: Research and Applications*, *8*(1), 2–11.

Balbontin, A. (2000). New product development practices in American and British firms. *Technovation*, *20*, 257–274. doi:10.1016/S0166-4972(99)00136-4

Barba, E. (2001). *Ingeniera Concurrente. Gua parasuImplantacio'n enla Empresa*. Barcelona: Diagnostico y Evaluacion Gestion.

Barber, E. (2009). How to measure the value in the value chains. *International Journal of Physical Distribution & Logistics Management*, *38*(9), 685–698. doi:10.1108/09600030810925971

Briere-Cote, A., Rivest, L., & Desrochers, A. (2010). Adaptive generic product structure modelling for design reuse in engineer-to-order. *Computers in Industry*, *61*, 53–65. doi:10.1016/j.compind.2009.07.005

Calantone, R. J., & Di Benedetto, C. A. (2000). Performance and time to market: Accelerating cycle time with overlapping stages. *IEEE Transactions on Engineering Management*, *47*(2), 232–244. doi:10.1109/17.846790

Cameron, N. S., & Braiden, P. M. (2004). Using business process re-engineering for the development of production efficiency in companies making engineered to order products. *International Production Economics*, *89*, 261–273. doi:10.1016/S0925-5273(02)00448-6

Campbell, S., & Mohun, V. (2007). *Mastering enterprise SOA with SAP Netweaver and mySAP ERP*. Indianapolis, IN: Wiley Publishing, Inc.

Chen, C.-S. (2006). Concurrent engineer-to-order operation in the manufacturing engineering contract industries. *International Journal of Industrial and Systems Engineering*, *1*(1-2), 37–58. doi:10.1504/IJISE.2006.009049

Chopra, S., & Meindl, P. (2001). *Supply chain management, strategy, planning and operation*. Upper Saddle River, NJ: Prentice-Hall.

Combs, L. (2004). The right channel at the right time. *Industrial Management (Des Plaines)*, *46*(4), 8–16.

Conner, M. (2004). The supply chain's role in leveraging PLM. *Supply Chain Management Review*, *8*(2), 36–43.

Cooper, R. G., & Edgett, S. J. (2003). *Best practices in product innovation: What distinguishes top performers*. Ancaster, Canada: Product Development Institute Inc.

Demeter, K., & Mateusz, Z. (2011). The impact of lean practices on inventory turnover. *International Journal of Production Economics*, *133*, 154–163. doi:10.1016/j.ijpe.2009.10.031

Elfving, J. (2003). *Exploration of opportunity to reduce lead time for engineered-to-order products*. PhD Dissertation, University of California, Berkeley.

Gao, J., X., *et al.* (2000). Implementation of concurrent engineering in the suppliers to the automotive industry. *Journal of Materials Processing Technology*, *107*, 201–208. doi:10.1016/S0924-0136(00)00669-5

Gosling, J., & Naim, M. M. (2009). Engineer-to-order supply chain management: A literature review and research agenda. *International Journal of Production Economics*, *122*, 741–754. doi:10.1016/j.ijpe.2009.07.002

Gunasekaran, A., Lai, K. C., & Cheng, T. C. (2008). Responsive supply chain: A competitive strategy in networked company. *International Journal of Management Science*, *36*, 549–564.

Hendericks, K. B. (2007). The impact of enterprise systems on corporate performance: A study of ERP, SCM and CRM system implementations. *Journal of Operations Management*, *25*(1), 65–82. doi:10.1016/j.jom.2006.02.002

Herder, P. M., & Weijnen, M. P. C. (2000). A concurrent engineering approach to chemical process design. *International Journal of Production Economics*, *64*, 311–318. doi:10.1016/S0925-5273(99)00068-7

Holweg, M. (2005). The three dimensions of responsiveness. *International Journal of Operations & Production Management*, *25*(7), 603–622. doi:10.1108/01443570510605063

Ketchen, D. J., Hult, T. M., Rebarick, W., & Meyer, D. (2008). Best value supply chains: A key competitive weapon for the 21st century. *Business Horizons*, *51*, 235–243. doi:10.1016/j.bushor.2008.01.012

Kim, B. (2005). *Mastering business in Asia: Supply chain management*. Singapore: Wiley.

Koufteros, X. (2001). Concurrent engineering and its consequences. *Journal of Operations Management*, *19*, 97–115. doi:10.1016/S0272-6963(00)00048-6

Kumar, A., Fantazy, K. A., & Kumar, U. (2006). Implementation and management framework for supply chain flexibility. *Journal of Enterprise Information, 19*(3), 303–319. doi:10.1108/17410390610658487

Lee, H. L. (2004). The triple-A supply chain. *Harvard Business Review, 82*(10), 102–112.

Li, S. H., Rao, S. S., Nathan, R. T., & Nathan, B. R. (2006). The impact of supply chain management practices on competitive advantage and organizational performance. *Omega, 34*, 107–124. doi:10.1016/j.omega.2004.08.002

Li, X. P. (2002). *Optimization methods of multilevel hierarchical planning architecture of engineer-to-order enterprises*. PhD Dissertation, Harbin Institute of Technology, Harbin, China.

MEEP. (2009). *Concurrent engineering materials*. The Manufacturing Education Partnership. Penn State University of Puerto Rico-Mayaguez & University of Washington Sandia National Lab.

Mo, J. P. T. (2009). The role of lean in the application of information technology to manufacturing. *Computers in Industry, 60*, 266–276. doi:10.1016/j.compind.2009.01.002

O'Marah, K. (2003). The business case for PLM. *Supply Chain Management Review, 7*(6), 16–18.

O'Marah, K., & Hofman, D. (2010). *The AMR supply chain top 25 for 2010*. Stamford, CT: Gartner Research Publication.

Pandit, A., & Yimin, Z. (2007). An ontology based approach to support decision-making for the design of ETO (Engineer-To-Order) products. *Automation in Construction, 16*, 759–770. doi:10.1016/j.autcon.2007.02.003

Patel, A. (2008). *Best practices in front-end design*. A Bentley White Paper, design and FEED applications.

Porter, M. E. (1990). The competitive advantage of nation. *Harvard Business Review, 68*(2), 73–93.

Portioli-Staudacher, A., *et al.* (2003). *Implementation of concurrent engineering: A survey in Italy and Belguim.*

Reichhart, A., & Holweg, M. (2007). Creating the customer-responsive supply chain: A reconciliation of concepts. *International Journal of Operations & Production Management, 27*(11), 1144–1172. doi:10.1108/01443570710830575

Riezebos, J., Klingenberg, W., & Hicks, C. (2009). Lean production and Information Technology: Connection or contradiction? *Computers in Industry, 60*, 237–247. doi:10.1016/j.compind.2009.01.004

SAP AG. (2003). *Manufacturing strategy: An adaptive perspective.* SAP White Paper by SAP SCM.

Swafford, P., Gosh, S., & Murthy, N. (2006). A framework for assessing value chain agility. *International Journal of Operations & Production Management, 26*(2), 118–140. doi:10.1108/01443570610641639

Tennant, C., & Roberts, P. (2000). A faster way to create better quality products. *International Journal of Project Management, 19*, 353–362. doi:10.1016/S0263-7863(00)00010-7

Teresko, J. (2004). The PLM revolution. *Industry Week, 253*(2), 32–36.

Tsinopoulos, K., & Bell, K. (2008). Supply chain integration systems by small engineer to order companies: The challenge of implementation. *Journal of Manufacturing Technology Management, 21*(1), 50–62. doi:10.1108/17410381011011489

Umemoto, K., Endo, A., & Machaco, M. (2004). From Sashimi to Zen-in. The evolution of concurrent engineering at Fuji Xerox. *Journal of Knowledge Management, 8*(4), 89–99. doi:10.1108/13673270410548504

Valle, S., & Vazquez-Bustelo, D. (2009). Concurrent engineering performance: Incremental versus radical innovation. *International Journal of Production Economics*, *119*, 136–148. doi:10.1016/j.ijpe.2009.02.002

Wang, Z., Zhan, D., & Xu, X. (2006). Service-oriented infrastructure for collaborative product design in ETO enterprises. *Proceedings of 10th International Conference on Computer Supported Cooperative Work in Design.*

Womack, J., & Jones, D. T. (2003). *Lean thinking: Banish waste and create wealth in your corporation* (2nd ed., pp. 15–36). New York, NY: Free Press.

Yassine, A., & Braha, D. (2003). Four complex concurrent engineering and the design structure matrix method. *Concurrent Engineering: Research and Applications*, *11*(3), 165–176. doi:10.1177/106329303034503

Zhou, H., & Benton, W. C. (2007). Supply chain practice and information sharing. *Journal of Operations Management*, *25*, 1348–1365. doi:10.1016/j.jom.2007.01.009

KEY TERMS AND DEFINITIONS

Concurrent Engineering: Concurrent engineering in this sense is moderate collaborative engineering approach that is much more focused on the engineering product design process of concurrent cross-functional partner organizations together in order to create products that are much better, much affordable and with a much reduced lead-time.

Customer Oriented Supply Chains Management: This is where the entire supply chain management is geared or focused towards cordinating events for the full satisfaction of the end customer.

Engineer-to-Order: ETO is a product development process, which starts with a product specification and finishes with an engineering design as its deliverable.

ETO-CE Best Practice Approach: The ETO-CE operational process is termed as the "best practice" approach in this chapter.

ETO-CE Operational Process Model: An ETO process flow model which utilizes the concurrent engineering operational principle in improving ETO supply chains.

ETO-CE SCM Integration Process: This is where some ERP / IT systems are integrated in the ETO-CE supply chains to enhance effective and efficient improvement in the entire ETO supply chain management.

Supply Chain: a system of technology, activities, information, people as well as organizations and resources involved in moving a product or service from supplier to customer at the right place and at the right time.

Supply Chain Management: Supply Chain Management is the management of the entire interconnected chain of an organization including the activities, technology, information, the people as well as the all the other resources involved.

APPENDIX

ATO	Assemble To Order
BOM	Bill Of Materials
BTO	Build To Order
CAD	Computer Aided Design
CAE	Computer Aided Engineering
CAM	Computer Aided Manufacture
CE	Concurrent Engineering
ERP	Enterprise Resource Planning
ESA	Enterprise Service Architecture
ETO	Engineer To Order
IDA	Institute for Defense Analysis
IPD	Integrated Product development
JIT	Just In Time
LM	Lean Manufacture
MTS	Make To Stock
NPI/D	New Product Introduction / Development
PLC	Product Life Cycle
R&D	Research & Development
SC	Supply Chain
SCM	Supply Chain Management
SOA	Service Oriented Architecture
XML	Extensible Mark-up Language

Chapter 8
Total Quality Management in the Global Supply Chain

Janet H. Sanders
East Carolina University, USA

ABSTRACT

This chapter provides an overview of the importance of total quality management in supply chain management. It provides a summary of the evolution of quality and how supply chain management fit into the evolution. It then discusses the importance of quality for each entity of the value chain and how the reduction of variability along the entire supply chain is critical to optimum delivery performance. The latter sections of the chapter discuss how quality and continuous improvement tools and methodologies can be mapped with supply chain management strategies to optimize the performance of the entire supply chain.

THE EVOLUTION OF QUALITY

What is quality? Quality has many definitions but, its primary definition is determined by the perspective of the user. The American Society of Quality Control (ASQ) defines quality as: "A subjective term for which each person or sector has its own definition" (ASQ, 2011). Quality is not a new concept in the modern business world; however, the concepts and principles evolved over the years. The stones of the pyramids built back in the fifteenth century B.C. show evidence of the importance of quality. The stones were cut so precisely that even today, it is nearly impossible to get a knife blade between them. (Evans & Lindsay, 2008).

Before the days of mass production, the artisan served as both the manufacturer and inspector (ASQ, 2011; Evans & Lindsay, 2008; Summers, 2006). These skilled craftsmen completed individual products and inspected them prior to providing them to the customer. If the customer

DOI: 10.4018/978-1-4666-0246-5.ch008

was dissatisfied with the product, he/she communicated directly with the artisan. This approach to quality was followed by manufacturing in the industrialized world until early in the nineteenth Century.

The factory system approach which emphasized product inspection started in Great Britain in the mid-1750s. This model was a product of the Industrial Revolution in Europe. It divided the craftsmen trade into specialized tasks. Quality was ensured through skilled laborers and was supplemented by inspections and audits. Non-conforming product was reworked or scrapped. Prior to the onset of mass production, the concept of interchangeable parts evolved. In the middle of the eighteenth century, Honoré Le Blanc, a French gunsmith, developed a system for manufacturing muskets to a standard pattern using interchangeable parts (Evans and Lindsay, 2008). After learning about this idea, Thomas Jefferson brought it to America. As a result, the United States government awarded Eli Whitney a contract in 1798 to supply muskets to the armed forces (Evans and Lindsay, 2008). The need for interchangeable parts as well as, the need from random matching of mating parts created the necessity for the control of quality.

Quality in the Twentieth Century

Early in the twentieth century, the Unites States drifted from the European approach to quality and adopted the efficiency improvement approach developed by Frederick W. Taylor (ASQ, 2011; Evans and Lindsay, 2008; Turner, et. al, 1993). Taylor's approach was to improve the method of performing work, reduce the time required to complete tasks, and set standard time for the work. This method led to significant and rapid increases in productivity but negatively affected quality. Because this method segmented jobs into specific work tasks and focused on increasing efficiency, inspection departments were created to keep defective product from reaching the customer. Quality became the responsibility of inspectors and inspection became the primary means of quality control. This approach to quality resulted in the development of separate quality departments. Quality became primarily the responsibility of the quality departments.

As the shift of responsibility for quality continued, the fundamentals of total quality were developed by Henry Ford, Sr. however; the Bell System was credited as the leader in early modern history of industrial quality assurance. The Bell System achieved its noteworthy quality through the inspection department in its Western Electric Company in the early 1900s. From this group, employees were transferred to the Bell Telephone Laboratories. The focus of this group was the development of new theories and methods of inspection to improve and maintain quality. Several of the quality assurance pioneers – Walter Shewhart, Harold Dodge, George Edwards, Joseph Juran, and W. Edwards Deming (who coined the phrase "quality assurance") – were members of this group.

An output of the era of quality assurance (QA) was quality control (QC). Quality control went beyond inspection. It referred to the use of specifications and inspection to design, produce, review, sustain, and improve the quality of products and service (Summers, 2006). After the United States (U.S.) entered World War II in 1941, legislation was enacted to steer the civilian economy to military production. During this time of high demand, the U.S. military helped suppliers improve quality and statistical quality control (SQC) became widely known and gradually adopted throughout manufacturing industries.

After World War II ended, during the late 1940s and early 1950s, the shortage of civilian goods in the U.S. made production a top priority. In the push for high short-term profitability and high production levels, quality was neglected and little interest was placed in quality improvement. It was during this time that Dr. Joseph Juran and Dr. W. Edwards Deming introduced SQC to the Japanese to help them rebuild their country. Overtime, the emphasis on quality shifted from that of inspection and detection to the prevention of poor quality. Statistical Process Control (SPC) emphasized the prevention of defects. SPC techniques also tried to limit the variation present in the product produced or service provided.

In the 1950s and 1960s, Japanese products had the reputation of inferior exports and were shunned by international markets. U.S. consumers purchased domestic goods and accepted quality without question. To change this perception, Japanese organizations explored new ways of thinking about quality. With the help of Juran and Deming, the Japanese focused on educating upper management about the importance of quality, integrating quality throughout their organizations, and developing a culture of continuous improvement. This approach led to continuous and steady improvement in the quality of Japanese products. Twenty years later, the quality of Japanese products exceeded that of Western manufacturing. Because of the higher quality levels, by the 1970s, Japanese companies' penetration into the Western markets was significant. In a few short years, Japanese companies made significant inroads into markets that were previously dominated by American companies – i.e. computer chip and automobile industries. By the 1980s, the US steel, consumer electronics, and banking industries also recognized the impact of Japanese competition.

Increased global competition, the appearance of higher quality foreign products, extensive U.S. product recalls and the Challenger space shuttle disaster increased the U.S. consumer's awareness of the importance of quality. In response to this awareness, the chief executive officers of major U.S. companies personally initiated corporate-wide quality improvement programs. This was the birth of Total Quality Management (TQM).

In 1987, the ISO 9000 quality-management standards were published and the Malcolm Baldrige National Quality Award was established by the U.S. Congress. Companies continued to make significant strides toward improved quality. By the early 1990's the gap between the quality of U.S. automakers and Japanese automakers had narrowed significantly. It was also during these years that companies realized that the approaches they used to manage quality were also needed for quality management. The historical scope of quality activities primarily placed emphasis on the quality of physical products in manufacturing industries. It was called "little Q" (ASQ Glossary, 2011; Evans and Lindsay, 2008; Gyrna, et. al., 2007). The scope began to expand to the application of quality concepts to all products, goods, and services, to all functional activities, and to all industries – i.e. manufacturing, service, government, and non-profit.

Quality in the Twenty-First Century

As the twenty-first century began, new interest in fundamental quality principles began to emerge. Continuous Improvement (CI) was one of the new approaches. CI's primary focus was to continuously improve processes to enable companies to give customers what they wanted the first time and every time. An extension of CI was the Six Sigma methodology. This approach to quality differed from the previous ones in that it focused on project selection that would deliver bottom line output reductions in customer requirements with measurable and documented results to the goal of no more than 3.4 defects per million opportunities (Allen, 2010; Ehrlich, 2002).

Shortly after the emergence of Six Sigma, came the re-emergence of the Toyota Total Production Systems (TPS) approaches in the form of Lean manufacturing. Lean manufacturing is a business philosophy that was originally developed at Toyota Motor Company. Toyota referred to it as TPS and its objective was the elimination of all forms of waste in the production process. Seven waste categories were originally identified (Womack and Jones, 2003; Ehrlich, 2002). The number of categories was later increased to eight by Tiichi

Ohno (Ohno,1988). Overtime, the Lean and Six Sigma methodologies were merged to form Lean Six Sigma.

It was during this era of continuous improvement when companies had reduced manufacturing costs as much as possible that they began to realize that the next logical area to target for increased market share and profit was the supply chain. Supply chain management (SCM) was birthed. Simchi-Levi, et. al. (2003, pg. 1) defined supply chain management as "A set of approaches utilized to efficiently integrate suppliers, manufacturers, warehouses, and stores, so that merchandise is produced and distributed at the right quantities, to the right locations, and at the right time, in order to minimize system-wide costs while satisfying service level requirements." Overtime, the Lean and SCM concepts were combined to form Lean Supply Chain Management. The primary goals of Lean SCM was to focus on the customer, provide a pull based flow, minimize waste in inventory and create value with growth. Its approach followed the 5R's of logistics (Craig, 2006).

Today, companies continue their continuous improvement approaches through a variety and mixture of the improvement methodologies described in this section and the pursuit of the best practices that maximizes the quality of their products or services.

QUALITY AND THE VALUE CHAIN

The supply chain is a dynamic system composed of a complex network of resources, operations, and organizations dispersed over a large geographical area. The various facilities within the supply chain may have different and conflicting objectives. Synchronization of the various resources is critical to the optimum delivery performance. The reduction of variability along the entire supply chain is an intelligent strategy for properly synchronizing the constituent entities along the network (Garg, et. al, 2004). Variability is reduced by controlling quality. The following discussion focuses on the perspective of quality from the viewpoint of customers, distributors, suppliers, marketing, design, and manufacturing.

From the viewpoint of a pull system, product is not produced until requested by a customer. To create loyal and satisfied customers, companies must identify the customers' needs, design products and services that meet those needs and measure the customers' satisfaction. Statistics show that growth in market share is strongly correlated with customer satisfaction. Additionally, customer needs and wants drive competitive advantage. As a result, it is critical for companies to competently and correctly identify customer needs, wants, and expectations. Customer quality may be characterized in three different ways – expected, actual, and perceived (Evans and Lindsay, 2008). Expected quality is quality that the customer assumes will be received from the product as their needs and expectations are translated into product or service specifications. Actual quality is the quality that is delivered to the customer and it is the yield from the production process. It is imperative that designers of products and services accurately record the customer needs and expectations from marketing and develop the specifications accordingly. Perceived customer quality is a measure of the expected quality to the actual quality. If the expected quality exceeds the actual quality, then the customer will probably be unhappy and dissatisfied. If on the other hand, the expected quality exceeds the actual quality then the customer will be satisfied or delighted.

The organization within the value chain that is key to accessing the customer quality expectations is marketing. There are numerous methods of obtaining customer needs, expectations, and wants. Marketing may utilize surveys, focus groups, direct customer contact, complaint monitoring, internet traffic, or field intelligence. But since perceived quality drives consumer behavior, the marketing group must carefully and accurately gauge customer requirements and communicate them to the organization.

Like the marketing organization, the design organization must correctly translate the customer requirements to the organization. They do so in the form of functional product specifications. The design of a quality product or service should include two layers, product and process design. The product design should focus on the development of product characteristics as defined by the customer. An important component of this transfer of the customer specification is information quality. The specifications must be correctly communicated to designers so that they can correctly develop the engineering specifications. Similarly, the information quality must be correct for the design of manufacture or assembly of a product. The design organization refers to customer quality and engineering quality as the foundations for robust product design. Otto and Wood (2001) refer to customer quality as the minimization of performance variation for all environment and user conditions and engineering quality as assurance that the product functions as it is intended according to the implicit customer's expectations. Engineering quality can also be termed as the customer's expected quality.

Supplier quality is an important input into the product or service production organization. The goals and requirements of the supplier must be closely aligned with the other entities in the value chain. To ensure proper alignment, an organization's buyer may need to communicate the specifications of the final product and the specifications of the material to the supplier. Several approaches may be utilized in the maintenance of supplier quality. A company may use lot acceptance sampling as a means to monitor and verify supplier quality. Statistical process control on specific product characteristics may be used to monitor and verify supplier quality. Outsourcing may be used. Supplier certification may be used. The primary intent of supplier certification is to minimize or eliminate the need for incoming testing or inspection of material. As another option, suppliers could be certified at different quality levels. The receiving company could develop specific criteria and classify the supplier at specific levels – i.e. Level 1, 2, 3 or A, B, or C – according to the specifics of each criteria. As another example, an "approved" supplier could mean that the supplier would meet the minimum quality requirements with an overall compliance of 90% or a "preferred" supplier would produce better than minimum quality with a higher level of compliance and for consecutive time intervals over a specified time interval. Another approach may be a supplier quality rating system in which supplier quality is quantified over a period of time. The units of measure will differ among companies; however, the measures may include percentage of nonconforming product, overall product quality, economic analysis, and a measure of the delivery against the schedule, price, or other categories. Some companies use the supplier rating to determine the market share of future purchases given to each supplier. Regardless, of which single or combination approach that is utilized, supplier quality must be effectively quantified and monitored to effectively synchronize the supply chain.

Manufacturing quality can be implemented through a host of methods and methodologies. Automated manufacturing, cellular manufacturing, computer-integrated manufacturing, flexible manufacturing, and group technology are a few of the tangible methods used to minimize product variation and maximize product quality. In regards to manufacturing methodologies, the list includes any of the continuous improvement methodologies that have evolved over the years including Total Quality Management, Six Sigma, and Lean. More details about the synchronization of these methodologies and SCM will be discussed later in this chapter. Another component of manufacturing quality is the management of the manufacturing processes. This involves the planning and administering of activities necessary to achieve a high level of performance in the key business processes and the monitoring and identification of opportunities for improving product quality and manufacturing performance. The activities may include continuous improvement activities, process and product audits, benchmarking of best practices, innovation, reengineering, and quality planning, control, and improvement.

Like suppliers, distributor quality is critical in the optimum delivery performance of the supply chain. Quality must be monitored and controlled at the physical distribution sites as well as for the distribution processes. Product identification, handling, expiration, rotation, and availability are all components of product quality at the physical distribution sites. The quality of product identification can be implemented by various means. One recent implementation of product identification and tracking that has a high degree of accuracy and that is becoming increasing valuable in the supply chain is the radio frequency identification (RFID) tag. RFID is an improvement over the bar code, because it can carry much more information, has read and write capabilities, and will allow tracking in real time (Bonsor and Keener, 2011). These tags can be a key method for managing and coordinating the movement of product between distribution sites.

The quality of product handling is exercised in the physical handling of the product such that it is not damaged and also in the management of the loading, unloading, and sorting activities. In the case of companies that use the closely located distribution centers to more quickly restock store shelves or those that use virtual inventory strategies for product distribution, quality and product accuracy must be maintained as the product is moved between warehouses or between shipping docks (Blanchard, 2007). Another method for maintaining the quality of the distribution process is the automation of product information. The elimination of the paper-based inventory system in favor of the computer integrated bar code scanner can significantly reduce data input errors and improve inventory accuracy and information quality. Voice recognition technology is an increasingly popular distribution best practice. It is an improvement over the bar code reader in that it receives and executes spoken commands (Blanchard, 2007).

Additional distribution practices that could affect product quality in the supply chain include data accuracy and integrity relative to stock levels and lead times. Any combination of RFID, voice recognition technology and automated conveyor systems can be utilized to manage the stock levels, lead times, product expiration and rotation, and material movement. A holistic approach for effectively controlling these components is a warehouse management system (WHS). A WHS is a system that controls, manages, and regulates the physical activities of product movement, including product receipt, material movement and storage, and order selection (Blanchard, 2007; Bowersox, et.al. 2002). It can be linked to other distribution operations – i.e. like vendor managed inventory systems (Blanchard, 2007; Bowersox, et.al. 2002; Lambert, 2008) – to manage and monitor the control of product.

Although the various entities within the supply chain may have different and sometimes conflicting objectives, in order to optimize quality and delivery performance, quality must be addressed at each level and maximized globally.

SUPPLY CHAIN MANAGEMENT AND QUALITY TOOLS

As noted in the beginning of this chapter, quality evolved from the total functional responsibility of the tradesperson to a level where quality is everyone's job, the big Q. However, a transition to this level of quality awareness is a process that must be rooted by a sound organizational focus on quality. As companies embark on this transition, they must embrace a paradigm shift in the way in which they view their customers, human resources, manufacturing and service processes, and all fundamental business activities. This shift must include the embedding of quality principles throughout the supply chain.

Earlier, supply chain management (SCM) was generally defined as an approach to efficiently integrate multiple entities so that the right product is produced and distributed to the right locations at the right time. Process improvement methodologies and tools that have been utilized in the manufacturing sector can be used to facility these goals. Inevitably, in the process of integrating the multiple entities of the supply chain, problems evolve. If a problem is defined as the gap between the current level of a process, product, or service and the desired performance level, then problem solving methodologies can be utilized to close the gap. There is a multitude of problem solving methodologies that could be utilized; some that were developed by quality "experts" and others that were developed by individual companies. A few of the more common ones include:

- Classical Approach (Identify, Define, Investigate, Analyze, Solve, Confirm)
- Six Sigma's DMAIC process (Define, Measure, Analyze, Improve, Control)
- Kepner-Tregoe Problem Analysis
- Shanin Problem Solving
- Eight Disciplines (8-D) at Ford Motor Co.
- IDEA (Investigate, Design, Execute, Adjust)

The procedure for using these methodologies may vary from three to eight steps; however, the foundation for these methodologies was Deming and Shewhart's, Plan Do Check Act and Plan Do Study Act methodologies. All of the methodologies listed have a common starting point – the recognition that a problem exists – and a common ending point – an innovative solution to the problem. Another common element of the methodologies is the tools used. Quality pioneer Kaoru Ishikawa believed that ninety-five percent of the quality problems in the workplace could be solved by using what are known as the seven quality control tools: histograms, flow charts, control charts, check sheets, pareto diagrams, cause and effect diagrams, and scatter diagrams (Evans and Lindsay, 2008; Evans, 2008, Gyrna, 2007; Summers, 2006). A closer look at the pairing of each of these quality tools and their application in SCM may yield the same ninety-five percent improvement in supply chain performance. Table 1 shows each tool, its application in the quality area, and how it can be utilized to monitor or improve the quality of the supply chain.

The histogram is a type of bar chart that visually displays the classes on the horizontal axis and the class frequencies on the vertical axis. The height of the bars represents the class frequencies. This tool can provide a compact visual presentation of data about the overall performance of the supply chain or about an individual entity's performance. One potential application is the display of the distribution of products in a supply chain. As shown in Figure 1, if a SC contained products A, B, C, & D, a histogram could be used to graphically display the distribution of the products. A similar chart could be used to display the distribution of a problem in the supply chain – for example, the graph could display on-time delivery data for the supply chain.

A different variety of the bar chart is the Pareto diagram. Like the histogram, it shows the relative frequency for the specified classes however; it shows the classes in the descending quantity of occurrence. It is very useful in identifying the class with the most impact on the characteristic investigated. It is based on the Pareto principle that 20% of the sources cause 80% of the problems. Using the same data as that from Figure 1, Figure 2 shows that Product B has the greatest impact on the characteristic displayed. If this chart was a display of defect data, the Pareto principle suggests that Products B and C cause 80% of the problems. If the number of defects can be reduced for these products, the overall performance of the characteristic would be greatly improved.

Table 1. Mapping of the seven basic quality tools with supply chain management

Quality Tool	Quality Application (Tague, 2004)	Possible SCM Application
Histogram	Provides a graphical summary of frequency distribution of data. It shows which values occur most frequently, as well as, the spread of the data.	▪ Display the distribution of product among Supply Chain (SC) entities ▪ Display the distribution of problems within the SC or entities ▪ Display the variability of products, services, or problems within the SC or entities
Flow Chart	Provides a graphical representation of all the steps involved in an entire process or a segment of a process. It shows the actual flow or sequence of events in a process.	▪ Graph the flow of products and services in the SC ▪ Graph the flow of product or service within the SC entities ▪ Graph the flow of entities along the SC
Control Chart	A graphical tool used to monitor the activity of an ongoing process. A powerful tool for analyzing variation in processes and how a process changes over time.	▪ Monitor the change of a SC metric, for example, critical to quality, critical to delivery, or critical to cost metrics
Check Sheet	A tool used to systematically collect and compile data so that patterns and trends can be clearly detected and shown.	▪ Collect data about a SC entity or metric ▪ Collect data about a product or service
Pareto Diagram	A tool used to find the "vital few" causes that create the majority of problems. Shows their relative frequency and size in a descending bar graph.	▪ Identify the products or services in the SC or within an entity that cause the most quality problems ▪ Identify the entities in the SC that cause the most quality problems
Cause and Effect Diagram	Used to identify possible causes for an effect or problem and sort the ideas into useful categories. Can be used to help identity the root cause of a problem.	▪ Identity potential causes of problems with SC products, services, or entities ▪ Help identity strategies for addressing the problems in the SC
Scatter Diagram	A graphical technique used to analyze the relationship between two different variables. It graphs pairs of numerical data, one variable on the x-axis and one on the y-axis, to display any relationship between the two.	▪ Identify correlations between and among SC entities and SC metrics, for example, correlation between on-time-delivery and distance between distributor and retail site or correlation between cost and SC improvements or inventory management methods

Figure 1. Supply chain histogram

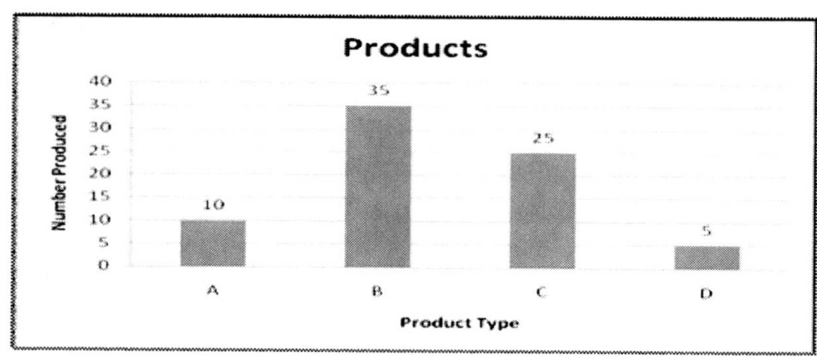

A great way to collect detailed data about a SC entity, a product, or a service is with a check sheet. The check sheet is a data recording device with a list of categories that is used to record the number of times a particular event occurs. The data from the sheet could be summarized, compiled, and presented in visual formats like Figures 1 and 2.

Once the data has been summarized and the patterns or trends have been identified, a flow chart could be used to show the details of the process related to the data. The flow chart provides a visual display of the actual flow or sequence of events in a process. This tool can be used to identify unexpected complexity, problems areas, redundancy, unnecessary loops, and opportunities for simplification or standardization. Example applications in SCM include the mapping of the entire flow of products or services in an entire supply chain or within a specific entity. After the actual flows are displayed, areas of improvement could be identified.

The cause and effect diagram is a tool that could be used to help identity the causes of a problem. A team of individuals could use this tool to create a graphical display of all of the possible causes of a problem. This tool encourages a team to focus on the causes, not the symptoms of a problem, by using specific cause categories – i.e. methods, materials, people, environment or information, machines, and measurement. Since the Pareto chart in Figure 2 showed that Product B caused of 47% of the problem, a cause and effect diagram could be used to list the specific causes of the problem. Next, the team could rank the causes and determine the root cause that needs to be eliminated in order to eliminate the problem.

The scatter diagram could be used by the team to display data on potential causes identified by the cause and effect diagram. This tool displays pairs of numerical data and can be used to analyze the relationship between the data pairs. If for example, the cause of the problem was delinquent on-time deliveries, the scatter diagram could be analyzed for correlations between the delivery time and distance metrics, cost metrics, or quality metrics.

After a problem has been identified, the control chart tool could be used to monitor, control, or improve the performance of the respective process. This tool could be used to determine if variation in process is or is not normal. If abnormal variation, trends, or cycles are detected, corrective action should be taken to eliminate the problem. This tool could be used for any measured metric for a specific entity or along the entire supply chain.

Figure 2. Supply chain Pareto

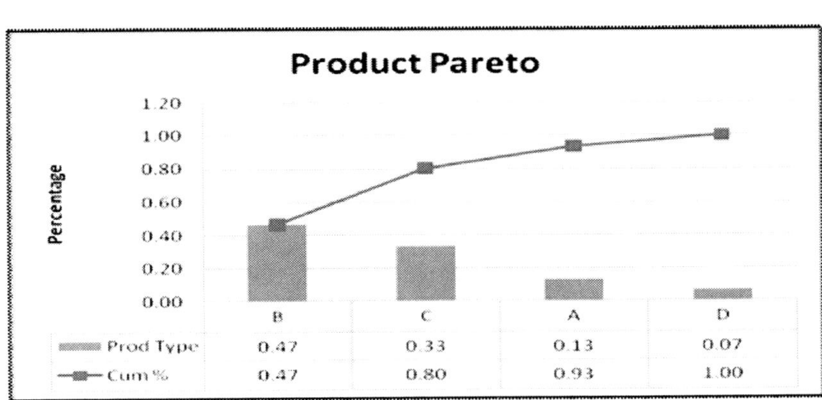

SUPPLY CHAIN MANAGEMENT AND LEAN TOOLS

Just as the seven quality tools can be utilized to facility supply chain management, so can continuous improvement methodologies like Lean and Six Sigma. The Lean methodology could be used in multiple applications. The primary objective of Lean is the use of less work and waste to get more value (Allen, 2010; Sayer, 2007; Womack, 2003). Elements of waste are present wherever a product is produced, a material is processed, or a service is provided. Like the basic quality tools, basic Lean tools can be matched with SCM. Table 2 lists the fundamental Lean tools and how they can be paired with SCM to optimize the supply chain.

In respect to supply chain management, an initial Lean tool that should be utilized to access the current state of a process and the value stream is value stream mapping. The value stream is the

Table 2. Mapping of the lean tools with supply chain management

Lean Tool	Lean Application (MacInnes, 2009; Gryna, 2007; Sayer, 2007; George, et. al., 2005)	Possible SCM Application
Value Stream Mapping	A graphical display of the sequence of activities, flow of information, identification and alignment of resources, identification of value creation and waste, and lead time of activities	• Produce a graph of the flow of services, demand characteristics, resources, information, waste, and lead times for a supply chain. • Evaluate the current- state map against a desired future-state map
Kaizen Event	A two to five day structured team-based process improvement effort where resources focus on delivering an immediate solution to a problem	• Conduct a session with a team from various entities of the Supply Chain (SC) to immediately resolve a delivery, product quality, or service problem
Visual Management	The use of visual cues to signal or alert people of a problem.	• Provide alert cues for data trends for critical to quality, critical to delivery, or critical to cost metrics • Provide proactive alerts to SC entities about product or service problems occurring with other entities
5 S Process	A program that mandates that resources be provided in the required location and be available as needed to support work activities. Implemented through five steps: sort, straighten, scrub, systemize, standardize.	• Maintain organized computer files for the various SC entities, products, or services • Provide standard locations for databases, operating procedures, specifications, references, etc. • Designate a regular routine for specific meetings, data transfers, inventory counts or turnovers, fiscal quarters or years, etc.
Waste Elimination	A structured approach to eliminating waste. Waste is any activity that consumes resources but produces no added value to the product or service.	• For each waste category, identify specifics instances in SC processes and among SC entities. Use lean and quality tools to minimize or eliminate the waste.
Continuous Flow	The sequencing of activities in the process with one piece at a time to minimize delays, reduce lead time and reduce work-in-progress.	• Reduce storage and transportation costs by producing a product or service at the rate that it's requested by the customer • Optimize the sequence of product flow along the SC using the one piece concept
Error Proofing	A structured approach to catching a mistake before it is translated into a nonconforming product or service.	• Maximize supplier certification to minimize incoming and source inspection. • Validate data transmitted between SC entities, i.e. phone number formats, product code and their formats, etc. • Implement bar codes or RFID tags on products • Automate processes to minimize human error

stream of activities used to create a product or service that the customer values. The value stream map (VSM) is like a flow chart on steroids. VSM uses simple graphics and icons to display the sequence and movement of information, materials, and actions in a value stream. Additionally, it provides a visual display of the specific activities, information, timing, and events. It's cupboard of icons include those to depict (MacInnes, 2002):

- Production flow of manufacturing process, customers, suppliers, data boxes, and employee numbers
- Material flow for push or pull movement of materials, automated movement of materials, first in first out inventory movement, rail, truck, or air shipments, inventory count, storage, and emergency stock
- Information flow of manual or electronic information, information type, production, withdrawal, or signal Kanban, Kanban card post, and load leveling
- Manufacturing icons for visual management, error proofing, quick changeover, product or process standards, stretch objectives, performance boards, and constraining operations.

For the supply chain, value stream mapping is ideal for displaying the flow of sales orders, production data, manufacturing, purchasing, shipping, and accounting processes for the overall supply chain or the activities within an entity. In the application of this tool, the current state value stream is mapped and analyzed for waste. Next, an ideal state VSM is completed to show the value stream with only value-added activities.

As noted, one of the primary purposes of Lean is the elimination of waste. In the process of transitioning from the current state value stream to the ideal state, one of the key ways of improving the health of the value stream is the elimination of waste. Waste is typically categorized into seven or eight different forms: transportation, motion or movement, waiting, overproduction, inventory, extra processing, defects, or underutilization of resources or people. Waste is also classified as Type 1 Muda (non-value-added but deemed necessary for the company or Type 2 Muda (non-value-added and not necessary for the company). Type 2 wastes are the first targets for elimination (MacInnes, 2009; Sayer, 2007; George, et. al., 2005; Womack and Jones, 2003). By listing, categorizing, and classifying the wastes in the value chain, the SC could be strategically optimized by removing the non-value adding activities.

The kaizen event is a Lean method that could be utilized to focus on an immediate solution to a problem. The kaizen event is a team-based improvement effort in which actual changes are implemented (MacInnes, 2009). It typically lasts two to five days and specific resources are assembled to focus on a targeted area. For the supply chain, the target area could be product delivery, quality, or service or it could be a specific problem within an entity in the SC.

Within the various supply chain entities and along the entire SC, visual management methods could be utilized to help maintain awareness about the product and its movement and to monitor the product or service's performance. Within the physical workplace, visual tools could include sensors to indicate the movement or presence of product, display boards, charts, or pictograms. For the virtual SC workplace, similar electronic and computer tools and dashboards could be used to present, monitor, or red flag critical to quality, delivery, or cost metrics. The electronic signals could be utilized for the SC entities to signal product or service movement or provide alerts about problems.

A similar visual management tool is the 5 S method. The primary objective of this tool is workplace organization. For the physical workplace, this method could ensure that the appropriate resources are provided in the required location and be available as needed to support work activities. For the virtual SC, this method could manifest through standardized information management, organized and standardized electronic files names and structures, standardized electronic forms, specific and standardized locations for databases, standardized operating procedures, standardized file and system back-ups, or specifications. Additionally, standards and protocol could be established for data transfer and exchanges.

The 5 S method could be the foundation for error proofing of processes and systems. Error proofing is a fact-based problem-solving approach for ensuring quality in work processes by eliminating the cause of errors. Errors are the cause of defects in products or services. In addition to source inspection, final inspection, and process monitoring, error proofing could include physical and electronic constraints and signals, sensors, counters, data validation, and immediate feedback methods.

In the Lean methodology, continuous flow refers to the sequencing of activities through the entire process one task or unit at a time. In the application of this method, as soon as one task is completed, the next task is immediately started. This method helps to reduce elapsed time between a customer's order and the product or service delivery, it prevents wait times, it reduces excess backlog of work, and it reveals problems early in the delivery process. It could be implemented in the hand-off of activities and services between supply chain entities and within the entities.

Like the quality toolbox, the Lean methodology contains a host of tools that can be used to improve the supply chain. The integration of these tools and SCM methods will lead to significant quality improvement along the entire supply chain.

SUPPLY CHAIN MANAGEMENT AND SIX SIGMA TOOLS

The cousin to Lean and the quality toolbox is Six Sigma. Like Lean, the definition of Six Sigma has grown to represent a number of concepts. Its definitions include: (Allen 2010; Evans and Lindsay, 2008; Gedyrna, 2007; Brue, 2006; George, et. al, 2005; Gygi, 2005; Ehrlich, 2002)

- A quality management philosophy
- A methodology that blends together many of the key elements of past quality initiatives
- A business philosophy of focusing on continuous improvement by understanding customers' needs, analyzing business processes, and instituting proper measurement methods.
- A methodology that an organization uses to ensure that it is improving its key processes
- A statistical concept that measures a process in terms of defects
- A statistical concept that represents the amount of variation present in a process relative to customer requirements or specifications

Regardless of how it's defined, Six Sigma's primary goal is to minimize mistakes and maximize value by focusing on the customer requirements. It too can be paired with supply chain management methodologies to optimize the supply chain. Table 3 lists a mapping of Six Sigma tools with SCM applications.

The five step Define, Measure, Analyze, Improve, and Control (DMAIC) method is the most recognized Six Sigma methodology. The DMAIC method is used to improve the current capabilities of an existing process (Six Sigma Academy, 2002). In the define phase, the project is defined, the customer needs are stated and the processes or products to be improved are defined. In the measure phase, the baseline and target performance levels are determined, the input and output variables are defined, and the measurement systems are validated. In the analyze phase, the key process inputs that affect the process outputs are established and the root cause(s) of the defects is determined. In the improve phase, solutions that

Table 3. Mapping of the Six Sigma methodology with supply chain management

Six Sigma Tool	Six Sigma Application	Possible SCM Application
DMADV Method	A 5-Step method used to help create or redesign a process, product, or service to meet customer requirements	•Use the 5-Step method to design the Supply Chain processes to meet Six Sigma quality.
DMAIC Method	A 5-Step method used to improve the current capabilities of an existing process	• Use define phase tools to help quantify critical to quality, critical to delivery, or critical to cost SC measures • Use the 5-Step process to maximize a quality or service metric
Process Sigma Level	A metric used to indicate the performance (sigma level) of a measured characteristic	• Use the DPO or DPU method to calculate the sigma level of critical to quality, critical to delivery, or critical to cost SC measures (Sanders and Pagliari, 2009) • Use quality tools to move the quality level toward the 6 sigma level of performance

address and eliminate the root cause(s) of the defects are developed, tried out, and implemented. In the control phase, documenting, standardizing, and monitoring activities are implemented to maintain the gains achieved in the earlier phases. This method could be used to improve the performance of critical to quality, critical to delivery, or critical to cost metrics within the SC entities or to maximize these metric for the entire supply chain. (Bandyopadhyay and Jenicke, 2007; Garg, Narahari, & Viswanadham, 2004)

The five step Define, Measure, Analyze, Design, Verify (DMADV) method is a variant of the Define for Six Sigma (DFSS) method (Brue, 2006). This method is used to help create a process, product, or service to meet customer requirements or to complete a redesign because the process, product, or service is consistently incapable of meeting a customer requirement. For the supply chain, this method could be used in the early development of processes within an entity and in the establishment of a supply chain. Additionally, it could be used in the redesign efforts for a SC metric that is consistently missed.

Regardless of the six sigma methodology used, the primary goal is to produce a product of service that meets the customer requirements and delivers no more than 3.4 defects per million observations (DPMO). As the DPMO decreases, the process sigma level increases. The route to this goal can take two different paths. The DPMO calculation can be completed using the defects per unit (DPU) or the defects per observation (DPO) (Sanders and Pagliari, 2009). The DPU method calculates the defective rate for the unit of product or service. The DPO method calculates the defective rate as a function of the complexity of the product or service – i.e. per defect opportunity. The DPU method is the one most often utilized but the DPO method levels the playing field by incorporating the product's or service's complexity into the calculation. In the final analysis, the DPU for a specific critical metric for different entities may be the same however; the processes or methods for producing the products or services within the entities could be more or less complex. Whereas, with the DPO method, if different entities had the same number of defects, the less complex entity would have a higher DPO than the more complex one. The applicable process sigma level would be lower and more attention would be directed to the entity which is truly producing more defects. These differences in calculating the process sigma for a metric for an entity and especially for the overall supply chain should be taken into consideration in the optimization of the supply chain.

QUALITY AND THE FUTURE OF THE SUPPLY CHAIN

Total quality, Lean, and Six Sigma are often viewed as cousin process improvement methodologies and supply chain management should be adopted into the family. Actually, the integration of the quality and SCM methodologies is still in its infancy and will continue to mature. The optimization of supply chains using methods like DPO entity optimization, waste elimination, VSM, lean supply chains, and six sigma will continue to develop (Sanders and Pagliari, 2009; Hau L. Lee_, Seungjin Whang, 2005; Garg, 2004; Stratton and Warburton, 2003). Additionally, other methodologies native to manufacturing – i.e. flexible manufacturing (Garavelli, 2003), enterprise resource planning (ERP) systems, customer supplier relationship management – will be integrated by SCM. Also, innovative approaches to supply (Arshinder, Arun Kanda, S.G. Deshmukh, 2008) and value chain management (Al-Mudimigha, A. S. et. al., 2004) and service quality (Stanley and Wisner, 2001) will continue to mature

CONCLUSION

This chapter covered the evolution of quality from the perspective of the tradesperson through the transitions from quality assurance to quality control to total quality management to continuous improvement. Regardless of the era in which a company finds itself, a common and consistent requirement for the quality focused organization is a total commitment from management. Just like the Japanese did in the 1950s and 1960s, companies must focus globally on educating upper management about the importance of quality, integrating quality throughout their organizations, and developing a culture of continuous improvement. The focus must never return to the little Q, but continue to expand the possibilities of the big Q. With the numerous quality methodologies and tools available, the total quality of the customer-oriented global supply chain should be maximized and optimized at every level.

REFERENCES

Al-Mudimigha, A. S., Zairib, M., & Ahmed, A. M. (2004). Extending the concept of supply chain: The effective management of value chains. *International Journal of Production Economics*, *87*, 309–320.

Alcrecht, K. (1992). *The only thing that matters*. New York, NY: Harper-Collins.

Allen, T. (2010). *Introduction to engineering statistics and lean sigma* (2nd ed.). New York, NY: Springer. doi:10.1007/978-1-84996-000-7

American Society of Quality Control (ASQ). (2011). *Definition of quality*. Retrieved January 25, 2011, from http://asq.org/glossary/q.html

American Society of Quality Control (ASQ). (2011). *Definition of big Q, little q*. Retrieved February 1, 2011, from http://asq.org/ glossary/b.html

American Society of Quality Control (ASQ). (2011). The history of quality – Overview. Retrieved January 25, 2011, from http://asq.org/learn-about-quality/ history-of-quality/overview/overview.html

Arshinder, A. K., & Deshmukh, S. G. (2008). Supply chain coordination: Perspectives, empirical studies and research directions. *International Journal of Production Economics*, *115*, 316–335. doi:10.1016/j.ijpe.2008.05.011

Bandyopadhyay, J. K., & Jenicke, L. O. (2007). Six Sigma approach to quality assurance in global supply chains: A study of United States automakers. *International Journal of Management*, *24*(1).

Blanchard, D. (2007). *Supply chain management best practices*. Hoboken, NJ: John Wiley & Sons, Inc.

Bonsor, K., & Keener, C. (2011). *How RFID works*. Retrieved February 3, 2011, from http://electronics.howstuffworks.com/gadgets/high-tech-gadgets/ rfid.htm/printable

Bowersox, D. J., Closs, D. J., & Cooper, M. B. (2002). *Supply chain logistics management*. New York, NY: McGraw-Hill Companies.

Brue, G., & Howes, R. (2006). *Six Sigma, The McGraw Hill 36-hour course*. New York, NY: McGraw- Hill Companies.

Craig, T. (2006). *Lean SCM – More essentials*. Retrieved February 15, 2011, from http://www.scmnews.com/ scmnews-66-20060718LeanSCMMoreEssentials.html

Ehrlich, B. H. (2002). *Transactional Six Sigma and lean servicing*. Boca Raton, FL: St. Lucie Press. doi:10.1201/9781420000337

Evans, J. R., & Lindsay, W. M. (2008). *Managing for quality and performance excellence* (7th ed.). Mason, OH: South-Western Cengage Learning.

Garavelli, C. A. (2003). Flexibility configurations for the supply chain management. *International Journal of Production Economics*, *85*, 141–153. doi:10.1016/S0925-5273(03)00106-3

Garg, D., Narahari, Y., & Viswandham, N. (2004). Design of Six Sigma supply chains. *IEEE Transactions on Automation Science and Engineering*, *1*(1). doi:10.1109/TASE.2004.829436

George, M. L., Rowlands, D., Price, M., & Maxey, J. (2005). *The lean Six Sigma pocket toolbook*. New York, NY: McGraw Hill.

Gryna, F. M., Chua, R. C. H., & Defeo, J. A. (2007). *Juran's quality planning & analysis for enterprise quality* (5th ed.). New York, NY: The McGraw-Hill Companies, Inc.

Gygi, C., DeCarlo, N., & Williams, B. (2005). *Six Sigma for dummies*. Indianapolis, IN: Wiley Publishing, Inc.

Hau, L., & Whang, S. (2005). Higher supply chain security with lower cost: Lessons from total quality management. *International Journal of Production Economics*, *96*, 289–300. doi:10.1016/j.ijpe.2003.06.003

Kojima, M., Nakashima, K., & Ohno, K. (2008). Performance evaluation of SCM in JIT environment. *International Journal of Production Economics*, *115*, 439–443. doi:10.1016/j.ijpe.2007.11.017

Lambert, D. M. (Ed.). (2008). *Supply chain management process, partnerships, performance* (3rd ed.). Sarasota, FL: Supply Chain Management Institute.

MacInnes, R. L. (2002). *The lean enterprise memory jogger*. Salem, NH: GOAL/QPC.

MacInnes, R. L. (2009). *The lean enterprise memory jogger for service*. Salem, NH: GOAL/QPC.

Ohno, T. (1988). *The Toyota production system – Beyond large scale production*. Portland, OR: Productivity Inc.

Otto, K. N., & Wood, K. L. (2001). *Product design techniques in reverse engineering and new product development*. Upper Saddle River, NJ: Prentice Hall.

Sander, J. H., & Pagliari, L. (2009). *A bi-level approach for applying Six Sigma's DPMO to supply chain management*. Presented at the 2009 IERC Conference, Miami, FL.

Sayer, N. J., & Williams, B. (2007). *Lean for dummies*. Hoboken, NJ: Wiley Publishing, Inc.

Simchi-Levi, D., Kamisky, P., & Simchi-Levi, E. (2003). *Designing & managing the supply chain* (2nd ed.). New York, NY: The McGraw-Hill Companies.

Six Sigma Academy. (2002). *The black belt memory jogger*. Salem, NH: Goal/QPC.

Stanley, L. L., & Wisner, J. D. (2001). Service quality along the supply chain: Implications for purchasing. *Journal of Operations Management, 19*, 287–306. doi:10.1016/S0272-6963(00)00052-8

Strattona, R., & Warburton, R. D. H. (2003). The strategic integration of agile and lean supply. *International Journal of Production Economics, 85*, 183–198. doi:10.1016/S0925-5273(03)00109-9

Summers, D. C. S. (2006). *Quality*. Upper Saddle River, NJ: Pearson Education, Inc.

Tague, N. R. (2004). *The quality toolbox* (2nd ed.). Milwaukee, WI: ASQ Quality Press.

Turner, W. C., Mize, J. H., Case, K. E., & Nazemetz, J. W. (1993). *Introduction to industrial and systems engineering*, 3rd ed. Englewood, Cliffs, NJ: Prentice Hall.

Womack, J. P., & Jones, D. T. (2003). *Lean thinking: Banish waste and create wealth in your corporation*. New York, NY: Free Press.

ADDITIONAL READING

Brassard, M., & Ritter, D. (1994). *The memory jogger™ II*. Salem, NH: GOAL/QPC.

The, W. Edwards Deming Institute. (n.d.). *Website*. Retrieved from www.deming.org

The Juran Institute. (n.d.). *Website*. Retrieved from www.juran.com

KEY TERMS AND DEFINITIONS

Continuous Improvement (CI): A philosophy that focuses on incremental change that may be small and gradual or a breakthrough with large & rapid improvement to enable a company to give customers what they want the first time, every time (Evans and Lindsay, 2008; Summers, 2006).

Lean: An improvement methodology that uses a systematic approach for identifying and eliminating waste (non-value-added activities) through continuous improvement by flowing the product at the pull of the customer, in pursuit of perfection (Sayer, 2007; Ehrlich, 2002).

Quality: The characteristics of a product or service that bear on its ability to satisfy stated or implied needs; A product or service free of deficiencies (ASQ, 2011).

Quality Assurance (QA): Is planned and systematic activities directed toward providing customers with goods and services of appropriate quality (Evans and Lindsay, 2008).

Quality Control (QC): The use of specifications and inspection to design, produce, review, sustain, and improve the quality of products and service (Summers, 2006).

Six Sigma: A business philosophy that focuses on continuous improvement by understanding customers' needs, analyzing business processes, and instituting proper measurement methods. It seeks to improve quality through reduced variation for every product, process, or transaction in a company, with the ultimate goal of eliminating all defects (Summers, 2006).

Statistical Quality Control (SQC): Statistical data is collected, analyzed, and interpreted to solve problems and monitor production and parts inspection (Summers, 2006).

Statistical Process Control (SPC): The use of statistical methods to prevent defects and control the process (Summers, 2006).

Total Quality Management (TQM): People-focused management system that focuses on increasing customer satisfaction and reducing costs; a systems approach that integrates organizational functions and the entire supply chain and stresses learning and adaptation to change as the keys to success (Evans and Lindsay, 2008).

Value Chain: All of the activities that a company must do to design, order, produce, and deliver a product or service to its customers (MacInnes, 2002).

Chapter 9
Supply Chain Management and the Other Half

Kaninika Bhatnagar
Eastern Illinois University, USA

ABSTRACT

Supply Chain Management operations have traditionally been a gendered career. The role of a diverse workforce, particularly women, is reexamined from the perspective of maximizing the bottom-line and profit sharing in the logistics industry. The unique and problematic diversity issues that underlie both practices and policy in the industry are discussed. These include the more obvious inequities in salaries, to the more insidious and often invisible assumptions that may underlie policy. The net result is detrimental for both business and the basic ethical imperative of equity. The narrative places the discussion of logistics business operations and decision-making in the context of the current research on gender differences, and examines possible ways to create more equitable enterprises, while maintaining and improving the bottom-line.

INTRODUCTION

The chapter examines the role of women in supply chain management, in the context of management practices, education, and HR issues. There is need for an interdisciplinary approach to review a content heavy domain such as supply chain management to avoid too much 'inbreeding' as it were. A new lens often serves to shed new light on an old theme. This chapter provides just such an outlook to reassess practices and operations from a different place and perspective. It may seem a bit trivial, and/or irrelevant to discuss this area through a gender lens. However, it should soon become apparent that the field of SCM, as is perhaps all business, commerce, production, and manufacturing, is deeply gendered in ways that may impede know-how, and the bottom-line,

DOI: 10.4018/978-1-4666-0246-5.ch009

besides being on the wrong side of ethical and moral imperatives. The counter-argument to the above position stems from the assumption that content areas, professional domains, and fields of expertise are neutral by definition. One can posit that it is indeed so, but only in an ideal world. In the world we live in, however, the reality is far from so. There are numbers to prove the existing disparity, however, the discussion needs to move beyond numbers to the deeper problematic that lies underneath.

The issue of gender role assignments is critical in this context. Arguably the role of women in most if not every culture has been that of a nurturer. A nurturer by definition is a secondary role. It implies care giving, support, and servicing functions. Professions such as teachers and health professionals, the nurturers, and caregivers, still constitute the bulk of workforce where women are employed. Men on the other hand, are typically not assigned to or associated with a nurturing role. Without falling into the trap of triviality, it is perhaps safe to assert that gender roles have traditionally worked along the lines of 'primary' and 'secondary' functions. Our social system frames men's work as 'primary'. Engineers, scientists, politicians, stockbrokers, and business personnel are for instance all involved in a 'primary' rather than a 'secondary' occupation. Doubtless, these are stereotypes, and there are contrary instances on either side. Having said that though, women in such roles are still an exception rather than the rule, and often battle unspoken yet deep-seated biases we do not know we have.

It is necessary to delve on this seemingly oft beaten track in a book about business process and strategy, because business forms a 'primary' occupational description. It has traditionally been the male domain, and for good reason. Commerce has formed the underlying lifeline of money, power, and control in various communities, and been fundamentally antithetical to women's traditional role in the societal schema. Today for instance, 15 of the Fortune 500 CEOs are women (CNNMoney, 2010). However, I would venture to state that women make upwards of 80% or more of secretarial staff in those very same companies. The distinction between the primary and secondary roles is starkly visible.

The gender issue in supply chain dynamic must be contextualized along this overall duality. The statistics support the social schema outlined above. Women formed only 15% of all Supply Chain Management VP positions across the country in 2010 (Payscale, 2010). According to the U. S. Census Bureau (2010), women-owned firms accounted for only 28.7% of all non-farm businesses in the U.S. in 2007. This was a mere 6.4% of total employment, and only 4% of total receipts. Equity in position is further compounded by pay scale disparities. Salary gap as reported by Payscale (2010), for a Supply Chain Analyst for instance, can vary from $13.00 to $24.83 an hour for male employees, and $15.50 to $21.68 an hour for female employees. The variance is higher for male employees, however the mean is also higher. According to Logistics, UK, the fastest growing logistics organization in the world, the boards of the UK's 350 top companies all have more male directors than women. Almost half have no women at all. This discrepancy is reflected in the overall numbers where women hold fewer than 10% of the managerial roles in logistics. Moreover women account for a mere 22% of the logistics workforce in the UK, compared with 46% in other sectors. Helms and Guffey (1997) note that from 1980 to 1987 over three million jobs were gained by women that were previously held by men, however, the rise in jobs has not meant equality in wages, benefits and opportunities. This difference in pay and earnings is accounted for by the highly segregated nature of the labor market with women concentrated in what is generally referred to as the "secondary" labor market. Typically, the secondary market is poorly organized, consisting of low pay, low status, and part-time or temporary employment.

This is further compounded by the rapid expansion of the service sector, where women predominate.

Although the gender gap is disappearing in many industries, occupations, roles etc. where women commonly hold leadership positions, "the upper echelon of the supply chain ranks - whether it is transportation, logistics, or warehousing and distribution - has remained the near-exclusive domain of men" (Solomon, 2010). A survey of women in transportation and warehousing by Catalyst, a New York based organization that promotes women's advancements in business, found that there were no female CEOs at the companies polled, moreover only 11% of the firms had women board members and 12.6% had what Catalyst termed female "executive officers". According to Solomon (2010), overall women represented only about 24% of the total labor force at the firms surveyed. Thus the increasing numbers of women in the workforce are not adequately reflected in the higher echelons, the boardrooms and the executive suites of business enterprises where strategy is set, and power resides. This may seem anachronistic for results reported in 2010. These numbers though are only a symptom, and reveal the underlying problematic that ails our economy and social makeup in profound ways.

SCM TODAY: TECHNOLOGY VS. PEOPLE

The supply chain management practices have been undergoing a sea change during the past decade. Local to global trends, and the inevitable morphs of simple to complex networks are ubiquitous. Innovation is perhaps the most salient attribute among the 21st century high technology industries. High tech startups, lean operations, typically university setting incubations that are strong on knowledge capital, form a unique set of emerging technology firms. Although this is only one sector of the supply chain pie, it is an increasingly significant one, both in terms of the dollar value, as well as the research and development imperative. Innovation calls for a fundamentally different supply chain model. Moreover, new technology products may lead to untapped markets requiring innovative supply chain configurations, modeled on lean management and agility rather than stable processes based on predictability and cost efficiency (Lee, 2002). Sebastiao & Golicic, (2008) propose an emerging supply chain mode, focusing on the development and management of highly innovative, early stage technology firms. New product development calls for a flexible model that must effectively create and respond to markets through an iterative trial and error process (Christensen, 2003). The system must have inbuilt resilience and responsiveness in the face of tremendous market variability.

The workforce numbers cited earlier, coupled with the snapshot of a rapidly evolving supply chain industry landscape create a reset, and rethink scenario in terms of policy and practice fundamentals. It is easy to argue that a volatile market, demand unpredictability, coupled with a host of emerging product-base, all call for a technological solution. Companies must invest huge amounts in IT in order to ensure efficient supply chains, necessary to gain competitive advantage. Numerous ways to improve companies' supply chain performance have been proposed (Cook & Greenspan, 2003). More technology is presented as the panacea for all market ills.

Research, however, tends to say otherwise. The human resource issue, or the *people factor* in supply chain management is cited by many as the most overlooked, and critical factor in supply chain competitiveness (McCarter, Fawcett, & Magnan, 2005; Smagalla, 2004; Cook & Greenspan, 2003). It is reported that there is still a bias towards quick IT fixes. Organizations tend to easily embrace technology, yet the effort investing in human resources is poor by comparison. "We know how to invest in technology, but we're at a loss when it comes to investing in people" (Smagalla, 2004, p90). Kakati, (2002) pointed out the need to go beyond technology when looking for monetary gain, and competitive advantage. Organizational change is the super-set within which all technological change must and can happen. Zeleny (2002) describe an organization's IT infrastructure in terms of the human ability to use and apply the technology for users' benefit. Further studies point to the need for investigating people management in SCM research (Gunasekarana & Ngai, 2005; McCarter, Fawcett, & Magnan, 2005). In other words IT is not independent of people. The inclusion of women and diversity in the supply chain workforce must be contextualized within this overall human resource framework. This chapter seeks to investigate issues that are unique to women within the argument for greater human resource efficiency.

SCM Workforce and Diversity: A Gendered Perspective

Diversity is by definition the notion of the 'other'. Arguably there are any number of manifestations of the 'other'-ness: age, ethnicity, class, color, and gender being just some. This chapter investigates the role of gender with respect to issues related to the SCM workforce. The choice although limiting, has been made to ensure a deep rather than a broad discussion of the issues at hand. It must be emphasized though, that the diversity argument is the 'big tent' discourse. Moreover, with changing demographics in the 21st century, the whole notion of diversity must also be reexamined. According to the U.S. Census Bureau, by the year 2050, the minorities of today will together constitute a majority of the country's population (CNN articles, 2008). It may then become necessary to reexamine the debate on diversity from new perspectives. However, even so a part of the diversity question exists within a mental schema of age old established norms and unspoken conventions. That framework is likely to continue even though the narratives of numbers may tell a different story. According to the 2010 U.S. Census, women make up 50.6% of the U.S. population. Women also form the majority of students graduating from our schools. Women receive 6 out of 10 college degrees. According to Education Week's Diplomas Count 2010, about 67% of male students and 74% of female students graduate high school in the U.S. (Education Week, 2010). However, the number of women holding corporate offices and CEO positions in Global Fortune 500 companies is a measly 2.6% (Ibarra & Hanson, 2009).

Business careers are not the most often sought after positions among graduating class of women undergraduates. But then again why should we care? Besides such occupational 'segregation' by gender occurs all the time. Nursing is a predominantly female profession, so is ballet for instance, and there are no complaints in the gender lobby about those. What then is the issue with business as a whole being predominantly male? Clearly there are two ways to look at this question: the more fundamental moral imperative of gender equity, but also the potential gains for the industry as a whole. In the following sections these conceptual categories are discussed in the context of several pertinent issues that may be responsible for reframing the current debate on this subject.

Gender Debate: Context and Subtext

Background

Arguably "Supply Chain Management" is a fancy phrase for optimal distribution of goods and services for maximizing profit, and minimizing waste. SCM has existed as an indispensable industry arm in days well before computers and the global information superhighway. As long as 'for profit transactions' or commerce served the human need for financial gain, some form of SCM was needed for managing effective logistics operations. The question of gender appears quite extraneous. In fact the industry did quite well without the other half up until now. So what does it stand to gain by greater female participation? Perhaps the answer lies to some degree in the changing nature of the SCM industry itself.

In the past ten-fifteen years, the world has shrunk remarkably. Rules have changed repeatedly. Young startup ventures such as Google, and Facebook have defied conventional wisdom and 'taken over the world' in a manner of speaking. In the ancient world of mid-20th century, business required significant capital investment, experience, connections, and an existing brick and mortar establishment. If your family owned a midsize manufacturing facility, where your father, and grandfather before him, was the CEO, it was a high probability, that as a son you were likely to inherit, continue and expand family business. As a daughter you probably visited the factory seldom, if at all, and focused your attention on finding the most eligible bachelor for marriage, or pursue the more 'suitable' professions like teaching, or nursing. Doubtless this is only a caricature of reality at best. There were plenty of exceptions, some well known, most not as much, but they are not the subject of this chapter.

There have been some remarkable and fundamental changes to business during the last ten-fifteen years; notwithstanding the social, and societal conventions or expectations. For instance, if we consider a startup venture today, there is no longer the need for significant capital investment. Access is not dictated by the power of connections. Moreover experience becomes irrelevant when technology and business models are changing so rapidly. A young person today has in fact an advantage in the technology savvy world that his or her grandfather with sizable capital still may not. Notice too that business has become more neutral than it ever was, in gender terms. A young man or woman has access to the same technology tools, and expertise. More importantly technology is more critical than any amount of muscle power. The 'bigness' is suddenly irrelevant in this arena to a very large extent. There is thus a transformational change in prospective demographics for business as a whole, and women as a group are well positioned to take advantage of these fundamental shifts in ways business is conducted.

Transformative Processes

Today supply chains are global, and information intensive, where knowledge management plays a critical role in maintaining one's competitive advantage. A widely accepted definition of SCM describes it as "a set of approaches utilized to efficiently integrate suppliers, manufacturers, warehouses, and stores so that merchandise is produced and distributed in the right quantities, to the right locations and at the right time in order to minimize system-wide costs while satisfying service level requirements of the customers in the entire supply chain" (Mehta, 2004, p.842). With Walmart, for instance, retailing in the United States, and manufacturing in China and Taiwan, the integration of suppliers, manufacturers, warehouses, and stores becomes a global enterprise. The key SCM operations, moreover, become very closely linked to the overall production chain. Warehouse management, inventory control, and product design, for instance, must be carried out within the framework of IT decision support system and the integration of various supply chains by strategic partnering. The critical skills to manage such a complex system are strategic, operational, as well as tactical.

At this point it is interesting to step back a little, and examine what women as a group may bring to this complex operation. In the management of a home or a 'domestic unit' per se, generally it is the woman who performs the 'supply chain' functions. In a traditional home setting the man tends to be the 'producer/manufacturer/supplier' unit, while the woman's role is 'warehouse management/ inventory control/ and the ultimate supply chain integration and distribution'. Far be it perceived as a way to trivialize complex operations, and global systems, nonetheless, it is easy to see that women have been traditionally performing supply chain functions albeit in much smaller and simpler settings. McCarter et al. (2005), lay out a detailed list of skills necessary and valued the most for efficient SCM operation:

- System evaluation and selection
- Negotiation
- Systems thinking and analysis
- Team building and management
- Tradeoff analysis
- Quality Control
- Benchmarking
- Problem solving
- Computer (basic programs to Web Design)
- New product development
- Relationship management
- Process improvement and integration
- Brand management
- Customer Service
- Costing – ABC, target, and total
- Six Sigma
- Outsourcing and the use of 3PLs
- Process integration
- Cycle time reduction

- Value analysis/ value engineering (p. 203)

Beyond the procedural and operational issues, each of the above skills can be categorized along the following triad:

1. Technical
2. Behavioral
3. Managerial

While there is no inherent gender difference in terms of one's capacity to master any of these three sets, however, in many instances women may bring a new approach to the table. For example, according to Park & Krishnan (2005), women approach decision making differently from men. The differences may be critical and complementary. Research also points to a crucial difference among men and women in management skills. Female managers with leadership positions in organizations are seen to be equally effective as their m male counterparts (Eagly & Johnson, 1990), however, in some ways they tend to be more participative and exhibit greater interpersonal skills as leaders than men. According to Byron, (2007), a significant interactive effect was found for female managers who more accurately perceived nonverbal emotional expressions, received higher performance ratings from their supervisor and higher satisfaction ratings from their subordinates. Female managers tend to involve others in decision-making, and seek their input resulting in a collaborative and democratic leadership model (Manning & Robertson, 2010; Eagly & Karau, 1995; Jurma & Powell, 1994). Surely upper management positions in supply chain industry can benefit from such a perspective on decision-making.

It is the thesis of this researcher that sometimes (over)simplification is a necessary tool in the interest of clarity. The tripartite division outlined above may be somewhat broad but it illustrates the need for a strategic negotiation of matching priorities, skills, and capacities among the SCM workforce. Finally, perceptions play a key role in women's education, and career choices. Negative perceptions about what a profession entails, often act as the ultimate gatekeepers, grades and ability notwithstanding (Bhatnagar & Brake, 2010). However, it is also necessary to examine issues beyond perceptions that may be responsible for women's lower participation in this sector.

Gender Equity: The Moral Imperative

Remuneration Structures

It is an open debate whether systemic barriers are worse than barriers of perception, or the other way round. However, the compensation structure is, and has been a systematic impediment. As exhibit-one, it is one of the most blatant instances of disparity between male and female employees.

However, the inequity in pay is a function of job description, more than a result of any employee demographic characteristics. More women are occupied in lower paying jobs down the promotion ladder, and more men are employed in upper income bracket, upper management and CEO positions. Some broad figures quoted in the beginning of this chapter paint this picture all too well. The discrimination, if we can call it that, exists not so much between two equally qualified individuals being offered the same job, and pay. It is instead, the larger and subtler segregation of job levels by gender. More men are CEOs and more women are secretaries. Obviously as an aggregate men make more than women do.

Gender differences in job descriptions and promotion opportunities have been documented along a wide spectrum of fields, and the job market in SCM companies is no exception to the overall trend. Early research literature on this subject includes discussions of organizational structures, and bureaucratic processes that generate and sustain discrimination (Bielby & Baron, 1984; Bergmann, 1986). Women entering the job market at lower wages, also help keep maintaining high wages for men (Bergmann, 1986). To some extent the same argument can be applied to other minorities as well. It was also found that income disparity increased with establishment size (Bielby & Baron, 1984). Ransom & Oaxaca (2005) report a pattern of intra-firm mobility and job assignment that generally penalized women. Hierarchical discrimination is also reported to be at the basis of occupational segregation between men and women, where men are reported to dislike supervision by female managers (Neuman & Oaxaca, 2003; Baldwin, Butler, & Johnson, 2001). Although to be fair, the reported disparity is as much a function of job assignment, and opportunities, as it is that of personal choice and preferences.

The 'secondary' perception of women workforce as discussed in previous sections of this chapter, further aggravates the problem of salary differences. In a 'traditional' family, although the role models are changing there as well, men have always been the primary wage earners and providers. They put food on the table, as it were, while womenfolk engaged in the endless litany of service roles. The problem with secondary wage earners makes women more dispensable than not, especially in trying economic times. Moreover from the employers' point of view dispensable workers are likely to be lower paid compared to their regular workforce. Thus the issues relating to workforce salary are severally intertwined, and gender often acts as a divisory fulcrum. Salary inequities may however, only be a symptom of the larger policy issues that are both more fundamental, and therefore the more immoveable pieces of this jigsaw.

Policy Problems

'Policy' is a delightfully vague term. Whether it is government regulatory policies, legislative initiatives, state and federal 'think tank' recommendations, or private business best practices, in almost each of these cases the assumptions that underlie the newly minted policies are often invisible. These assumptions are also more likely than not, a product of times, conditions, and context that is no longer current. This is especially true of the super fast world of today. One can make the case that there is an inherent lag of at least five to ten years between the implementation of a policy, and the conditions it was designed for.

An instructive and relevant case from the European Union (EU) can be discussed here. The EU economic policy defines 'value' as moving up the value chain, and articulates it as an economic objective (Browne, Moylan, & Scaife, 2010). Promoting and rewarding innovation and risk takers in business start-ups is a core value of EU economic policy. There are no arguments about the laudable economic goal of moving up the value chain, which in turn should lead to promotion and development of higher value jobs. However, as

Browne et al. (2010) point out, an unanticipated consequence of this objective is the exclusion of female entrepreneurs, who typically tend to be self-employed, and located within the low-tech micro-enterprise within the service sector. The objective as stated implies an expectation of high level of technical skills, competence, and knowledge from its potential workforce. Low-tech micro enterprises would tend to be set-aside in this policy framework. It is reasonable to extend Browne et al.'s argument closer to home. Low-tech startups typically exhibit limited growth potential. Female entrepreneurs more often than not tend to move towards low-tech ventures. It is of course easy to assign causality here. However, the operative factor is the assessment of risk, and risk taking behaviors. Women in general tend to exhibit lower risk taking behaviors. The reasons may be a diversion into historical and sociological gender debate, however, familial responsibilities forming the biggest piece of most women's plate, external risk taking tends to be moderate to low. Moreover, raising funds for starting their own business continues to be a greater challenge for women. Service sector presents a less expensive alternative, where home-based, low technology startups are possible. This is a self-perpetuating pattern that contributes in part to locating women in low income, low technology, and low growth sectors.

This is an illustration of ways in which behavioral and traditional gender role assignments have historically diminished women's inclination and capacity for engaging in high-risk behaviors. There is a clear mismatch between entrepreneurial drive, and realities at home. Policy initiatives can exacerbate such mismatch. The previously cited EU example illustrates how female entrepreneurs in Europe risk being doubly disadvantaged. Browne et al. discuss this notion, where on the one hand women's acquired skill set through employment lacks critical business acumen. Moreover, as a group they tend to move to low-tech service sector with potential of limited growth. The well-meaning government policy thus ends up contributing to the perpetuation of disadvantaged groups.

The solution for this particular instance could be twofold. Firstly, the policy makers in government can acknowledge the importance and key role of service sector to regional economy. Such a determination is exclusive of any discriminatory argument. Both technical and service sectors must be equally promoted to create a healthy economic environment. Secondly, the underlying and often invisible reasons that propel women into service sector and away from technical enterprises must be examined at a policy level. Many reasons are vestiges from the past, a function of our collective historic memory rather than reflective of any reality on the ground per se.

Linear vs. Life-Course Career Pathways

There are some fundamental differences between male and female life course pathways, objectives, and priorities. The age-old dualism of career vs. family is alive and well in the 21st century. These differences translate differently for different careers, some more than others. So for instance, the conventional career pathway of a teacher or a nurse is more aligned with not only the supposed inclination and interest, but also with the variety of life course changes a woman is likely to go through; marriage and childcare being the most critical of these. So for instance careers that typically require a lot of travel, relocation, longer hours, and/or unpredictable schedules may not work with a woman's constant and predictable obligations at home.

When we examine business career pathways in the context mentioned above, it becomes clear how male and female entrepreneurs may have very different goals. It is critical to understand this difference that may drive male and female business persons in unique ways. For instance, McMurray (2002) suggests that the emphasis on growth may not be compatible with the goals and objectives of female entrepreneurs, where businesswomen may require a more flexible model that can accommodate a number of exit and reentry routes. Businessmen on the other hand, are more likely to focus on a sustained growth pattern. Thus a male oriented business model is likely to be more linear in nature, with predetermined steps or stages determined by the business life cycle. A typical entrepreneurial business venture tends to go through a sequence of stages according to the business life cycle. A majority of female entrepreneurs however, may be turned away by the highly structured nature of this business model, and may "need to take a different type of 'journey' to that of their male counterparts for family related reasons" (Browne, Moylan, & Scaife, 2010, p114).

Research findings reported by the Kaufmann Foundation (2009) reinforce this theme. The study found that women who achieved fast growth for their firms had taken a more varied path to business ownership than their male counterparts. It was also found that female executives were less likely to have relevant managerial or executive experience, although increasingly they were likely to have a professional background (Mattis, 2000). It is important to recognize and acknowledge this disparity, in order to fully appreciate women's role and contributions to today's business processes. A parallel schema is reported by research in science and technology education (Bhatnagar & Brake, 2010; Eccles, 1994), where the more traditional education and career pathways tend to be linear and male dominated, while alternate life-course trajectories offer possibilities for women in closing the gender gap.

It is important to note that the so-called gender difference lies essentially in the implementation, rather than the substance of any business format. As all business has traditionally been male dominated, the 'time-tested', established models for successful business practices are linear or favor a male framework. It is however possible to cast these very same processes in a different mold, favoring a female framework which may turn out to be more lateral and flexible, rather than linear and rigid. Children and family domain, traditionally a woman's responsibility, are more likely to be addressed in such a framework. A strictly linear model on the other hand, will risk distancing a majority of female entrepreneurs.

The preceding discussion on career pathways has addressed business in general, without focusing on SCM operations in particular. However, the operating criteria are almost identical in terms of the linear, and rigid framework of work, as well as the inherent systemic unpredictability. All business is driven by factors that are external, and therefore unknowns to a large degree: the economies of supply and demand, and the variability of customer behavior for example. SCM must be fine tuned in real time, as must all other business operations. This inherent flux in the very nature of all business or commerce creates a problematic gender dynamic.

ETHICAL IMPERATIVE VS. BUSINESS OBJECTIVES

Discussions on business strategies and goals may often overlook ethical factors; after all the idea is to maximize profit, where notions of moral good may seem a bit anachronistic and irrelevant. However, I would argue that the diversity and gender factor in any business tends to work in the favor of furthering the economic bottom-line of any enterprise. So let us put ethics aside for a moment, and examine business practices more closely. According to a study commissioned by the London Central Learning and Skills Council, and the London Human Resource Group, a more diverse workforce improves business performance. It allows companies to tap into new customer groups (Newsdesk, 2004). Reported benefits included higher retention rates, reduction in recruitment costs, greater customer satisfaction, access to a wider customer base, better supply chain management and access to new ideas on process and product improvements. There is no doubt a 'wrong' way of 'doing diversity', where being a diverse workplace becomes a matter of fulfilling quota requirements without any thought towards business strategy. All too often the need for a diverse workplace is not adequately integrated at higher levels of business goals, and objectives where a strategic partnership can be structured to benefit the business as a whole.

The diversity directive needs to be practiced *inwards*. So in other words, if a business actively promotes values, practices, and environment that invite people with diverse backgrounds, instead of creating an artificial diversity by fulfilling regulatory imperatives, it is more likely to ensure increased profits, as well as structure a more welcoming work environment. Senior managers can structure the business in a way that makes it more open to women. Having said that though, one cannot overlook the more fundamental imperative of being equitable and just. Creating business environments that are more conducive and open to women not only makes for a sound managerial strategy, but also contributes to the long overdue directives of fairness and equal opportunity. Our law books have had these for sometime; however, translation in the real world requires substantial reframing, and restructuring of current practices, policies, and assumptions.

FUTURE RESEARCH DIRECTIONS AND RECOMMENDATIONS

Clearly there is a need for moving beyond the moral argument towards greater inclusion, profitability and success. A strategic plan that incorporates the goals outlined in this chapter, in order to translate theory to practice is sorely needed. Future research can focus on identifying measurable objectives that can serve as the evaluation criteria to achieve these goals. One such set of recommendations is the inclusion of women and diversity when appointing senior board members of logistics companies was outlined by the UK Financial Reporting Council (FRC) (Logistics & Handling, June 2010). Although the report addresses a different market, the ideas are quite relevant for us here in the United States as well. The strategies outlined in this report for promoting diversity in logistics companies serve to reinforce, and extend the discussion we have engaged in this chapter.

According to FRC a successful diversity initiative will come from the top leadership, rather than being an HR program. Lasting change comes from within where senior sponsorship can firmly embed the change within the organization. Welcoming women in senior ranks goes beyond policy initiative to reframing the cultural norms of a company. Hiring must go hand in hand with retention. Not only must businesses be more open to hiring diverse candidates, but once in the pool ways to actively engage, encourage, and incentivize talent must be practiced. From the business partners' point of view such initiatives are not likely to be cost intensive. Reforming business practices to welcome more women for instance, will be an exercise in revisiting established policies to create more flexible programming & leave and benefits package, and a more open environmental culture. The critical idea is to point the diversity directive in any business or organization inwards. Best practices must however, be encoded in some sort of measurable language, with a clear translation from goals to performance objectives and accountability, where 'success' can be defined by a set of evaluation criteria.

CONCLUSION

This chapter has attempted to highlight various issues pertaining to the role of diversity in general, and women in particular in the supply chain management operations today. Barriers to entry, and advancement are twofold. From the point of view of the entrant, the female employee, or prospective employee, the barriers of perception become the initial gatekeepers. These are compounded by the inherent nature of work, which may be cyclical, unpredictable, often creating hostile environment from the point of view of the woman worker who will typically have different life goals and priorities. Government directives may further complicate matters by formulating policies often based on invisible societal assumptions that unintentionally disadvantage one group over another.

Furthermore, it has also been shown that diversity is good for business. Several studies mentioned previously attest to the fact that diversity tends to improve the bottom-line, provided it is structured as an integral open business environment, and not an unrelated attempt to shore up the 'numbers'. It is a good idea solely as a business strategy, the moral and ethical imperative notwithstanding. Actionable recommendations based on the FRC diversity initiative have been emphasized. However, any similar proposal can succeed if it has been integrated into the company culture, and strategic goals.

Lastly a note on the nature of business itself, there has been a seismic shift towards more agile supply chains spanning complex business operations that are global in scope. The role of the Internet and digital revolution has made for unprecedented changes in the supply chain cycle. Boundaries are fading. The nature of work and the employee demographic is changing. It is an ideal time to revisit the issue of diversity in supply chain workforce, and examine ways in which a more diversified personnel can contribute uniquely to the business processes.

REFERENCES

Baldwin, M. L., Butler, R. J., & Johnson, W. G. (2001). A hierarchical theory of occupational segregation and wage discrimination. *Economic Inquiry*, *39*(1), 94–110. doi:10.1093/ei/39.1.94

Bergmann, B. R. (1986). *The economic emergence of women*. New York, NY: Basic Books.

Bhatnagar, K., & Brake, M. (2010). Gender differences in technology perceptions of high school students and their intent to choose technology college majors. *Journal of Engineering Technology*, *27*(2), 8–16.

Bielby, W. T., & Baron, J. N. (1984). A woman's place is with other women: Sex segregation within organizationsIn Reskin, B. (Ed.), *Sex segregation in the workplace* (pp. 27–55). Washington, DC: National Academy Press.

Browne, J., Moylan, T., & Scaife, A. (2010). Female entrepreneurs – Out of the frying pan, into the fire? *Irish Journal of Management*, *28*(2), 109–133.

Byron, K. (2007). Male and female managers' ability to 'read' emotions: Relationships with supervisor's performance ratings and subordinates' satisfaction ratings. *Journal of Occupational and Organizational Psychology*, *80*(4), 713–733. doi:10.1348/096317907X174349

Christensen, C. M. (2003). *The innovator's dilemma*. New York, NY: Harper Collins Publishers.

CNN. (2008). *Minorities expected to be majority in 2050*. Retrieved from http://articles.cnn.com/2008-08-13/us/census.minorities_1_hispanic-population-census-bureau-white-population?_s=PM:US

Cook, M., & Greenspan, N. (2003). Why companies fail the supply chain basics. *European Business Journal*, *15*(2), 74–78.

Eagly, A. H., & Johnson, B. T. (1990). Gender and leadership style: A meta-analysis. *Psychological Bulletin*, *108*(2), 233–256. doi:10.1037/0033-2909.108.2.233

Eagly, A. H., & Karau, S. J. (1995). Gender and the effectiveness of leaders: A meta-analysis. *Psychological Bulletin, 117*(1), 125–145. doi:10.1037/0033-2909.117.1.125

Eccles, J. S. (1994). Understanding women's educational and occupational choices. *Psychology of Women Quarterly, 18*, 585–609. doi:10.1111/j.1471-6402.1994.tb01049.x

Education Week. (June 2, 2010). *Graduation by the numbers*. Retrieved from http://www.edweek.org/ ew/articles/2010/06/ 10/34execsum.h29.html

Gunasekarana, A., & Ngai, E. W. T. (2005). Build-to-order supply chain management: A literature review and framework for development. *Journal of Operations Management, 23*(5), 423–451. doi:10.1016/j.jom.2004.10.005

Helms, C., & Guffey, C. (1997). The role of women in Europe. *European Business Review, 97*(2), 80–85. doi:10.1108/09555349710162580

Ibarra, H., & Hanson, M. (2009, December 21). Women CEOs: Why so few? *Harvard Business Review*. Retrieved from http://blogs.hbr.org/ cs/2009/12/women_ceo_why_so_few.html

Jurma, W. E., & Powell, M. L. (1994). Perceived gender roles of managers and effective conflict management. *Psychological Reports, 74*(1), 104–106. doi:10.2466/pr0.1994.74.1.104

Kakati, M. (2002). Mass customization - needs to go beyond technology. *Human Systems Management, 21*, 85–93.

Kaufmann Foundation. (2009). *Characteristics of new firms: A comparison by gender: Third in a series of reports using data from the Kaufmann Firm survey*. Kaufmann, the Foundation of Entrepreneurship, January 2009, Retrieved from http://www.kauffman.org/ uploadedfiles/kfs_gender_020209.pdf

Lee, H. L. (2002). Aligning supply chain strategies with product uncertainties. *California Management Review, 44*(3), 105–119.

Logistics Handling. (June 8, 2010). *Diversity and inclusion in logistics: Why bother?* International Institute for Material Handling and Logistics. Retrieved from http://www.LogisticsHandling.com

Manning, T., & Robertson, B. (2010). Seniority and gender differences in 360-degree assessments of influencing, leadership and team behaviors. Part 1: Introduction and seniority differences. *Industrial & Commercial Training, 42*(3), 139–146. doi:10.1108/00197851011038123

Mattis, M. (2000). Women entrepreneurs in the United StatesIn Davidson, M. J., & Burke, R. (Eds.), *Women in management: Current research issues* (*Vol. 11*). London, UK: Sage.

McCarter, M. W., Fawcett, S. E., & Magnan, G. M. (2005). The effect of people on the supply chain world: Some overlooked issues. *Human Systems Management, 24*, 197–208.

McMurray, A. (2002). *Mapping the support provision for women in enterprise in Northern Ireland and a strategic framework for the future*. Ann McMurray Consulting Ltd.

Mehta, J. (2004, July-August). Supply chain management in a global economy. *Total Quality Management, 15*(5-6), 841–848. doi:10.1080/14783360410001680279

Money, C. N. N. (2010). *Fortune 500: Women CEOs*. Retrieved from http://money.cnn.com/ magazines/fortune/ fortune500/2009/womenceos/

Neuman, S., & Oaxaca, S. (2003). Gender versus ethnic wage differentials among professionals: Evidence from Israel. *Annales d'Economie et de Statistique, 71-72*, 267–292.

Newsdesk. (March 2004). Employers raising the bottom line through diversity. *Management Services, 48*(3), 6.

Park, D., & Krishnan, H. (2005). Gender differences in supply chain management practices. *International Journal of Management and Enterprise Development*, *2*(1), 27–37. doi:10.1504/IJMED.2005.006022

Payscale.com. (2010). *Salary snapshot of VP, supply chain management jobs*. Retrieved from http://www.payscale.com/research/US/Job=Vice_President_(VP),_Supply_Chain_Management/Salary

Payscale.com. (2010). *Hourly rate snapshots of supply chain analysts' jobs*. Retrieved from http://www.payscale.com/ research/US/Job=Supply_Chain_Analyst/ Hourly_Rate/by_Gender

Ransom, M., & Oaxaca, R. (2005). Intrafirm mobility and sex differences in pay. *Industrial & Labor Relations Review*, *58*(2).

Sebastiao, H. J., & Golicic, S. (2008). Supply chain strategy for nascent firms in emerging technology markets. *Journal of Business Logistics*, *29*(1), 75–91. doi:10.1002/j.2158-1592.2008.tb00069.x

Smagalla, D. (2004). Supply-chain culture clash. *MIT Sloan Management Review*, *46*(1), 6.

Solomon, M. B. (June 3, 2010)/ Women shattering logistics/ glass ceilings. *DcVelocity.com.* Retrieved from http://www.dcvelocity.com/articles/20100603_women_shattering_logistics_glass_ceiling

U.S. Census Bureau. (2010). *Survey of business owners - Women owned firms: 2007.* Retrieved from http://www.census.gov/ econ/sbo/get07sof.html?8

Zeleny, M. (2002). Knowledge of enterprise: Knowledge management or knowledge technology? *International Journal of Information Technology and Decision Making*, *1*(2), 181–207. doi:10.1142/S021962200200021X

ADDITIONAL READING

Albelda, R. P. (1986). Occupational segregation by race and gender, 1958-1981. *Industrial & Labor Relations Review*, *39*(3), 404–411. doi:10.2307/2524099

Bayard, K., Hellerstein, J. K., Neumark, D., & Troske, K. R. (2003). New evidence on sex segregation and sex differences in wages from matched employee-employer data. *Journal of Labor Economics*, *21*(4), 887–992. doi:10.1086/377026

Bender, P. S. (2000). Debunking five supply chain myths. *Supply Chain Management Review*, *4*(1), 52–58.

Beth, S., Burt, D. N., Copacino, W., Gopal, C., Lee, H., & Lynch, R. P. (2003). Supply chain challenges: Building relationships. *Harvard Business Review*, *81*(7), 64–73, 117.

Boraas, S., & Rodgers, W. M. (2003). How does gender play a role in earnings gap? An update. *Monthly Labor Review*, March, 2003. U.S. Department of Labor, Bureau of Labor Statistics. Retrieved from http://www.bls.gov/ opub/mlr/2003/03/art2full.pdf

Brake, M., & Bhatnagar, K. (2008). Gender differences in high school students' views of technology. *American Society of Engineering Education (ASEE) Conference Proceedings*, June 2008, Pittsburgh, PA

Brush, C., Carter, N., Gatewood, E., Greene, P., & Hart, M. (2004). *Clearing the hurdles: Women building high-growth businesses*. London, UK: FT Prentice Hall, Pearson Education Inc.

Dejardin, A. (2008, September). *Gender dimensions of globalization.* Discussion paper presented at the meeting on Globalization – Decent Work and Gender, the Oslo Conference on Decent Work – A key to Social Justice for a Fair Globalization, International Labor Organization. Retrieved from http://www.ilo.org/ wcmsp5/groups/public/-dgreports/-integration/ documents/meetingdocument/wcms_100856.pdf

Gattorna, J. (2010). *Dynamic supply chains: Delivering value through people*. New York, NY: Pearson Financial Times

Hisrich, R., & Brush, C. (1996). *The women entrepreneur: Starting, financing and managing a successful new business*. Lexington, MA: Lexington Books.

Kaufmann Foundation. (2010). *Sources of financing for new technology firms: A comparison by gender*. Kaufmann Firm Survey. Retrieved from http://www.kauffman.org/ research-and-policy/ sources-of-financing-for-new-technology-firms-a-comparison-by-gender.aspx

Kaufmann Foundation. (2010). *Gatekeepers of venture growth: The role and participation of women in the venture capital industry.* Kaufmann Firm Survey. Retrieved from http://www.kauffman.org/ research-and-policy/gatekeepers-of-venture-growth.aspx

Kovács, G., & Tatham, P. (2009). Humanitarian logistics performance in the light of gender. *International Journal of Productivity and Performance Management*, *58*(2), 174–187. doi:10.1108/17410400910928752

Lee, H. L. (2004). The triple-A supply chain. *Harvard Business Review*, *82*(10), 102–112.

Liker, J. K., & Choi, T. Y. (2004). Building deep supplier relationships. *Harvard Business Review*, *82*(12), 104–113.

Marlow, S., & Carter, S. (2004). Accounting for change: Professional status, gender disadvantage and self employment. *Women in Management Review*, *19*(1), 5–17. doi:10.1108/09649420410518395

McAfee, M. B., Glassman, M., & Honeycutt, E. D. Jr. (2002). The effects of culture and human resource management policies on supply chain management strategy. *Journal of Business Logistics*, *23*(1), 1–18. doi:10.1002/j.2158-1592.2002.tb00013.x

Miller, M. (2010). Humanitarian logistics and WISE (Women's Institute for Supply Chain Excellence). *Logistics and Transport.* Retrieved from http://www.insidecareers.co.uk/ __802574D80054B660.nsf/idlive/7QUEFBTDEN!opendocument

Moore, D., & Buttner, P. (1997). *Women entrepreneurs: Moving beyond the glass ceiling.* Thousand Oaks, CA: Sage.

Narayanan, V. G., & Raman, A. (2004). Aligning incentives in supply chains. *Harvard Business Review*, *82*(11), 94–102.

Selko, A. (2008). Supply chain salary survey: Survey confirms professional credentials, gender make a difference. *Industry Week.* Retrieved from http://www.industryweek.com/ articles/supply_chain_salary_survey_16419.aspx

Slone, R. E. (2004). Leading a supply chain turnaround. *Harvard Business Review*, *82*(10), 114–121.

Still, L. V., & Timms, W. (2000). Women's business: The flexible alternative workstyle for women. *Women in Management Review*, *15*(5/6), 272–283. doi:10.1108/09649420010372931

Stoica, M., Liao, J., & Welsch, H. (2004). Organizational culture and patterns of information processing: The case of small and medium-sized enterprises. *Journal of Developmental Entrepreneurship*, *9*(3), 251–266.

Tompkins, J. A. (2000). *No boundaries: Moving beyond supply chain management*. Relaigh, NC: Tompkins Press.

United Nations. (2010). *On business & human rights: Gender discussion.* Special Representative of the Secretary-General. Retrieved from http://www.srsgconsultation.org/ index.php/main/discussion?discussion_id=17

Winn, J. (2004). Entrepreneurship: Not an easy path to top management for women. *Women in Management Review*, *19*(3), 143–153. doi:10.1108/09649420410529852

KEY TERMS AND DEFINITIONS

Behavioral Skills: In the context of this chapter, the behavioral skills needed for an efficient SCM operation may include, but not be limited to negotiation, team building, relationship management, customer service, & process improvement and integration skills.

Diversity: The notion of 'other'-ness, where a diverse group may exhibit variations including, but not limited to ethnicity, gender, age, culture, socioeconomic profile, and lifestyle. Diversity is referenced against a supposed 'norm'-al demographic profile, which may represent the majority community in a given context.

Entrepreneur: In the context of this chapter, a business entrepreneur can be defined as an individual engaged in a commercial for-profit enterprise; who may exhibit high-risk taking behavior, self-sustaining financial capacity, and likely have irregular and unpredictable work hours.

Gender Roles: The social consensus on various roles and responsibilities pertaining to male and female gender that typically results in occupational segregation

Global Supply Chains: Trans-national business processes leading to a high degree of supplier, manufacturer, and distributor integration in knowledge-management and information intensive global network.

Linear vs. Life-Course Pathways: Career pathways are defined in terms of direct vs. indirect, circuitous route to career goals. Career responsibilities are matched with familial obligations to correlate jobs to gender roles.

Primary vs. Secondary Occupations: Categorizing job descriptions by 'production' (manufacturing/ operations/ management), vs. 'support' (servicing/ secretarial) duties.

Chapter 10
Identifying the Determinants of Customer Retention in a Developing Country Context

Norizan Mohd Kassim
University Technology Malaysia, Malaysia

ABSTRACT

This chapter investigates how image, perceived service quality, and satisfaction determine customer retention in the retail banking industry in Malaysia. Data was obtained using a self-administered survey involving a convenience sample of 134 retail banking customers in Malaysia. The results show that image is both directly and indirectly related to retention through satisfaction, while perceived service quality is indirectly related to retention through satisfaction. The chapter concludes that satisfaction is not the sole determinant of retention in retail banking. Some managerial implications of this research find that the interrelationships between the determinants (image, quality, and satisfaction) allow bank managers to better understand the dynamics of customer retention formation.

INTRODUCTION

The financial landscape is undergoing transformation, driven by financial liberalization and consolidation, economic transformation, and more discerning consumers. These developments have been reinforced by technological advancements, which have allowed the developments of new and more efficient delivery and processing channels as well as more innovative products and services. Against this backdrop, a number of challenges have emerged. Foremost amongst these is intensified competitive pressures, spurred by financial liberalization and technology revolution. Banking institutions are facing competition not only from each other but also from non-traditional competi-

DOI: 10.4018/978-1-4666-0246-5.ch010

tors such as non-bank financial intermediaries as well as from alternative sources of financing, such as the capital markets. Another strategic challenge facing banking institutions today is the growing and changing needs and expectations of consumers in tandem with increased education levels and growing wealth. Consumers are becoming increasingly discerning and have become more involved in their financial decisions. For this reason, they are demanding a broader range of products and services at more competitive prices through more efficient and convenient channels. As such the need to enhance the competitiveness of the banking sector to withstand forces of change and compete in this more liberalization environment becomes even more pressing. Successful institutions will be the ones with the agility to adapt swiftly and respond to the changing market needs through-innovative and differentiated product offerings; excellent service quality; and superior level of efficiency. Moreover, to meet the challenge from more discerning and demanding consumers, it is equally important for banking institutions to complement the richer and more customized range of product offerings with higher levels of service performance. Of important is the enhancement on customer relationship management and development of 'front-office' strategy that is aligned with the customer-centric value proposition to improve customer satisfaction and retention.

Therefore, what seems vital is a deep understanding of the *factors influencing customer retention*. In particularly, the first primary objective of this research was to investigate the impact of image on consumers' perception of the service quality and their satisfaction with that service. Secondly, the paper aims at determining the relationship between consumers' satisfaction and consumers' retention. The research is undertaken within the context of the retail banking services in a developing country, i.e. Malaysia, one of the most important economies in the South East Asia. It is hoped that the findings of this study will be useful to other countries with similar environment and level of economic development.

LITERATURE REVIEW

Importance of Service Retention

Retention of current customers or loyalty is of interest to many researchers (Broyles, 2009; de Matos, Henrique & de Rosa, 2009; Dowling & Uncle 1997; Ganguli & Roy, 2011; Ganesh et. al., 2000; Mittal & Lassar 1998). The emphasis on customer retention is justified by the lesser cost of retaining a customer than obtaining a new one (Fornell 1992; Fornell & Wernerfelt, 1987; Keaveney, 1995; Reichheld & Kenny, 1990; Reichheld & Sasser, 1990). For instance, by retaining its customers, a company might avoid or reduce its costs of advertising to entice new customers, costs of a personal selling pitch to new prospects, costs of setting up new accounts, costs of explaining business procedures to new clients, and costs of inefficient dealings during the customer's learning process (Barsky, 1994; Mittal & Lassar 1998; Peppers & Rogers, 1993; Reichheld & Sasser, 1990). Furthermore, it was argued that a company can presumably increase its revenues and profits (Palmatier & Gopalakrishna, 2005) by inducing its existing customers to increase their *usage* (Danaher & Rust, 1996). For example, retaining customers and trying to encourage them into more profitable states for their banks seems an appropriate customer service strategy (Colgate et al., 1995; Dawes & Swailes, 1999; Palmatier & Gopalakrishna, 2005). This profitability is assumed to result from quality because higher quality leads to satisfied customers (Anderson et al., 1994; Cronin & Taylor, 1992; Danaher & Rust, 1996; Parasuraman et al., 1988) and satisfied customers tend to use more of a service or product (Danaher & Rust, 1996).

Retention may be demonstrated in multiple ways; for example, by expressing preference for a company over others, by continuing to purchase from it or by increasing its business in the future through continued purchasing (Rahman & Azhar, 2011; Zeithaml et. al., 1996). However, where measures of customer retention have been sought, operationalization has proven difficult because customer retention involves behavior over *time*. Moreover, loyalty is a separate construct to those of repurchase intention and customer satisfaction/dissatisfaction towards an organization. These latter aspects of a customer relationship are subjected to contingencies and do not necessarily predict future behavior (Madden, 2000). Furthermore, service industries present a more difficult setting to understanding customer retention or loyalty than manufactured goods industries because the basis of consumer choice and continued patronage are less obvious (Mittal & Lassar, 1998). Services are intangible and they cannot be completely standardized and they vary according to the mood of the service provider and service customer at the moment of service delivery. Thus, in service businesses, what is given and received is relatively intangible which will result in customer evaluation criteria being less well articulated, and the appraisal of the value received to be much more subjective (Keaveney, 1995; Lovelock, 1991; Zeithaml et al., 1993).

Service Quality and Satisfaction

Kassim (2006) found that both customer satisfaction and customer perceptions of service quality were important predictors of customer retention in telecommunication services. Bloemer et al (1998) have identified similar relationship; both customer satisfaction and customer perceptions of service quality were important predictors of loyalty in retail banking services.

Indeed, a positive relationship between service quality and satisfaction has been well established in the banking sector (Ganguli & Roy, 2011; Jamal & Naser, 2002; Hooi Ting, 2004). In the retail banking services area, most models of customer evaluations of services focus on the comparative judgment of expectations versus perceived performance resulting in the two major evaluative judgments of perceived service quality and customer satisfaction (Bloemer et al., 1998; Kanning & Bergmann, 2009; Murphy, 1996; Smith, 1995). For example, customers assess service quality by comparing their expectations prior to their service encounter with a bank (employee), they develop perceptions during the service delivery process and then they compare their perceptions to their expectations with the actual service received from the bank employee. However, some researchers argue that comparison of perceived performance against expectations may not explain the customer satisfaction/dissatisfaction formation adequately without considering post consumption evaluations that dominate perceived performance. Thus, perceived performance alone may be the best predictor of satisfaction (Kanning & Bergmann, 2009). Moreover, perceived performance has been modeled frequently in the literature as directly affecting the satisfaction decision (Cronin & Taylor, 1992; Churchill & Suprenant, 1982; Halstead et al., 1994; Oliver & DeSarbo, 1988; Patterson & Johnson, 1993; Tse & Wilton, 1988). Performance can be defined as the perception of a customer's judgment of the service offered by the organization (Llosa et al., 1998). Thus, in this research, we used perceived performance as the measurement of perceived service quality and it is comprehensively defined as 'the subjective evaluation made by customer over a certain period of time after a service encounter.' Therefore, satisfaction can be considered as the customer's evaluation of the service received.

The Relationship between Image, Quality, Satisfaction, and Retention

It has been suggested that image has been viewed as a critical aspect of a company's ability to maintain its market share position. The reason being that image has been related to core aspects of organizational success such as customer patronage (Bloemer et al. 1998; Granbois, 1981; Kassim et al., 2010; Kargaonkar et al., 1985). Previous research also reported that image significantly affects consumers' perception of quality (Bloemer et al. 1998; Hildebrandt, 1988; Mazursky & Jacoby, 1986). Bloemer et al. (1998) found that both quality and satisfaction were important predictors of loyalty, but satisfaction in fact had the strongest relationship with loyalty (de Matos, Henrique and de Rosa, 2009; Ganguli and Roy, 2011; Pont & McQuilken, 2005). Meanwhile, quality has both direct and indirect (through satisfaction) impact on loyalty. They also found that while image does not have a direct positive or indirect effect (via satisfaction) on loyalty, it nevertheless has an impact on satisfaction via quality. The relationship between retention and image, however, remained unclear as to whether there is a direct relationship between image and retention or whether this relationship is mediated by, for example, quality and satisfaction (see Figure 1).

Based on the above theoretical background, we propose the following hypotheses:

- H_1: Image has a direct positive effect on customer retention
- H_2: Image has an indirect positive effect on customer retention via customer satisfaction
- H_3: Image has a direct positive effect on quality
- H_4: Quality has a direct positive effect on customer retention
- H_5: Quality has an indirect positive effect on retention via satisfaction
- H_6: Satisfaction has direct positive effect on retention

RESEARCH METHOD

Questionnaire Design

A cross-sectional survey design was adopted which questioned respondents on a range of banking services. The design of the questionnaire was based on multiple-item (quality) and single-item measurement (image, satisfaction and retention) scales. The reliability tests for these single-item measures are good (as described in the following paragraphs) and thus for this reason, we believe that the measures are adequate (Mittal et al., 1998). Items related to image of the bank measurements

Figure 1. The relationship between image, quality, satisfaction, and retention and their linkages

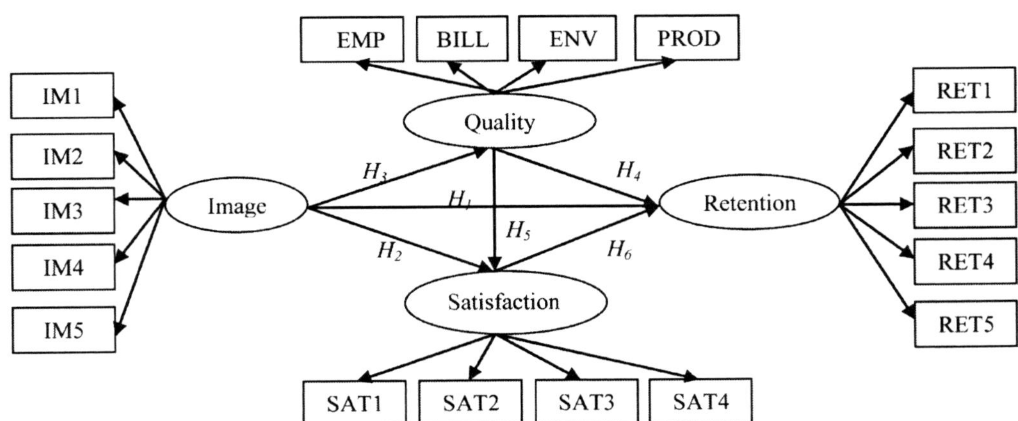

were taken from a previous research (Bloemer et. al., 1998). These items were adapted to the specific characteristics of our research setting. Five image items in the questionnaire were selected and measured on a four-point Likert scale, ranging from 1 = disagree to 4 = agree. This scale was pre-tested and found to be valid and reliable with Cronbach alpha equal to 0.83 (see Table 1).

Items related to perceived service quality were based on the service quality literature by Parasuraman et al., 1988. These items were modified to suit this research, i.e. in a retail banking setting with Cronbach alpha equals to 0.95. Regarding customer satisfaction with the bank services, the current study referred to Patterson and Smith's (2003) research, and identified four satisfaction-related items. These were measured on a four-point Likert scale ranging from 1 = disagree to 4 = disagree. This scale was found valid and reliable with Cronbach alpha of 0.90 (see Table 1).

The second part of the questionnaire addressed the issue of retention. Only the favorable measures established in the literature were used (for example, Boulding et al., 1993; Danaher and Rust, 1996; Heskett et al., 1994; Levesque and McDougall, 1996; Zeithaml et. al., 1996). Respondents were asked about their preference for the current service provider, intention of recommending the service to others, intention of continuing using the service, intention of increasing the usage of the service and intention not to switch to other bank. Recommending the service to others will attract new customers through the mechanism of positive word-of-mouth comments that will subsequently reduce the marketing costs the company must spend to get additional customers (Danaher and Rust, 1996; Parasuraman et. al., 1988, 1991; Zeithaml et. al., 1996; Zeithaml, 2000). Preferring the service to others (Woodside et.al., 1989; Zeithaml, 2000) indicates that the experiences that customers had with the service provider influenced their decision not to defect or switch to others (Bhote, 1997). Continuing to use the service and having no intention to switch indicate that customers will have the strongest levels of retention intentions and the weakest to switch (Danaher and Rust, 1996; Zeithaml et. al., 1996). Five retention-related items were identified and measured on a four-point Likert scale (ranging from 1 = disagree to 4 = agree). The Cronbach alpha for this was 0.86.

The last part of the questionnaire consisted of a series of respondents' demographic and socio-economic characteristics such as ethnicity, gender, age, marital status, education, occupation and income. This information was asked at the end of the questionnaire because of its private and personal nature (Aaker et al., 2000; Malhotra, 1993; Sekaran, 2000).

Table 1. Summary of descriptive statistics of the variables

Construct Variables[a]	Image	Quality				SAT	RET
		EMP	BILL	ENV	PROD		
Mean	2.92	2.65	2.89	2.78	2.65	2.74	2.85
Std. Dev.	0.69	0.68	0.62	0.60	2.70	0.63	0.63
CA	0.83	0.94	0.86	0.88	0.92	0.90	0.86
CR	0.83	0.94	0.87	0.88	0.94	0.90	0.86

Note: [a] EMP = Bank employee, BILL = Billing integrity, ENV = Banking environment, PROD = Products and services; SAT = Satisfaction; RET = Retention; CA = Cronbach Alpha; CR = Composite reliability

Sample

An empirical study was conducted among the retail banking customers of a major banks in Malaysia. A data set to test the proposed model came from a self-administered and telephone survey of a convenient sample of retail banking customers in the southern region of Peninsula Malaysia. Of the 400 questionnaires distributed, 134 were retained as useable. Normal methods of testing for non-response bias could not be used in this research nor could the respondents be compared with the population from which the sample was drawn, because there are no other surveys or data about the population of retail banking customers available in Malaysia.

The composition of the sample comprised respondents of between 22 to 40 years of age (71.2 percent) and those less than 21years (12.1 percent). About 55.2 percent of the respondents were single with 62.7 percent being female. Of the sample, 70.7 percent of the respondents had at least a diploma and 33.1 percent were in teaching profession. Finally, 14.2 percent of the respondents had monthly salary of less than RM1,000 about 74.4 percent had a monthly salary of between RM1,001 and RM5,000 and 3.0 percent had a monthly salary of above RM10.001. Please note that 1USD$ is equivalent to RM3.00.

RESULTS

Preliminary Analyses

Data were primarily analyzed using SPSS 13.0 and Amos 4.0. Descriptive statistics such as means and standard deviation were obtained for the interval-scaled independent and dependent variables. The results are summarized in Table 1.

Initially, we used exploratory factor analysis (EFA) and Cronbach's alpha on the quality item measurements. EFA results indicated that only four factors should be grouped for service quality items (see Table 1). The factors also presented internal consistency levels. We then adjusted the factors labels to account for the items' integration and to determine the different factors of quality: Banking employee (twelve items), Billing integrity (five items), Banking environment (eleven items) and Product and services (five items).

To further refine and validate the measurements we used CFA, which is also used to test their convergent, and discriminant validities (Janssens et al. 2008). Table 2 summarizes the results of CFA. The maximum likelihood (ML) estimation was chosen for this research because of the robustness of ML estimation against the violation of assumption of least squares multivariate normality in a moderately sized sample (Diamantopoulos, 1994; Kline, 1998: Janssens, 2008).

To evaluate the fit of the confirmatory factor analysis (CFA) and structural equation modeling (SEM), goodness of fit indicators were used including, chi-squared statistics (χ^2), comparative fit index (CFI), standardized root mean residual (SRMR) and root mean square error of approximation (RMSEA). CFI was used over other fit indices because it is able to avoid underestimation of fit in a small sample (Bentler, 1990; Chang and Cheung, 2001; Babin et. al., 2010). A CFI value of over 0.95 or better is desirable as it indicates a good fit of the model to data (Bentler, 1992; Doll et. al., 1994; Chang & Cheung, 2001; Babin et. al., 2010). Table 2 details the four types of quality measurement.

The bank employee scale contains items that represent the degree of reliability, responsiveness and empathy in delivering the service to the customer. The results indicated that the factor loadings ranged from 0.67 to 0.86 explaining 63.4% of the variance and the internal reliability estimate (Cronbach alpha) was 0.94 indicating high internal reliability. The confirmatory factor analysis reflects a good fit to the data, χ^2 = 54.55 and CFI = 0.97.

The billing integrity factor contains items that represent the degree of accuracy and procedures

Table 2. Properties of measurements

Construct and its indicator variables	Mean	Std. Dev.	Factor loadings	R^2
Bank Employee (EMP)				
EMP1	2.75	0.79	0.70	0.45
EMP2	2.79	0.82	0.72	0.56
EMP3	2.67	0.92	0.81	0.63
EMP4	2.75	0.83	0.75	0.65
EMP5	2.72	0.89	0.86	0.68
EMP6	2.68	0.90	0.82	0.74
EMP7	2.66	0.88	0.81	0.56
EMP8	2.53	0.95	0.80	0.66
EMP9[a]	Deleted			
EMP10[a]	Deleted			
EMP11	2.54	0.82	0.75	0.52
EMP12	2.11	0.88	0.67	0.49
Billing integrity (BILL)				
BILL1	2.82	0.78	0.73	0.63
BILL2[a]	Deleted			
BILL3	2.93	0.71	0.77	0.71
BILL4	2.90	0.73	0.84	0.84
BILL5	2.93	0.70	0.79	0.79
Banking environment (ENV)				
ENV1[a]	Deleted			
ENV2[a]	Deleted			
ENV3	2.63	0.85	0.65	0.44
ENV4	2.96	0.79	0.62	0.45
ENV5	2.77	0.78	0.79	0.48
ENV6	2.79	0.81	0.81	0.43
ENV7	2.87	0.78	0.66	0.65
ENV8	2.81	0.82	0.69	0.63
ENV9	2.57	0.94	0.67	0.38
ENV10	2.80	0.74	0.67	0.42
ENV11[a]	Deleted			
Bank products and services(PROD)				
PROD1	2.70	0.76	0.88	0.70
PROD2	2.60	0.74	0.95	0.90
PROD3	2.66	0.76	0.84	0.78
PROD4[a]	Deleted			
PROD5[a]	Deleted			

Note: R^2 = Squared multiple correlations; [a] = These items were deleted with low factor loadings of less than 0.50 (Babin et. al., 2010) in handling customer account. The results indicate that the factor loadings ranged from 0.73 to 0.84 explaining 71.1% of the variance. The internal reliability estimate was 0.86 indicating high internal reliability and consistency. The fit of the confirmed model resulted in a $\chi^2 = 9.09$ and CFI = 0.97.

The banking environment factor contains items that represent the degree of the bank's efficiency and accessibility. The reliability estimate was 0.88 indicating high internal reliability and consistency. Factor loadings ranged from 0.62 to 0.81 explaining 54.9% of the variance. The factor was then subjected to the confirmatory factor analysis and had a very good fit with $\chi^2 = 30.46$ and CFI = 0.97.

The products and services factor contains items that represent the degree of banks' effectiveness in providing updated information about their banking products and services. However, the *just identified*, three-indicator model shown in Table 2 was appropriate–the number of data parameters perfectly reproduce the sample covariance matrix, and the chi-square statistic and the degrees of freedom are equal to zero. This finding suggests that the model fit the sample data well (Blunch, 2008; Byrne, 2001; Kline, 1998; Tabachnick and Fidell, 2001). The factor analysis resulted in loadings ranging from 0.84 to 0.95 explaining 86.1% of the variance. Furthermore, the internal reliability was 0.92 indicating high internal reliability and consistency.

In Table 3 we present an overview of the correlations between the variables: quality, image, satisfaction and retention.

As shown in Table 3, all the correlation coefficients are significant ($p< 0.01$). There is a positive relationship between quality and image (between $r = 0.33$ to 0.49), image and satisfaction ($r = 0.68$), image and retention ($r = 0.69$), quality and satisfaction (between $r = 0.36$ to 0.62), quality and retention (between $r = 0.37$ to 0.59), and satisfaction and retention ($r = 0.77$). Discriminant validity is demonstrated when a measure is adequately distinguishable from related constructs; average variance extracted (AVE) of each individual constructs should be greater than the share variances (square correlation) between the constructs when compared (Fornell and Larcker, 1981; Babin et. al., 2010). The results in Table 3 show that the AVE of each individual constructs were greater than the share variances between the constructs. Thus, this supports the discriminant validity of the constructs.

Table 3. Pearson correlations and discriminant validity of the measurements

Constructs		**Image**	**Quality**				**SAT**	**RET**
Variables[a]			**EMP**	**BILL**	**ENV**	**PROD**		
		0.50						
Image Quality:	EMP	0.49	**0.49**					
	BILL	0.33	0.51	**0.62**				
	ENV	0.46	0.66	0.33	**0.48**			
	PROD	0.35	0.37	0.35	0.42	**0.79**		
SAT		0.68	0.62	0.36	0.56	0.39	**0.70**	
RET		0.69	0.59	0.39	0.46	0.37	0.77	**0.50**

Note: Diagonal represents the average variance extracted (AVE), while the other matrices represent the shared variances. [a] EMP = Bank employee, BILL = Billing integrity , ENV = Banking environment, PROD = Product and services; SAT = Satisfaction; RET = Retention; Correlation is significant at $p< 0.01$ level (two-tailed)

Next we used structural equation modeling to test the adequacy of our model. The results of the structural model are depicted in Figure 2. Figure 2 shows the results of the model.

Using maximum likelihood estimation, the model provides a good fit to the data with a χ^2 (degree of freedom = 128, N = 134) = 201.17, *p* <0.001, RMSEA = 0.07 and CFI value of 0.95 (Hair et. al., 2010). Figure 2 presents the standardized structural model coefficients along the arrows in the model. The patterns of causal relationships are consistent with those predicted in the model. As shown in Figure 2, image has a significantly positively influence on quality (χ^2=0.67, p<0.00), satisfaction (χ^2 = 0.55, p<0.00) and both direct (χ^2=0.28, p<0.05) and indirect (through satisfaction) on retention. Image explained 45.0 per cent of the quality's variance, 70.0 per cent of satisfaction's variance and 82.0 per cent of retention's variance. Therefore, H_1, H_2 and H_3 can be accepted.

We expected that quality has a direct positive effect on retention via satisfaction and that satisfaction will have a direct positive effect on retention. Based on the analysis presented above, we conclude that quality has insignificant impact on retention (β = 0.17). Therefore, H_4 has to be rejected. On the other hand, quality has an indirect effect on retention via satisfaction (β = 0.35) and that satisfaction has a direct effect on retention (β = 0.54). Therefore, H_5 and H_6 can be accepted on the basis of our analysis.

The research hypotheses were confirmed and disconfirmed through SEM in order of their presentations as summarised in Table 4. Five of the hypotheses were fully supported. The discussion, implications and limitations of these results are described in the following sections.

DISCUSSION

With a confirmatory design, we used structural equation modeling to assess the adequacy of our model. Our analysis shows that image has both direct and indirect (through quality) relationships with satisfaction. In brief, this study disconfirms a previous research that the effect of image on satisfaction is mediated only by quality (see Bloemer et. al., 1998). Hence, we are able to capture a more detailed insight into the relationship between image and quality on one hand and satisfaction on

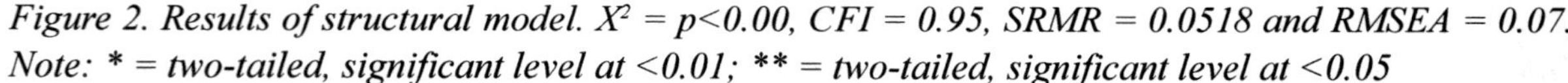
*Figure 2. Results of structural model. X^2 = p<0.00, CFI = 0.95, SRMR = 0.0518 and RMSEA = 0.07. Note: * = two-tailed, significant level at <0.01; ** = two-tailed, significant level at <0.05*

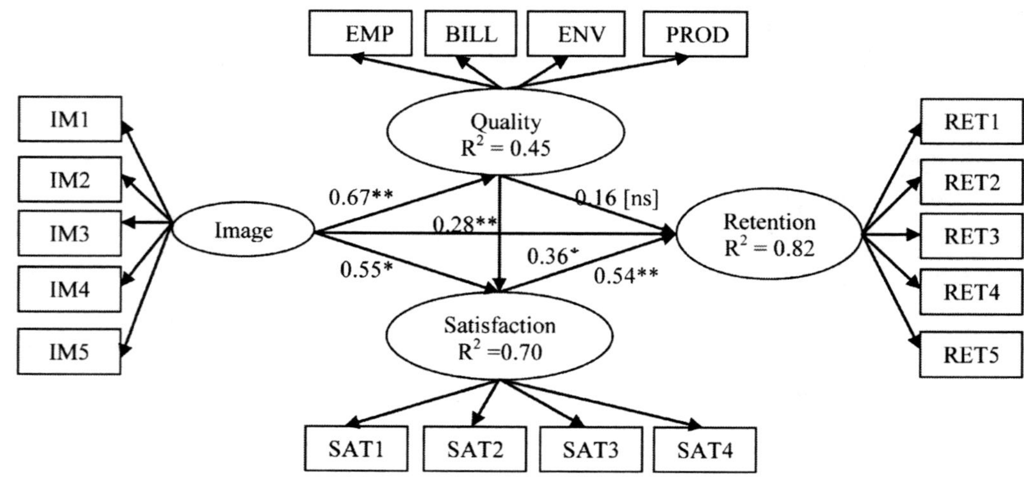

Table 4. Summary of results of hypotheses

Hypothesis		Supported
H_1:	Image has a direct positive effect on retention	Accepted
H_2:	Image has an indirect positive effect on retention via satisfaction	Accepted
H_3:	Image has a direct positive effect on quality	Accepted
H_4:	Image has an indirect positive effect on retention via quality	Rejected
H_5:	Quality has an indirect positive effect on retention via satisfaction	Accepted
H_6:	Satisfaction has direct positive effect on retention	Accepted

the other hand. Our study also shows that satisfaction has a direct positive effect on retention and is consistent with the previous studies conducted by Ganguli and Roy (2011), Kassim (2006) and Rust and Zahorik (1993). This result seems to validate the importance of customer satisfaction in formulating customer retention in other service settings (for example, retail banking). Thus, customer satisfaction plays an important role in customer retention formation but not quality. A possible explanation for this could be that what is given and received is relatively intangible which will result in customer evaluation criteria being less well articulated and the appraisal of the value received to be much more subjective (Keaveney, 1995; Lovelock, 1991; Zeithaml et. al., 1993). Moreover, customer retention involves behavior over time. The current study shows also that image has direct and indirect (through satisfaction) effects on retention. Thus, image could be viewed as an important determinant in formulating both satisfaction and retention evaluations.

PRACTICE IMPLICATIONS

The findings of this research have some implications for managerial decision making in the area of customer satisfaction, especially for managers of retail banking services. First, given that satisfaction plays a dominant role in formulating retention assessments, marketers should continuously provide services that satisfy and delight customers. Second, this research identifies that satisfaction is not the sole determinant of customer retention. Caution should be taken with regards to the impact of image on retention. Image seems to be a construct that has a relatively important role too. Therefore, good customer contacts, the use of corporate advertisement and innovative products and services, society-driven (commitment to society and individual, financial advices on investment, financing, etc) and finally, competitive prices in terms of interest rates, service charges and so on will create the perception of a strong financial institution. Finally, although quality seems to be a construct that has a negative direct impact on retention, this construct warrants further examination because it still has an indirect effect on retention via satisfaction. Thus, bank managers should invest resources to enhance overall satisfaction. Management and employees should strive to find out what customers expect (in terms of reliability, responsiveness, empathy, accuracy, procedure handling, efficiency, accessibility and updated information about products and services) when designing strategies to enhance overall satisfaction. This implies an extensive and continuous training program a bank needs to carry out for its employees.

FUTURE RESEARCH DIRECTIONS

There are a few limitations in our study that should be considered when interpreting the results and implications. First of all, our sample size is adequate but on the low side for structural equation modeling. As a result, CFI was used to assess the model to avoid potential bias. Large sample may be used in future studies. Secondly, the sampling procedure of this study was not random. Moreover, there were no data about the population of retail banking users available or published. This precluded testing for non-response. Finally, it may be fruitful to replicate our study in a similar research setting in other countries and to other services (for examples, health services, leisure services, etc.).

CONCLUSION

To conclude, this study shows how image may be linked to perceived service quality, satisfaction and retention. We are able to identify that image plays an important role in determining customer retention in retail banking. This study also shows the interrelationships between the determinants which gives us a better understanding of the dynamics of customer retention formation. In essence, our conclusion is that all the three constructs (image, quality and satisfaction) exert an influence on customer retention.

REFERENCES

Aaker, D., Kumar, V., & Day, G. S. (2000). *Marketing research*. New York, NY: John Wiley & Sons, Inc.

Anderson, E. W., Fornell, C., & Lehman, D. R. (1994). Customer satisfaction, market share and profitability: Findings from Sweden. *Journal of Marketing*, *58*(July), 53–66. doi:10.2307/1252310

Babin, B. J., Hair, J. F. Jr, Anderson, R. E., & Black, W. C. (2010). *Multivariate data analysis*. Upper Saddle River, NJ: Pearson Education Inc.

Barsky, J. (1994). *World-class customer satisfaction*. Burr Ridge, IL: Irwin Professional Publishing.

Bentler, P. M. (1990). Comparative fit indexes in structural equation models. *Psychological Bulletin*, *107*(2), 238–246. doi:10.1037/0033-2909.107.2.238

Bentler, P. M. (1992). On the fit of models to covariance and methodology to the bulletin. *Psychological Bulletin*, *112*(3), 400–404. doi:10.1037/0033-2909.112.3.400

Bhote, K. R. (1997). What do customers want anyway? *American Management Association*, (March), 36-40.

Bloemer, J., de Ruyter, K., & Peeters, P. (1998). Investigating drivers of bank loyalty: The complex relationship between image, service quality and satisfaction. *International Journal of Bank Marketing*, *16*(7), 276–286. doi:10.1108/02652329810245984

Boulding, W., Kalra, A., Staelin, R., & Zeithaml, V. (1993). A dynamic process model of service quality: from expectations to behavioral outcomes. *JMR, Journal of Marketing Research*, *30*(February), 7–27. doi:10.2307/3172510

Broyles, S. A. (2009). Loyalty's influence on satisfaction in cross-cultural settings. *Journal of Product and Brand Management*, *18*(6), 414–424. doi:10.1108/10610420910989730

Byrne, B. M. (2001). *Structural equation modeling with AMOS: Basic concepts, applications and programming*. London, UK: Lawrence Erlbaum Associates.

Chang, M. K., & Cheung, W. (2001). Determinants of the intention to use Internet/WWW at work: A confirmatory study. *Information & Management*, *39*, 1–14. doi:10.1016/S0378-7206(01)00075-1

Churchill, G. A., & Suprenant, C. (1982). An investigation into the determinants of customer satisfaction. *JMR, Journal of Marketing Research*, *19*(November), 491–504. doi:10.2307/3151722

Colgate, M., Stewart, K., & Kinsella, R. (1995). Customer defection: A study of the student market in Ireland. *International Journal of Bank Marketing*, *14*(8), 23–29.

Cronin, J. J., & Taylor, S. A. (1992). Measuring service quality: A re-examination and extension. *Journal of Marketing*, *56*, 55–68. doi:10.2307/1252296

Danaher, P. J., & Rust, R. T. (1996). Indirect benefits from service quality. *Quality Management Journal*, *3*(2), 63–85.

Dawes, J., & Swailes, S. (1999). Retention sans frontiers: Issues for financial service retailers. *International Journal of Bank Marketing*, *17*(1), 36–43. doi:10.1108/02652329910254037

de Matos, C. A., Henrique, J. L., & de Rosa, F. (2009). The different roles of switching costs on satisfaction-loyalty relationship. *International Journal of Bank Marketing*, *27*(7), 506–523. doi:10.1108/02652320911002331

Doll, W. J., Xia, W., & Torkzadeh, G. (1994). A confirmatory factor analysis of the end-user computing satisfaction instrument. *Management Information Systems Quarterly*, *18*(4), 453–661. doi:10.2307/249524

Dowling, G., & Uncle, M. (1997). Do customer loyalty programs really work? *Sloan Management Review*, (Summer): 71–82.

Fornell, C. (1992). National customer satisfaction barometer: The Swedish experience. *Journal of Marketing*, *56*(January), 6–21. doi:10.2307/1252129

Fornell, C., & Larcker, D. F. (1981). Evaluating structural equation models with unobservable variables and measurement error. *JMR, Journal of Marketing Research*, *18*, 39–50. doi:10.2307/3151312

Fornell, C., & Wernerfelt, B. (1987). Defensive marketing strategy by customer complaint management: A theoretical analysis. *JMR, Journal of Marketing Research*, *24*, 337–346. doi:10.2307/3151381

Ganesh, J., Arnolds, M. J., & Reynolds, K. E. (2000). Understanding the customer base of service providers: an examination the differences between switchers and stayers. *Journal of Marketing*, *64*(July), 65–87. doi:10.1509/jmkg.64.3.65.18028

Ganguli, S., & Roy, S. K. (2011). Generic technology-based service quality dimensions in banking: impact on customer satisfaction and loyalty. *International Journal of Bank Marketing*, *29*(2), 168–189. doi:10.1108/02652321111107648

Granbois, D. (1981). An integrated view of the choice/patronage processIn Monroe, K. B. (Ed.), *Advances in consumer research* (*Vol. 8*, pp. 693–695). Ann Arbor, MI: Association for Consumer Research.

Halstead, D., Hartman, D., & Schmidt, S. L. (1994). Multisource effects on the satisfaction process. *Journal of the Academy of Marketing Science*, *22*, 114–129. doi:10.1177/0092070394222002

Heskett, J. L., Jones, T. O., Loveman, G. W., Sasser, W. E., & Schlesinger, L. A. (1994). Putting the service profit chain to work. *Harvard Business Review*, *72*(March-April), 164–174.

Hildebrandt, L. (1988). Store image and the prediction of performance on retailing. *Journal of Business Research*, *17*, 91–100. doi:10.1016/0148-2963(88)90026-4

Hooi Ting, D. (2004). Service quality and satisfaction perceptions: Curvilinear and interaction effect. *International Journal of Bank Marketing, 22*(6), 407–420. doi:10.1108/02652320410559330

Jamal, A., & Naser, K. (2002). Customer satisfaction and retail banking: An assessment of some of the key antecedents of customer satisfaction in retail banking. *International Journal of Bank Marketing, 20*(4/5), 146–161. doi:10.1108/02652320210432936

Kanning, P. U., & Bergmann, B. (2009). Predictors of customer satisfaction: Resting the classical paradigms. *Managing Service Quality, 19*(4), 377–390. doi:10.1108/09604520910971511

Kargaonkar, P. K., Lund, D., & Price, B. (1985). A structural equations approach toward examination of store attitude and store patronage behavior. *Journal of Retailing, 61*(Summer), 39–60.

Kassim, N. M. (2006). Telecommunications industry in Malaysia: Demographics effect on customer expectations, performance, satisfaction and retention. *Asia Pacific Business Review, 12*(4), 437–363. doi:10.1080/13602380600571401

Kassim, N. M., Najdawi, M. K., Al-Azmeh, Z., & Sidiq, H. (2010). Effects of institutional reform on corporate image and value in a developing country context. *Measuring Business Excellence, 14*(2), 32–45. doi:10.1108/13683041011047849

Keaveney, S. M. (1995). Customer switching behavior in service industries: An exploratory study. *Journal of Marketing, 59*, 71–82. doi:10.2307/1252074

Kline, R. B. (1998). *Principles and practice of structural equation modeling*. New York, NY: Guildford Press.

Levesque, T., & McDougall, G. H. C. (1996). Determinants of customer satisfaction in retail Banking. *International Journal of Bank Marketing, 14*(7), 12–20. doi:10.1108/02652329610151340

Llosa, S., Chandon, J.-L., & Orsingher, C. (1998). An empirical study of SERVQUAL's dimensionality. *The Service Industries Journal, 18*(2), 16–44. doi:10.1080/02642069800000017

Lovelock, C. H. (1991). *Services marketing*. Upper Saddle River, NJ: Prentice-Hall, Inc.

Madden, K. M. (2000). *The role of communication in building customer relationships in the Australian financial services industry: an in-depth study*. Unpublished doctoral dissertation, university of Southern Queensland, Toowomba, Australia.

Malhotra, N. K. (1993). *Marketing research: An applied orientation*. Englewood Cliffs, NJ: Prentice-Hall Inc.

Mazursky, D., & Jacoby, J. (1986). Exploring the development of store image. *Journal of Retailing, 62*, 145–165.

Mittal, B., & Lassar, W. M. (1998). Why do customer switch? The dynamics of satisfaction versus loyalty. *Journal of Services Marketing, 12*(3), 177–194. doi:10.1108/08876049810219502

Mittal, V., Rose, W. T., & Baldasare, P. M. (1998). The asymmetric impact of negative and positive attribute-level performance on overall satisfaction and repurchase intention. *Journal of Marketing, 62*(January), 33–47. doi:10.2307/1251801

Murphy, J. A. (1996). Retailing bankingIn Buttle, F. (Ed.), *Relationship marketing, theory and practice* (pp. 74–90). London, UK: Paul Chapman.

Oliver, R. L., & DeSarbo, W. S. (1988). Response determinants in satisfaction judgments. *The Journal of Consumer Research, 14*, 495–506. doi:10.1086/209131

Palmatier, R. W., & Gopalakrishna, S. (2005). Determining the payoff from relationship marketing programs. In *MSI Reports: Marketing Science Institute Working Paper Series, 1*(5), 49-70.

Parasuraman, A., Berry, L. L., & Zeithaml, V. A. (1991). Refinement and reassessment of the SERVQUAL scale. *Journal of Retailing*, *67*(4), 420–430.

Parasuraman, A., Zeithaml, V. A., & Berry, L. L. (1988). SERVQUAL: A multiple item scale for measuring consumer perceptions of service quality. *Journal of Retailing*, *64*(Spring), 12–40.

Patterson, P. G., & Johnson, L. W. (1993). Disconfirmation of expectations and the gap model of service quality: An integrated paradigm. *Journal of Consumer Satisfaction, Dissatisfaction, and Complaining Behavior*, *8*, 22–31.

Patterson, P. G., & Smith, T. (2003). A cross-cultural study of switching barriers and propensity to stay with service provider. *Journal of Retailing*, *79*, 107–120. doi:10.1016/S0022-4359(03)00009-5

Peppers, D., & Rogers, M. (1993). *The one to one future: Building relationship one customer at a time*. New York, NY: Doubleday.

Pont, M., & McQuilken, L. (2005). An empirical investigation of customer satisfaction and loyalty across two divergent bank segments. *Journal of Financial Services Marketing*, *9*(4), 344–359. doi:10.1057/palgrave.fsm.4770165

Rahman, S., & Azhar, S. (2011). Xpressions of generation Y: Perceptions of the mobile phone service industry in Pakistan. *Asia Pacific Journal of Marketing Logistics*, *23*(1), 91–107. doi:10.1108/13555851111100012

Reichheld, F. F., & Kenny, D. W. (1990). The hidden advantages of retention. *Journal of Retail Marketing*, *12*(4), 19–23.

Reichheld, F. F., & Sasser, W. E. (1990). Zero defections: quality comes to services. *Harvard Business Review*, (September-October): 105–111.

Rust, R. T., & Zahorik, A. (1993). Customer satisfaction, customer retention, and market share. *Journal of Retailing*, *69*(2), 193–215. doi:10.1016/0022-4359(93)90003-2

Sekaran, U. (2000). *Research method for business: A skill building approach*. New York, NY: John Wiley & Sons, Inc.

Smith, A. M. (1995). Measuring service quality: Is SERVQUAL now redundant? *Journal of Marketing Management*, *111*(1-3), 257–276. doi:10.1080/0267257X.1995.9964341

Tabachnick, B. G., & Fidell, L. S. (1996). *Using multivariate statistics*. New York, NY: HarperCollins.

Tabachnick, B. G., & Fidell, L. S. (2001). *Using multivariate statistics*. Boston, MA: Allyn & Bacon.

Tse, D., & Wilton, P. (1988). Models of consumers' satisfaction formation: An extension. *JMR, Journal of Marketing Research*, *25*, 204–212. doi:10.2307/3172652

Woodside, A., Frey, L., & Daly, R. (1989). Linking service quality, customer satisfaction and behavioral intentions. *Journal of Health Care Marketing*, *9*(December), 5–17.

Zeithaml, V. A. (2000). Service quality, profitability and the economic worth of customers: What we know and what we need to learn. *Journal of the Academy of Marketing Science*, *28*(1), 67–85. doi:10.1177/0092070300281007

Zeithaml, V. A., Parasuraman, A., & Berry, L. L. (1993). The nature and determinants of customer expectations of service. *Journal of the Academy of Marketing Science*, *21*(1), 1–12. doi:10.1177/0092070393211001

Zeithaml, V. A., Parasuraman, A., & Berry, L. L. (1996). The behavioral consequences of service quality. *Journal of Marketing*, *49*(Spring), 33–46.

KEY TERMS AND DEFINITIONS

Customer Retention: Customer retention refers to both attitudinal loyalty (e.g., recommending the service to others) and behavioral loyalty (e.g., increase usage).

Customer Satisfaction: Satisfaction is the customer's evaluation of the service received.

Image: Image is the reception of an organization in its surroundings.

Malaysia: Malaysia is a developing country with multi-ethnic and multi-cultural mix of the population and one of the most important economies in South East Asia.

Perceived Service Quality: Perceived service quality is the subjective evaluation made by customer over a certain period of time after a service encounter.

Retail Banking: Retail banking is banking that provides direct services to individual customers.

Structural Equation Modeling: Structural equation modeling is a statistical technique used to examine the measurement and structural properties of a theoretical model.

Chapter 11
Adopting and Integrating Cloud Computing

Tugrul Daim
Portland State University, USA & University of Pretoria, South Africa

Marc Britton
Portland State University, USA

Ganesh Subramanian
Providence Health Systems, USA

Rubyna Brenden
University of Western States, USA

Nuttavut Intarode
SCG Cement, Thailand

ABSTRACT

Cloud Computing has been around in the background in some shape or form for decades now. Yet people still ask – what is cloud computing? What can it do, and why should it be considered for growing technology needs? In the past, businesses have integrated cloud computing partially to meet their technology needs due to skepticism, reliability, and cost of the concept. However, the era is approaching where this could be a feasible solution that meets technology needs and assists businesses in meeting their goals in a reliable and efficient way. Can businesses be convinced yet? (O'Donnell, 2009). In a nutshell, cloud computing has grown over the last ten years and is still growing but making waves in the industry now more than ever, but why all this hype? Perhaps because cloud computing is seen as a viable replacement of enterprise owned local IT infrastructure (Francis, 2009).

DOI: 10.4018/978-1-4666-0246-5.ch011

INTRODUCTION

With technology innovation in mind, we researched various aspects of cloud computing. The objective of our study is to predict the adoption rate of Cloud Computing in the future with a soft timeline using a scenario-based forecasting model. In the course of our research, we identified key barriers preventing this transition, created a roadmap to outline the basics of cloud computing, identification of key areas for technology integration, performed a barrier analysis, and plotted a business adoption model. We concluded with recommendations and predictions in the next few years which could serve as a tool that businesses could use to determine if cloud computing is the right step in meeting their technology and business needs.

In order to highlight the multi aspects of Cloud Computing and all that it has to offer in the next ten years. A graphical roadmap was designed to explain Cloud Computing and all it encompasses. (refer to Figure 1) The roadmap is a high level overview of cloud computing, we identified market drivers, services, providers and the underlying technology components, which distinguish them in this area. Following this, we conducted surveys with experts in the Industry. We concluded that there are three key barriers from the surveys that would impact businesses in the next ten years. This assisted us in analysis throughout the paper. We then derived a business adoption model in respect to the data collected from the surveys, and categorized businesses into four main categories and predicted the adoption rate according to a time line and cost. This analysis led to the trend analysis section of this paper, and highlighted ma-

Figure 1. Research methodology

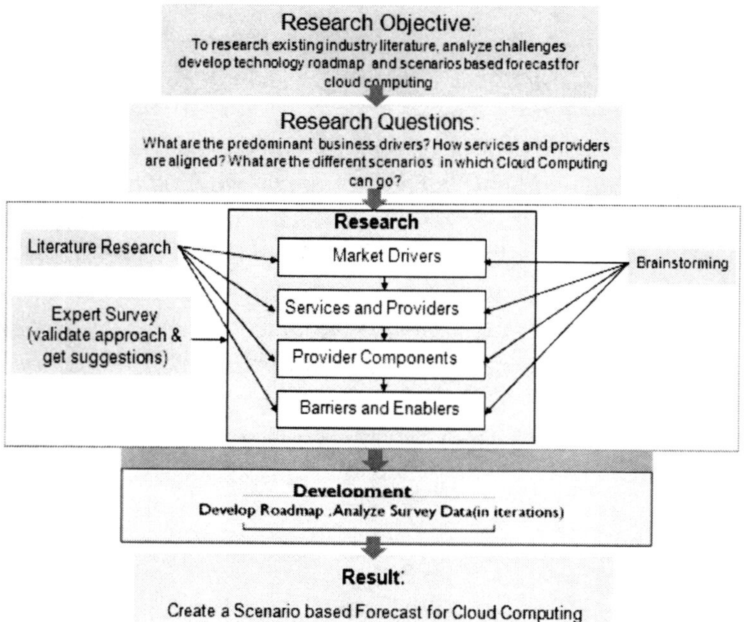

jor trends in the industry, barriers and the impact of these barriers on businesses. We then studied the data and plotted a scenario-base forecasting model to predict the adoption of Cloud Computing in relation to business adoption and technology Integration which is the focal point of our study.

Within this report we set out to answer the following questions:

1. What are the predominant market drivers of cloud computing?
2. How is cloud computing services and providers aligned?
3. What possible scenarios could play out in the future of cloud computing?

Within the report we used several methods to clearly answer these questions. We first researched the marked drivers, services and providers, provider components, and barriers and enablers of cloud computing through literature research, group brainstorming, and an expert survey. With our research we developed a roadmap of cloud computing to summarize the complexities in a visually meaningful way.

For expert survey, we used scoring method for giving and ranking the scores of each question (Uzoka and Ijatuyi, 2005; Robert and Sharif, 2008). This methodology is a simple method to rate or weight the preferences based on experts' opinions. It is not a complicated method to calculate the data and get the results of the evaluation (Schoemaker, 1995). It uses the number that has high value to rate the most significant parameters and the lower number to rate the less significant ones.

Next, we analyzed our survey data to find out what experts think about the barriers, enablers, and future timeline of cloud computing with respect to large and small businesses. We found that the survey data fit nicely with our literature research we had compiled and verified our thoughts on the barriers and adoption rate of small and large businesses.

Finally, from our data we extracted four scenarios to forecast the future of cloud computing. These four scenarios show how the cloud computing market will react depending on how the current barriers are or are not overcome adequately.

BACKGROUND

Overview of Cloud Computing

Cloud computing heralds an evolution of business that is no less influential than e-business, according to Gartner Inc. Gartner maintains that the very confusion and contradiction that surrounds the term "cloud computing" signifies its potential to change the status quo in the IT market (Reynolds and Bess, 2009). "During the past 15 years, a continuing trend toward IT industrialization has grown in popularity as IT services delivered via hardware, software and people are becoming repeatable and usable by a wide range of customers and service providers," said Daryl Plummer, managing vice president and Gartner. The commoditization, standardization of technologies binding IT and the popularity of the internet along with the rise of virtualization and service-oriented software architectures, have all changed the dynamics of how IT is delivered. The three major factors which drive the IT services are hardware, software, and people. Businesses that use those services today have to focus on how to host these services and what kind of an IT structure they need to host them. They have to consider how some of these services are implemented. Together, these three major trends constitute the basis of a discontinuity that will create a new opportunity and shape the relationship between those who are utilizing these services and those who are selling them. The worry of how the Services are set up is fading away and the focus for consumers is slowly shifting with what services are required for them to successfully utilize IT to drive business goals. We also found that contrary to popular belief, cloud computing's security benefits outweigh its security risks (Andriole, 2009). The types of IT services that can be provided through a cloud are wide-ranging.

According to NIST, Cloud Computing is defined as a model for enabling convenient, on-demand network access to a shared pool of configurable computing resources (e.g., networks, servers, storage, applications, and services) that can be rapidly provisioned and released with minimal management effort or service provider interaction (Hall, 2009; Mell and Grance, 2009). Even though the above definition attempts to explain the cloud there are other varying definitions. According to Deloitte, there are 22 ways we can define cCloud cComputing (Callewaert et al., 2009).

Even though there is some ambiguity on what constitutes the cloud, the lack of clear definition doesn't preclude the benefits of cloud from people in realizing the value of it. We hope to convey the value of cloud computing and at the same time minimize the confusion behind it, we will also consider the providers view and services in parts of our research (Reynolds and Bess, 2009). According to our lLiterature review, we find there is some level of consensus emerging around the characteristics of the cloud. We see that there are some capabilities that must be adhered to in considering cCloud cComputing. We found that the best way to interpret the data from our literature review is to align them in a Technology Roadmap.

Overview of Scenarios

Since the sixties, scenarios have become a major concept and methodology in future researches but it goes back further than that. Projecting courses of action or describing future events is not limited to contemporary authors. Ancient civilizations speculated about the future (Roubelat and Godet, 2000; Becker, 1983). Although speculating about the future predates current times, Scenario planning is a tool that has gained increased attention during the last 20 years as an effective method for examining future uncertainties and investigating assumptions in organizations (Chermack, 2005).

One thing on which we can all agree is that the future is uncertain. So why do we find it useful to discuss and study it? There can only be one response: we consider at least something in the future predictable. If that is so, a disciplined approach towards separating the predictable from the uncertain is clearly helpful for understanding. This is what the scenario technique aims to do (Van Der Heijden, 2000).

Scenarios are not an end in themselves. They are a management tool to improve the quality of executive decision making and are especially effective in dealing with uncertainties (Wilson, 2000; Postma and Liebl, 2005). A number of scenario generation procedures have been proposed and may all be appropriate in particular circumstances. These procedures differ in regard to their approach to structure, the nature of the scenario elements used, their handling of the time dimension, their approach to scenario probabilities, the scope or size of the scenarios, and a few other aspects (Mitchell et al., 1979).

Overview of Roadmap

Technology road mapping is one of flexible and efficient tools which are vastly exploited in many organizations such as industry, government, and academia to support their strategic moves, improving short-, medium-, and long-term planning processes and making a decision for the future (Phaal et al., 2004; Kostoff and Schaller, 2001; Lee and Park, 2005; Rinne, 2004). This visualize approach furnishes the companies to explore and communicate the correlation between each hierarchical structure of the roadmap (drivers: i.e. law

& regulation and market, products, technologies, and other supporting infrastructures: i.e. R&D etc.) based on time horizon. It also assists the organizations in balancing between market "pull" and technology "push" (Phaal and Muller, 2008; Daim and Oliver, 2008; Holmes and Ferril, 2005). Adoption of technology roadmap can provide the visibility of strategic intent in the multiple views of businesses. For example, companies can focus on technological trajectories by combining technology roadmapping, information technology (IT) and supply chain management to ensure its sustainability for new product development decisions (Patrick and Echols, 2008). In addition, the holistic approach of technology roadmapping can help technology consumers play the technology selection game. They can take into account the technology landscape and select the best choice of technologies for their companies. If nothing is promising, they can cruise over the roadmapping architecture to dig down into new promising technologies of other virtual node (Rinne, 2004). With numerous benefits of the technology roadmapping, not only does it assisting the companies in enabling to survive in the fast-paced and unpredictable business circumstances, but it also furnishes the advantageous information to track the performance of individual or set of disruptive technologies so as to enhance the competitive edge of the organization in the long run (Lee et al., 2007). For this paper we wanted to use the same model of creating a Technology Roadmap, develop a Service Roadmap, and include all of the tTechnologies involved with the cCloud cComputing. Here the consumers demand to drive down the cost of the current IT model creates a mMarket pull which is met by the tTechnology pPush from the providers in delivering innovative services to consumers. The next few sections are dedicated to the individual areas of the roadmap. We have given a comprehensive summary of the roadmap in the end.

MARKET DRIVERS

Cost

Cost is a key driver for consumers to switch to cloud computing, capital expenditure is transferred to oOperating expense. Since the Cloud model is based on pay as you go, the overall upfront cost involved in setting up the Infrastructure is reduced considerably. The cost per transaction is low in a Cloud Model due to the providers focus in creating Energy Efficient Datacenters, Volume Licensing, and Shared IT solution for multiple consumers and the ability to move resources from one consumer to another depending upon the load of individual. IT administrative overhead exists for the current in house model. The procurement, staging and setting up of the infrastructure in house every time is eliminated if switched over to the cloud model. Cost involved in IT maintenance, upgrades and huge licensing costs are much lower in a cloud model for a consumer due to the large-scale deployment of the provider reducing the expenses.

Business

Looking at the business perspective, the last 15 years has been focused on how IT can enhance value of the organizations. Today we are at crossroads where the cost to set up IT Infrastructure is on par or higher than the utility it can provide. Companies have to set up multiple departments within the organization to manage IT. For most of these companies, IT may not fall under their core competency, but they are unable to ignore IT due to their dependency. Switching over to cloud for these companies enables them to focus on their core competency but at the same time still leverage the use of IT. We have seen from our research that for Geo-Eye (Callewaert et al., 2009), a commercial satellite provider for US-Dept of Defense and Intelligence have eliminated the use of multi-processor super computers by switching over to a Cloud Provider. Similarly bBusinesses will find convenience using IT as needed instead of planning an Infrastructure for a need that may or may not exist in the future. The advantage of scaling up and down based on the Business need is also a key factor, as IT is completely in sync with the varying cycles of the individual business. From the perspective of the providers who are pushing the Cloud Technology already, we are seeing a huge opportunity to the different variants of the Technology.

The current Software as a Service (SAAS) market is at $8 billion and growing to a projected $20 billion market in the next five years due to new emerging vendors providing innovative and on demand solutions. Companies like Oracle, SAP and Microsoft are investing heavily and are triggering continuous growth in this area. Infrastructure as a Service (IAAS) is expected to grow due to the awareness it has created in the Industry. Moreover IAAS is one area where companies do not need to worry about the customization which exists at the application level. Research shows that the IAAS market is projected to hit $6 billion in 2013. Platform as a Service (PAAS) is still in its nascent stage with lack of standards and is still not expected to grow compared to the other two providing technologies. Overall, the cloud industry is projected to grow at a compound annual growth rate of 24% for the 2008-2013 periods (Callewaert et al., 2009).

Environmental

There are regulations today as to how IT waste is managed by organizations. There is also corporate responsibility for every organization to monitor, control and reduce the emission they produce. According to Lawrence Berkley National Laboratory, the IT industry is estimated to have produced 2% of the overall global CO2 emission from the period 2000-2005, which is equivalent to the emissions produced by the Airline Industry. Factors like the ones mentioned here, forces Organizations to look at how IT assets are handled to reduce waste and its effect on the environment (Callewaert et al., 2009). Cloud computing provides an alternative where the assets are managed by the provider. Consumers use a pc or other client device to access their applications remotely. As mentioned in the cost section of the market drivers, the provider can design and maintain a state of art energy efficient datacenter resulting in lower CO2 emissions and will have global processes to manage IT waste.

Legal

With regards to legalities, there are still gaps. On one hand there are lack of regulations for moving the data to a cloud. This is an inhibitor to the adoption of the cloud model. On the other hand there is a lack of knowledge about Security within organizations. There are several organizations where Security Engineering is done by IT System Administrators and Network Administrators whose primary job is to manage the Servers and Networks.

Today there are several regulations such as PCI, where companies are required to meet security standards. Do these organizations have the technical know how to implement security solutions to address these regulations? Moreover, small business are unable to afford state of art tools. Security as a Service is a solution for these companies to move their data to a cloud model in order to enhance their security. Research shows that companies such as IBM and Amazon have understood the importance of security and have made that one of their core competencies. Engaging the providers to deliver Security solutions can help mitigate some of the Security concerns that they have with an in-house Security model. These providers can design proprietary security solutions to suit individual consumers' compliance and regulation needs. Since there are apprehensions about moving data to the cloud, this area will continue to evolve in the coming years with comprehensive solutions developed by providers to meet the regulations.

SERVICES

The Roadmap includes the key services that are provided by Cloud Vendors. We have classified each service based on the standard prevalent in the industry. Based on what services are provided by a particular Cloud Provider, a classification is done in the Industry. Even though service providers are identified by the type of service they deliver, there are certain commonalities expected among all vendors. The service provided by any vendor must have subscription model where the consumer procures the service independently. In other words, it is delivered as self-service. They provide an array of services with a pay per use option. The services are created for all consumers they serve; which shouldn't be confused for a hosted model where a provider dedicates part of a service to a particular consumer. By pursuing a shared service model, providers keep the cost down. In addition to procuring the initial service, the provider has the functionality setup automatically, where a consumer can scale the services up or down depending on his requirement at any point of time. Depending on the usage they are billed automatically. In addition to touching the various services provided in the Industry, we have also emphasized the importance of Private Cloud in the roadmap where the Consumer and Provider reside within the same Organization. The Hybrid cloud which blends both the Private Cloud and Public Cloud is also portrayed in the roadmap.

SAAS

This service uses a multitenant architecture where a single application is delivered to thousands of customers using a browser. There are several variants of applications that come under Software as a Service. We have identified them under the Technology Components in the Roadmap. Both the provider and consumers benefit from SAAS. On the provider it is easy to host one application for several consumers, on the consumer side they save on server cost for hosting the application in-house and the licensing cost involved in using the application. The strongest segments involved in SAAS are CRM, Web conferencing and E-learning.

Integration as a Service

Enterprise Application Integration is a framework used to enable Integration of systems and applications across the Enterprises. Cloud offers Integration as a Service to replace EAI. Integration as a Service or known as IntAAS is the ability to deliver a complete integration stack required for consumers. IntAAS includes Integration with Applications, Semantic Mediation, flow control and Integration design. Most of the function used in EAI (Enterprise Application Integration) is included in the IntAAS however they are delivered as a service. Today IntAAS market according to Gartner is $1.5billion (Hall, 2009). Companies have spent that much in 2008 for Enterprise Applications Integration. Even though IntAAS offers huge market opportunity the growth is expected to be low due maturity of on premise applications that are currently integrated and the cost is required to switch over.

IAAS

One of the success stories of Cloud Computing is its ability to deliver Infrastructure as a Service. Today Companies are constantly facing the battle of obsolete hardware, inefficient infrastructure, customer demand to deliver superior service and increase in IT budget due to high operating cost. IAAS offers a solution to switch the companies infrastructure to a cloud provider. There are several services that are offered under IAAS. Namely, Network as a Service, Storage as a Service, and Server as a Service are all part of IAAS. It offers an excellent choice for customers to switch their capital Data Center cost into an Operating IAAS cost. A simple mapping of how the utility model for power works can be substituted for IAAS. Unlimited scalability, sizeability, superior performance and low cost make it a great offering for Businesses to switch their Infrastructure to a Cloud model.

PAAS

A complete Platform consists of application development, interface development, database development, storage and testing are provided remotely by a Cloud Provider, known as Platform as a Service or PAAS. Enterprise class applications are created using PAAS for local use but using the full capability of the cloud model. Even though it has generated considerable interest in the Industry, according to Delloid, PAAS is still in its early stage in the market (Callewaert et al., 2009). With PAAS, the system features can be changed and upgraded seamlessly. PAAS is also known as "cloudware" as a result of moving resources from privately owned computers to a cloud model (Mitchell, 2008).

Security as a Service

Core Security has to be emphasized in the age of Identity thefts and corporate hacks of sensitive information. Organizations find it difficult to run an effective Security Infrastructure due to the frequent changes in technology, regulations and new services like Identity Management. If those services are delivered over the Internet, then Security is being deployed as a Service.

Private Cloud

Private cloud (also called internal cloud or corporate cloud) is a marketing term for a proprietary computing architecture that provides hosted services to a limited number of people behind a firewall. Advances in virtualization and distributed computing have allowed corporate network and datacenter administrators to effectively become service providers that meet the needs of their "customers" within the corporation. In a Private Cloud, some of the services mentioned above like SAAS, PAAS, IAAS are all offered within the organizations IT capabilities but in a Cloud Model. That is, the services are offered on-demand like the Public Cloud. However, both the consumers and providers reside within the organization.

Hybrid Cloud

When an organization utilizes both its private cloud and public cloud provided by external service providers, then they are part of a hybrid cloud model. The Cloud Infrastructure comprises of two or more Clouds. Merging a private cloud to a public cloud is one way of creating a Hybrid cloud. They remain as unique entities but are bound together by a standardized or proprietary technology that enables data and application portability. Although cloud computing is often said to be the future of the industry, the hybrid model is more prevalent for a number of reasons. Large enterprises often already have substantial investments in the infrastructure required to provide resources in-house. Furthermore, many organizations would prefer to keep sensitive data under their own control to ensure security. A hybrid model provides answers to these concerns by balancing both the benefits offered by a public cloud model and mitigates the risks prevalent due to internal compliance and governance requirements.

PROVIDERS AND COMPONENTS

Both the area of providers and components are merged in this section to identify the providers as well as explain the unique underlying components, which makes their services successful. Today, we have several providers in the Industry who have their proprietary cloud solutions for various services required by the consumers. In this area, we have split the providers into the individual areas of specialization.

Infrastructure

A variety of vendors were chosen who provide IAAS as the service. All of these vendors use some of the traditional and modern technologies used in non-cloud environments today. In addition, they also use High Density Servers with Blade Technology and Virtualization, Open source servers to reduce the cost of licensing, Disk de-duplication, and San replication for redundancy and Ethernet MPLS for superior Network performance. We have also shown certain specific innovations by selective vendors who deploy Infrastructure with their own-patented technologies. Namely Amazon Web services S3/EC2 having their Elastic IP addressing for quick resources deployment and IBMs Web sphere Cloud burst appliance specifically targeted for Private Cloud. The IBMs appliance, works on a model of signing up services within the organization that meets most of the criteria of a public cloud service setup in house. They also use the Virtualized Blade servers with self service and chargeback metering in. We see a keen interest of deploying Cloud burst appliance in business analytics and organizations use it for testing and development.

Integration

Two vendors were chosen in the area of Integration as a Service. CastIron using its own cloud library TIP has one of the most innovative service/business models to target companies of all size. Castiron strength lays in extensive domain experience with enterprise integration and flexible SAAS integration. Bhoomi uses an open source service bus architecture is the first provider to target IN-Taas to specifically target SAAS providers. Their Visual Integration process editor solution target small and mid size companies.

Platform

It is imperative to define what the boundaries of platform are. A platform layer of a cloud can be related to a middleware where the connections between the software and the cloud database tools are managed. Microsoft Azure, Google App Engine and Force.com are the 3 providers have been chosen for the PAAS area. The Azure platform (Azure) is Microsoft's first attempt at a cloud services platform and their take on implementing Platform as a Service (PaaS)-style functionality (Meader, 2009). Azure includes an operating system (Windows Azure) and several collections of developer, communication and data services intended to simplify the creation and hosting of Windows-based applications in the cloud. Google's App Engine cloud offering is targeted at web developers and web hosting applications. App Engine is essentially a hosted version of a CGI handler; it would normally be operated as part of a web server application, and its applications can be accessed via only HTTP/HTTPS on a standard port. The only programming languages currently supported by the App Engine are Python and Java (Nolle, 2009). Force.com cloud is designed to integrate with Salesforce.com's application tools. The cloud is built on Salesforce.com's Apex On-Demand Platform and the Apex language is used to create hosted applications (Maddison, 2009).

Software Applications The providers who come under software applications primarily deliver SAAS. Their market landscape is further divided into sub segments like digital content creation, web collaboration, content, communication and collaboration and supply chain management. (see Table 1) Individual vendors were picked based on literature research in order to see that they are relatively mature in the market, provide significant investment in the services they can provide, are experienced with technology to succeed in the evolving cloud market and their partnership and alliance which would make them successful in business. The underlying components were also

Table 1. Areas of SAAS services

Service	Area	SASS Providers
CRM	Customer Relationship Management	SalesForce
SCM	Supply Chain Management	Ariba
CCC	Content Communication and Collaboration	Cisco, IBM
DCC	Digital Content Creation	Youtube

identified in the roadmap at a much broader level that shows them providing successful delivery of the service.

Security

There are several areas under security which would be beneficial for organizations to move their Infrastructure to the cloud model. The prominent providers we have picked here are Cisco, Trend Micros Systems and McAfee. They all provide security services like web protection, email protection, vulnerability assessment and threat mitigation. It is also foreseen that these vendors continue to work and produce several services in the coming years to handle other enforced compliance regulations and legal frameworks which might come as a standard down the road.

CLOUD COMPUTING ROADMAP

Roadmap-Overview

The challenge of this topic is how to comprehend the vast information available about cloud technology. It was felt that the strength of this Project report lies in how successfully we portray the different layers in cloud computing and also the players who are driving these technologies. In addition, the current challenges faced by the consumers needed to be shown. The solution was to convert literature research into a form of meaningful information using a Technology Roadmap. The Technology Roadmap illustrates how the cloud industry has evolved over the last 10 years and where it could possibly be heading in the next 5 years with respect to the stakeholders in the Industry.(refer to Figure 2) Appended is of the methods of constructing the Technology Roadmap. The time period chosen for this roadmap is from the year 2000 to 2015.

The Road Map has 4 levels starting with Market Drivers, followed by Services, Providers and Provider Components respectively. At the provider components level of the roadmap there are 5 categories, Infrastructure, Platform, Software Applications, Integration and Security. The methodology used to construct this portion of the Roadmap is to first show what the unique provider components are with respect to a particular category. The concept of cloud computing is more of an innovation which happened at a service level as apposed to a technology, but driven by specific individual technologies. In the roadmap there are certain components that are innovations that happened at the technology level leading different providers to use the technology. For example, in virtualization there are some components that are unique for a particular provider. The Providers are linked above the Components level then, depending upon a particular service they provide, they are classified in their own area of specialization.

The next area of the roadmap is services. This area is named services instead of products unlike other roadmaps because here the topic we have chosen is classified as a service as apposed as a product. In the services area, common cloud services were chosen that are prevalent today.

Figure 2. Cloud computing technology roadmap

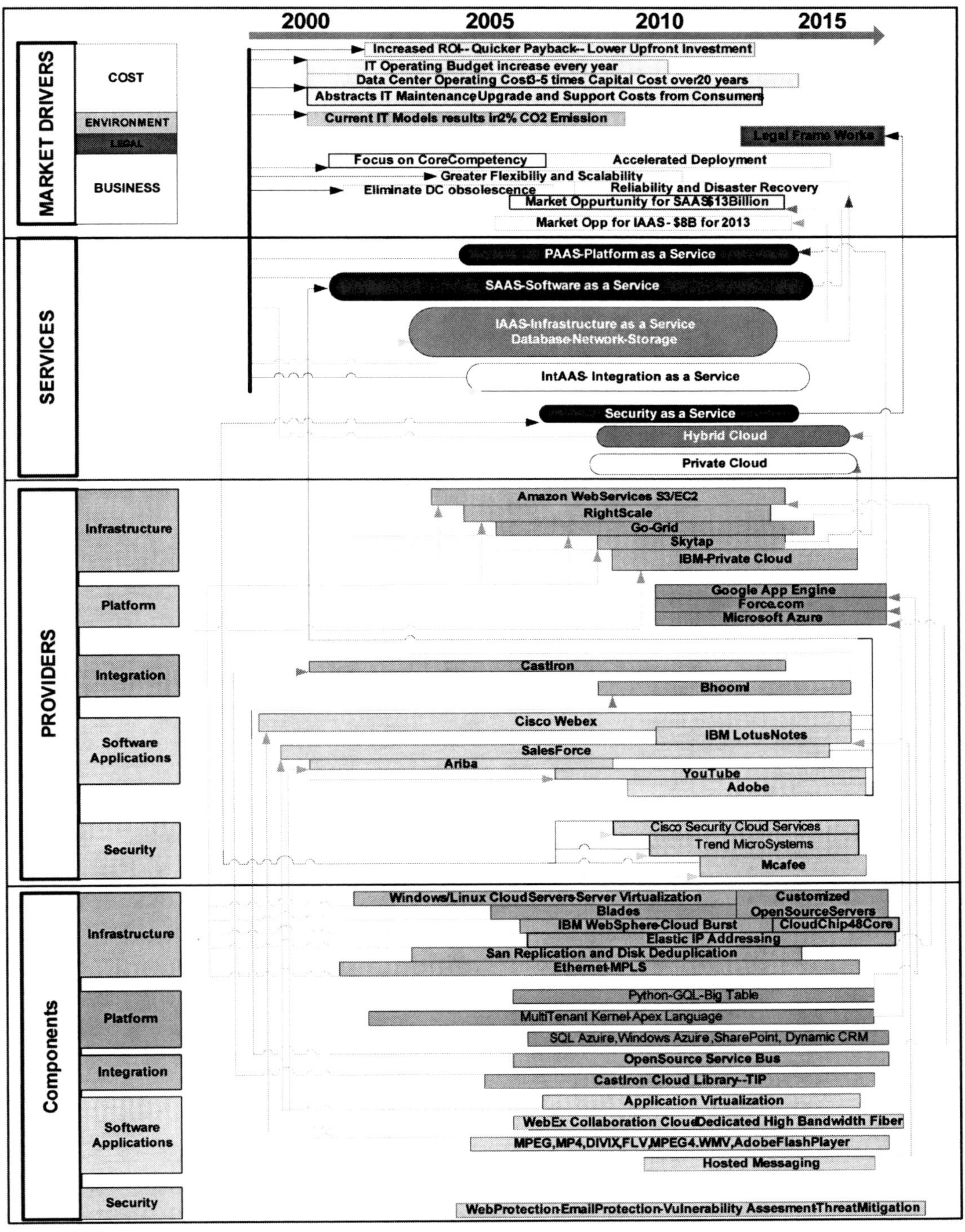

These seven different service levels make up the different types of Cloud services available today. Finally, the seven different services align with their respective Market Drivers.

This Roadmap was constructed based on a 15 year time line. The linkages and connections were arrived from detailed research with respect to functionality, facts and future assumptions in the respective areas. At the lower level you see the provider components coded with appropriate colors with respect to each category. The same colors were used at the Provider level to depict the linkages between the components and the providers who use those components. We have used discrete colors to depict the services layers. The same colors were used from the services level for the lines that connect the providers to the service. Finally, the services are connected to each market driver by suitable arrows. Highlighted is each line going from a particular service and meeting a unique market driver by its own service color. We also see multiple services meeting the same set of Market Drivers. They are highlighted with a thick black backbone line on the left side resulting in the completion of the Roadmap. We followed the conventional method of drawing a Roadmap and connected services to its respective market drivers. That is, a unidirectional arrow starting from the service layer reaching its appropriate market driver. The combination of using color-coded boxes, lines and arrows with color identification should help those unfamiliar with roadmaps in understanding the concept.

Roadmap-Summary

The services road map shows the options available so anyone can understand what the current services offered are in a particular area of specialization and how it translates to driving a particular market need. As with any other roadmap, this roadmap provides a current snapshot at this point in time. There are many changes happening that could affect the roadmap since cloud computing is still in an infant stage. The changes, both at the consumer level as well as at the provider level can lead to another set of parallel services offered in the next few years. The same is true from a consumer perspective looking at other drivers which would be prevalent in future.

The only thing certain about technology is that it frequently changes. The roadmap user should bear in mind that roadmaps have to be constantly updated with due consideration given to these changes. In addition to the point above, bare in mind that this roadmap is a bird's eye view of the Cloud technologies, the major providers, etc.. There should always be a constant endeavor to traverse this roadmap alongside with the individual technology roadmaps. This would help all understand where the technology is headed, as well as predict disruptive technology that is going to affect the overall roadmap in future.

EXPERT OPINION

The objective of this questionnaire here is to validate our understanding about the current drivers and inhibitors to cloud computing. In addition to it our purpose of the survey is to gather data that can be mapped into different scenarios for the consumers and providers. Scenario planning can be used in many different ways. For the purpose of this paper we are using it as a forecasting model to predict the future of cloud computing and what small, medium and large companies could expect in the future. For our model we generated a survey asking some basic questions about the future of cloud computing directed to industry experts from small and large business perspectives. The questions and a tally of the results can be seen in Table 2.

The questions were asked to 5 IT experts from a variety of backgrounds. The first question "Who should switch to cloud computing" gives an idea of the size of business that will switch to could computing first. Most experts picked small busi-

Table 2. Expert survey

Question	Small	Medium	Large
1. Who should switch to cloud computing	3	2	1
2. What are the enablers Key decisions:	Cost	Efficiency	State of the art tools
Score:	5	1	0
3. What are the barriers Key decisions:	Security	Customized Application	Performance
Score:	4	3	4
4. How soon will the company adopt cloud computing Adoption rate:	1-2 years	3-5 years	5-10 years
Score:	0	4	0

Note: Survey asked to 5 industry experts

ness for the reasoning that there is lower startup cost and typically fewer infrastructures needs. They are also not as heavily invested in their current data management so the switch is easier.

The second question "In your view what are the enablers" shows that cost is the main driver behind cloud computing. All industry experts agreed that lowering IT cost would be the benefit to companies. This relates back to question 1 where small businesses would be the first to adopt cloud computing because of the lower initial cost.

The third question "What are the barriers" had fairly evenly distributed answers between security, customized application, and performance. Some of the experts thought that all three were important while others picked one or two. This could be due to the range of experts that were surveyed. Someone from a small business may not think that security is a big issue while someone from a large business may think it is the biggest issue. This result shows that security, customized applications, and performance are important factors to different people looking to make the switch to cloud.

The fourth and final question "How soon will the company adopt cloud computing" shows that cloud computing is in the near future in the minds of IT professionals. All respondents agreed that the transition will happen in the next 3-5 years with the exception of one who did not think the transition will happen.

The adoption rate will differ for large and small businesses and is based on question 4. In this paper we will analyze when small and large business will likely adopt cloud computing depending on their needs as a business. The adoption rate will vary depending on how cloud computing adapts to the barriers from the survey (security, custom applications, and performance) of different industries.

SURVEY IMPLICATIONS

The key factors which emerged from the survey data are the technical parameters like performance, customized applications and emphasis on a Business to be complaint in protecting the data they currently hold in their in house data centers. We would like to look at the perspective of how these 3 parameters can affect businesses irrespective of their size and also look at what would be the difference between consumers who are dependent on these barriers vs. consumers who are not dependent on these barriers. The survey gave us insights to focus down to the key factors which enable cloud computing. One is the adoption rate of Small and Large Business and the other is about the influence of barriers in the adoption of cloud model irrespective of the segment they belong to. We wanted to validate these insights by providing two different analyses to look at these factors closely so that it will help us in the Scenario based Forecasting in the end.

Analysis of Barriers on Cloud Computing

As discussed in the previous section the 3 parameters Compliance requirements, Custom Applications and Performance influence the adoption of cloud computing. The data from these barriers has driven our Analysis of Barriers. Businesses could use this as a decision matrix based on their Individual IT Infrastructure and identified barriers. We also found that based on this analysis we forecast that performance, customized applications, and Compliance will progress accordingly within the next ten years, eliminating these factors as barriers of switching to Cloud Computing in this time frame.

It is important to look at each one of them separately and understand its importance from the perspective of the consumers.

Custom Applications

The idea behind cloud itself is consolidation of applications, so naturally the transition from on-site to a cloud model depends on how dependant they are on custom applications. Having more Custom Applications was a concern expressed by the experts with respect to the adoption of Cloud. Even though it is a concern now, there are companies who act as developers and integrators that will mitigate this problem in future by acting as a liaison between provider and consumer and help companies move to a cloud model. Moreover integration, support, and management are given a high value by the end user. It is seen that a lot of improvement and R&D is being done in this area from big industry players down to single proprietary owners. That said, various new applications are being developed with web-based integration in mind that will also meet the need of the end user. Research on "open-platforms" to support these legacy applications are also being developed by Industry leaders.

Performance

There is a lot of R&D focused on improving materials and technologies currently used to transmit data and voice in the telecommunication companies, specifically to yield higher performance. In consideration of these advances and proven improvement in the past ten years, it is foreseen that performance will not be a barrier after three years.

Compliance Requirements

Lastly, compliance is the laggard in this Industry. Consumers are concerned that there are no Legal Frameworks that is universally adoptable across moving their data from Consumer owned Infrastructure to a Cloud Provider. Based on their feedback this factor will play a decisive role for a concerned consumer who is bound by legal requirements to not move their data to the Cloud. Moreover, it is of utmost concern to Industries like Health Care, Government, Education, Banking, etc. Furthermore, compliance concerns will take longer to overcome but there is tremendous effort from government and Industry leaders to overcome this barrier. Compliance also ties into security and how data is stored, protected, and transferred. Security has improved dramatically over the years but is still not perfected. There are new concerns being raised with Cloud Computing. For example, there are issues in relation to data storage overseas and International Law and the risks that are associated. Compliance is predicted as one of the highest barriers for those wanting to make the shift to cloud computing. This is not believed to happen in the next 10 years.

Barriers Analysis

We have taken 3 time periods for our analysis. They are 3years, 5years and 10 years. We are assigning a High or Low value for the 3 parameters namely Compliance, Custom Applications and performance. Since we have 3 values there could be 8 possibilities. Out of these 8 possibilities there could be one unique possibility applicable to a company. On the first iteration, when we start assigning a value of Low for all 3, we predict the adoption is going to take less than 3 years. For a company that requires average performance, Low Compliance and minimum Custom Applications, the chances that they will move to a Cloud Model are high and we see that they could adopt within the next 3 years. Another example seen in the chart below is companies who can manage with average performance and minimal custom applications but have higher compliance requirements and to move their data to a cloud model is expected to take a longer time of 10 years. All the iterations are shown in the next page along with the Figure 3.

The next step in our analysis is to shift our focus on consumer segments. Do these barriers influence consumers depending upon their size? What would be their adoption to cloud computing with respect to these barriers? All of these are explained in the Business Adoption model below.

Business Adoption Model

The model below forecasts the adoption of Cloud Computing in four categorized businesses with respect to time and cost. The model is driven by data collected from questionnaires and literature research on current trends. We want to focus this analysis based on Small Businesses and Large Businesses who are specialized and not specialized.

To simplify the model the businesses were categorized into four possible common groups as follows:

- **Small Businesses (SB):** These are standard small businesses that require basic technology Infrastructure ex: email, standard industry applications, files sharing, telecom, and Internet connectivity.
- **Small-Specialized Businesses (SB-S):** These are small businesses that require all standard technologies identified above in (SB), and in addition have a need for customized proprietary applications, high data performance and bandwidth needs, and compliance regulations. In other words these businesses have specialized needs.
- **Large Businesses (LB):** These are standard large businesses that require basic technology Infrastructure. For example, email, standard industry applications, files sharing, telecom, and Internet connectivity.
- **Large Specialized Businesses (LB-S):** These are large businesses that require all standard technologies identified above in (LB), and in addition have a need for customized proprietary applications, high data performance and bandwidth needs, and compliance regulations.

Adoption Rate

In relation to the (SB) adoption above in Figure 4, It was found that none of these barriers will affect this category, therefore putting it in the higher adoption rate within three to four years bracket - cloud computing currently meets all of SB's needs. Large Businesses (LB)–proves to have a higher adoption rate within the next five to six years however will incur a higher cost compared to (SB) in the initial switch over but proves to yield a lower overall cost in the long run.

However (SB-S), Figure 4, has an elevated concern with all three barriers, which puts them in the Mid-Adoption rate within the next seven to eight years bracket. Large Specialized businesses (LB-S) will be the slowest in comparison with the three identified business categories above

Figure 3. Three key technical parameters of clouded computing adoption

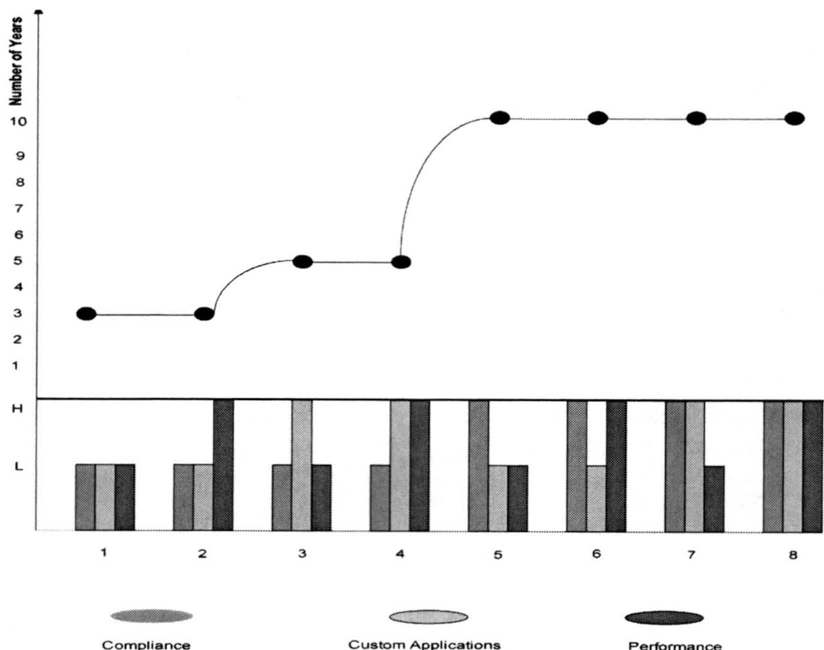

in adopting cloud computing. They fall in the mid-adoption rate as well. All three barriers affect these groupings the most, as indicated be the previous Barrier Analysis, there is a higher forecasted switch over in the next 10 years in consideration of (LB-S) barriers.

DISCUSSION

The summary of both the Barrier Analysis and the Business Adoption models provide headway in how much consumers have to weigh their current environment in terms of size due to the investments in their Infrastructure and how critical these barriers are influencing them in making the decision to switch over to Cloud Computing. Providers equally have a decisive role to play. The reason why the provider's role is important is to clear some of the ambiguity related to these barriers as well as to create concrete action plans to resolve the real issues affecting the adoption of cloud computing. This it is critical for them. Provider's responsibilities lie in creating an environment where the consumer is able to see the roadmap of how and when they should consider switching over to cloud computing. How the individual barriers maybe be overcome and what are the costs involved in the switchover will be clear once the providers are able integrate their solution to meet the consumers expectations. The providers are challenged here in creating a universal solution for the issues faced by consumers. Providers are also divided here by the areas of services they provide; there can never be a uniform framework which can provide the path of transformation, here is where the question may no longer be simply whether technology is adopted or provided, but rather which technology is adopted (Francis, 2009).The idea of Cloud Developers or Integrators is mooted to address the gaps that providers should understand the gaps better so that consumers can move forward cautiously with their help. When it comes to predicting the forecasting

Figure 4. General time line and cost

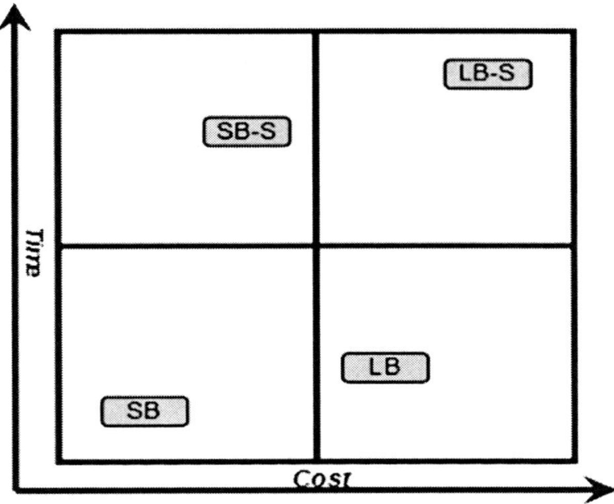

of any technology in addition with the variability involved, in a multitude of areas, it is difficult to create an accurate forecasting model pointing in only a particular direction where the Industry can head. In considering the above, while legacy enterprise software can simply be installed and run on instances on the cloud using cloud based infrastructure services, maximum benefits are realized by end users when these applications itself are provided as a service in the form of a platform or software (Bickering, 2009).

We focused on predicting multiple scenarios, where the Industry could potentially head in the coming years. A particular scenario is a compilation of the states of various players in the Industry and continuous internal and external changes can take them into different direction in the future. We will now explain the Scenario based forecasting method that will give you a better understanding of where the various stages that providers and consumers can be in the future, and what would be the roles of developers and integrators in helping them to reach a successful transformational state to cloud computing.

CLOUD SCENARIOS

Scenario Planning

Scenario planning is an approach that assists organizations in making effective decisions today for an uncertain future. The aim of scenario planning is to portray a range of possible consequences of strategic decisions by taking into account both internal and external aspects of the organizations. It predicts the possible outcomes of each decision that might happen after prospective future developments unfolded (Borjeson et al., 2006). This approach is often exploited with other forecasting technologies in order to expand the future perspectives and also help the organizations better prepare themselves for unforeseen events. Furthermore, it likewise assists them in carving through the future issues. As a result, scenario planning becomes a promising tool that is applied to a variety of industries (Zegras et al., 2004; Sager, 2001; Bradfield, 2005; Borjeson and Hojer, 2006). With a set of plausible assumption about the key uncertainties that might effect to the organization, a set of scenarios is carefully selected to reflect the range of possible future events. Thus, the time period used in scenario planning should reflect the time horizon of the most significant decision movement (Porter, 1985).

Scenario Model

Technology Integration and Business Adoption

Four scenarios were chosen based on two factors to help predict the future of cloud computing. One parameter is Technology Integration and the other is Business Adoption. The integration of cloud computing with current IT infrastructure is a general concern for businesses and there are barriers to just cross the Chasm for them on the Organization's perspective to get comfortable with Cloud Computing technology. The other parameter is the Technical Integration where how quickly providers educate consumers about the value of the Cloud computing. These 2 key factors yield four scenarios for Cloud computing starting from the Present State to a Fully Matured model for Organizations to adopt Cloud Computing. The 4 scenarios we have depicted here starts with the "Present State", and can go either in the direction "Just Crossed the Chasm" or "Acceptance Chasm". Finally the most desirable state for the Industry is landing into the "Acceptance Wonderland" where both the Business Adoption and Technical Integration are high. All details are depicted in figure 5.

Present State

Low Adoption and Low Integration

In this scenario, the cloud model lacks clarity to justify organizations concerns in the area of Interoperability and Latency issues revolved around the performance of Cloud Computing. It is particularly a decisive factor for large organizations that have invested substantially in their current infrastructure. Moreover there is always resistance to change. Organizations are not clear about the Transformation to see their IT moving from in-house to a cloud model. Legal Frameworks are not prevalent today to deal with the Compliance and Governance regulations businesses might have to comply with after moving to a Cloud Model. From our research we see this can considerably delay getting the consumers into the Chasm or extending the Chasm to a long time. By and large the present time frame is marred by a confused state in organizations and they are not ready to move to the Cloud model.

Just Crossed the Chasm

High Adoption and Low Integration

Cost is the main driver in this scenario. Organizations simply find their current model of owning IT, resulting in replacement of Servers and other underlying infrastructure components every few years is Unsustainable in the longer run increasing their IT budget year after year. Although there are still many issues with the cloud, many consumers adopt with high hopes for the future. The cost savings resulting due to a "pay as you use" model offered by Cloud, favor Businesses to do the switch. Potential emissions reductions efforts by the government help to urge people to partake in the model through possible tax incentives. Businesses large and small have ways to sidestep the issues in order to keep afloat. Those which don't switch to cloud here may not be able to stay competitive. On the provider side, we predict there may be several initiatives to create independent bodies to address some of the challenges faced by Cloud from the legal, compliance and governance perspective. We expect new frame works to have emerged addressing the concerns mentioned above.

Acceptance Chasm

Low Acceptance and High Integration

In this scenario, companies are uneasy about moving to cloud computing. The adoption is generally not taken off although the technology has been highly integrated. The cloud industry has made a significant push and there has been a lot of money put into the integration of cloud computing with companies. Consumers don't realize the Technological enhancements transform into Business Value for them to make the switch. Uncertain Economic Climate will play a decisive factor as consumers may hesitate to switch their IT from a provisioning model to an on-demand model due to risks involved in the switchover in-spite of the cost savings provided by Cloud.

Acceptance Wonderland

High Acceptance and High Integration

A scenario with high acceptance and high integration is win-win for consumers and providers of cloud computing. This means that the technology push for cloud computing succeeded in removing any concerns with the barriers. The products that are on the market are safe, secure, and highly affordable making it easy to integrate a small or large business into the cloud. In this case many leaps and bounds have happened over existing technology on the cloud market. New roles like Cloud Integrators and Cloud Developers would have emerged. Their role would be to make a smooth transition to a cloud model whether it is a Public or Private. In addition to that they constantly provide feedback for providers to improve some of the service offerings to the consumers. Surprises may occur that drive the market as new technologies emerge within this realm.

CONCLUSION

We observe based on our research and the analysis done for this paper that Cloud computing has some unique features which can be attractive for Businesses. At the same time it also comes with its own share of challenges equally. Since reliability, interoperability and security is a barrier, it is still uncertain whether the Businesses are comfortable moving their mission critical applications to cloud. Consumers need to realign their IT model as a precursor to move to cloud. Standardization of processes, understanding their internal service level agreements, careful evaluation of their compliance requirements all will pave way for easy transformation to cloud whenever they are ready. Careful consideration should be given by Businesses to decide what would be the Business impact of loosing data, user disruptions as they are at the mercy of providers now. They also have to carefully prepare appropriate legal contracts to meet the losses due to the disruption which are beyond their control. The Second factor related to cloud computing is the real value of cost savings a consumer can achieve by moving to cloud. Even though Cloud Providers at a macro level aim at providing superior computing service at a low cost, their ultimate business motive is to sell services. They are going to provide a range of features at different levels of price and consumers should understand the aspects of services they utilize. Selection of features which are applicable to them will ensure that their move to cloud is resulted at a cost lower than the current model. Since cloud offers the provision for instant scaling it is imperative that consumers demand transparency from providers in tracking the costs occurred depending on their usage. Another impact organizations will face is there might be some realignment with the current organization structure to suit the cloud model. Some of their current management and technical workforce will vanish due to the adoption to cloud; some new positions will also be created. Businesses

Figure 5. Scenarios of cloud computing

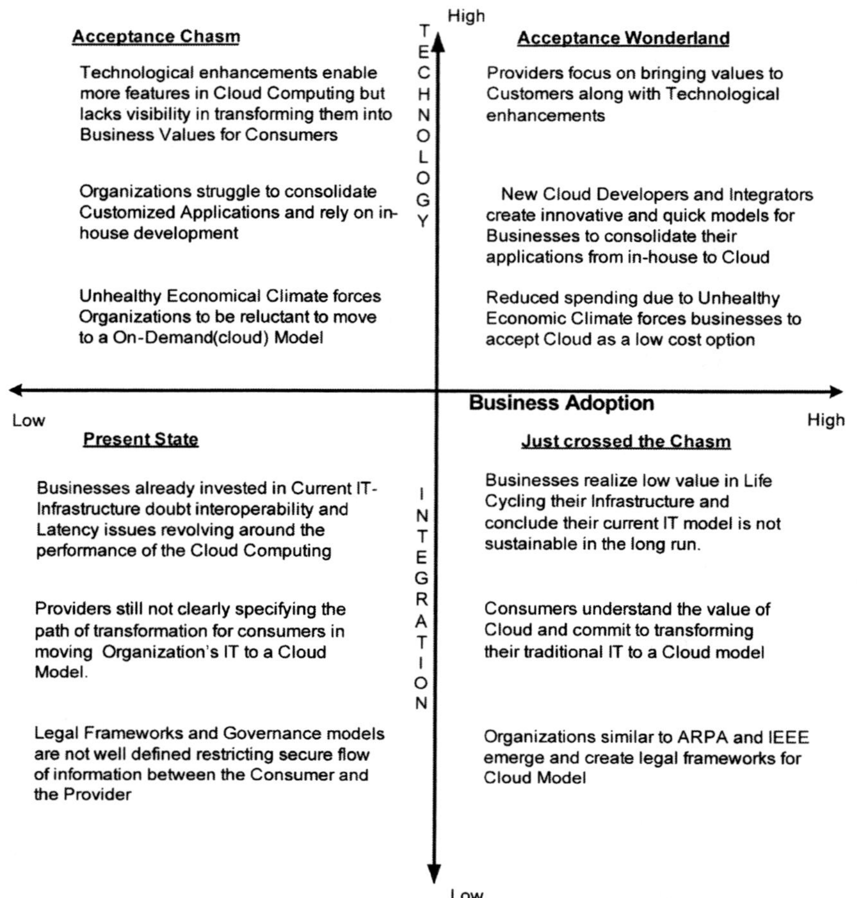

need to have a careful assessment of the impact from this perspective to ensure that they are able to provide the same level of service they have provided with the old structure. Our objective as stated in the beginning of the paper is to forecast the integration of providers into the consumers' acceptance domain so that the Technology can move from the present nascent state to the successfully adopted future state. We have shown in our report the detailed study of the technologies and services that are going to form the Technology Integration. We also explored the report from the consumer side by analyzing the barriers and the size of the consumers. Is cloud technology going to be adopted like the past innovations similar to Mainframe computing, Client Server Technology or the latest web technologies, using the Internet extensively? We conclude in the end that cloud computing has the potential to change the way in which IT is managed today. The extent of adoption will place the Industry in one of four scenarios outlined in this paper.

REFERENCES

Andriole, S. (2009). Entering the cloud: Phased adoption to computing nirvana. *Cutter IT Journal*, *22*, 32–37.

Becker, H. S. (1983). Scenarios: A tool of growing importance to policy analysts in government and industry. *Technological Forecasting and Social Change*, *23*, 95–120. doi:10.1016/0040-1625(83)90049-5

Bickering, E. (2009). An empirical assessment of technology adoption as a choice between alternatives. *Information Resources Management Journal*, *22*(4).

Borjeson, L., & Hojer, M. (2006). Scenario types and techniques: Towards a user's guide. *Futures*, *38*, 723–739. doi:10.1016/j.futures.2005.12.002

Borjeson, L., Hojer, M., Dreborg, K. H., Ekvall, T., & Finnveden, G. (2006). Scenario types and techniques: Towards a user's guide. *Futures*, *38*, 723–739. doi:10.1016/j.futures.2005.12.002

Bradfield, R. (2005). The origins and evolution of scenario techniques in long range business planning. *Futures*, *37*, 795–812. doi:10.1016/j.futures.2005.01.003

Callewaert, P., Robinson, P. A., & Blatman, P. (2009). *Cloud computing forecasting change*. Retrieved February 14, 2010, from www.deloitte.com/ assets/Dcom.../ ie_Consulting_CloudComputing_09.pdf

Chermack, T. J. (2005). Studying scenario planning: Theory, research suggestions and hypotheses. *Technological Forecasting and Social Change*, *72*, 59–73.

Daim, T. U., & Oliver, T. (2008). Implementing technology roadmap process in the energy services sector: A case study of a government agency. *Technological Forecasting and Social Change*, *75*, 687–720. doi:10.1016/j.techfore.2007.04.006

Francis, L. (2009). *Cloud computing: implications for enterprise software vendors (ESV)*. Thesis (S.M.), Massachusetts Institute of Technology, System Design and Management Program.

Hall, C. (2009). *Satisfaction with on-demand/ cloud-based business intelligence and data warehousing remains high*.

Holmes, C., & Ferril, M. (2005). The application of operation and technology roadmapping to aid Singaporean SMEs identify and select emerging technologies. *Technological Forecasting and Social Change*, *72*, 349–357. doi:10.1016/j.techfore.2004.08.010

John, M. (2009). *Cloud based security as a service*. Retrieved February 14, 2010, from http:// cloudsecurity.trendmicro.com/ the-security-as-a-service-model/

Kostoff, R. N., & Schaller, R. R. (2001). Science and technology roadmaps. *IEEE Transactions on Engineering Management*, *48*(2). doi:10.1109/17.922473

Lee, S., Kang, S., Park, Y., & Park, Y. (2007). Technology roadmapping for R&D planning: The case of the Korean parts and materials industry. *Technology (Elmsford, N.Y.)*, *27*, 433–445.

Lee, S., & Park, Y. (2005). Customerization of technology roadmaps according to roadmapping purposes: Overall process and detailed modules. *Technological Forecasting and Social Change*, *72*, 567–583. doi:10.1016/j.techfore.2004.11.006

Meader, P. (2009). *An introduction to developing for Microsoft Azure*. Retrieved February 14, 2010, from http://searchcloudcomputing.techtarget.com/ generic/0,295582,sid201_gci1366241,00.html

Mell, P., & Grance, T. (2009). *The NIST definition of cloud computing*. Retrieved February 14, 2010, from http://csrc.nist.gov/ groups/SNS/ cloud-computing/ index.html

Mitchell, D. (2008). *Defining platform as a service*. Retrieved February 14, 2010, from http://blogs.bungeeconnect.com/2008/02/18/defining-platform-as-a-service-or-paas

Mitchell, R., Tydeman, J., & Georgiades, J. (1979). Structuring the future-application of a scenario-generation procedure. *Technological Forecasting and Social Change*, *14*, 409–428. doi:10.1016/0040-1625(79)90038-6

Nolle, T. (2009). *Platform as a service: Google and Force.com.* Retrieved February 14, 2010, from http://searchcloudcomputing.techtarget.com/ tip/0,289483,sid201_gci1355986,00.html

O'Donnell, A. (2009). Hot technologies: While insurers often are cautious in their adoption of emerging technologies, carriers are investing in solutions that are just too transformative to ignore, including cloud computing, mobile capabilities, risk assessment solutions and social media. *Insurance & Technology*, *35*, 24–28.

Patrick, I. J., & Echols, A. E. (2008). Technology roadmapping in review: A tool for making sustainable new product development decisions. *Technological Forecasting and Social Change*, *71*, 81–100. doi:10.1016/S0040-1625(03)00064-7

Phaal, R., Farukh, C. J. P., & Probert, D. R. (2004). Technology roadmapping–A planning framework for evolution and revolution. *Technological Forecasting and Social Change*, *71*, 5–26. doi:10.1016/S0040-1625(03)00072-6

Phaal, R., & Muller, G. (2008). An architectural framework for roadmapping: towards visual strategy. *Technological Forecasting and Social Change*, *76*(1).

Porter, M. E. (1985). *Competitive advantage – Creating and sustaining superior performance*.

Postma, T., & Liebl, F. (2005). How to improve scenario analysis as a strategic management tool? *Technological Forecasting and Social Change*, *72*, 161–173.

Reynolds, E., & Bess, C. (2009). Clearing up the Cloud: Adoption strategies for cloud computing. *Cutter IT Journal, June*.

Rinne, M. (2004). Technology roadmaps: Infrastructure for innovation. *Technological Forecasting and Social Change*, *71*, 67–80. doi:10.1016/j.techfore.2003.10.002

Robert, W., & Sharif, N. (2008). A concept framework for ranking R&D project. *IEEE Transactions on Engineering Management*, *55*, 267–278. doi:10.1109/TEM.2008.919725

Roubelat, F., & Godet, M. (2000). Scenario planning: An open future. *Technological Forecasting and Social Change*, *65*, 1–2.

Sager, B. (2001). Scenarios on the future of biotechnology. *Technological Forecasting and Social Change*, *68*, 109–129. doi:10.1016/S0040-1625(00)00107-4

Schoemaker, P. J. H. (1995). Scenario planning: a tool for strategic thinking. *Sloan Management Review*, *36*, 25–40.

Stevens, H., & Petty, C. (2008). *Risks of cloud computing*. Retrieved February 14, 2010, from http://www.gartner.com/ it/page.jsp?id=707508

Uzoka, F. M. E., & Ijatuyi, O. A. (2005). Decision support system for library acquisition: A framework. *The Electronic Library*, *23*, 453–462. doi:10.1108/02640470510611517

Van Der Heijden, K. (2000). Scenarios and forecasting: Two perspectives. *Technological Forecasting and Social Change*, *65*, 31–36. doi:10.1016/S0040-1625(99)00121-3

Wilson, I. (2000). From scenario thinking to strategic action. *Technological Forecasting and Social Change*, *65*, 23–29. doi:10.1016/S0040-1625(99)00122-5

Chapter 12
Radio Frequency Identification in the Smart Supply Chain

Albert Lozano-Nieto
The Pennsylvania State University, USA

ABSTRACT

Radio Frequency Identification (RFID) is a relatively new technology that has emerged from the works of automated identification. RFID is based on the exchange of information between a device called a tag and a device called a reader after the reader queries the tag. The tags can be attached to specific items, boxes of these items, pallets of these boxes, or a combination of the previous, thus enabling the transmission of their contents. Once this information is detected and processed, it can be used as needed by the specific application. Among the different uses of RFID in the supply chain, this chapter focuses on those related to inventory control and the detection of counterfeited products.

INTRODUCTION

It is undeniable that the introduction of barcodes and their acceptance by all industry several years ago resulted in a revolution in the supply chain. We are now facing a similar transformation with the introduction of Radio Frequency Identification (RFID). The use of RFID allows the introduction of an additional level of intelligence in the management of products as they move through the different steps in the supply chain. Of particular interest are the possibilities to track inventory on real time as well as to introduce techniques to detect and prevent counterfeited products. These two characteristics in turn, result in a decrease of losses and a reduction in processing time and labor.

The goal of this chapter is to provide the reader with an introduction to the basic principles of RFID as well as to illustrate how this technology is being currently used to increase the efficiency in the supply chain as well as to fight the counterfeit of products that are critical to our society.

DOI: 10.4018/978-1-4666-0246-5.ch012

The counterfeiting of goods is an increasingly widespread problem through the industrialized and developing world. Recent estimates put the effect of counterfeiting between 5% to 7% of total world trade (Kim and Kim, 2005). The US defines counterfeiting as an item that is a copy or a substitute of a legal item without the right to do so, or whose materials, performance or characteristics are knowingly misrepresented by the manufacturer, supplier or vendor (US Department of Energy, 2004). While counterfeiting evokes the image of products imitating luxury watches, designer purses and other high-end items, the real impact of counterfeited items is more serious and may have extreme consequences. This is especially important as counterfeited products are increasingly appearing in critical systems such as the electronic components used for defense systems, pharmaceutical products and parts used for repair and maintenance of aircraft.

Counterfeiting of Electronic Products

The counterfeit of electronic components happens in different ways such as the remarking of electronic components to make them appear different from what they originally are, selling defective parts staged for disposal by the original manufacturer or parts that result from reselling components taken from electronic boards that were scheduled for destruction or simply knowingly selling components that are not operational (Livingston, 2007). While in this last case components may have been at one time real components, they have been obtained without any quality control procedures and at the very least, they have aged considerably.

The effects of counterfeited electronic components is more worrisome when they are used in critical systems such as avionics, flight controls or defense systems. To make the problem worse, it can be extremely difficult to link the crash of a military aircraft, for example, to counterfeited electronic parts and especially to identify the part that failed as complex systems tend to fail in complex ways. We need to keep in mind that counterfeited electronic products may work correctly for some time, or as long as they do not exceed some operational parameters unknown to the user. A different concern comes from counterfeited electronics products, having a backdoor that can be used to disrupt a service. The use of counterfeited computer processors in systems that control critical missions of critical assemblies, for example the power grid or the control of electrical stations can enable a third party to have access to otherwise secure systems without being known by their legitimate users.

If counterfeited electronic products are difficult to detect after a failure, it is extremely difficult, almost impossible to detect them at the time of use or when assembling the subsystems. It is possible to find several reasons to explain the increase in the counterfeit of electronic products, specifically electronic components. Our society is used to, and demands, lower costs in electronic products. To most users, the only difference between a legally manufactured and a counterfeited cell phone battery is only their cost, especially before there are widespread news of failures and their consequences. The reason for the spread of counterfeited integrated circuits in avionics and military products is double. First, in an effort to save costs, the Department of Defense started an initiative several years ago focused on purchasing electronic components off the shelf instead of having electronic components specifically designed and manufactured by approved manufacturers. In addition, the electronic components tend to remain in service in military ships or airplanes for 10 or 20 years after being discontinued by the manufacturer. This forces military purchasers to use small brokerage firms who buy and sell integrated circuits without knowing who is making them. In turn, this opens the door to counterfeited or defective components to be used in our nation's defense systems. As a response to recent incidents of detecting counterfeited components in these critical systems, the military is requiring documentation about conformance and traceability before purchasing parts. However, this is just a very short-term measure that can be easily circumvented by dedicated counterfeiters. It is then, necessary, to rethink the global electronics supply chain in an effort to ensure the validity of any electronic parts used in critical or defense electronic equipment.

Counterfeiting of Pharmaceutical Products

The pharmaceutical supply chain is in principle, not different from the chain for any other goods as it involves a large number of raw materials and finished products. However, due to its intrinsic characteristics, the pharmaceutical supply chain must be viewed with special attention. Counterfeited pharmaceutical products are medicines that are deliberately and fraudulently mislabeled with respect to their identity as well as their source. The effect of counterfeited pharmaceutical products compromises the safety of patients, causes economic losses to established drug manufacturers and becomes a threat to the national security of countries. While the percentage of counterfeited pharmaceutical products is estimated between the 5% to 7%, which is common to any product, experts in the field have seen a marked increase in the last few years.

A reason for the increase in counterfeited pharmaceutical products is the access by counterfeiters to cheap and effective printing technology. It is now possible to illicitly reproduce any label even those that incorporate additional security marks. In addition, the last few years have witnessed an increase in the number of small wholesalers who buy and sell pharmaceutical products. This phenomenon creates a large secondary market that allows the ease introduction of counterfeited pharmaceutical products as pharmaceutical products change hands many times before reaching the end user. Coupled to this situation is the number of expensive drug therapies that attract counterfeiters due to the potential large economic benefits they may obtain.

The pharmaceutical industry has tried to develop techniques to combat the counterfeit of its products although they have not found a totally effective technique. Most of the efforts are carried out by manually inspection of drugs to check for evidence of counterfeit. Unfortunately, if a counterfeited drug is detected, it is very difficult to trace it back to the point it was introduced in the pharmaceutical supply chain.

Inventory Inaccuracies

The accuracy of inventory is essential for a business dealing with physical assets. However, it is well known that large discrepancies may exist between inventory and the goods available. Most of these discrepancies are due to the break between data flow (inventory data) and the flow of goods. Studies of inventory inaccuracies show a strong reduction in profits between 10% and 25% (Fleisch and Tellkamp, 2005). The four major factors that contribute to these inaccuracies are theft, unsalable products, misplaced items and incorrect deliveries. The last two causes are the direct result of poor process quality control practices that can therefore be improved with existing or new technologies for which RFID emerges a very valuable candidate.

RADIO FREQUENCY IDENTIFICATION (RFID) USE IN THE SUPPLY CHAIN

RFID is a technology that uses radio frequency for communication between a tag – also known as the transponder- and a reader – also known as the interrogator-. The transponder carries a unique identification number that is sent to the interrogator every time that the transponder is queried. The identification number can then be referenced against a database to retrieve additional information on the object that was tagged. RFID technology is in this way, functionally similar to the bar codes that appear in almost all products marketed in the United States and a large number of countries. They differ in the way that the information is read: by optical means in the case of bar codes and by radiofrequency in the case of RFID.

Although the widespread use of this technology is recent, it was first developed during World War II in order to identify friend or foe aircraft. After several years, and following the advances in the development of personal computer, personal communications and microelectronics in general, the technology is now mature enough to be mass-marketed at competitive costs. In this environment RFID has emerged as a viable solution to the problem of remotely identifying objects in different situations and in different locations.

Any RFID system can be divided into four subsystems:

- The tag that is affixed to the item being tracked
- The reader that is used to capture the information emitted by the tag and in some cases to write new information to the tag if necessary
- The antennas that are used to couple energy between the transponder and interrogator
- A host computer that is used to transmit commands to the interrogator, process the data that the reader has received and hosts the software for data management

Tag Classification

Each one of these subsystems can be classified depending on the technology used or other parameters. Tags can be classified depending on the source of energy they use to transmit the information to the reader:

- Passive tags. These tags do not contain any source of power and therefore they are the most simple and least expensive tags. The energy required to energize its internal circuits is harvested from the electromagnetic field generated by the reader. They have a low read range, less than 10 feet but are extremely inexpensive with costs around 2 cents or less.
- Semi-passive tags: These tags contain batteries used to power electronic systems other than those required for the communication with the reader. These systems are normally sensors and transducers. Because they also harvest the energy from the field for communication with the reader, they have the same read range as passive tags. The cost of these tags exceeds $20 per unit.
- Active tags contain batteries that are used to energize the electronics required to communicate with the interrogator. In this type of tag, the communication can be initiated even when the tag is far away from the interrogator, 100 feet or more. These tags can be produced for around $20 a piece. While passive tags have an ideally infinite life, the life of the active tags is limited to the life of their batteries.

It is necessary to point out that with the exception of very specific applications (for example, the E-Z pass system for toll payment in highways that use active tags in order to have a useful read range), the great majority of RFID systems today employ passive tags.

Tags can also be classified on the amount of information that they can hold as well as if this information is fixed or can be re-written by the appropriate reader. Using this approach, tags can be classified as:

- Class 0: These tags can only be read by the interrogator. The data in these tags is an alphanumeric identification string, preprogrammed by the manufacturer. The RFID system cannot overwrite or modify this code.

- Class 1: The identification string from these tags can be programmed by the manufacturer or by the RFID system, but it can only be written once. Once the data is written it cannot be overwritten or modified. These tags are known as WORM tags (Write Once Read Many).
- Class 2: These tags can be re-written by the interrogator many times. A typical application would be in a production line in which the tag is updated after each step of production is completed. These tags have more memory and can hold more information than Class 0 and Class 1 tags hold.

As technology progresses, the number of Class 2 tags used in commercial products is steadily increasing.

A final classification of tags is based on the frequency of the signal used to transmit information between the tag and the reader. The selection of a specific frequency has clear engineering implications as it determines the type of technology used to design the whole system, the dimensions of the antennas used as well as the cost of the system. However, the selection of the operating frequency has more important implications for the focus of this chapter as it determines the type or types of products that can be tagged. In other words, different types of products require the use of different operating frequencies. With this in mind, tags can be classified depending on their operating frequency as:

- Low-Frequency (LF) RFID systems, operating in the 125 kHz to 140 kHz range. These tags are used by a large number of systems as the technology for this frequency range is well developed and so it has a low cost. Because LF waves work well around metals or objects with high water content, one of the main applications of this frequency range is its use for animal tracking. These tags can only support low data rates. In addition, they are relatively large in size due to their antenna requirements.
- High Frequency (HF) systems, operating at 13.56 MHz. This frequency is also well developed and therefore HF systems present a low cost, comparable to LF systems. These systems are less sensitive to noise than LF systems, supporting a higher transmission speed and a smaller antenna. Therefore, the tags can be smaller than tags used for LF system. The HF systems however, do not work well if the tags have to be attached to metallic objects or used in materials with high water content. Both LF and HF systems have a limited read range of below 10 feet because they only use passive tags.
- Ultra-High Frequency (UHF) systems that operate in the 860 MHz to 930 MHz frequency range. Tags in this frequency range can be active tags. However, because of the attenuation due to water content, these systems do not work well in moist environments, and because of wave reflections, they do not work well around metallic objects either. UHF systems are slowly growing in their commercial use as new generations of UHF RFID systems can read up to 1,500 tags per second in good conditions.
- Microwave systems operating at 2.45 GHz and at 5.8 GHz. These systems support much higher read speeds and a read range slightly below UHF systems. Their main drawback is the higher attenuation by atmospheric moisture and the interference from other devices in this unregulated frequency range. These systems are still under development and we should see more of them being introduced commercially in the next years.

RFID systems operating in the LF and HF ranges have spearheaded the development and acceptance of RFID systems worldwide. However, the majority of systems being placed today are UHF RFID systems. The increased read rates of the UHF RFID plus the additional information they can store, put them at the forefront of the development of this technology. For example, a 96-bit data code stored in the memory of a tag can uniquely identify 10^{29} objects. To put this in perspective, this means that it can uniquely identify 10^{19} different objects for every human that is alive today (Glidden et al, 2004). Therefore, these type of systems offer extreme advantages for the traceability of goods that cannot be compared to other systems.

Reader Classification

Readers can also be divided into different classes. Here, the classification is based on their functionality and operation:

- Fixed Interrogators are the types used in warehouses and other large facilities where the are mounted on walls, doors or other structures. These types of interrogators need an external power source and can accommodate several antennas.
- Handheld Interrogators, are much smaller than fixed interrogators. The interrogators have an antenna built into the unit and are battery operated. Some of these interrogators can also read barcodes, increasing their functionality. The communication between handheld interrogators and their main system can be either tethered or by wireless methods.
- Mobile Interrogators that can be connected to a laptop port, PDAs or cellphones, or even mounted in forklifts or clamp trucks. These interrogators usually have wireless connections and are powered by their host.

Other Sub-Systems

The last two sub-systems of the RFID chain, the antennas and the host computers are less flexible in terms of choosing their different elements. The antennas used by both interrogators and tags are mainly constrained by the frequency of the RFID signal as well as the desired read range between interrogator and tags. The power used by the system has also an influence on the dimensions of the antennas, especially the electrical conductors used in the design of the interrogators.

Finally, the host computers can be as varied as they are available in the industry. The database and the interface between the database and the user are determined by the application. Therefore, the interface can be customized for each specific case.

RFID SYSTEMS IN THE SUPPLY CHAIN

RFID as a method for collecting data in the supply chain presents several advantages when compared to traditional methods such as bar codes. First, RFID does not have the necessity of optical line of sight. In fact, several materials are transparent to radiofrequency signals. Secondly, the newer RFID systems allow the tags to be rewritten several times, updating the information that stored while bar codes are a fixed asset at the time of them being printed. Finally, RFID tags do not have the limitations of bar codes being able to be defaced or spoofed by an individual or organization printing new, fake codes. In order to rewrite a RFID tag, it is necessary to have a password, thus validating the new information stored in the tags.

RFID helps eliminate the problems related to unaccounted inventory. An unaccounted excess of inventory results in overstocking and an increase in the labor costs. Conversely, stock-out issues result in empty shelves and unsatisfied customers that translates in losing current and future sales.

Another important application of RFID systems in the supply chain is for ensuring product authentication either at a single item level or at the aggregate item level. Furthermore, RFID is a technology that can be applied to the global supply chair or just to some specific parts. For example, when focused on shipping and distribution, the technology allows the suppliers to accurately determine the location of a pallet as well as to track how it travels through the supply chain.

An emerging area of interest in the use of RFID is in cattle and food production due to the requirements by the United States as well as the European Union to provide better trace of food sources. The use of RFID can also help to reduce costs at the time of recalling specific products (Attaran, 2007).

The traceability of goods in the food supply chain is becoming critical to the survival of this sector. Recent events related to specific food contamination have resulted in dramatic drops in the sale of similar products from all producers and distributors. Most of the logistics associated with tracking and tracing products in the food supply chain can be solved using RFID systems and simple, personal computers (Kelepouris et al, 2000). Using these systems, companies can accurately trace product lots that need to be recalled, thus substantially decreasing the costs of the process as well as minimizing the damage to their corporate image. Furthermore, the use of traceability can be exploited as a marketing tool to gain new customers.

The standards for RFID use in the supply chain have been mostly developed through the work of EPCGlobal. Its standard is aimed towards improving the visibility of the supply chain end-to-end. In this model, products are tagged at the case and pallet level at the manufacturer's facility. As the pallets leave the warehouse, the readers gather information from the pallets without needing any additional effort. This information, in turn, is sent to a computer that filters the data and sends it to the appropriate applications. These applications don't have to reside in the same computer. In fact, the software allows to retrieve detailed information from any object stored in a network similar to the Internet that is using the EPC code. With this information, the system knows the location in which an object was produced and when and can make it accessible to a distributor after it reads the tags of the pallets after receiving them. This allows the distributor to route the good to the appropriate trucks or other methods of transportation. Once the products arrive to the retailer, their tags are read at the docks, and the inventory information is updated. If the shelves were to have their own readers, it would be possible to automatically produce replenishment orders.

RFID as a Tool for Counterfeiting Prevention

RFID is considered as a technique to complement the more commonly used anti-counterfeit approaches in the pharmaceutical industry. It presents that advantage of allowing immediate verification of a drug at any moment or location. It also allows the establishment of robust track and trace, thus providing true pedigree information about drugs. All this is based on individually identifying drugs at the package level. An additional advantage of RFID systems compared to traditional systems such as barcodes is that RFID has the ability to acquire and store relevant environmental information, for example the range of temperatures during the transportation process.

The different techniques for current authentication using RFID can be divided in those that do not authenticate the information sent by the tag and those that authenticate this information. The first method is simpler and less expensive although it is less robust. The second method has more robustness at the price of being more complex.

The simplest for identifying a specific product is by using the unique serial associated to a specific tag. This approach is based on the assumption that different products will be given different serial numbers. A specific product can be identified as a valid product by comparing the serial number stored in its tag with a list of valid numbers stored in a secure server. The weakness of this approach is that if counterfeiters can guess how the serial numbers are assigned to products, they can store valid serial numbers into counterfeited products as this method does not authenticate the data stored in the tag. A more refined process without data authentication is known as track and trace. This method comes like a natural evolution of the simple serial number, and is based on storing dynamic information as the goods move through the supply chain. The tag then presents a history of the steps that the product has taken as it was moved through the distribution process. In addition to authentication of the product, the track and trace method provides the pedigree of the product.

The previous two approaches are susceptible to data cloning as the information between tag and reader is interchanged in the open. To prevent this, it is possible to use cryptography techniques to allow for reliable authentication while keeping the critical information secret. Because increasing concerns about data security in several applications using RFID systems, there are several protocols based on this approach. The review of these protocols is beyond the scope of this paper and can be easily located in the literature. In any case the costs associated with authentication must be taken into account when considering the use of RFID systems.

RFID as Tool to Increase the Efficiency in the Supply Chain

RFID systems have also been proposed to increase the efficiency of the supply chain when dealing with goods that have a short shelf life and prevent, for example, spoilage of certain goods. This last problem is typically due from excess stock and inefficient stock rotation. Although bar codes have been tried for the identification of these goods, the effectiveness of this approach is seriously limited. First, reading barcodes involves almost always manual handling of these goods, making data capture difficult and time consuming. Also, the readability of the barcodes is sometimes compromised due to dirt, bending or other conditions that prevent reading the barcode. In these applications, RFID present several advantages compared to barcodes, such as being able to read the tags associated to the goods automatically as the goods move through a specific portal.

Karkkainen (2003) discusses the improvement in the efficiency in using RFID versus other methods in short shelf goods. A company that was using barcodes to track their short shelf products decided to develop a trial run using RFID to study the potential benefits of this technology. In particular, the goal was to quantify the reduction in labor costs associated to monitoring and counting the stock as well as to quantify the reduction in spoilage of their goods through the supply chain. This trial used RFID tags applied to plastic crates. The tags contained information regarding the description of products in the crate, the quantity of products, the use-by date of the products as well as a unique identifier for each crate. The tags were programmed with this information at the end of the production line. The first time that tags were read was at the door of the depot for these goods. The use of a portal reader allowed to read all the tags while the crates were being transported inside the depot without requiring any additional efforts. The second time the tags were read was at the point of exiting the depot in destination to the stores. These two read processes resulted in the increase in the accuracy of the inventory that was placed in the chilling area of the depot. In addition, the company reported that the bulk of the benefits of using RFID for their goods happened at the retail store level. This technology resulted in savings related to retail store replenishment productivity due to the increase in the visibility of their assets. They also noted a reduction of losses in their stock due to an increase in inventory accuracy that gave them a better control over stock rotation.

Ferrer et al (2010) present several case studies of using RFID systems to increase the efficiency of the system. The authors have shown that simple RFID tags attached to beer kegs have decreased the number of kegs being lost or stolen by 4%. Further, using RFID tags that can measure and record the weight of each keg upon delivery and return has decreased the distributor's tax liability as these are typically levied by the volume of beer distributed. The authors also describe the increase efficiency in locating railcars as they move through the railroad network thus improving the speed and reliability of delivery. The concept of Real Time Location Systems (RTLS) by using active tags applied to prison inmate tracking is also described in the same study. In this case, inmates are issued bracelets with active tags carrying their identity number. A central database tracks the movement of inmates through the prison alerting officers when they come close to off-limits areas or when certain inmates come close to each other if the database determines they have a history of violent acts.

CONCLUSION

Radio Frequency Identification is a new technology that will enable new and powerful features to tomorrow's supply chain. RFID is emerging as a powerful tool used to fight the counterfeit of critical goods such as pharmaceutical products, electronic components used in defense systems and replacement parts in the aerospace industry. This technique allows the authentication of these diverse components and presents the ability to trace how they moved through their own supply chain. Another advantage of using RFID in the supply chain resides on its ability to improve the efficiency of inventory, locate critical parts and in summary, decrease logistics costs.

Although the use of RFID applied to the supply chain is still in its infancy, we cannot but expect a strong increase in its presence in the coming years. It is therefore critical that those professionals involved in supply chain management and operations to have at least a basic knowledge of the capabilities –as well as limitations- of this technique.

REFERENCES

Attaran, M. (2007). RFID: An enabler of supply chain operations. *Supply Chain Management: An International Journal*, *12*(4), 249–257. doi:10.1108/13598540710759763

Ferrer, G., Dew, N., & Apte, U. (2010). When is RFID right for your service? *International Journal of Production Economics*, *124*, 414–425. doi:10.1016/j.ijpe.2009.12.004

Fleisch, E., & Tellkamp, C. (2005). Inventory inaccuracy and supply chain performance: A simulation study of a retail supply chain. *International Journal of Production Economics*, *95*, 373–385. doi:10.1016/j.ijpe.2004.02.003

Glidden, R., Bockoric, C., Cooper, S., Diorio, C., Dressler, D., & Gutnik, V. (2004). Design of ultra-low-cost UHF RFID tags for supply chain applications. *IEEE Communications Magazine*, (August): 140–151. doi:10.1109/MCOM.2004.1321406

Karkkainen, M. (2003). Increasing efficiency in the supply chain for short shelf life goods using RFID tagging. *International Journal of Retail & Distribution Management*, *31*, 529–536. doi:10.1108/09590550310497058

Kelepouris, T., Pramatari, K., & Doukidis, G. (2007). RFID-enabled traceability in the food supply chain. *Industrial Management & Data Systems*, *107*, 183–200. doi:10.1108/02635570710723804

Kim, J., & Kim, J. H. (2005). Anti-counterfeiting solution employing mobile RFID environment. *Proceedings of the World Academy of Science, Engineering and Technology, 8,* (pp. 141-145).

Livingston, H. (2007). Avoiding counterfeit electronic components. *IEEE Transactions on Components and Packaging Technologies*, *30*, 187–189. doi:10.1109/TCAPT.2007.893682

US Department of Energy. (2004). *Process guide for the identification and disposition of suspect/counterfeit or defective items at Department of Energy facilities*. Office of Environment, Safety and Health, United States Department of Energy.

KEY TERMS AND DEFINITIONS

Active RFID: RFID systems in which the tags have their own battery source.

Authentication: The process of validating the authenticity of the data being transmitted by the RFID system.

Counterfeit: The illicit making of copies of products that may or may not have the characteristics of the items being copied. Reader: Systems that generates the power necessary to energize the transponder and detects its messages. Also known as interrogator.

RFID: Radio Frequency Identification.

Passive RFID: RFID systems in which the tags do not have a separate source of energy. They are energized by the electromagnetic field generated by the reader.

Tag: System attached to the items being tracked consisting of an antenna, memory and additional circuits. Also known as transponder.

Chapter 13
The Role of Human Collaboration in Supply Chain Management

Kenneth A. Saban
Duquesne University, USA

John Mawhinney
Duquesne University, USA

ABSTRACT

This chapter discusses the importance human collaboration in supply chain management. Supply chain performance is often equated with acquiring the best technology or process. However, current studies suggest that supply chain performance also requires human collaboration. To change conventional thinking, this chapter proposes a holistic approach to achieving human collaboration among distributed partners, clarifies the forces that facilitate human collaboration, and identifies the steps management can take to create more collaborative team members.

INTRODUCTION

Advances in Information Technology (IT) coupled with the creation of the World Wide Web (WWW) and Internet have not only generated a more efficient means for manufacturers to interact with customers, but also for customers to access competitive products. This latter change has, in many ways, shifted the power from the seller to the buyer. As a result, manufacturers are transforming their supply chains to provide more value laden products and services. Supply chains represent the material and information interchanges stretching from acquisition of raw materials to delivery of finished products, and consists of vendors, service providers, and customers (Chopra and Meindl, 2001; McAdam and McCormick, 2001; Council of Supply Chain Management Professionals, 2010).

To help with this transformation, many manufacturers have adopted the latest best in class

DOI: 10.4018/978-1-4666-0246-5.ch013

strategies like Customer Relationship Management, Supplier Relationship Management, and versions of Collaborative Planning Forecasting and Replenishment (Lapide, 2010). While 48 percent of U.S. businesses have implemented these approaches and their associated tools, only nine percent are considering future updates, with the remaining 91 percent not sure how to proceed (Forrester, 2005). This finding suggests that adopting the latest supply chain program does not guarantee success. Success also requires the support of the people responsible for implementing such programs.

This paper will review the challenges associated with transforming supply chains, and discuss the factors that facilitate human collaboration as well as the managerial implications to achieve supply chain collaboration.

SUPPLY CHAIN CHALLENGES

There are a number of challenges with transforming today's supply chain. Foremost is the trap of becoming more enamored with the technology than its implementation (Mills, Schmitz, and Frizelle, 2004). Too often, (CIOs) hear about a new technology and think 'we have to have one of those' without stopping to think about whether or not this is true (Gain, 2005). Information systems and technology are major enablers of many best in class Supply Chain Management (SCM) firms. However, selecting enablers without a clear vision of business goals and understanding of the role that people play makes any decision a risky proposition. There is strong evidence that SCM information systems and technology investments have the largest positive impact on business competitiveness when they are focused on enabling supply chain collaboration (Fawcett, et al. 2011).

Bowersox, Closs and Drayer (2005) contend that lasting supply chain performance can only be achieved when an organization develops an integrated approach to SCM. A good example is IBM. After deciding to transform the company into an adaptive organization that could profitably respond to customer needs, Sam Palmisano, CEO, developed a multi-dimensional supply chain transformation program shaped by five insights:

1. Cultural transformation access when leaders walk the talk
2. CEO backing and trust are keys to sustained cross-unit integration
3. Customer focus must permeate end-to-end supply chain processes
4. Employees must be measured and rewarded for end-to-end efforts
5. Technology deployment must be backed by sound IT governance

IBM's strategic transformation netted: a savings of about $27 million per day; 38.6% more time for IBM's sales force to spend time with customers; helped reduce IBM services businesses' costs by more than $3 billion between 2002-2004; and improved the company's ability to sell integrated solutions made-up of IBM hardware, software and services (Gartner 2005). This case underscores the importance of dealing with human behavior, the right technology and business processes as integrated and dependent factors.

Another challenge is that vendors and suppliers may not have the resources and expertise to deal with advanced supply chain management initiatives. This is especially true with Small and Medium Enterprises (SMEs) who can constitute a large percentage of a supplier base (Chan, 2004; Emiliani and Stec, 2004). Having limited resources and expertise, SMEs tend to focus on internal operational issues - unless forced to comply (Morrell and Ezingeard, 2001; Estrin, Foreman and Garcia, 2003; Harney, 2005; Archer, Wang and Kang, 2008; Celuch, Walz,

Saxby, and Ehlen, 2010). When pressured to comply, many SMEs simply walk away. Ohno (1988) found that only nine percent of SMEs saw reverse auctions as an opportunity. This behavior can be linked to a mindset which is to keep the ship afloat by selling as much as possible (Davidow and Malone, 1992). Toyota dealt with these shortcomings by providing technical support and on-site training which increased profits for both the company and its suppliers.

A third challenge is not to overlook the strategic role that people play in implementing an advanced supply chain strategy (National Research Council, 2000; Handfield and Nichols, 2002; Russell and Hoag, 2004; Maku and Collins, 2005). There are specific costs with underestimating social and organizational issues. Ernst & Whinney (1987) found that companies that did not place a strong emphasis on training performed lower than companies who made employee development a priority. Michigan State University (Bowersox, Droge, Rogers and Wardlow, 1989), Pennsylvania State University (Novack, Langly and Rinehart, 1995), and Fawcett and Magnan (2005) also found that human resource development plays a major role in supply chain performance. After surveying 358 executives from leading manufacturers and service providers, Gowen and Tallon (2003) concluded that proper human resource management enhances the "value added" of supply chains by providing more effective resources in terms of better trained employees and enthusiastic employees and managers, which can equate to a more efficient and effective supply chain and one that is hard to emulate.

Social and organizational issues are especially important when dealing with virtual supply chain's which is often defined as groups of people who work interdependently with shared purpose across space, time, and organizational boundaries using technology to communicate and collaborate (Lipnack and Stamps, 1997; Kirkman, Rosen, Gibson, Tesluk and McPherson, 2002). Sabre, Inc., the inventor of electronic commerce for the travel industry, overcame this problem by building trust among their partners distributed around the globe (Kirkman et al., 2002). The company processes over 400 million travel bookings annually and is used by more than 60,000 travel agents in 114 countries. Building trust in virtual partnerships is often very difficult to achieve for two reasons. First, due to the unique nature of virtual enterprises, managers cannot rely on traditional trust-building methods based on social interaction, face-to-face meetings, and direct observations of fellow team member commitment. Second, while managers can generally dictate how employees interact and work in their own enterprise, directing transactions outside company boundaries is quite challenging to say the least (Welty and Becerra-Fernandez, 2001).

This discussion has highlighted three human challenges with transforming today's supply chain; management being more enamored with technology than its implementation, the lack of expertise among vendors and suppliers to implement today's advanced supply chain management methods, and not overlooking the strategic role that people play. Each challenge underscores the various ways people (professionals and management) impact supply chain collaboration. It is therefore important to develop a better understanding of human collaboration.

HUMAN COLLABORATION

This discussion will define human collaboration, introduce relevant organizational theory that supports human collaboration, and discuss the particular factors that facilitate human collaboration.

One way to think about human collaboration is to consider a large philharmonic orchestra. If each orchestra member were to use a different sheet of music and play independently, the performance would be chaotic. However, when you employ the same sheet of music and add a conductor to organize individual play, real harmony is achieved (McClellan, 2003). Through harmonization, individuals, teams, organizations direct their respective talents in such a fashion that they achieve an outcome that can go beyond their own limited vision of what is possible (Gray, 1989). The same can be said about supply chains.

"What is the best way to get all the members in a supply chain to collaborate?" To some, supply chain collaboration is achieved when information technology systems are in place and operational (Barrat, 2004; Sanders and Premus, 2005). While this approach works well for the transfer of explicit information, it does little to facilitate the transfer of tacit information which is critical to complex problem solving (Dyer, 2000; Handfield and Nichols, 2002; Davis and Spekman, 2004; Russell and Hoag, 2004; Cohen and Roussel, 2005; Joia and Lemos, 2010). These topics will be discussed in greater detail under "communications". A more suitable approach is to employ a strategy that aligns people, technologies and processes in such a fashion as to be able to address the many nuances of each supply chain partnership (Bal and Teo, 2000, 2001, 2001a). We call this the "Human-Technology-Process Linkage" whereby human collaboration facilitates technology adoption which in turn facilitates the supply chain processes in place (refer to Figure 1).

This linkage is based upon contingency theory - which from a supply chain point of view – suggests that managers recognize change in the marketplaces and then reconfigure their supply chains to meet and/or exceed those challenges. For example, increased competition, shortened technology cycles, and heightened customer demands requires companies to collaborate more up and/or down the supply chain. This contingent response toward collaboration shifts the competitive focus from firms competing against each other to supply chains competing against supply chains.

Figure 1. People-technology-process linkage

For the purposes of this paper, we modified Fawcett, Magnan and McCarter's (2008) contingency framework (See Figure 2) to understand how supply chain collaboration is achieved. Our framework contains four components. The first component represents the forces that drive change. For example, changing customer demands, increased competition, shortened product life-cycles, etc. The second component represents the people-technology-process assets that create network collaboration. It is important that these assets are aligned and engaged. Resisting forces, the third component, represent those forces that encourage people to resist communicating with others, adopting new technologies/processes, working toward common goals and strategies, etc. Managers must deal with these resisting forces by employing the right collaboration strategy. The fourth component represents the desired collaborative performance such as improved innovation, abbreviated new product launches, and better problem solving. By removing resisting forces, a higher degree of collaboration can be generated between supply chain partners which translates into better operating performance.

"What factors facilitate human collaboration?" Our review of the literature generated a large number of factors that were linked to supply chain collaboration. To validate these factors, we developed a focus group of 10 regional supply chain executives (representing Fortune 500 corporations as well as consulting organizations). The attendees were asked to rate the relevance of each factor based on their day-to-day business experience. This event resulted in the identification of six factors that facilitate human collaboration.

Trust

Grenier and Metes, 1995; Kumar, 2000; Chopra and Meindl, 2001; Jonsson and Zineldin, 2003; Ryssel, Ritter and Gemunden, 2004 agree that building trust among supply chain partners is a critical starting point. Studies have shown that trust has a significant impact of the level and depth of collaboration and when collaboration exists it produces positive supply chain efficiency results (Ha, Park, and Cho, 2011). In addition, Wagner, Coley, and Lindemann (2011) found that trust developed between suppliers and buyers during complex project collaboration has a more significant impact on future relations than do economic considerations. However, trust is often the most difficult collaboration factor to achieve. The reason is managers often assume personal relationships will fall into place due to the implementation of today's collaborative technology. However, this is far from the truth. Building trusting relationships where each party has confidence in the other members' capabilities and actions requires more than the right technology and processes, it also requires building personal relationships. Some executives believe that supply chain management is one of the most emotional experiences in which they have ever participated. There have been so many methodologies that have developed over the years, people blaming other people for their problems, based on some incident that may or may not have occurred sometime in the past. Once you get everyone together into the same room, you begin to realize the number of false perceptions that exist. People are still very reluctant to let someone else make decisions within their area. It becomes especially tricky when you show people how "sub-optimizing" their functional area can "optimize" the entire supply chain. (Handfield and Nichols, 2002).

Trust also requires linking the belief systems of individuals and teams such that each is interested in the other partner's welfare and would not take any action without considering its impact on the other partner (Fukuyama, 1996). Consider this example: a supplier has been brought in by a

Figure 2. Understanding supply chain collaboration

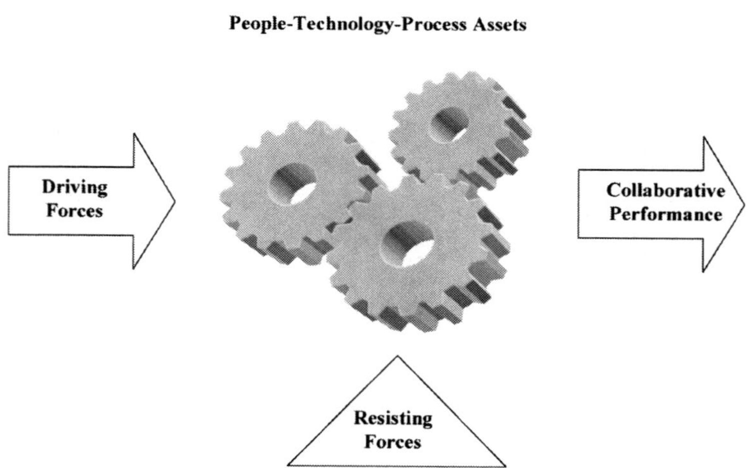

manufacturer to provide the aluminum wings for an airplane. However, late in the design process, it is discovered that a composite wing will better suite the customer. In addition, the supplier does not have the ability to make composite wings, and has sunk considerable costs into the project. In a trust-based relationship, the supplier has to trust that the manufacturer will treat them fairly whether they decide to stay with the aluminum wing or go with the composite wing. The manufacturer must also trust that each supplier will optimize the enterprise, even when it reduces or eliminates its own role (Goranson, 1999).

Beliefs

Collaboration requires that partners from different organizations not only trust each other, but also believe that the whole is as important as the individual pieces – especially as it relates to meeting the needs of others. A good example is the Kariya Number 1 plant of Aisin Seiki - a major Japanese supplier of brake fluid-proportioning valves to Toyota. Within hours after the plant burned to the ground, Aisin engineers met with their counterparts at Toyota and their other tier one suppliers and passed along their blueprints for valves to any supplier that requested them and distributed whatever undamaged tools, raw materials, and work in process that could be saved. To everyone's surprise, Kyoritsu Sangyo – a small tier two supplier of welding electrodes – delivered 1,000 production-quality values within 85 hours after the accident (Evans and Wolf, 2005).

To be able to work in this fashion, individual/team/organizational beliefs must be aligned. Beliefs are the lenses through which workers see their purpose and responsibilities, set expectations for success and reward, and generally make sense of their place in this environment. Belief system alignment is especially critical when forging virtual supply chains (Grenier and Metes, 1995):

- Beliefs about working with networked information: selecting electronic information over paper information, being more comfortable working in distant locations over traditional office settings, proactively seeking information over reacting to information sent you, and sharing information over hoarding information.
- Beliefs about work processes: virtual processes are simultaneous, people need to think more about solving the problem now not working on it later. When they plan their work, people need to think about getting the right mix of people together over where do these people work.
- Beliefs about teaming: people need to trust other stakeholders they may have not worked with before. You are finished only when everyone's work is done and recognition and rewards are distributed for team performance over individual performance.
- Beliefs about communications: just because a meeting ends, communications does not end, even if I cannot see someone I can still communicate with them 24/7.
- Beliefs about learning: you learn as much from success as you do failure. Learning is not a one-time experience, rather a series of personal experiences from which to draw upon.

Once belief systems are aligned, people are more inclined to share information about one's self as well as process knowledge and domain specific knowledge; for example developing a working knowledge of given protocols to communicate electronically with other team members (Cleland, Bidinda, and Chung, 1995). Based on these observations we posit that beliefs and knowledge contribute to individuals, teams and organizations ability to collaborate.

Communications

While the essence of collaboration is the interaction between two parties, it is communication that links individuals and companies. Jonsson and Zineldin (2003) call communications the "factory" of human society, as it is people and not accounting systems, computer terminals or trading agreements that can communicate effectively with each other. While technology plays an increasingly important role in the transfer of information between organizations, it is still an enabler and not the driver of success (Cohen and Roussel, 2005).

Therefore, it is important to understand the types of information that are exchanged in any relationship. Most researchers divide information into two types. Explicit information i.e., facts and figures is easily codified and can be transmitted across computer networks. Tacit information i.e., know-how involves knowledge that is complex and difficult to codify. To facilitate both exchanges, Toyota formed its supplier association (*Kyohokia*) which focused on: 1) information exchange between suppliers and Toyota, 2) mutual training and development of suppliers, and 3) establishing socializing events. This has allowed Toyota to develop superior knowledge transfer capabilities which in turn allows all supply chain members to understand each others goals and coordinate their efforts to achieve common goals while maintaining a satisfactory working relationship (Dyer, 2000).

Culture

By aligning trust, beliefs, and communications, organizations are able to establish a culture which supports decision-making and work. Organizational culture is often referred to as a pattern of basic assumptions that are commonly applied to various business problems and as such are passed along to new hires and new partners as the way to address similar problems (Schien 1985). This view suggests that culture resides both inside the company and with external partners. While problems with internal integration typically revolve around power/status, leadership and standards, external integration issues normally entail external environments [obtaining a shared understanding of key actors in the environment], mission [developing consensus on who are we, why are we here, and what are our strengths and weaknesses] and correction [developing consensus on how external issues should be solved] (Schultz, 1994). As noted earlier, IBM recognized that if they were going to regain their market dominance, the company had to change their culture that was out-of-sync with its customers (Forrester, 2005). IBM took a number of corrective actions:

- The company appointed some 400 top supply chain executives as "evangelists" to "walk the talk"
- The company communicated its supply chain strategy anchored around four imperatives [Drive focus-flexibility-quality-cost competitiveness, roll-out IBM's core strategic processes across the globe, extend supply chain principles to IBM's labor-based businesses, provide industry leading solutions integration and delivery capability].
- The company secured bottom-line support by changing success metrics
- The company stayed the course no matter if the strategy changed

Because each supply chain partnership has unique qualities, the possibility exists that management may be confronted with a wide-range of assumptions pertaining to the value of collaboration. By educating front-line managers as to the nuances of creating a collaborative culture, the company will increase the probability that individuals and teams will be more supportive of the networks mission and goals.

Reward Systems and Metrics

To maintain a collaborative culture, it is critical that the proper reward systems and metrics be established as they reinforce certain types of behavior. It is therefore important that manufacturers pay considerable attention to the reward systems that are in place for both their employees as well as the employees of their suppliers (Harrington and Harrington, 1995). The reason for doing so is that these programs not only reward individuals and teams on how they improve corporate performance, but also recognize individuals and teams that deliver high customer value (Forrester, 2005). Therefore, when designing a supply chain reward system, managers need to: a) focus on what is valued, b) demonstrate a clear connection between behavior, the rewards and metrics, and c) recognize that changes in behavior patterns – such as the adoption of new supply chain technology and processes – may require different types of incentives.

The second requirement is to establish the right metrics. Cohen and Roussell (2005) argue that any effective metrics program must include:

1. Internally focused metrics that address such items as the cost of goods sold, labor rates, and asset turns
2. Financial and non-financial metrics that address such items as production quality and flexibility, and forecast accuracy
3. Customer metrics that address such items as on-time delivery, order-fulfillment, and fill rates
4. Innovation and collaborative metrics that address such items as bringing innovative products to market in record time, developing break-through technology, and solving complex business issues

It is important to periodically review one's reward systems and metrics to insure they support the current mission and objectives of the supply chain network.

Synergy

To maintain ongoing collaboration, a number of synergistic activities must take place (Harrington, Hefner and Cox, 1995). For example, making sure that the flow of information between and among partners is maintained. While team interactions within an office are easy to arrange and manage, interactions among virtual teams can be more complex. Therefore, it is important that team building exercises be included in virtual situations coupled with formal exercises like creating charters, mission statements, goals, and operating norms (Kirkman et al., 2002). Another activity is to encourage team members to accept and utilize the dynamics of the team, thus eliminating the traditional view that "I am right and you are wrong." The Toyota Group's *kyson kyoei* (co-existence and co-prosperity) philosophy underscores the view that what is good for the extended enterprise is good for me, and what is good for me is good for the extended enterprise (Dyer, 2000). The next activity involves internalization. That is, team members must learn to tolerate ambiguity, modify their own views and belief systems, and be receptive to new ways to make group decisions (Goldman, Nagel and Preiss, 1995). The last activity requires that the team implement their plans and strategies from which they will learn, grow and become more synergistic.

This discussion suggests that trust, beliefs, communications, culture, reward systems/ metrics, and synergy encourage people to collaborate and as such become the elements or teeth of the human collaboration gear that engages the technology and processes in place (see Figure 3). Each element drives harmonious behavior which leads to great supply chain collaboration and improved performance.

Figure 3. Human collaboration gear

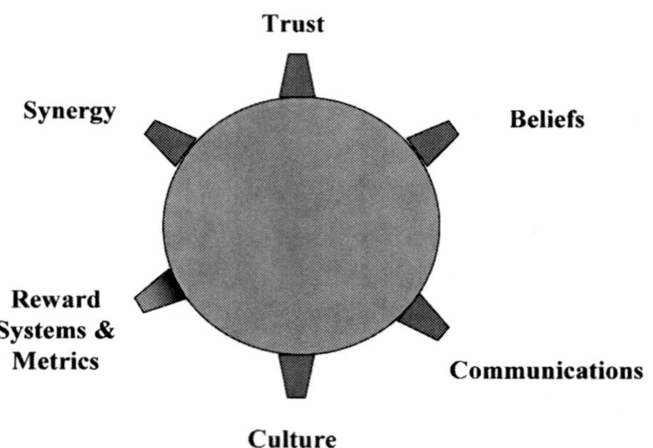

MANAGERIAL IMPLICATIONS

While technology can be tested to ensure performance to specifications and processes can be mapped to confirm the expected results, human collaboration is more difficult to develop and maintain. There are four steps management can take to transform their conventional supply chains into more collaborative networks.

First Step

The starting point is to recognize that to be competitive the company will: a) require an ongoing stream of innovations, b) have to realize that the innovations required may reside outside corporate boundaries, and c) in order to access those capabilities, the company will have to become more collaborative with external partners. A study conducted by IBM (2006) of some 750 global CEOs shows that only about half of the operations were capable of collaboration within their own boundaries - let alone with external partners. Recognizing the criticality of collaboration is a starting point on which to build a collaborative organization. After conducting 51 in-depth interviews across various supply chain positions, Fawcett, Magnan and McCarter (2008) concluded that managers must recognize the importance of collaboration if they are going to be able to compete in the 21st Century. They also reported that performance improvement hinged on a company's ability to improve collaboration with its supply chain partners. Likewise, a study of supply chain collaboration in a segment of the apparel industry identified the most significant barrier to internal and external collaboration success was lack of supply chain vision and understanding (Ramesh, Banwet and Shankar, 2010).

Therefore, the first step is for the leadership of the organization is to make collaboration and supply chain integration critical strategies for the company's competitive success. This will often require a culture that is able to change through the introduction of new processes and technology. With this commitment in place the following three steps will provide a roadmap to success.

Second Step

After recognizing the importance of supply chain collaboration, supply chain managers must then alter their views about achieving it. That is, management needs to realize that all supply chain collaborations are not equal because the products and services purchased can vary significantly in terms of value and criticality. For example, the relationship with a supplier of jet engines will be viewed differently than one with a supplier of cleaning products. As jet engines are more complex to make, have a higher value, and more critical to the success of operating an airplane than cleaning products, a higher degree of collaboration will be required with the jet engine manufacturer. It is important to employ a framework to understand and be able to deal with the different types of collaborative arrangements. After studying numerous supply leaders, Cohen and Rousel (2005) concluded that each recognize that every supply chain relationship required different attention. To which, they suggest that collaborative arrangements can be grouped into one of four categories:

1. Transactional collaborations occur when low risk and low value purchases are made. These partnerships require little collaboration as the purchases are normally straight or modified rebuys.
2. Cooperative collaborations demand a higher level of information exchange because the products or services are more critical to the manufacturer. As the level of information increases so to does the level of collaboration.
3. Coordinated collaborations require that manufacturers and suppliers work much closer due to the higher criticality of the products. Due to the functionality of the products, more collaboration is required between the manufacturer and the supplier.
4. Synchronized collaborations occur when manufacturers and suppliers invent and/or co-engineer a new product. As these tasks are very complex and timely, extensive collaboration is required between the partners.

By developing this understanding, managers can determine the level of collaboration required with each supply chain relationship and devise a plan to achieve the desired collaboration required through the proper alignment of people, processes and technology (Fung, Fung and Wind, 2007). This is an important step as it reduces the many problems associated the "one size fits all" approach to supply chain management (Stonebraker and Afifi, 2004).

Given the differentiation of suppliers based on complexity, risk, and cost, the foundation is set to develop the specific goals and plans expected from a collaborative approach. It is important to recognize that all suppliers identified in target categories can be included in a collaborative initiative at one time. Therefore, it is important to develop a collaborative plan.

Third Step

The next step is to develop a collaborative plan that aligns the network's mission, goals, collaborative strategies, and structure. Mission and goals not only drive investments, but also social networks. Therefore, before a collaborative network can be created, the leadership must insure that its mission and goals are sound. Garrett Engine Boosting Systems Inc, a supplier to the automotive industry, set-out to improve both the quality of their products and reduce costs through improved supplier collaboration and integration. Garrett's leadership team established a goal to synchronize planning with their suppliers to meet the rapid changes in the automotive industry. This was achieved by aligning people with collaborative supply chain technology, processes, and metrics. By providing the technology and process to allow people to better communicate, develop stronger relationships, and work together creatively, Garrett achieved a reduction in change notice cycle time of 50 percent and the quality of finished product improved 600 percent (Rockstroh, 2002). This case underscores the importance of incorporating the human collaboration in one's mission and goals.

Collaborative strategies should not only deal with technology and process implementation, but also human integration. The employees hired by the company – as well as its partners – need to have a strong degree of trust, a common belief system, good communication skills, team synergy, a collaborative culture, and the proper reward systems and metrics in place (Andraski, 1998; Rutherford, 2000; Collins, 2001; Nelson, Moody, and Stegner, 2001; Burt, Dobler and Starling, 2003; Gowen and Tallon, 2003; Koulikoff-Souviron and Vida, 2005).

After interviewing supply chain executives from six medium/large size firms in the information/electronic industry, Hsu (2005) came to the same conclusion. That is, supply chain collaboration is contingent upon a number of things such as mission and goals, leadership, reward systems, culture, trust, and beliefs.

An appropriate recommendation then would be to assess how well each critical partner that is targeted for collaborative integration in your supply chain is contributing to the overall mission of the network. Those not providing the level of support and performance required to meet the network goals would be candidates for collaboration review. This first requires establishing minimum requirements for the six collaboration factors described earlier. With this baseline in place an assessment of the current status of the non-conforming critical partner's collaboration factors can be conducted. By then benchmarking the collaborative practices of supply chain leaders in the deficient areas, plans for change and improvement can be established (Brandmeier and Rupp, 2010). This gap analysis will not only demonstrate the importance of human collaboration, but also pinpoint areas of strength and weakness.

With the collaborative goals and strategies in place including areas of weakness to be improved, the next step is to establish specific metrics to monitor improvement and goal achievement.

Fourth Step

Given the proper people and/or partners are "on the bus," it is also important to develop the right controls to ensure that the company's mission and goals can be met. Controls normally take two forms: reward systems and metrics. Reward systems represent the formal and informal mechanisms by which employee performance is defined, evaluated, and rewarded. Reward systems are important as they affect attitudes, behaviors and motivation which influence technology and process adoption that eventually impacts the execution of Key Performance Indicators (KPIs). Metrics which are internally, financial/nonfinancial, customer, and innovation/collaboration focused provide a way to monitor progress toward a particular outcome or set of goals (Manetti, 2001). Benchmarking supply chain leaders is a good place to start to insure that you have the right metrics in place (Leenders, Johnson, Flynn and Fearon, 2006). Therefore, it is incumbent that reward systems and metrics be aligned.

After surveying supply chain professionals across 11 different industries, Lockamy and McCormack (2004) found that delivery process measures – on inter-relationships and supply chain processes - have a significant impact on supply chain performance. These measurements are best used to reward and recognize the process participants.

In short, to make your supply chain more collaborative, management must not only employ the right technology and processes, but also manage the human resources distributed across the network. This is achieved by embracing the strategic role of human collaboration, altering conventional thinking about the role of people, developing plans geared to leveraging one's human resources, and establishing controls that facilitate and not deter supply chain collaboration.

SUMMARY

Supply chain performance is often equated with acquiring the best technology or process. However, current studies suggest that supply chain performance also requires human collaboration. To change conventional thinking, this paper has: a) proposed a holistic approach to supply chain management – one that links human, technology and processes and b) identified six factors (trust, beliefs, communications, culture, reward systems/ metrics, and synergy) that facilitate human collaboration, and c) identified the four steps management can take to create a more collaborative network.

While the literature on supply chain management is quite robust, less attention has been given to the role of human collaboration. This void has left many CEOs questioning how they are going to make their supply chain networks more collaborative given the extreme pressure for innovative products and services. We believe that the holistic approach outlined herein, will allow manufacturers to better leverage their technology and process investments by producing the type of collaboration necessary to meet if not exceed customer expectations.

As a next step, the authors plan on conducting a comprehensive field study to validate the impact of the six collaborative factors, and by doing so validate not only validate the factors that drive human collaboration, but also the strategic role of human collaboration in supply chain management.

REFERENCES

Andraski, J. C. (1998). Leadership and the realization of supply chain collaboration. *Journal of Business Logistics*, *19*(2), 9.

Archer, N., Wang, S., & Kang, C. (2008). Barriers to the adoption of online supply chain solutions in small and medium enterprises. *Supply Chain Management: An International Journal*, *13*(1), 73. doi:10.1108/13598540810850337

Bal, J., & Teo, P. K. (2000). Implementing virtual team working: Part 1 - A literature review of best practice. *Logistics Information Management*, *13*(6), 346. doi:10.1108/09576050010355644

Bal, J., & Teo, P. K. (2001). Implementing virtual team working: Part 2 - A literature review. *Logistics Information Management*, *14*(3), 208. doi:10.1108/09576050110390248

Bal, J., & Teo, P. K. (2001a). Implementing virtual team working: Part 3 – A methodology for introducing virtual team working. *Logistics Information Management*, *14*(4), 276. doi:10.1108/EUM0000000005722

Barrat, M. (2004). Understanding the meaning of collaboration in the supply chain. *Supply Chain Management*, *9*(1), 30. doi:10.1108/13598540410517566

Bowersox, D. J., Closs, D. J., & Drayer, R. W. (2005, January 1). The digital transformation: Technology and beyond. *Supply Chain Management Review*, *9*, 22–30.

Bowersox, D. J., Daugherty, P. J., Droge, C. L., Rogers, D. S., & Wardlow, D. L. (1989). *Leading-edge logistics: Competitive positioning for the 90s*. Oak Brook, IL: Council of Logistics Management.

Brandmeier, R., & Rupp, F. (2010). Benchmarking procurement functions: causes for superior performance. *Benchmarking: An International Journal*, *17*(1), 5. doi:10.1108/14635771011022299

Burt, D. N., Dobler, D. W., & Starling, S. L. (2003). *World class supply management: The key to supply chain management* (7th ed.). Boston, MA: McGraw-Hill Irwin.

Celuch, K., Walz, A. M., Saxby, C., & Ehlen, C. (2011). Understanding SME intention to use the internet for managing supplier information. *New England Journal of Entrepreneurship*, *14*(1), 9.

Chan, H. (2004). The supply-chain squeeze. *Optimize*, (February).

Chopra, S., & Meindl, P. (2001). *Supply chain management: Strategy, planning and operation*. Upper Saddle River, NJ: Prentice Hall.

Cleland, D. I., Bidanda, B., & Chung, C. A. (1995). Human issues in technology integration – Part 1. *Industrial Management (Des Plaines)*, *37*(4), 22.

Cohen, S., & Roussel, J. (2005). *Strategic supply chain management*. New York, NY: McGraw-Hill.

Collins, J. (2001). *Good to great*. New York, NY: Harper Business.

Council of Supply Chain Management Professionals. (2010). *Glossary of supply chain and logistics terms and glossary*. Retrieved from http://www.cscmp.org

Davidow, W. H., & Malone, M. S. (1992). *The virtual corporation*. HarperBusiness.

Davis, E. W., & Spekman, R. E. (2004). *The extended enterprise*. Upper Saddle River, NJ: Prentice Hall.

Dyer, J. H. (2000). *Collaborative advantage*. Oxford University Press.

Emiliani, M. L., & Stec, D. J. (2004). Aerospace parts suppliers' reaction to online reverse auctions. *Supply Chain Management*, *9*(2), 139. doi:10.1108/13598540410527042

Ernst & Whinney. (1987). *Corporate profitability & logistics*. Oak Brook, IL: Council of Logistics Management.

Estrin, L., Foreman, J. T., & Garcia, S. (2003). *Overcoming barriers to technology adoption in small manufacturing enterprises (SMEs)*. White paper Carnegie Mellon University, Software Engineering Institute (June).

Evans, P., & Wolf, B. (2005). Collaboration rules. *Harvard Business Review*, *83*(7/8), 96.

Fawcett, S. E., & Magnan, G. M. (2005). *Achieving world-class supply chain alignment: Benefits, barriers, and bridges*. White paper Center for Advanced Purchasing Studies. Retrieved from http://.www.capsresearch.org

Fawcett, S. E., Magnan, G. M., & McCarter, M. W. (2008). A three-stage implementation model for supply chain collaboration. *Journal of Business Logistics*, *29*(1), 93. doi:10.1002/j.2158-1592.2008.tb00070.x

Fawcett, S. E., Wallin, C., Allred, C., Fawcett, A. M., & Magnan, G. M. (2011). Information Technology as an enabler of supply chain collaboration: A dynamic-capabilities perspective. *Journal of Supply Chain Management*, *47*(1), 38. doi:10.1111/j.1745-493X.2010.03213.x

Forrester. (2005). *APAC study chain apps spending outlook*. Retrieved from http://www.forrester.com

Fukuyama, F. (1996). *Trust: The social virtues and the creation of prosperity*. New York, NY: Free Press.

Fung, V. K., Fung, W. K., & Wind, Y. (2007). *Competing in a flat world*. Upper Saddle River, NJ: Wharton School Publishing.

Gain, S. (2005). *Perfect projects*. ITP Technology. Retrieved from http://.www.itp.net

Gartner (2005). *IBM transforms its supply chain to drive growth*. Retrieved from http://www.gartner.com

Goldman, S. L., Nagel, R. N., & Preiss, K. (1995). *Agile competitors and virtual organizations*. New York, NY: Van Nostrand Reinhold.

Goranson, H. T. (1999). *The agile virtual enterprise*. Westport, CT: Quorum Books.

Gowen, C. R., & Tallon, W. J. (2003). Enhancing supply chain practices through human resource management. *Journal of Management Development, 22*(1-2), 32.

Grenier, R., & Metes, G. (1995). *Going virtual*. Upper Saddle River, NJ: Prentice Hall.

Gray, B. (1989). *Negotiations: Arenas for reconstructing meaning*. Unpublished working paper, Pennsylvania State University, Center for Research in Conflict and Negotiation, University Park, PA.

Ha, B.-C., Park, Y.-K., & Cho, S. (2011). Suppliers' affective trust and trust in competency in buyers: Its effect on collaboration and logistics efficiency. *International Journal of Operations & Production Management, 31*(1), 56. doi:10.1108/01443571111098744

Hanfield, R. B., & Nichols, E. L. Jr. (2002). *Supply chain redesign*. Upper Saddle River, NJ: Prentice Hall.

Harney, J. (2005). Enterprise content management for SMBs. *AIIM E-Doc Magazine, 19*(3), 59.

Harrington, H. J., & Harrington, J. S. (1995). *Total quality management*. New York, NY: McGraw-Hill, Inc.

Harrington, H. J., Hefner, M. B., & Cox, C. K. (1995). *Environmental change plans: Best practices for improvement planning and implementation. Harrington and Harrington's Total Improvement Management*. New York, NY: McGraw-Hill, Inc.

Hsu, L. (2005). SCM system effects on performance for interaction between suppliers and buyers. *Industrial Management (Des Plaines), 105*(7), 857.

IBM. (2006). *Expanding the innovation horizon*. Somers, NY: IBM Global Services.

Joia, L. A., & Lemos, B. (2010). Relevant factors for tacit knowledge transfer within organisations. *Journal of Knowledge Management, 14*(3), 210. doi:10.1108/13673271011050139

Jonsson, P., & Zineldin, M. (2003). Achieving high satisfaction in supplier-dealer working relationships. *Supply Chain Management, 8*(3-4), 224.

Kirkman, B. L., Rosen, B., Gibson, C. B., Tesluk, P. E., & McPherson, S. O. (2002). Five challenges to virtual team success: Lessons from Sabre, Inc. *The Academy of Management Executive, 16*(3), 67. doi:10.5465/AME.2002.8540322

Koulikoff-Souviron, M., & Pascal, V. (2005). A dose of collaboration. *European Business Forum, 22*, 59.

Kumar, N. (2000). *The power of trust in manufacturer-retailer relationships. Harvard Business Review: Managing The Value Chain*. Boston, MA: HBS Publishing.

Lapide, L. (2010). A history of CPFR. *The Journal of Business Forecasting, 29*(4), 29.

Leenders, M. R., Fraser, J. P., Flynn, A. E., & Fearson, H. E. (2006). *Purchasing and supply management* (13th ed.). Boston, MA: McGraw-Hill Irwin.

Lipnack, J., & Stamps, J. (1997). *Virtual teams: reaching across space, time, and organizations with technology*. New York, NY: John Wiley and Sons.

Lochamy, A. III, & McCormack, K. (2004). Linking SCOR planning practices to supply chain performance. *International Journal of Operations & Production Management*, *24*(11/12), 1192.

Maku, T. C., & Collins, T. R. (2005). The impact of human interaction on supply chain management practices. *Performance Improvement*, *44*(7), 26. doi:10.1002/pfi.4140440708

Manetti, J. (2001). How technology is transforming manufacturing. *Production and Inventory Management Journal, 42*(1).

McAdam, R., & McCormack, D. (2001). Integrating business processes for global alignment and supply chain management. *Business Process Management*, *7*(2), 113. doi:10.1108/14637150110389696

McClellan, M. (2003). *Collaborative manufacturing*. New York, NY: St. Lucie Press.

Mills, J., Schmitz, J., & Frivol, G. (2004). A strategic view of supply networks. *International Journal of Operations & Production Management*, *24*(9/10), 1012. doi:10.1108/01443570410558058

Morrell, M., & Ezingeard, J. (2001). Revisiting adoption factors of inter-organizational information systems in SMEs. *Logistics Information Management*, *15*(1-2), 46.

National Research Council. (2000). *Surviving supply chain integration*. Washington, DC: National Academy Press.

Nelson, D., Moody, P. E., & Stegner, J. (2001). *The purchasing machine*. New York, NY: The Free Press.

Novack, R. A., Langly, C. J. Jr, & Rinehart, L. M. (1995). *Creating logistics value: themes for the future*. Oak Brook, IL: Council on Logistics Management.

Ohno, T. (1988). *Toyota production system*. Portland, OR: Productivity Press.

Ramesh, A., Banwet, D. K., & Shankar, R. (2010). Modeling the barriers of supply chain collaboration. *Journal of Modeling in Management*, *5*(2), 176. doi:10.1108/17465661011061014

Rockstroh, J. (2002). Achieving quality ROI across the supply chain. *Quality*, *41*(6), 54.

Rogers, S. (2004). *Supply chain management: Six elements of superior design*. Retrieved from http://www.manufacturing.net

Russell, D. M., & Hoag, A. M. (2004). People and information technology in the supply chain: Social and organizational influences on adoption. *International Journal of Physical Distribution & Logistics Management*, *34*(1-2), 102. doi:10.1108/09600030410526914

Rutherford, T. D. (2000). Re-embedding, Japanese investment and the restructuring buyer-supplier relations in the Canadian automotive components industry during the 1990s. *Regional Studies*, *34*(8), 739. doi:10.1080/00343400050192838

Ryssel, R., Ritter, T., & Gemunden, H. G. (2004). The impact of information technology deployment on trust, commitment and value creation in business relationships. *Journal of Business and Industrial Marketing*, *19*(3), 197. doi:10.1108/08858620410531333

Sanders, N. R., & Premus, R. (2005). Modeling the relationship between firm IT capability, collaboration, and performance. *Journal of Business Logistics*, *26*(1), 1. doi:10.1002/j.2158-1592.2005.tb00192.x

Schein, E. H. (1985). *Organizational culture and leadership*. San Francisco, CA: Jossey-Baas Publishers.

Schultz, M. (1994). *On studying organizational culture*. New York, NY: Walter de Gruyter.

Simatupang, T. M., & Sridharan, R. (2004). Benchmarking supply chain collaboration: An empirical study. *Benchmarking*, *11*(5), 484. doi:10.1108/14635770410557717

Stonebraker, P. W., & Afifi, R. (2004). Toward a contingency theory of supply chains. *Management Decision*, *42*(9), 1131. doi:10.1108/00251740410565163

Wagner, S. M., Coley, L. S., & Lindemann, E. (2011). Effects of suppliers' reputation on the future of buyer-supplier relationships: The mediating roles of outcome fairness and trust. *Journal of Supply Chain Management*, *47*(2), 29. doi:10.1111/j.1745-493X.2011.03225.x

Welty, B., & Becerra-Frenandez, I. (2001). Managing trust and commitment in collaborative supply chain relationships. *Communications of the ACM*, *44*(6), 67. doi:10.1145/376134.376170

KEY TERMS AND DEFINITIONS

Business Metrics: a variety of business assessments designed to monitor performance of specific aspects of business operations.

Collaborative Planning, Forecasting, and Replenishment (CPFR): A business process for value chain partners to coordinate plans in order to reduce the variance between supply and demand

Contingency Theory: is a subset of organizational theory that argues that because oorganizations are complex entities management needs to deal with the variety of external forces i.e., increased competition, shortened technology cycles, heightened customer demands when developing any business strategy.

Customer Relationship Management (CRM): is a business strategy with a focus on understanding, anticipating and managing the needs of an organization's current and potential customers.

Human Collaboration: is a condition whereby the management and employees from autonomous organizations agree to collaborate in a harmonious fashion to achieve a common set of goals.

Key Performance Indicators (KPIs): are business metrics specifically selected to monitor performance of operations that are deemed critically important to success, and are designed to maintain or improve operational performance.

Reward System: is the process and rules by which benefits and/or compensation are allocated to employees or business partners who meet or exceed prescribed standards of performance.

Small and Medium Enterprises (SME): defines companies whose head count is less than a prescribed number of employees. Specific number of employees varies by country or measuring organization; in the USA small enterprises generally are those with less than 100 employees and medium enterprises are those with less than 500 employees.

Supplier Relationship Management (SRM): is a business strategy with a focus on improving relationships with suppliers, enhancing supply management practices, and meeting business goals through greater visibility of supplier performance, value contribution, and processes.

Supply Chain: is a system of organizations, people, processes, information systems and technologies involved in moving material, products, services, and information from originating suppliers to final customers.

Supply Chain Management: is the management of a network of autonomous yet interconnected organizations whose purpose is to collaborate in the development of a product or service that meets/exceeds customer expectations.

Chapter 14
Evaluation of Key Metrics for Performance Measurement of a Lean Deployment Effort

Edem G. Tetteh
Paine College, USA

Ephrem Eyob
Virginia State University, USA

Yao Amewokunu
Virginia State University, USA

ABSTRACT

To meet customer's needs for high-quality goods and avoiding risks of product-liability, global firms continually evaluate the performance of their supply chain for optimum design. Lean management is one of the key techniques businesses adopt in redesigning their processes. The technique is a vital strategy to increase productivity and effectiveness with respect to the movement of goods. Multivariate Analysis of Variance (MANOVA) was utilized to evaluate the performance of work cell, shift, worker's experience, and kaizen event participation level during a lean enterprise deployment effort at a multinational organization. The significance of the effects of these variables were assessed based on various lean supply chain factors such as First In First Out (FIFO), Setup Wheel System (SWS), Standard Operating Procedures (SOP), Clip System(CS), and Key Performances Indicators (KPI). The results support the criticality of metrics and their impact in implementing a lean manufacturing process in a global supply chain environment.

DOI: 10.4018/978-1-4666-0246-5.ch014

INTRODUCTION

Lean manufacturing has been shown to improve the competitiveness of organizations. The concept of lean started first with the Toyota Production System (TPS). Then, the idea was expanded by a research group at Massachusetts of Institute of Technology (Womack & Jones, 1996). The philosophy of lean uses a process of waste reduction, thus producing higher quantity and better quality products with the least resources possible. The goals are zero lead time, zero inventory, and zero defects, resulting in higher customer satisfaction (Tapping, Luyster, & Shuker, 2002).

Lean manufacturing strives for continuous improvement towards an ideal through relentless reduction of waste, where ideal means delivering what the customer requests on time, on demand, and free of defects (Miller, 2005). Lean process can be traced back to the early 1900s, when Henry Ford introduced the notion of mass production in 1913 (Miller, 2005). However, according to Soderquist and Motwani (1999), Taiichi Ohno was the first to present lean manufacturing to eliminate production waste at Toyota (Soderquist & Motwani, 1999). Source of wastes identified by Ohno include: errors that require recertification, product defects, process steps that are not needed, goods or employee movement without any purpose, goods and services that don't meet the needs of the customers, and any waiting time due to bottlenecks. Taiichi Ohno classified these wastes into seven basic types: overproduction, transportation, process waste, operator movement, inventory, idle time, bad quality (Bateman & David, 2002). Continuous improvement with a focus on the seven wastes is part of lean manufacturing.

It uses a team focused methodology requiring knowledge to be pulled from everyone (from the hourly worker to the upper management), and driven by continuous improvement (Kaizen). The team focuses on continuous improvements and uses tools and techniques to identify and eliminate wastes. Harris and Donatelli (2005) stated that value-stream mapping is the foundational tool used by any company that is on the cutting edge of transformation from a traditional organization to a lean enterprise. Value-stream mapping of products was started through the Toyota production system of lean manufacturing. Ninety-four percent of manufacturing errors or problems belong to systems, and lean manufacturing attacks these systems with the common goal of cost reduction or improvement of production (Deming, 1986).

Kaizen events are ways of accelerating improvements to worker productivity. These events help management to find new ways to gain substantial savings in time, space and labor output (Alukal & Manos, 2006). During Kaizen events, worker's ideas are highly encouraged for frequent and small improvements. This results in shrunken lead times, dramatic reduction in work-in-process, and reduction of scrap and defects, while minimizing the need for capital expenditures (Mika, 2005). They are important because they provide an excellent return on investments of financial and human resources. Furthermore, continued improvements will compound the return, since Kaizen never really ends (Mika, 2005). The events often eliminate the need for costly overtime by improving processes while collapsing lead times, and dramatically reducing work-in-process. It helps focus on improving material flow, information flow, and process quality of a business.

The rest of the chapter will cover the following sections: First, a description of lean techniques is covered. Next, various lean enterprise tools are discussed. Finally, a case study of a firm is presented. The research method, data collection, analyzes, and results are covered.

LEAN TECHNIQUES

One of the primary lean techniques is Poke Yoke. It was developed by Shingo Shigeo in the 1960's, and can be seen as the art of error proofing (Elbadawi, McWilliams and Tetteh, 2010). The process is designed to make it hard to make mistakes or at least easy to be detected and corrected. According to the authors, Shingo explained that a mistake is something a human cannot avoid, but a defect is allowing such a mistake to reach the customer. Therefore, defects are totally avoidable. Poke Yoke utilizes set-up devices or inspection techniques to ensure that the process is done correctly. Standardized works set a foundation that facilitates future change and continuous improvement (Zimmerman, 2010). In many organizations, work procedures called standardized work are written with highly detailed descriptions, but still holding their simplicity (Emiliani, 2008). These work procedures remove unneeded variation and confusion, allowing the process to flow smoothly.

Another technique used by companies to tackle waste is quick changeover. It's the act of changing from the last good piece of a product run to the first good piece of the next run. Quick changeover minimizes the time that operators use during changeover operations, since the excess time doesn't add any value to the products or process. The goal is to spend less time changing from one job to the other. This allows new employees to comprehend complicated operations easily and cover other operations that are not their specialization (Shingo, 1985). The technique helps achieve a smooth flow of value on a production line of different products. One more lean technique that goes along with quick changeover is 5S. It's a series of lean manufacturing standards used to improve the work place (Cross, 2008). 5S are cleansing methods that provide workers with a comfortable and efficient workspace enabling them to perform at their most effective level.

Furthermore, Total Productive Maintenance (TPM), another lean technique, was introduced by Seiichi Nakajima in the late 1970's (Elbadawi, McWilliams & Tetteh, 2010). It aims to ensure the effectiveness of production equipment. TPM focuses on ridding time loss due to breakdowns and stoppages. The origin of TPM is Nipponese, a Japanese manufacturer of automotive electrical parts. The method exerted a major influence over the economic progress made by Japanese manufacturers in the late 1970's. It's based on a continuous improvement strategy that embraces all aspects of the organization maximizing the productivity of the equipment. It also contributes to a successful strategy towards zero breakdowns, zero defect, and lower cost, which can be achieved by observing the equipment's life span. The most popular performance measure in TPM is the Overall Equipment Effectiveness (OEE) defined as follows (Smith & Hawkins, 2004):

OEE= Equipment Availability × Performance Efficiency × Rate of Quality

The world-class level of OEE starts at 85% based on the following values: 90% equipment availability, 95% performance efficiency, and 99% quality rate (Evan & Lindsay, 2004). This is achievable in concordance with Total Quality Management (TQM). Evan & Lindsay (2004) described TQM as the integration of all functions and processes within an organization to achieve a continuous improvement in the quality of goods and services. The technique is used to improve continuously all areas of a company's operation to satisfy customers' requirements (Liang, 2010).

Kanban is a key element in a just-in-time system (Widyadana, 2010). It's a signaling system that gives instructions on when to manufacture or supply a component based on the actual usage of the material. It also informs on what, when and how much should be produced. However, the technique can cause dramatic spikes in demand with the influx of new orders. Kaizen events can be used to minimize the disruption. It's a technique that focuses on structured improvement projects, using a dedicated cross-functional team to improve a targeted work area, with specific goals, in an accelerated timeframe (Farris et al., 2009). Six Sigma methodology and Lean management tools are utilized to find the root causes of issues in many areas of an organization. This provides

Figure 1. FIFO sign with 18 reels maximum

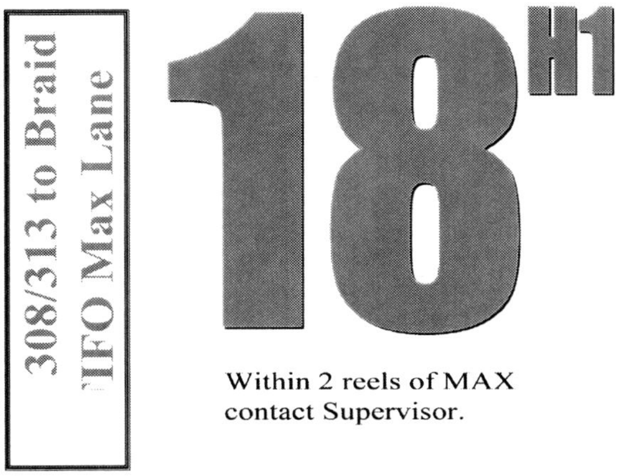

organizations with management tools needed to make their processes more efficient and effective to serve customers better.

LEAN ENTERPRISE TOOLS

First In First Out (FIFO) is a useful lean tool when dealing with logistics and inventory management. It facilitates order sequencing and control approach in fulfilling demands. It prevents earlier orders from being delayed in favor of newer commands. FIFO is used to help operators to complete orders in the sequence that they are received, and up to the maximum. An example of an application of FIFO is displayed in Figure 1. This allows the company to ensure that customer's orders received first are completed and shipped first.

For a maximum efficiency of FIFO, a customized tool namely setup wheel was designed. As illustrated in Figure 2, this tool was based on a set of racks used to stop the reels from moving freely. The tool facilitates the organization of work area by physically straightening up the reels to reflect the sequences in the orders. Prior to use of this tool, it was difficult for operators to prevent the reels to roll or move to undesired locations.

Standard Operating Procedures (SOPs) are written instructions that outline the steps or tasks needed to complete a task operate a piece of machinery or plant. SOPs are effective parts of a quality system with a purpose to assist workers to carry out operations correctly and consistently. The tool enables the workers in the study plant to understand the steps in performing their task. As shown on Form 1, the instructions were written in a brief manner with simple language that all operators are able to read and understand.

One additional tool that helped the implementation of the FIFO is the clip system. It consists of customized color coded clips designed to signify the maximization of the FIFO lanes when they are at full capacity. One of its main goals is to prevent the overflow of the setup wheel system, and help the management of the orders. The colors were used to identify bathes. For example, the color red can be used to identify the first order of twenty reels on a thirty reels maximum FIFO lane and the yellow color will be used for a second set of ten reels on the same lane. Other basic customer information such as customer's names, locations, order and cell numbers, and operator's identification were printed on the clip.

All the lean tools discussed in the previous paragraphs constituted the key performance indicator (KPI). In lean manufacture, KPI is a useful tool for measuring and developing metrics that support and facilitate the achievement of the critical goals of the organization (Vorne, 2011). Key performance indicators are important for understanding and improving manufacturing performance both from lean manufacturing perspective of eliminating waste and from corporate point of view of achieving strategic goals. The tool can be highly effective for exposing, quantifying and visualizing muda, the lean term for waste (Vorne, 2011). To be efficient, the measures must provide meaningful, reliable, and accurate information. They are to be as specific as possible based on data collected. Companies' goals and desires are

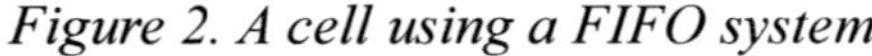

Figure 2. A cell using a FIFO system

often vague, but KPIs are to craft them to be very specific.

STUDY METHOD

Study Settings

The study was conducted at a world-class manufacturing plant that makes signal transmission products primarily for the entertainment, residential, industrial and security markets. The plant is located in one of the Midwestern States of the United States, and it is home to one of the firm's global manufacturing divisions along with a distribution and an engineering center. At the site, workers design, manufacture, and market various product types such as cables, ethernet switches, and industrial connectivity for the following markets: industrial; audio and video; security; networking; and communications.

The company is one of the largest U.S. based manufacturers of high-speed electronic cables with specialty on electronics and data networking products. It has presence in the following four segments: Americas segment, Europe, Middle East, and Africa (EMEA) segment, Asia Pacific segment, and the Wireless segment.

The Americas segment contributed approximately 54%, 52%, and 57% of the company consolidated revenues consecutively in 2009, 2008, and 2007 respectively with an industrial market to include applications ranging from advanced industrial networking and robotics to traditional instrumentation and control systems. Their cable products are used in discrete manufacturing and process operations involving the connection of computers, programmable controllers, robots, operator interfaces, motor drives, sensors, printers, and other devices. They also cover other industrial environments, such as petrochemical and other harsh-environment operations, which require cables with exterior armor or jacketing to endure physical abuse, exposure to chemicals, extreme temperatures, and outside elements.

Procedure

The goal of the study was to assess performance metrics through a worker's level of satisfaction and learning after a 30 days deployment of a lean enterprise effort. During a month long intervention that preceded the survey, an audit form shown in Figure 3 was used to collect the work cells level of compliance with the FIFO, Setup Wheel, Standard Operating Procedures (SOP), Clip, and KPI systems.

The tasks consisted of the shift supervisors conducting a walk-through every hour to assess the following for compliance:

A. Is the number of reels exceeding the requirement on the FIFO sign?
B. Are the reels stored in an orderly manner on the tracks/lanes provided?
C. Are all colored clips accounted for? (All 10 clips for each color should either be on a reel or on a stack.)
D. Are any reels in the FIFO track/lane without an attached colored clip?

In the case of non-compliance, a shift supervisor would proceed to provide feedback to the operators in the work cell in question, providing them instructions on how to avoid a non-conformance in the future. The same evaluation course of action was repeated every hour during the three shifts for thirty days. Along with the short guidance provided by the shift supervisors for non-compliances, workers participated in many Kaizen events during the entire time of the study. At the conclusion of the 30 days intervention period, a learning and satisfaction assessment survey was given to the workers. One of the work cells in the plant, the "R cell", was used as a control group: workers assigned to that cell didn't participate in any kaizen events, and received no feedback or instructions from their shift supervisors.

Analysis and Results

The independent variables (IV) were cell at four levels (C cells, H cell, M cells, and R cell); shift at three levels (1st, 2nd and 3rd shifts); worker's experience at five levels(Less than a year, 1-5 years, 6-15 years, 16-30 years, and more than 30 years); and worker's participation in Kaizen events at two levels (participation and non-participation. As illustrated in Table 1, the dependent variables (DV) were the work cell performance scores in the learning and satisfaction with lean tools such as FIFO, Setup Wheel, SOP, Clip System, and KPI.

SAS 9.1 software was used to analyze the data with the alpha level set at *0.05*. Tests were conducted to determine if there are statistical differences between and among the performance in work cell assignment, shift, experience, and worker's kaizen event participation based of the cell performance on the following lean tools: FIFO, Setup wheel system, SOP, Clip System, and KPI.

A multivariate analysis of variance (MANOVA) was performed since there are five performance measures, some or all of which may be correlated.

The results showed that the MANOVA test is significant for *cell,* Λ=.72, $F(15, 339.95) = 2.89, p < .001$, and for *kaizen*, Λ=.86, $F(5, 123) = 3.98, p = .002$ as illustrated in Table 2. All the four cells are statistically different based on the variables FIFO, Setup wheel, SOP, Clip system, and KPI. This can be interpreted as people who participated in Kaizen events and those who did not significantly differ from each other.

On the basis of the previous results, another MANOVA was performed to test the main and interaction effects of variables *cell* and *kaizen.* They are found to be the only two dependent variables that significantly affect the set of variables under question 5. The results shown in Table 3 demonstrated that the interaction is not significant Λ=.93, $F(15, 353.75) = .62, p = .86$. There were only main MANOVA effects of Kaizen and cell on the set of dependent variables

Figure 3. FIFO audit form for the H cell

	Item	H2 FIFO MAX Audit Auditor:______ Week:______	1	2	3	4	5
PE 303 to Cabler 313 (Ceeco) FIFO MAX	1	Number of reels does not exceed FIFO MAX.					
	2	Reels are stored in an orderly manner on the tracks/lanes provided.					
PE 303 to Cabler 319 (Cook) FIFO MAX	3	Number of reels does not exceed FIFO MAX.					
	4	Reels are stored in an orderly manner on the tracks/lanes provided.					
Cabling to PE 310 FIFO Max	5	Number of reels does not exceed FIFO MAX.					
	6	Reels are stored in an orderly manner on the tracks/lanes provided.					
	7	All Colored Clips are accounted for. (All 10 Clips for each Color should either be on a reel or on a stack.)					
	8	No Reels should be in the FIFO MAX track/lane without a Colored Clip attached.					
OVERALL		**Total Possible Score**	10	10	10	10	10
		Score Out of Total Possible					
		Green (100%) or Red (<100%) Of Possible					

Next Page For Countermeasures

Item (1-10) Missed	Countermeasure	Responsible

Table 1. Description of the variables

Variable	N	Mean Score	Standard Deviation	Min	Max
FIFO	147	54.198318	40.283943	0	100
Setup Wheel	147	40.477961	40.115235	0	100
SOP	147	40.080056	38.956114	0	100
Clip System	147	42.507987	41.473942	0	100
KPI	147	36.457426	35.543168	0	100

under consideration. More specifically, cells means on FIFO, Setup wheel, SOP, Clip system, and KPI, as a set, are not equal, Λ=.75, F(15, 353.75) = 2.63, $p < .001$. Furthermore, the results show a significant association between participation in kaizen events and the same set of variables, Λ=.91, F(5, 128) = 2.62, $p < .05$. This can be interpreted as the performance of people who participate in Kaizen events differed significantly from employees who didn't take advantage of the training.

Since significant results were found in MANOVA, a Univariate analysis, namely an unbalanced two-way ANOVA, followed by multiple comparison procedure, was performed as a follow-up to verify which of the independent variable(s) is (are) associated with *cell* and *kaizen* respectively. The results show that the cells significantly differ on Clip system, F(3, 132) = 5.17, $p < .01$) whereas the differences between the cells are statistically non significant with regard to FIFO, Setup wheel, SOP, and KPI. The multiple comparison analysis based on Dunnett procedure, reveals that cell R (the control group) differs from cell C and cell H but not from cell M. Contrary to what could be expected, theses groups know about lean tools better than the control group as illustrated in Figure 4.

Two models of MANOVA were tested. In the first model, Question 8 and Question 10 were included separately (or count as individual variables) in the set of the dependent variables. In the second model, the two variables were merged to create one variable called *cell performance*. To create *cell performance* we took the mean of Question 8 and Question 10 after Question 10 score was reversed. The results of these analyses are shown in Table 4.

The result for the first model show that MANOVA test is significant, Λ=.85, F(12, 365.41) = 1.94, $p < .05$ as illustrated in Table 5; meaning that all the four cells have not equal means on the set of the variables comprising Question 7-Question 10.

As in the case of the lean tools, a univariate analysis of variance using GLM method was performed to identify which, if any, of the in dependent variables were associated with the variable *cell*. The univariate analysis results including multiple comparison show that the cells

Table 2. MANOVA test for cell, shift, experience and kaizen effects on lean tools

	Λ	F	dl	p	η^2
cell	.72	2.89	15, 339.95	<.001	.28
shift	.93	.91	10, 246	.525	.07
exp	.83	1.21	20, 408.89	.240	.17
kaizen	.86	3.98	5, 123	.002	.14

Table 3. MANOVA test for cell and kaizen effects on lean tools

	Λ	*F*	*dl*	*p*	η^2
cell	.75	2.63	15, 353.75	<.001	.25
kaizen	.91	2.62	5, 128	.027	.09
Cell*kaizen	.93	.62	15, 353.75	.86	.07

differ with regard to Question 7, $F(3, 141) = 4.18$, $p < .01$ and Q9 $F(3, 141) = 4.23$, $p < .01$.

The control group tends on average to be more satisfied by the way FIFO was implemented than the group in cell M. The two groups also differ with regard to Question 9, with cell R more likely to avoid confusion than cell M. Compared to the two remaining groups (cell C and cell H) the differences are not statistically significant. These facts were expected because, by not having a direct participation in the lean effort at the plant, the workers in cell R were satisfied with the lean implementation effort. Cell R didn't have enough exposure and involvement to provide a good assessment of the FIFO system implementation.

The results of the second model are similar to the previous ones, except that cell performance is associated with cell. Thus MANOVA test is significant, Λ=.88, $F(9, 338.44) = 2.11$, $p < .05$ as shown in Table 6.

The univariate analysis of variance shows that each of the three independent variables is associated to variable *cell*. The results demonstrate that the means of the four cells regarding Question 7 are not all equal $F(3, 141) = 4.18$, $p < .01$and the same is true for Q9 $F(3, 141) = 4.23$, $p < .01$ and variable *cell performance* $F(3, 141) = 2.64$, $p = .05$.

Nonetheless, the multiple comparison results for the *cell performance* do not yield significant differences between the four groups. This is not a

Figure 4. Main effect for clip system

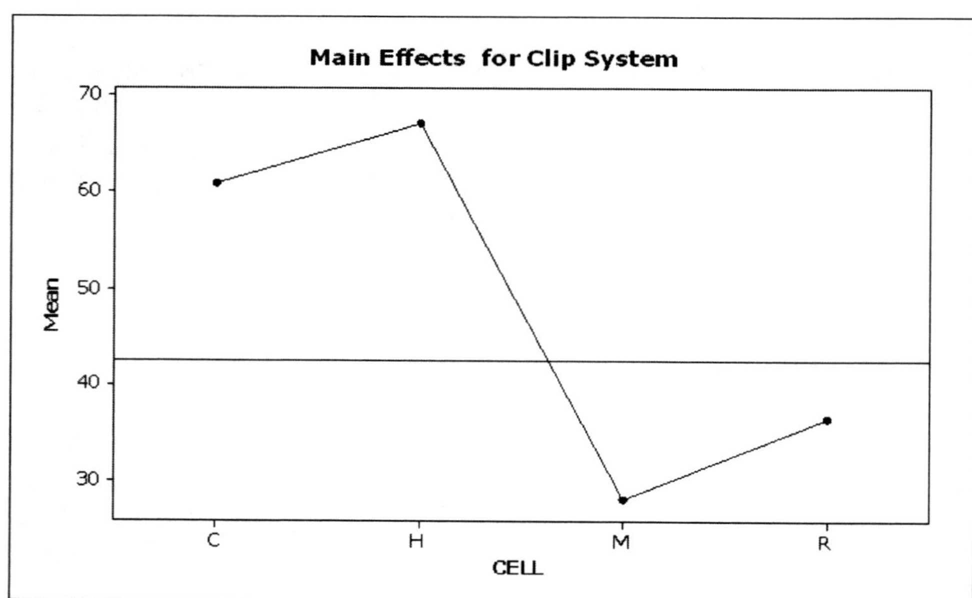

Table 4. MANOVA test for cell, and kaizen effects on lean tools

	Λ	F	dl	p	η^2
cell	.75	2.63	15, 353.75	<.001	.25
kaizen	.91	2.62	5, 128	.027	.09
Cell*kaizen	.93	.62	15, 353.75	.86	.07

Table 5. MANOVA test for cell effect on Q7-Q10

	Λ	F	dl	p	η^2
cell	.85	1.94	12, 365.41	.03	.15

Table 6. MANOVA test for cell effect on Q7, Q9 and cell performance

	Λ	F	dl	p	η^2
cell	.88	2.11	9, 338.44	.03	.12

big surprise, since the exact *p* value for the omnibus test is .052, and the likelihood of finding significant differences through multiple comparisons was very slim. As for the results for Question 7 and Question 9, they remain unchanged.

CONCLUSION

The purpose of a lean system is to increase the throughput of an organization to meet customers' product demands. This will provide any firms with what they want, when they want it, and at the same time meets their customers' quality expectations. In a global supply chain environment, the identification of key performance measures and their assessment is critical to improve processes continuously. The results of this study showed that the reliance on systematic strategies using lean tools and principles as well as the emphasis on training are the key elements to a successful lean enterprise deployment in a global supply chain environment.

REFERENCES

Alukal, G., & Manos, A. (2006). *Lean kaizen: A simplified approach to process improvements*. Milwaukee, WI: American Society of Quality Press.

Bateman, N., & David, A. (2002). Process improvement programmes: A model for assessing sustainability. *International Journal of Operations & Production Management*, *22*(5), 515–526. doi:10.1108/01443570210425156

Condi, C. (2009). *Lean reaches rural hospital*. Institute of Industrial Engineers. Retrieved March 2, 2009, from http://www.iienet2.org/ Details.aspx?id=10808

Deming, E. (1986). *Out of the crisis*. MIT Press.

Emiliani, M. (2008). *Practical lean leadership: A strategic leadership guide for executives*. Kensington, CT: The CLBM, LLC.

Evans, J. R., & Lindsay, W. M. (2005). *An introduction to Six Sigma & Process improvement*. Cincinnati, OH: Thomson Southwestern Publishing Company.

Farris, J., Van Aken, E., Doolen, T., & Worley, J. (2009). Critical success factors for human resource outcomes in Kaizen events: An empirical study. *International Journal of Production Economics, 117*(1), 42–65. doi:10.1016/j.ijpe.2008.08.051

Food and Agriculture Oorganization. (1999). Guidelines for quality management in soil and plant laboratories. *FAO Soil Bulletin, 74*. National Resources Management and Environment Department. Retrieved June 28, 2011, from http://www.fao.org/ docrep/w7295e/w7295e04.htm

Harris, G., & Donatelli, A. (2005). *Value-stream mapping as a lean management tool*. Huntsville, AL: University of Alabama.

Isam, E., McWilliams, D., & Tetteh, E. (2010). Enhancing lean manufacturing learning experience through hands-on simulation. *Simulation and Gaming, 41*(4). Sage Publications.

Karen Martin & Associations. (2011). *Lean terminology*. Retrieved June 28, 2011, from http://www.ksmartin.com/ resources/terminology.html#f

Laraia, A., Moody, P., & Robert, R. (1999). *The kaizen blitz: Accelerating breakthroughs in productivity and performance*. John Wiley & Sons Inc.

Liang, K. (2010). *Aspects of quality tools on total quality management*. Academic Search Complete.

Martin, K., & Osterling, M. (2007). *The kaizen event planner: Achieving rapid improvement in office, service, and technical environments*.

Mika, G. (2005). *Kaizen event implementation manual*. Society of Manufacturing Engineers.

Miller, J. (2005). *Introduction to lean and value-stream mapping*. Gemba Research.

Quick Changeover. (2010, August 23). *A lean journey*. Retrieved June 28, 2011, from http://www.aleanjourney.com/ 2010/08/quick-changeover.html

Shingo, S. (1985). *A revolution in manufacturing: The SMED system*. Productivity Press.

Smith, R., & Hawkins, B. (2004). *Lean maintenance: Reduce costs, improve quality, and increase market share*. Elsevier Science Life Cycle Engineering Series.

Soderquist, K., & Motwani, J. (1999). Quality issues in lean production implementation: A case study of a French automotive supplier. *Total Quality Management, 10*(8), 1107–1122. doi:10.1080/0954412997091

Tapping, D., Luyster, T., & Shuker, T. (2002). *Value stream management*. New York, NY: Productivity Press.

Tpslean. (2011). *Throughput solutions*. Retrieved June 28, 2011, from http://tpslean.com/ glossary/ fifodef.htm

Vorne. (2011). *Key performance indicators (KPIs)*. Retrieved June 28, 2011, from http://www.vorne.com/ learning-center/kpi.htm

Widyadana, G. A., Wee, H. M., & Chang, J.-Y. (2010). Determining the optimal number of Kanban in multi-products supply chain system. *Journal of International of Systems Science, 41*(2). Taylor & Francis.

Womack, J. P., & Jones, D. T. (1996). *Lean thinking* (2nd ed.). New York, NY: Simon & Shuster.

Zimmerman, B. (2010). What do we mean by empowerment? *Policy & Practice*, 68.

KEY TERMS AND DEFINITIONS

First In First Out: Is an inventory management strategy enacted to ensure that quality is upheld on all shipped products and components.

Global Supply Chain: Refers to the network created among different worldwide companies producing, handling, and distributing specific goods and/or products.

Kaizen Event: Is a short, focused project aimed at eliminating production waste in a particular area of an organization.

Lean Manufacturing: Is a manufacturing strategy that seeks to produce a high level of throughput with a minimum of inventory.

Metrics: Meaningful measures that target continuous process improvement actions.

Quality: Is the customer's perception of how a good or service is fit for their purpose and how it satisfies stated and implicit specifications.

Standard Operation Procedures: Is a document containing instructions on how to perform a task. It ensures that routine jobs get performed safely and in compliance with applicable regulations.

Chapter 15
Design for Sustainment:
Challenges and Theoretical Issues in Product and Global Supply Chain Management

Benedict M. Uzochukwu
North Carolina A & T State University, USA

Silvanus J. Udoka
North Carolina A & T State University, USA

ABSTRACT

The purpose of this chapter is to chronicle and analyze existing challenges and theoretical issues in the domain of product, system, and the emerging area of global supply chain sustainment. These challenges encompass the provision of reliable, efficient, cost-effective, and quality services by key players and major stakeholders in product and global supply chain. The authors argue that sustainment concept serves as a vehicle for elevating the rate of product and system utilization. This will have a tremendous impact at reducing the burden of product or system's operational issues thereby allowing for the leveraging of the enormous potentials of sustainment. Both contemporary as well as classical journal papers and publications are included in this study to trace and describe the development, state of sustainment perspectives, available tools, and methodologies in product and global supply chain system sustainment.

INTRODUCTION

Designers of products or systems are often saddled with the responsibility of designing sustainable products or systems despite well-known recurring problems. While improvement in design processes seems to have been ameliorated, some of these problems and challenges are still in existence. SCDigest Editorial Staff (2010) identified five challenges of today's global supply chain as supply chain volatility and uncertainty, complexity of managing increased supply chain globalization, the critical nature of cost-optimized supply chain,

DOI: 10.4018/978-1-4666-0246-5.ch015

global risk management and the issue of global supply chain integration. There is also the dearth of robust systems or frameworks that captures pertinent and verifiable life time data, the lack of consensus among product or system designers about how to go about achieving sustainment, difficulty arising from various product usage environments, complexity of product or system design options and lack of coherent method for defining design parameters, and so on, still loom large.

Castillo (2010) discussed the changes that took place in the distribution of large volume of gasoline during the early days of the United States Army's Operation Iraqi Freedom (OIF) in 2003 and cited the need for more collaboration among strategic partners due to the increased storage and distribution requirements for gasoline and other petroleum products. Shaked and Jolliet (2011) stated that with increasing globalization, goods are now produced outside their area of consumption. To ensure progress is sustained, the authors noted that it is becoming crucial to assess and minimize all the global environmental health impacts associated with global production chains and consumption in those different areas. To address this challenge, they identified lifecycle assessment (LCA) as a veritable decision support tool that can address this issue.

These issues confronting product and global supply chain system appears to be founded theoretically but in practice, a major challenge will be predicated on how best to design sustainable products and systems using real time data in dynamic operational environment. These unresolved problems will continue to be the subject matter for future research undertakings. In the short run, the current research efforts are critiqued to create a basis for establishing a methodology that will guide the design of sustainable products and systems in varied dynamic operational environments.

Sustainability is bio-centric in nature. As a result, it recognizes the interplay of various socio-economic and ecological systems on a short rather than on a long term basis. Cutcher-Gershenfeld et al (2004) defined sustainability with respect to trade-offs among economic development and social and environmental goals. It is generally a broad concept not just viewed as the environment and resources any longer. The authors advocate that systems must be sustainable on environmental, economic, developmental and social and political dimensions In essence, sustainability robustly relates to the capability to replenish or retain major characteristics, resources and inputs over a period of time. As more organizations commit to supply chain sustainability, there is urgent need to devise long term sustainment strategies as against short term, quick fix or stop gap strategies offered by current practices. This will require the incorporation of lessons learned throughout a product or system's operational lifecycle in the early design stage decisions and utilize them in the design of global supply chain sustainment framework. This proactive strategy can substantially enhance global supply chain long term sustainment through reduction in lifecycle costs, information access and operational efficiency and effectiveness.

The primary focus of this research is on product and global supply chain system supportability practices and how these practices can apply to the sustainment of product and global supply chain systems operational performance. The remaining paper is organized as follows. The next section gives an overview of the concept of sustainment and sustainability as well as the historical background of sustainment concept. The subsequent section presents a brief review of related literature on various sustainment frameworks, practices and challenges confronting product and global supply chain dominated-systems. Sustainment and product design parameters are introduced in the next section. Next, design for sustainment stakeholders is discussed. This is followed by a description of high-level design for sustainment. Challenges facing product and global supply chain sustainment are highlighted. Finally, the summary section makes a case for discussion and inclusion of the concept of sustainment in the overall product and global supply chain framework by incorporating engineering design and technology tools to address various lifecycle, management, logistical and supportability challenges.

Overview of the Concept of Sustainment and Sustainability

It is necessary to make an attempt at distinguishing between the concept of sustainment and the concept of sustainability for the purpose of this paper. The reason is that sustainment and sustainability have been used inter-changeably by researchers, authors and practitioners alike. In short, the two concepts seem to be intertwined in their meaning, usage and context. Sustainability primarily relates to the interrelationships of human objects and their environment. On the other hand, sustainment refers to all activities necessary to keep an existing product or system operational in order to successfully meet an objective. The emphasis is on the mission-readiness objective of the product or system. Therefore, product or system sustainment in the context of this paper can be described as those activities designed to meet the operational and performance readiness requirements of products or systems in a cost effective and efficient manner. In this context, sustainment lays emphasis on the assembly, reliability, maintenance, manufacture and increase in product performance. Sustainment programs involving complex durable products, such as military weapon systems, require smart processes and technologies, and a new mindset regarding the provision of desired support to designed and manufactured products.

BACKGROUND

The vast majority of literature in the field of sustainment is linked to the military as an organization and the United States Department of Defense (DOD) as an entity within the organization. When DOD addresses sustainment, it is usually in terms of the weapons programs, which include test equipment and product support for the aging military weapon systems platform that continuously need upgrade and maintenance. Over the past decade, emphasis has been placed on the study of sustainment strategies for military systems, test engineering, supply chain management, applications and processes. These areas are still evolving. Published literature on sustainment on aforementioned areas is therefore still in its relative infancy.

The challenges faced by the DOD are also similar to the ones faced by global supply chain practitioners. The burden of ensuring that sustainment overheads in the supply chain inventory adhere to supportability design guidelines is enormous. Some of these foremost challenges include the task of transforming existing global supply chain management systems as well as designing new ones with minimal sustainment footprints. Another key area of concern in designing for sustainment is providing relevant data to the design function to remove product or system sustainment disablers. These disablers ultimately stop the supply chain assets from performing their intended functions or reaching their full designed potentials. As more and more of legacy products and systems deteriorate with age, they typically carry significant maintenance and overhead costs. In addition to sustaining older assets and replacing outdated components, the high costs to repair, as well as a desire for enhanced performance of the legacy and new systems have heightened the desire for improved product sustainment within the global supply chain network. These apparent problems and deterioration are a result of poor early design decisions during the product or system developmental stage. Limited knowledge of and forethought about sustainment issues by design engineering has led to reactive, instead of proactive sustainment solutions.

LITERATURE REVIEW

This section reviews numerous attempts by practitioners, authors and researchers to define the subject matter of sustainment. In the succeeding section, some of these attempts are discussed within the context of supply chain, product design, decision support, technology as well as lifecycle management. An important goal of reviewing related literature is to identify existing contexts in the area of sustainment and how the term is addressed in those specific areas. This review will also give an insight into other existing research work in the domain of sustainment.

Mathaisel (2006) defined sustainment as the maintenance, repair and overhaul (MRO) practices that keep systems operating and up-to-date through new designs and upgrades throughout their entire lifecycle. In essence, sustainment is any action taken proactively on a new product or reactively on an existing product to meet new and existing objectives of continual performance. The 2000 Joint Publication 4-0, which is Doctrine for Logistic Support of Joint Operations, states that sustainment in the military, for example, is the provision of personnel, logistic, and other support required to maintain and prolong operations or combat until the successful accomplishment or revision of a mission. The Defense Acquisition Guidebook (2004) and the Brundtland Commission (1987) have offered various definitions of sustainment which fall within the context of this research. With respect to the military environment, the Reliability Analysis Center (2004) indicates that sustainment is all the activities required to keep a weapon system operational in both peacetime and wartime.

Chestnutwood and Levin (1999) are of the view that actions occur during the life of a system to overcome the cost and performance driven problems that are inherent in every system and become visible as the system ages and technology advances. According to the authors, the actions that occur during a system's lifecycle are based on decisions made using available information. Sustainment therefore represents a significant fraction of the lifecycle costs associated with the operation of typical complex durable products such as the military weapons systems.

The Advanced Technology Institute (2001) submits that over the past several years, the DOD has published several documents that describe the vision that the leadership has for the defense posture of the future. The DOD also described other mission scenarios it expects over the next decade. Those scenarios and experiences from recent campaigns have led to additional visionary documents like the Future Logistic Enterprise, Force Transformation, Performance Based Logistics, and End to End Logistics. The theme that emerges from these initiatives is a military that is moving substantially toward the concepts of flexibility, agility, and rapid reconfigurability of forces capable of quick tailored responses to threats or missions.

In a position paper on sustainment before the United States House Armed Services Committee, the Commander USAR Materiel Command, Lyles (2001) called for the identification of critical breakthroughs and changes in the paradigm of maintenance, repair and overhaul support for the 21st century for the military. Repairs on demand, resource loading and scheduling, material and parts availability are some sustainment activities that can support this paradigm. The main concern in sustaining weapons systems efficiently and effectively should be geared towards reducing the cost of sustainment. This could be achieved by cutting down on product cycle times and the development of low-cost processes for maintaining and improving the reliability of new and existing weapons systems. In 1997, the DOD budget for operations and maintenance was approximately twice as large as the budget for procurement and represented approximately 36% of the total defense budget (OMB, 1998). The budget document reiterates that current events in the United

States military call for efficient weapon systems management.

Various Sustainment Frameworks

Several research publications within the past two decades have identified some sustainment practices for maintenance of products or systems. These best in class sustainment practices are discussed in this section.

Sustainment and Global Supply Chain Development

Wang et al., (2011) discussed the increasing attention towards incorporating sustainability into global supply chain system. The authors proposed a framework for evaluating the sustainability of a detergent supply chain through the integration of supply chain dynamic simulation and environmental and societal Life Cycle Assessment (LCA). It is the view of the authors that the social dimension of sustainability, when compared to the economic and environmental dimensions, has not yet been well-defined by practitioners due to the difficulties in quantifying social themes into metric indicators. Gravier & Swartz (2009) identified the problem of technological obsolescence in vendor supplied parts in the new product development process. The authors specifically alluded to both the rapid pace of technological advance and increasingly disintegrated supply chains. The consequence is that products with high degree of technology and long life cycles have become problematic. In this research, the authors also analyzed the implications for supply chain evolution and obsolescence management.

Supply-chain coordination depends on the availability of timely and precise information that is visible to all players in the supply chain network. The authors undertook a case study of three automotive supply chains that face such new demands resulting from the introduction of an order-driven supply-chain strategy (Holweg and Pil, 2008). Wognuma et al (2011) discussed lifecycle assessment in the supply chain. In their article, they analyzed the various stages that a food product passes through and identified opportunities to reduce environmental impact and measures taken to address these impacts utilizing verifiable, usable and relevant product lifecycle information for improved lifetime operational performance.

Typically, life cycle assessment (LCA) can be a veritable tool for assessing and identifying various environmental impacts of products in the global supply chain by investigating the entire lifecycle of these products from beginning of life to end of life with all different material flows that are relevant for that product's long term operational performance. Deploying LCA can be used to improve a product's overall environmental lifecycle balance as well as assist in comparing with benchmarks in the entire global supply chain network.

Challenges of Sustainment-Dominated Global Supply Chain Systems

Flint (2004) addressed the challenges inherent in a world moving quickly toward competition among global supply chain network of firms. The author focuses on four critical challenges marketing strategists face in global supply chain management. These challenges relate to customer value and value delivery. The challenges faced by global supply chain strategists are: understanding what customers value within supply chains across critical market segments throughout the globe, understanding changes in environments and customer value perceptions throughout global supply chains, delivering value in an environment where a never-before-seen level of marketplace uncertainty created by the accelerating pace of change at a global level is coupled with a drive towards supply chain management, and creating and staying committed to processes over ad hoc decision making for addressing these issues.

The question of obsolete technology and lack of innovation has become particularly challenging for products and systems with high level of technology and long term operational life cycles within the framework of design and supportability of products in the global supply chain. This is aggravated by the quick tempo of technological advancement and the increasing level of disintegration in the global supply chain system. Goodall et al., (2002) discussed the pace of technological turnover for electronics embedded in many new products. Tewary & Wang (2005) noted that the risk of technological or market failure and capital investment in an electronic chip fabrication plant will be on the threshold of rising to $10 billion by 2015. Modern business practices aggravate the problem. Craighead et al (2007) identified reduced supply bases, global sourcing, and reliance on supply clusters as issues that can increase an organization's vulnerability to parts obsolescence. The authors noted that a disruption to one supply source can affect many buyers.

Gulledge (2010) researched on how the evolution of enterprise services has changed the approach for enabling Product Lifecycle Management (PLM) and Supply Chain Management (SCM) business processes. The authors demonstrates how the new technologies can be used to enable a critical process that links vehicle health maintenance to PLM by using composite application design to integrate condition-based maintenance (CBM) and PLM. Critical processes of product improvement process were identified and the authors aligned the same information with enterprise business systems for supporting more traditional business processes. In turn, this information is shared with the original equipment manufacturer for product data management which completed the extended supply chain for the example product.

Global supply chains are faced with the phenomenon of hyper-competition (Hulsmann, 2008) thereby necessitating the need for global supply chains to build up competitive advantage in order to survive. However, (Piplani et al., 2007) stated that under hyper-competition, sustainable competitive advantage is hard to achieve due to fast-moving action on the part of competitors. A typical example to buttress this point lies in producing new generation of products as well as increased service level. Organizations no longer have to deal with only on managing their internal and linear-supply chains, but they are also confronted with multiple demands engineered by worldwide stakeholders and global structures and processes of supply, production, and distribution (Muller-Christ & Hulsmann, 2003)

Piplani et al., (2007) also added that more and more companies have begun to out-source non-core activities to the cheapest locations and focus only on their core operations which they have comparative advantage thereby resulting in increasing globalization of supply chains. According to the authors, "globalization also leads to the customer order fulfillment process being no longer controlled by a single, integrated organization, but by a number of decentralized and independent firms collaborating together." The effectiveness of any supply chain depends largely on the successful alignment of its decisions making strategies towards addressing specific customer requirements. Therefore, supply chains need to re-align themselves to adjust to this trend if the goal of achieving optimal utilization of resources can be achieved.

BEST IN SUSTAINMENT CLASS PRACTICES

Garmon et al. (2001) identified a sustainment philosophy which calls for component redesign whenever the inventory for an obsolete component is depleted. Mathaisel et al. (2004) focused on six enabling practices categorized under technology insertion management (TIM). The primary focus of this research was on maintenance, repair and overhaul (MRO) practices and how those practices can help the military operations. One major practice being advocated is the rapid Commercial off-the-Shelf (COTS) insertion which can extend a product's life. The author catalogued and documented the linkages to where these best sustainment practices may reside with the hope that others can learn and avoid costly and time-consuming mistakes. Some of the sustainment best in class practices are shown in Figure 1.

An Analysis of Sustainment Challenges and Issues in Military Supply Chain System

Attempts have been made in the military to optimize the sustainment cost against the backdrop of system lifecycle costs associated with maintenance and operation of weapon systems. The private sector and the government, through the DOD, have made efforts to form alliances and partnerships to bring some resolution to this crisis. Highly visible among these efforts is the U.S Army modernization through spares program (Kros, 1999), flexible sustainment (Performance-based business environment, 1997), and the lean sustainment initiative (Agripino et al, 2001). As could be seen from these efforts, attention was directed mainly to specific elements of the sustainment system instead of addressing the entire spectrum of the organization in a coordinated and effective manner.

Cordesman (2000) stated that the DOD has reduced its budget by 29% since 1990. This reduction has greatly impacted weapon system acquisition and in-service support. According to the author, reduced budgets have forced the various branches of military to seek ways to extend the life of aging/legacy weapon systems currently in service with significant reductions in acquisition of replacement systems. Gansler (1999) stated that as sustainment costs increase, there is less funding available to procure replacement systems. The author also states that an analysis conducted by DOD concluded that, unless mission requirements and the operational tempo are reduced, or there are significant increases in the budget, the operational maintenance cost portions of the budget will equal the total current budgets by the year 2024. The threats posed by emerging nuclear nations, the ongoing war on terror on Iraq, Afghanistan and Africa as major fronts, the events of 911 in the United States, the Madrid train bombing, the British train terror attack, attacks on US embassies in Kenya and Tanzania, and the bombings in Bali in Indonesia have given added impetus on the sustainment strategy by the United States military.

In order to fully address these emerging needs, the military must have the capability to produce a range of desired effects by bringing together the right blend of assets at the place and time most favorable to success. This way, the military can achieve the necessary destruction or suppression of enemy forces with fewer forces, reducing the

Figure 1. Classification of best sustainment practices (Adapted from Mathaisel, 2004)

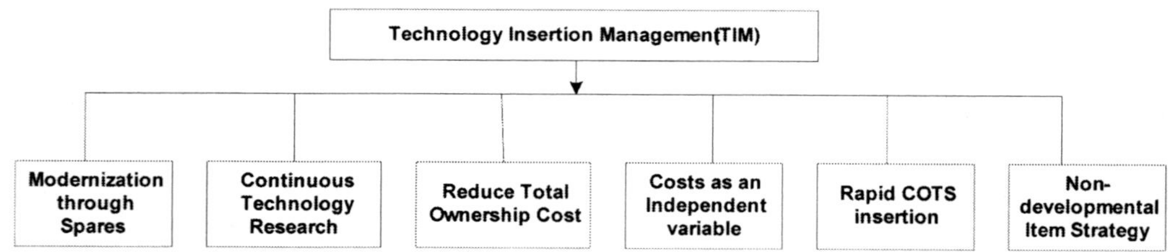

need for time-consuming and risky massing of people and equipment. With over 60% of the total aircraft system life-cycle cost associated with operations and aircraft maintenance, and as aircraft systems age, there is great opportunity to optimize sustainment costs (Blanchard, 1998).

Aging systems, increased maintenance costs, diminished readiness, deferred modernization and other related factors referred to as the death spiral (Gansler, 1999), make it imperative for DoD to find innovative solutions to support legacy systems that are cost effective and flexible as illustrated in Figure 2.

According to Jones, (1995) and Blanchard, and Verma (1995), the Designated Overhaul Point (DOP) performs various maintenance functions like servicing, inspection, testing, adjusting/aligning, removing, replacing, reinstalling, troubleshooting, calibrating, repairing, modifying and overhauling of various weapons systems and associated components.

Blanchard (1998) noted that the Integrated Logistics Support function is a composite of all support considerations (system design for sustainability and logistics infrastructure) necessary to ensure effective and economic well-being of the system throughout its existing lifecycle. The primary objective of these maintenance activities is to maintain the military readiness objective.

Agripino et al. (2001) illustrate that the current military sustainment model is inefficient and complex; the costs outweigh its usefulness. Even though, the model has proved to be good for the support of large slowly changing platforms and systems, several negative characteristics have been identified. Apart from containing uncoupled processes, the model is not responsive in today's maintenance, repair and overhaul environment.

Figure 2. Sustainment death curve (Agripino et al., 2002)

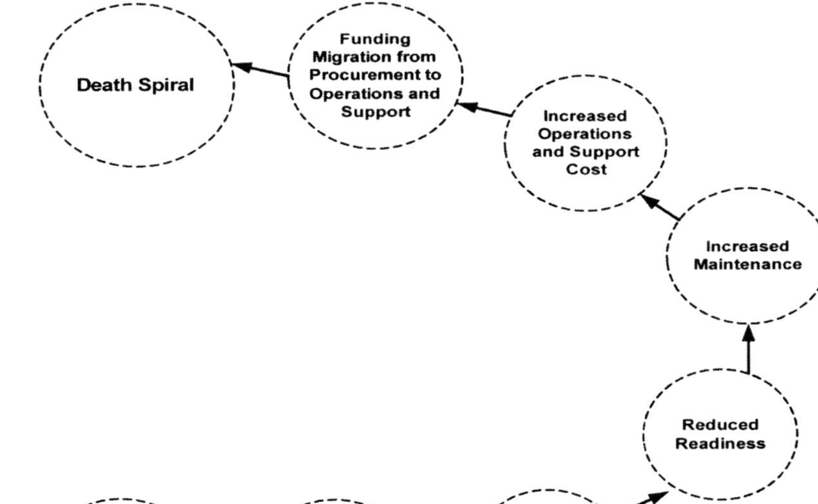

Maintenance, Repair, and Overhaul (MRO)

Current research efforts on maintenance repair and overhaul operations (MRO) focus on individual elements of this sustainment system. Agripino et al. (2002) advocated solving the sustainment problem by conducting research that should impact the whole enterprise, from raw material suppliers to final product delivery. To accomplish this objective, the authors developed a new lean framework for military systems sustainment. The goal of this model is to minimize non-value-added activities throughout the entire enterprise. Nightingale (2000) advocated that lean is focused on value added activities in terms of performance, flexibility, capability, quality and added long-term competitive success.

The Lean Sustainment Enterprise Model (LSEM) developed by Agripino (2002) calls for the consolidation and integration of the sustainment functions. The overall goal is to achieve significant customer service levels while reducing total ownership costs. The new organizational framework allows close coordination between the operational community and the supporting sustainment network required to meet evolving lifecycle support requirements. Mathaisel (2009) proposed a sustainment transformation framework. This entails changes in repair processes, material support, financial accounting systems as well as the mindset of the management. The intent is to overhaul the industrial space needed to function with commercial efficiency in the mold of lean manufacturing. The author identified two major issues that work against the current sustainment goals. In the first place, current systems are designed and arranged as separate entities. Secondly, past performance improvement efforts were concerned with the process instead of the product.

The author submitted that a transformation plan is needed to confront and adequately respond to increased and unpredictable demand for mission ready resources. Their focus was on mainly increasing throughput and customer support, with a benefit of increasing capacity, availability and productivity. Their research led to the Air force material command's depot maintenance MRO transformation. These methods and practices have facilitated increased capacity, higher quality and productivity and cost reduction in the organization.

Cognitive Engineering Approach

Goh and Coleman (2003) presented a novel cognitive engineering approach to creating a framework that more fully captures the decision support needs of commercial aircraft gas turbine engine maintenance, repair and overhaul (MRO) organizations. They developed a broader set of computer-based decision support tools to meet various other decision support needs of the engine MRO community. Some of these needs are fault prognostics, maintenance planning, scope of work, and generation and configuration management. Using field studies of various airlines, engine MRO providers and engine manufacturers across North America, Asia-Pacific and Europe, the analyses presented in their paper offer a thorough understanding of the cognitive needs and the decision-making process in engine MRO organizations.

Sustainment through Consolidation

Ellmyer (2006) explored why the Air Force should consolidate the operational function of supply support, why it is needed, and what to do about it. Consolidation will provide a stable infrastructure when conflicts go from peace time to war time operations. They insist that the Air Force must create a supply chain management enterprise that makes operations more efficient, more effective, and reduce costs while providing sustained levels of weapon system availability.

Obsolescence Planning for Design for Product Sustainment

The key input that enables planning for design for sustainment is obsolescence forecasting. Most electronic part obsolescence forecasting is based on the development of models for the products' lifecycle. Singh and Sandborn (2006) discussed the impact of technology on the system. They noted that the short product lifecycle associated with fast moving technology changes can become both a problem and an opportunity for manufacturers and systems integrators to explore. The authors also identified two major obsolescence mitigation approaches. One is reactive in nature, focusing on minimizing the costs of obsolescence mitigation; that is, minimizing the cost of resolving the problem after it has occurred. The other is the proactive oriented methodology, which has larger sustainment cost avoidance because of the forward looking approach.

This problem is especially prevalent in the military systems, where systems often encounter obsolescence problems before they are fielded. Hamilton and Chin (2001) stated that obsolescence began to emerge as a problem in the 1980s when the end of the Cold War accelerated pressure to reduce military outlays. While Stogdill (1999) reported the existence of part obsolescence mitigation strategies, Tilton (2006) targeted enterprise-wide solutions by tracking obsolete parts. This method ensures that the lowest cost options for mitigating obsolescence are pursued and achieved. According to Sing and Sandborn (2006), "sustainment problems are going to get worse, not better in the future and are going to become significant lifecycle and cost drivers in numerous product sectors" (p. 13). Therefore, the lifecycle and operational cost components makes a strong case for laying the foundation for designing for sustainment.

The future sustainment relationships are envisaged to be linked and design integration focused. In this connection, the major categories of resources required in the design for sustainment system are discussed in the next section. In Table 1, a summary of existing sustainment frameworks are presented.

SUSTAINMENT AND PRODUCT DESIGN

The scope of design cuts across a variety of subject domains and faces a myriad of daunting challenges that range from design complexity and specifications to integration and maintenance/supportability. Typically, design output can range from design of products and systems, to designs of processes and services. Product design is a multi-stage process. These stages begin with requirement analysis, followed by preliminary and subsequently detailed design. Generally, experience has shown that design is an open ended process and, therefore, continues to evolve until the final design is approved. Goel and Craw (2006), for example, stated that a design problem may be underspecified and its specification may need to be completed as the design process progresses. In another example, a design problem may be over-constrained and some constraints may need to be relaxed to find a satisfactory design solution.

Design practices are changing globally. Designer's preparedness to respond in a timely and innovative manner to changing customer demands has the advantage of offering products with higher performance and greater overall customer appeal. Kamrani (2001) therefore suggested that to be competitive, organizations need to make products that can be easily configured to offer distinctive capabilities in the areas of product or system development and design, manufacturing engineering, material, and maintenance.

Sustainment and Product Design Decisions

Articulating sound design decisions is a cornerstone upon which product sustainment and sup-

Table 1. Summary of some existing research framework on product or system sustainment

Author	Research	Framework	Goal
Wang et al. (2011)	Integrating Economic, Environmental and Social Indicators for Sustainable Supply Chains	Supply chain dynamic simulation and Life Cycle Assessment	Focus on evaluating the sustainability of a detergent supply chain through integration of supply chain dynamic simulation and environmental- and societal- Life Cycle Assessment (LCA).
Gulledge et al (2010)	Condition-based Maintenance and the product improvement process	Approaches for enabling Product Lifecycle Management (PLM) and Supply Chain Management (SCM) business processes	Focus is on integrating condition-based maintenance (CBM) and PLM through composite application design.
Mathaisel (2009)	Lean Transformation	Architecture for Lean Transformation	Change in repair processes, material support, financial accounting systems and management mindset
Piplani et al (2008)	Sustainable supply chain management	A Review Paper	Focus is on new developments and stimulation of further discussions in the domain of global supply chains
Ellmyer (2006)	Sustainment through consolidation	Command and Control of Sustainment	Focus is on more efficient operations, more effective and cost reduction
Mathaisel et al. (2004)	Best Sustainment Practices	Classification of Best sustainment practices	Focus is on identifying, classifying and implementing a set of best practices for the sustainment of US military systems
Goh and Coleman (2003)	Cognitive Engineering	Cognitive Engineering approach to sustainment	Framework captures decision support needs for MRO organizations
Agripino et al. (2002)	Maintenance Repair and Overall (MRO)	LEAN Sustainment Enterprise Model (LSEM)	Consolidation and integration of sustainment functions
Wilson et al. (2002)	Sustainment through Innovation	Product Innovation Sustainment Model	Focus on activity model for front-end innovation

portability processes are based. Several design decisions that can greatly impact sustainment are depicted in Figure 3. These decisions will provide a unified perspective on what sustained performance requirements are and how appropriate data is gathered for making the requisite design decisions to ensure sustainment and supportability of the product when deployed.

Baldwin and Clarke (2000) divide the definition of modularity into two concepts namely: (a) the module and (b) the notions of abstraction, information hiding and interface. By implication, the larger system connecting its constituent modules should provide a structure that allows the modules to retain their independence and yet integrate to deliver the desired system level value. Groover (2001) advocates that products be designed in such ways that consists of several modules that can be readily assembled to create the finished items. Shah (2004) states that for the design of complex durable product, the degree of freedom available to the designer after several iterations becomes very small. Once convergence occurs, the designer is so constrained by the interdependencies of prior choices. This allows for minimal changes to be made to the design later on. This paralyzing complexity leads to an inability of designers to adapt to a changing environment because they cannot capture the emerging trend nor take advantage of new technological innovations. Jamshidi (2005) stated that the United States military, through the DOD, uses the system of systems approach to underscore the DOD's preferred modular approach to development, acquisition and sustainment. Typically, every subsystem (product or part) should be de-

Figure 3. Major product and system design decisions to enhance sustainment

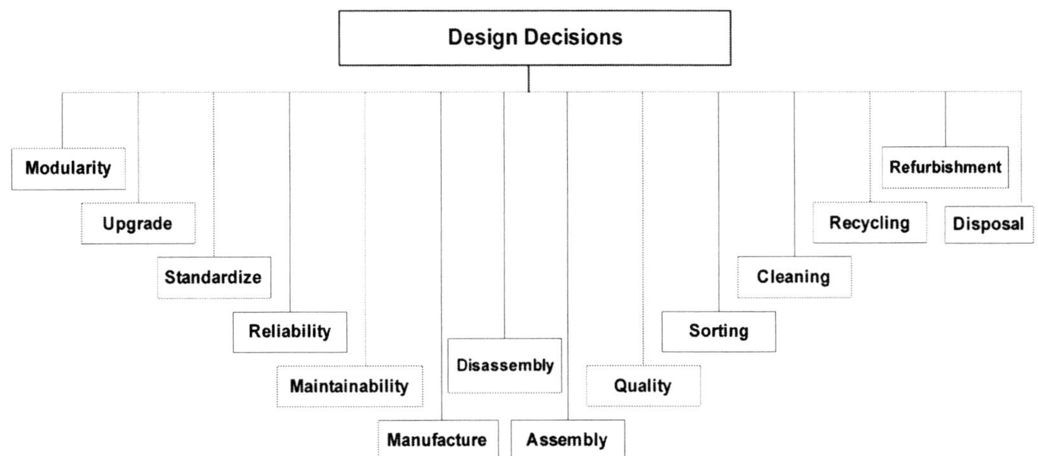

signed so that maintenance, upgrades and repair have a minimal impact on the total system's operational effectiveness.

Sustainment and Upgradeability

Groover (2001) emphasized the necessity of designing and developing products that are upgradeable. This highlights the need for more effective strategies to accomplish these upgrades more quickly and at a cost effective manner, while at the same time, ensuring that the upgraded subsystems are more sustainable themselves.

Sustainment and Standardization

Various aspects of design standardization have been discussed in the published literature. Tarondeau (1998) discussed various ramifications of standardization on product or system design. Standardization can typically result in higher productivity sustainment. Standardization could also reduce the number of reference points to be maintained for efficient operational performance. According to Agard and Kusiak (2004), the unnecessary cost of robustness may be balanced by sustained productivity and decrease in product and process control. Lee and Tang (1997) developed a mathematical model to determine the best compromise between the investment necessary for the standardization and the profit resulting from the economy of scale. Hyer and Wemmerlov's (1984) approach involves grouping parts, products, and processes that are similar, and therefore can be readily applied to standardization.

The overarching concept behind standards is to provide predictable building blocks for others to build upon so that the need for re-invention is minimized. This process is required to lower the costs of creation and innovation, and reap the benefits of shared infrastructure. Product standardization is a technique in engineering design that aims to reduce the variety of parts within a product. According to Agard and Kusiak (2004), it necessitates designing an overly robust product or the use of a robust process that is often more flexible. Product design standardization makes it possible for the maximum number of items to be made with the fewest number of basic parts.

Sustainment and Design for Manufacture (DFM)

Stoll (1990) defined design for manufacture as the integration of full range of policies, techniques, practices, and attitudes that cause a product to be designed for the optimum manufacturing cost, the optimum achievement of manufactured quality. This can assure the optimum achievement of overall operational lifecycle sustainment and supportability. Accordingly, sustainment can be achieved by the ability to identify product concepts that are inherently easy to manufacture, focus on component design for ease of manufacture and assembly, and integrate manufacturing process design and product design to ensure the best matching of needs and requirements.

The chances that redesign may become necessary to make production of the product feasible can result in high costs and disappointing operational performance. The sustainment of the designed product will therefore be jeopardized. This situation reveals the need for a well thought out design and the need for considering and addressing manufacturing and sustainment issues at the early design stages (Kuo & Hong-Chao Zhang, 1995). Some of the basic principles to follow in design for manufacture are listed by McBride (2003) as follows: simplification and reduction in the number of parts, standardization and use of common parts and materials, designing for parts orientation and handling to minimize non value-added manual effort and so on.

Sustainment and Reliability

Sitaraman and Pang (2001) state that designing for reliability is achieved when a product performs the functions for which it is designed. This ties into the overall concept of sustainment which emphasizes a product's continued lifecycle operational performance. Typical issues of concern in reliability design includes the product's service life, failure rate, reliability testing requirements, type of material used in the product, tolerances and specifications. In the past, especially in the defense industry, as soon as a product met the customer's detailed specification, it was shipped. It did not matter whether it met the customer's requirement or not. In today's production environment, customers rely on manufacturers to understand their needs and to anticipate what is needed. This is a major shift in the thinking of many manufacturers in the defense industry (Crowe & Feinberg, 2001). Batson and Elam (2002) offer alternative ways to build reliability rather than depending on maintenance (preventive, predictive or corrective) activities to restore equipment or product function in order to guarantee reliability and enhance sustainment. The authors recognize that design decisions that achieve desired reliability are better than solutions implemented after a product has been finished and launched.

Ghodrati and Kumar (2005) give a review of reliability characteristics of any product or equipment. The authors state that system reliability characteristics and factors such as mean time to failure (MTTF) and mean time to repair (MTTR) for both the component and the whole system are required for reliability analysis. A list of system operating factors such as dust, temperature, humidity, pollution and vibration are significant in the context of system reliability analysis.

Sustainment and Robustness

Fowlkes and Clyde (1995) indicate that a product is said to be robust when it is insensitive to the effects of sources of variability, even though the sources themselves are still present in the system. A good example is the USAF Thunderbolt II, often called the Warthog. This typically ensures that a product reaches its full potential during its operational lifecycle. Baston and Elam (2002) define robust design as an optimization approach that uses a series of experiments to find parameter settings for the design that yields predicted targeted performance, and is as insensitive to noise as possible. This method provides a systematic and efficient approach for finding a near-optimum combination of design parameters, generating a product that is functional, exhibits a high level of product operational performance, and is insensitive or robust to noise factors. A robust design steps are depicted in Figure 4.

Designing for robustness of a product requires identifying design features that are potentially vulnerable to various physical effects that can lead to a degraded product performance as the product goes through its operational lifecycle. This typically ties into the ability to sustain and support that particular product which according to Sobe et al. (2007) is similar to design for yield and manufacturing. The robust design approach can be applied using Taguchi's method in order to find parameter settings for the product design that is able to yield the targeted predicted performance (George, 2002). Several robust design performance issues are user, design, environmental, production and operational variation based.

The author suggests that incorporating the robust design approach can minimize warranty returns by making random product failures less likely or nonexistent. Therefore, robust reliability design and robust sustainment design can analyze failure times to identify significant factors, and their optimal settings for reliability and sustainability using statistically designed experiments.

Figure 4. Steps for robust design implementation

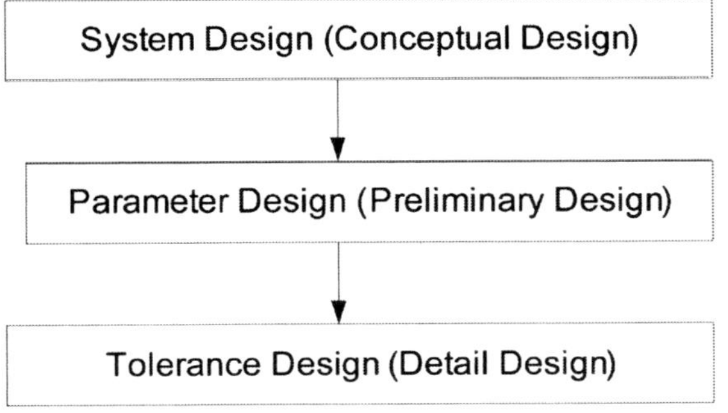

Jayatilleka and Okogbaa (2001) state that Accelerated Life Tests (ALT) are useful in identifying potential failure modes and normal operational stress levels of products at the design stage of product development. Early failures detected in a product are bound to have adverse effects on its sustainment during its operational lifecycle. In the same study, the authors stated that prior ALT studies showed early failures in the journal bearings. In one such study, the positioning of the bearing window was found to be a critical design parameter that affected proper lubrication, which ultimately determine the life of the motor. The ALT was designed to determine the optimal position of the window that produces the maximum life for the motor. This was done by carrying out tests at higher loads and at different bearing window positions. In recent years, Taguchi's robust design method has been widely used to achieve high quality by improving product design Yang and Yang (1998). As soon as a product is deployed in environment of use or application, environmental stresses are the main noise factors that will be encountered. This underscores the need to make products robust against environmental stresses. Environmental stress testing (EST) usually conducted in the design cycle is a value-added process in terms of product reliability improvement.

Currently, many environmental stress tests (ESTs) are performed routinely and not carefully planned Caruso (1996) which limits EST added value. Yang and Yang in their actual case study show that products produced with optimum levels of design parameters are more robust and reliable when exposed to environmental stresses. It is envisaged that if the same principles are implemented in design for sustainment, similar results can be achieved.

Figure 5. A model for operations and maintenance (adapted from Lundin, 1999)

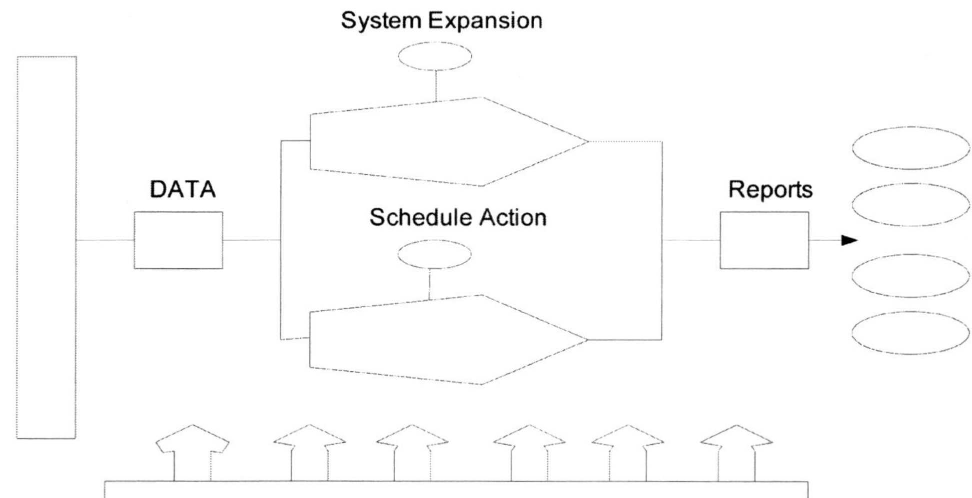

Sustainment and Maintainability

Maintainability should be a designed-in capability and not an add-on option Schaeffer (2003). In essence, it pertains to the ease, accuracy, safety and economy in performing maintenance actions. A system should be designed such that it can be maintained without large investments of time, cost or other resources (e.g., personnel, materials, facilities, test equipment) and without adversely affecting system mission success. Maintainability is a measure of the ability of an item to be maintained, whereas maintenance constitutes a series of actions taken to restore or retain an item in an effective operational state. Lundin (1999) proposed a general model describing the operations and maintenance processes presented in Figure 5.

The model is divided into two parallel parts. The two separate main processes are intended for two different user categories of the system namely: Operations (used by personnel using the system day to day for corrective action) and Maintenance (Personnel using the system to perform tests and analysis for preventive action. The main concern of the operations component is about the good and efficient performance of the product or system while the maintenance component is concerned with the several tasks associated with the maintenance component. In modeling the aging process and maintenance actions, Sugier and Anders (2007) listed three major factors that contribute to the aging behavior of equipment as physical characteristics, operating practices and the maintenance policy in place.

Sugier and Anders (2007) also employed a technique called first passage time (FPT) between states, which provides the average times for first reaching any state from any other state. If the end-state is F , the FPT's are the mean remaining lifetimes from any of the initiating states.

Then for all states $s = 1 \ldots K$.

$$P^{s0} + \sum_{r} P^{sr} = 1 \qquad (2.1)$$

where

K represents number of deterioration states

R represents number of repairs in the model under consideration.

P^{so} represents probability of selecting maintenance r in the s and

P^{sr} represents probability of returning to state Ds from inspection Is (situation when no maintenance is scheduled as a result of the inspection).

Without the design for maintainability process, many of the features that make a product maintainable might not be realized during the product development stage. An important benefit of maintainability design is the reduction in maintenance costs and time taken to keep a product up and running.

The maintenance phase in the complete product lifecycle is often the most expensive and time-consuming of all product lifecycle phases. According to Misra (2005), as the product development progresses in its lifecycle through the phases of requirements analysis, design, implementation, testing, and maintenance, the complexity and the cost of the product increase. Because of its cost, product sustainment and supportability remain a major challenge in product design and quality engineering studies. Indications of the impact of design considerations concerning maintainability in the relatively early phases (design or implementation) of product development should help the design engineer to improve design with the hope of reducing the recurring sustainment footprints that could otherwise occur due to poor design.

DESIGN FOR SUSTAINMENT SYSTEM STAKEHOLDERS

In Figure 6, a schematic of the major stakeholders in design for sustainment of complex products and systems, such as the military weapon system, is depicted. The first group comprises people and the organizations they work for. In the military environment, for example, this group is made up of department of defense personnel and private sector stakeholders (contractors).

In a manufacturing environment, the stakeholders are made up of the product designers, the manufacturing and the production engineers. The organizational management is also interested in what happens within and outside the system. Another important group is the technology and strategy group. In this group, key issues are the application of appropriate automatic identification technologies like RFID, bar codes or commercial off-the-shelf (COTS) to support sustainment initiatives.

DECOMPOSITION OF DESIGN FOR SUSTAINMENT

A high-level design for sustainment decomposition framework is proposed. This is depicted in Figure 7. The framework consists of two primary components: the design component and the sustainment component. The design component consists of the environment that the product will operate in, the product itself and the design model. The sustainment section consists of the operations/maintenance and the retirement models. This decomposition is necessary to distinguish between the front-end and back-end activities of the design for sustainment process. The design section lays the groundwork for the product's continued performance to maintain or prolong operations, and it is critical to the process of satisfying the constraints imposed by the product operational and usage environment with the understanding that as designed products go through their operational life, they deteriorate over time.

CHALLENGES FACING DESIGN FOR SUSTAINMENT

A variety of issues confront the sustainment of global supply chain as well as designed products

Figure 6. Sustainment triangle showing the interdependency of the three key groups

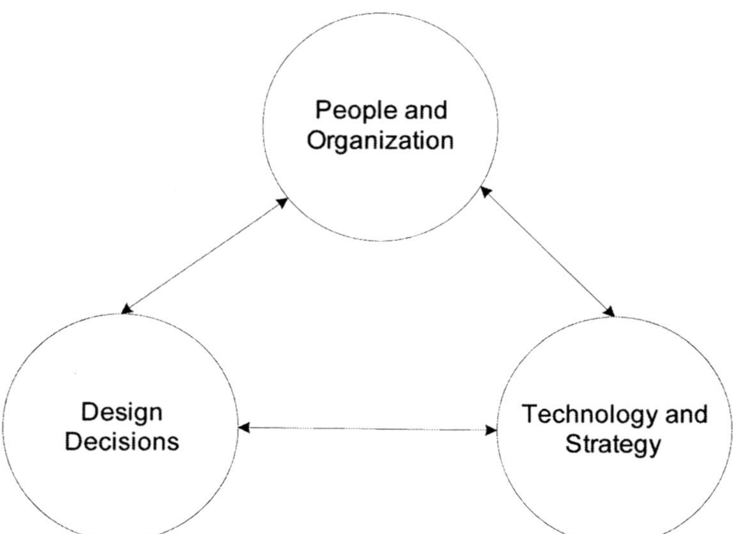

or systems. One of the major issues discovered during the course of developing this article is that various organizations and institutions have limited knowledge and understanding of what sustainment is. There are no clearly defined roadmaps or standards for defining sustainment. As a result, the concept of sustainment remains a work in process. Furthermore, the concept of sustainment and technology interweave with each other. The absence of requisite technology adds to the current major challenges. Under these conditions, supporting designed products or systems becomes a very complicated issue which completely negates the idea of sustainment. During the product or system development stage, sustainment requirements may be consigned to the background or even deferred which later affects the effective and efficient performance of the product or system. If sustainment requirements are not provided for; even a well designed product or system may not be deemed economically and functionally sustainable. This invariably increases the burden of maintenance with all related cost implications.

A sustainment strategy demands that adequate information be filtered from product or system performance and the knowledge transferred to the designers to address peculiar product characteristics that enhance their sustainment. To this end, a matrix of best practices and framework need to be developed to drive and support design for sustainment. These innovative ideas will provide actionable design insights in addressing sustainment related issues.

CONCLUSION

The concept of sustainment has been embraced with much rhetorical flourish and it remains to be seen what the general consensus comes out to be with respect to the realization of anticipated results or outcomes. It is in the realization of this need that this paper chronicles the current research and strategies on sustainment. It is clear that the concept of Sustainment represents basic and critical transformational change designers of products and global supply chain systems must embrace as a panacea for continued efficient operational performance.

Figure 7. High-level decomposition of sustainment highlighting design and sustainment components

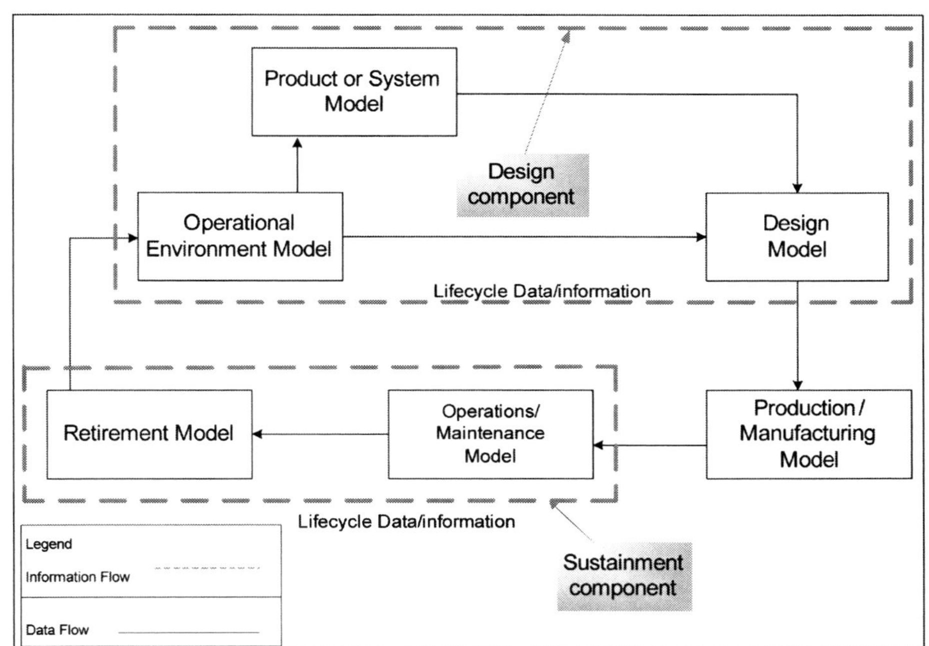

The attainment of an enduring product and global supply chain sustainment includes the challenge of providing strategic cost-effective benefits throughout a product or system's operational lifecycle operations. The achievement of mission readiness objective of designed products and systems typically involves designing an enduring support as well as supporting the design. This entails institutionalizing sound, safe and quality global logistical support. Expertise in sustainment engineering, good maintenance practices, sustainable supply chain management, targeted innovative solutions, technology are panacea to achieving mission readiness objective of product and global supply chain requirements. There is therefore the urgent need of discussing and including sustainment in the overall global supply chain framework using engineering design and technological tools or concepts. There is currently little effort to address the global supply chain sustainment challenges and how environmental and operational lifecycle related data or information ought to be integrated into early design, engineering, technology, management, logistical, supportability and service issues for product and global supply chain transformation.

REFERENCES

Advanced Technology Institute. (2001). *Defense sustainment consortium. Strategic Investment Plan, Contract: N00140-01-C-L622* (p. 29418). SC: North Charleston.

Agard, B., & Kusiak, A. (2004). *A standardization of components, products and processes with data mining.* International Conference on Production Research Americas, Santiago, Chile, August 1-4.

Agripino, M., Cathcart, T., & Mathaisel, D. F. X. (2002). A lean sustainment enterprise model for military systems. *Acquisition Review Quarterly, August*, 274-297.

Agripino, M., Cathcart, T., & Mathaisel, D. (2002). A lean sustainment model for military Systems. *Acquisition Review Journal, Fall*, 274-297.

Baldwin, C., & Clark, K. (2000). *Design rules, Vol. 1: The power of modularity*. MIT Press. ISBN 0-262-024667

Batson, R. G., & Elam, M. E. (2002). *Robust design: An experiment-based approach to design for reliability conference*. MARCON.

Blanchard, B. S. (1998). *Logistics engineering and management*. Upper Saddle River, NJ: Prentice Hall.

Blanchard, B. S., Verma, D., & Peterson, E. L. (1995). *Maintainability*. New York, NY: Wiley-Interscience.

Brundtland Commission. (1987). *Our common future*. World Commission on Environment and Development.

Caruso, H. (1996). An overview of environmental reliability testing. *Proceedings of the Annual Reliability and Maintainability Symposium,* (pp. 102–109).

Castillo, J. A. (2010). OIF fuel distribution challenges. *Army Sustainment*, *42*(2), 8–9.

Chestnutwood, M., & Levin, R. (1999). *Technology assessment and management methodology - An approach to system life sustainment and supportability*. ISBN: 0-7803-5749-3/99/0

Cordesman, A. H. (2000). *Trends in US defense spending: The size of funding, procurement, and readiness problems*. Washington, DC: Center for Strategic and International Studies.

Craighead, C. W., Blackhurst, J., Rungtusanatham, M. J., & Handfield, R. B. (2007). The severity of supply chain disruptions: Design characteristics and mitigation capabilities. *Decision Sciences*, *38*(1), 131–156. doi:10.1111/j.1540-5915.2007.00151.x

Crowe, D., & Feinberg, A. (2001). *Design for reliability*. Boca Raton, FL: CRC.

Cutcher-Gershenfeld, J., Field, F., Hall, R., Kirchain, R., Marks, D., Oye, K., & Sussman, J. (2004). Sustainability as an organizing design principle for large-scale engineering systems. *Engineering Systems Monograph, March,* 29-31.

Defense Acquisition Guidebook. (2004, November 01). *United States defense acquisition technology and logistics (Defense AT & L).*

Ellmyer, E. G. (2006). Centralized supply chain management: Command and control of sustainment. A Research Report, Maxwell Air Force Base, Alabama. AU/ACSC/8009/AY06.

Fowlkes, W. Y., & Creveling, C. M. (1995). *Engineering methods for robust product design: Using Taguchi methods in technology and product development*. Prentice Hall.

Gansler, J. S. (1999). *Acquisition Reform Update, January.* U.S. Department of Defense, USD (A&T), Office of the Secretary of Defense, acquisition & technology.

Garmon, P. J., Gary, M. J., Laughlin, L. L., Sjoberg, E. S., Lasater, D., Calloway, S., & Robins, W. (2001). Just-in-time sustainment. *The 20th Conference on Digital Avionics Systems,* Vol. 1, 14-18 October.

George, M. L. (2002). *Lean Six Sigma: Combining Six Sigma quality with lean speed.* New York, NY: McGraw-Hill.

Ghodrati, B., & Kumar, U. (2005). Applications and case studies: Reliability and operating environment-based spare parts estimation approach. *Journal of Quality in Maintenance Engineering*, *11*(2), 169–184. doi:10.1108/13552510510601366

Goel, A. K., & Craw, S. (2006). Design, innovation and case-based reasoning. . *The Knowledge Engineering Review*, *20*(03), 271–276. doi:10.1017/S0269888906000609

Goh, S., & Coleman, S. (2003). *Sustainment of commercial aircraft gas turbine engines: An organizational and cognitive engineering approach*. AIAA's 3rd Annual Aviation Technology, Integration, and Operations (ATIO) Tech 17 – 19 November, Denver, CO.

Goodall, R., Fandel, D., Allan, A., Landler, P., & Huff, H. R. (2002). Long term productivity mechanisms of the semiconductor industry. *American Electrochemical Society Semiconductor Silicon Conference,* Vol. 2, (pp. 125–143).

Gravier, M. J., & Swartz, S. M. (2009). The dark side of innovation: Exploring obsolescence and supply chain evolution for sustainment-dominated systems. *The Journal of High Technology Management Research*, *20*(2), 87–102. doi:10.1016/j.hitech.2009.09.001

Groover, P. G. (2001). *Automation, production systems, and computer-integrated manufacturing* (2nd ed., p. 609). Prentice-Hall.

Gulledge, T., Hiroshige, S., & Iyer, R. (2010). Condition-based maintenance and the product improvement process. *Journal of Computers in Industry*, *61*, 813–832. doi:10.1016/j.compind.2010.07.007

Hamilton, P., & Chin, G. (2001). Military electronics and obsolescence part 1: The evolution of a crisis. *COTS Journal*, March, 77–81.

Holweg, M., & Pil, F. K. (2008). Theoretical perspectives on the coordination of supply chains. *Journal of Operations Management*, *26*(3), 389–406. doi:10.1016/j.jom.2007.08.003

Hulsmann, M., Grapp, J., & Li, Y. (2008). Strategic adaptivity in global supply chains-Competitive advantage by autonomous cooperation. *International Journal of Production Economics*, *114*, 14–26. doi:10.1016/j.ijpe.2007.09.009

Hyer, N., & Wemmerlov, U. (1984). Group technology and productivity. *Harvard Business Review*, (July- August): 140–149.

Jamshidi, M. (2005). *System-of-systems engineering: A definition*. Hawaii: IEEE SMC.

Jayatilleka, S., & Okogbaa, G. O. (2001). Accelerated life test for identifying potential failure modes and optimizing critical design parameters in a journal bearing. *IEEE Proceedings of Annual Reliability and Maintainability Symposium.*

Jones, J. (1995). *Integrated logistic support handbook*. New York, NY: MacGraw Hill.

Kamrani, A. K., & Salhieh, S. M. (2001). *Product design for modularity* (p. 224). doi:10.1007/978-1-4615-1725-2

Kuo, T. C., & Zhang, H. (1995). *Design for manufacturability and design for "X": Concepts, applications, and perspectives*. IEEEiCPMT International Electronics Manufacturing Technology Symposium.

Kros, T. C. (1999). *Modernization through spares: An analysis of implementation at the U.S. Army aviation and missile command*. Retrieved from http://www.nps.navy.mil/ code36/krostc.html

Lee, H. L., & Tang, C. S. (1997). Modeling the costs and benefits of delayed product differentiation. *Management Science*, *43*(1), 40–53. doi:10.1287/mnsc.43.1.40

Lundin, O. (1999). *An operations and maintenance process model for energy management* (pp. 1–7). IEEE.

Lyles, L. L. (2001, 23 March). *Commander, USAR material command before the House Armed Services Committee.*

Mathaisel, D. F. X. (2006). *Sustaining the military enterprise: An architecture for a lean transformation*. Babson Park, MA: Babson College.

Mathaisel, D. F. X., Cathcart, T., & Comm, C. (2004). A framework for benchmarking, classifying, and implementing best sustainment practices. *Journal of Benchmarking, 11*(4), 403–417. doi:10.1108/14635770410546791

Mathaisel, D. M. X. (2009). *The lean enterprise: An architecture for lean transformation.* Auerbach Publications, Taylor and Francis Group.

McBride, D. (2003). *Design for manufacturability*. EMS Consulting Group. Retrieved from http://www.emsstrategies.com

Misra, S. C. (2005). Modeling design/coding factors that drive maintainability of software systems. *Software Quality Journal, 13*, 297–320. doi:10.1007/s11219-005-1754-7

Muller-Christ, G., & Hulsmann, M. (2003). Quo vadis Umweltmanagement? Entwicklungsperspektiven einer nachhaltigkeitsorientierten Managementlehre. *Die Betriebswirtschaft, 63*, 257–277.

Nightingale, D. (2000). *Integrating the lean enterprise*. MIT Presentation. Retrieved from http://lean.mit.edu

Office of Management and Budget. (1998). *Budget of the United States Government: Historical tables*. Washington, DC: U.S. Government Printing Office.

Performance-Based Business Environment. (1997, January 23). *Flexible sustainment guide*. Retrieved from http://dsp.dla.mil/ sustainment/ flexguide2.pdf

Piplani, R., Pujawan, N., & Ray, S. (2007). Sustainable supply chain management. *International Journal of Production Economics, 111*(2), 193–194. doi:10.1016/j.ijpe.2007.05.001

Reliability Analysis Center. (2004)..*Journal of the Reliability Analysis Center, 10*(2).

Digest Editorial Staff, S. C. (2010, August 12). Supply chain news: The five challenges of today's global supply chains. *Supply Chain Digest.* Retrieved from http://www.scdigest.com/ ASSETS/ ON_TARGET/ 10-08-12-3.php?cid=3649

Schaeffer, M. (2003). *Designing and assessing supportability in DOD weapon systems: A guide to increased reliability and reduced logistics footprint*. Office of Secretary of Defense.

Shah, N. B. (2004). *Modularity as an enabler for evolutionary acquisition.* MS Thesis Science in Aeronautics and Astronautics at the Massachusetts Institute of Technology (MIT).

Shaked, S., & Jolliet, O. (2011). Global life cycle impacts of consumer productsIn Nriagu, J. (Ed.), *Encyclopedia of environmental health* (pp. 1002–1014). doi:10.1016/B978-0-444-52272-6.00397-4

Singh, P., & Sandborn, P. (2006). Obsolescence driven design refresh planning for sustainment-(n.d). dominated systems. *The Engineering Economist, 51*(2).

Sitaraman, S. K., & Pang, J. H. L. (2001). *Fundamentals of design for reliability*. The McGraw-Hill Companies, Inc.

Sobe, U., Rooch, K. H., Ripp, A., & Pronath, M. (2009). Robust analog design for automotive applications by design centering with safe operating areas. *IEEE Transactions on Semiconductor Manufacturing, 22*(2), 217–224.doi:10.1109/TSM.2008.2011628

Stogdill, R. C. (1999). Dealing with obsolete parts. *IEEE Design & Test of Computers, 16*(2), 17–25. doi:10.1109/54.765200

toll, H. W. (1990). Design for manufacturing. In C. W. Allen (Ed.), Simultaneous engineering. (pp. 23-29). SME Press.

Sugier, J., & Anders, G. J. (2007). Modeling changes in maintenance activities through fine-tuning Markov models of ageing equipment. *2nd International Conference on Dependability of Computer Systems* (pp. 336–343).

Tewary, A., & Wang, N. (2005). *Semiconductors*. Standard and Poor's Industry Surveys.

Tilton, J. R. (2006). *Obsolescence management Information System (OMIS)*. Keyport, WA: Navy Underwater Warfare Center. Retrieved from. http://www.dmsms.org/ file.jsp?storename=OMIS_article1.pdf

Tarondeau, J.C. (1998). De nouvelles formes d'organisation pour l'entreprise. La gestion par lesrocessus. *Cahier Français, Management et organisation des entreprises, 287*. Paris, France: La Documentation Française.

Wang, P. C., Halim, I., Arief, A., & Rajagopalan, S. (2011). Integrating economic, environmental and social indicators for sustainable supply chains. *Journal of Computer Aided Chemical Engineering, 29*, 1220–1224. doi:10.1016/B978-0-444-54298-4.50023-4

Wognuma, P. M., Bremmers, H., Trienekens, J. H., van der Vorst, G. A. J., & Bloemhof, J. M. (2011). Systems for sustainability and transparency of food supply chains – Current status and challenges. *Journal of Advanced Engineering Informatics, 25*(1), 65–76. doi:10.1016/j.aei.2010.06.001

Yang, K., & Yang, G. (1998). Degradation reliability assessment using severe critical values. *International Journal of Reliability Quality and Safety Engineering, 5*, 85–95. doi:10.1142/S0218539398000091

KEY TERMS AND DEFINITIONS

Commercial Off-the-Shelf: Any Item or software that is commercially and openly available over the counter which requires no specific modification over its lifecycle operations.

Disablers: Any issue that will prevent the product or system from performing intended function.

Footprint: The smallest amount of maintenance effort that will keep a product continuously operational.

Reliability: Achieved when a product performs the functions for which it is designed.

Robustness: The ability of a product to perform in spite of environmental encumbrances.

Stakeholder(s): The interest group(s) without whose support a product or system cannot deliver intended results.

Sustainment: The continuous operational performance of a product or system throughout its lifecycle.

Chapter 16
Inventory Cost Share for Supply Chain Coordination by Means of Contracts

Alejandra Gomez-Padilla
Center of Exact Sciences and Engineering, University of Guadalajara, Mexico

ABSTRACT

This chapter highlights the importance of contracts for coordination between companies in a supply chain. It considers a dyadic situation, with a supplier and a retailer. Coordination is achieved by two types of decisions: economic (concerning prices established and stated over a contract), and physical exchange of products (concerning the inventory that is going to be held by the retailer). First one contract with a simple pricing scheme is considered, and then two contracts with inventory holding cost shared among the companies of the supply chain. The former is presented to explain the general situation and the two last ones to explain different schemes of inventory cost share. A numerical example is also shown. The objective is to illustrate that a supply chain may be efficiently coordinated if the companies establish contracts with inventory holding cost share.

INTRODUCTION

The study of dyadic supply chains has experienced a growing interest the last decade, and it has been approached from different points of view. One of the approaches is, like the one of this document: cooperation, as Liu and Wang (2007) who revealed the importance of cooperation among members of a supply chain concluding that actual competition is between supply chains, not between companies. Other of the approaches is partnership. Tyan and Wee (2003) identify four strategies of retailer-supplier partnership and consider that vendor managed inventory (VMI) is the highest level

DOI: 10.4018/978-1-4666-0246-5.ch016

of partnership. "VMI partnerships occur when downstream supply chain customers choose to partner with their suppliers. Agreements are made as to where the inventory is stored, either at the supplier site or the customer site, and when the billing for the inventory will take place, either upon shipment to the customer or upon use of the part. Further, the supplier will often take control of actually managing inventory levels for the customer. In some cases, a customer representative may be located at the supplier's site to help manage the activity, or vice versa, as in the retail store. The advantage to the supply chain is that transactions are often automated and redundancies in paperwork are reduced." APICS, 2009 (p.57). VMI has also growing interested, and many approaches are found on literature, going from the conditions for adoption (Dong et al., 2007) to operational decisions for cost reduction (Yao et al., 2007; van der Vlist et al., 2007). VMI should not be confused with a buy back contract; under a VMI scheme the supplier will manage the inventory and in the approach of this document under a buy back contract scheme the retailer manage the inventory.

"Optimal supply chain performance requires the execution of a precise set of actions. Unfortunately, those actions are not always in the best interest of the members in the supply chain, i.e., the supply chain members are primarily concerned with optimizing their own objectives, and that self-serving focus often results in poor performance. However, optimal performance can be achieved if the firms coordinate by contracting on a set of transfer payments such that each firm's objective becomes aligned with the supply chain's objective" Cachon (2004). A contract is an agreement between two or more parties that creates for each party a duty to do something (e.g., to provide goods at a certain price according to a specified schedule) or a duty not to do something (e.g., to divulge an employer's trade secrets or financial status to third parties); (Britannica Concise Encyclopedia online, July 2011). It is a business arrangement for the supply of goods or services at a fix price (Merriam Webster dictionary online; July 2011). A contract may be oral or written. Contracts explain the financial flows and the physical flows generated among contracting companies, this is the reason why our attention is centered on contracts.

This work centers on identifying, for the companies of a dyadic supply chain related under a given contract, what are the decisions to be taken considering his own interests of profit. Each company knows that these decisions are going to influence the decisions that the other company will take and will impact the coordination of the chain. The interest of this work is on financial flows and physical flow. Attending the financial flows, the analysis is in terms of price and in terms of the reasons that activate a monetary transfer between the companies. Attending the physical flows, the interest is in terms of quantities of the exchanged product. A financial flow may occur by several reasons. A very clear reason for a financial flow is that a company buys a product from his supplier, but there exist other reasons depending on the contract, two examples are: when the company sells a quantity of products over the final market, or when the company doesn´t sell all the products and has to hold them as stock. Physical flows occur when one a company orders a quantity of products, so the ordered quantity will be physically transferred, and this units will be either sold, kept in stock or put aside as unsold.

From an economic point of view, the contracts will determine the behavior of each company taking into account its objectives of profitability (profit maximization). The economic conditions of the exchanges specified over contracts, determine the behavior of the companies and thus the effectiveness of coordination of the supply chain.

The document first presents a literature review concerning coordination and contracts and then the general model is introduced. This general model is not considering the type of contract, and specifies the profit maximization functions for the retailer and the supplier. With the general model it is also possible to specify the base stock level (inventory decision) that maximizes the expected profit for the supply chain as a whole. The document continues by explaining how a wholesale price contract works, with its profit maximization functions, and the same is done for a quantity flexibility contract and a buy back contract. Finally, conclusions are presented. For simplicity, in this document, as in Cachon (2004), the retailer will be referred as "he" and the supplier as "she".

LITERATURE REVIEW

In the contract several decisions will be established. These decisions arise from the needs of the companies: supply and order quantities of a product, and pay or be paid, this is, receive the economic amounts agreed for the product. The companies take these decisions looking forward to attain certain goals each company has. When the decisions established in a contract satisfy both companies simultaneously corresponds to a "coordination" situation according to several authors (Anupindi and Bassok, 2002; Cachon, 2004; Larivière, 2002; Tsay, 1999; Weng, 1999; Liang et al., 2011). Supply chain coordination has been a main issue of research in the last years (Axsater, 2001; Tayur et al., 2003; De Kok and Grave, 2004; Liang et al., 2011). If the contract does not allow at least one of the companies to carry out its objective, there is no coordination. When the companies are in this non coordination situation, then forced compliance exist. Forced compliance implies that the contractual arrangements will be accomplished even though they do not satisfy the objectives of at least one the two companies; they will be accomplished because they are registered in the contract.

Further than the question concerning the existence of coordination, it is important to deepen on the effectiveness of the coordination if it exists. In other words, it is important to study if the independent decisions taken by the contracting companies are compatible (and then coordinate the supply chain) and correspond to the maximization of the profit not only for each company, but for the whole supply chain. Each company is expecting that the contract is settled in terms that its own profit will be maximized. Liang et al. (2011) study coordination and revenue share, with a game theory approach, for a manufacturer with several retailers and a company of third party logistics; they consider a decentralized model, small alliances and a large scale alliance, and show that for the latter coordination is possible. This document study a dyadic system, so it is possible to consider these two companies independently trying to maximize their own profit, and also as one entity, or supply chain, which also seeks to maximize his profit. In this last situation the two companies share the whole profit of this supply chain (as a single unit). Consequently it will be possible to stand out that what defines the share of profit between the companies is the contract, and that it is also the contract what induces (especially induces) the maximization or not of the profit of the chain. Before centering our attention on the economic dimension and the physical flow derived from the contract on the literature review, it is important to highlight that the study of contracts is also studied by management and social sciences (Froehlichner and Vendemini, 1999; Tirole, 1988), and that the approaches to the study of contracts are very vast.

Literature concerning contracts may be coarsely divided in two groups: newsvendor situation and multi period situation. The newsvendor situation is characterized by the fact that the supplied products may not be kept on stock, this is, the products must be sold in one period of time. For a newsvendor situation it has been found that for a wholesale price contract, it is possible to coordinate the supply chain for buy back contracts (Pasternack, 1985) and quantity flexibility contracts (Tsay, 1999). Arshinder et al. (2009) and Yang and Qi (2009) propose a framework to design coordinating contracts for the newsvendor case. In a multi period situation, unsold units at one period may be stored to be sold later. In this situation the supplier and/or the retailer will hold a stock of units and take in charge the costs induced by this (like the inventory holding cost). Inventory holding under a base stock policy, as the approach of this document, has been widely considered in literature. A theoretical analysis is the one of El Sodany (2011) who studies a situation with a safety stock when inventory holding cost is an expected value. A practical analysis was handled by Praharsi et al. (2010) who propose a heuristic for joint replenishment to minimize inventory holding costs and ordering cost and Tseng et al. (2011) propose an algorithm to reduce bullwhip effect and consequently also reduce inventory holding costs. Sepehri (2011) shows that for a multi product and multi agent situation, inventory holding cost has an impact on the performance of the supply chain. Wang et al. (2010) study retroactive holding cost, that increases or decreases according to storage time and selling period. Zhang (2010) studies a situation of integrated inventory model for a dyadic chain; he shows that by integrating the decisions of reorder point, order quantity and number of shipments, costs is reduced and proposes that the companies share this savings.

Anupindi and Bassok (2002) analyze the multi period situation for wholesale contracts between two agents. They pay attention to the conditions for the committed quantity per period and they propose how to accomplish the contract agreements. Lian and Deshmukh (2009) have a similar approach, with the difference of discounts for commitments in advance. In this paper the interest is not in accomplishing the contract agreements but rather in establishing the contract conditions that will coordinate the supply chain. Some interesting complementary approaches are the ones of Kamrad and Siddique (2004), who analyze the situation where order levels change due to exchange rate fluctuations, Scandizzo and Ventura (2010) with an analysis of concession contracts under uncertainty, and Crespo Marquez and Blanchar (2004), who study portfolios of contracts mainly for electronic industry. Schneeweiss et al. (2004) center their attention on inventory holding costs and purchase cost of parts.

Tsay (1999) consider a supplier and a retailer engaged by a quantity flexibility contract, where a quantity flexibility contract commits the supplier and the retailer in a minimum and maximum ordered and delivered quantities respectively. Tsay and Lovejoy (1999) analyze a particular case with lead time and demand forecast actualization. Eppen and Iyer (1997) study a similar situation and call it backup agreement. Wu (2005) consider a model where quantity flexibility is related to final demand forecast and not to inventory. Vaish and Garg (2011) propose a model to determine, for a retailer, the optimal order quantity and the optimal display quantity (units of stock displayed for the customers) to transport form the warehouse to the display area. Xiao et al. (2010) study a dyadic chain, where the decisions are the order quantity and the advertising investment; they consider second ordering which is the possibility for the retailer to pass a second order of unsatisfied demand. This should not be confused with quantity flexibility. In most of the related literature, quantity flexibility corresponds to a flexibility commitment in the final command. In this work, a quantity flexibility contract is relative to inventory holding cost share, as in Cachon (2004).

Berstain and Ferguson (2005) and Nakade et al. (2011), with a game theoretical approach, consider a wholesale price with buy back contract, this is, they consider a newsvendor situation where the supplier buys back the un sold product to the multiple retailers, who compete among them by the offered prices to the supplier. This buy back situation is also identified in literature as return policies, like Qin and Xue (2010) who analyze coordination in a dyadic supply chain with return policies considering different scenarios of risk aversion preference of the companies. Cachon (2004), Emmons and Gilbert (1998) and Pasternack (1985) have studied a buy back contract under a newsvendor situation, and Padmanaghan and Png (1997) have studied this contract for multi periods. Wang and Zipkin (2009) study buy back contracts performance based on agents incentives in a dyadic supply chain. Donohue (2000) also studies a multi period under the assumption that demand forecast is updated across the time. Hou et al. (2010) consider a situation when a manufacturer has two suppliers: a main supplier, for which they define order quantity, and backup supplier, for which they define back up price. In this document, the buy back contract operates in a different way than the one in previous works for multi periods. In previous works a buy back contract correspond to a physical flow of un-sold units from the retailer to the supplier. In this work, as in Gomez-Padilla (2009) and (2011), the un-sold units are always physically at the warehouse of the retailer, but the supplier contributes to inventory holding cost by a "buy back amount". This document presents the same approach that the former ones but with actualized survey and enhanced with a numerical example.

GENERAL MODEL

It is modeled a multi-period situation where a supplier, (identified with a sub index s) supplies a product to a retailer (identified with a sub index r). The retailer controls his inventory by a base stock policy; the supplier has no capacity restrictions and the delivery lead time is null. The supplier has a production cost per unit $\mathbf{c_s}$. The retailer faces a demand over the final market and the price of the product over this final market is **p**; he has a production cost per unit $\mathbf{c_r}$. The retailer passes a command at the end of each period for the quantity necessary to complete his base stock level. The inventory holding cost per unit is $\mathbf{h_r}$. The selling price over the final market is bigger than the sum of inventory holding and production costs of the retailer ($\mathbf{p > h_r + c_r}$) and the price over the final market is bigger than the sum of production costs of the retailer and the supplier ($\mathbf{p > c_r + c_s}$).

This is the sequence of events: the supplier receives an order for a number of units. The supplier sends these units immediately to the retailer. Since they are on a situation of symmetrical information, all information is shared, so the supplier knows the price over the final market, the inventory holding cost and the production cost of the retailer, and the retailer knows the production cost of the supplier. After demand is observed, two situations may present: either demand was bigger or the same than the base stock level, so the inventory is empty, or either demand was smaller than the base stock level and there are some units in stock. In this work, unsatisfied demand or stockout are lost sales. In a lost sales context, the unsatisfied demand at one period cannot be satisfied in further periods.

In this work, demand is a stochastic stationary process. This means that the distribution of the demand is independent; the expected demand is noted $\boldsymbol{\mu}$. This variable has a density function f(y) and a distribution function F(y), where:

$$\mu = \int_0^\infty yf(y)dy$$

With the stationary hypothesis, the expected inventory level is the same at each period of time. The base stock level of the retailer is noted $\boldsymbol{Q}$. This expected stock depends on the base stock level, noted *I(Q)* and defined by:

$$I(Q) = \int_0^Q F(y)dy$$

Sales have been defined as the minimum between the expected demand and the base stock, its expected value, noted *S(Q)*, is defined by:

$$S(Q) = Q - \int_0^Q F(y)dy$$

It is possible to see that the base stock level corresponds to the sum of expected sells and expected stock.

$$Q = S(Q) + I(Q)$$

The expected stockout $B_r(Q)$ under a stationary regime is given by:

$$B_r(Q) = \mu - Q + \int_0^Q F(y)dy$$

The amount (in monetary units) transferred from the retailer to the supplier will be given by the contract, and depends on the ordered quantity at that period. The ordered quantity will actually be the physical flow since the supplier has no production capacity constraints. The flow, in number of units, will be for the number of units sold during the previous period. Since the contract has not yet been defined, it is not possible to explicit the financial transfer. At this point it is only known that the transfer is function of the base stock level Q. Its expectance will be represented as $ET(Q)$.

PROFIT MAXIMIZATION

Now it is possible to present the expected profit in a stationary regime for the retailer (noted $\pi_r(Q)$), for the supplier (noted $\pi_s(Q)$) and the expected profit for the whole supply chain (noted $\Pi(Q)$), where Q is the base stock level of the retailer.

The benefit is the difference from the incomes and the expenses. In this approach, the incomes of the retailer are the revenues from sales, and his expenses are the costs (holding inventory and production) and the financial transfer to the supplier. The revenue is calculated by the price over the final market p, and the expected sales $S(Q)$. The revenue is then: $p\,S(Q)$. The expenses are given from the holding cost of inventory ($h_r I(Q)$), production cost of units sold ($c_r S(Q)$) and the financial transfer for the units sent by the supplier ($ET(Q)$). The expected profit for the retailer $\pi_r(Q)$ is:

$$\pi_r(Q) = (p - c_r)S(Q) - h_r I(Q) - ET(Q) \qquad (1)$$

In this model, the incomes of the supplier come from the transfer from the retailer. Her only expense is the production cost of units ordered by retailer. The quantity ordered to the supplier will be for the units sold by the retailer $S(Q)$. This expectance depends on the base stock level Q fixed by the retailer. The expected profit of the supplier $\pi_s(Q)$ will be:

$$\pi_s(Q) = ET(Q) - c_s S(Q) \qquad (2)$$

The expected profit for the chain $\Pi(Q)$, is the sum of the expected profits of both companies, the retailer and the supplier:

$$\Pi(Q) = \pi_r(Q) + \pi_s(Q)$$

The expected global profit is:

$$\Pi(Q) = (p - c_r - c_s)\,S(Q) - h_r I(Q) \qquad (3)$$

The global profit is independent of the contract. The retailer and the supplier may take decisions focusing their individual benefit maximization, which may not correspond with the decisions that will maximize the profit of the whole supply chain seen as a single unit.

At this moment, without having information about the contract between the retailer and the supplier, it is possible to analyze the expected profit of the chain. The price over the final market is bigger than the sum of production cost of the retailer and the supplier ($p > c_r + c_s$). The second derivate of the expected profit of the chain is then negative and the expected profit of the chain is concave. It exist a base stock level that maximizes the expected benefit for the chain, noted $Q°$ and it corresponds to the point where the first derivate is null:

$$(p - c_r - c_s)(1 - F(Q°)) - h_r F(Q°) = 0$$

The base stock level of the retailer, which maximizes the expected profit of the chain, is the unique solution of:

$$F\left(Q^{\circ}\right) = 1 - \frac{h_r}{\left(p - c_r + h_r\right) - c_s} \qquad (4)$$

It is at this point that the financial transfer from the retailer to the supplier may be presented as a function of the contract. The objective of each company is to maximize its own profit. The decision variable of the retailer in this model is the base stock level Q. The supplier can influence this decision by intervening on the parameters of the contract.

First the situation of a simple pricing scheme contract will be presented: wholesale price. The results from a wholesale price contract will be then used to compare with two other contracts: quantity flexibility and buy back. These two contracts have in common that the supplier contributes with the inventory holding cost. In each case it is optimized the expected benefit of the retailer as a function of the base stock level Q, and the expected benefit of the supplier as a function of the contract parameters. It is analyzed the possibility of efficiently coordinate the chain, this is, the possibility of simultaneously maximize the expected benefit of the retailer, the supplier and the whole supply chain.

WHOLESALE PRICE CONTRACT

Description

A wholesale price contract is one of the simplest contracts between two companies: the retailer pays the supplier a price w per ordered unit.

The usual assumptions about the price over the final market and the transfer price are considered. The price over the final market is bigger than the sum of transfer price and the production cost of the retailer ($p > w + c_r$), to ensure that the retailer is not losing. The transfer price is bigger than the production cost of the supplier ($w > c_s$), to ensure a positive profit for the supplier.

In this contract the retailer takes the inventory holding cost in charge.

The expected transfer for a wholesale price contract is:

$$ET(Q) = w\,S(Q) \qquad (5)$$

In this section it will be studied the behavior of the retailer and the supplier under a wholesale price contract. From the side of the retailer, his decision variable is the base stock level, and he wants to optimize his expected profit. Next it is going to be studied the point of view of the supplier, who wants to optimize her own profit. In order to do so, she may intervene over the transfer price per unit w.

Retailer Decision: Base Stock Level

As it was previously explained, the behavior of the retailer under a stationary regime is as follows: he has one decision variable, which is the base stock level Q, and he wants to maximize his expected profit. His expected profit is expressed as a function of the expected sales and the expected stock.

$$\pi_r(Q) = (p - c_r - w)S(Q) - h_r I(Q) \qquad (6)$$

Given the condition that the price over the final market is bigger than the sum of the transfer price and the production cost of the retailer (***p* > *w* +** c_r), the second derivate of the expected profit is negative. It exists then a base stock level for the retailer under a wholesale price contract Q_r* that will maximize his expected profit defined by the repartition function of demand:

$$F\left(Q_r *\right) = 1 - \frac{h_r}{\left(p - c_r + h_r\right) - w} \quad (7)$$

Comparing this expression with the base stock level that maximizes the expected benefit of the whole supply chain *F(Q°)*, and given that the price per unit is bigger than the production cost of the retailer $w > c_s$, it is possible to realize that: ***F(Q$_r$*) < F(Q°)***.

In other words, with a wholesale price contract the retailer will decide to hold a base stock level smaller than the base stock that maximizes the expected profit of the supply chain. Under this situation it is the retailer who takes in charge the inventory holding costs. It is important to highlight that both base stock levels (the one optimal for the retailer *F(Q*)*, and the one optimal for the supply chain *F(Q°)*) may be equal if the transfer price ***w*** is equal to the production cost c_s of the supplier (comparing Equations 4 and 7), but then the supplier will have a null profit.

Supplier Decision: Wholesale Price

$$\pi_s(Q,w) = (w - c_s)\ S(Q) \quad (8)$$

The profit of the supplier increases if the retailer orders more (if the quantity ordered by the retailer increases). She maximizes her profit if the base stock level corresponds to the maximal expected demand over the final market. With a wholesale price contract there are no inventory holding costs for the supplier, so she wants the retailer to always have enough units in stock to satisfy demand. It was possible to see that the retailer will not do so because he will not want to increase his inventory holding costs. Since information is symmetrical, the supplier knows that the retailer will decide his base stock level from (7). The supplier will be able to influence the decision of the retailer by intervening over the price *w*. The relation between the transfer price and the optimal base stock level *Q* for the retailer is:

$$w\left(Q\right) = p - c_r - h_r \frac{F\left(Q\right)}{1 - F\left(Q\right)} \quad (9)$$

The supplier may then determine *Q* (and also *w*) in order to optimize her own profit. The optimal quantity will null the derivate of:

$$\pi_s\left(Qw\left(Q\right) = p - c - h_r \frac{F\left(Q\right)}{1 - F\left(Q\right)} - c_s\right) S\left(Q\right) \quad (10)$$

The optimal base stock level (to be hold by the retailer) for the supplier solves this equation:

$$(p - c_r - c_s)(1 - F(Q)\ )^3 - h_r F(Q)(1 - F(Q))^2$$
$$-h_r\left(Q - \int_0^Q F\ (y)dy\right)\frac{\partial}{\partial Q}F(Q) = 0 \quad (11)$$

The supplier will fix her optimal transfer price

$$w* = p - c_r - h_r \frac{F\left(Q^*\right)}{1 - F\left(Q^*\right)}$$

knowing that the retailer will decide his base stock level from this price.

Coordination of a Wholesale Price Contract

In the case of a wholesale contract, the retailer and the supplier will arrive to coordinate but this coordination will not be efficient since this will not correspond to the profit maximization of the chain. As it was previously seen, since the wholesale price is smaller than the production cost of the retailer, the optimal base stock level for the retailer will not be the same than the optimal base stock level for the supplier. The supplier will not accept to offer a wholesale price equal to her production cost per unit since her profit would then be zero.

QUANTITY FLEXIBILITY

Description

With a quantity flexibility contract, the price asked by the supplier is w* (the optimal transfer price in the case of a wholesale price contract), but she will pay the inventory holding cost for as much as δQ of the stock (where $\delta \in [0,1]$). The supplier will take in charge the inventory holding cost of part of the units in stock.

The expected transfer is:

$$ET(Q) = w * S(Q) - h_r \int_{(1-\delta)Q}^{Q} F(y) dy \tag{12}$$

The expected transfer depends on the base stock level and on the parameter $\boldsymbol{\delta}$. The particular case where $\boldsymbol{\delta=0}$ corresponds to the wholesale price contract already analyzed. In the case where $\boldsymbol{\delta}=1$, the supplier completely takes in charge the inventory holding cost.

Retailer Decision: Base Stock Level

The expected profit for the retailer with the expected transfer for a quantity flexibility contract will be,

$$\pi_r(Q) = (p - c_r) S(Q) - h_r 1(Q)$$

for a stationary regime:

$$-w * S(Q) + h_r \int_{(1-\delta)Q}^{Q} F(y) dy \tag{13}$$

The second derivate of the expected profit is negative for Q and δ.

If $\boldsymbol{\delta=0}$, the base stock level which maximizes the expected profit of the retailer for a quantity flexibility contract $Q^F_{r\ \delta=0}$ is the same calculated for a wholesale price contract. If $\boldsymbol{\delta=1}$, all the inventory holding cost will be taken in charge by the supplier; in this situation the retailer will want to have a base stock equal to the maximum expected demand so that he will completely satisfy demand. In the other cases ($0 < \delta < 1$), the equation that will solve considering δ and Q is:

$$(p - c_r - w^*)(1 - F(Q)) - h_r (1-\delta) F((1-\delta)Q) = 0 \tag{14}$$

Supplier Decision: Quantity in Stock for Which to Pay Holding Cost

Under a context of quantity flexibility contract the expected profit for the supplier is:

$$\pi_s(Q) = w * S(Q) - h_r \int_{(1-\delta)Q}^{Q} F(y) dy - c_s S(Q) \tag{15}$$

It will now be analyzed, as previously done for a retailer for a fix transfer price per unit w^*

(wholesale price contract), the base stock level to be held by the retailer that is better for the supplier. If ***δ=0***, which corresponds to a wholesale price contract, the base stock level that maximizes the expected profit of the supplier is the one that allows the retailer to satisfy the maximal demand (defined by $F(Q_{r\ \delta=0}^{F}) = 1$). Indeed, in this case the entire inventory holding cost is assumed by the retailer. If ***δ=1***, for a fix transfer price w^*, the base stock level that maximizes the expected profit of the supplier is lower than the maximal demand ($F(Q_{r\ \delta=1}^{F}) < 1$), since the supplier takes in charge all the inventory holding costs. For a quantity flexibility contract, and for a fix transfer price w^* per unit, the supplier will be interested in that the retailer will not hold too much stock, since now she will participate of this cost.

Coordination of a Quantity Flexibility Contract

In the wholesale price contract, for a fix unitary price w^*, the retailer was interested in holding an inventory base stock smaller than the one that was convenient for the supplier, and the supplier wanted the retailer to hold enough stock to satisfy de maximal demand.

The optimal base stock levels in terms of profit maximization for the supplier and the retailer are respectively solution of the first derivate of (13) and (15), and are function of δ.

The supplier must consider the behavior of the retailer and must offer a δ that will make that both profit expectances (for retailer and supplier) will be simultaneously maximized. This is, a δ that: $F(Q_s^F) = F(Q_r^F)$ and $F((1-\delta)\ Q_s^F) = F((1-\delta)\ Q_r^F)$.

The system of two equations formed by the first derivate of (13) and (15) when they are equal to 0, conducts to:

$$(p - c_r - c_s + h_r)\ (1 - F(Q_s^F)) - h_r F(Q_s^F) = 0 \quad (16)$$

In the case when a δ exist that satisfies previous equations, the expected profit of the chain is optimized. This is that $F(Q_r^F) = F(Q_s^F) = F(Q°)$, or in specific base stock level $Q_r^F = Q_s^F = Q°$, this way the base stock level that optimizes the profit of the retailer and the supplier also optimizes the expected profit for the whole chain:

$$\left(1-\delta\right)F\left(\left(1-\delta\right)Q^{\circ}\right) = \frac{p - c_r - w^*}{p - c_r - c_s + h_r} \quad (17)$$

The equation has one solution for δ over [0 ;1]. In fact, the function defined by $\delta \rightarrow (1-\delta)\ F((1-\delta)Q)$, is continuous and decreasing over [0 ;1]. Then for $\delta \in [0\ ;1]$, the expression varies from $F(Q°)$ to 0. This is that

$$0 \le \frac{p - c_r - w^*}{p - c_r - c_s + h_r} \le F\left(Q^{\circ}\right)$$

and then the equation admits a unique solution noted δ^*.

The supplier may then propose a way to share inventory holding cost that will efficiently coordinate the chain.

BUY BACK CONTRACT

Description

In the case of a quantity flexibility contract, the chain is efficiently coordinated by the supplier participating on the total inventory holding cost of part of the stock. In a buy back contract, it is explored the case where the supplier supports partially the inventory holding sock for the whole stock. It is important to not to confuse this situation with the one of a quantity flexibility contract for δ=1, which is the case where the supplier takes completely in charge the inventory holding cost for the whole stock. From a wholesale price w^* known, the supplier will try to decide the "buy back" price that will represent her contribution to inventory holding cost and that will allow her to maximize her profit.

In a buy back contract the unitary price to pay to the supplier is w^*, but the supplier pays to the retailer an amount b per unit in stock. Remember that $(p > w^* + c_r)$ and $(w^* > c_s)$. The inventory holding cost of the retailer is bigger than the contribution of the supplier to the holding cost in order to avoid that holding cost become an income to the retailer $(h_r > b)$.

The transfer is given by the price w^* per unit ordered minus the amount b per un-sold units resting in stock. Under the stationary hypothesis, the expected units to order is equal to the expected sales $S(Q)$, and the expected inventory $I(Q)$ is independent of the period of time. The expected transfer for the buy back contract is:

$$ET\left(Q\right) = w * S\left(Q\right) - bI\left(Q\right) \qquad (18)$$

Next there will be analyzed the expected profit for the retailer and the supplier.

Retailer Decision: Base Stock Level

The expected profit for the retailer for a buy back contract is:

$$\pi_r(Q) = (p - c_r - w^*)S(Q) - (h_r - b)\, I(Q) \qquad (19)$$

The second derivate of the expected profit of the retailer is negative for a buy back price b smaller than $p - c_r - w^* + h_r$; it exist then a base stock level Q_r^B for the retailer that maximizes his expected profit. This level, for a fix unitary price w^* is:

$$F\left(Q_r^B\right) = 1 - \frac{h_r - b}{\left(p - c_r + h_r\right) - \left(w^* + b\right)} \qquad (20)$$

Knowing that $(w^*+b) > c_s$, and $(h_r - b) < h_r$, it is not possible to make general conclusions about $F(Q_r^B)$ and $F(Q°)$. In the particular case of a quantity flexibility contract for $\delta=1$, the base stock level of a buy back contract $F(Q_r^B)$ is smaller than the base stock level obtained from a quantity flexibility contract $F(Q_r^F)$ (when $\delta=1$). Indeed, for a quantity flexibility contract with $\delta=1$ the supplier supports all the inventory holding cost and in a buy back contract, the supplier contributes with inventory holding cost. For this reason the retailer is interested in having a smaller base stock with a quantity flexibility contract than for a buy back contract.

Supplier Decision: Buy Back Price

The expected profit for the supplier as a function of the base stock level is:

$$\pi_s(Q) = (w^* - c_s)\, S(Q) - b\, I(Q) \qquad (21)$$

The second derivate is negative and the base stock level Q_s^B that maximizes the expected profit of the supplier is, for a unitary price w^*:

$$F\left(Q_s^B\right) = 1 - \frac{b}{w^* - c_s + b} \qquad (22)$$

For a fix unitary price w^*, the base stock level of the retailer that maximizes the expected profit of the supplier is smaller than the maximal demand level because the supplier shares the holding cost with the retailer. If compared with $F(Q_s^F)$ of a quantity flexibility contract for $\delta=1$, the base stock level of a buy back contract $F(Q_s^B)$ is bigger. In fact, in a quantity flexibility contract for $\delta=1$, it is the supplier who takes in charge all the inventory holding stock, while in a buy back contract the supplier just takes in charge a part of this cost.

Coordination of a Buy Back Contract

It will be possible to efficiently coordinate the chain under certain conditions.

The base stock levels that will maximize the expected profit for the supplier and the retailer are respectively solution of (20) and (22), and are function of buy back price ***b***. The supplier must take into account the behavior of the retailer and propose a buy back price ***b*** so that both expected profits (of retailer and supplier) will be simultaneously maximized; this is a ***b*** for which $Q_s^B = Q_r^B$.

The profit of the chain is maximized if $Q_r^B = Q_s^B = Q°$, so the supplier may fix a buy back price b that will incite the retailer to establish $Q°$ as his base stock level.

Deducing from (20):

$$b = h_r - \frac{(p - c_r - w^*)(1 - F(Q°))}{F(Q°)} \tag{23}$$

Then, by substitution of $F(Q°)$ from (4), the unitary buy back price that maximizes the expected profit of the chain and that allows to efficiently coordinate the chain is:

$$b = h_r(1 - \frac{p - c_r - w^*}{p - c_r - c_s}) \tag{24}$$

For a buy back contract as presented in this document, it is possible to efficiently coordinate the supply chain, and in this way simultaneously maximize the expected profit for the supplier, the retailer and the chain.

NUMERICAL EXAMPLE

In order to illustrate the previous results, a numerical analysis is handled. The costs considered were as follows: price of the product over final market: **p**= 16; production cost per unit for supplier: $\mathbf{c_s}$ = 2; production cost per unit for retailer: $\mathbf{c_r}$ = 1; inventory holding cost per unit for retailer: $\mathbf{h_r}$=2.

With this information, the supplier will have to determine the price w that she will offer to the retailer. For simplicity we are considering a uniformly distributed demand, going from 0 to 1, this is:

$$F(Q) = \frac{Q. - a}{b - a} for\ a \leq Q \leq b$$

It is considered b=1 and a=0 so that the base stock may be interpreted as a percentage of the maximum possible finite demand (which will be 1 in this case).

The next figure (Figure 1) show the analysis handled by the supplier. Over de horizontal axis the base stock is represented, and over the vertical axis, the profit for the supplier, the retailer and the chain as a function of the wholesale price. The wholesale price depends on the base stock level of the retailer, this is: w(Q).

The maximum profit for the supplier is attaint if w=12.12, and by offering this price, the retailer will have a base stock corresponding to the 60% of the maximum possible demand. For the retailer, the lower the price is, the more his profit increase and the bigger the base stock he will carry. The maximum profit for the chain will be attaint if the supplier fixes w=3.67 and the optimal base stock will correspond to the 85% of the maximum possible demand. As previously explained, it is important to attend the efficiency of this coordination.

The supplier will ask the retailer w=12.12; Figure 2 shows the analysis that will be done by the supplier after receiving the information of the price.

As previously explained, the supplier will then decide to hold a base stock level Q=60% of the maximum possible demand.

When the dyadic chain works under a quantity flexibility contract, the supplier will pay the inventory holding cost for δ Q. If the supplier and the

Figure 1. Analysis to determine the wholesale price

Figure 2. Analysis to determining the base stock for w=12.12

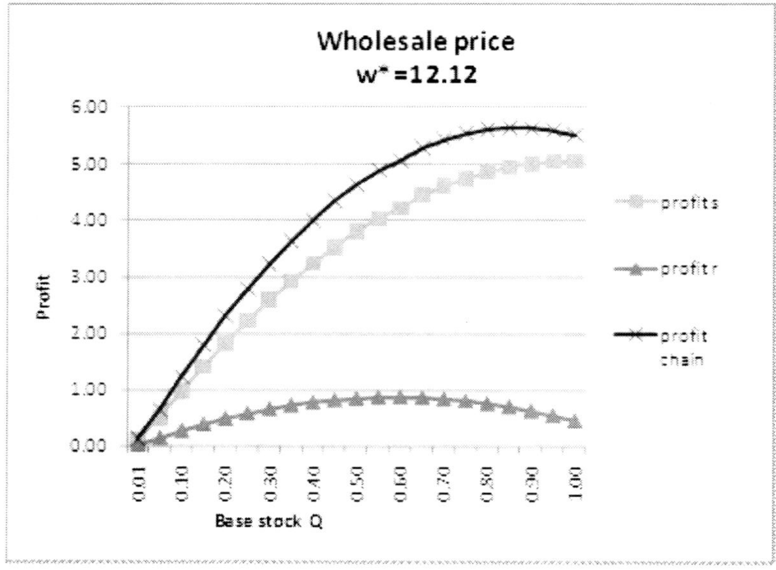

retailer agree on δ=0.53, the retailer will modify the base stock to Q=90% of the maximum expected demand, and the chain will be coordinated. This is, the retailer, the supplier and the chain will simultaneously maximize their profits. This is shown over Figure 3.

If operating with a buy back contract, the supplier will pay part of the inventory holding stock. If the companies agree on b=1.55 (Figure 4), as

Figure 3. Coordination for quantity flexibility contract

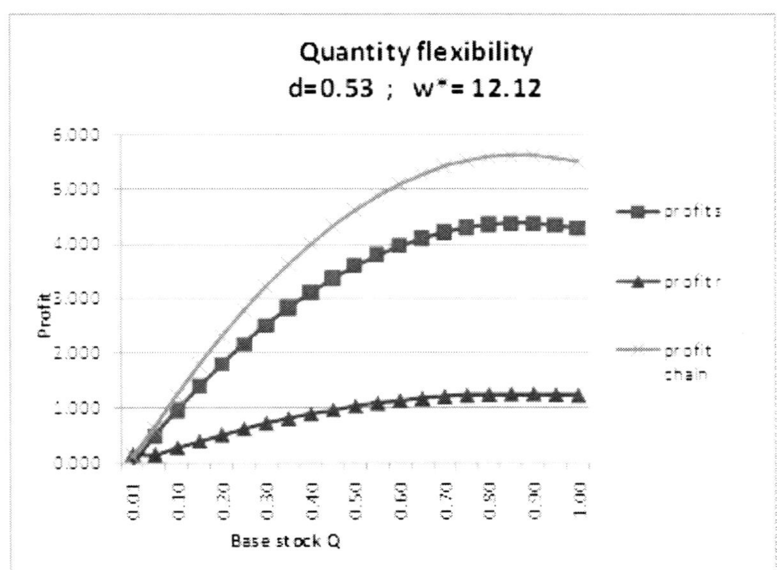

Figure 4. Coordination for buy back contract

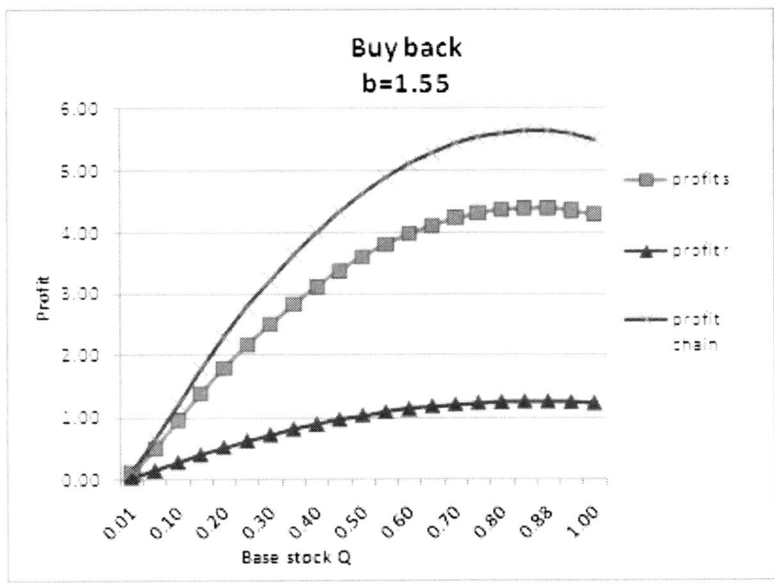

with the quantity flexibility contract, the retailer will increase the base stock and the chain will achieve coordination.

The two contracts may then coordinate the chain. With both contracts the supplier, the retailer and the chain will maximize simultaneously their profit, but the supplier will always have a significantly higher benefit that the retailer since it is she who fixes the price.

CONCLUSION

With the approach presented on this document, it was possible to highlight the impacts that the contract conditions have over the companies and on the coordination of the dyadic supply chain. The general model was presented without considering the type of contract. The base stock level for the retailer that maximizes the expected profit for the chain was next determined. The study continued with an analysis of a wholesale price contract. In this contract the supplier fix the price and the retailer decide his base stock level. The supplier had complete information about the retailer, so she fixed a price that would make the retailer fix a base stock level that will maximize her own profit. The base stock level fixed by the retailer is different than the base stock level that maximizes the supply chain expected profit. It was possible to conclude that a wholesale price contract will coordinate the chain by forced compliance, but it will not efficiently coordinate the chain. Next, two contracts where the supplier shares the inventory holding cost were presented and analyzed: quantity flexibility and buy back. The difference of the contracts relies on how the supplier will participate of the inventory holding cost. In a wholesale price contract the supplier will not worry about this cost and retailer completely take it in charge. In the quantity flexibility contract: quantity flexibility the supplier engages to assume the inventory holding cost for a maximum limit of the base stock level. With a quantity flexibility contract, it is possible to propose a maximum limit of the base stock level to be paid by the supplier. This limit will simultaneously maximize the expected benefits for the retailer, the supplier and the whole supply chain. In a buy back contract, the supplier engages to pay part of the inventory holding cost for the entire inventory being held by the retailer. It is possible to propose a buy back sum that will maximize the expected revenue for the supplier and the retailer, efficiently coordinating the supply chain. The sequence of events was explained with a numerical example.

It was shown that contracts where inventory holding cost is shared between the members of the chain may efficiently coordinate a supply chain when information is symmetrical and by establishing the contract parameters that will maximize their profit.

REFERENCES

Anupindi, R., & Bassok, Y. (2002). Supply contracts with quantity commitments and stochastic demandIn Tayur, S., Ganeshan, R., & Magazine, M. (Eds.), *Quantitative models for supply chain management* (pp. 197–232). Kluwer Academic Publishers. doi:10.1007/978-1-4615-4949-9_7

APICS. (2009). *Operations management body of knowledge framework* (2nd ed.). The Association for Operations Management.

Arshinder, K. A., & Deshmukh, S. G. (2009). A framework for evaluation of coordination by contracts: A case of two-level supply chains. *Computers & Industrial Engineering*, *56*(4), 1177–1191. doi:10.1016/j.cie.2008.03.014

Axsater, S. (2001). A framework for decentralized multi-echelon inventory control. *IIE Transactions*, *33*, 91–97. doi:10.1080/07408170108936810

Bernstein, F., & Federgruen, A. (2005). Decentralized supply chains with competing retailers under demand uncertainty*Management Science*, *51*, 18–29. doi:10.1287/mnsc.1040.0218

Cachon, G. P. (2004). Supply chain coordination with contractsIn De Kok, A. G., & Grave, S. C. (Eds.), *Handbooks in operations research and management science, 11: Supply chain management: Design, coordination and operation* (pp. 229–339). Elsevier B.V.

Crespo-Marquez, A., & Blanchar, C. (2004). The procurement of strategic parts: Analysis of a portfolio of contracts with suppliers using a system dynamics simulation model. *International Journal of Production Economics*, *88*, 29–49. doi:10.1016/S0925-5273(03)00177-4

De Kok, A. G., & Grave, S. C. (Eds.). (2004). *Handbooks in operations research and management science, 11: Supply chain management: design, coordination and operation*. Elsevier B.V.

Dong, Y., Xu, K., & Dresner, M. (2007). Environmental determinants of VMI adoption: An exploratory analysis. *Transportation Research Part E, Logistics and Transportation Review*, *43*(4), 355–369. doi:10.1016/j.tre.2006.01.004

Donohue, K. (2000). Efficient supply contracts for fashion goods with forecast updating and two production modes. *Management Science*, *46*(11), 1397–1411. doi:10.1287/mnsc.46.11.1397.12088

El Sodany, N. H. (2011). Periodic review probabilistic multi-item inventory system with zero lead time under constraint and varying holding cost. *Journal of Mathematics and Statistics*, *7*(1), 12–19. doi:10.3844/jmssp.2011.12.19

Emmons, H., & Gilbert, S. (1998). Return policies in pricing and inventory decisions for catalogue goods. *Management Science*, *44*(2), 276–283. doi:10.1287/mnsc.44.2.276

Eppen, G., & Iyer, A. (1997). Backup agreements in fashion buying: The value of upstream flexibility. *Management Science*, *43*(11), 1469–1484. doi:10.1287/mnsc.43.11.1469

Froehlichner, T., & Vendemini, S. (1999). *Connivences d'acteurs, contrats, coopération interentreprises et métamorphose des organizations*. Paris, France: Presses Universitaires de Nancy.

Gomez-Padilla, A. (2009). Supply chain coordination by contracts with inventory holding cost share. *International Journal of Information Systems and Supply Chain Management*, *2*(2), 36–47. doi:10.4018/jisscm.2009040103

Gomez-Padilla, A. (2011). Contracts based on inventory cost share for supply chain coordinationIn Wang, J. (Ed.), *Supply chain optimization, management and integration: Emerging applications* (pp. 126–138). Hershey, PA: IGI Global. doi:10.4018/978-1-60960-135-5.ch009

Hou, J., Zeng, A. Z., & Zhao, L. (2010). Coordination with a backup supplier through buy-back contract under supply disruption. *Transportation Research Part E: Logistics and Transportation*, *46*(6), 881–895. doi:10.1016/j.tre.2010.03.004

Kamrad, B., & Siddique, A. (2004). Supply contracts, profit sharing, switching, and reaction options. *Management Science*, *50*(1), 64–82. doi:10.1287/mnsc.1030.0157

Lariviere, M. A. (2002). Supply chain contracting and coordination with stochastic demandIn Tayur, S., Ganeshan, R., & Magazine, M. (Eds.), *Quantitative models for supply chain management* (pp. 233–268). Kluwer Academic Publishers. doi:10.1007/978-1-4615-4949-9_8

Lian, Z., & Deshmukh, A. (2009). Analysis of supply contracts with quantity flexibility. *European Journal of Operational Research*, *196*(2), 526–533. doi:10.1016/j.ejor.2008.02.043

Liang, Y., Zuo, X., & Lei, H. (2011). Research on supply chain coordination of TPL supplier participation. *Journal of Service Science and Management*, *4*(1), 1–7. doi:10.4236/jssm.2011.41001

Liu, L., & Wang, L. (2007). Management strategy of materials supply for manufacturing organizations. *Computers & Industrial Engineering*, *53*(2), 326–349. doi:10.1016/j.cie.2007.06.026

Nakade, K., Tsubouchi, S., & Sediri, I. (2010). Properties of Nash equilibrium retail prices in contract model with a supplier, multiple retailers and price-dependent demand. *Journal of Software Engineering and Applications*, *3*(1), 27–33. doi:10.4236/jsea.2010.31003

Padmanabhan, V., & Png, I. P. L. (1997). Manufacturer's returns policy and retail competition. *Marketing Science*, *16*(1), 81–94. doi:10.1287/mksc.16.1.81

Pasternack, B. (1985). Optimal pricing and returns policies for perishable commodities. *Marketing Science*, *4*(2), 166–176. doi:10.1287/mksc.4.2.166

Praharsi, Y., Purnomo, H. D., & Wee, H. M. (2010). An innovative heuristic for joint replenishment problem with deterministic and stochastic demand. *International Journal of Electronic Business Management*, *8*(3), 223–230.

Qin, Z., & Xue, X. (2010). Risk averse members coordination with extended buy-back contract. *Journal of Service Science and Management*, *3*(1), 23–32. doi:10.4236/jssm.2010.31003

Scandizzo, P. L., & Ventura, M. (2010). Sharing risk through concession contracts. *European Journal of Operational Research*, *207*(1), 363–370. doi:10.1016/j.ejor.2010.04.008

Schneeweiss, C., Zimmer, K., & Zimmermann, M. (2004). The design of contracts to coordinate operational interdependencies within the supply chain. *International Journal of Production Economics*, *92*, 43–59. doi:10.1016/j.ijpe.2003.10.005

Sepehri, M. (2011). Cost and inventory benefits of cooperation in multi-period and multi-product supply. *Scientia Iranica Transactions EIndustrial Engineering (American Institute of Industrial Engineers)*, *18*(3).

Tayur, S., Ganeshan, R., & Magazine, M. (Eds.). (2003). *Quantitative models for supply chain management* (6th ed.). Kluwer Academic Publishers.

Tirole, J. (1988). *The theory of industrial organization*. Cambridge, MA: M.I.T. Press.

Tsay, A. A. (1999). The quantity flexibility contract and supplier-costumer incentives. *Management Science*, *45*(10), 1339–1358. doi:10.1287/mnsc.45.10.1339

Tsay, A. A., & Lovejoy, W. S. (1999). Quantity flexibility contracts and supply chain performance. *Manufacturing and Service Operations Management*, *1*(2), 89–111. doi:10.1287/msom.1.2.89

Tseng, L. T., Tseng, L. F., & Chen, H. C. (2011). Exploration of the bullwhip effect based on the evolutionary least mean square algorithm. *International Journal of Electronic Business Management*, *9*(2), 160–168.

Tyan, J., & Wee, H. M. (2003). Vendor managed inventory: A survey of the Taiwanese grocery industry. *Journal of Purchasing and Supply Management*, *9*(1), 11–18. doi:10.1016/S0969-7012(02)00032-1

Vaish, B., & Garg, G. (2011). Optimal ordering and transfer policy for an inventory system with time dependent holding cost and three component demand rate. *Journal of Mathematics Research*, *3*(2), 212–223. doi:10.5539/jmr.v3n2p212

van der Vlist, P., Kuik, R., & Verheijen, B. (2007). Note on supply chain integration in vendor-managed inventory. *Decision Support Systems*, *44*(1), 360–365. doi:10.1016/j.dss.2007.03.003

Wang, K. H., Tung, C. T., Chien, C. L., & Hung, F. C. (2010). A deteriorating two-item inventory model with continuously decreasing demand and retroactive holding cost. *Journal of International Management Studies*, *5*(1), 10–18.

Wang, Y., & Zipkin, P. (2009). Agents' incentives under buy-back contracts in a two-stage supply chain. *International Journal of Production Economics*, *120*(2), 525–539. doi:10.1016/j.ijpe.2009.04.008

Weng, Z. K. (1999). The power of coordinated decisions for short life cycle products in a manufacturing and distribution supply chain. *IIE Transactions*, *31*(11), 1037–1049. doi:10.1080/07408179908969905

Wu, J. (2005). Quantity flexibility contracts under Bayesian updating. *Computers & Operations Research*, *32*(5), 1267–1288. doi:10.1016/j.cor.2003.11.004

Xiao, T., Yan, X., & Zhao, J. (2010). Coordination of a supply chain with advertising investment and allowing the second ordering. *Technology and Investment*, *1*(3), 191–200. doi:10.4236/ti.2010.13022

Yang, J., & Qi, X. (2009). On the design of coordinating contracts. *International Journal of Production Economics*, *122*(2), 581–594. doi:10.1016/j.ijpe.2009.06.002

Yao, Y., Evers, P. T., & Dresner, M. E. (2007). Supply chain integration in vendor-managed inventory. *Decision Support Systems*, *43*(2), 663–674. doi:10.1016/j.dss.2005.05.021

Compilation of References

Aaker, D., Kumar, V., & Day, G. S. (2000). *Marketing research*. New York, NY: John Wiley & Sons, Inc.

Advanced Technology Institute. (2001). *Defense sustainment consortium. Strategic Investment Plan, Contract: N00140-01-C-L622* (p. 29418). SC: North Charleston.

Agard, B., & Kusiak, A. (2004). *A standardization of components, products and processes with data mining.* International Conference on Production Research Americas, Santiago, Chile, August 1-4.

Agarwal, A., Shankar, R., & Tiwari, M. K. (2007). Modeling agility of supply chain. *Industrial Marketing Management*, *36*(4), 443–457. doi:10.1016/j.indmarman.2005.12.004

Agripino, M., Cathcart, T., & Mathaisel, D. F. X. (2002). A lean sustainment enterprise model for military systems. *Acquisition Review Quarterly, August*, 274-297.

Ahgren, B. (2010). Mutualism and antagonism within organisations of integrated health care. *Journal of Health Organization and Management*, *24*(4), 396–411.

Ainscough, M., & Yazdani, B. (2000). Concurrent engineering within British industry. *Concurrent Engineering: Research and Applications*, *8*(1), 2–11.

Ajmal, M. M., Helo, P., & Kekäle, T. (2010). Critical factors for KM in project business. *Journal of Knowledge Management*, *14*(1), 156–168. doi:10.1108/13673271011015633

Akkermans, H. A., Bogerd, P., Yucesan, E., & van Wassenhove, L. N. (2003). The impact of ERP on supply chain management: Exploratory findings from European Delphi study. *European Journal of Operational Research*, *146*, 284–301. doi:10.1016/S0377-2217(02)00550-7

Alcrecht, K. (1992). *The only thing that matters*. New York, NY: Harper-Collins.

Allee, V. (2002). *The future of knowledge: Increasing prosperity through value networks*. Boston, MA: Butterworth-Heinemann.

Allen, T. (2010). *Introduction to engineering statistics and lean sigma* (2nd ed.). New York, NY: Springer. doi:10.1007/978-1-84996-000-7

Al-Mudimigha, A. S., Zairib, M., & Ahmed, A. M. (2004). Extending the concept of supply chain: The effective management of value chains. *International Journal of Production Economics*, *87*, 309–320.

Alukal, G., & Manos, A. (2006). *Lean kaizen: A simplified approach to process improvements*. Milwaukee, WI: American Society of Quality Press.

American Society of Quality Control (ASQ). (2011). *Definition of quality*. Retrieved January 25, 2011, from http://asq.org/glossary/q.html

American Society of Quality Control (ASQ). (2011). The history of quality – Overview. Retrieved January 25, 2011, from http://asq.org/ learn-about-quality/ history-of-quality/overview/ overview.html

Anderson, E. W., Fornell, C., & Lehman, D. R. (1994). Customer satisfaction, market share and profitability: Findings from Sweden. *Journal of Marketing*, *58*(July), 53–66. doi:10.2307/1252310

Anderson, E., & Weitz, B. (1992). The use of pledges to build and sustain commitment in distribution channels. *JMR, Journal of Marketing Research*, *29*(1), 18–35. doi:10.2307/3172490

Anderson, J., & Narus, J. (1990). A model of distributor firm and manufacturer firm working partnerships. *Journal of Marketing*, *54*(1), 42–58. doi:10.2307/1252172

Andraski, J. C. (1998). Leadership and the realization of supply chain collaboration. *Journal of Business Logistics*, *19*(2), 9.

Andriole, S. (2009). Entering the cloud: Phased adoption to computing nirvana. *Cutter IT Journal*, *22*, 32–37.

Anthony, M. K., & Hudson-Barr, D. (2004). A patient-centered model of care for hospital discharge. *Clinical Nursing Research*, *13*(2), 117–136. doi:10.1177/1054773804263165

Anton, B. B., Schafer, J. J., Micenko, A., Wolf, D. M., DiNucci, S., & Donovan, P. (2009). Clinical decision support. How CDS tools impact patient care outcomes. *Journal of Healthcare Information Management*, *23*(1), 39–45.

Anupindi, R., & Bassok, Y. (2002). Supply contracts with quantity commitments and stochastic demandIn Tayur, S., Ganeshan, R., & Magazine, M. (Eds.), *Quantitative models for supply chain management* (pp. 197–232). Kluwer Academic Publishers. doi:10.1007/978-1-4615-4949-9_7

APICS. (2009). *Operations management body of knowledge framework* (2nd ed.). The Association for Operations Management.

Archer, N., Wang, S., & Kang, C. (2008). Barriers to the adoption of online supply chain solutions in small and medium enterprises. *Supply Chain Management: An International Journal*, *13*(1), 73. doi:10.1108/13598540810850337

Arshinder, A. K., & Deshmukh, S. G. (2008). Supply chain coordination: Perspectives, empirical studies and research directions. *International Journal of Production Economics*, *115*, 316–335. doi:10.1016/j.ijpe.2008.05.011

Arshinder, K. A., & Deshmukh, S. G. (2009). A framework for evaluation of coordination by contracts: A case of two-level supply chains. *Computers & Industrial Engineering*, *56*(4), 1177–1191. doi:10.1016/j.cie.2008.03.014

Atkinson, W. (2008). 12 steps to more effective supplier relationships. *Purchasing*, *137*(5), 17.

Attaran, M. (2007). RFID: An enabler of supply chain operations. *Supply Chain Management: An International Journal*, *12*(4), 249–257. doi:10.1108/13598540710759763

Axsater, S. (2001). A framework for decentralized multi-echelon inventory control. *IIE Transactions*, *33*, 91–97. doi:10.1080/07408170108936810

Aydin, M. E., & Fogarty, T. C. (2004). A simulated annealing algorithm for multi-agent systems: A job shop scheduling application. *Journal of Intelligent Manufacturing*, *15*(6), 805–814. doi:10.1023/B:JIMS.0000042665.10086.cf

Aytug, H., Lawley, M. A., McKay, K., Mohan, S., & Uzsoy, R. (2005). Executing production schedules in the face of uncertainties: A review and some future directions. *European Journal of Operational Research*, *161*(1), 86–110. doi:10.1016/j.ejor.2003.08.027

Babin, B. J., Hair, J. F. Jr, Anderson, R. E., & Black, W. C. (2010). *Multivariate data analysis*. Upper Saddle River, NJ: Pearson Education Inc.

Bakar, A. H. A., Hakim, I. L., Chong, S. C., & Lin, B. (2009). Measuring supply chain performance among public hospital laboratories. *International Journal of Productivity and Performance Management*, *59*(1), 75–97. doi:10.1108/17410401011006121

Baker, G. R., Norton, P. G., Flintoft, V., Blais, R., Brown, A., & Cox, J. (2004). The Canadian adverse events study: The incidence of adverse events among hospital patients in Canada. *Canadian Medical Association Journal*, *170*(11), 1678–1686. doi:10.1503/cmaj.1040498

Balbontin, A. (2000). New product development practices in American and British firms. *Technovation*, *20*, 257–274. doi:10.1016/S0166-4972(99)00136-4

Baldwin, C., & Clark, K. (2000). *Design rules, Vol. 1: The power of modularity*. MIT Press. ISBN 0-262-024667

Baldwin, M. L., Butler, R. J., & Johnson, W. G. (2001). A hierarchical theory of occupational segregation and wage discrimination. *Economic Inquiry*, *39*(1), 94–110. doi:10.1093/ei/39.1.94

Bal, J., & Teo, P. K. (2000). Implementing virtual team working: Part 1 - A literature review of best practice. *Logistics Information Management*, *13*(6), 346. doi:10.1108/09576050010355644

Bal, J., & Teo, P. K. (2001). Implementing virtual team working: Part 2 - A literature review. *Logistics Information Management*, *14*(3), 208. doi:10.1108/09576050110390248

Bal, J., & Teo, P. K. (2001a). Implementing virtual team working: Part 3 – A methodology for introducing virtual team working. *Logistics Information Management*, *14*(4), 276. doi:10.1108/EUM0000000005722

Ballé, M., & Régnier, A. (2007a). From cars to catheters: Adapting lean principles within a healthcare environment. *Development and Learning in Organizations*, *21*(4), 28–30. doi:10.1108/14777280710758871

Ballé, M., & Régnier, A. (2007b). Lean as a learning system in a hospital ward. *Leadership in Health Services*, *20*(1), 33–41. doi:10.1108/17511870710721471

Ballou, R. H., Gilbert, S. M., & Mukherjee, A. (2000). New managerial challenges from supply chain opportunities. *Industrial Marketing Management*, *29*(1), 7–18. doi:10.1016/S0019-8501(99)00107-8

Bandyopadhyay, J. K., & Jenicke, L. O. (2007). Six Sigma approach to quality assurance in global supply chains: A study of United States automakers. *International Journal of Management*, *24*(1).

Barba, E. (2001). *Ingeniera Concurrente. Gua parasuImplantacio'n enla Empresa*. Barcelona: Diagnostico y Evaluacion Gestion.

Barber, E. (2009). How to measure the value in the value chains. *International Journal of Physical Distribution & Logistics Management*, *38*(9), 685–698. doi:10.1108/09600030810925971

Barrat, M. (2004). Understanding the meaning of collaboration in the supply chain. *Supply Chain Management*, *9*(1), 30. doi:10.1108/13598540410517566

Barsky, J. (1994). *World-class customer satisfaction*. Burr Ridge, IL: Irwin Professional Publishing.

Bateman, N., & David, A. (2002). Process improvement programmes: A model for assessing sustainability. *International Journal of Operations & Production Management*, *22*(5), 515–526. doi:10.1108/01443570210425156

Batson, R. G., & Elam, M. E. (2002). *Robust design: An experiment-based approach to design for reliability conference*. MARCON.

Baum, J. A. C., & Ingram, P. (1998). Survival-enhancing learning in the Manhattan hotel industry, 1898-1980. *Management Science*, *44*(7), 996–1016. doi:10.1287/mnsc.44.7.996

Becker, H. S. (1983). Scenarios: A tool of growing importance to policy analysts in government and industry. *Technological Forecasting and Social Change*, *23*, 95–120. doi:10.1016/0040-1625(83)90049-5

Bentler, P. M. (1990). Comparative fit indexes in structural equation models. *Psychological Bulletin*, *107*(2), 238–246. doi:10.1037/0033-2909.107.2.238

Bentler, P. M. (1992). On the fit of models to covariance and methodology to the bulletin. *Psychological Bulletin*, *112*(3), 400–404. doi:10.1037/0033-2909.112.3.400

Benton, W. C., & Maloni, M. (2005). The influence of power driven buyer/seller relationships on supply chain satisfaction. *Journal of Operations Management*, *23*, 1–22. doi:10.1016/j.jom.2004.09.002

Bergmann, B. R. (1986). *The economic emergence of women*. New York, NY: Basic Books.

Bernstein, F., & Federgruen, A. (2005). Decentralized supply chains with competing retailers under demand uncertainty *Management Science*, *51*, 18–29. doi:10.1287/mnsc.1040.0218

Bertrand, K. (1986). Crafting "win-win" situations in buyer-supplier relationships. *Business Marketing*, (June), 24-30.

Besterfield, D. H., Besterfield-Michna, C., Besterfield, G., & Besterfield-Sacre, M. (2002). *Total quality management* (3rd ed.). Prentice Hall.

Bhatnagar, K., & Brake, M. (2010). Gender differences in technology perceptions of high school students and their intent to choose technology college majors. *Journal of Engineering Technology*, *27*(2), 8–16.

Bhote, K. R. (1997). What do customers want anyway? *American Management Association*, (March), 36-40.

Bickering, E. (2009). An empirical assessment of technology adoption as a choice between alternatives. *Information Resources Management Journal*, *22*(4).

Bieda, B. (2007). *The use of life cycle assessment (LCA) conception of Mittal steel Poland SA energy generation – Krakow plant case study*. First International Conference on Energy and sustainability. Wessex Institute of Technology Press.

Bielby, W. T., & Baron, J. N. (1984). A woman's place is with other women: Sex segregation within organizationsIn Reskin, B. (Ed.), *Sex segregation in the workplace* (pp. 27–55). Washington, DC: National Academy Press.

Blanchard, B. S. (1998). *Logistics engineering and management*. Upper Saddle River, NJ: Prentice Hall.

Blanchard, B. S., Verma, D., & Peterson, E. L. (1995). *Maintainability*. New York, NY: Wiley-Interscience.

Blanchard, D. (2007). *Supply chain management best practices*. Hoboken, NJ: John Wiley & Sons, Inc.

Blank, J. L. T., & Merkies, A. H. Q. M. (2004). Empirical assessment of the economic behaviour of Dutch general hospitals. *Health Economics*, *13*(3), 265–280. doi:10.1002/hec.824

Bloemer, J., de Ruyter, K., & Peeters, P. (1998). Investigating drivers of bank loyalty: The complex relationship between image, service quality and satisfaction. *International Journal of Bank Marketing*, *16*(7), 276–286. doi:10.1108/02652329810245984

Bonel, E., & Rocco, E. (2007). Coopeting to survive: Surviving coopetition. *International Studies of Management & Organization*, *37*(2), 70–96. doi:10.2753/IMO0020-8825370204

Bonner, J., & Calantone, R. (2004). Buyer attentiveness in buyer-supplier relationships. *Industrial Marketing Management*, *34*, 53–61.

Bonsor, K., & Keener, C. (2011). *How RFID works*. Retrieved February 3, 2011, from http://electronics.howstuffworks.com/ gadgets/high-tech-gadgets/ rfid.htm/printable

Borjeson, L., & Hojer, M. (2006). Scenario types and techniques: Towards a user's guide. *Futures*, *38*, 723–739. doi:10.1016/j.futures.2005.12.002

Borjeson, L., Hojer, M., Dreborg, K. H., Ekvall, T., & Finnveden, G. (2006). Scenario types and techniques: Towards a user's guide. *Futures*, *38*, 723–739. doi:10.1016/j.futures.2005.12.002

Boubekri, N. (2001). Technology enablers for supply chain management. *Integrated Manufacturing Systems*, *12*(6), 394–399. doi:10.1108/EUM0000000006104

Boulding, W., Kalra, A., Staelin, R., & Zeithaml, V. (1993). A dynamic process model of service quality: from expectations to behavioral outcomes. *JMR, Journal of Marketing Research*, *30*(February), 7–27. doi:10.2307/3172510

Bovet, D., & Martha, J. (2000). *Value nets: Breaking the supply chain to unlock hidden profits*. New York, NY: Wiley.

Bowersox, D. J., Closs, D. J., & Cooper, M. B. (2002). *Supply chain logistics management*. New York, NY: McGraw-Hill Companies.

Bowersox, D. J., Closs, D. J., & Cooper, M. B. (2002). *Supply chain logistics management*. Boston, MA: McGraw-Hill/Irwin.

Bowersox, D. J., Closs, D. J., & Drayer, R. W. (2005, January 1). The digital transformation: Technology and beyond. *Supply Chain Management Review*, *9*, 22–30.

Bowersox, D. J., Daugherty, P. J., Droge, C. L., Rogers, D. S., & Wardlow, D. L. (1989). *Leading-edge logistics: Competitive positioning for the 90s*. Oak Brook, IL: Council of Logistics Management.

Bradfield, R. (2005). The origins and evolution of scenario techniques in long range business planning. *Futures*, *37*, 795–812. doi:10.1016/j.futures.2005.01.003

Bradley, A. (2005). The ups and downs of relationships. *Supply Management*, *10*(21), 15.

Brandao de Souza, L. (2009). Trends and approaches in lean healthcare. *Leadership in Health Services*, *22*(2), 121–139. doi:10.1108/17511870910953788

Brandenburger, A., & Nalebuff, B. J. (1996). *Co-opetition*. New York, NY: Doubleday.

Brandmeier, R., & Rupp, F. (2010). Benchmarking procurement functions: causes for superior performance. *Benchmarking: An International Journal*, *17*(1), 5. doi:10.1108/14635771011022299

Brandon-Jones, A., Ramsay, J., & Wagner, B. (2010). Trading interactions: Supplier empathy, consensus and bias. *International Journal of Operations & Production Management*, *30*(5), 453–487. doi:10.1108/01443571011039588

Brennan, R. W., Balasubramanian, S., & Norrie, D. H. (1997). *Dynamic control architecture for advanced manufacturing system.* International Conference on Intelligent Systems for Advanced Manufacturing, Pittsburgh, PA, USA.

Brennan, P., & Turnbull, P. (1999). Adaptive behavior in buyer-seller relationships. *Industrial Marketing Management*, *28*, 481–495. doi:10.1016/S0019-8501(99)00057-7

Briere-Cote, A., Rivest, L., & Desrochers, A. (2010). Adaptive generic product structure modelling for design reuse in engineer-to-order. *Computers in Industry*, *61*, 53–65. doi:10.1016/j.compind.2009.07.005

Broekhuis, M., & Donk, D. P. v. (2011). Coordination of physicians' operational activities: a contingency perspective. *International Journal of Operations & Production Management*, *31*(3), 251–273. doi:10.1108/01443571111111919

Browne, J., Moylan, T., & Scaife, A. (2010). Female entrepreneurs – Out of the frying pan, into the fire? *Irish Journal of Management*, *28*(2), 109–133.

Brown, S. A., & Venkatesh, V. (2003). Building a successful business: The FedEx story. *Communications of the ACM*, *46*(4), 84–89. doi:10.1145/641205.641210

Broyles, S. A. (2009). Loyalty's influence on satisfaction in cross-cultural settings. *Journal of Product and Brand Management*, *18*(6), 414–424. doi:10.1108/10610420910989730

Brue, G., & Howes, R. (2006). *Six Sigma, The McGraw Hill 36-hour course*. New York, NY: McGraw- Hill Companies.

Brundtland Commission. (1987). *Our common future*. World Commission on Environment and Development.

Burt, D. N., Dobler, D. W., & Starling, S. L. (2003). *World class supply management: The key to supply chain management* (7th ed.). Boston, MA: McGraw-Hill Irwin.

Burt, D. N., Petcavage, S. D., & Pinkerton, R. L. (2010). *Supply management* (8th ed.). Boston, MA: McGraw-Hill/Irwin.

Busato, A., Matter, P., Künzi, B., & Goodman, D. C. (2010). Supply sensitive services in Swiss ambulatory care: An analysis of basic health insurance records for 2003-2007. *BMC Health Services Research*, *10*, 315–315. doi:10.1186/1472-6963-10-315

Byrne, B. M. (2001). *Structural equation modeling with AMOS: Basic concepts, applications and programming*. London, UK: Lawrence Erlbaum Associates.

Byron, K. (2007). Male and female managers' ability to 'read' emotions: Relationships with supervisor's performance ratings and subordinates' satisfaction ratings. *Journal of Occupational and Organizational Psychology*, *80*(4), 713–733. doi:10.1348/096317907X174349

Cachon, G. P. (2004). Supply chain coordination with contractsIn De Kok, A. G., & Grave, S. C. (Eds.), *Handbooks in operations research and management science, 11: Supply chain management: Design, coordination and operation* (pp. 229–339). Elsevier B.V.

Calantone, R. J., & Di Benedetto, C. A. (2000). Performance and time to market: Accelerating cycle time with overlapping stages. *IEEE Transactions on Engineering Management*, *47*(2), 232–244. doi:10.1109/17.846790

Callewaert, P., Robinson, P. A., & Blatman, P. (2009). *Cloud computing forecasting change*. Retrieved February 14, 2010, from www.deloitte.com/ assets/Dcom.../ ie_Consulting_CloudComputing_09.pdf

Cameron, N. S., & Braiden, P. M. (2004). Using business process re-engineering for the development of production efficiency in companies making engineered to order products. *International Production Economics*, *89*, 261–273. doi:10.1016/S0925-5273(02)00448-6

Campbell, S., & Mohun, V. (2007). *Mastering enterprise SOA with SAP Netweaver and mySAP ERP*. Indianapolis, IN: Wiley Publishing, Inc.

Carlson, G., & Greeley, H. (2010). Is the relationship between your hospital and your medical staff sustainable? *Journal of Healthcare Management / American College of Healthcare Executives, 55*(3), 158-173.

Carr, A. S., & Pearson, J. N. (1999). Strategically managed buyer-supplier relationships and performance outcomes. *Journal of Operations Management, 17*(5), 497–519. doi:10.1016/S0272-6963(99)00007-8

Caruso, H. (1996). An overview of environmental reliability testing. *Proceedings of the Annual Reliability and Maintainability Symposium,* (pp. 102–109).

Castillo, J. A. (2010). OIF fuel distribution challenges. *Army Sustainment, 42*(2), 8–9.

Celuch, K., Walz, A. M., Saxby, C., & Ehlen, C. (2011). Understanding SME intention to use the internet for managing supplier information. *New England Journal of Entrepreneurship, 14*(1), 9.

Chan, H. (2004). The supply-chain squeeze. *Optimize,* (February).

Chan, F. T. S., & Kumar, N. (2005). Global supplier development considering risk factors using fuzzy extended AHP based approach. *Omega: The International Journal of Management Science, 37*(4), 417–431.

Chang, M. K., & Cheung, W. (2001). Determinants of the intention to use Internet/WWW at work: A confirmatory study. *Information & Management, 39,* 1–14. doi:10.1016/S0378-7206(01)00075-1

Chase, R. L. (1997). A knowledge based organization: An international survey. *Journal of Knowledge Management, 1*(1), 38–49. doi:10.1108/EUM0000000004578

Chen, G. S. (2010). *On the supply chain management of public hospital materials.* Paper presented at the 2010 International Conference on E-Product E-Service and E-Entertainment, ICEEE2010, Henan.

Chen, C.-S. (2006). Concurrent engineer-to-order operation in the manufacturing engineering contract industries. *International Journal of Industrial and Systems Engineering, 1*(1-2), 37–58. doi:10.1504/IJISE.2006.009049

Chen, F., Drezner, Z., Ryan, J. K., & Simchi-Levy, D. (2000). Quantifying the bullwhip effect in a simple supply chain: The impact of forecasting, lead times, and information. *Management Science, 46*(3), 436–443. doi:10.1287/mnsc.46.3.436.12069

Chermack, T. J. (2005). Studying scenario planning: Theory, research suggestions and hypotheses. *Technological Forecasting and Social Change, 72,* 59–73.

Chestnutwood, M., & Levin, R. (1999). *Technology assessment and management methodology - An approach to system life sustainment and supportability.* ISBN: 0-7803-5749-3/99/0

Ching-Torng, L., Hero, C., & Yi-Hong, T. (2005). Agility evaluation using fuzzy logic. *International Journal of Production Economics, 101*(2), 353–368.

Chiuc, C., & Yih, Y. (1995). A learning based methodology for dynamic scheduling in distributed manufacturing systems. *International Journal of Production Research, 33*(11), 3217–3232. doi:10.1080/00207549508904870

Chopra, S., & Meindl, P. (2001). *Supply chain management: Strategy, planning and operation.* Upper Saddle River, NJ: Prentice Hall.

Chopra, S., & Meindl, P. (2010). *Supply chain management: Strategy, planning, and operation* (4th ed.). Boston, MA: Pearson.

Chow, S., & Holden, R. (1997). Toward an understanding of loyalty: The moderating role of trust. *Journal of Managerial Issues, 9*(3), 275–298.

Christensen, C. M. (2003). *The innovator's dilemma.* New York, NY: Harper Collins Publishers.

Christopher, M. (1998). *Logistics and supply chain management: Strategies for reducing cost and improving service.* Prentice-Hall.

Christopher, M., & Towill, D. R. (2000). Supply chain migration from lean and functional to agile and customised. *Supply Chain Management: An International Journal, 5*(4), 206–213. doi:10.1108/13598540010347334

Chryssolouris, G., & Subramaniam, V. (2001). Dynamic scheduling of manufacturing job shops using genetic algorithms. *Journal of Intelligent Manufacturing, 12,* 281–293. doi:10.1023/A:1011253011638

Chung, W.-C., Fan, P.-L., Chiu, H.-C., Yang, C.-Y., Huang, K.-L., & Tzeng, D.-S. (2010). Operating room cost for coronary artery bypass graft procedures: does experience or severity of illness matter? *Journal of Evaluation in Clinical Practice*, *16*(6), 1063–1070. doi:10.1111/j.1365-2753.2009.01251.x

Churchill, G. A., & Suprenant, C. (1982). An investigation into the determinants of customer satisfaction. *JMR, Journal of Marketing Research*, *19*(November), 491–504. doi:10.2307/3151722

Claro, D. P., Claro, P. B., & Hagelaar, G. (2006). Coordinating collaborative joint efforts with suppliers: The effects of trust, transaction specific investment and information network in the Dutch flower industry. *Supply Chain Management*, *11*(3), 216–224. doi:10.1108/13598540610662112

Cleland, D. I., Bidanda, B., & Chung, C. A. (1995). Human issues in technology integration – Part 1. *Industrial Management (Des Plaines)*, *37*(4), 22.

CNN. (2008). *Minorities expected to be majority in 2050*. Retrieved from http://articles.cnn.com/ 2008-08-13/us/census.minorities_1_hispanic-population-census-bureau-white-population?_s=PM:US

Cohen, S., & Roussel, J. (2005). *Strategic supply chain management*. New York, NY: McGraw-Hill.

Cohen, S., & Roussel, J. (2005). *Strategic supply chain management: The five disciplines for top performance*. New York, NY: McGraw-Hill.

Cohen, W. M., & Levinthal, D. A. (1990). Absorptive capacity: A new perspective on learning and innovation. *Administrative Science Quarterly*, *35*(1), 128–152. doi:10.2307/2393553

Colgate, M., Stewart, K., & Kinsella, R. (1995). Customer defection: A study of the student market in Ireland. *International Journal of Bank Marketing*, *14*(8), 23–29.

Collins, J. (2001). *Good to great*. New York, NY: Harper Business.

Combs, L. (2004). The right channel at the right time. *Industrial Management (Des Plaines)*, *46*(4), 8–16.

Condi, C. (2009). *Lean reaches rural hospital*. Institute of Industrial Engineers. Retrieved March 2, 2009, from http://www.iienet2.org/ Details.aspx?id=10808

Conner, M. (2004). The supply chain's role in leveraging PLM. *Supply Chain Management Review*, *8*(2), 36–43.

Contractor, F. J., & Lorange, P. (2002). The growth of alliances in the knowledge-based economyIn Contractor, F. J., & Lorange, P. (Eds.), *Cooperative strategies and alliances* (pp. 3–24). Oxford, UK: Pergamon. doi:10.1016/S0969-5931(02)00021-5

Cook, M., & Greenspan, N. (2003). Why companies fail the supply chain basics. *European Business Journal*, *15*(2), 74–78.

Cooper, M. C., Lambert, D. M., & Pagh, J. D. (1997). Supply chain management: More than a new name for logistics. *The International Journal of Logistics Management*, *8*(1), 1–14. doi:10.1108/09574099710805556

Cooper, R. G., & Edgett, S. J. (2003). *Best practices in product innovation: What distinguishes top performers*. Ancaster, Canada: Product Development Institute Inc.

Cordesman, A. H. (2000). *Trends in US defense spending: The size of funding, procurement, and readiness problems*. Washington, DC: Center for Strategic and International Studies.

Council of Supply Chain Management Professionals. (2010). *Glossary of supply chain and logistics terms and glossary*. Retrieved from http://www.cscmp.org

Cowling, P. I., & Johansson, M. (2002). Using real time information for effective dynamic scheduling. *European Journal of Operational Research*, *139*(2), 230–244. doi:10.1016/S0377-2217(01)00355-1

Cowling, P. I., Ouelhadj, D., & Petrovic, S. (2003). A multi-agent architecture for dynamic scheduling of steel hot rolling. *Journal of Intelligent Manufacturing*, *14*, 457–470. doi:10.1023/A:1025701325275

Craig, T. (2006). *Lean SCM – More essentials*. Retrieved February 15, 2011, from http://www.scmnews.com/scmnews-66-20060718LeanSCMMoreEssentials.html

Craighead, C. W., Blackhurst, J., Rungtusanatham, M. J., & Handfield, R. B. (2007). The severity of supply chain disruptions: Design characteristics and mitigation capabilities. *Decision Sciences*, *38*(1), 131–156. doi:10.1111/j.1540-5915.2007.00151.x

Crespo-Marquez, A., & Blanchar, C. (2004). The procurement of strategic parts: Analysis of a portfolio of contracts with suppliers using a system dynamics simulation model. *International Journal of Production Economics*, *88*, 29–49. doi:10.1016/S0925-5273(03)00177-4

Cronin, J. J., & Taylor, S. A. (1992). Measuring service quality: A re-examination and extension. *Journal of Marketing*, *56*, 55–68. doi:10.2307/1252296

Crosby, L., Evans, K., & Cowles, D. (1990). Relationship quality in services selling: An interpersonal influence perspective. *Journal of Marketing*, *54*(3), 68–81. doi:10.2307/1251817

Crowe, D., & Feinberg, A. (2001). *Design for reliability*. Boca Raton, FL: CRC.

Cutcher-Gershenfeld, J., Field, F., Hall, R., Kirchain, R., Marks, D., Oye, K., & Sussman, J. (2004). Sustainability as an organizing design principle for large-scale engineering systems. *Engineering Systems Monograph, March*, 29-31.

Dacosta-Claro, I. (2002). The performance of material management in health care organizations. *The International Journal of Health Planning and Management*, *17*(1), 69–85. doi:10.1002/hpm.653

Dacosta-Claro, I., & Lapierre, S. D. (2003). Benchmarking as a tool for the improvement of health services' supply departments. *Health Services Management Research*, *16*(4), 211–223. doi:10.1258/095148403322488919

Daim, T. U., & Oliver, T. (2008). Implementing technology roadmap process in the energy services sector: A case study of a government agency. *Technological Forecasting and Social Change*, *75*, 687–720. doi:10.1016/j.techfore.2007.04.006

Danaher, P. J., & Rust, R. T. (1996). Indirect benefits from service quality. *Quality Management Journal*, *3*(2), 63–85.

Darr, E., Argote, L., & Epple, D. (1995). The acquisition, transfer, and depreciation of knowledge in service organizations: Productivity in franchises. *Management Science*, *41*(11), 1750–1762. doi:10.1287/mnsc.41.11.1750

Dath, T. N. S., Rajendran, C., & Narashiman, K. (2010). An empirical study on supply chain management: The perspective of logistics service providers. *International Journal of Logistics Systems and Management*, *6*(1), 1–22. doi:10.1504/IJLSM.2010.029718

Davenport, T. H., & Prusak, L. (1998). *Working knowledge: How organizations manage what they know*. Boston, MA: Harvard Business School Press.

Davidow, W. H., & Malone, M. S. (1992). *The virtual corporation*. HarperBusiness.

Davis, E. W., & Spekman, R. E. (2004). *The extended enterprise*. Upper Saddle River, NJ: Prentice Hall.

Dawe, N., & Ryan, K. (2003). The faulty three legged stool model of sustainable development. *Conservation Biology*, *17*(5), 1458–1460. doi:10.1046/j.1523-1739.2003.02471.x

Dawes, J., & Swailes, S. (1999). Retention sans frontiers: Issues for financial service retailers. *International Journal of Bank Marketing*, *17*(1), 36–43. doi:10.1108/02652329910254037

Day, A. (2009). Supplier relationship management. *Supply Management*, *14*(16), 25–27.

Day, G. S., & Klein, S. (1987). Cooperative behaviour in vertical markets: The influence of transaction costs and competitive strategiesIn Houston, M. I. (Ed.), *Review of marketing* (pp. 39–66).

De Kok, A. G., & Grave, S. C. (Eds.). (2004). *Handbooks in operations research and management science, 11: Supply chain management: design, coordination and operation*. Elsevier B.V.

de Matos, C. A., Henrique, J. L., & de Rosa, F. (2009). The different roles of switching costs on satisfaction-loyalty relationship. *International Journal of Bank Marketing*, *27*(7), 506–523. doi:10.1108/02652320911002331

de Treville, S., Shapiro, R. D., & Hameri, A.-P. (2004). From supply chain to demand chain: The role of lead time reduction in improving demand chain performance. *Journal of Operations Management*, *21*(6), 613–627. doi:10.1016/j.jom.2003.10.001

Defense Acquisition Guidebook. (2004, November 01). *United States defense acquisition technology and logistics (Defense AT & L)*.

Demeter, K., & Mateusz, Z. (2011). The impact of lean practices on inventory turnover. *International Journal of Production Economics*, *133*, 154–163. doi:10.1016/j.ijpe.2009.10.031

Deming, E. (1986). *Out of the crisis*. MIT Press.

Dickson, E. W., Anguelov, Z., Vetterick, D., Eller, A., & Singh, S. (2009). Use of lean in the emergency department: A case series of 4 hospitals. *Annals of Emergency Medicine*, *54*(4), 504–510. doi:10.1016/j.annemergmed.2009.03.024

Digest Editorial Staff, S. C. (2010, August 12). Supply chain news: The five challenges of today's global supply chains. *Supply Chain Digest.* Retrieved from http://www.scdigest.com/ASSETS/ON_TARGET/10-08-12-3.php?cid=3649

Disney, S. M. (2003). The effect of vendor managed inventory (VMI) dynamics on the bullwhip effect in supply chains. *International Journal of Production Economics*, *85*, 199–215. doi:10.1016/S0925-5273(03)00110-5

Doll, W. J., Xia, W., & Torkzadeh, G. (1994). A confirmatory factor analysis of the end-user computing satisfaction instrument. *Management Information Systems Quarterly*, *18*(4), 453–661. doi:10.2307/249524

Dong, Y., Xu, K., & Dresner, M. (2007). Environmental determinants of VMI adoption: An exploratory analysis. *Transportation Research Part E, Logistics and Transportation Review*, *43*(4), 355–369. doi:10.1016/j.tre.2006.01.004

Donohue, K. (2000). Efficient supply contracts for fashion goods with forecast updating and two production modes. *Management Science*, *46*(11), 1397–1411. doi:10.1287/mnsc.46.11.1397.12088

Dowling, G., & Uncle, M. (1997). Do customer loyalty programs really work? *Sloan Management Review*, (Summer): 71–82.

Dubinsky, A. J., & Ingram, T. N. (1982). Salespeople view buyer behavior. *Journal of Purchasing and Materials Management*, *18*(3), 6–11.

Dwyer, A. J. (2010). Medical managers in contemporary healthcare organisations: A consideration of the literature. *Australian Health Review*, *34*(4), 514–522. doi:10.1071/AH09736

Dyer, J. F., & Nobeako, K. (2000). Creating and managing a high performance knowledge-sharing network: The Toyota case. *Strategic Management Journal*, *21*, 345–367. doi:10.1002/(SICI)1097-0266(200003)21:3<345::AID-SMJ96>3.0.CO;2-N

Dyer, J. H. (2000). *Collaborative advantage*. Oxford University Press.

Dyer, J., & Chu, W. (2003). The Role of trustworthiness in reducing transaction costs and improving performance: Empirical evidence from the United States, Japan and Korea. *Organization Science*, *14*(1), 57–68. doi:10.1287/orsc.14.1.57.12806

Eagly, A. H., & Johnson, B. T. (1990). Gender and leadership style: A meta-analysis. *Psychological Bulletin*, *108*(2), 233–256. doi:10.1037/0033-2909.108.2.233

Eagly, A. H., & Karau, S. J. (1995). Gender and the effectiveness of leaders: A meta-analysis. *Psychological Bulletin*, *117*(1), 125–145. doi:10.1037/0033-2909.117.1.125

Eccles, J. S. (1994). Understanding women's educational and occupational choices. *Psychology of Women Quarterly*, *18*, 585–609. doi:10.1111/j.1471-6402.1994.tb01049.x

Education Week. (June 2, 2010). *Graduation by the numbers*. Retrieved from http://www.edweek.org/ ew/articles/2010/06/ 10/34execsum.h29.html

Ehrlich, B. H. (2002). *Transactional Six Sigma and lean servicing*. Boca Raton, FL: St. Lucie Press. doi:10.1201/9781420000337

Eisenhardt, K. M., & Santos, F. M. (2002). Knowledge-based view: A new theory of strategy? In Pettigrew, A., Thomas, H., & Whittington, R. (Eds.), *Handbook of strategy and management*. Thousand Oaks, CA: Sage Publications.

Eisenhardt, K., & Galunic, D. C. (2000). Coevolving at last, a way to make synergies work. *Harvard Business Review*, •••, 91–101.

Eisnehardt, K., & Martin, J. A. (2000). Dynamic capabilities: What are they? *Strategic Management Journal*, *21*, 1105–1121. doi:10.1002/1097-0266(200010/11)21:10/11<1105::AID-SMJ133>3.0.CO;2-E

El Sodany, N. H. (2011). Periodic review probabilistic multi-item inventory system with zero lead time under constraint and varying holding cost. *Journal of Mathematics and Statistics*, *7*(1), 12–19. doi:10.3844/jmssp.2011.12.19

Elfving, J. (2003). *Exploration of opportunity to reduce lead time for engineered-to-order products*. PhD Dissertation, University of California, Berkeley.

Elg, M., Stenberg, J., Kammerlind, P., Tullberg, S., & Olsson, J. (2011). Swedish healthcare management practices and quality improvement work: Development trends. *International Journal of Health Care Quality Assurance*, *24*(2), 101–123. doi:10.1108/09526861111105077

Elinor, R. (2005). Study shows SRM leaders. *Supply Management*, *10*(25), 10.

Ellmyer, E. G. (2006). Centralized supply chain management: Command and control of sustainment. A Research Report, Maxwell Air Force Base, Alabama. AU/ACSC/8009/AY06.

Ellram, L. M. (1991). Supply chain management: The industrial organisation perspective. *International Journal of Physical Distribution & Logistics Management*, *21*(1), 13–22. doi:10.1108/09600039110137082

Emiliana, M. L. (2010). Historical lessons in purchasing and supplier relationship management. *Journal of Management History*, *16*(1), 116–136. doi:10.1108/17511341011008340

Emiliani, M. (2008). *Practical lean leadership: A strategic leadership guide for executives*. Kensington, CT: The CLBM, LLC.

Emiliani, M. L., & Stec, D. J. (2004). Aerospace parts suppliers' reaction to online reverse auctions. *Supply Chain Management*, *9*(2), 139. doi:10.1108/13598540410527042

Emmons, H., & Gilbert, S. (1998). Return policies in pricing and inventory decisions for catalogue goods. *Management Science*, *44*(2), 276–283. doi:10.1287/mnsc.44.2.276

Eppen, G., & Iyer, A. (1997). Backup agreements in fashion buying: The value of upstream flexibility. *Management Science*, *43*(11), 1469–1484. doi:10.1287/mnsc.43.11.1469

Epstein, R. M., Fiscella, K., Lesser, C. S., & Stange, K. C. (2010). Why the nation needs a policy push on patient-centered health care. *Health Affairs (Project Hope)*, *29*(8), 1489–1495. doi:10.1377/hlthaff.2009.0888

Ernst & Whinney. (1987). *Corporate profitability & logistics*. Oak Brook, IL: Council of Logistics Management.

Estrin, L., Foreman, J. T., & Garcia, S. (2003). *Overcoming barriers to technology adoption in small manufacturing enterprises (SMEs)*. White paper Carnegie Mellon University, Software Engineering Institute (June).

Evans, J. R., & Lindsay, W. M. (2005). *An introduction to Six Sigma & Process improvement*. Cincinnati, OH: Thomson Southwestern Publishing Company.

Evans, J. R., & Lindsay, W. M. (2008). *Managing for quality and performance excellence* (7th ed.). Mason, OH: South-Western Cengage Learning.

Evans, P., & Wolf, B. (2005). Collaboration rules. *Harvard Business Review*, *83*(7/8), 96.

Fabius, R. J. (2007). The broadening horizon for physician executives: The six constituencies of health care. *Physician Executive*, (May-June): 72–74.

Farris, J., Van Aken, E., Doolen, T., & Worley, J. (2009). Critical success factors for human resource outcomes in Kaizen events: An empirical study. *International Journal of Production Economics*, *117*(1), 42–65. doi:10.1016/j.ijpe.2008.08.051

Fatholahi, A. (2009). A scientific approach to buying decisions: Value-based purchasing takes hints from evidence-based processes. *Hospital Materials Management*, *34*(4), 5–7.

Fawcett, S. E., & Magnan, G. M. (2005). *Achieving world-class supply chain alignment: Benefits, barriers, and bridges*. White paper Center for Advanced Purchasing Studies. Retrieved from http://.www.capsresearch.org

Fawcett, S. E., Magnan, G. M., & McCarter, M. W. (2008). A three-stage implementation model for supply chain collaboration. *Journal of Business Logistics*, *29*(1), 93. doi:10.1002/j.2158-1592.2008.tb00070.x

Fawcett, S. E., Magnan, G. M., & McCarter, M. W. (2008). Benefits, barriers, and bridges to effective supply chain management. *Supply Chain Management: An International Journal*, *13*(1), 35–48. doi:10.1108/13598540810850300

Fawcett, S. E., Wallin, C., Allred, C., Fawcett, A. M., & Magnan, G. M. (2011). Information Technology as an enabler of supply chain collaboration: A dynamic-capabilities perspective. *Journal of Supply Chain Management*, *47*(1), 38. doi:10.1111/j.1745-493X.2010.03213.x

Feeley, T. W., Fly, H. S., Albright, H., Walters, R., & Burke, T. W. (2010). A method for defining value in healthcare using cancer care as a model. *Journal of Healthcare Management*, *55*(6), 399–411.

Fenies, P., Gourgand, M., & Rodier, S. (2006, Oct. 2006). *A decisional model for the performance evaluation of the logistic process: Application to the hospital supply chain.* Paper presented at the 2006 International Conference on Service Systems and Service Management.

Ferber, J. (1999). *Multi-agent systems: An introduction to distributed artificial intelligence*. London, UK: Addison-Wesley.

Ferenc, J. (2010). Time well spent? Assessing nursing-supply chain activities. *Materials Management in Health Care*, *19*(2), 12–16.

Ferman, J. H. (2009). Healthcare reform and a VBP program. Value-based purchasing concepts continue to evolve through the legislative process. *Healthcare Executive*, *24*(2), 56–59.

Ferrer, G., Dew, N., & Apte, U. (2010). When is RFID right for your service? *International Journal of Production Economics*, *124*, 414–425. doi:10.1016/j.ijpe.2009.12.004

Fillingham, D. (2007). Can lean save lives? *Leadership in Health Services*, *20*(4), 231–241. doi:10.1108/17511870710829346

Fine, C. H. (1998). *Clockspeed: Winning industry control in the age of temporary advantage*. Reading, MA: Perseus Books.

Fine, C. H. (2000). Clockspeed-based strategies for supply chain design. *Production and Operations Management*, *9*(3), 213–221. doi:10.1111/j.1937-5956.2000.tb00134.x

Fischer, K., Muller, J. P., Heimig, I., & Scheer, A. W. (1996). Intelligent agents in virtual enterprises. *First International Conference on Practical Applications of Intelligent Agents and Multi-Agent Technology (PAAM)*, London, (pp. 205–223).

Fisher, M. L. (1997). What is the right supply chain for your product? *Harvard Business Review*, *75*(2), 105–116.

Fleisch, E., & Tellkamp, C. (2005). Inventory inaccuracy and supply chain performance: A simulation study of a retail supply chain. *International Journal of Production Economics*, *95*, 373–385. doi:10.1016/j.ijpe.2004.02.003

Flowers, W. P., Tomlinson, D., Levy, E., Deponio, M., & Rosenbaum, M. (2009). Optimizing hospital supply chain processes for savings. *Healthcare Financial Management: Journal of the Healthcare Financial Management Association*, *63*(2), 1–4.

Food and Agriculture Oorganization. (1999). Guidelines for quality management in soil and plant laboratories. *FAO Soil Bulletin, 74.* National Resources Management and Environment Department. Retrieved June 28, 2011, from http://www.fao.org/ docrep/w7295e/w7295e04.htm

Ford, C. M. (2002). The futurity of decisions as a facilitator of organizational creativity and change. *Journal of Organizational Change Management*, *15*(6), 635–646. doi:10.1108/09534810210449541

Fornell, C. (1992). National customer satisfaction barometer: The Swedish experience. *Journal of Marketing*, *56*(January), 6–21. doi:10.2307/1252129

Fornell, C., & Larcker, D. F. (1981). Evaluating structural equation models with unobservable variables and measurement error. *JMR, Journal of Marketing Research*, *18*, 39–50. doi:10.2307/3151312

Fornell, C., & Wernerfelt, B. (1987). Defensive marketing strategy by customer complaint management: A theoretical analysis. *JMR, Journal of Marketing Research*, *24*, 337–346. doi:10.2307/3151381

Forrester. (2005). *APAC study chain apps spending outlook*. Retrieved from http://www.forrester.com

Foss, N. J., Husted, K., & Michailova, S. (2010). Governing knowledge sharing in organizations: Levels of analysis, governance mechanisms, and research directions. *Journal of Management Studies*, *47*(3), 455–482. doi:10.1111/j.1467-6486.2009.00870.x

Fowlkes, W. Y., & Creveling, C. M. (1995). *Engineering methods for robust product design: Using Taguchi methods in technology and product development*. Prentice Hall.

Fox, M. S., Chionglo, J. F., & Barbuceanu, M. (1993). *The integrated supply chain management system. Internal Report*. Dept. of Industrial Engineering, University of Toronto.

Francis, L. (2009). *Cloud computing: implications for enterprise software vendors (ESV)*. Thesis (S.M.), Massachusetts Institute of Technology, System Design and Management Program.

Frank, L. K. (1925). The significance of industrial integration. *The Journal of Political Economy*, *33*(2), 179–195. doi:10.1086/253662

Frith, L. (1999). Priority setting and evidence based purchasing. *Health Care Analysis*, *7*(2), 139–151. doi:10.1023/A:1009497307073

Froehlichner, T., & Vendemini, S. (1999). *Connivences d'acteurs, contrats, coopération inter-entreprises et métamorphose des organizations*. Paris, France: Presses Universitaires de Nancy.

Fukuyama, F. (1996). *Trust: The social virtues and the creation of prosperity*. New York, NY: Free Press.

Fung, V. K., Fung, W. K., & Wind, Y. (2007). *Competing in a flat world*. Upper Saddle River, NJ: Wharton School Publishing.

Gain, S. (2005). *Perfect projects*. ITP Technology. Retrieved from http://.www.itp.net

Ganesan, S. (1994). Determinants of long-term orientation in buyer-seller relationships. *Journal of Marketing*, *58*(2), 1–19. doi:10.2307/1252265

Ganesh, J., Arnolds, M. J., & Reynolds, K. E. (2000). Understanding the customer base of service providers: an examination the differences between switchers and stayers. *Journal of Marketing*, *64*(July), 65–87. doi:10.1509/jmkg.64.3.65.18028

Ganguli, S., & Roy, S. K. (2011). Generic technology-based service quality dimensions in banking: impact on customer satisfaction and loyalty. *International Journal of Bank Marketing*, *29*(2), 168–189. doi:10.1108/02652321111107648

Gansler, J. S. (1999). *Acquisition Reform Update, January*. U.S. Department of Defense, USD (A&T), Office of the Secretary of Defense, acquisition & technology.

Gao, J., X., *et al.* (2000). Implementation of concurrent engineering in the suppliers to the automotive industry. *Journal of Materials Processing Technology*, *107*, 201–208. doi:10.1016/S0924-0136(00)00669-5

Garavelli, C. A. (2003). Flexibility configurations for the supply chain management. *International Journal of Production Economics*, *85*, 141–153. doi:10.1016/S0925-5273(03)00106-3

Garg, D., Narahari, Y., & Viswandham, N. (2004). Design of Six Sigma supply chains. *IEEE Transactions on Automation Science and Engineering*, *1*(1). doi:10.1109/TASE.2004.829436

Garmon, P. J., Gary, M. J., Laughlin, L. L., Sjoberg, E. S., Lasater, D., Calloway, S., & Robins, W. (2001). Just-in-time sustainment. *The 20th Conference on Digital Avionics Systems*, Vol. 1, 14-18 October.

Gartner (2005). *IBM transforms its supply chain to drive growth*. Retrieved from http://www.gartner.com

Garvin, D. (1987). Competing on eight dimensions of quality. *Harvard Business Review*, *6*, 101–109.

Gattorna, J. (2006). *Living supply chains: How to mobilize the enterprise around delivering what your customers want*. Harlow, UK: Financial Times-Prentice Hall.

George, M. L. (2002). *Lean Six Sigma: Combining Six Sigma quality with lean speed*. New York, NY: McGraw-Hill.

George, M. L., Rowlands, D., Price, M., & Maxey, J. (2005). *The lean Six Sigma pocket toolbook*. New York, NY: McGraw Hill.

Georgiadis, P., Vlachos, D., & Iakovou, E. (2005). A system dynamics modeling framework for the strategic supply chain management of food chains. *Journal of Food Engineering*, *70*(3), 351–364. doi:10.1016/j.jfoodeng.2004.06.030

Germain, R., Claycomb, C., & Dröge, C. (2008). Supply chain variability, organizational structure, and performance: The moderating effect of demand unpredictability. *Journal of Operations Management*, *26*(5), 557–570. doi:10.1016/j.jom.2007.10.002

Ghodrati, B., & Kumar, U. (2005). Applications and case studies: Reliability and operating environment-based spare parts estimation approach. *Journal of Quality in Maintenance Engineering*, *11*(2), 169–184. doi:10.1108/13552510510601366

Glidden, R., Bockoric, C., Cooper, S., Diorio, C., Dressler, D., & Gutnik, V. (2004). Design of ultra-low-cost UHF RFID tags for supply chain applications. *IEEE Communications Magazine*, (August): 140–151. doi:10.1109/MCOM.2004.1321406

Gobeli, D. H., Koeing, H. F., & Mishra, C. S. (2002). Strategic value creationIn Phan, P. (Ed.), *Technology entrepreneurship* (pp. 3–16). Greenwich, CT: Information Age Publishing.

Goel, A. K., & Craw, S. (2006). Design, innovation and case-based reasoning. *The Knowledge Engineering Review*, *20*(03), 271–276. doi:10.1017/S0269888906000609

Goetsch, D. L., & Davis, S. B. (2010). *Quality management for organizational excellence: Introduction to total quality* (6th ed.). Upper Saddle River, NJ: Prentice Hall.

Goh, S., & Coleman, S. (2003). *Sustainment of commercial aircraft gas turbine engines: An organizational and cognitive engineering approach*. AIAA's 3rd Annual Aviation Technology, Integration, and Operations (ATIO) Tech 17 – 19 November, Denver, CO.

Goldman, S. L., Nagel, R. N., & Preiss, K. (1995). *Agile competitors and virtual organizations*. New York, NY: Van Nostrand Reinhold.

Gomez-Padilla, A. (2009). Supply chain coordination by contracts with inventory holding cost share. *International Journal of Information Systems and Supply Chain Management*, *2*(2), 36–47. doi:10.4018/jisscm.2009040103

Gomez-Padilla, A. (2011). Contracts based on inventory cost share for supply chain coordinationIn Wang, J. (Ed.), *Supply chain optimization, management and integration: Emerging applications* (pp. 126–138). Hershey, PA: IGI Global. doi:10.4018/978-1-60960-135-5.ch009

Goodall, R., Fandel, D., Allan, A., Landler, P., & Huff, H. R. (2002). Long term productivity mechanisms of the semiconductor industry. *American Electrochemical Society Semiconductor Silicon Conference,* Vol. 2, (pp. 125–143).

Goranson, H. T. (1999). *The agile virtual enterprise*. Westport, CT: Quorum Books.

Gorelick, D. (1998). New rationale in buyer/seller relations. *Graphic Arts Monthly*, *70*(8), 81.

Gosling, J., & Naim, M. M. (2009). Engineer-to-order supply chain management: A literature review and research agenda. *International Journal of Production Economics*, *122*, 741–754. doi:10.1016/j.ijpe.2009.07.002

Gowen, C. R., & Tallon, W. J. (2003). Enhancing supply chain practices through human resource management. *Journal of Management Development*, *22*(1-2), 32.

Granbois, D. (1981). An integrated view of the choice/patronage processIn Monroe, K. B. (Ed.), *Advances in consumer research* (*Vol. 8*, pp. 693–695). Ann Arbor, MI: Association for Consumer Research.

Grant, D. B. (2010). Integration of supply and marketing for a blood service. *Management Research Review*, *33*(2), 123–133. doi:10.1108/01409171011015810

Gravier, M. J., & Swartz, S. M. (2009). The dark side of innovation: Exploring obsolescence and supply chain evolution for sustainment-dominated systems. *The Journal of High Technology Management Research*, *20*(2), 87–102. doi:10.1016/j.hitech.2009.09.001

Gray, B. (1989). *Negotiations: Arenas for reconstructing meaning*. Unpublished working paper, Pennsylvania State University, Center for Research in Conflict and Negotiation, University Park, PA.

Grenier, R., & Metes, G. (1995). *Going virtual*. Upper Saddle River, NJ: Prentice Hall.

Groover, P. G. (2001). *Automation, production systems, and computer-integrated manufacturing* (2nd ed., p. 609). Prentice-Hall.

Grove, A. L., Meredith, J. O., MacIntyre, M., Angelis, J., & Neailey, K. (2010). UK health visiting: Challenges faced during lean implementation. *Leadership in Health Services*, *23*(3), 204–218. doi:10.1108/17511871011061037

Gryna, F. M., Chua, R. C. H., & Defeo, J. A. (2007). *Juran's quality planning & analysis for enterprise quality* (5th ed.). New York, NY: The McGraw-Hill Companies, Inc.

Guanghui, Z., Jiang, P., & Huang, G. Q. (2009b). A game-theory approach for job scheduling in networked manufacturing. *International Journal of Advanced Manufacturing Technology*, *41*(9-10), 972–985. doi:10.1007/s00170-008-1539-9

guide to increased reliability and reduced logistics footprint. Office of Secretary of Defense.

Gulledge, T., Hiroshige, S., & Iyer, R. (2010). Condition-based maintenance and the product improvement process. *Journal of Computers in Industry*, *61*, 813–832. doi:10.1016/j.compind.2010.07.007

Gunasekaran, A., Lai, K. C., & Cheng, T. C. (2008). Responsive supply chain: A competitive strategy in networked company. *International Journal of Management Science*, *36*, 549–564.

Gunasekarana, A., & Ngai, E. W. T. (2005). Build-to-order supply chain management: A literature review and framework for development. *Journal of Operations Management*, *23*(5), 423–451. doi:10.1016/j.jom.2004.10.005

Gygi, C., DeCarlo, N., & Williams, B. (2005). *Six Sigma for dummies*. Indianapolis, IN: Wiley Publishing, Inc.

Ha, B.-C., Park, Y.-K., & Cho, S. (2011). Suppliers' affective trust and trust in competency in buyers: Its effect on collaboration and logistics efficiency. *International Journal of Operations & Production Management*, *31*(1), 56. doi:10.1108/01443571111098744

Hagedoorn, J. (1993). Understanding the rationale of strategic technology partnering: Inter-organizational modes of cooperation and sectoral differences. *Strategic Management Journal*, *14*, 371–385. doi:10.1002/smj.4250140505

Haldin-Herrgard, T. (2000). Difficulties of diffusion of tacit knowledge in organizations. *Journal of Intellectual Capital*, *1*(4), 357–365. doi:10.1108/14691930010359252

Hall, C. (2009). *Satisfaction with on-demand/cloud-based business intelligence and data warehousing remains high*.

Hallen, L., Johanson, J., & Seyed-Mohamed, N. (1991). Interfirm adaptation in business relationships. *Journal of Marketing*, *55*(2), 29–37. doi:10.2307/1252235

Halstead, D., Hartman, D., & Schmidt, S. L. (1994). Multisource effects on the satisfaction process. *Journal of the Academy of Marketing Science*, *22*, 114–129. doi:10.1177/0092070394222002

Hamel, G., Doz, Y. L., & Prahalad, C. K. (1989). Collaborate with your competitors-and win. *Harvard Business Review*, *67*(1), 133–139.

Hamilton, P., & Chin, G. (2001). Military electronics and obsolescence part 1: The evolution of a crisis. *COTS Journal*, March, 77–81.

Hanfield, R. B., & Nichols, E. L. Jr. (2002). *Supply chain redesign*. Upper Saddle River, NJ: Prentice Hall.

Hannon, D. (2005). Supplier relationships key to future success. *Purchasing*, *134*(10), 21–25.

Harney, J. (2005). Enterprise content management for SMBs. *AIIM E-Doc Magazine*, *19*(3), 59.

Harrington, H. J., & Harrington, J. S. (1995). *Total quality management*. New York, NY: McGraw-Hill, Inc.

Harrington, H. J., Hefner, M. B., & Cox, C. K. (1995). *Environmental change plans: Best practices for improvement planning and implementation. Harrington and Harrington's Total Improvement Management*. New York, NY: McGraw-Hill, Inc.

Harris, C., & Streeter, C. (2010). A new purchasing philosophy. *Industrial Engineer*, *42*(9), 42–46.

Harris, G., & Donatelli, A. (2005). *Value-stream mapping as a lean management tool*. Huntsville, AL: University of Alabama.

Hau, L., & Whang, S. (2005). Higher supply chain security with lower cost: Lessons from total quality management. *International Journal of Production Economics*, *96*, 289–300. doi:10.1016/j.ijpe.2003.06.003

Haywood, T. (2010). The cost of confusion: healthcare reform and value-based purchasing. *Healthcare Financial Management: Journal of the Healthcare Financial Management Association*, *64*(10), 44–48.

Heide, J., & John, G. (1990). Alliances in industrial purchasing: The determinants of joint action in buyer-supplier relationships. *JMR, Journal of Marketing Research*, *27*(1), 24–37. doi:10.2307/3172548

Helms, C., & Guffey, C. (1997). The role of women in Europe. *European Business Review*, *97*(2), 80–85. doi:10.1108/09555349710162580

Hendericks, K. B. (2007). The impact of enterprise systems on corporate performance: A study of ERP, SCM and CRM system implementations. *Journal of Operations Management*, *25*(1), 65–82. doi:10.1016/j.jom.2006.02.002

Hendriks, P. (1999). Why share knowledge? The influence of ICT on the motivation of knowledge sharing. *Knowledge and Process Management*, *6*(2), 91–100. doi:10.1002/(SICI)1099-1441(199906)6:2<91::AID-KPM54>3.0.CO;2-M

Herder, P. M., & Weijnen, M. P. C. (2000). A concurrent engineering approach to chemical process design. *International Journal of Production Economics*, *64*, 311–318. doi:10.1016/S0925-5273(99)00068-7

Herroelen, W., & Leus, R. (2005). Project scheduling under uncertainty: Survey and research potentials. *European Journal of Operational Research*, *165*(2), 289–306. doi:10.1016/j.ejor.2004.04.002

Heskett, J. L., Jones, T. O., Loveman, G. W., Sasser, W. E., & Schlesinger, L. A. (1994). Putting the service profit chain to work. *Harvard Business Review*, *72*(March-April), 164–174.

Hildebrandt, L. (1988). Store image and the prediction of performance on retailing. *Journal of Business Research*, *17*, 91–100. doi:10.1016/0148-2963(88)90026-4

Hill, A., & Hill, T. (2009). *Manufacturing operations strategy* (3rd ed.). Basingstoke, UK: Palgrave Macmillan.

Hoffmann, M., & Schubert, K. (2009). Material flow management at the university hospital in Jena. *Stoffstrommanagement am Universitätsklinikum Jena, 11*(10), 38-41.

Hoffman, W. (2003). Missing links. *PM Network*, *17*(6), 50–54.

Hofman, D., & Cecere, L. (2005). The agile supply chain. *The Supply Chain Management Review, November,* 18-19.

Holmes, C., & Ferril, M. (2005). The application of operation and technology roadmapping to aid Singaporean SMEs identify and select emerging technologies. *Technological Forecasting and Social Change*, *72*, 349–357. doi:10.1016/j.techfore.2004.08.010

Holweg, M. (2005). The three dimensions of responsiveness. *International Journal of Operations & Production Management*, *25*(7), 603–622. doi:10.1108/01443570510605063

Holweg, M., & Pil, F. K. (2008). Theoretical perspectives on the coordination of supply chains. *Journal of Operations Management*, *26*(3), 389–406. doi:10.1016/j.jom.2007.08.003

Hooi Ting, D. (2004). Service quality and satisfaction perceptions: Curvilinear and interaction effect. *International Journal of Bank Marketing*, *22*(6), 407–420. doi:10.1108/02652320410559330

Horvath, L. (2001). Collaboration: The key to value creation in supply chain management. *Supply Chain Management: An International Journal*, *6*(5), 205–207. doi:10.1108/EUM0000000006039

Hou, J., Zeng, A. Z., & Zhao, L. (2010). Coordination with a backup supplier through buy-back contract under supply disruption. *Transportation Research Part E: Logistics and Transportation*, *46*(6), 881–895. doi:10.1016/j.tre.2010.03.004

Howells, J. R. L. (2002). Tacit knowledge, innovation and economic geography. *Urban Studies (Edinburgh, Scotland)*, *39*(5/6), 871–884. doi:10.1080/00420980220128354

Hsu, L. (2005). SCM system effects on performance for interaction between suppliers and buyers. *Industrial Management (Des Plaines)*, *105*(7), 857.

Hsu, T.-H., Su, H.-Y., & Liao, P.-P. (2010). Enhancing value creation of device vendors in the medical service industry: A relationship perspective. *The Service Industries Journal*, *30*(11), 1787–1801. doi:10.1080/02642060802624316

http://www.dmsms.org/ file.jsp?storename=OMIS_article1.pdf

Hughes, C. (2009). *Using clinical decision support to improve health and achieve cost savings*. San Diego, CA: Anvita Health Inc.

Hulsmann, M., Grapp, J., & Li, Y. (2008). Strategic adaptivity in global supply chains-Competitive advantage by autonomous cooperation. *International Journal of Production Economics*, *114*, 14–26. doi:10.1016/j.ijpe.2007.09.009

Hult, G. T. M., Ketchen, D. J., & Arrfelt, M. (2007). Strategic supply chain management: Improving performance through a culture of competitiveness and knowledge development. *Strategic Management Journal*, *28*(10), 1035–1052. doi:10.1002/smj.627

Humphreys, M., Williams, M., & Meier, R. (1996). Product quality, interpersonal process quality and their relationships to overall customer satisfaction. *Proceedings of the 1996 NAIT Convention*, Los Angeles, CA.

Humphreys, M., Williams, M. R., & Goebel, D. J. (2008). Toward an enhanced definition and measurement of purchasing's strategic role in buy-supplier relationships. *Journal of Business-To-Business Marketing*, *15*(3), 323–353. doi:10.1080/15470620802059307

Humphreys, M., Williams, M. R., & Goebel, D. J. (2009). The mediating effect of supplier oriented purchasing on conflict in inter-firm relationships. *Journal of Business and Industrial Marketing*, *24*(3/4), 198–206. doi:10.1108/08858620910939741

Humphreys, M., Williams, M., & Meier, R. (1997). Leveraging the total market offering in the agile enterprise. *Quality Management Journal*, *97*(5), 60–74.

Hyer, N., & Wemmerlov, U. (1984). Group technology and productivity. *Harvard Business Review*, (July- August): 140–149.

Ibarra, H., & Hanson, M. (2009, December 21). Women CEOs: Why so few? *Harvard Business Review*. Retrieved from http://blogs.hbr.org/ cs/2009/12/women_ceo_why_so_few.html

IBM. (2006). *Expanding the innovation horizon*. Somers, NY: IBM Global Services.

in Aeronautics and Astronautics at the Massachusetts Institute of Technology (MIT)

Ipe, M. (2003). Knowledge sharing on organizations: A conceptual framework. *Human Resource Development Review*, *2*(4), 337–359. doi:10.1177/1534484303257985

Isam, E., McWilliams, D., & Tetteh, E. (2010). Enhancing lean manufacturing learning experience through hands-on simulation. *Simulation and Gaming, 41*(4). Sage Publications.

Jain, K., Nagar, L., & Srivastava, V. (2006). Benefit sharing in inter-organizational coordination. *Supply Chain Management: An International Journal*, *11*(5), 400–406. doi:10.1108/13598540610682417

Jamal, A., & Naser, K. (2002). Customer satisfaction and retail banking: An assessment of some of the key antecedents of customer satisfaction in retail banking. *International Journal of Bank Marketing*, *20*(4/5), 146–161. doi:10.1108/02652320210432936

Jamshidi, M. (2005). *System-of-systems engineering: A definition*. Hawaii: IEEE SMC.

Janda, S., & Seshadri, S. (2001). The influence of purchasing strategies on performance. *Journal of Business and Industrial Marketing*, *16*(4), 294–308. doi:10.1108/EUM0000000005502

Jap, S. (1999). Pie-expansion efforts: Collaboration processes in buyer-supplier relationships. *JMR, Journal of Marketing Research*, *36*(4), 461–475. doi:10.2307/3152000

Jayatilleka, S., & Okogbaa, G. O. (2001). Accelerated life test for identifying potential failure modes and optimizing critical design parameters in a journal bearing. *IEEE Proceedings of Annual Reliability and Maintainability Symposium.*

Jeong, K.-C., & Kim, Y.-D. (1998). A real-time scheduling mechanism for a flexible manufacturing system: Using simulation and dispatching rules. *International Journal of Production Research*, *36*(9), 2609–2626. doi:10.1080/002075498192733

Jeong, S. J., Lim, S. J., & Kim, K. S. (2005). Hybrid approach to production scheduling using genetic algorithm and simulation. *International Journal of Advanced Manufacturing Technology*, *28*(1-2), 126–136.

Jiao, Y. Y., Li, K., & Jiao, R. J. (2008, 21-24 Sept. 2008). *A case study of hospital patient discharge process re-engineering using RFID.* Paper presented at the Management of Innovation and Technology, 2008. ICMIT 2008. 4th IEEE International Conference on.

John, M. (2009). *Cloud based security as a service.* Retrieved February 14, 2010, from http://cloudsecurity.trendmicro.com/ the-security-as-a-service-model/

Johnston, D., McCutcheon, D., Stuart, F., & Kerwood, H. (2004). Effects of supplier trust on performance of cooperative supplier relationships. *Journal of Operations Management, 22*(5), 23–38. doi:10.1016/j.jom.2003.12.001

Joia, L. A., & Lemos, B. (2010). Relevant factors for tacit knowledge transfer within organisations. *Journal of Knowledge Management, 14*(3), 210. doi:10.1108/13673271011050139

Jones, C., Hesterly, W. S., & Borgatti, S. P. (1997). A general theory of network governance: Exchange conditions and social mechanisms. *Academy of Management Review, 22*(4), 911–945.

Jones, J. (1995). *Integrated logistic support handbook.* New York, NY: MacGraw Hill.

Jonsson, P. (2008). *Logistics and supply chain management.* London, UK: McGraw-Hill.

Jonsson, P., & Zineldin, M. (2003). Achieving high satisfaction in supplier-dealer working relationships. *Supply Chain Management, 8*(3-4), 224.

Jurma, W. E., & Powell, M. L. (1994). Perceived gender roles of managers and effective conflict management. *Psychological Reports, 74*(1), 104–106. doi:10.2466/pr0.1994.74.1.104

Jüttner, U., Christopher, M., & Baker, S. (2007). Demand chain management-integrating marketing and supply chain management. *Industrial Marketing Management, 36*(3), 377–392. doi:10.1016/j.indmarman.2005.10.003

Kaihara, T. (2003). Multi-agent based supply chain modeling with dynamic environment. *International Journal of Production Economics, 85*, 263–269. doi:10.1016/S0925-5273(03)00114-2

Kakati, M. (2002). Mass customization - needs to go beyond technology. *Human Systems Management, 21*, 85–93.

Kamrad, B., & Siddique, A. (2004). Supply contracts, profit sharing, switching, and reaction options. *Management Science, 50*(1), 64–82. doi:10.1287/mnsc.1030.0157

Kamrani, A. K., & Salhieh, S. M. (2001). *Product design for modularity* (p. 224). doi:10.1007/978-1-4615-1725-2

Kannan, V. R., & Tan, K. C. (2006). Buyer-supplier relationships: The impact of supplier selection and buyer-supplier engagement on relationship and firm performance. *International Journal of Physical Distribution & Logistics Management, 36*(10), 755–775. doi:10.1108/09600030610714580

Kanning, P. U., & Bergmann, B. (2009). Predictors of customer satisfaction: Resting the classical paradigms. *Managing Service Quality, 19*(4), 377–390. doi:10.1108/09604520910971511

Karen Martin & Associations. (2011). *Lean terminology.* Retrieved June 28, 2011, from http://www.ksmartin.com/resources/terminology.html#f

Kargaonkar, P. K., Lund, D., & Price, B. (1985). A structural equations approach toward examination of store attitude and store patronage behavior. *Journal of Retailing, 61*(Summer), 39–60.

Karkkainen, M. (2003). Increasing efficiency in the supply chain for short shelf life goods using RFID tagging. *International Journal of Retail & Distribution Management, 31*, 529–536. doi:10.1108/09590550310497058

Kassim, N. M. (2006). Telecommunications industry in Malaysia: Demographics effect on customer expectations, performance, satisfaction and retention. *Asia Pacific Business Review, 12*(4), 437–363. doi:10.1080/13602380600571401

Kassim, N. M., Najdawi, M. K., Al-Azmeh, Z., & Sidiq, H. (2010). Effects of institutional reform on corporate image and value in a developing country context. *Measuring Business Excellence, 14*(2), 32–45. doi:10.1108/13683041011047849

Kaufmann Foundation. (2009). *Characteristics of new firms: A comparison by gender: Third in a series of reports using data from the Kaufmann Firm survey.* Kaufmann, the Foundation of Entrepreneurship, January 2009, Retrieved from http://www.kauffman.org/ uploadedfiles/kfs_gender_020209.pdf

Keaveney, S. M. (1995). Customer switching behavior in service industries: An exploratory study. *Journal of Marketing, 59*, 71–82. doi:10.2307/1252074

Kelepouris, T., Pramatari, K., & Doukidis, G. (2007). RFID-enabled traceability in the food supply chain. *Industrial Management & Data Systems*, *107*, 183–200. doi:10.1108/02635570710723804

Ketchen, D. J., Hult, T. M., Rebarick, W., & Meyer, D. (2008). Best value supply chains: A key competitive weapon for the 21st century. *Business Horizons*, *51*, 235–243. doi:10.1016/j.bushor.2008.01.012

Khan, A., Bakkappa, B., Metri, B. A., & Sahay, B. S. (2009). Impact of agile supply chains' delivery practices on firms' performance: Cluster analysis and validation. *Supply Chain Management: An International Journal*, *14*(1), 41–48. doi:10.1108/13598540910927296

Kim, J., & Kim, J. H. (2005). Anti-counterfeiting solution employing mobile RFID environment. *Proceedings of the World Academy of Science, Engineering and Technology, 8,* (pp. 141-145).

Kim, B. (2005). *Mastering business in Asia: Supply chain management*. Singapore: Wiley.

Kim, H. (2002). Predicting how ontologies for the semantic web will evolve. *Communications of the ACM*, *45*(2), 48–54. doi:10.1145/503124.503148

Kirkman, B. L., Rosen, B., Gibson, C. B., Tesluk, P. E., & McPherson, S. O. (2002). Five challenges to virtual team success: Lessons from Sabre, Inc. *The Academy of Management Executive*, *16*(3), 67. doi:10.5465/AME.2002.8540322

Kline, R. B. (1998). *Principles and practice of structural equation modeling*. New York, NY: Guildford Press.

Kogut, B., & Zander, U. (1992). Knowledge of the firm, combinative capabilities, and the replication of technology. *Organization Science*, *3*(3), 383–397. doi:10.1287/orsc.3.3.383

Kojima, M., Nakashima, K., & Ohno, K. (2008). Performance evaluation of SCM in JIT environment. *International Journal of Production Economics*, *115*, 439–443. doi:10.1016/j.ijpe.2007.11.017

Kostoff, R. N., & Schaller, R. R. (2001). Science and technology roadmaps. *IEEE Transactions on Engineering Management*, *48*(2). doi:10.1109/17.922473

Koufteros, X. (2001). Concurrent engineering and its consequences. *Journal of Operations Management*, *19*, 97–115. doi:10.1016/S0272-6963(00)00048-6

Koulikoff-Souviron, M., & Pascal, V. (2005). A dose of collaboration. *European Business Forum*, *22*, 59.

Kros, T. C. (1999). *Modernization through spares: An analysis of implementation at the U.S. Army aviation and missile command*. Retrieved from http://www.nps.navy.mil/ code36/krostc.html

Kumar, A., Fantazy, K. A., & Kumar, U. (2006). Implementation and management framework for supply chain flexibility. *Journal of Enterprise Information*, *19*(3), 303–319. doi:10.1108/17410390610658487

Kumar, N. (2000). *The power of trust in manufacturer-retailer relationships. Harvard Business Review: Managing The Value Chain*. Boston, MA: HBS Publishing.

Kumar, S. (2010). Specialty hospitals emulating focused factories: A case study. *International Journal of Health Care Quality Assurance*, *23*(1), 94–109. doi:10.1108/09526861011010703

Kumar, S., & Aldrich, K. (2010). Overcoming barriers to electronic medical record (EMR) implementation in the US healthcare system: A comparative study. *Health Informatics Journal*, *16*(4), 306–318. doi:10.1177/1460458210380523

Kuo, T. C., & Zhang, H. (1995). *Design for manufacturability and design for "X": Concepts, applications, and perspectives*. IEEEiCPMT International Electronics Manufacturing Technology Symposium.

Kwon, O. B., & Lee, K. C. (2002). MACE: Multi-agents coordination engine to resolve conflicts among functional units in an enterprise. *Expert Systems with Applications*, *23*, 9–21. doi:10.1016/S0957-4174(02)00023-4

Lambert, D. J., Stock, J. R., & Ellram, L. M. (1998). *Fundamentals of logistics management*. McGraw-Hill.

Lambert, D. M. (Ed.). (2008). *An executive summary of supply chain management: Processes, partnerships, performance* (3rd ed.). Sarasota, FL: Supply Chain Management Institute.

Lambert, D. M. (Ed.). (2008). *Supply chain management process, partnerships, performance* (3rd ed.). Sarasota, FL: Supply Chain Management Institute.

Lapide, L. (2010). A history of CPFR. *The Journal of Business Forecasting*, *29*(4), 29.

Laraia, A., Moody, P., & Robert, R. (1999). *The kaizen blitz: Accelerating breakthroughs in productivity and performance*. John Wiley & Sons Inc.

Lariviere, M. A. (2002). Supply chain contracting and coordination with stochastic demandIn Tayur, S., Ganeshan, R., & Magazine, M. (Eds.), *Quantitative models for supply chain management* (pp. 233–268). Kluwer Academic Publishers. doi:10.1007/978-1-4615-4949-9_8

Larsson, R., Bentsson, L., Henriksson, K., & Sparks, J. (1998). The inter-organizational learning dilemma: Collective knowledge development in strategic alliances. *Organization Science*, *9*(3), 285–305. doi:10.1287/orsc.9.3.285

Lawson, C., & Lorenz, E. (1999). Collective learning, tacit knowledge and regional innovative capacity. *Regional Studies*, *33*(4), 305–317. doi:10.1080/713693555

Lee, H., & Whang, S (2001). *E-business and supply chain integration*. Stanford Global Supply Chain Management Forum.

Lee, C. K. M., Ho, W., Ho, G. T. S., & Lau, H. C. W. (2011). Design and development of logistics workflow systems for demand management with RFID. *Expert Systems with Applications*, *38*(5), 5428–5437. doi:10.1016/j.eswa.2010.10.012

Lee, H. L. (2002). Aligning supply chain strategies with product uncertainties. *California Management Review*, *44*(3), 105–119.

Lee, H. L. (2004). The triple-A supply chain. *Harvard Business Review*, *82*(10), 102–112.

Lee, H. L., & Tang, C. S. (1997). Modeling the costs and benefits of delayed product differentiation. *Management Science*, *43*(1), 40–53. doi:10.1287/mnsc.43.1.40

Leenders, M. R., Fraser, J. P., Flynn, A. E., & Fearson, H. E. (2006). *Purchasing and supply management* (13th ed.). Boston, MA: McGraw-Hill Irwin.

Lee, S., Kang, S., Park, Y., & Park, Y. (2007). Technology roadmapping for R&D planning: The case of the Korean parts and materials industry. *Technology (Elmsford, N.Y.)*, *27*, 433–445.

Lee, S., & Park, Y. (2005). Customerization of technology roadmaps according to roadmapping purposes: Overall process and detailed modules. *Technological Forecasting and Social Change*, *72*, 567–583. doi:10.1016/j.techfore.2004.11.006

Lessard, D. R., & Zaheer, S. (1996). Breaking the silos: Distributed knowledge and strategic responses to volatile exchange rates. *Strategic Management Journal*, *17*(7), 513–543. doi:10.1002/(SICI)1097-0266(199607)17:7<513::AID-SMJ832>3.0.CO;2-P

Levesque, T., & McDougall, G. H. C. (1996). Determinants of customer satisfaction in retail Banking. *International Journal of Bank Marketing*, *14*(7), 12–20. doi:10.1108/02652329610151340

Li, C. (2009). Agile supply chain: Coming in volatile markets. *Management Science and Engineering*, *3*(2).

Li, X. P. (2002). *Optimization methods of multilevel hierarchical planning architecture of engineer-to-order enterprises*. PhD Dissertation, Harbin Institute of Technology, Harbin, China.

Liang, K. (2010). *Aspects of quality tools on total quality management*. Academic Search Complete.

Liang, Y., Zuo, X., & Lei, H. (2011). Research on supply chain coordination of TPL supplier participation. *Journal of Service Science and Management*, *4*(1), 1–7. doi:10.4236/jssm.2011.41001

Lian, Z., & Deshmukh, A. (2009). Analysis of supply contracts with quantity flexibility. *European Journal of Operational Research*, *196*(2), 526–533. doi:10.1016/j.ejor.2008.02.043

Lilley, K. (2008). An integrated strategy for e-procurement: The case for Leeds teaching hospitalsIn Hübner, U., & Elmhorst, M. A. (Eds.), *E-business in healthcare* (pp. 177–195). London, UK: Springer.

Lin, F., & Shaw, M. J. (1998). Reengineering the order fulfillment process in supply chain networks. *International Journal of Flexible Manufacturing Systems*, *10*(3), 197–229. doi:10.1023/A:1008069816606

Lipnack, J., & Stamps, J. (1997). *Virtual teams: reaching across space, time, and organizations with technology*. New York, NY: John Wiley and Sons.

Li, S. H., Rao, S. S., Nathan, R. T., & Nathan, B. R. (2006). The impact of supply chain management practices on competitive advantage and organizational performance. *Omega*, *34*, 107–124. doi:10.1016/j.omega.2004.08.002

Li, S., Rao, S. S., Ragu-Nathan, T. S., & Ragu-Nathan, B. (2005). Development and validation of a measurement instrument for studying supply chain management practices. *Journal of Operations Management*, *23*(6), 618–641. doi:10.1016/j.jom.2005.01.002

Liu, L., & Wang, L. (2007). Management strategy of materials supply for manufacturing organizations. *Computers & Industrial Engineering*, *53*(2), 326–349. doi:10.1016/j.cie.2007.06.026

Livingston, H. (2007). Avoiding counterfeit electronic components. *IEEE Transactions on Components and Packaging Technologies*, *30*, 187–189. doi:10.1109/TCAPT.2007.893682

Llosa, S., Chandon, J.-L., & Orsingher, C. (1998). An empirical study of SERVQUAL's dimensionality. *The Service Industries Journal*, *18*(2), 16–44. doi:10.1080/02642069800000017

Lochamy, A. III, & McCormack, K. (2004). Linking SCOR planning practices to supply chain performance. *International Journal of Operations & Production Management*, *24*(11/12), 1192.

Lodge, A., & Bamford, D. (2007). Health service improvement through diagnostic waiting list management. *Leadership in Health Services*, *20*(4), 254–265. doi:10.1108/17511870710829364

Logistics Handling. (June 8, 2010). *Diversity and inclusion in logistics: Why bother?* International Institute for Material Handling and Logistics. Retrieved from http://www.LogisticsHandling.com

Lovelock, C. H. (1991). *Services marketing*. Upper Saddle River, NJ: Prentice-Hall, Inc.

Lundin, O. (1999). *An operations and maintenance process model for energy management* (pp. 1–7). IEEE.

Lu, Q., & Wood, L. (2006). The refinement of DFM: Inclusion of process design. *International Journal of Operations & Production Management*, *26*(10), 1123–1145. doi:10.1108/01443570610691102

Lyles, L. L. (2001, 23 March). *Commander, USAR material command before the House Armed Services Committee.*

MacInnes, R. L. (2002). *The lean enterprise memory jogger*. Salem, NH: GOAL/QPC.

MacInnes, R. L. (2009). *The lean enterprise memory jogger for service*. Salem, NH: GOAL/QPC.

Madden, K. M. (2000). *The role of communication in building customer relationships in the Australian financial services industry: an in-depth study*. Unpublished doctoral dissertation, university of Southern Queensland, Toowomba, Australia.

Madhavan, R., & Grover, R. (1998). From embedded knowledge to embodied knowledge: New product development as knowledge management. *Journal of Marketing*, *62*(4), 1–12. doi:10.2307/1252283

Mahendrawathi, E. R., Pranantha, D., & Johansyah Dwi, U. (2010, 5-7 Dec. 2010). *Development of dashboard for hospital logistics management.* Paper presented at the Open Systems (ICOS), 2010 IEEE Conference on.

Maione, G., & Naso, D. (2003). A soft computing approach for task contracting in multi agent manufacturing control. *Computers in Industry*, *52*, 199–219. doi:10.1016/S0166-3615(03)00127-1

Maku, T. C., & Collins, T. R. (2005). The impact of human interaction on supply chain management practices. *Performance Improvement*, *44*(7), 26. doi:10.1002/pfi.4140440708

Malhotra, N. K. (1993). *Marketing research: An applied orientation*. Englewood Cliffs, NJ: Prentice-Hall Inc.

Maloni, M., & Benton, W. C. (2000). Power influences in supply chain. *Journal of Business Logistics*, *21*(1), 49–73.

Manetti, J. (2001). How technology is transforming manufacturing. *Production and Inventory Management Journal*, *42*(1).

Manning, T., & Robertson, B. (2010). Seniority and gender differences in 360-degree assessments of influencing, leadership and team behaviors. Part 1: Introduction and seniority differences. *Industrial & Commercial Training*, *42*(3), 139–146. doi:10.1108/00197851011038123

Martin, K., & Osterling, M. (2007). *The kaizen event planner: Achieving rapid improvement in office, service, and technical environments.*

Martin, N. (2004). Supplier relationship management. *Interactive Marketing*, *6*(1), 34–43. doi:10.1057/palgrave.im.4340266

Maruster, L., & Jorna, R. J. (2005). From data to knowledge: A method for modeling hospital logistic processes. *IEEE Transactions on Information Technology in Biomedicine*, *9*(2), 248–255. doi:10.1109/TITB.2005.847194

Mathaisel, D. M. X. (2009). *The lean enterprise: An architecture for lean transformation.* Auerbach Publications, Taylor and Francis Group.

Mathaisel, D. F. X. (2006). *Sustaining the military enterprise: An architecture for a lean transformation.* Babson Park, MA: Babson College.

Mathaisel, D. F. X., Cathcart, T., & Comm, C. (2004). A framework for benchmarking, classifying, and implementing best sustainment practices. *Journal of Benchmarking*, *11*(4), 403–417. doi:10.1108/14635770410546791

Mattis, M. (2000). Women entrepreneurs in the United StatesIn Davidson, M. J., & Burke, R. (Eds.), *Women in management: Current research issues* (*Vol. 11*). London, UK: Sage.

Mazursky, D., & Jacoby, J. (1986). Exploring the development of store image. *Journal of Retailing*, *62*, 145–165.

McAdam, R., & McCormack, D. (2001). Integrating business processes for global alignment and supply chain management. *Business Process Management*, *7*(2), 113. doi:10.1108/14637150110389696

McBride, D. (2003). *Design for manufacturability*. EMS Consulting Group. Retrieved from http://www.emsstrategies.com

McCarter, M. W., Fawcett, S. E., & Magnan, G. M. (2005). The effect of people on the supply chain world: Some overlooked issues. *Human Systems Management*, *24*, 197–208.

McClellan, M. (2003). *Collaborative manufacturing*. New York, NY: St. Lucie Press.

Mcclure, W. M., & Faraj, S. (2005). Why should I share? Examining social capital and knowledge contribution in electronic networks of practice. *Management Information Systems Quarterly*, *29*(1), 35–57.

McGinnis, M. A., & Vallopra, R. M. (1999). Purchasing and supplier involvement in process improvement: A source of competitive advantage. *Journal of Supply Chain Management*, *35*(4), 42–50. doi:10.1111/j.1745-493X.1999.tb00243.x

McKenna, M. K. L., & Murray, W. E. (2002). Jungle law in the orchard: Comparing globalization in the New Zealand and Chilean apple industries. *Economic Geography*, *78*(4), 494–514. doi:10.1111/j.1944-8287.2002.tb00197.x

McMurray, A. (2002). *Mapping the support provision for women in enterprise in Northern Ireland and a strategic framework for the future*. Ann McMurray Consulting Ltd.

Meader, P. (2009). *An introduction to developing for Microsoft Azure*. Retrieved February 14, 2010, from http://searchcloudcomputing.techtarget.com/generic/0,295582,sid201_gci1366241,00.html

MEEP. (2009). *Concurrent engineering materials.* The Manufacturing Education Partnership. Penn State University of Puerto Rico-Mayaguez & University of Washington Sandia National Lab.

Mehta, J. (2004, July-August). Supply chain management in a global economy. *Total Quality Management*, *15*(5-6), 841–848. doi:10.1080/14783360410001680279

Mehta, S. V., & Uzsoy, R. (1999). Predictable scheduling of a single machine subject to breakdowns. *International Journal of Computer Integrated Manufacturing*, *12*(1), 15–38. doi:10.1080/095119299130443

Meier, R., Humphreys, M., & Williams, M. (1998). The role of purchasing in the agile enterprise. *International Journal of Purchasing & Materials Management*, *34*(4), 39–45.

Mell, P., & Grance, T. (2009). *The NIST definition of cloud computing*. Retrieved February 14, 2010, from http:// csrc.nist.gov/ groups/SNS/cloud-computing/ index.html

Meyr, H., Rohde, J., & Stadtler, H. (2002). Basic for modelingIn Stadtler, H., & Kilger, C. (Eds.), *Supply chain management and advanced planning: Concepts, models, software and case studies* (2nd ed., pp. 45–70). Berlin, Germany: Springer – Verlag.

Mika, G. (2005). *Kaizen event implementation manual*. Society of Manufacturing Engineers.

Miller, J. (2005). *Introduction to lean and value-stream mapping*. Gemba Research.

Mills, J., Schmitz, J., & Frivol, G. (2004). A strategic view of supply networks. *International Journal of Operations & Production Management*, *24*(9/10), 1012. doi:10.1108/01443570410558058

Min, S. (2001). Inter-functional coordination in supply chain managementIn Mentzer, J. T. (Ed.), *Supply chain management* (pp. 371–390). Thousand Oaks, CA: Sage Publications.

Mintzberg, H. (1997). Toward healthier hospitals. *Health Care Management Review*, *22*(4), 9–18.

Mintzberg, H. (2002). Managing care and cure - Up and down, in and out. *Health Services Management Research*, *15*(3), 193–206. doi:10.1258/095148402320176639

Misra, S. C. (2005). Modeling design/coding factors that drive maintainability of software systems. *Software Quality Journal*, *13*, 297–320. doi:10.1007/s11219-005-1754-7

Mitchell, D. (2008). *Defining platform as a service*. Retrieved February 14, 2010, from http://blogs.bungeeconnect.com/ 2008/02/18/defining-platform-as-a-service-or-paas

Mitchell, R., Tydeman, J., & Georgiades, J. (1979). Structuring the future-application of a scenario-generation procedure. *Technological Forecasting and Social Change*, *14*, 409–428. doi:10.1016/0040-1625(79)90038-6

Mittal, B., & Lassar, W. M. (1998). Why do customer switch? The dynamics of satisfaction versus loyalty. *Journal of Services Marketing*, *12*(3), 177–194. doi:10.1108/08876049810219502

Mittal, V., Rose, W. T., & Baldasare, P. M. (1998). The asymmetric impact of negative and positive attribute-level performance on overall satisfaction and repurchase intention. *Journal of Marketing*, *62*(January), 33–47. doi:10.2307/1251801

Modi, S., & Mabert, V. A. (2007). Supplier development: improving supplier performance through knowledge transfer. *Journal of Operations Management*, *25*(1), 42–64. doi:10.1016/j.jom.2006.02.001

Moeller, S., Faassnacht, M., & Klose, S. (2006). A framework for supplier relationship management. *Journal of Business-To-Business Marketing*, *13*(4), 69–94. doi:10.1300/J033v13n04_03

Mohammed, J., & Sadique, A. (2010). *Lean value stream manufacturing for sustainability*. 8th Global Conference for Sustainable Manufacturing, Abu Dhabi, UAE.

Mo, J. P. T. (2009). The role of lean in the application of information technology to manufacturing. *Computers in Industry*, *60*, 266–276. doi:10.1016/j.compind.2009.01.002

Monczka, R. M., Handfield, R. B., Giunipero, L., & Patterson, J. (2009). *Purchasing and supply chain management*. Mason, OH: South-Western Cengage Learning.

Money, C. N. N. (2010). *Fortune 500: Women CEOs*. Retrieved from http://money.cnn.com/ magazines/fortune/ fortune500/2009/womenceos/

Monostori, L., Váncza, J., & Kumara, S. R. T. (2006). Agent-based systems for manufacturing. *CIRP Annals - Manufacturing Technology*, *55*(2), 697-720.

Monostori, L., Márkus, A., Van Brussel, H., & Westkämper, E. (1996). Machine learning approaches to manufacturing. *Annals of the CIRP*, *45*(2), 675–712.

Morgan, R., & Hunt, S. (1994). The commitment-trust theory of relationship marketing. *Journal of Marketing*, *58*(3), 20–39. doi:10.2307/1252308

Morrell, M., & Ezingeard, J. (2001). Revisiting adoption factors of inter-organizational information systems in SMEs. *Logistics Information Management*, *15*(1-2), 46.

Muller-Christ, G., & Hulsmann, M. (2003). Quo vadis Umweltmanagement? Entwicklungsperspektiven einer nachhaltigkeitsorientierten Managementlehre. *Die Betriebswirtschaft*, *63*, 257–277.

Munier, N. (2005). *Introduction to sustainability: Road to a better future*. Springer Publications.

Murphy, J. A. (1996). Retailing bankingIn Buttle, F. (Ed.), *Relationship marketing, theory and practice* (pp. 74–90). London, UK: Paul Chapman.

Nachtmann, H., & Pohl, E. A. (2009). *The state of healthcare logistics: Cost and quality improvement opportunities*. Fayetteville, AR: Center for Innovation in Healthcare Logistics, University of Arkansas.

Nakade, K., Tsubouchi, S., & Sediri, I. (2010). Properties of Nash equilibrium retail prices in contract model with a supplier, multiple retailers and price-dependent demand. *Journal of Software Engineering and Applications*, *3*(1), 27–33. doi:10.4236/jsea.2010.31003

Narang, R. (2011). Determining quality of public health care services in rural India. *Clinical Governance: An International Journal*, *16*(1), 35–49. doi:10.1108/14777271111104574

National Research Council. (2000). *Surviving supply chain integration*. Washington, DC: National Academy Press.

Nelson, D., Moody, P. E., & Stegner, J. (2001). *The purchasing machine*. New York, NY: The Free Press.

Neuman, K., O'Connor, C., & Myles, L. (2000). Communication key to supply chain efficiency. *Hospital Materials Management*, *25*(4), 11–13.

Neuman, S., & Oaxaca, S. (2003). Gender versus ethnic wage differentials among professionals: Evidence from Israel. *Annales d'Economie et de Statistique*, *71-72*, 267–292.

Newsdesk. (March 2004). Employers raising the bottom line through diversity. *Management Services, 48*(3), 6.

Nightingale, D. (2000). *Integrating the lean enterprise*. MIT Presentation. Retrieved from http://lean.mit.edu

Nolle, T. (2009). *Platform as a service: Google and Force.com.* Retrieved February 14, 2010, from http://searchcloudcomputing.techtarget.com/ tip/0,289483,sid201_gci1355986,00.html

Nonaka, I. (1994). A dynamic theory of organizational knowledge creation. *Organization Science*, *5*(1), 14–37. doi:10.1287/orsc.5.1.14

Nonaka, I., & Takeuchi, H. (1995). *The knowledge-creating company: How Japanese companies create the dynamics of innovation*. New York, NY: Oxford University Press.

Noordewier, T., John, G., & Nevin, J. (1990). Performance outcomes of purchasing arrangements in industrial buyer-vendor relationships. *Journal of Marketing*, *54*(4), 80–94. doi:10.2307/1251761

Novack, R. A., Langly, C. J. Jr, & Rinehart, L. M. (1995). *Creating logistics value: themes for the future*. Oak Brook, IL: Council on Logistics Management.

O'Marah, K., & Hofman, D. (2010). *The AMR supply chain top 25 for 2010*. Stamford, CT: Gartner Research Publication.

O'Toole, T., & Donaldson, B. (2000). Managing buyer-supplier relationship archetypes. *Irish Marketing Review*, *13*(1), 12–20.

Oakden, R., & Leonaite, K. (2011). *A framework for supply chains: Logistics operations in the Asia-Pacific region*. North Ryde, Australia: McGraw-Hill Australia.

O'Donnell, A. (2009). Hot technologies: While insurers often are cautious in their adoption of emerging technologies, carriers are investing in solutions that are just too transformative to ignore, including cloud computing, mobile capabilities, risk assessment solutions and social media. *Insurance & Technology*, *35*, 24–28.

Office of Management and Budget. (1998). *Budget of the United States Government: Historical*

Ohno, T. (1988). *The Toyota production system – Beyond large scale production*. Portland, OR: Productivity Inc.

Ohno, T. (1988). *Toyota production system*. Portland, OR: Productivity Press.

Oliver, R. L., & DeSarbo, W. S. (1988). Response determinants in satisfaction judgments. *The Journal of Consumer Research*, *14*, 495–506. doi:10.1086/209131

O'Marah, K. (2003). The business case for PLM. *Supply Chain Management Review*, *7*(6), 16–18.

Otto, K. N., & Wood, K. L. (2001). *Product design techniques in reverse engineering and new product development*. Upper Saddle River, NJ: Prentice Hall.

Ouelhadj, D., Cowling, P. I., & Petrovic, S. (2003b). Utility and stability measures for agent-based dynamic scheduling of steel continuous casting. In *Proceedings of the IEEE International Conference on Robotics and Automation* (175–180). Taipei, Taiwan.

Ouelhadj, D., Cowling, P. I., & Petrovic, S. (2003a). Contract net protocol for cooperative optimisation and dynamic scheduling of steel productionIn Ibraham, A., Franke, K., & Koppen, M. (Eds.), *Intelligent systems design and applications* (pp. 457–470). Berlin, Germany: Springer.

Ouelhadj, D., & Petrovic, S. (2009). A survey of dynamic scheduling in manufacturing systems. *Journal of Scheduling, 12*, 417–431. doi:10.1007/s10951-008-0090-8

Ozkil, A. G., Zhun, F., Dawids, S., Aanes, H., Kristensen, J. K., & Christensen, K. H. (2009, 5-7 Aug. 2009). *Service robots for hospitals: A case study of transportation tasks in a hospital.* Paper presented at the IEEE International Conference on Automation and Logistics, ICAL '09.

Padmanabhan, V., & Png, I. P. L. (1997). Manufacturer's returns policy and retail competition. *Marketing Science, 16*(1), 81–94. doi:10.1287/mksc.16.1.81

Palmatier, R. W., & Gopalakrishna, S. (2005). Determining the payoff from relationship marketing programs. In *MSI Reports: Marketing Science Institute Working Paper Series, 1*(5), 49-70.

Pandit, A., & Yimin, Z. (2007). An ontology based approach to support decision-making for the design of ETO (Engineer-To-Order) products. *Automation in Construction, 16*, 759–770. doi:10.1016/j.autcon.2007.02.003

Pannowitsch, S. (2009). Institutionalized healthcare reform in Germany? Error correction or political strategy? *German Policy Studies, 5*(1), 141–168.

Panteli, N., & Sockalingam, S. (2005). Trust and conflict within virtual inter-organizational alliances: A framework for facilitating knowledge sharing. *Decision Support Systems, 39*, 599–617. doi:10.1016/j.dss.2004.03.003

Pappas, J. M., Flaherty, K. E., & Wooldridge, B. (2004). Tapping into hospital champions-strategic middle managers. *Health Care Management Review, 29*(1), 8–16.

Parasuraman, A., Berry, L. L., & Zeithaml, V. A. (1991). Refinement and reassessment of the SERVQUAL scale. *Journal of Retailing, 67*(4), 420–430.

Parasuraman, A., Zeithaml, V. A., & Berry, L. L. (1988). SERVQUAL: A multiple item scale for measuring consumer perceptions of service quality. *Journal of Retailing, 64*(Spring), 12–40.

Park, J., Shin, K., Chang, T., & Park, J. (2010). An integrative framework for supplier relationship management. *Industrial Management + Data Systems, 110*(4), 495-515.

Park, D., & Krishnan, H. (2005). Gender differences in supply chain management practices. *International Journal of Management and Enterprise Development, 2*(1), 27–37. doi:10.1504/IJMED.2005.006022

Park, S. H., & Ungson, G. R. (2001). Interfirm rivalry and managerial complexity: A conceptual framework of alliance failure. *Organization Science, 12*(1), 37–53. doi:10.1287/orsc.12.1.37.10118

Pasternack, B. (1985). Optimal pricing and returns policies for perishable commodities. *Marketing Science, 4*(2), 166–176. doi:10.1287/mksc.4.2.166

Patel, A. (2008). *Best practices in front-end design.* A Bentley White Paper, design and FEED applications.

Patrick, I. J., & Echols, A. E. (2008). Technology roadmapping in review: A tool for making sustainable new product development decisions. *Technological Forecasting and Social Change, 71*, 81–100. doi:10.1016/S0040-1625(03)00064-7

Patterson, P. G., & Johnson, L. W. (1993). Disconfirmation of expectations and the gap model of service quality: An integrated paradigm. *Journal of Consumer Satisfaction, Dissatisfaction, and Complaining Behavior, 8*, 22–31.

Patterson, P. G., & Smith, T. (2003). A cross-cultural study of switching barriers and propensity to stay with service provider. *Journal of Retailing, 79*, 107–120. doi:10.1016/S0022-4359(03)00009-5

Payscale.com. (2010). *Hourly rate snapshots of supply chain analysts' jobs.* Retrieved from http://www.payscale.com/ research/US/Job=Supply_Chain_Analyst/Hourly_Rate/by_Gender

Payscale.com. (2010). *Salary snapshot of VP, supply chain management jobs.* Retrieved from http://www.payscale.com/ research/US/ Job=Vice_President_(VP),_Supply_Chain_Management/ Salary

Pelletier, J. (1996). *A Delphi study to define the domain and identify the key characteristics of supplier-oriented purchasing behavior*. Unpublished Master's thesis, Illinois State University, Normal.

Peppers, D., & Rogers, M. (1993). *The one to one future: Building relationship one customer at a time*. New York, NY: Doubleday.

Performance-Based Business Environment. (1997, January 23). *Flexible sustainment guide*.

Phaal, R., Farukh, C. J. P., & Probert, D. R. (2004). Technology roadmapping–A planning framework for evolution and revolution. *Technological Forecasting and Social Change*, *71*, 5–26. doi:10.1016/S0040-1625(03)00072-6

Phaal, R., & Muller, G. (2008). An architectural framework for roadmapping: towards visual strategy. *Technological Forecasting and Social Change*, *76*(1).

Pieters, A., Oirschot, C. v., & Akkermans, H. (2010). No cure for all evils: Dutch obstetric care and limits to the applicability of the focused factory concept in health care. *International Journal of Operations & Production Management*, *30*(11), 1112–1139. doi:10.1108/01443571011087350

Ping, L., Zhou, Z., & Chen, Y. (2005). Study on coordination in multi-agent-based agile supply chain management. *The Fourth International Conference on Machine Learning and Cybernetics,* Guangzhou, (pp. 18-21).

Piplani, R., Pujawan, N., & Ray, S. (2007). Sustainable supply chain management. *International Journal of Production Economics*, *111*(2), 193–194. doi:10.1016/j.ijpe.2007.05.001

Podolny, J. M., & Page, K. L. (1998). Network forms of organization. *Annual Review of Sociology*, *24*, 57–76. doi:10.1146/annurev.soc.24.1.57

Polanyi, G. (1966). *Tacit dimension*. London, UK: Routledge & Kegan Paul.

Pont, M., & McQuilken, L. (2005). An empirical investigation of customer satisfaction and loyalty across two divergent bank segments. *Journal of Financial Services Marketing*, *9*(4), 344–359. doi:10.1057/palgrave.fsm.4770165

Porter, M. E. (1985). *Competitive advantage – Creating and sustaining superior performance*.

Porter, M. (1998). Clusters and the new economics of competition. *Harvard Business Review*, *76*(6), 77–90.

Porter, M. (2003). The economic performance of regions. *Regional Studies*, *37*(6 & 7), 549–578.

Porter, M. E. (1990). The competitive advantage of nation. *Harvard Business Review*, *68*(2), 73–93.

Porter, M. E., & Teisberg, E. O. (2004). Redefining competition in health care. *Harvard Business Review*, *82*(6), 64–76.

Portioli-Staudacher, A., *et al.* (2003). *Implementation of concurrent engineering: A survey in Italy and Belguim.*

Postma, T., & Liebl, F. (2005). How to improve scenario analysis as a strategic management tool? *Technological Forecasting and Social Change*, *72*, 161–173.

Powell, W. W., & Brantley, P. (1992). Competitive cooperation in biotechnology: Learning through networksIn Nohria, N., & Eccles, R. G. (Eds.), *Networks and organizations*. Boston, MA: Harvard Business School Press.

Powell, W. W., Koput, K. W., & Smith-Doerr, L. (1996). Interorganizational collaboration and the locus of innovation: Networks of learning in biotechnology. *Administrative Science Quarterly*, *41*(1), 116–145. doi:10.2307/2393988

Powers, T. L., & Reagan, W. R. (2007). Factors influencing successful buyer-seller relationships. *Journal of Business Research*, *60*, 1234–1242. doi:10.1016/j.jbusres.2007.04.008

Prahalad, C. K., & Ramaswamy, V. (2004). *The future of competition*. Harvard Business Press.

Praharsi, Y., Purnomo, H. D., & Wee, H. M. (2010). An innovative heuristic for joint replenishment problem with deterministic and stochastic demand. *International Journal of Electronic Business Management*, *8*(3), 223–230.

Project Management Institute (PMI). (2008). *A guide to the project management body of knowledge* (4th ed.). Newtown Square, PA: Project Management Institute.

Qin, Z., & Xue, X. (2010). Risk averse members coordination with extended buy-back contract. *Journal of Service Science and Management*, *3*(1), 23–32. doi:10.4236/jssm.2010.31003

Quick Changeover. (2010, August 23). *A lean journey.* Retrieved June 28, 2011, from http://www.aleanjourney.com/ 2010/08/quick-changeover.html

Rahimnia, F., & Moghadasian, M. (2010). Supply chain leagility in professional services: How to apply decoupling point concept in healthcare delivery system. *Supply Chain Management: An International Journal*, *15*(1), 80–91. doi:10.1108/13598541011018148

Rahman, S., & Azhar, S. (2011). Xpressions of generation Y: Perceptions of the mobile phone service industry in Pakistan. *Asia Pacific Journal of Marketing Logistics*, *23*(1), 91–107. doi:10.1108/13555851111100012

Ramesh, A., Banwet, D. K., & Shankar, R. (2010). Modeling the barriers of supply chain collaboration. *Journal of Modeling in Management*, *5*(2), 176. doi:10.1108/17465661011061014

Ransom, M., & Oaxaca, R. (2005). Intrafirm mobility and sex differences in pay. *Industrial & Labor Relations Review*, *58*(2).

Rauen, C. A., Makic, M. B. F., & Bridges, E. (2009). Evidence-based practice habits: Transforming research into bedside practice. *Critical Care Nurse*, *29*(2), 46–59. doi:10.4037/ccn2009287

Reichhart, A., & Holweg, M. (2007). Creating the customer-responsive supply chain: A reconciliation of concepts. *International Journal of Operations & Production Management*, *27*(11), 1144–1172. doi:10.1108/01443570710830575

Reichheld, F. F., & Kenny, D. W. (1990). The hidden advantages of retention. *Journal of Retail Marketing*, *12*(4), 19–23.

Reichheld, F. F., & Sasser, W. E. (1990). Zero defections: quality comes to services. *Harvard Business Review*, (September-October): 105–111.

Reliability Analysis Center. (2004).. *Journal of the Reliability Analysis Center*, *10*(2).

Renna, P. (2009). A performance comparison between efficiency and pheromone approaches in dynamic manufacturing schedulingIn Chiong, R. (Ed.), *Intelligent systems for automated learning and adaptation* (pp. 273–298). Hershey, PA: Information Science Reference. doi:10.4018/978-1-60566-798-0.ch012

Renna, P. (2011). Multi-agent based scheduling in manufacturing cells in a dynamic environment. *International Journal of Production Research*, *49*(5), 1285–1301. doi:10.1080/00207543.2010.518736

Retrieved from http://dsp.dla.mil/ sustainment/ flex-guide2.pdf

Revere, L., Black, K., & Zalila, F. (2010). RFIDs can improve the patient care supply chain. *Hospital Topics*, *88*(1), 26–31. doi:10.1080/00185860903534315

Reynolds, E., & Bess, C. (2009). Clearing up the Cloud: Adoption strategies for cloud computing. *Cutter IT Journal, June*.

Riezebos, J., Klingenberg, W., & Hicks, C. (2009). Lean production and Information Technology: Connection or contradiction? *Computers in Industry*, *60*, 237–247. doi:10.1016/j.compind.2009.01.004

Rinne, M. (2004). Technology roadmaps: Infrastructure for innovation. *Technological Forecasting and Social Change*, *71*, 67–80. doi:10.1016/j.techfore.2003.10.002

Robertson, P. L., & Yu, T., F. (2001). Firm strategy, innovation and consumer demand: A market process approach. *Managerial and Decision Economics*, *22*, 183–199. doi:10.1002/mde.1016

Robert, W., & Sharif, N. (2008). A concept framework for ranking R&D project. *IEEE Transactions on Engineering Management*, *55*, 267–278. doi:10.1109/TEM.2008.919725

Rockstroh, J. (2002). Achieving quality ROI across the supply chain. *Quality*, *41*(6), 54.

Rogers, S. (2004). *Supply chain management: Six elements of superior design*. Retrieved from http://www.manufacturing.net

Roubelat, F., & Godet, M. (2000). Scenario planning: An open future. *Technological Forecasting and Social Change*, *65*, 1–2.

Russell, D. M., & Hoag, A. M. (2004). People and information technology in the supply chain: Social and organizational influences on adoption. *International Journal of Physical Distribution & Logistics Management*, *34*(1-2), 102. doi:10.1108/09600030410526914

Rust, R. T., & Zahorik, A. (1993). Customer satisfaction, customer retention, and market share. *Journal of Retailing*, *69*(2), 193–215. doi:10.1016/0022-4359(93)90003-2

Rutherford, T. D. (2000). Re-embedding, Japanese investment and the restructuring buyer-supplier relations in the Canadian automotive components industry during the 1990s. *Regional Studies*, *34*(8), 739. doi:10.1080/00343400050192838

Rutledge, V., Huber, D., & Mathews, J. (2010). Progression of strategies used by a healthcare system preparing for healthcare reform: past and present. *Frontiers of Health Services Management*, *27*(1), 13–27.

Ryssel, R., Ritter, T., & Gemunden, H. G. (2004). The impact of information technology deployment on trust, commitment and value creation in business relationships. *Journal of Business and Industrial Marketing*, *19*(3), 197. doi:10.1108/08858620410531333

Sager, B. (2001). Scenarios on the future of biotechnology. *Technological Forecasting and Social Change*, *68*, 109–129. doi:10.1016/S0040-1625(00)00107-4

Samuel, C., Gonapa, K., Chaudhary, P. K., & Mishra, A. (2010). Supply chain dynamics in healthcare services. *International Journal of Health Care Quality Assurance*, *23*(7), 631–642. doi:10.1108/09526861011071562

Sander, J. H., & Pagliari, L. (2009). *A bi-level approach for applying Six Sigma's DPMO to supply chain management*. Presented at the 2009 IERC Conference, Miami, FL.

Sanders, N. R., & Premus, R. (2005). Modeling the relationship between firm IT capability, collaboration, and performance. *Journal of Business Logistics*, *26*(1), 1. doi:10.1002/j.2158-1592.2005.tb00192.x

SAP AG. (2003). *Manufacturing strategy: An adaptive perspective*. SAP White Paper by SAP SCM.

Sarac, A., Absi, N., & Dauzère-Pérès, S. (2010). A literature review on the impact of RFID technologies on supply chain management. *International Journal of Production Economics*, *128*(1), 77–95. doi:10.1016/j.ijpe.2010.07.039

Sayer, N. J., & Williams, B. (2007). *Lean for dummies*. Hoboken, NJ: Wiley Publishing, Inc.

Scandizzo, P. L., & Ventura, M. (2010). Sharing risk through concession contracts. *European Journal of Operational Research*, *207*(1), 363–370. doi:10.1016/j.ejor.2010.04.008

Schaeffer, M. (2003). *Designing and assessing supportability in DOD weapon systems: A*

Schein, E. H. (1985). *Organizational culture and leadership*. San Francisco, CA: Jossey-Baas Publishers.

Schneeweiss, C., Zimmer, K., & Zimmermann, M. (2004). The design of contracts to coordinate operational interdependencies within the supply chain. *International Journal of Production Economics*, *92*, 43–59. doi:10.1016/j.ijpe.2003.10.005

Schoemaker, P. J. H. (1995). Scenario planning: a tool for strategic thinking. *Sloan Management Review*, *36*, 25–40.

Schultz, M. (1994). *On studying organizational culture*. New York, NY: Walter de Gruyter.

Scott, I. (2009). What are the most effective strategies for improving quality and safety of health care? *Internal Medicine Journal*, *39*(6), 389–400. doi:10.1111/j.1445-5994.2008.01798.x

Sebastiao, H. J., & Golicic, S. (2008). Supply chain strategy for nascent firms in emerging technology markets. *Journal of Business Logistics*, *29*(1), 75–91. doi:10.1002/j.2158-1592.2008.tb00069.x

Sekaran, U. (2000). *Research method for business: A skill building approach*. New York, NY: John Wiley & Sons, Inc.

Sepehri, M. (2011). Cost and inventory benefits of cooperation in multi-period and multi-product supply. *Scientia Iranica Transactions EIndustrial Engineering (American Institute of Industrial Engineers)*, *18*(3).

Setijono, D., Naraghi, A. M., & Ravipati, U. P. (2010). Decision support system and the adoption of lean in a Swedish emergency ward: Balancing supply and demand towards improved value stream. *International Journal of Lean Six Sigma*, *1*(3), 234–248. doi:10.1108/20401461011075026

Shah, N. B. (2004). *Modularity as an enabler for evolutionary acquisition.* MS Thesis Science

Shaked, S., & Jolliet, O. (2011). Global life cycle impacts of consumer productsIn Nriagu, J. (Ed.), *Encyclopedia of environmental health* (pp. 1002–1014). doi:10.1016/B978-0-444-52272-6.00397-4

Sharma, A., & Sheth, J. N. (1997). Supplier relationships: Emerging issues and challenges. *Industrial Marketing Management*, *26*(2), 91–100. doi:10.1016/S0019-8501(96)00153-8

Shaw, M. J. (1988). Dynamic scheduling in cellular manufacturing systems: A framework for network decision making. *Journal of Manufacturing Systems*, *13*, 13–94.

Shen, W., Norrie, D. H., & Xue, D. (1998). *An agent-based manufacturing enterprise infrastructure for distributed integrated intelligent manufacturing system.* In PAAM'98.

Shen, W., Norrie, D. H., & Barthes, J. P. A. (2001). *Multi-agent systems for concurrent intelligent design and manufacturing*. London, UK: Taylor & Francis.

Shi, H. (2010). *Research on supply management in hospital based on VMI.* Paper presented at the 17th International Conference on Industrial Engineering and Engineering Management, IE and EM2010, Xiamen.

Shingo, S. (1985). *A revolution in manufacturing: The SMED system*. Productivity Press.

Simatupang, T. M., & Sridharan, R. (2004). Benchmarking supply chain collaboration: An empirical study. *Benchmarking*, *11*(5), 484. doi:10.1108/14635770410557717

Simchi-Levi, D., Kaminsky, P., & Simchi-Levi, E. (2008). *Designing and managing the supply chain: Concepts, strategies, and case studies* (3rd ed.). Boston, MA: McGraw-Hill/Irwin.

Simchi-Levi, D., Kamisky, P., & Simchi-Levi, E. (2003). *Designing & managing the supply chain* (2nd ed.). New York, NY: The McGraw-Hill Companies.

Simonet, D. (2010). Healthcare reforms and cost reduction strategies in Europe: The cases of Germany, UK, Switzerland, Italy and France. *International Journal of Health Care Quality Assurance*, *23*(5), 470–488. doi:10.1108/09526861011050510

Singh Gaur, S., Xu, Y., Quazi, A., & Nandi, S. (2011). Relational impact of service providers' interaction behavior in healthcare. *Managing Service Quality*, *21*(1), 67–87. doi:10.1108/09604521111100252

Singh, P., & Sandborn, P. (2006). Obsolescence driven design refresh planning for sustainment-(n.d). dominated systems. *The Engineering Economist*, *51*(2).

Sitaraman, S. K., & Pang, J. H. L. (2001). *Fundamentals of design for reliability*. The McGraw-Hill Companies, Inc.

Siwamogsatham, V., & Saygin, C. (2004). Auction-based distributed scheduling and control scheme for flexible manufacturing systems. *International Journal of Production Research*, *42*, 547–572. doi:10.1080/00207540310001613683

Six Sigma Academy. (2002). *The black belt memory jogger*. Salem, NH: Goal/QPC.

Sladek, R. M., Bond, M. J., & Phillips, P. A. (2010). Do doctors, nurses and managers have different thinking styles? *Australian Health Review: A Publication of the Australian Hospital Association*, *34*(3), 375-380.

Smagalla, D. (2004). Supply-chain culture clash. *MIT Sloan Management Review*, *46*(1), 6.

Smeltzer, L. R. (1997). The meaning and origin of trust in buyer-supplier relationships. *International Journal of Purchasing and Materials Management*, *33*(1), 40–48.

Smith, A. M. (1995). Measuring service quality: Is SERVQUAL now redundant? *Journal of Marketing Management*, *111*(1-3), 257–276. doi:10.1080/0267257X.1995.9964341

Smith, P. (2005). More than a beautiful friendship. *Supply Management*, *10*(3), 22–25.

Smith, R. G. (1980). The contract net protocol: High-level communication and control in distributed problem solving. *IEEE Transactions on Computers C*, *29*(12), 1104–1113. doi:10.1109/TC.1980.1675516

Smith, R., & Hawkins, B. (2004). *Lean maintenance: Reduce costs, improve quality, and increase market share*. Elsevier Science Life Cycle Engineering Series.

Snell, P. (2008). Tackle aggression toward suppliers. *Supply Management*, *13*(23), 10.

Sobe, U., Rooch, K. H., Ripp, A., & Pronath, M. (2009). Robust analog design for automotive applications by design centering with safe operating areas. *IEEE Transactions on Semiconductor Manufacturing*, *22*(2), 217–224. doi:10.1109/TSM.2008.2011628

Sobrero, M., & Schrader, S. (1998). Structuring inter-firm relationships: A meta-analytic approach. *Organization Studies*, *19*(4), 585–615. doi:10.1177/017084069801900403

Soderquist, K., & Motwani, J. (1999). Quality issues in lean production implementation: A case study of a French automotive supplier. *Total Quality Management*, *10*(8), 1107–1122. doi:10.1080/0954412997091

Sohal, A. S., Power, D. J., & Terziovski, M. (2003). Integrated supply chain management from the wholesaler's perspective: Two Australian case studies. *International Journal of Physical Distribution & Logistics Management*, *32*(2), 96–109. doi:10.1108/09600030210421714

Solomon, M. B. (June 3, 2010)/ Women shattering logistics/ glass ceilings. *Dc Velocity.com.* Retrieved from http:// www.dcvelocity.com/ articles/20100603_women_shattering_logistics_glass_ceiling

Stank, T., Brzica, M., & Ficenec, J. (2009). The benefits of supply chain integration using a third-party integrator. *Transfusion*, *49*(11 Pt 2), 2536–2538. doi:10.1111/j.1537-2995.2009.02472.x

Stanley, L. L., & Wisner, J. D. (2001). Service quality along the supply chain: Implications for purchasing. *Journal of Operations Management*, *19*, 287–306. doi:10.1016/ S0272-6963(00)00052-8

Steffen, M. (2010). The french health care system: Liberal universalism. *Journal of Health Politics, Policy and Law*, *35*(3), 353–387. doi:10.1215/03616878-2010-003

Stevens, H., & Petty, C. (2008). *Risks of cloud computing*. Retrieved February 14, 2010, from http://www.gartner.com/ it/page.jsp?id=707508

Stevens, G. C. (1989). Integrating the supply chain. *International Journal of Physical Distribution & Logistics Management*, *19*(8), 3–8. doi:10.1108/EUM0000000000329

Stock, J. R., Boyer, S. L., & Harmon, T. (2010). Research opportunities in supply chain management. *Journal of the Academy of Marketing Science*, *38*, 32–41. doi:10.1007/ s11747-009-0136-2

Stock, J. R., & Lambert, D. M. (2001). *Strategic logistics management* (4th ed.). Boston, MA: McGraw-Hill/Irwin.

Stogdill, R. C. (1999). Dealing with obsolete parts. *IEEE Design & Test of Computers*, *16*(2), 17–25. doi:10.1109/54.765200

Stonebraker, P. W., & Afifi, R. (2004). Toward a contingency theory of supply chains. *Management Decision*, *42*(9), 1131. doi:10.1108/00251740410565163

Strattona, R., & Warburton, R. D. H. (2003). The strategic integration of agile and lean supply. *International Journal of Production Economics*, *85*, 183–198. doi:10.1016/ S0925-5273(03)00109-9

Stratton, R., & Knight, A. (2010). Managing patient flow using time buffers. *Journal of Manufacturing Technology Management*, *21*(4), 484–498. doi:10.1108/17410381011046599

Sugier, J., & Anders, G. J. (2007). Modeling changes in maintenance activities through fine-tuning Markov models of ageing equipment. *2nd International Conference on Dependability of Computer Systems* (pp. 336–343).

Summers, D. C. S. (2006). *Quality*. Upper Saddle River, NJ: Pearson Education, Inc.

Sun, P. Y.-T., & Scott, J. L. (2005). An investigation of barriers to knowledge transfer. *Journal of Knowledge Management*, *9*(2), 75–90. doi:10.1108/13673270510590236

Supply Chain Management Terms and Glossary(2010). Retrieved on December, 3, 2010, from http://cscmp.org/ digital/glossary/glossary.asp

Swafford, P., Gosh, S., & Murthy, N. (2006). A framework for assessing value chain agility. *International Journal of Operations & Production Management*, *26*(2), 118–140. doi:10.1108/01443570610641639

Swaminathan, J. M., Smith, S. F., & Sahed, N. M. (1996). *A multi-agent framework for supply chain dynamics*. NSF Research Planning Workshop on AI & Manufacturing.

Szulanski, G. (1996). Exploring internal stickiness: Impediments to the transfer of best practice within the firm. *Strategic Management Journal, 17*(Winter Special Issue), 27-43.

Tabachnick, B. G., & Fidell, L. S. (1996). *Using multivariate statistics*. New York, NY: HarperCollins.

Tabachnick, B. G., & Fidell, L. S. (2001). *Using multivariate statistics*. Boston, MA: Allyn & Bacon.

tables. Washington, DC: U.S. Government Printing Office.

Tague, N. R. (2004). *The quality toolbox* (2nd ed.). Milwaukee, WI: ASQ Quality Press.

Tangpong, C., Michalisin, M. D., & Melcher, A. J. (2008). Toward a typology of buyer-supplier relationships: A study of the computer industry. *Decision Sciences, 39*(3), 571–593. doi:10.1111/j.1540-5915.2008.00203.x

Tapping, D., Luyster, T., & Shuker, T. (2002). *Value stream management*. New York, NY: Productivity Press.

Tarokh, M. J., & Mehryar, M. (2006). Multi-agent based framework for agile supply chain management. *Proceedings of the 2006 IEEE International Conference on System of Systems Engineering,* Los Angeles, CA, USA.

Tarondeau, J.C. (1998). De nouvelles formes d'organisation pour l'entreprise. La gestion par lesrocessus. *Cahier Français, Management et organisation des entreprises, 287*. Paris, France: La Documentation Française.

Tayur, S., Ganeshan, R., & Magazine, M. (Eds.). (2003). *Quantitative models for supply chain management* (6th ed.). Kluwer Academic Publishers.

Teichgräber, U. K., & de Bucourt, M. (2011). Applying value stream mapping techniques to eliminate non-value-added waste for the procurement of endovascular stents. *European Journal of Radiology*.

Teisberg, E. O., Porter, M. E., & Brown, G. B. (1994). Making competition in health care work. *Harvard Business Review, 72*(4), 131–141.

Tennant, C., & Roberts, P. (2000). A faster way to create better quality products. *International Journal of Project Management, 19*, 353–362. doi:10.1016/S0263-7863(00)00010-7

Teresko, J. (2004). The PLM revolution. *Industry Week, 253*(2), 32–36.

Tewary, A., & Wang, N. (2005). *Semiconductors*. Standard and Poor's Industry Surveys.

Tilton, J. R. (2006). *Obsolescence management Information System (OMIS)*. Keyport, WA: Navy Underwater Warfare Center. Retrieved from.

Tipman, M. (2005, January/February). Projects and procurement. *Summit, 8*, 20–21.

Tirole, J. (1988). *The theory of industrial organization*. Cambridge, MA: M.I.T. Press.

toll, H. W. (1990). Design for manufacturing. In C. W. Allen (Ed.), Simultaneous engineering. (pp. 23-29). SME Press.

Towill, D. R. (1997). The seamless supply chain – The predator's strategic advantage. *International Journal of the Techniques of Manufacturing, 13*(1), 37–56.

Towill, D. R. (2009). Frank Gilbreth and health care delivery method study driven learning. *International Journal of Health Care Quality Assurance, 22*(4), 417–440. doi:10.1108/09526860910964861

Tpslean. (2011). *Throughput solutions*. Retrieved June 28, 2011, from http://tpslean.com/ glossary/fifodef.htm

Travaglia, J. F., Debono, D., Spigelman, A. D., & Braithwaite, J. (2011). Clinical governance: A review of key concepts in the literature. *Clinical Governance: An International Journal, 16*(1), 62–77. doi:10.1108/14777271111104592

Trentesaux, D., Pesin, P., & Tahon, C. (2000). Distributed artificial intelligence for FMS scheduling control and design support. *Journal of Intelligent Manufacturing, 11*, 573–589. doi:10.1023/A:1026556507109

Trerise, B. (2010). Establishing an organizational culture to enable quality improvement. *Leadership in Health Services, 23*(2), 130–140. doi:10.1108/17511871011040715

Trybou, J., Gemmel, P., & Annemans, L. (2011). The ties that bind: An integrative framework of physician-hospital alignment. *BMC Health Services Research*, *11*(1), 36. doi:10.1186/1472-6963-11-36

Tsay, A. A. (1999). The quantity flexibility contract and supplier-costumer incentives. *Management Science*, *45*(10), 1339–1358. doi:10.1287/mnsc.45.10.1339

Tsay, A. A., & Lovejoy, W. S. (1999). Quantity flexibility contracts and supply chain performance. *Manufacturing and Service Operations Management*, *1*(2), 89–111. doi:10.1287/msom.1.2.89

Tse, D., & Wilton, P. (1988). Models of consumers' satisfaction formation: An extension. *JMR, Journal of Marketing Research*, *25*, 204–212. doi:10.2307/3172652

Tseng, L. T., Tseng, L. F., & Chen, H. C. (2011). Exploration of the bullwhip effect based on the evolutionary least mean square algorithm. *International Journal of Electronic Business Management*, *9*(2), 160–168.

Tsinopoulos, K., & Bell, K. (2008). Supply chain integration systems by small engineer to order companies: The challenge of implementation. *Journal of Manufacturing Technology Management*, *21*(1), 50–62. doi:10.1108/17410381011011489

Tucker, A. L., Singer, S. J., Hayes, J. E., & Falwell, A. (2008). Front-line staff perspectives on opportunities for improving the safety and efficiency of hospital work systems. *Health Services Research*, *43*(5), 1807–1829. doi:10.1111/j.1475-6773.2008.00868.x

Turner, W. C., Mize, J. H., Case, K. E., & Nazemetz, J. W. (1993). *Introduction to industrial and systems engineering*, 3rd ed. Englewood, Cliffs, NJ: Prentice Hall.

Tyan, J., & Wee, H. M. (2003). Vendor managed inventory: A survey of the Taiwanese grocery industry. *Journal of Purchasing and Supply Management*, *9*(1), 11–18. doi:10.1016/S0969-7012(02)00032-1

U.S. Census Bureau. (2010). *Survey of business owners - Women owned firms: 2007*. Retrieved from http://www.census.gov/ econ/sbo/get07sof.html?8

Umemoto, K., Endo, A., & Machaco, M. (2004). From Sashimi to Zen-in. The evolution of concurrent engineering at Fuji Xerox. *Journal of Knowledge Management*, *8*(4), 89–99. doi:10.1108/13673270410548504

Umscheid, C., Williams, K., & Brennan, P. (2010). Hospital-based comparative effectiveness centers: Translating research into practice to improve the quality, safety and value of patient care. *Journal of General Internal Medicine*, *25*(12), 1352–1355. doi:10.1007/s11606-010-1476-9

US Department of Energy. (2004). *Process guide for the identification and disposition of suspect/counterfeit or defective items at Department of Energy facilities*. Office of Environment, Safety and Health, United States Department of Energy.

Uzoka, F. M. E., & Ijatuyi, O. A. (2005). Decision support system for library acquisition: A framework. *The Electronic Library*, *23*, 453–462. doi:10.1108/02640470510611517

Vaish, B., & Garg, G. (2011). Optimal ordering and transfer policy for an inventory system with time dependent holding cost and three component demand rate. *Journal of Mathematics Research*, *3*(2), 212–223. doi:10.5539/jmr.v3n2p212

Valckenaers, P., & Van Brussel, H. (2005). Holonic manufacturing execution systems. *CIRP Annals - Manufacturing Technology*, *54*(1), 427-432.

Valle, S., & Vazquez-Bustelo, D. (2009). Concurrent engineering performance: Incremental versus radical innovation. *International Journal of Production Economics*, *119*, 136–148. doi:10.1016/j.ijpe.2009.02.002

Van Brussel, H., Wyns, J., Valckenaers, P., Bongaerts, L., & Peeters, P. (1998). Reference architecture for holonic manufacturing systems: PROSA. *Computers in Industry*, *37*, 255–274. doi:10.1016/S0166-3615(98)00102-X

Van de Castle, B., & Szymanski, G. (2008). Supply chain management on clinical unitsIn Hübner, U., & Elmhorst, M. A. (Eds.), *E-business in healthcare* (pp. 197–217). London, UK: Springer.

Van Der Heijden, K. (2000). Scenarios and forecasting: Two perspectives. *Technological Forecasting and Social Change*, *65*, 31–36. doi:10.1016/S0040-1625(99)00121-3

van der Valk, W. (2009). Effective buyer-supplier interaction patterns in ongoing service exchange. *International Journal of Operations & Production Management*, *29*(8), 807–833. doi:10.1108/01443570910977706 van der Vlist, P., Kuik, R., & Verheijen, B. (2007). Note on supply chain integration in vendor-managed inventory. *Decision Support Systems*, *44*(1), 360–365. doi:10.1016/j.dss.2007.03.003

Váncza, J., & Márkus, A. (2000). An agent model for incentive-based production scheduling. *Computers in Industry*, *43*, 173–187. doi:10.1016/S0166-3615(00)00066-X

VanVactor, J. D. (2011). A case study of collaborative communications within healthcare logistics. *Leadership in Health Services*, *24*(1), 51–63. doi:10.1108/17511871111102526

Vieira, G. E., Hermann, J. W., & Lin, E. (2003). Rescheduling manufacturing systems: A framework of strategies, policies and methods. *Journal of Scheduling*, *6*(1), 36–92. doi:10.1023/A:1022235519958

Vieira, G. E., Herrmann, J. W., & Lin, E. (2000). Analytical models to predict the performance of a single machine system under periodic and event-driven rescheduling strategies. *International Journal of Production Research*, *38*(8), 1899–1915. doi:10.1080/002075400188654

Von Hippel, E. (1966). *The sources of innovation*. New York, NY: Oxford University Press.

Von Hippel, E. (1994). Sticky information and the locus of problem solving: Implications for innovation. *Management Science*, *40*(4), 429–439. doi:10.1287/mnsc.40.4.429

Vorne. (2011). *Key performance indicators (KPIs)*. Retrieved June 28, 2011, from http://www.vorne.com/learning-center/kpi.htm

Wagner, S. M., Coley, L. S., & Lindemann, E. (2011). Effects of suppliers' reputation on the future of buyer-supplier relationships: The mediating roles of outcome fairness and trust. *Journal of Supply Chain Management*, *47*(2), 29. doi:10.1111/j.1745-493X.2011.03225.x

Walters, D. (2008). Demand chain management+response management=increased customer satisfaction. *International Journal of Physical Distribution and Logistics Management*, *38*(9), 699–725. doi:10.1108/09600030810925980

Wang, Z., Zhan, D., & Xu, X. (2006). Service-oriented infrastructure for collaborative product design in ETO enterprises. *Proceedings of 10th International Conference on Computer Supported Cooperative Work in Design.*

Wang, K. H., Tung, C. T., Chien, C. L., & Hung, F. C. (2010). A deteriorating two-item inventory model with continuously decreasing demand and retroactive holding cost. *Journal of International Management Studies*, *5*(1), 10–18.

Wang, P. C., Halim, I., Arief, A., & Rajagopalan, S. (2011). Integrating economic, environmental and social indicators for sustainable supply chains. *Journal of Computer Aided Chemical Engineering*, *29*, 1220–1224. doi:10.1016/B978-0-444-54298-4.50023-4

Wang, Y., & Zipkin, P. (2009). Agents' incentives under buy-back contracts in a two-stage supply chain. *International Journal of Production Economics*, *120*(2), 525–539. doi:10.1016/j.ijpe.2009.04.008

Waring, J. J., & Bishop, S. (2010). Lean healthcare: Rhetoric, ritual and resistance. *Social Science & Medicine*, *71*(7), 1332–1340. doi:10.1016/j.socscimed.2010.06.028

Webster, S. (2008). *Principles and tools for supply chain management*. Boston, MA: McGraw-Hill/Irwin.

Welty, B., & Becerra-Frenandez, I. (2001). Managing trust and commitment in collaborative supply chain relationships. *Communications of the ACM*, *44*(6), 67. doi:10.1145/376134.376170

Wen, Y., Liu, Z., & Liu, J. (2010, 9-10 January). *Logistics mode reengineering of hospital materials based on JIT theory.* Paper presented at the Logistics Systems and Intelligent Management, 2010 International Conference on.

Weng, Z. K. (1999). The power of coordinated decisions for short life cycle products in a manufacturing and distribution supply chain. *IIE Transactions*, *31*(11), 1037–1049. doi:10.1080/07408179908969905

Widyadana, G. A., Wee, H. M., & Chang, J.-Y. (2010). Determining the optimal number of Kanban in multi-products supply chain system. *Journal of International of Systems Science*, *41*(2). Taylor & Francis.

Willoughby, K. A., Chan, B. T. B., & Strenger, M. (2010). Achieving wait time reduction in the emergency department. *Leadership in Health Services*, *23*(4), 304–319. doi:10.1108/17511871011079010

Wilson, I. (2000). From scenario thinking to strategic action. *Technological Forecasting and Social Change*, *65*, 23–29. doi:10.1016/S0040-1625(99)00122-5

Wognuma, P. M., Bremmers, H., Trienekens, J. H., van der Vorst, G. A. J., & Bloemhof, J. M. (2011). Systems for sustainability and transparency of food supply chains – Current status and challenges. *Journal of Advanced Engineering Informatics*, *25*(1), 65–76. doi:10.1016/j.aei.2010.06.001

Womack, J. P., & Jones, D. T. (1996). *Lean thinking* (2nd ed.). New York, NY: Simon & Shuster.

Womack, J. P., & Jones, D. T. (2003). *Lean thinking: Banish waste and create wealth in your corporation*. New York, NY: Free Press.

Womack, J., & Jones, D. T. (2003). *Lean thinking: Banish waste and create wealth in your corporation* (2nd ed., pp. 15–36). New York, NY: Free Press.

Wonga, T. N., Leunga, C. W., Maka, K. L., & Fungb, R. Y. K. (2006). Dynamic shopfloor scheduling in multi-agent manufacturing systems*Expert Systems with Applications*, *31*(3), 486–494. doi:10.1016/j.eswa.2005.09.073

Wood, L. C. (2010a). *Effective horizontal coordination in clusters: Bridging the barriers to effective supply chain management*. Doctoral Thesis, The University of Auckland, Auckland.

Wood, L. C. (2010b). *The role of clusters in creating value in supply chains: Evidence from the examination of clusters with RBV*. Paper presented at the ANZAM 2010: The 24th Australian and New Zealand Academy of Management, Adelaide, South Australia.

Woodside, A., Frey, L., & Daly, R. (1989). Linking service quality, customer satisfaction and behavioral intentions. *Journal of Health Care Marketing*, *9*(December), 5–17.

Wooldridge, M. (1999). Intelligent agentsIn Weiss, G. (Ed.), *Multiagent systems*. Cambridge, MA: MIT Press.

Wooldridge, M., & Jennings, N. R. (1995). Intelligent agents: Theory and practice. *The Knowledge Engineering Review*, *10*(2), 115–152. doi:10.1017/S0269888900008122

Wu, J. (2005). Quantity flexibility contracts under Bayesian updating. *Computers & Operations Research*, *32*(5), 1267–1288. doi:10.1016/j.cor.2003.11.004

Wu, L., Yue, X., & Sim, T. (2006). Supply clusters: A key to China's cost advantage. *Supply Chain Management Review*, *10*(2), 46–51.

Xiao, T., Yan, X., & Zhao, J. (2010). Coordination of a supply chain with advertising investment and allowing the second ordering. *Technology and Investment*, *1*(3), 191–200. doi:10.4236/ti.2010.13022

Yang, J., & Qi, X. (2009). On the design of coordinating contracts. *International Journal of Production Economics*, *122*(2), 581–594. doi:10.1016/j.ijpe.2009.06.002

Yang, K., & Yang, G. (1998). Degradation reliability assessment using severe critical values. *International Journal of Reliability Quality and Safety Engineering*, *5*, 85–95. doi:10.1142/S0218539398000091

Yao, Y., Evers, P. T., & Dresner, M. E. (2007). Supply chain integration in vendor-managed inventory. *Decision Support Systems*, *43*(2), 663–674. doi:10.1016/j.dss.2005.05.021

Yassine, A., & Braha, D. (2003). Four complex concurrent engineering and the design structure matrix method. *Concurrent Engineering: Research and Applications*, *11*(3), 165–176. doi:10.1177/106329303034503

Yeo, K. (2006). Managing uncertainty in major equipment procurement in engineering projects. *European Journal of Operational Research*, *171*(1), 123–134. doi:10.1016/j.ejor.2004.06.036

Yousri, T. A., Khan, Z., Chakrabarti, D., Fernandes, R., & Wahab, K. (2011). Lean thinking: Can it improve the outcome of fracture neck of femur patients in a district general hospital? *Injury*, *42*(11). doi:10.1016/j.injury.2010.11.024

Zeithaml, V. A. (2000). Service quality, profitability and the economic worth of customers: What we know and what we need to learn. *Journal of the Academy of Marketing Science*, *28*(1), 67–85. doi:10.1177/0092070300281007

Zeithaml, V. A., Parasuraman, A., & Berry, L. L. (1993). The nature and determinants of customer expectations of service. *Journal of the Academy of Marketing Science*, *21*(1), 1–12. doi:10.1177/0092070393211001

Zeithaml, V. A., Parasuraman, A., & Berry, L. L. (1996). The behavioral consequences of service quality. *Journal of Marketing*, *49*(Spring), 33–46.

Zeleny, M. (2002). Knowledge of enterprise: Knowledge management or knowledge technology? *International Journal of Information Technology and Decision Making*, *1*(2), 181–207. doi:10.1142/S021962200200021X

Zhou, B., Wang, S., & Xi, L. (2008). Agent-based decision support system for dynamic scheduling of a flexible manufacturing system. *International Journal of Computer Applications in Technology*, *32*(1), 47–62. doi:10.1504/IJCAT.2008.019489

Zhou, H., & Benton, W. C. (2007). Supply chain practice and information sharing. *Journal of Operations Management*, *25*, 1348–1365. doi:10.1016/j.jom.2007.01.009

Zhou, R., Nee, A. Y. C., & Lee, H. P. (2009a). Performance of an ant colony optimisation algorithm in dynamic job shop scheduling problems. *International Journal of Production Research*, *47*(11), 2903–2920. doi:10.1080/00207540701644219

Zikmund-Fisher, B. J., Couper, M. P., Singer, E., Ubel, P. A., Ziniel, S., & Fowler, F. J. (2010). Deficits and variations in patients' experience with making 9 common medical decisions: The DECISIONS survzey. *Medical Decision Making*, *30*(5), 85S–95S. doi:10.1177/0272989X10380466

Zimmerman, B. (2010). What do we mean by empowerment? *Policy & Practice*, ▪▪▪, 68.

About the Contributors

Ephrem Eyob is a Professor in the Department of Technology in the Logistics Program at Virginia State University. Prior to that he was Professor and Chair for the Department of Computer Information Systems, School of Business, at the same university. His research interest is in Information Systems and supply chains areas, primarily in Web-based functional integration, ERP applications, business intelligence, optimization of supply chain networks, and Information Technology applications in supply chains. He served as the guest editor for the *International Journal of Management and Decision Making, International Journal of Economics Management and Services* and edited two books. Currently, he is serving as a member of the editorial board member for six journals. He has published over one hundred refereed articles, book chapters, and proceedings in major journals and conferences.

Edem G. Tetteh is an Assistant Vice President for Academic Affairs and Associate Professor at Paine College. He has previously held a faculty position in the Industrial and Logistics Technology (INLT) program in the Department of Technology at Virginia State University. He received his BS in Manufacturing Systems and MS in Industrial Engineering both from North Carolina Agricultural and Technical State University. He received his PhD in Technology from Purdue University-West Lafayette. Dr. Tetteh has authored a book entitled *Engineering Approach to Work Design: Issues for the Obese Workers*. He also has several publications in the areas of Ergonomics & Human Factors and Logistic & Supply Chain. He directed the self study leading to the accreditation of the Industrial and Logistics Technology program by the Association of Technology Management and Applied Engineering (ATMAE).

* * *

Richard Addo-Tenkorang is currently a researcher and a doctoral student in Industrial Management at the University of Vaasa, Finland. He holds MSc. in Digital Enterprise Management and a BEng (Hons) degree in Mechanical Engineering from the Universities of Westminster, UK and Wolverhampton, UK, respectively. His research interests are in the area of ERP systems and concurrent engineering for new product introduction/development (NPI/D), as well as logistics and supply chain management. He has 5 years working experience in the areas of engineering systems, new product introduction and development, design for manufacture, project management, and quality management.

Mian M. Ajmal is currently working as Assistant Professor of Management at Abu Dhabi University, Abu Dhabi, UAE and also continuing as researcher at Oulu Business School, University of Oulu, Finland.

He holds D.Sc. (Economics & Business Administration) and MBA degrees. He has been involved in several research projects in last few years. His research interests pertain to knowledge, project and supply chain management, entrepreneurship, internationalization of firms along with organizational behavior, and culture. He has been publishing his research articles in several international journals and conferences.

Ali Alavizadeh is an Assistant Professor in the MCET Department at Indiana University- Purdue University Fort Wayne. He has taught in George Washington University (Washington, DC), and Morehead State University (Morehead, KY) in Engineering Management and in Industrial and Engineering Technology. His industrial experience is in the field of enterprise architecture, systems analysis, and software engineering for private, governmental, and nongovernmental organizations. His research interests include complex systems modeling and simulation, enterprise architecture, and nonlinear dynamical systems. He is a member of the Association of Enterprise Architects (AEA) and International Council on Systems Engineering (INCOSE).

Yao Amewokunu is an Assistant Professor of Management in the Department of Management and Marketing at Virginia State University. He earned a MBA in International Management and a Ph.D. in Management from Laval University (Canada). Dr. Amewokunu's research interests include strategic management, entrepreneurship, and SME management. He is greatly involved in his research activities and is an author and a co-author of several publications in refereed journals and many peer-reviewed conferences.

Kaninika Bhatnagar is an Assistant Professor in the School of Technology at Eastern Illinois University, Charleston IL. She earned her Ph.D. in Technology from Eastern Michigan University, and an MS in Architecture from the University of Michigan, Ann Arbor. Kaninika teaches a variety of applied engineering technology courses at both undergraduate and graduate levels. She has been published in the *Journal of Engineering Technology*, and the *American Society of Engineering Education (ASEE) Proceedings,* among others. Her primary research interest is the interaction of diversity in general, and gender in particular, with science and technology issues in the new century.

Rubyna Brenden is a Systems Analyst at University of Western States in Portland, Oregon. She has BS in Computer Science from London Metropolitan University and an MS in Engineering and Technology Management from Portland State University.

Marc Britton received his MS in Engineering and Technology Management from Portland State University. He had worked at Precision Cast Parts as a Production Engineer.

Dan Brown is a Professor in the Technology Department at Illinois State University. His teaching responsibilities include project team leadership, training implementation, and evaluation of training programs. He is Coordinator of Graduate Studies for the Department of Technology. He is a member of the Project Management Institute, the Association of Technology Management and Applied Engineering, and the American Society for Training & Development.

Tugrul Daim is an Associate Professor and PhD Program Director in the Department of Engineering and Technology Management at Portland State University. He has been recently appointed as Extraordinary Professor at the Graduate School of Technology Management at University of Pretoria. He received his BS in Mechanical Engineering from Bogazici University in Turkey, MS in Mechanical Engineering from Lehigh University in Pennsylvania, MS in Engineering Management from Portland State University, and PhD in Systems Science: Engineering Management from Portland State University in Portland, Oregon.

Reza Djavanshir is an Associate Professor at The Johns Hopkins University Carey Business School. He graduated from the University of Tabriz, followed by a Master's degree in Industrial Engineering and Operations Research, and his Doctorate in Systems Engineering both from the George Washington University (USA). His research interests include technology strategy architecture, meta-systems, global sourcing & supply chains, and infrastructure upgrades and catalectic technology strategies in developing and transitioning economies. Dr. Djavanshir started his career in the early 80s as an engineer by joining the R&D Division of the BBN/GTE Telenet. He was also a lead scientist with MITRE / MITRE-TEK, where he worked on R&D Projects for NASA Systems Engineering projects. Prior to joining Johns Hopkins in 2002, he served as Sr. Technologist and Vice President of Citicorp's Citgroup Global Information Networks.

Alejandra Gomez-Padilla is Associate Professor at the Department of Industrial Engineering of the Center of Exact Sciences and Engineering (CUCEI) at University of Guadalajara. Graduated as Industrial Engineer in 1998 from the Technological Institute of Superior Studies of Occident (Mexico), she received a M.Sc. degree in Industrial Engineering (2001) from the Department of Mathematics and Industrial Engineering at the Ecole Polytechnique de Montreal She obtained a Ph.D. in Industrial Engineering from GILCO research laboratory at the Institut National Polytechnique de Grenoble in France (2005). Prior to her graduate studies she worked in product and process engineering for an international company, a leader in the electronic industry. Her research interests are on modeling and optimizing flows in supply chains. She is member of the Association for Operations Management (APICS) and of the Institute of Industrial Engineers (IIE). She has leaded research projects on optimization, logistic and supply chain management.

Nuttavut Intarode received his B.S. in Industrial Chemistry from Chiang Mai University in Thailand and an M.S. in Engineering and Technology Management from Portland State University. He is the Technology Commercialization Officer of the SCG Cement Company.

Norizan Mohd Kassim is Professor of Marketing at the International Business School, International Campus, University Technology Malaysia. She received her PhD in Marketing from Southern Cross University, Australia. Her publications have appeared, among others, in *Journal of Business Research, Singapore Management Review, Asia Pacific Business Review, International Journal of Bank Marketing, European Journal of Marketing, Electronic Markets, Journal of Financial Service Marketing, Asia Pacific Journal of Marketing and Logistics*, and *Measuring Business Excellence.*

Yohanes Kristianto is a Researcher in Industrial Management at University of Vaasa, Finland. Dr. Kristianto research interests are in the area of supply-chain strategy/management and production/operations management. He has 11 years of working experiences in the area of quality management, logistics, and process engineering.

Albert Lozano-Nieto is Professor of Engineering at the Pennsylvania State University. His main teaching responsibilities are focused on the Baccalaureate degree in Electrical Engineering Technology at the Wilkes-Barre campus. A native of Barcelona, Spain, he joined Penn State in 1996. Dr. Lozano-Nieto received his Doctoral degree in Electrical Engineering in 1994 and his Baccalaureate degree in Telecommunication Engineering in 1988, both by the Polytechnic University of Catalonia, Barcelona, Spain. He is also a RFID+ Certified Professional awarded by CompTIA since 2008. Dr. Lozano's interests are focused on new technologies, the study of bioelectrical impedance, and the use of high altitude balloons for undergraduate research activities.

John Mawhinney is Executive Assistant Professor of Supply Chain Management in the Palumbo/Donahue Schools of Business, Duquesne University. He possesses 37 years of supply chain industry, consulting, and academic experience. Dr. Mawhinney earned a B.S. in Logistics and Marketing at Ohio State University, an MBA from the University of Pittsburgh, and a Doctorate in Education from Duquesne University.

Ron Meier is a Professor in the Technology Department at Illinois State University. His teaching responsibilities include project initiation & planning, project implementation & control, lean Six Sigma, and quality management systems. He is a member of the Project Management Institute, the American Society for Quality (ASQ), and the Association of Technology Management and Applied Engineering. He is currently the Vice-Chair of e-based initiatives for the Quality Management Division of ASQ.

Jaby Mohammed is an Assistant Professor in the Petroleum Institute in Abu Dhabi. Prior to this position, he was the Director for the graduate program in Technology and an Assistant Professor at Purdue University (Fort Wayne campus). He also has worked at Morehead State University, Kentucky, USA. Dr. Mohammed is a senior member of the Society of Manufacturing Engineers (SME) and Institute of Industrial Engineers (IIE). His area of research includes new product development and rapid prototyping; supply chain management, Six Sigma, and lean manufacturing.

Véronique Nabelsi is an Assistant Professor of Technology Management at Université du Québec en Outaouais, Canada. She has consulted on ERP, RFID, and process optimization in such diverse sectors as industrial product development and healthcare. She received a Ph.D. in Industrial Engineering, specialized in Technology Management, from École Polytechnique in Montréal.

Rocco Padalino received his "*Laurea*" degree from the University of Basilicata in Mechanical Engineering in 2005. He took Ph.D. degree at University of Basilicata in Industrial and Innovation Engineering. He was appointed Research Visitor at Hungarian Academy of Sciences Computer and Automation Research Institute, MTA SZTAKI advised by Professor Vancza. His academic research principally deals with the development of innovative negotiation for manufacturing scheduling in dynamic environment.

Paolo Renna is an Assistant Professor at Department of Environmental Engineering and Physics in the Engineering Faculty of Basilicata University (Italy). He took Ph.D. degree at Polytechnic of Bari in Advanced Production Systems. His academic researches principally deal with the development of innovative negotiation and production planning in distributed environments and manufacturing scheduling in dynamic environment. Several contributions have been presented on design multi agent architecture and test by discrete event simulation in business to business environment. Among the contributions, he is co-author of two research books about e-marketplaces and production planning in production networks. Moreover, he has developed coordination approaches in multi-plant production planning environment and innovative scheduling approaches in flexible and reconfigurable manufacturing systems.

Kenneth A. Saban is Associate Professor of Marketing in the Palumbo/Donahue Schools of Business, Duquesne University. He possesses 39 years of commercial and academic experience. Dr. Saban earned a B.S.B.A. from Youngstown State University, a M.S.J. from Northwestern University, and a Doctorate from the University of Pittsburgh. He has developed a particular expertise in the area of *business collaboration* through a wide-range of research projects, grants and industry partnerships. Dr. Saban has published over 22 articles/book chapters and given numerous academic and industry presentations.

Janet H. Sanders is an Assistant Professor in the Department of Technology at East Carolina University where her research focus is quality, statistics, lean Six Sigma, and virtual reality technology. She earned a B.S. in Ceramic Engineering, an M.S. in Industrial Management from Clemson University, and a Ph.D. in Industrial Engineering from North Carolina A & T State University. She has over 20 years of manufacturing experience in various industries. Janet's certifications include ASQ certified Quality Auditor, Quality Engineer, and Six Sigma Black Belt. She is also a consultant and trainer for problem solving, root cause analysis, and lean Six Sigma.

Ganesh Subramanian is a Lead Infrastructure Architect at Providence Health Systems. He had been involved in design, engineeringm and implementation of several IT infrastructure projects at Providence. Ganesh completed his Master's in Engineering and Technology Management at the Portland State University in Oregon.

Mohammad J. Tarokh is an Associate Professor at K.N Toosi Technology University (Tehran, Iran). After his graduation from the Sharif Technology University, he obtained his Master's and Doctoral degrees in Industrial Engineering, both from the Bradford University in the UK.

Silvanus J. Udoka, PhD, is a LANGURE Senior Fellow, Department of Management Chair and Associate Professor with joint appointment in the Department of Management and the Department of Industrial and Systems Engineering at North Carolina A&T State University. He earned a Ph. D. in Industrial Engineering and Management from Oklahoma State University. His research interests are in the areas of Interactive Visualization and Visual Depiction, Immersive 3-D (I-3D) Environments; Robotics applications, Automation and Integrated Manufacturing Systems Engineering; Design for Sustainment; and Six Sigma and Lean Enterprises. He is an active member of Society of Manufacturing Engineers (SME), Institute of Industrial Engineers (IIE) American Society of Engineering Education (ASEE), Alpha Pi Mu, Tau Beta Pi, Phi Kappa Phi, and the Order of the Engineer.

Benedict M. Uzochukwu received his Doctoral degree in Industrial Engineering from the North Carolina A & T State University, Greensboro. His research interests include design for sustainment, lifecycle systems, systems integration, and management of technology systems. He has several peer reviewed publications to his credit. Dr. Uzochukwu is a member of Institute of Industrial Engineers (IIE), Society for Engineering Management (SEM), Society for Health Systems (SHS), Alpha Pi Mu, and Phi Kappa Phi.

Robertus Wahyu Nayan Nugroho obtained Master's degree from Department of Nonwovens, Technical University of Liberec, Czech Republic. His research interests are in the area of nanoscience, fiber technology, and electrochemistry. He has 5 years of working experiences in the area of food processing and nanoscience.

Lincoln Wood is a Lecturer in Logistics and Supply Chain Management at Curtin University of Technology in Perth, Australia. He earned his PhD at the University of Auckland and received the CSCMP Young Researcher Award in 2009. He has published in journals including *Transportation Research Part B: Methodological* and the *International Journal of Operations & Production Management* and has authored many conference papers and book chapters. His research interests include strategic SCM, SCM in clusters and SMEs, and service operations.

Index

D

E

F

G

H

I

J

K

S

T

V

W

CPSIA information can be obtained at www.ICGtesting.com
Printed in the USA
BVOW041616041112

304496BV00007B/30/P

9 781466 602465

Turn Left at Alpha Centauri

Section 1

BLASTOFF!

If you like science fiction, you have probably watched dozens of movies and TV shows about space travel and life on distant worlds. Would you like to travel through space? What would you be thinking as you looked back on the planet Earth?

Would you have to bring along all the food, water, and oxygen you would need, or could you grow food and produce oxygen in your spacecraft? The force of gravity is almost nonexistent in space. How could you eat, move around, and exercise once you escaped Earth's gravity? If objects are weightless, could you play catch with something as big as a refrigerator? Could you celebrate your first day in space with a candlelight dinner, or would that be too dangerous? Is fire even possible without gravity? These are some of the questions you will investigate in Section 1.

What's out in space?

What makes a star shine? How long would it take you to travel to a star? How did the universe begin, and how is it changing? In Sections 2–3 you will learn how to interpret clues that can tell you a lot about places where no one has gone before.

Freeze Frame

Now that you have watched the video segment, discuss the following on-screen questions with the other students in your class.

1. For astronauts in weightless conditions, how are eating and drinking different from on Earth?
2. How could you recycle food and oxygen in the closed system of a spacecraft?

INVESTIGATION 1

Living High

Ever Wonder?

If you were going camping in the mountains, how would you prepare for your trip? You would want to know about the camping area: What kinds of animals live there? Is water available? How cold will it get at night? You would need the right kinds of food and clothing, and you would need to know what to do in an emergency. Good planning might save your life.

If planning is important for a camping trip, think how much more important it is for a trip into space. In this investigation you will probe some of the questions facing the people who build life-support systems for missions in space.

Materials List

- Large clear jar with metal lid (screw top)
- Masking tape
- Gravel
- Dechlorinated water
- Pond water and sediment
- Aquarium plants
- Aquatic snails
- Pond invertebrates
- pH paper or pH meter
- Thermometer
- Wax
- Hot plate
- 2 beakers (200 mL)
- Colored pencils
- Safety goggles
- Thermal gloves

STEP-BY-STEP   

Day 1

1. Write your group members' names and today's date on a piece of tape. Attach the tape to the lid of the jar.
2. Place about 4 cm of gravel in the jar.
3. Half-fill the jar with dechlorinated water.
4. Add about 150 mL of pond water and sediment to the jar. Be sure to include some of the muddy substance at the bottom of the container of pond water.
5. Add some aquatic plants to your jar. If possible, use more than one species. If the plants have roots, anchor them in the gravel. In your logbook, record the numbers and types of plants that you put in the jar.
6. Gently add three or four snails and a few other pond invertebrates to your jar. (Do not overload the ecosystem with too many animals.) Record the numbers and kinds of animals that you add.
7. Put on your safety goggles and thermal gloves. Half-fill a beaker with wax, and place it on the hot plate. Turn the hot plate on "medium."
8. If necessary, add enough dechlorinated water to the jar to bring the total volume up to 4 cm from the top. In your logbook, record the depth of the water.
9. Add a thermometer to your jar.
10. Test the pH of the water, and record it in your logbook.
11. Tightly screw the lid onto your jar. When the wax in your beaker has melted, pour the wax carefully on top of the lid to seal the hole. (During the next two weeks, you may need to uncover the hole to provide a vent if too much gas builds up in the jar.)
12. In your logbook, use colored pencils to sketch the biosphere in your jar. Label all the items that you placed in the jar.
13. Place the biosphere in a well-lit area that your teacher assigns. When moving the biosphere, be careful not to shake or disturb it.
14. In your logbook, record the temperature in the jar and the temperature in the classroom.

The planet Earth itself has a biosphere. When seen from outer space, as in this view from a space shuttle, Earth looks small and fragile. This makes it easy to see how a delicate biosphere can be damaged.

Days 2–10

15 Without opening or disturbing your biosphere, observe it carefully for nine more class days.

16 In your logbook, keep a daily record of the temperatures in the jar and classroom. Be sure to date each entry. Also record any changes you observe in the biosphere.

17 At least twice a week, draw a sketch to show how the appearance of your biosphere changes.

Final Day

18 After 10 class days, carefully open the jar and examine the contents of your biosphere.

19 Count how many plants and animals of each type are in the biosphere. Record the number and condition of each type in your logbook.

20 Test the pH of the water, and record it in your logbook. Also record your other observations of the contents of the jar.

21 Follow your teacher's directions for disposing of your materials and cleaning up the work area.

CAREER LINKS

Agriculture and Natural Resources

U.S. Forest Service

AQUACULTURIST

Aquaculturists breed, raise, and market a variety of plants and animals that live in water. These water organisms serve as food, as bait, or as stock for recreational fishing. Some of them are sold to aquarium owners and to laboratory researchers. In the future, aquaculturists may help supply and maintain a food source for space travelers. Aquaculturists raise organisms in controlled environments. They carefully monitor the temperature, acidity, and dissolved-oxygen and waste levels of the water in these environments. Aquaculturists must also understand the reproductive cycle, the disease resistance, and the nutritional requirements of each species they breed.

To pursue this career, you will need a bachelor's degree in aquaculture or biology. An advanced degree is necessary for research positions. For more information, write:

World Aquaculture Society
SC Sea Grant Consortium
287 Meeting Street
Charleston, SC 29401
http://www.ansc.purdue.edu/aquanic/was

Related occupations: marine biologist, hydroponics engineer, conservationist, zoologist, agricultural scientist

Talk It Over

Work with the other members of your group to answer the following questions.

1. What was the energy source for the living things in your biosphere? Did some species serve as the energy source for others? Explain your ideas.
2. What were the nutrient sources for the plants in your biosphere? What were the nutrient sources for the animals in your biosphere?
3. What happened to waste and dead material in your biosphere? How did this process affect the nutrition of the plants and animals?
4. How did the animals in your biosphere obtain oxygen? Explain your idea.
5. What are the living and nonliving factors that affected your biosphere?
6. What could you have done differently to increase the growth of the plants or animals in your biosphere? Explain your ideas.
7. How would your biosphere look in two months if you kept it going? Give the reasons for your prediction.

Spread the Word

Work with the other members of your group to present your findings to the rest of the class. Tell what you learned about the ways your biosphere (an enclosed ecosystem) recycled nutrients and survived. Also describe the living and nonliving factors that affect the health of an enclosed system.

A good way to begin your presentation would be to display your biosphere and tell how you set it up. Use your visual aids: Show the sketches you made of your biosphere at different times. Explain what you think occurred inside the biosphere. Then describe any changes you could make to help the organisms in it grow and survive longer. Explain how the organisms in your biosphere recycled nutrients. Finally, imagine you must design an ecosystem to support life in a new space station for several years. Display a preliminary plan for a balanced biosphere that could survive a long stay in space. Conclude your presentation by describing some types of workers who need to understand how biospheres work.

Read All about It!

World in a Jar

CREATING a closed system of living things that will maintain itself for a long time is a difficult and complex task. In Investigation 1 you and your classmates created several small systems of living things in sealed environments. Each "world in a jar" was a self-contained biosphere. The planet Earth itself has a **biosphere**. This includes the entire region where all of Earth's organisms live.

Earth's biosphere has sustained itself for billions of years. Some of the artificial biospheres that you and other students set up would not last very long. Is it possible to create a large biosphere that would last a long time? One group of people has been trying to do this since the 1980s. They built a large glass structure called Biosphere 2 in the desert near Tucson, Arizona. (Why "Biosphere 2"? Because Earth is Biosphere 1.) Each section of the building contains a different environment: ocean, desert, grassland, and tropical and temperate forests. Eight people entered the biosphere in 1991 and lived there for two years. They had planned to eat only the food they would grow inside and to recycle all wastes. However, because of technical problems, they eventually needed food and oxygen from outside. Because of this, some scientists have criticized the experiment.

No Deliveries

The ideas that shaped Biosphere 2 have influenced the designers of the International Space Station. Designing a biosphere for a space station is a tough challenge. It must be a completely self-contained unit that recycles everything except sunlight or some other source of energy. Designers must be careful to select only those plants, animals, and other organisms that will benefit the

A World of One's Own

Where could you walk out your door in the morning and visit a rain forest, a desert, and an ocean—and still be home in time for lunch?

In Biosphere 2.

Located in Arizona, Biosphere 2 is the largest closed ecological system in the world. The glass and steel structure covers more than three acres and is more than 25 m tall in some places. All air, water, and nutrients recycle within the system. Its ecological areas—or biomes—include a rain forest, a desert, an "ocean," a marsh, a savannah, an agricultural area, and a human habitat.

One team of eight researchers spent two years inside the structure. The nonhuman residents are diverse—nearly 4,000 living species. People no longer inhabit Biosphere 2, but since 1996 Columbia University has conducted classes and research there. Visitors are also allowed inside.

Life in such a small space required the Biospherians to improve the ways they interacted with the environment. Because they recycled everything, researchers learned much about reusing water and waste products and about controlling pollution. Agricultural science has gained from Biosphere 2, where one-half acre of land produced a two-year, pesticide-free food supply. Endangered species and habitats may also benefit from the project. The knowledge that scientists gained about living in a closed environment may prove valuable for long-term space travel and life on space stations.

astronauts. The system must provide enough water and nutrients to keep the astronauts alive for long periods. Once the system is sealed, no new supplies may arrive for months or even years.

Before building a space biosphere, designers must answer many questions. How many plants and animals should it contain, and what kinds should they be? How much water and oxygen should the space station carry? Will the biosphere recycle water and oxygen quickly enough to meet the needs of its people, animals, and plants? How can the astronauts produce clean, safe water? Designers must consider the size of the biosphere to determine how much space to allow for crops, food animals, and people. Scientists need to consider what each crop will produce, along with its requirements for temperature, light, water, nitrogen, and mineral nutrients. Some plants require a short day to flower and produce fruits, while others need more hours of sunlight. Some crops, such as wheat, require a cool season before harvest.

The Right Blend

To meet so many different needs, the biosphere must maintain safe levels of oxygen (O_2) and carbon dioxide (CO_2) in the air. Both plant and animal cells consume O_2 and produce CO_2. Plants also absorb CO_2 from the air to produce food substances. Earth's atmosphere contains roughly 79% nitrogen, 21% oxygen, and 0.03% carbon dioxide. Any major change in these amounts could affect life in the biosphere. Designers must make sure the biosphere maintains a proper balance of these gases.

In Earth's atmosphere, the levels of these gases depend on all the living things that produce and consume them. The level of carbon dioxide also depends on the fact that it dissolves easily in water. Large quantities of CO_2 dissolve in the oceans, and this helps to keep the amount of CO_2 in the air fairly constant. For example, much of the "extra" CO_2 that enters the air from factories, engines, and fires dissolves in the oceans. On the other hand, if CO_2 production fell, some of the carbon dioxide in ocean water would diffuse back into the atmosphere. (To "diffuse" means to move from an area of high concentration to an area of low concentration.)

Large quantities of CO_2 dissolve in the oceans, and this helps to keep the amount of CO_2 in the air fairly constant.

Could space-station planners design a system that would recycle CO_2 in this way? How much water would it need? Water is very dense. Getting heavy tanks of water into orbit would use extra rocket fuel. Would it be worth the expense? Is there a cheaper way to provide water? All these questions must be answered before construction of the space station begins.

Besides oxygen and carbon dioxide, many other nutrients cycle through Earth's biosphere. The most important ones are nitrogen, which is part of the proteins in all living things, and the minerals calcium, phosphorus, potassium, sulfur, and iron. Most of Earth's nitrogen exists in the form of chemical compounds that make up certain rocks. As a result, it is not easily available to living things. But the nitrogen gas (N_2) that makes up most of the atmosphere is easily available. The space-station biosphere must be able to provide the nitrogen and other nutrients that plants and animals need. In other words, designers must find a way to cycle nitrogen and other nutrients.

GET THIS . . .

An **ion** is an atom that has a positive or negative charge because it has lost or gained an electron.

ROUND AND ROUND

Here's how the nitrogen cycle works on Earth. Lightning and some kinds of soil bacteria and other microscopic organisms cause chemical reactions that convert N_2 to ions, such as ammonium (NH_4^+) and nitrate (NO_3^-). An **ion** is an atom or molecule that has a positive or negative electrical charge because it has lost or gained an electron. Such reactions also occur in factories that produce nitrogen fertilizers for farms and gardens. Plants and bacteria can use these forms of nitrogen to make proteins, but animals and fungi cannot.

When animals, such as deer and grasshoppers, eat plants, they digest the plant's proteins and use them to make their own proteins. Predators, such as wolves, obtain protein from their prey. Animal wastes and dead plants and animals are consumed and broken down by large numbers of organisms, including worms, insects, bacteria, and fungi. Some of the nitrogen in the wastes and dead material becomes protein in the bodies of these decomposers. Bacteria also break down some of the nitrogen further, converting it back to NH_4^+ and NO_3^- ions, which the roots of plants may absorb. Some of the nitrogen returns to the atmosphere as N_2 (see Figure 1).

LOTS OF QUESTIONS

How could a space-station biosphere cycle enough nitrogen to take care of all its inhabitants? This is a major problem now facing space scientists. Before they can solve it, they must answer several other questions. Must the biosphere contain a large amount of air that is rich in N_2? **Legumes** (plants such as peas, beans, and peanuts) have nodules on their roots that nourish and protect the bacteria that convert N_2 to usable forms. Would it be important to grow such plants in the space station? If so, can astronauts also harvest and eat them? Should there be birds, such as chickens, to supply protein-rich meat and eggs? Should there be larger animals, such as sheep and goats? Should there be an aquarium for fish? If so, which fish can grow most quickly and produce the least waste? If the biosphere must last for several years, will inbreeding in the small animal populations affect the health and productivity of the animals? . . .

Unlike nitrogen, the cycles of mineral nutrients—calcium, iron, and others—do not involve a gaseous form, such as N_2. As rocks break down on Earth, they release minerals that dissolve in water in the soil. Like nitrogen, these minerals enter the biosphere when plants absorb this water through their roots. Many minerals build up in animal tissues over time. For example, bones and teeth are mostly a compound of calcium and phosphorus. Also like nitrogen, the minerals in wastes and dead matter return to the soil and water. This replenishes the supply of plant nutrients.

How would this process work in space? Would astronauts have to fertilize the plants, or would they simply take mineral pills? Some minerals are harmful to plants and people when consumed in large quantities.

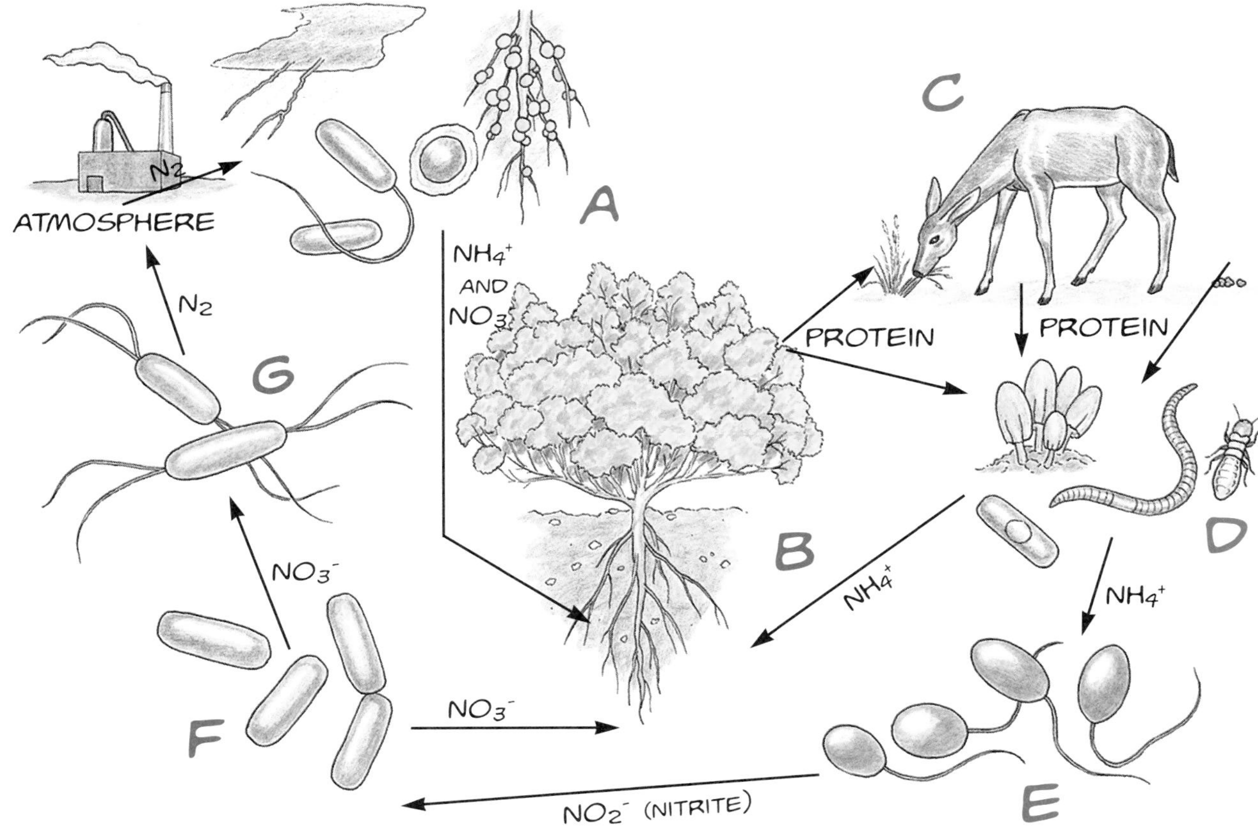

Figure 1: The nitrogen cycle

Note: Lightning, fertilizer factories, and bacteria in soil and the roots of certain plants convert N_2 gas from the atmosphere to NH_4^+ and NO_3^- ions (A), which plants (B) absorb through their roots and convert to protein. Animals (C) consume plant protein. Decomposers (D) break down dead plant and animal material and animal wastes, converting protein back into NH_4^+. Soil bacteria (E, F) convert NH_4^+ to NO_3^-, which may be used by plants or returned to the atmosphere by other soil bacteria (G).

How could the people on the space station check and adjust mineral levels? How often should they do these things? Scientists do not know the answers to many of these questions. Before people can leave Earth and live in an artificial biosphere for long periods, scientists must do a lot more research. Once the biosphere is in orbit, it may be difficult to correct mistakes. Good research and good planning are critical to success.

On Your Own

Answer the following questions based on "World in a Jar."

1 Why do you think the people who designed Biosphere 2 chose glass for its domed roof instead of steel or some other common building material?

2 How could bacteria that obtain energy by carrying out chemical reactions on sulfur, iron, or other minerals be useful in the biosphere of a space station? Would the bacteria fill the same roles as plants, animals, or decay organisms, such as fungi? Explain your ideas.

3 Suppose you wanted to speed up the production of food for astronauts in a space-station biosphere. Would it help to add to the soil the nutrients that earthworms, bacteria, and other decomposers need? Explain your answer.

Off the Scale

Ever Wonder?

Suppose you are an astronaut floating inside a space shuttle that is orbiting Earth. How does it feel to be weightless? You are still the same size you were on the ground, but your weight is gone. Where did it go? What does it mean to be weightless? If objects in space have no weight, could you move a large communication satellite as easily as you could pick up a notebook?

In this investigation you will learn about a more accurate concept than weight to describe and compare objects in space. You will also learn how astronauts can "weigh" themselves even when they are weightless.

These "weightless" astronauts learn that it isn't easy to pose for a group picture while they float inside a space shuttle that is orbiting Earth.

Materials List

- Spring scale
- Dual pan balance
- Set of masses and forceps for handling them
- Metal meter stick with 2 wooden blocks attached
- 2 C-clamps
- Plastic 35-mm film canister
- Foam rubber
- Masking tape
- 10 pennies
- 1 nickel
- Stopwatch or wristwatch with second hand
- Graph paper
- Safety goggles

STEP-BY-STEP

1. Examine the dual pan balance and spring scale. Use each one to weigh 10 pennies. In your logbook, record the weight of the pennies as measured by each device.

2. Sketch the balance and the scale. Record a brief description of how each device works. Be sure to explain how gravity is involved with each one.

3. Put on your safety goggles.

4. Use one or two C-clamps to attach the end of the meter stick with the wooden blocks to the top of your table. The other end of the stick should extend away from the tabletop so that it is free to vibrate horizontally (see Figure 2). *Caution: Make sure the meter stick does not block an aisle.*

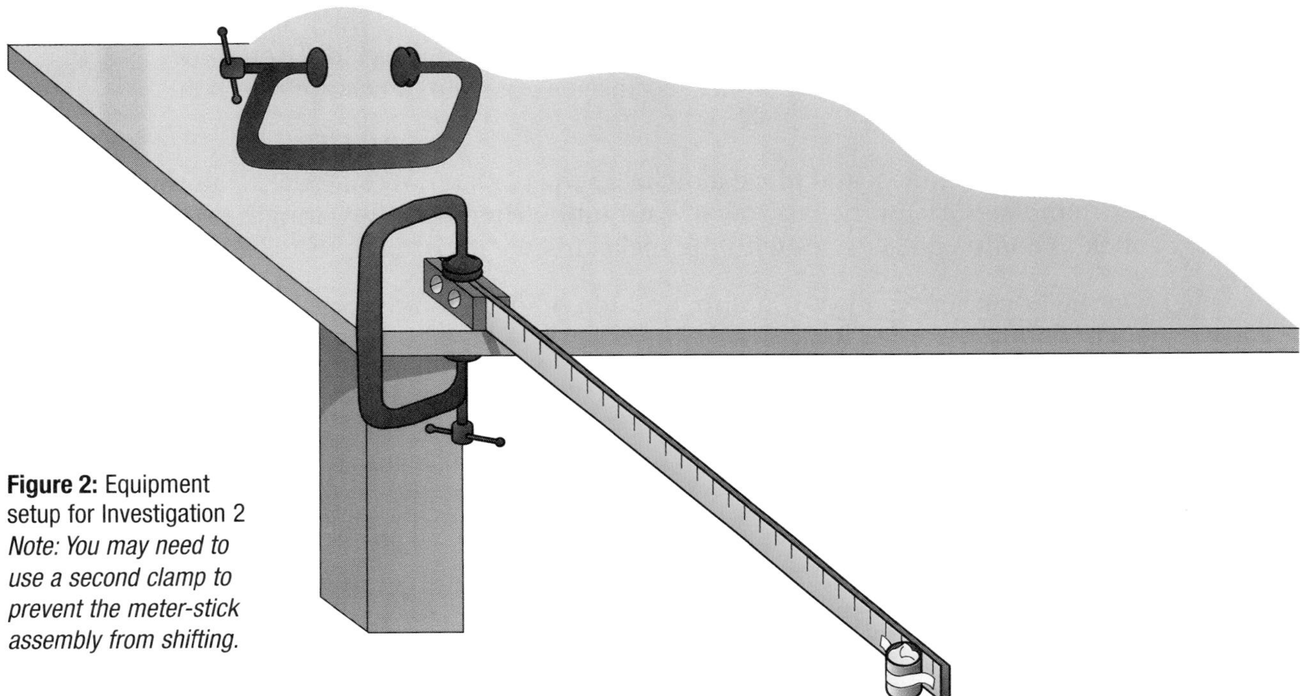

Figure 2: Equipment setup for Investigation 2
Note: You may need to use a second clamp to prevent the meter-stick assembly from shifting.

5. Insert a piece of foam rubber into a film canister. Tape the canister to the free end of the meter stick. Then put the cover on the canister.

6. In your logbook, set up a data table with two columns and the headings shown in the following sample. The sample shows three blank rows, but your table will need 12 blank rows.

Number of pennies	Time for 25 vibrations (sec)

7. Test your mechanism by pulling the end of the meter stick to the right side and releasing it. The stick will swing back and forth. Every time it moves from the right to the left and back to the right is one cycle. Stop the stick.

8. Using a stopwatch, measure the number of seconds it takes for the stick to complete 25 cycles with no pennies in the canister. Record the results in the first row of your data table.

9. Place one penny in the canister. Use the piece of foam rubber to prevent the coin from moving. Measure how many seconds it takes for the stick to complete 25 cycles. Record the result in the second row of your table.

10. Conduct nine more trials as in Step 9. For each trial, add one penny to the canister and record the results on the next line of your data table.

11. On a piece of graph paper, make a line graph of your data. (**Math tip:** Knowing how to make graphs is an important math skill. For this graph, you should show the number of pennies on the x-axis and the number of seconds on the y-axis. Mark all your data as points on the grid. Then draw a line or smooth curve that comes as close as possible to each of the data points.)

12. Remove the pennies, and place a nickel in the canister. Write "Nickel" in the left-hand column of the last row of your table. Then time how long it takes the stick to complete 25 cycles with the nickel inside. Record the result.

13. On the line or curve in your graph, find the point that matches the number of seconds you recorded for the nickel in Step 12. Follow a vertical line downward from that point to find the number of pennies that weigh the same as your nickel. Record this weight in your logbook.

14. In Step 1 you determined the weight of 10 pennies with a dual pan balance. Now figure the weight of one penny by dividing the total weight by 10. Record this weight.

15. Figure the weight of the nickel by multiplying the number of pennies that you recorded in Step 13 by the weight of one penny.

16. Use the dual pan balance to determine the weight of the nickel. Record this measurement in your logbook.

TALK IT OVER

Work with the other members of your group to answer the following questions.

1. How close was the weight you calculated for the nickel to your actual measurement with the dual pan balance? How could you make the measurement with the vibrating stick more accurate? Explain your thinking.

2. As you added more pennies, what happened to the vibration time? Would you expect the same thing to happen in space, where all objects are weightless? Give the reasons for your answer.

World Bank

Intensive Care/Critical Care Nurse

A nurse who works in the field of intensive or critical care treats patients who are seriously ill or badly injured. Patients in an intensive-care unit may have had major surgery, severe burns, organ transplants, or serious heart or lung problems. These medical conditions often require patients to be in highly controlled and monitored environments with life-support services. Premature babies who have complications at birth also need special environments. Some nurses specialize in caring for such infants. Others specialize in working with older children in pediatric care. To work in intensive care, you will need at least a four-year nursing degree. After graduation, you will need to receive special training and certification. For more information, write:

American Nurses Foundation
600 Maryland Avenue, S.W., Suite 100 West
Washington, DC 20024
http://www.ana.org/anf

Related occupations: surgery nurse, respiratory therapist, cardiovascular invasive specialist, emergency medical technician, nurse anesthetist

3 Suppose you traveled to Mars and collected some rocks there. On your way back to Earth, which would be the best device—a spring scale, a dual pan balance, or a vibrating stick—for measuring how much rock you collected? Explain your answer.

4 Do all three measuring devices depend on gravity to work? If any of them do not, what do they measure? Is it weight, or is it something else? Explain your answer.

RESULTS

Spread the Word

Work with the other member(s) of your group to share your findings with the rest of the class. Your main goal should be to explain what you learned about the difference between the weight of an object and the "amount" of matter in it. Show an enlarged copy of your graph, and tell how you estimated the weight of the nickel. Then explain how astronauts who want to "weigh" themselves in space could apply what you have learned. Be sure to give the reason that each of the three devices you investigated would or would not work in space.

Describe a situation in which astronauts on a space shuttle need to work with a large, weightless object. Explain why moving such an object may be difficult even though it has no weight in space.

Is spaceflight hazardous to your health? Do plants and animals grow normally in space? The next video segment will help you answer these questions. As you watch it, think about how weightlessness affects living things. Then discuss the video segment with the other students in your class. After your discussion, read "Weighty Matters."

Read All about It!

Weighty Matters

Because you live on Earth, you are used to the benefits of gravity. You can enjoy a drink without having it float out of the glass into your face. If you drop a book, it falls to the floor. You can walk with your feet on the ground. Earth's gravity is pulling on you. You know Earth's gravity makes it possible for you to walk around town without having to worry about falling off the planet. But did you also know that your own gravity is pulling on Earth?

Gravity is a force that all matter exerts on all other matter in the universe. Every object pulls on every other one. Right now, Earth's gravity is pulling on you, holding you to the surface. The force that the planet's gravity exerts on your body is your **weight**. At the same time, your body is pulling Earth toward you with equal force. (Just as Earth pulls on every gram of your body, every gram of your body pulls on Earth. The forces of gravity are equal.)

What's the Matter?

The strength of the pull between any two objects depends on the amount of matter in each one. You and the planet pull on each other with the same force, but the force between Earth and an object that has more matter than you do would be greater. For example, your school building contains more matter than your body. As a result, Earth pulls the school with a stronger force (the school has more weight than you) and the school exerts a stronger force on Earth. What if you were on the Moon, which has only one-sixth as much matter as Earth? The Moon pulls only one-sixth as hard on objects. You would weigh only one-sixth as much as on Earth.

The amount of matter in an object is not the only factor that determines the force of gravity. The distance between objects is another factor. The farther apart two objects are, the smaller the force of gravity is between them. Suppose you went to a very

low place, such as Death Valley, California, and weighed yourself. Then suppose you climbed a high mountain, such as Mount Wilson, and weighed yourself again. You would weigh slightly less on the mountain because you would be farther away from most of the Earth when you are in a high place. For another example of how distance affects the force of gravity, think about Jupiter. Largest planet in the solar system, Jupiter contains far more matter than Earth. But Jupiter is so far away that it exerts much less pull on you than Earth does.

Gravity made it possible for you to use a spring scale and a dual pan balance to measure weights during Investigation 2. The attraction between Earth and the coins produced a weight force that pulled them closer together. The spring scale measured how far the weight of the coins stretched a spring. The balance measured how much weight was needed to equal the downward force of the coins' weight. But the vibrating meter stick moved sideways, not downward with the force of gravity. How did that "scale" work?

How Much Would You Weigh on Pluto?

If you weigh 120 pounds (54.43 kg) at sea level, your mass is 54.43 kg wherever you go. However, your weight will decrease at higher altitudes on Earth. Your weight would also be different on the Moon and on other planets. Weight depends on the force of gravity. Here are some examples of how your weight would differ in various places:

Location	**Weight (lb)**
Boston, MA (sea level)	120.000
Pittsburgh, PA (235 m above sea level)	119.965
Denver, CO (1,638 m above sea level)	119.903
Moon	19.918
Mars	45.600
Jupiter	312.000
Pluto	4.800

Note: Jupiter has 318 times the mass of Earth, but the force of gravity on the surface of Jupiter is only 2.6 times greater than the force of gravity on Earth. You would not weigh 318 times as much on Jupiter because that planet is so large that most of its mass would be too far away from you to exert such a strong pull. In the same way, Pluto has only 0.002 (1/500th) the mass of Earth, but the force of gravity on the surface of Pluto is 0.04 (1/25th) the force of gravity on Earth. Your weight on Pluto would not be 1/500th of your weight on Earth because that planet is so small that all of its mass would be closer to you.

Mass 50, Weight 0

The vibrating stick did not measure weight. It measured **mass**, the amount of material in an object. An object's mass does not depend on gravity. If your mass on Earth is 50 kg, your mass on the Moon or anywhere else would still be 50 kg. Your mass does not change unless you gain or lose matter (for example, by eating or dieting).

Weight and mass are related. The weight of any object depends on its mass and its distance from other objects. Away from all other masses, any object will be weightless. If another object is located nearby, the weight of each object depends on how much mass each one has and how close they are to each other. A spacecraft is never truly weightless, no matter where it is in the solar system. Even when it is far from Earth, it will experience small gravitational forces from the Sun, Earth, and the other planets.

It's Hard to Change

Objects have another property that depends on mass: The more mass an object has, the more energy it takes to start moving or to change speed or direction. Objects tend to resist changes in their motion. An object at rest tends to stay at rest, and an object in motion tends to stay in motion. **Newton's First Law of Motion** deals with this property of matter, which is called **inertia**. The more mass an object has, the greater its inertia. The vibrating stick is an example of an **inertial balance**, a device that does not depend on gravity to measure masses. Astronauts use an inertial balance to check their masses in space.

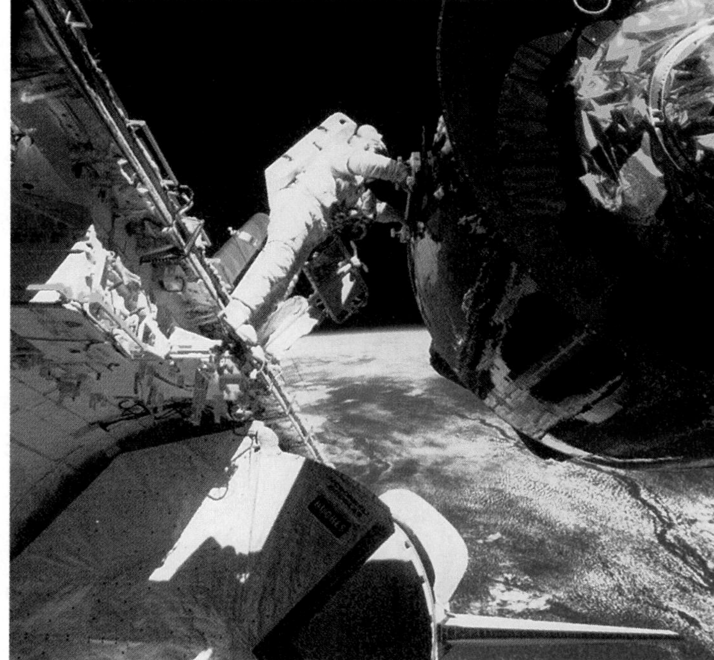

Inertia is very important in space. It helps to keep the shuttle, astronaut, and satellite in this photograph in orbit. If the satellite is given a strong push, it will continue to move away in a straight line, with constant speed.

Every time you added a penny to your inertial balance in the investigation, you increased its mass. This gave it more inertia, and so you had to apply more energy to make the stick vibrate. Your graph showed the connection between the mass (number of pennies) and the speed of the vibrations (number of seconds). The graph served the same purpose as the markings on the spring scale, which showed the relation between the weight on the scale and the distance that the spring stretched. You used your graph as a tool to measure a different mass, the nickel.

Quick Escape

To launch a rocket, it is necessary to overcome two things: the rocket's inertia (tendency to stay at rest on the launchpad) and Earth's gravity. A rocket is a very heavy object, partially because it must carry a lot of fuel to overcome inertia and gravity. As a rocket rises, gravity slows it down and pulls it back. But if the rocket moves fast enough, it will soon be far away, where the pull of Earth's gravity is weaker. The rocket also becomes lighter as it burns its fuel, and this helps it move faster. When a rocket reaches **escape speed** (11.6 km per second), it can outrun Earth's gravity. In other words, when a rocket is rising at this speed, Earth's gravity is weakening too quickly to pull it back (see Figure 3). Every planet has a different escape speed that depends on the planet's mass.

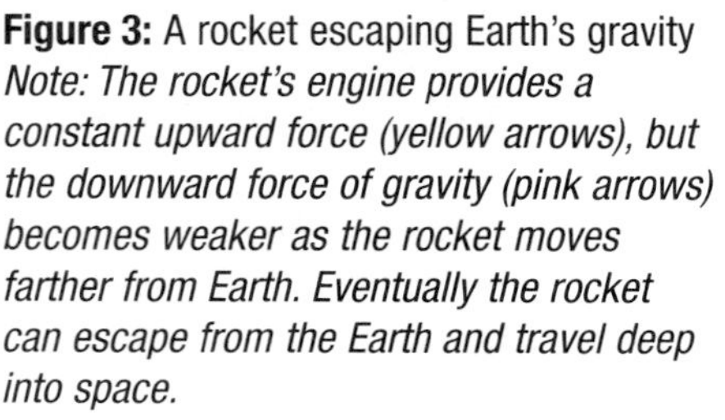

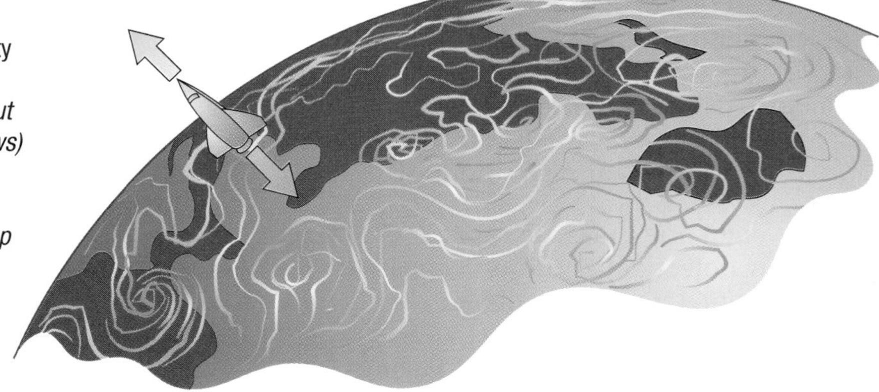

Figure 3: A rocket escaping Earth's gravity
Note: The rocket's engine provides a constant upward force (yellow arrows), but the downward force of gravity (pink arrows) becomes weaker as the rocket moves farther from Earth. Eventually the rocket can escape from the Earth and travel deep into space.

Artist's conception of the International Space Station

Far from Earth and other planets, space travelers would have to cope with the effects of weightlessness. Humans—and all other living things—have adapted to life on Earth, where gravity is nearly constant. The force of people's weight requires them to use their muscles to stand up and walk around. But floating astronauts have no weight to support against the force of gravity, and so their muscles tend to get weaker. Bones are another problem. On Earth, people's bones must support their weight. This stimulates the bones, keeping them dense and strong. The first astronauts who spent more than a few days in space discovered that their bones lost minerals and became weaker. To maintain healthy bones and muscles, space travelers must exercise often.

No More Ups and Downs

Other living things depend on gravity as much as humans do. Plants produce roots that grow downward and stems that grow upward. This is partly in response to gravity, although stems also grow toward light, which usually comes from above, and roots tend to grow toward moist soil, which usually is deeper than surface soil. But out in space, where there is no "up" or "down," roots and stems grow in wild curlicues. When the International Space Station is in orbit, scientists will place small animals in **artificial gravity**. A rotating device will create a force that feels like gravity. But don't confuse this with the real thing. Artificial gravity has nothing to do with weight.

The Fabric of Space

For about 200 years, scientists used Newton's Laws of Motion to explain how gravity works. According to Newton, gravity is a mysterious force that attracts objects to one another. But when Albert Einstein presented his general theory of relativity in 1915, he gave the world a new way to think of gravity. According to Einstein, gravity is just a way to describe the motions of objects in space.

To Einstein, space is not simply an empty vacuum. It is more like a continuous "fabric." Imagine a huge sheet of rubber, with balls of various sizes on top of it. The balls have various masses. All of them, even the smallest one, dents the rubber sheet as it moves. A large ball dents the sheet a great deal more than the small balls do. Because the sheet bends more toward the bowling ball, any of the small balls that come near the large one will roll toward it.

The rubber sheet represents the fabric of space. In the universe as Einstein saw it, the concept of gravity serves as a way to describe how every object in the universe bends or distorts the space around it, causing other objects to move toward it. Instead of saying that the gravitational force of the Sun attracts the less massive Earth, Einstein might have said that the Sun bends or distorts space, making Earth move toward it.

On Your Own

Answer the following questions based on "Weighty Matters."

1. What happens to the mass and weight of a spacecraft as it travels from Earth to the Moon?
2. Suppose you were on a huge spacecraft that had a large gym. If you wanted to play baseball there, would the catcher need a face mask or would the weightless ball be harmless? After a batter hit a line drive, how would the ball move?
3. Do you think escape speed is greater on Earth or on Jupiter? Explain.

Do you need gravity to walk? How would you get around in space? Would simple activities—eating lunch, lying in bed, using the bathroom—present special problems on a spaceship? Could you have a candlelight dinner, or would the danger of fire be too great in an enclosed spacecraft? Is a fire in space even possible? The next video segment will help you answer these questions. As you watch, think about some ways that living and working in weightless conditions is different from life on Earth. Then discuss the video segment with the rest of the class. After your discussion, read "Who's Pulling?"

Read All about It!

Who's Pulling?

ARE you falling right now? If you are reading this book, you're probably not skydiving or falling out of a tree. But how do you know you're not falling? What does it mean to fall down?

When you are standing, the planet Earth pulls your body down against the ground. At the same time, your body pulls Earth upward with equal force. You feel the upward pressure of Earth against your feet. This feeling is what people call "weight" (see Figure 4). But it is more accurate to say that weight is the force that pulls you down against the ground. If you are falling, you do not feel the force of the Earth against your body because your body is not pressing against the ground. While

Figure 4: Weight—felt and unfelt
Note: When you stand (left), your weight presses on the floor and you feel the floor's resistance force pushing back up. During free fall (right), you do not feel a resistance force; therefore, you feel "weightless," even though your weight is still the same.

falling, you are weightless. You can get a good sensation of weightlessness when an elevator begins to descend and the floor falls away from your feet—or when a roller-coaster reaches the top of a steep climb and starts to fall.

Astronauts in orbit are not truly weightless. They are still close enough to Earth for its gravitational force to pull them downward. But they feel weightless because their bodies do not feel the planet pushing against them. Yet even though they do not feel the force of Earth's gravity, it will gradually pull them back to Earth, but this could take months or even years.

Root Beer Floats—And So Does Everything Else

In such weak gravity, if an astronaut "drops" something, it does not fall to the floor—it floats. And because it is moving with the speed of the spacecraft, it continues to travel along with everything else in the ship. Anything that is not secured floats randomly. People tend to float horizontally, but if they lean forward, they begin turning somersaults. Normal walking is impossible. Without weight, astronauts get no traction with their feet. They must use handgrips to pull themselves around the cabin.

Even eating and sleeping pose special problems in space. Forget about rice or peas. They would float or roll right off your plate. Liquids would not stay in your glass. If you were eating a stalk of celery, you would want to hold onto it between bites, or else it would float away. Before going to sleep, astronauts must zip themselves into

Excuse Me . . . Is There a Restroom up Here?

It's a personal question, but NASA hears it all the time: "How do astronauts go to the bathroom?"

The microgravity in a spacecraft presents some tricky problems for personal cleanliness. Space-shuttle toilets, which both men and women use, have hand and foot restraints and seat belts. The toilets cannot use water. Instead, a powerful flow of air carries away the waste, which is packaged for disposal back on Earth. Filters remove bacteria from the contaminated air. After the air is purified, it recirculates throughout the ship.

The astronauts can wash their hands and brush their teeth in a washbasin. A fan at the back of the basin pulls any excess water down the drain. Because showers are not possible in microgravity, shuttle travelers must take sponge baths. This may all sound uncomfortable, but it is a big improvement over the early space flights, which had no bathrooms at all. Still, the Johnson Space Center in Houston is testing new facilities, including a shower, for space stations of the future. Researchers are also looking at ways to treat waste chemically and put it to use, instead of disposing of it on Earth or in space.

These astronauts are just waking up. They sleep in these narrow cubicles to avoid floating around and bumping into walls.

sleeping bags or strap themselves into their bunks.

Slow Burn

Could you have a birthday cake with candles in space? As you saw in the video, fires do not burn well in orbit. On Earth, the hot smoke and gases from a flame expand, becoming less dense. Because they are less dense than the surrounding air, the gases tend to rise, making room for fresh air around the flame. The continuous upward flow of air provides a steady supply of oxygen and gives the flame its typical teardrop shape. But out in space, no upward flow of air occurs because there is no "up." A flame in space has a rounded, almost spherical shape, and the gases that it produces do not float away as they do on Earth. Instead, the gases accumulate around the flame until they block the supply of air and suffocate the fire.

. . . out in space, no upward flow of air occurs because there is no "up." A flame in space has a rounded, almost spherical shape, and the gases that it produces do not float away as they do on Earth.

Good News

But don't feel too sorry for astronauts who don't get candles on their birthday cakes. The fact that it is hard to keep a fire going in a spacecraft is good news. An overheated electrical circuit is not likely to start a fire that could use up the crew's precious oxygen supply or destroy the ship.

On Your Own

Answer the following questions based on "Who's Pulling?"

1 Once a spacecraft is 300,000 km from Earth's surface, the planet's gravity can no longer pull it back. Would the spacecraft be completely weightless at that point?

2 On Earth you might exercise by doing push-ups, sit-ups, and jumping jacks. Which, if any, of these could you do to keep in shape while in orbit? What are some other kinds of exercise that you could do in orbit? Explain your answers.

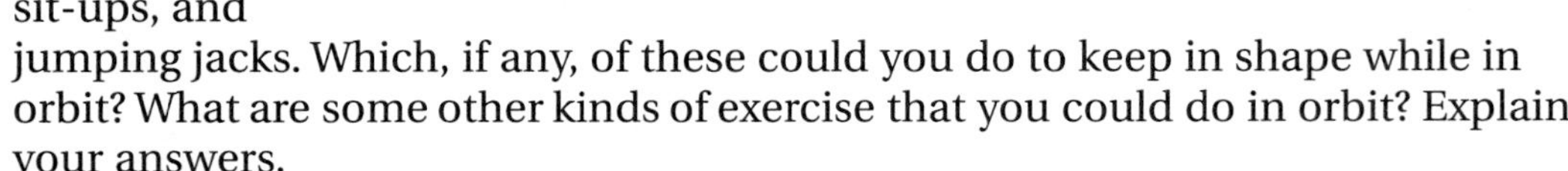

3 You can make popcorn by heating the kernels in cooking oil on the bottom of a covered pot. What problems would you have if you tried to do this in space? Explain what you think would cause the problems.

Section Wrap-up

First Orbit

10 . . . 9 . . . 8 . . . 7. . . . In a few seconds the rocket will blast off, carrying you into space for the first time. You're so nervous you feel as though the butterflies in your stomach are coming out of your ears.

3 . . . 2 . . . 1. . . . The rocket lifts off the launch pad on a column of flame. It climbs slowly at first but quickly picks up speed. The strong acceleration presses you down into your seat—that's the effect of inertia. Soon the rocket reaches escape speed, 11.6 km per second, and is outrunning Earth's gravity. You're going to make it into space.

Systems Check

As soon as the ship reaches orbit, you have work to do. You need to make sure that all the life-support systems survived the stress of the rocket ride. What was it like for the plants, animals, and equipment? It's time to check.

You unfasten your belts and stand up to walk back to the plants. That's a big mistake! Your first step pushes you off the floor, and your head is heading for the ceiling. For a second you forgot that you're in microgravity. You grab for the nearest handhold, but you pull yourself too hard and smack into the wall. Ow! You may be weightless up here, but you still have plenty of mass—you felt it when you hit the wall. Training. Training. Remember your training.

Counting on Plants

You float over to the plants. The potato plants look fine. That's good news, because you and the other members of the crew will be counting on them to provide oxygen and to convert carbon dioxide into nutritious food. The bean plants survived too. The nodules on their roots contain important bacteria that will convert some of the nitrogen in the air to amino acids, which these plants will use to grow protein-rich beans.

It will be interesting to watch the plants grow in microgravity. Will their roots grow toward the lights, and will their stems grow into the soil? This "soil" is not real earth, but it holds the nutrients and microorganisms the plants need.

Earthworms squirm frantically on and above the surface. You brought them along to help break down wastes and recycle nutrients to the plants, but they aren't used to weightless burrowing yet. That reminds you to take your calcium pill later. It will help strengthen your bones, which may get weaker in orbit, where they will not have to support your weight.

Staying in Shape

You also want to be sure to schedule some time on the exercise bike. Without exercise, it won't take long for you to lose your strength up here.

A light jump sends you safely across the cabin to a wall covered with dials and switches. You check the gas levels in the air: plenty of oxygen and not too much CO_2. The water supply looks good too, but you will have to keep an eye on it after everyone has had something to eat and drink and the waste-recycling system goes to work. Recycling waste will supply purified water both for drinking and for watering the plants.

Time to Eat

Thinking about food makes you hungry. It's time for your first meal in space. You look through the storage cabinets for something good to eat. There's no gas stove up here. It would be too dangerous, and it probably would not work very well without gravity to shape the flames so that fresh oxygen can replace burned gas. You find a packet of chili and a tube of juice. The chili sticks to your plate and spoon, but you can't pour the juice into a cup. It would float out and make a mess. Instead, you drink it through a straw.

While you eat, you look out at the Earth. It's a fantastic sight that few people have ever seen. Asia slides by, and soon you're over the Pacific Ocean. It won't be long before you will have circled the globe for the first time—the first of many times.

Pulling You Back

Earth's gravity, though very weak at this altitude, still has an effect on the spacecraft. Because you are circling the planet in a low orbit, in a matter of months Earth's gravity could pull you back into the atmosphere. But the pilot and Mission Control won't let that happen. They know when to use small rocket thrusters to boost the spacecraft into a higher and safer orbit.

Eventually, of course, you will have to drop out of orbit and return to the surface. But that moment is still in your future.

On Your Own

Answer the following questions based on "First Orbit."

1 The International Space Station is too large for NASA to launch in one piece. Astronauts must assemble it in orbit. Can workers floating in space toss big, weightless sections of the space station safely and easily to one another? Explain your answer.

Get This . . .

An object at rest tends to stay at rest, and an object in motion tends to stay in motion. This property of matter is called **inertia**.

2 The Earth's biosphere recycles water through evaporation followed by rain or snow. Is it possible to build a biosphere for weightless conditions that would recycle water in this way? Give the reasons for your answer.

3 Some people have suggested that it would be easier to send rockets into space if they were launched from an orbiting space station. Would you expect the necessary escape speed from orbit around the Earth to be greater, smaller, or the same as it is from a launch site on the surface? Explain.

Astronomer Carl Sagan referred to Earth as a "pale blue dot" in the vastness of space. The Galileo *spacecraft captured this computer-enhanced image of Earth and the Moon in 1992 from 6.2 million km out in space. The half-Earth is in the background.*

Section 2

OTHER WORLDS

HAVE you ever looked at pictures of the Moon? Its surface is pockmarked with craters. What caused all those craters?

What differences are there between a moon and a planet? Are the planets Venus and Mars like the Moon? Is there any way to learn about conditions on other planets without visiting them in a spaceship?

What is the solar system? What else is in the solar system besides the nine planets and their moons? What makes the planets travel around the Sun? Do they all move in the same direction that Earth does? Do they all lie in the same plane as Earth, or do they travel in different planes—like electrons around the nucleus of an atom? What keeps the solar system together? You will discover the answers to these questions as you complete all of the activities in this section.

As you watch the next video segment of this module, imagine the size of the solar system and think about the different kinds of objects that are in it.

FREEZE FRAME

Now that you have watched the video segment, discuss the following on-screen questions with the other students in your class.

1 How do planets stay in orbit around the Sun?

2 What are some types of differences between Earth and the other planets?

Balancing Act

EVER WONDER?

Have you ever wondered how Earth stays in orbit around the Sun? To complete its yearly orbit, Earth travels at a speed of 107,200 km per hour. What keeps it from shooting off into space? Does the Moon stay in orbit around Earth because of the same forces that keep Earth in orbit around the Sun? In this investigation you will discover how planets and moons in the solar system maintain their orbits year after year after year.

MATERIALS LIST

- String
- Scissors
- 2 rolls of masking tape (different sizes)
- Large spool
- 3 metal spoons of different masses
- Meter stick
- Felt-tipped marker
- Safety goggles

STEP-BY-STEP

1. Use the meter stick and scissors to measure and cut a piece of string 130 cm long.
2. Tie one end of the string to the smaller roll of masking tape. Mark a spot on the string 100 cm from the knot.
3. Thread the free end of the string through the spool. At the mark on the string, tie the string around the handle of the smallest spoon. Make sure the spoon and tape are tied securely.
4. Mark the string every 10 cm between the spoon and the tape.
5. In your logbook, set up a data table like this:

Spoon mass	Radius of orbit (cm) Small tape roll	Radius of orbit (cm) Large tape roll
Small		
Medium		
Large		

6. Put on your safety goggles.

7. One member of your team should be the orbiter. This person should hold the spool overhead in one hand and the roll of tape in the other hand. The other member of the team should stand at least 2 m away and serve as recorder. *Caution: No one should be closer than 2 m to the person doing the trial.*

8. Orbiter: Begin twirling the spoon overhead with a circular motion, as if spinning a lasso (see Figure 5). Keep a firm grasp on the spool, and do not hold the string. Move your arm and hand as little as possible so that the spoon swings in a horizontal circle. While spinning the spoon, gradually release the roll of tape.

9. Recorder: Observe the marks on the string, and estimate the length of string below the spool. Subtract this number from the length of string between the spoon and the tape (100 cm). Record the result in the first blank space of your data table.

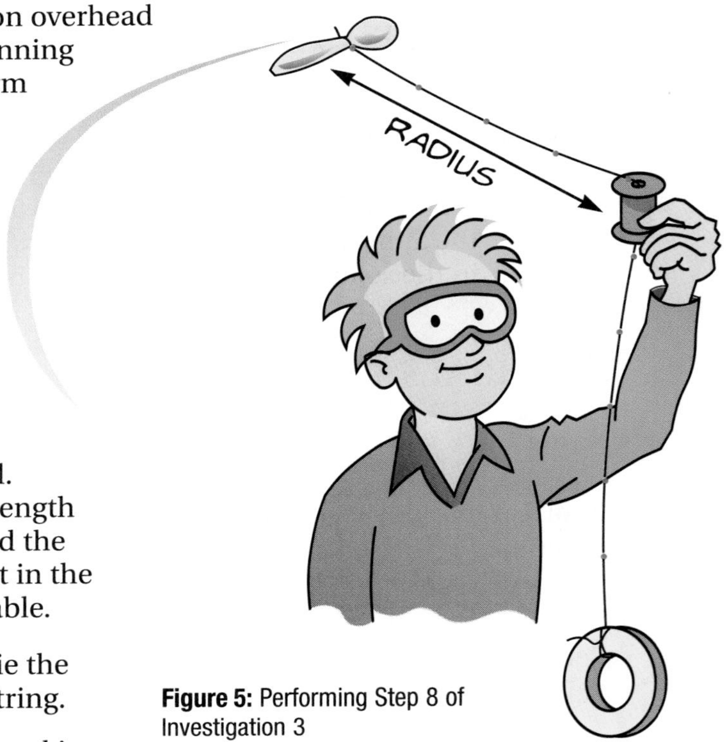

10. Remove the small spoon, and tie the medium-weight spoon to the string.

11. Repeat the procedure you followed in Steps 8 and 9. Each time you do a new trial, try to swing the spoon with the same force. Record the result in your data table.

12. Remove the second spoon, and attach the heaviest spoon to the string. Repeat the same procedure, and record the result.

13. Remove the small roll of tape, and replace it with the large one.

14. Perform a new series of trials, using each spoon. (Do not switch positions as orbiter and recorder.) Record the result each time in the appropriate space on the data table.

15. Clean up your work area, and return all the supplies to your teacher.

Figure 5: Performing Step 8 of Investigation 3

TALK IT OVER

Work with your partner to answer the following questions.

1. How did the radius of the spoon's orbit change when you released the roll of tape? What do you think caused the spoon and string to behave this way?

2. How did the spoon's mass affect the radius of its orbit? How could a difference in mass cause this change?

3. Think of the equipment you used in this investigation as a model of a planet orbiting the Sun. What does the string in this model represent? In what direction does it pull the orbiting spoon?

4. When you used a heavier roll of tape, how did it affect the orbits of the spoons? What does this suggest about how the Sun's mass affects the orbits of the planets?

5. What would happen if you cut the string while swinging the spoon? Which way would the spoon go? Explain.

6. Earth orbits the Sun in much the same way that your spoons orbited the rolls of tape. What factors keep Earth in a smooth orbit around the Sun? (Hint: Think about the items that you varied during the investigation.)

7. The Moon orbits the Earth just as the Earth orbits the Sun. If the Earth had less mass, do you think the Moon would still orbit the planet in the same way? If not, how might it change? Explain.

8. You may have heard people talk about a centrifugal (outward) force on objects in orbit. Was there a force pushing the orbiting spoon out away from the spool? If so, what was that force? If not, do you think centrifugal forces are real? Explain your thinking.

The Days Keep Getting Longer

Do you think you don't have enough hours in the day? Don't worry, your days are slowly growing longer—but the years are getting shorter.

You can thank the Moon for it. The Moon's gravitational pull is the chief cause of tides, creating tidal "bulges." This means that the water in the oceans is pulled outward at the equator. Scientists have long thought that these bulges should do two things: increase the velocity of the Moon and slow Earth's rotation. A slower rotation would mean that the length of a complete rotation—one full day—would grow longer.

Information from the Apollo lunar landings proved that the Moon is moving away from Earth at a rate of about 3.8 cm per year. It has been harder to prove that the days have been growing longer, but geologists recently found evidence in stones called "tidal rhythmites" or "tidalites." These stones formed along prehistoric shorelines. They contain microscopic bands of sand and silt that reflect the ebb and flow of tides.

By studying the thicknesses of these bands, scientists can calculate how long the monthly lunar cycle was in the ancient past. They have determined that 900 million years ago a day lasted about 18 hours. An 18-hour day would have made for a 487-day year.

RESULTS

Spread the Word

Work with your partner to present your results to the rest of the class. Share your conclusions about how objects, such as planets, stay in their orbits. You could begin by explaining how you set up and used your materials. Describe how the masses of the three spoons and the two rolls of tape affected the spoons' orbits. Then explain how these factors are similar to the forces that control the orbits of planets and moons. Tell the class how a change in one or more of these factors might affect the motion of the planets. Be sure to explain how your observations support your conclusions. Who needs to know about the forces that make objects travel in a circle? List several professions and everyday situations in which this information would be useful.

READ ALL ABOUT IT!

The Glue of the Universe

GRAVITY is the glue of the universe. It is the force that attracts objects to one another. Earth's gravity keeps you and everything else from flying off the planet. Gravity keeps the Moon in orbit around the Earth, the planets in orbit around the Sun, and the solar system in orbit around the center of a huge group of stars called a **galaxy**.

What causes one object to attract another? Scientists do not yet know the answer to this question—the force of gravity is still not completely understood. But a great deal is known about how gravity works.

The model you set up during Investigation 3 shows how gravity works when one object orbits another. The spoon traveled around the spool like a moon going around a planet. The string kept the spoon in orbit at the same speed and distance, preventing it from flying away. The weight of the tape pulled the string toward the spool with a constant force. The string pulled the spoon toward the center of its orbit with the same force. If the string had broken, the spoon would have flown off in a straight line (see Figure 6).

LIKE AN INVISIBLE STRING

The pull of the string was like the pull of gravity between Earth and the Moon. If Earth's gravity did not pull on the Moon, the Moon's inertia would carry it away in a straight line. But Earth's gravitational force, like an invisible string, continuously pulls the Moon inward, across the direction it is moving (see Figure 7). If you were standing on the Moon and facing in the direction that the Moon was traveling, you might say the Earth was pulling the Moon "sideways." Gravity pulls the Moon's path into a curve, a nearly circular orbit around Earth.

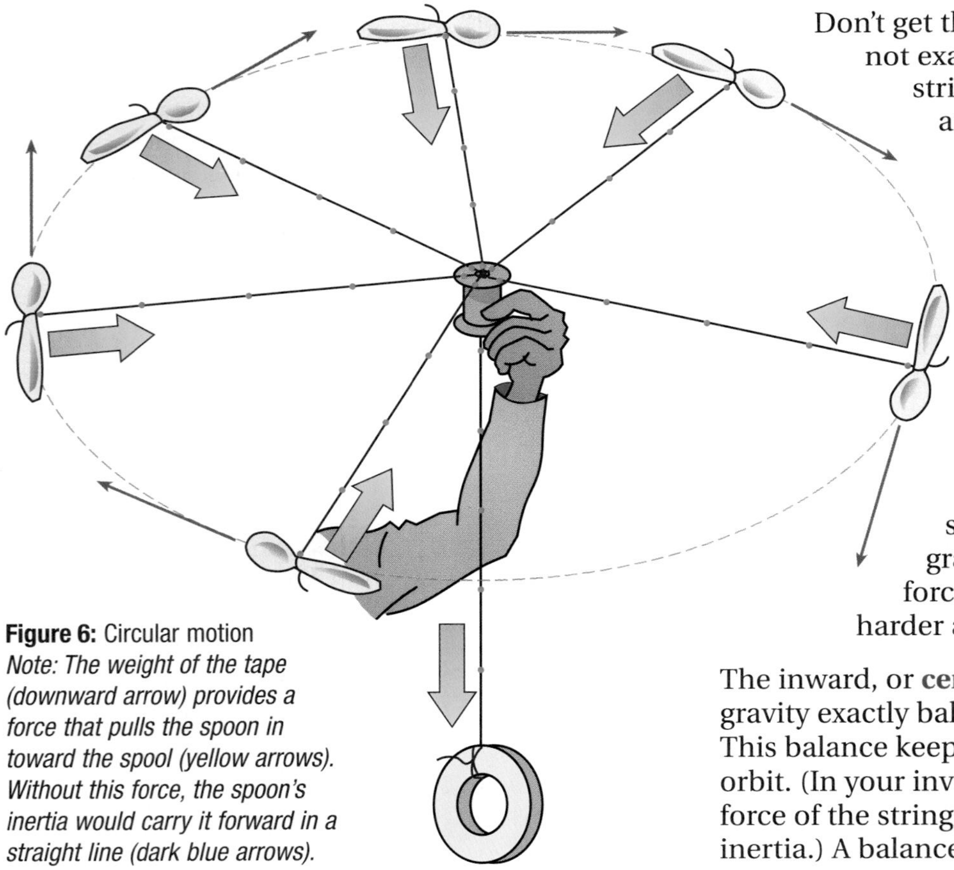

Don't get the wrong idea. Gravity is not exactly like the piece of string. You can *see* the string, and you can *move* it and *cut* it, but you can't see, move, or cut gravity. Also, the force of gravity between two objects, such as Earth and the Moon, becomes stronger as they come closer together, but when the spoon and the spool came closer together, the string, which represented gravity, did not exert more force. (The string did not pull harder as it got shorter.)

Figure 6: Circular motion
Note: The weight of the tape (downward arrow) provides a force that pulls the spoon in toward the spool (yellow arrows). Without this force, the spoon's inertia would carry it forward in a straight line (dark blue arrows).

The inward, or **centripetal**, force of Earth's gravity exactly balances the Moon's inertia. This balance keeps the Moon in a stable orbit. (In your investigation, the centripetal force of the string balanced the spoon's inertia.) A balance between gravity and inertia also keeps Earth in orbit around the Sun. The solar system contains nine known planets—Mercury, Venus, Earth, Mars, Jupiter, Saturn, Uranus, Neptune, and Pluto. Each of them is in a stable orbit around the Sun.

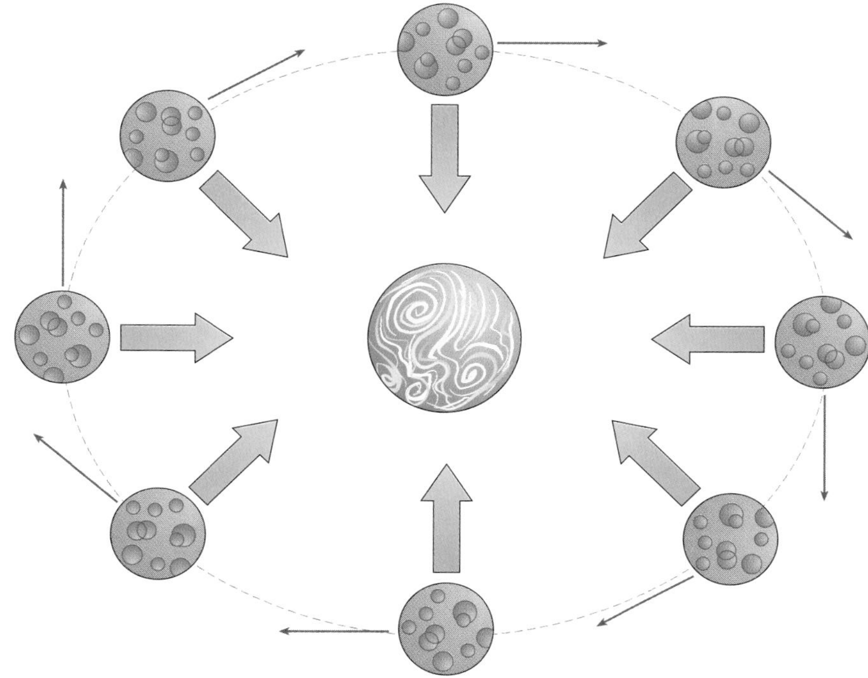

Figure 7: The Moon's orbit around Earth

Note: Like the weight of the tape (Figure 6), gravitational attraction between Earth and the Moon (yellow arrows) keeps the Moon from moving off in a straight line. Gravity constantly deflects the Moon into a curved orbit around Earth.

Far Out

Mercury is the nearest planet to the Sun, Pluto the most distant. Pluto is about 100 times farther from the Sun than Mercury is, but Pluto's orbiting speed is only about one-tenth as fast as Mercury's. Why does Pluto move so much more slowly? Far out on the edge of the solar system, Pluto experiences a much weaker pull from the Sun than Mercury does. Pluto is also less massive than Mercury; therefore, it has less inertia.

Just as the Sun's strong pull on Mercury balances Mercury's speed and mass, so also the Sun's weaker pull on Pluto balances Pluto's slower speed and smaller mass. As a result, both planets remain in stable orbits around the Sun. Mercury travels faster than any other planet (see Figure 8). If it did not, it would fall into the enormously massive Sun because the Sun's gravity would overwhelm Mercury's inertia.

Like the spoons in your investigation, every planet has a different mass. The more

Orbits of the Planets

Planet	Mass (times Earth's)	Average distance from Sun (million km)	Time to orbit Sun (Earth time)	Orbital speed (thousand km/hr)
Mercury	0.055	57.94	87.97 days	172.5
Venus	0.815	108.26	224.70 days	126.3
Earth	1.000	149.67	365.26 days	107.1
Mars	0.107	228.06	1.81 years	87.1
Jupiter	317.938	778.73	11.86 years	47.1
Saturn	95.181	1,427.71	29.46 years	34.6
Uranus	14.535	2,871.04	84.01 years	24.6
Neptune	17.147	4,498.86	164.79 years	19.6
Pluto	0.002	5,914.77	248.43 years	17.1

Figure 8: A table of planet statistics

massive planets, such as Jupiter and Saturn, have more inertia than the smaller ones, such as Mercury and Pluto. The Sun's gravity pulls harder on a more massive planet than it would pull on a less massive one at the same distance.

. . . if you throw a tennis ball and a baseball with the same amount of force, the tennis ball will accelerate faster than the baseball.

As you learned earlier, the centripetal pull of the Sun keeps each planet in orbit by continuously deflecting its motion from a straight line. Any change in the speed or direction of an object's motion is called an **acceleration**. Accelerations are caused by forces. The pull of the Sun's gravity is the force that accelerates a planet inward. How much the Sun accelerates a planet depends on that planet's mass. (Remember, the strength of the Sun's pull depends on the mass of a planet.)

Newton's Second Law

The relationship between acceleration, force, and mass is expressed in **Newton's Second Law of Motion**. This law states that when a force acts on an object (a mass), it causes an acceleration that is directly proportional to the force. In other words, the stronger the force is, the faster the object accelerates. If the same force is applied to two different masses, the less massive one

Wheeeee!

If you like to ride wild roller coasters, you know that when they go plunging down the slope, you feel pushed back in your seat. Maybe you prefer the carnival ride where you stand inside a large, rotating cylinder. As the cylinder spins faster, the floor drops out from under you—but you "stick" to the wall.

In both these cases, you perceive what is called a "fictitious force." What could be pushing you out against the wall in the barrel? There is nothing in front of you that could push you back. The wall is actually pushing you *inward*, but its pressure on your back makes it feel as though you are being pushed outward, against the wall.

People often say they feel "centrifugal force" when they move in a circle. "Centrifugal" means "away from the center." They feel themselves being pushed away from the center of the circle. A ride in a spinning cyclinder or on a roller coaster produces centripetal force. This force changes your course from a straight line to a curve. Centripetal force accelerates objects moving in a circle toward the circle's center. That's what makes you feel pushed into your seat on the roller coaster and against the wall of the spinning cylinder.

Newton's Best Friend

"My best friend is the truth," Isaac Newton wrote when he was a young university student. This open-minded attitude helped him become one of the greatest scientists in history.

Newton was born in England in 1643. His early life was difficult. His father had died before his birth, and Isaac was so sickly that he was not expected to live a single day. He spent his childhood reading, and when he grew up, he enrolled in Cambridge University. Cambridge was still teaching Aristotle's theory that the universe revolved around Earth. On his own, Newton studied a different view of the universe and a new mathematics. He came to believe that all matter was made of particles in motion, and he was especially interested in the motion of the Moon and the planets.

While a professor at Trinity College, Newton studied optics. Although he was wrong about the nature of light (he thought it was made of particles of matter), his discoveries about color were important. He also invented the reflector telescope.

Newton's personal life was often unhappy. Prone to fits of temper, he sometimes lived in isolation. But he put his solitude to good use. During one of these periods, he began to study attraction and repulsion. In 1686 he completed a work that became the basis for modern physical science: the *Philosophiae Naturalis Principia Mathematica*.

The *Principia* contains Newton's Three Laws of Motion: (1) that a body at rest tends to remain at rest, and that an object in motion tends to continue in a straight line with a constant velocity, unless acted on by a force; (2) that the acceleration of an object is directly proportional to the force acting upon it and inversely proportional to the object's mass; and (3) that every action produces an equal and opposite reaction. Newton also developed the law of universal gravitation, which became the dominant theory for the next 200 years.

will accelerate faster than the more massive one. For example, if you throw a tennis ball and a baseball with the same amount of force, the tennis ball will accelerate faster than the baseball. A simple equation sums up this relationship:

$$A = \frac{F}{M}$$

In this equation, A stands for acceleration, F for force, and M for mass. To determine the amount of acceleration, you divide the force by the mass. (The equation is sometimes written in a different form: $F = MA$.)

Planets in Balance

Your investigation helped you see how the pull of the Sun's huge mass accelerates a planet inward. When you switched to a heavier roll of tape, you increased the centripetal force on the spoon. Because you maintained the same force when swinging the spoons, the heavier roll pulled the spoon into a smaller orbit.

(By the way, the reason the large roll of tape pulled on the spoon with more force is that Earth's gravity pulled this roll down with more force. The large roll of tape did exert a tiny bit more gravitational attraction on the spoon, but the attraction was not enough to pull the spoon closer to the spool.)

Suppose you wanted to keep a spoon orbiting the large spool at the same distance it had orbited the small roll of tape. To do this, you would have to balance the greater force (large roll of tape) with a stronger swing that would increase the speed of the spoon. The Sun's gravitational force depends on its mass. If the Sun became more massive, the planets would have to move faster to stay in their present orbits—or else the Sun would pull them closer.

On Your Own

Respond to the following items based on "The Glue of the Universe."

1 Within the solar system are many chunks of rock called asteroids. Sometimes these objects collide with other planets, and sometimes they go into orbit around a planet. Describe several factors that would determine whether an asteroid goes into orbit around a planet or continues moving through space in a straight line.

Get This . . .

The inward, or centripetal, force of Earth's gravity exactly balances the Moon's inertia. This balance keeps the Moon in a stable orbit. A balance between gravity and inertia also keeps Earth in orbit around the Sun.

2 Tides are the rising and falling of large bodies of water twice a day. These regular tidal patterns support Newton's theory of gravity and reveal the influence of the Moon's pull on Earth. Explain how tides are related to gravity. (Hint: Think about what happens to a point on Earth as the planet rotates—and how distance affects the strength of gravity at that point.)

3 Suppose an outfielder on a baseball team has been missing a lot of fly balls. Do you think he could attract the ball to his glove better if he wore a much larger glove? Explain your thinking.

Weird Worlds

The universe contains billions of stars. Does this mean there are billions and billions of planets out there?

In the early 1990s, astronomers discovered a few Earth-sized planets orbiting stars called pulsars. It was not until 1995 that they found a planet orbiting a star that resembled the Sun. That discovery led to as much confusion as excitement.

What they found circling the star 51 Pegasi was a giant planet with about half the mass of Jupiter. But unlike Jupiter, this planet has a very small orbit—even smaller than Mercury's. The planet appears to be orbiting 51 Pegasi at a distance of about 8 million km. If this measurement is correct, then a year on the planet is only four Earth days long!

The planet's size and its close orbit are baffling because these features do not fit accepted theories about how planets form. A giant planet, as far as anyone knows, should not be able to form so near its parent star. Some observers think the object may not even be a planet. They suggest it may be a dwarf partner in a binary-star system. However, the eight other planets found since 1995 also include giants, and some of them have eccentric orbits, another mysterious feature.

It is hard to learn much about these planets. Astronomers detected them by the wobble they cause in a parent star. Nonetheless, researchers are exploring new ideas about how solar systems form, and they are hoping to find a way to see these planets through telescopes. These discoveries are also leading to new ideas about how Earth's solar system may have formed.

Creating Craters

Ever Wonder?

Have you ever looked at photos of the Moon and noticed the craters that cover its surface? What caused all those craters? Are other planets or moons in the solar system pockmarked with craters? Does Earth have some? If it does, why don't craters cover Earth's surface the same way they cover the Moon's? In this investigation you will make your own craters. This will help you discover what caused the craters on the Moon—and what craters can tell you about the history of the solar system.

Materials List

- Sheets of newspaper
- Plate
- Bowl (2 L)
- Large spoon
- Measuring spoons
- Soil
- Meter stick
- Safety goggles

Step-by-Step

1. Spread sheets of newspaper on the floor, and place the plate in the middle of the paper. Also cover nearby desks or walls with newspaper.
2. Half-fill the bowl with soil. Slowly add water, stirring constantly with the large spoon until the mud becomes a thick paste. (It should fall very slowly off the spoon.)
3. Fill the plate with mud. Smooth and flatten its surface.
4. Put on your safety goggles.
5. Use a tablespoon to scoop out a heaping glob of mud from the bowl. Hold the mud-filled tablespoon 50 cm above the plate, and let the glob fall onto the plate.
6. Observe what happens when the mud glob hits the plate of mud. Measure the distance between the edge of the glob and the farthest mud splatters.
7. In your logbook, draw a picture of the plate of mud and the pattern of splatters. Record the spoon size. Also record the height from which you dropped the mud, and note the measurements you made in Step 6.

8. Measure the depth and width of the crater. Record these figures in your logbook. Then remove the glob and return it to the bowl of mud.
9. Smooth out the surface of the mud on the plate.
10. Using the same spoon, scoop out another heaping glob of mud from the bowl. Try to make it the same size that you used before. Drop this glob from 100 cm above the plate.
11. Repeat Steps 6–9.
12. With the same spoon, scoop out a third glob of mud. Try to make it the same size as the first two. Drop it from a height of 150 cm.
13. Repeat Steps 6–9.
14. Repeat Steps 6–13 with each one of the remaining measuring spoons. Start with the spoon next in size below the tablespoon, and work your way down to the smallest one. Be sure to record the spoon size with each of your drawings.
15. Measure the dimensions—width, length, and depth—of each spoon you have used. Record these measurements in your logbook.
16. Clean up your work area, and return all supplies to your teacher. Before leaving the classroom, wash your hands with soap and warm water.

Dirty Snowballs from Space

A shower of "minicomets" may be raining down on Earth every day.

Cameras aboard NASA's orbiting Polar spacecraft have made ultraviolet images of Earth's atmosphere that show mysterious dark spots. These spots may have been caused by tons of water in the upper atmosphere—water that absorbs ultraviolet radiation and darkens the images.

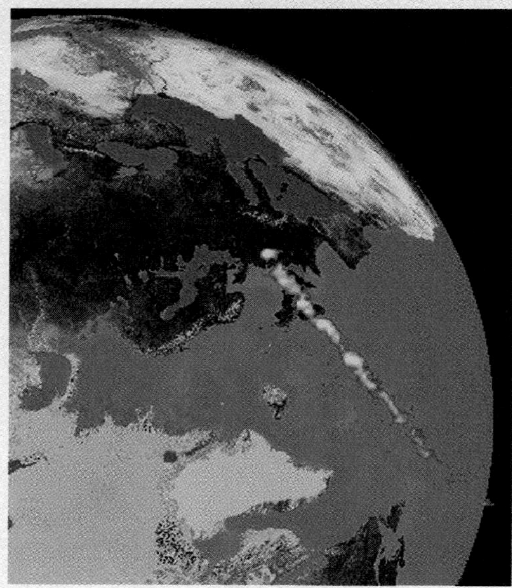

Some scientists believe that this water is the product of house-sized comets that break up in the upper levels of the atmosphere, about 2,000 km above Earth's surface. Comets are nicknamed "dirty snowballs" because they are made of rock, dirt, and ice. Some scientists think that about 20 comets speed into the atmosphere every minute.

Other scientists do not think that comets or tons of water are the cause of the dark spots. They ask why no one ever noticed such a rain of comets until now, and they point out that most of the inner planets in the solar system appear to be quite dry.

If the barrage of comets really exists, it could change people's ideas about the origin of the oceans. The standard explanation is that the oceans formed as Earth cooled and as water vapor, which escaped from inside the planet through volcanic vents, condensed. But over billions of years, dirty snowballs from space may have delivered the water in the oceans.

Talk It Over

Work with your partner to answer the following questions.

1. With each measuring spoon, the first drop was from 50 cm. How did the splatter pattern change when you dropped the mud from 100 cm and 150 cm? What was the reason that a higher drop changed the results in this way?
2. How did changing the spoon size affect the results of impact? What was the reason for this?
3. How did the size of the mud glob affect the size of the impact crater that it formed? Was each crater larger or smaller than the glob that formed it? How much larger or smaller? What other factors relate to the size of a crater?
4. If the mud globs were to fall on hard clay, would the craters be the same size as the ones you made? If you carried out the tests with hard clay on some other planet where everything weighed more, would the craters be the same size as they would on Earth? What if everything weighed less on the other planet? Explain.
5. How could the study of craters on Earth and on other planets and moons reveal facts about their past?

A Sea of Possibilities

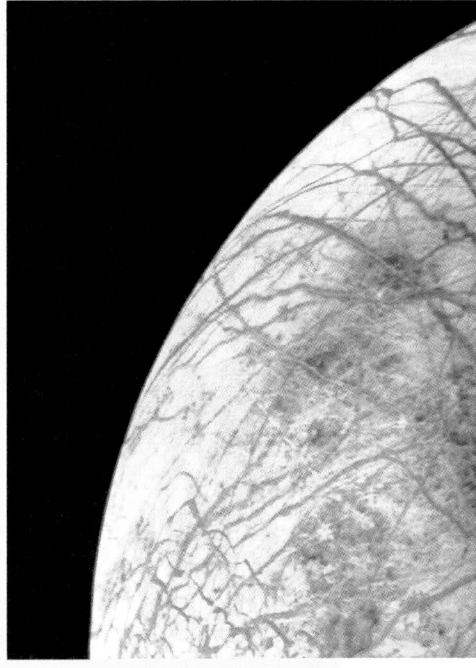

Earth may be the only planet in the solar system with oceans—but Europa may be the only moon that has some.

The Galileo spacecraft has been photographing Jupiter and its moons. Early photos of the moon Europa show what looked like an icy surface. Later photos taken closer to the surface—about 585 km above it—show cracks, fissures, and what seem to be large blocks of floating, moving ice. These could indicate a liquid ocean beneath the ice. If so, the oceans of Europa may have more water than all of Earth's oceans combined.

Because Europa has few known craters, it may be younger than previously thought. This means that Europa would be active geologically. The combination of water, heat from volcanic activity, and organic chemicals left by comets may provide an environment in which life could form. Perhaps life-forms similar to those that exist around hydrothermal vents in the Earth's oceans could thrive on Europa.

Researchers want to study Europa with robotic probes that could test the heat and composition of the water. In the meantime, plans are under way to use "cryobots" to study life in the frozen lakes of Antarctica. These devices are robots that can melt through thick ice. Such studies could help scientists prepare for similar tests on the surface of Europa.

Spread the Word

Work with your partner(s) to create a presentation that will show what you have learned in this investigation. Tell the class about the factors that affect the size of a crater and the pattern in which surface material splatters on impact. Organize your data into a table. List each drop, its size, the height of release, the size of the crater, and the distance that material splattered. Display your table as a large poster. You could also make enlarged copies of the drawings you made in your logbook. Outline your conclusions about the relationship between the size of an impact object and its effects. Explain how the study of craters on a planet or moon can reveal information about its history. List several professions in which it would be important to understand how craters form when objects collide.

Read All about It!

Cosmic Collisions

THE small mud balls that you dropped onto a plate of mud during Investigation 4 made some big craters. Mud from the balls themselves and from the flat surface splattered far from the point of impact. Imagine what might happen if the mud balls were large rocks or chunks of ice that smashed into a planet. Such an event actually took place in 1994 when the Shoemaker-Levy comet collided with Jupiter. (A **comet** is a ball of dust and ice that follows a long, oval orbit around the Sun. The orbit of a comet sometimes crosses the orbits of the planets.) Jupiter's strong gravity tore apart the Shoemaker-Levy comet some time before it struck, but the fragments still hit the planet with such force that they made huge black marks on the surface. Many people on Earth watched this series of impacts through telescopes.

Like Jupiter, the Moon shows evidence of cosmic collisions. If you look at the surface of the Moon, you will see many impact craters and dark spots. For billions of years, chunks of space rock called **meteoroids** have pounded the surface of the Moon. Meteoroids range in size from specks of dust to gigantic boulders. These rocks also fall to Earth. As a meteoroid passes through the atmosphere of

Collision with Jupiter

When a comet named Shoemaker-Levy 9 crashed into Jupiter in 1994, it showed the dangerous power of these long-tailed objects that are whizzing around the solar system.

Comets are irregular chunks of ice, rock, dirt, and frozen gases. They may be space debris that did not become part of planets when the solar system formed. Although a comet's tail can be millions of kilometers long, the head of a comet is rarely more than a few kilometers in diameter. Comets follow oval paths around the Sun. Their orbits are usually predictable. Some orbits take a few years to complete, while others take thousands of years.

The gravitational force of a large planet, such as Jupiter, can disturb a comet's orbit and may be strong enough to break up the comet. That is what happened to Shoemaker-Levy 9. Astronomers knew that it was likely to break up, and so they watched it closely for about two years before its impact.

Twenty-one fragments of the comet struck Jupiter over several days. Some made tremendous impacts, sending fireballs of exploding gases thousands of kilometers high.

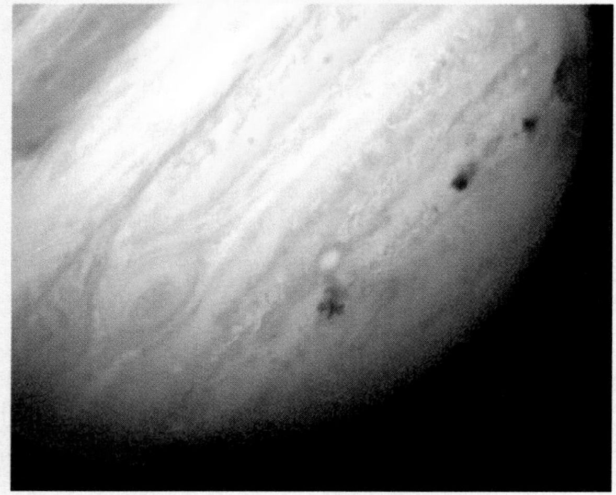

By studying these collisions, astronomers have learned more about Jupiter's atmosphere, surface, and dust rings. They have also learned more about comets themselves.

a planet or moon, it is called a **meteor**. If you look up on a starry night, you might see a meteor shoot across the sky, blazing briefly as it burns up in the atmosphere. (Any part of a meteor that reaches the surface without burning up is called a **meteorite**.)

Many meteoroids are fragments of asteroids. Leftovers from the birth of the solar system, **asteroids** range in size from a few meters to hundreds of kilometers. These space objects contain material that did not become part of a planet or moon, or they may be pieces of larger objects that collided or broke up millions of years ago.

As an asteroid or meteoroid travels through the solar system, it may come close to a planet or moon, whose gravity pulls on it. This starts a contest between the inertia of the smaller object and the gravitational pull of the planet or moon. The contest often ends with the asteroid or meteoroid crashing into the larger body as a meteor.

Battle Scars

Signs of such contests are visible on every planet and moon in the solar system. If a large meteor hits a planet or moon, it may make a large hole called a crater. As you saw in your investigation, a crater is usually much larger than the object that made it. The size of the crater depends on the speed and mass of the object that forms it. You made larger mud craters by dropping mud balls from higher points. This increased the speed of the mud balls, which then hit the surface with greater force. You also saw that larger mud balls made larger craters.

Like falling mud balls, larger meteors also make larger craters. Perhaps the largest crater on Earth is buried beneath the floor of the Caribbean Sea and southern Mexico. This crater is roughly 250 km wide. Researchers think the meteor that formed it was 10–30 km in diameter. The meteor's impact 65 million years ago may have led to the extinction of the dinosaurs and many other species.

Gravity supplied the force that accelerated your mud balls. As you learned from Newton's Second Law of Motion, a strong force will accelerate an object more quickly than a weak force will. Because Mars is less massive than Earth, the force of gravity is weaker on Mars. Because of this, falling meteors do not speed up as much on Mars as they do when they fall to Earth. On the other hand, because Jupiter is much larger and more massive than Earth, meteors accelerate more as they fall on that planet.

Get This . . .

Newton's Second Law of Motion states that the acceleration of an object is directly proportional to the force acting upon it and inversely proportional to the object's mass:

$$A = \frac{F}{M}$$

Rays

Besides making a crater when it collides with a moon or planet, a meteor scatters debris widely. Lines of scattered rock extend from some of the Moon's craters, such as the one named Copernicus (see Figure 9). These lines of rock are called **rays**. Gravity

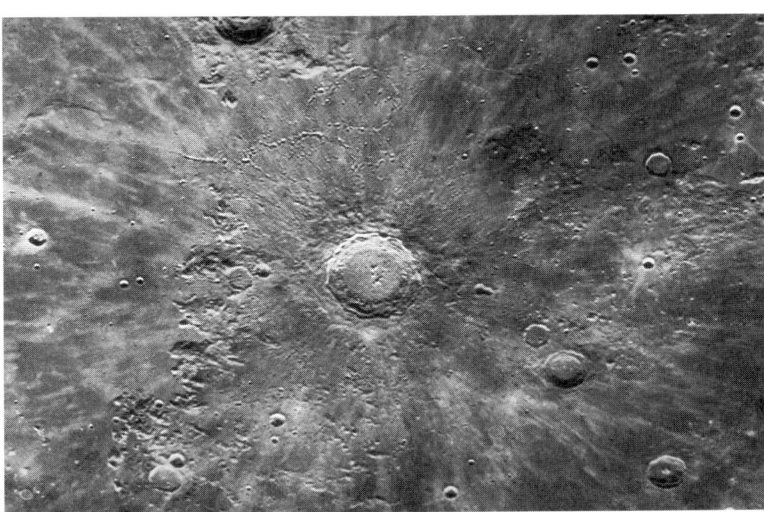

Figure 9: The crater Copernicus and its rays on the Moon
Note: The lines that extend outward from the crater are rays, lines of rocks that were expelled by the impact that formed the crater.

affects how the debris scatters. Earth's gravity is about six times stronger than the Moon's. Because of this, the debris that a meteor impact throws upward and outward is pulled back down much more quickly on Earth than on the Moon. If the meteor that produced the crater Copernicus had struck Earth, it would not have produced such long rays.

Because Earth is larger and more massive than the Moon, it is fair to conclude that Earth has received at least as many strikes as the Moon.

Gravity also affects whether a planet has an atmosphere. If a planet or moon has only a small mass, its gravity will be weak and gases will escape into space. The Moon has too little mass to keep an atmosphere. Without clouds and winds, the Moon has no rain or other weather. This explains why the Moon has so many more craters than Earth. Without water and wind to erode its surface, the Moon stays the same over long periods of time. Craters that were formed millions of years ago are still visible on its surface because nothing wears them away—except more meteoroids from space.

This crater near Flagstaff, Arizona, was formed by a meteor impact thousands of years ago. Because of dry desert conditions, the crater has not completely eroded.

Because the Moon has no atmosphere, there is no wind, rain, or other weather to erode craters or to erase astronauts' footprints.

Clues to the Past

Unlike the Moon, Earth has an atmosphere and weather. Storms and erosion wear away craters that meteors cause on Earth. A planet's atmosphere also serves as a shield against meteoroids. For example, when a meteoroid falls through Earth's atmosphere, friction between its surface and the air creates tremendous heat. As a result, most meteors burn up before reaching the ground. Because Earth is larger and more massive than the Moon, it is fair to conclude that Earth has received at least as many strikes as the Moon. But thousands of craters do not dot the surface of this planet. The atmosphere has either destroyed the meteors on the way down or eroded away most of the craters they formed.

Craters on a planet or moon can reveal a great deal about the history of its surface and atmosphere. For example, Mars has more craters than Earth but fewer than the Moon. This makes sense for a planet whose mass and gravity are in between those of Earth and the Moon. Some Martian craters are smoothed dents, while others are huge pits. Such features indicate slow weathering in a thin atmosphere. Mars also has many channels that look like dried-up riverbeds. This planet is too cold to have liquid water.

So how could these channels have formed? A possible explanation is that the meteors that hit Mars in the past may have created enough heat to melt its icy surface and create flowing water.

Cracks on Callisto

Meteors also collided with ice on Callisto, one of Jupiter's moons. Too small to keep an atmosphere, Callisto bears the marks of thousands of meteors that have pelted its icy surface (see Figure 10). When meteors hit the ice, they crack it the way a flying stone shatters a car's windshield.

Callisto's craters reveal its battered past. A huge crater called Valhalla is 20 km deep and the size of the state of Maine. The meteor that made this crater had such force that shock waves formed rings around the hole. The rings are like the splatters you made with your mud-ball meteors. Their distance from the crater is a measure of the force of impact. Callisto is so small that its gravity is not strong enough to accelerate a meteor very much; therefore, the shock rings and the size of the crater are the results of the meteor's huge size. The meteor was probably as big as the crater it made.

Figure 10: Meteor damage on Callisto
Note: This image of Callisto shows the marks left by some of the thousands of meteors that have crashed into its ice-covered surface. Callisto, one of the moons of Jupiter, resembles a cracked billiard ball.

On Your Own

Answer the following questions based on "Cosmic Collisions."

1 Mercury, the nearest planet to the Sun, has a surface covered with craters, just as Earth's moon does. Based only on this fact, what other characteristics would you expect Mercury to have? Explain your thinking.

2 One of Jupiter's moons, Europa, is covered with ice but is warmer than Callisto. Europa has few craters. Because Europa is too small to have much of an atmosphere, how would you explain the fact that it has few craters?

3 Suppose you analyzed a meteor that hit the Earth and determined that it came from a planet that is much younger than the Moon. Would you expect the planet from which the meteor came to be heavily cratered? Explain.

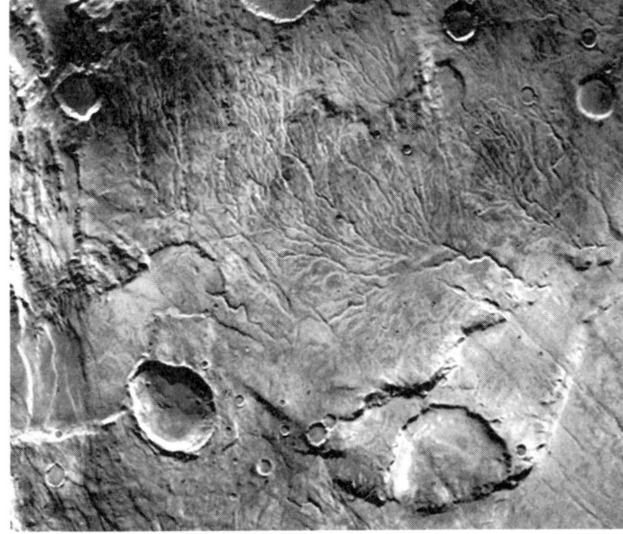

The surface of Mars has many channels that look like dry riverbeds—evidence that Mars may once have had flowing water.

Worlds of Color

EVER WONDER?

Mars is known as the "red planet." Have you ever seen pictures of Mars and wondered why it is red? Saturn is orange. What causes it to look orange? Why are planets different colors? Do the ones that look alike have certain things in common? Can the color of a planet reveal useful information? In this investigation you will learn how colors can provide clues to the minerals, gases, and other substances that make up planets.

MATERIALS LIST

- 2 plant misters
- Bunsen burner and jug (setup)
- Ringstand with clamp
- Rubber tubing for burner
- Cardboard with slit
- Diffraction grating
- Distilled water
- Solutions of lithium chloride, lithium nitrate, calcium chloride, strontium chloride, copper chloride, sodium chloride
- Unknown solution
- Matches
- Funnel
- Colored pencils
- Masking tape
- Pencil
- Safety goggles

STEP-BY-STEP

1. Put on your safety goggles. Secure the burner-and-jug setup with a ringstand and a clamp so that it will not tip over.
2. Light the burner. Adjust the air and gas intakes to produce a tall (about 10 cm) blue flame with no visible cone of flame inside it.
3. Turn out the lights.
4. Hold the cardboard with the slit between the flame and the diffraction grating. Look through the grating and the slit at the flame. *Caution: Do not hold the slit too close to the flame.*

5. In your logbook, describe the light from the flame as you see it through the slit and the diffraction grating. Then use colored pencils to draw a picture of the light from the flame.

6. In your logbook, describe the light from the flame as you see it without the slit and grating. Use colored pencils to draw a picture of the flame.

7. Using the funnel, fill one of the plant misters with distilled water. Write "Water" on a piece of masking tape, and attach it to this mister.

8. Using the funnel, pour one of the labeled solutions into the other mister. Do not use the sodium chloride solution at this time—save it for last.

9. Either you or your partner should carefully spray the solution through the "doorway" of the plastic jug into the burner's air intake while observing the flame. At the same time, the other partner should observe the flame through the slit and grating.

10. In your logbook, record the name of the solution and your observations of the flame. Also make a colored drawing of what you have observed. (The student who does the spraying should draw the flame itself. The other student should draw the light from the flame as observed through the slit and grating.)

11. Spray distilled water into the jug as you did with the solution in Step 9. This will clean out your equipment.

12. Empty the solution out of the mister according to your teacher's instructions. *Caution: Pour out the solution only where your teacher tells you.*

13. Thoroughly rinse the funnel and the empty mister with tap water several times. (Spray water through the nozzle and empty the mister into the sink each time.)

14. Using the funnel, pour a different solution into the clean mister. Repeat Steps 9–13. Continue this procedure until you have tested all six labeled solutions. After testing the fourth solution, you and your partner should trade places. (Don't forget: Test the sodium chloride solution last.)

15. Repeat Steps 9–13 with the unknown solution.

16. Copy your partner's notes and drawings in your logbook.

17. Clean up your work area, and return all materials to your teacher. Wash your hands with soap and warm water before leaving the room.

TALK IT OVER

Work with your partner to answer the following questions.

1. Compare your drawings of the results for the six known solutions. Are any drawings the same? If so, which ones? What might explain the similarity?

2. Compare your drawing of the light produced by the unknown solution with the drawings you made for the labeled solutions. What do you think the unknown solution contains? Explain your reasoning.

3. When you sprayed a solution into the flame, what did the flame add to the solution?

4. How could the light you saw through the diffraction grating help you identify a solution?

5. Compare your notes and drawings of the flame through the diffraction grating and without the grating. Do you see any connection between them? In other words, how are your results related?

6. Neon signs glow by applying electricity, a form of energy, to gases. What do you think makes a neon sign glow with a particular color? If you wanted to make a sign with a specific color, what would you do?

7. What do you think you would see through the diffraction grating if you mixed several solutions together and sprayed them into the flame? Explain your reasoning.

8. Scientists often use diffraction gratings to study the light from stars and planets. What kinds of information can they obtain about stars and planets by doing this?

No Little Green Men, But . . .

Did life ever exist on the planet Mars? Because of a meteorite found in Antarctica, some scientists think the answer is yes.

Twelve meteorites from Mars have been found on Earth. One of them, ALH84001, may be 4.5 billion years old. ALH84001 probably began its long journey to Earth when an asteroid collided with Mars, hurling pieces of rock into space. It probably landed in Antarctica 13,000 years ago, though scientists did not discover it until 1984.

The rock's mineral deposits—carbonates—provide three clues that suggest ancient Martian life. Three minerals in the deposits usually occur together only as a product of bacteria. Hydrocarbon molecules are also present, and these may show that at least organic molecules necessary for life existed on Mars. Finally, some structures in the carbonates appear to be fossilized bacteria. If these are signs that life once existed on Mars, it would be the first life detected on another world.

But some scientists question the evidence in ALH84001. They point out that the structures that look like bacteria also resemble some forms of magnetite that do not have a biological origin. The structures are also only about a thousandth the size of earthly bacteria—perhaps too small to have been able to live. And the meteorite may show evidence of a Martian environment that was too hot for life.

It is possible that life once existed on Mars, but it will take more rock samples to prove it.

Spread the Word

Design a presentation to show the class what your team has discovered about how colors can be used to identify chemical elements. Make a large, colored poster that displays how the flame looked with and without the diffraction grating. Label each of your illustrations with the name of the chemical element that you think was responsible for each color pattern you observed. Explain how you think the flame helped to produce the color patterns. Include the results you obtained with the unknown solution, and give your reasons for concluding that it contained a certain element. Describe how this procedure could be used to discover information about stars and planets. List situations in which this kind of information and the procedure you used would be helpful in everyday life. Describe some professions that use these techniques.

Career Links

IBM

Dyer/Finisher

Dyers and finishers work in the textile industry, which develops and produces yarns, fibers, fabrics, and clothing. These professionals match dye batches (called lots), improve dyes, and create new ones. They must understand fibers and know how different fabrics and fibers react to various dyes and inks. Dyers and finishers are trained in chemistry, and they operate both dyeing machinery and analytical instruments, such as those that measure spectrums. To work in this field, you will need a degree in textile engineering or textile chemistry. For more information, write:

American Association of Textile Chemists and Colorists
One Davis Drive
P.O. Box 12215
Research Triangle Park, NC 27709-2215
http://www.aatcc.org

Related occupations: apparel merchandiser, polymer chemist, textile technologist, print designer

Read All about It!

Fingerprints from Distant Worlds

You have probably heard that every man, woman, and child has a unique set of fingerprints, which can be used to identify them. Each chemical element—from aluminum to zinc—can also be identified by its own "fingerprint."

When you looked through the diffraction grating in Investigation 5, the lines of color that you saw were the chemical fingerprints of the solutions you sprayed into the flame. Like a prism, the grating spread out the colors in the light that came from the elements in the solution you sprayed into the flame.

Get This . . .

Every color of light has a different energy. The colors of the rainbow are arranged according to their energies—from red, which carries the lowest amount of energy, to violet, which carries the most.

For each solution you used, the grating produced a different series of lines of one or more colors of the rainbow. Every element produces a different series of colors—a different **spectrum**. Most of the light you saw in the spectrum came from hot, glowing atoms of the metal in each solution: calcium, copper, lithium, sodium, or strontium (see Figure 11). For example, sodium's spectrum contains two bright yellow lines. When you sprayed a sodium solution into the flame, you saw bright yellow light from the flame and bright yellow lines through the grating. Copper glows with a green flame—its spectrum contains three green lines. Strontium looked orange in the flame, but its spectrum contains several colors: bright red and orange lines, along with some green, blue, and violet ones. You did not see green, blue, and violet colors in the flame because the reds and oranges overwhelmed them. But they *were* there.

What caused the atoms to emit these colors? Every element's atoms have a specific energy level. Although the atoms can absorb additional energy, they tend to give up the extra energy quickly and return to their normal level. When you sprayed a solution into the burner, the flame gave the atoms in that solution more energy in the form of heat. The metal atoms in each solution absorbed the fire's energy but then returned to their normal energy level. This happened thousands of times every second. Whenever an atom fell back to its normal energy level, it released some energy in the form of light.

Why does every element produce a different series of colors? Atoms of each element can absorb energy only in several specific amounts. To understand how this works, suppose you want to climb a stone wall that has several handholds at unequal levels. Your arms need only a little energy to reach the first handhold, but if you want to skip the first handhold, they need more energy to pull you up to the second and third ones, which are higher. Like your arms grabbing for those handholds, the atoms in an element have specific energy levels that they can reach when they gain enough energy. If the atoms gain a small amount of energy, they can reach the first level. If they gain a larger amount, they can reach a higher level.

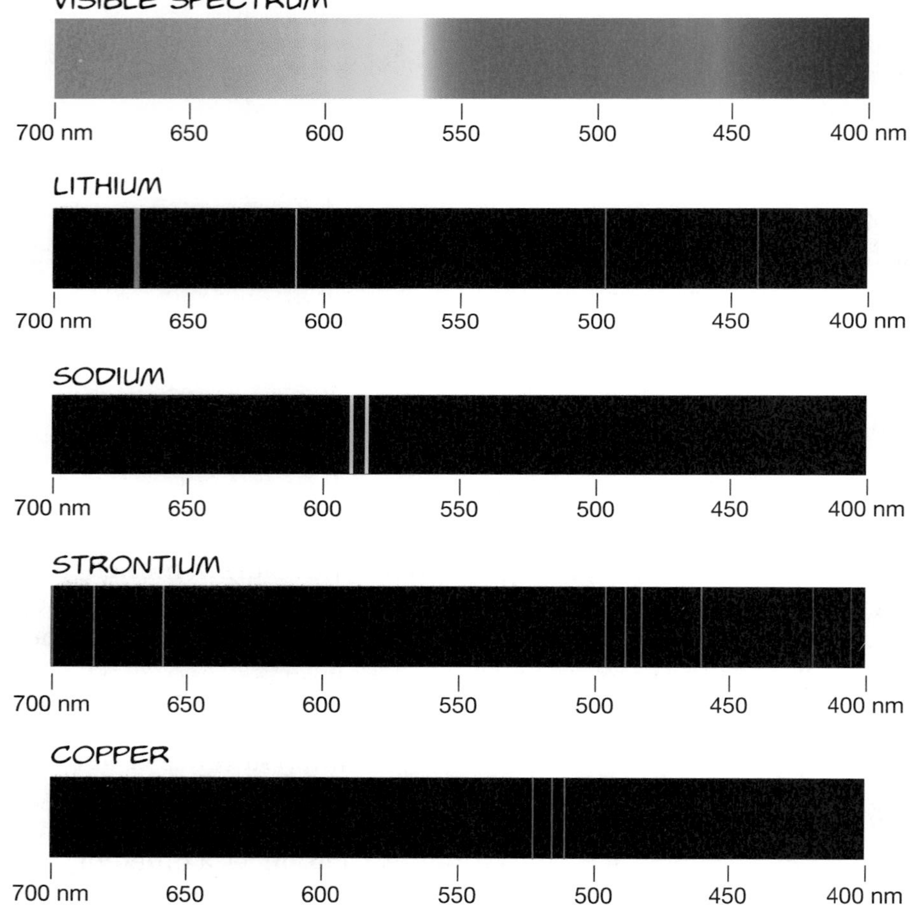

Figure 11: Spectrums of several metals
Note: Patterns of colored lines in a spectrum can be used to identify unknown materials. The numbers refer to the wavelengths of the light. Violet light has the shortest wavelength and the highest energy. Red light has the longest wavelength and the lowest energy. (The abbreviation nm stands for nanometer—1 nm is one millionth of a millimeter.)

Rainbow Arrangement

Atoms lose their extra energy by emitting light that contains the same amount of energy. Every color of light has a different amount of energy. The colors of the rainbow are arranged according to their energies. At one extreme is red, the color with the lowest amount. Then come orange, yellow, green, blue, indigo, and finally violet, which carries the most energy. Because elements absorb and release different amounts of energy, different elements produce different colors of light as they return to their normal states. The pattern of colored lines that you saw in each spectrum corresponds to the energy that atoms of each element lost as they returned to their normal state (see Figure 12).

In your daily life, most of the light you see is a mixture of many different colors, and each one of these colors has its own energy. For example, ordinary white light is composed of all the colors of the rainbow. If you see light that looks orange, that light has several different colors that have combined to produce orange. Part of each element's spectrum also includes energy levels that are too high or too low for human eyes to see. These kinds of "light" include ultraviolet, infrared, and radio waves.

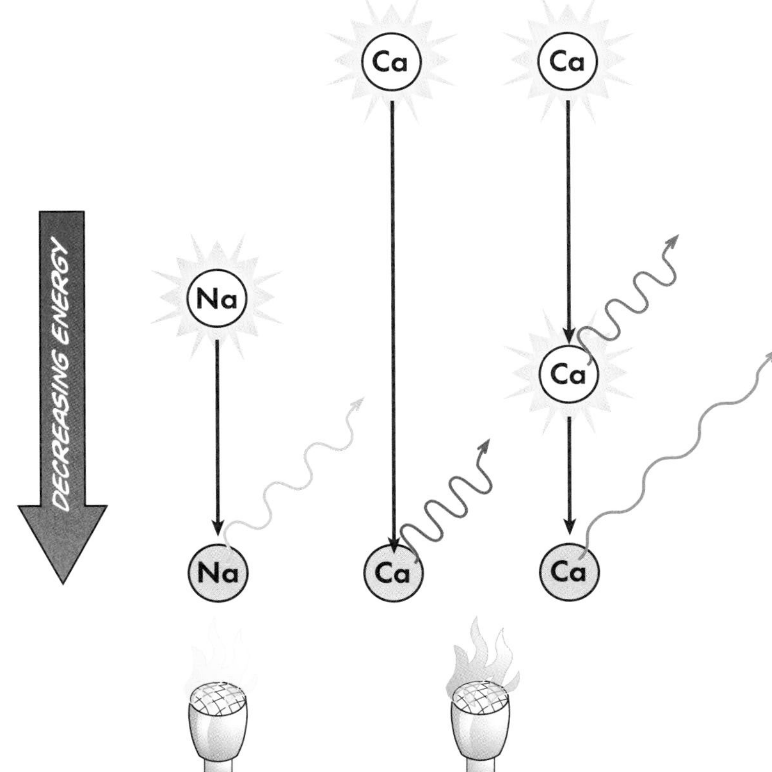

Figure 12: Sodium (Na) and calcium (Ca) atoms releasing energy
Note: Metal atoms absorb heat energy from the flames. They lose energy as they fall from one energy level to another and return to normal states. The color and energy of the light depend on how much energy they lose. A large loss (center) produces the violet line in the spectrum of calcium. Smaller losses produce calcium's blue and red lines (right) and sodium's yellow line (left).

Just as fingerprints can help police single out one criminal in a group of suspects, so also a spectrum can help you single out one element in a mixture.

Too Many to Count

To see the colors that make up an element's spectrum, you need to use a **spectroscope**. Your slit and diffraction grating were a kind of spectroscope. They revealed many colors that you may not have realized were in the colored flame. A real spectroscope breaks up every band of color into many fine lines of slightly different shades. In fact, you could see an almost countless number of colors through a high-quality spectroscope.

Spectrums are useful for identifying unknown substances. Recall how you identified your unknown solution: You used the slit and grating to produce its spectrum. Once you saw this spectrum, you could compare it with ones you saw earlier. When you found a matching spectrum, you knew that the unknown solution must contain the same substance as its spectrum twin. Just as fingerprints can help police single out one criminal in a group of suspects, so also a spectrum can help you single out one element in a mixture.

What does all this have to do with planets and stars? Think about it. . . . If you want to know what an unknown object is made of, all you have to do is look at its spectrum. For example, if you use a spectroscope to study a meteorite or a rock sample from the Moon or another planet, you will see a series of colored lines that can provide clues to which elements are present in your sample (see Figure 13).

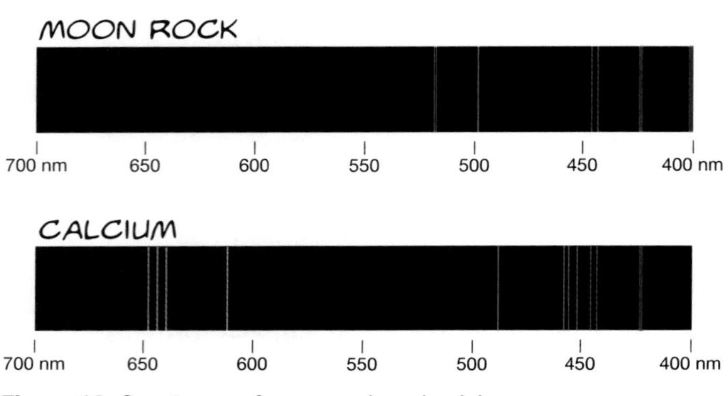

Figure 13: Spectrums of moon rock and calcium

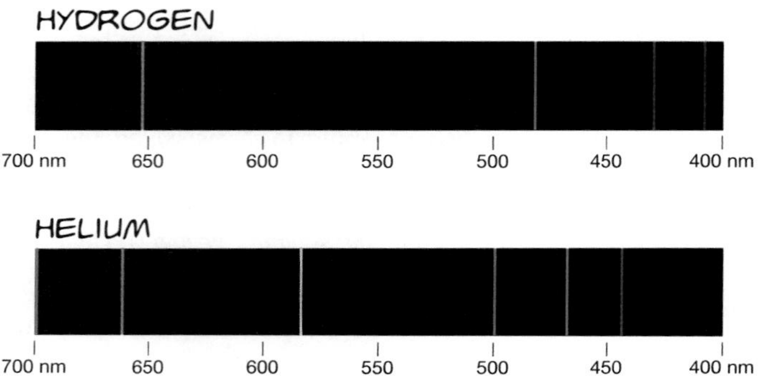

Figure 14: Spectrums of hydrogen and helium

The spectrums of space objects have helped people discover new elements. During a solar eclipse in 1868, an astronomer named P. Jules C. Janssen observed lines in the Sun's spectrum that no one had ever seen. He realized that an unknown element had caused them. This element was given the name helium, from Helios, the Greek name for the Sun (see Figure 14). A small amount of helium exists in the Earth's atmosphere, but it was not detected on Earth until 1895.

Pluto's Fingerprints

You can learn a lot about a planet or moon by looking at it through a telescope, but you can learn even more by looking at its spectrum. For example, Venus has a thick atmosphere of clouds, which in the past led people to think the planet might contain life-forms similar to those of Earth. But Venus's spectrum shows that its clouds are made of sulfuric acid, which is deadly to life on Earth. Another example is Pluto, the most distant planet from the Sun. Though Pluto is covered with solid ice, its spectrum shows that this ice is not frozen water but frozen methane (CH_4), which is a compound of carbon and hydrogen. In 1997 the Pathfinder mission to Mars used X-ray spectrums to determine the composition of rocks and soil on the surface of that planet.

The universe contains billions of stars, and it is likely that planets orbit many of them. Today's telescopes are not powerful enough for people to observe most of these stars and planets in detail. But the light that stars emit and planets reflect can reveal a wealth of information about these objects in space.

On Your Own

Answer the following questions based on "Fingerprints from Distant Worlds."

1. Is it possible for the spectrum of one planet to be exactly the same as the spectrum of another planet? If so, what would this mean? Explain your reasoning.

2. Could the spectrum of a star or planet change? If so, speculate on how this might happen. Explain your answer.

3. Suppose you examined the spectrum of a distant star and found lines that did not match the spectrum of any known element. How would you explain this?

Section Wrap-up

Homecoming

Over the intercom the captain announces, "We are now approaching Pluto." All eyes turn to the screen. It feels good to be back in the solar system. This is your first trip home after a year at the "10th Planet," the unofficial name of the new space observatory, which you have been helping to build. It's a long ride home. The observatory is so far out in space that the Sun looks no bigger than any other star from there. Pluto is 50 times farther from the Sun than Earth is, and so the Sun still looks small, but you are glad to see it is slightly larger than it looked back on the observatory.

The planets rarely line up one after another. That happens only once every 200 years, and so you won't see Uranus on this trip . . .

As you pass the bluish glow of Pluto, you use a spectroscope to break down its colors of light into lines associated with specific substances. The spectrum reveals that the glistening ice, which covers the entire surface of Pluto, is frozen methane. The methane gas froze into rocky shapes as it escaped from the planet's core. When Pluto reaches the point in its orbit that is as close as it ever gets to the Sun, a small amount of this ice warms up enough to become a gas again. For a short time, Pluto has a thin atmosphere. It shares this atmosphere with its huge moon, Charon, whose gravity is strong enough to attract some of the gas. Astronomers still do not know how Charon became Pluto's moon. Charon moves so fast that it can stay in a very close orbit around Pluto. Their gravitational pull on each other keeps them together in their long orbit around the Sun.

Caught by Neptune

The next planet is Neptune, one of the giant outer planets (see Figure 15). Its hazy blue clouds remind you of the clouds on Earth, but Neptune's spectrum tells you that these clouds contain poisonous methane, not water. The "fingerprints" of hydrogen and helium also show in its spectrum colors, and nitrogen shows up on its moon Triton. Triton is rich in elements, and this makes you wonder if Triton was originally a planet that was later pulled into orbit around Neptune. Trapped at a great distance from the Sun, Triton's riches are buried in solid ice. A small mining colony has been set up to extract rare minerals.

The planets rarely line up one after another. That happens only once every 200 years, and so you won't see Uranus on this trip—

Figure 15: Neptune

but you did see it on the outbound journey. Uranus is a beautiful aqua-colored giant. Its spectrum is very much like Neptune's, and its size and appearance confirm that they are made of similar material. The most unusual feature of Uranus is that it does not rotate the same way the other planets do. It spins on its side. It also has rings made of large, black rocks.

Inertia is one of several laws of motion that produce the spectacle you now see on the screen: the rings of Saturn.

The ship veers suddenly. "Sorry about that," the captain says. "We almost hit a small comet. That thing is really moving."

Liquid on the Loose

The sudden turn has sent loose objects floating through the cabin. Someone lost the lid on his cup, and now a gyrating blob of "spilled" soda pop is drifting toward the side wall. This is going to get messy. You think about inertia as you watch the soda float through the cabin. In a spaceship that is beyond the pull of gravity from a planet or moon, inertia is the main reason things move the way they do—the soda won't fall to the floor. It will splatter against the wall, and then thousands of droplets may be floating around like tiny planets. But somebody's using the old brain: Just before the soda hits the wall, a hand pokes up. The hand is holding a vacuum hose that slurps the liquid out of the air. Applause breaks out all over the cabin.

Inertia is one of several laws of motion that produce the spectacle you now see on the screen: the rings of Saturn. These rings are nothing like the dull, dark rings of Uranus or the thin rings of Neptune and Jupiter. Saturn's rings extend from 7,000 to 74,000 km away from the planet. They are made of thousands of bits of ice, rock, and dust, all orbiting the planet in a thin plane, which is only a few hundred meters thick. If you could pack the material in Saturn's rings into one solid mass, it would be only about 100 km across—a little bigger than the state of Rhode Island. Some bits shine deep red, like an iron-rich meteor. Others are blue. Most are yellow. The pulls of Saturn and its moons hold them in this flat, narrow band. Energy from the Sun makes the rings glow in different colors of light from the elements within them.

Figure 16: Saturn

A Star Isn't Born

Saturn itself glows yellow (see Figure 16). So does its neighbor, Jupiter (see Figure 17). Hydrogen and helium make up about 75% of each of these planets. This explains why they look yellowish, like the Sun. All three of these bodies are huge balls of gas held together by the sheer force of gravity. The Sun is big enough to create its own heat. Jupiter has starlike qualities. In fact, it may be a star that never formed. As enormous as Jupiter is, it is too small and cold to become a star. Its atmosphere is very active. A huge, red hurricane the size of two Earths swirls on its surface.

Figure 17: Jupiter

Lightning energizes its clouds, and its spectrum reveals the bright oranges, greens, and blues of many gases.

Several battered, icy moons orbit Jupiter. One of them, Callisto, looks like a snapshot of a thousand pebbles hitting the surface of a pond. Each "splash" is a crater, and each crater is the result of a meteor that crashed with such speed that the force of impact heated the nearby ice. The melted water splashed outward like splattered mud, and the surrounding ice cracked like a window.

As you approach Jupiter, the planet's tremendous gravity increases the speed of the ship. The captain takes advantage of this. He passes close to Jupiter—but not close enough to be pulled to the surface. The ship swings around the far side of the planet and shoots off in a new direction. You are traveling much faster now, thanks to a free boost from Jupiter's gravity.

Between Jupiter and Mars is a belt of asteroids. These asteroids may be material that never combined to form a planet in the early days of the solar system, or they may be parts of a planet that was shattered in some cosmic accident (see Figure 18). The captain steers clear of the asteroids. At the speed the ship is traveling, a collision with one of them would be disastrous.

Almost Home

You're almost home now. The next planet you will see is Mars. Its surface is scarred with many meteor impacts, but raging sandstorms have eroded many of the craters down to small dents. Its atmosphere is thinner than Earth's because its gravity is weaker. Once Mars had thick clouds of hydrogen and nitrogen like the white, fluffy ones on Earth, but these gases escaped because the red planet did not have enough gravitational pull to hold them. Even so, like Earth, Mars has enough atmosphere, gravity, and heat from the Sun to remain an active planet.

Many different elements exist on Mars. From its spectrum, you can tell that carbon dioxide makes up almost all of its atmosphere. Glaciers made of frozen carbon dioxide and a little frozen water cover its poles. The spectrum shows the lines of iron and sulfur minerals, indicating that Mars has rocks like some of Earth's.

The two moons of Mars are like the lifeless chunk of rock that orbits Earth. All three moons are dotted with craters. They serve as evidence of the many collisions that take place in space over millions of years. None

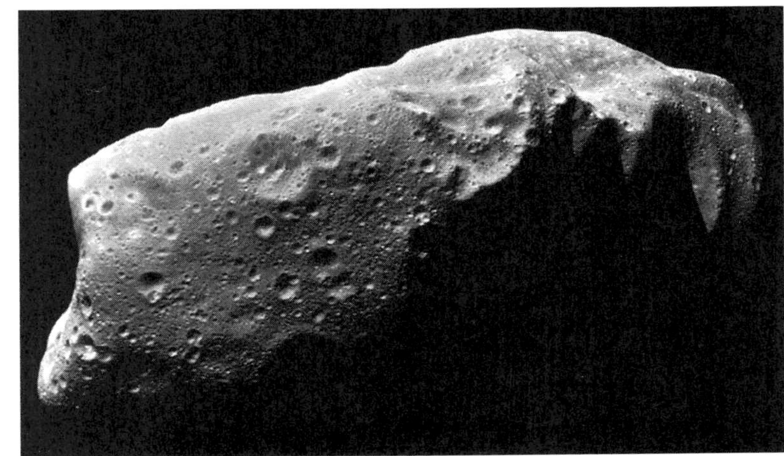

Figure 18: Asteroid 243 Ida

Figure 19: Artist's conception of the surface of Venus
Note: A dense atmosphere rich in carbon dioxide has produced a runaway greenhouse effect on Venus. The surface of the planet, which is hot enough to melt lead, burns up all but the largest meteors.

of these moons has enough mass to hold an atmosphere, and so the craters have not been worn away by wind and rain.

Hot Air

Soon you will be standing on Earth, the third planet from the Sun. You have never visited the two innermost planets, Venus and Mercury. Venus is a planet of raging storms (see Figure 19). Yellow-red clouds of sulfuric acid cover its surface. This thick, hot atmosphere blocks a direct view of the surface, but probes have found that the planet is rugged and rocky. Its carbon dioxide atmosphere, which is 90 times thicker than Earth's, presses down on the surface like a heavy blanket.

The thick atmosphere creates severe "air resistance," which has prevented meteor impacts from scattering debris very far. While most meteors burn up as they speed through Venus's atmosphere, the biggest ones do survive until impact. As a result, Venus has no small craters—but it does have large ones. Because these craters form in a very hard surface, they last a long time.

> **Get This . . .**
> Any change in the speed or direction of an object's motion is called an **acceleration.** Slowing down is also an acceleration—in a backward direction.

Even Venus's hot, corrosive weather does not erase them quickly.

Mercury is so close to the Sun that sheer heat melts away the scars of its craters. A few great craters reveal streaks of yellow material that splattered out when meteors collided with the planet. Mercury's spectrum shows that this yellow material must be one of many metals in the core of this small world. In the past, some of these metals melted from the inside and pushed up through the surface to form beautiful, golden "copper mountains."

The yellow Sun holds all these planets and moons in orbit around it. Although only a ball of gas, the Sun is so massive that it keeps all nine major planets moving in regular patterns. As your ship approaches Earth, it's nice to see the Sun looking like its old self again, big and bright and flooding the inner planets of the solar system with golden light.

On Your Own

Respond to the following items based on "Homecoming."

1. How could a low-speed collision with a chunk of rock push a spaceship into orbit around Uranus? Describe how this might happen.
2. Only the largest planets—Jupiter, Saturn, Uranus, and Neptune—have rings. What do you think is the reason for this?
3. Explain why craters on Venus do not have rays like those on the Moon.
4. How can studying a crater help you figure out what kind of object made it? Explain how this can also help you learn what that object was made of and where it came from.

Career Links

Engineering Technologies

IBM

Ink Chemist

Ink chemists develop and produce inks for a number of uses. Many of them work for printing companies, and some are employed in the garment industry, where they select or develop inks for clothing that carries logos, slogans, or other designs. Ink chemists often serve as expert witnesses in cases involving questionable documents. By examining the ink, they can tell when a document was written. They may also use this skill in the art world to determine the authenticity of a work created with inks. These chemists must understand the physical and chemical properties of inks. They must know how to produce the desired colors and how to match batches. They must also understand how inks react to different temperatures and lighting conditions. To work in this field, you will need a degree in chemistry. For more information, write:

American Chemical Society
1155 16th Street, N.W.
Washington, DC 20036
http://www.acs.org

Related occupations: printer, paint chemist, apparel designer, artist, graphic designer

Section 3

WHAT ELSE IS OUT THERE?

HAVE you ever thought about what lies beyond the solar system? The fastest space probe ever launched from Earth traveled about 35,000 km per hour. At that speed it would take nearly 20 years to reach Pluto. If it would take that long to cross the solar system, how long would it take to reach the stars you see in the sky? How long would it take to cross the entire Milky Way galaxy?

This galaxy contains billions of stars. How do stars form? What are they made of? Do they ever burn out? What is the reason that some stars look brighter than others? Is their brightness related to their temperature or their distance from Earth? How can you figure out how far away a star is?

The universe contains billions of galaxies. How did all these galaxies form? How big is the universe? Is it getting bigger or staying the same size? Will the universe last forever or come to an end? How can you explore the universe when so much of it is so far away? As you watch the next video segment, imagine what you could do to learn about stars and planets deep in space.

FREEZE FRAME

Now that you have watched the video segment, discuss the following on-screen questions with the other students in your class.

1. How can you find out what is beyond the solar system?
2. How did the universe form and reach its present state? What might happen to it someday?

New Information Is Changing Old Ideas about the Universe

Since the mid-1990s, a flood of new information from the Hubble Space Telescope and other spacecraft has challenged many old theories about the stars, planets, and other objects in space. Astronomers are now rethinking their ideas about the age and size of the universe, the possibility that life once existed on other planets, the origin of Earth's oceans, and other matters.

In this section of Module 10, you will learn about many of the objects that lie beyond the solar system. You will also learn two major theories about the origin and nature of the universe. These ideas are not likely to change in the near future. But technology is constantly improving the tools that astronomers use to observe the universe, and so even these long-accepted ideas may change someday. Space is full of surprises.

The Hourglass nebula

INVESTIGATION 6

What It Takes to Be a Star

Ever Wonder?

Have you ever wondered how the Sun formed? The universe contains billions of stars, many of them like the Sun. How did all these stars form? Are some stars older than others? Do they all use the same "fuel" to produce light and heat? Will the Sun and all the other stars ever burn out? What happens to a star when it dies? In this investigation you will learn how a star forms and how it changes during its long, dazzling lifetime.

Materials List

- Wide bowl or pan
- 10 small corks
- 10 magnetized pins

Step-by-Step

1. Run tap water into your pan until the water is several centimeters deep.
2. Insert a pin in the wide end of each cork. *Caution: Be careful not to stick yourself or a partner with a pin, but if you do, tell your teacher right away.*
3. Place one of the corks in the water. (Make sure you have enough water for the cork to float around freely.) Observe.
4. Think about what would happen if you put two corks in the water at opposite ends of the pan and waited. Describe in your logbook what you think would happen to the corks.
5. Place two corks at opposite ends of the pan. Observe what happens during a five-minute period.
6. In your logbook make a drawing that shows the paths the corks follow as they float in the pan. Record what happens as you watch the corks float.
7. Place five corks in the pan. Be sure to distribute them evenly. Observe what happens for five minutes.
8. Draw the paths that these corks follow as they float in the pan. Record what happens to them.
9. Describe in your logbook what you think would happen if 10 corks floated in the pan for five minutes. Compare what you think would happen with what actually took place when two and five corks were floating in the water. Record any ideas you have that may explain the movement of the corks.
10. Place 10 corks in the pan. Distribute them evenly, and observe what happens for five minutes.
11. Draw the path of the floating corks. Describe any patterns that you observe in their movement.
12. Remove all but three corks from the pan. Push the three remaining corks together at the center. Put the rest of the corks in the pan around the edges.
13. Draw the paths of the corks over a five-minute period. Describe any patterns that you observe.
14. Clean up your work area, and return all supplies to your teacher.

Talk It Over

Work with your partner(s) to answer the following questions.

1. What paths did the corks take when only two of them were in the water? Did their motions change when all 10 corks were floating? Describe what happened. How did their motions compare with your predictions of what would happen?
2. Did you see anything that was responsible for moving the corks? What force do you think caused their movement? Explain.

3 Do you think gravity caused the corks to move as they did? Give one or more reasons that gravity would be a good explanation for the corks' movement. Give one or more reasons that gravity would not be a good explanation.

4 Large clouds of dust and gas exist in space. How would you expect gravity to affect these clouds? What do you think would happen to them? Once the process started, how would it change?

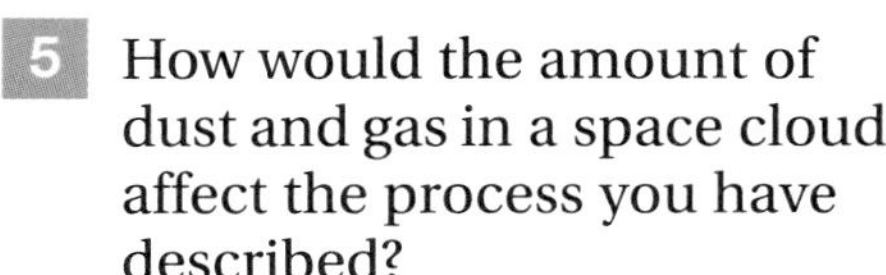

5 How would the amount of dust and gas in a space cloud affect the process you have described?

6 Suppose some force, such as the wind, broke up the clusters of corks and spread them apart. How would the corks behave after being separated? Would their distance from one another have any effect on their movement? If an asteroid passed through a cloud of space dust and scattered it, would the bits of dust behave the same as the corks? Explain your answer to each of these questions.

An Excuse for Dreaming

"Now, my suspicion is that the universe is not only queerer than we suppose, but queerer than we can suppose. . . . I suspect that there are more things in heaven and earth than are dreamed of in any philosophy. That is the reason why I have no philosophy myself, and must be my excuse for dreaming."

—J.B.S. Haldane, British biologist in *Possible Worlds* (1927)

Spread the Word

RESULTS

Work with your partner(s) to develop a presentation that will show the rest of the class what you have learned in this investigation. You could start by describing and explaining how the corks moved. Illustrate your ideas with a series of drawings. Then tell how the motions that you observed in the corks may help explain the way stars and planets form. Draw another series of pictures, perhaps in the form of a comic strip, to show several stages in this process.

List several professions in which people may use this kind of information. Also give some everyday examples in which gravitational attraction plays an important role.

Read All about It!

The Life of a Star

As you watched the floating corks drift slowly together during Investigation 6, you were watching a model of how a star forms. Because the pins in the corks were magnetized, they pulled the corks together in a clump. When several corks were in the same area, the pins' attractive force was even greater, and so they moved together more quickly. The magnetic force between the corks represents the effect of gravity on clouds of dust and gas floating in space. Like the corks, dust and gas particles in space

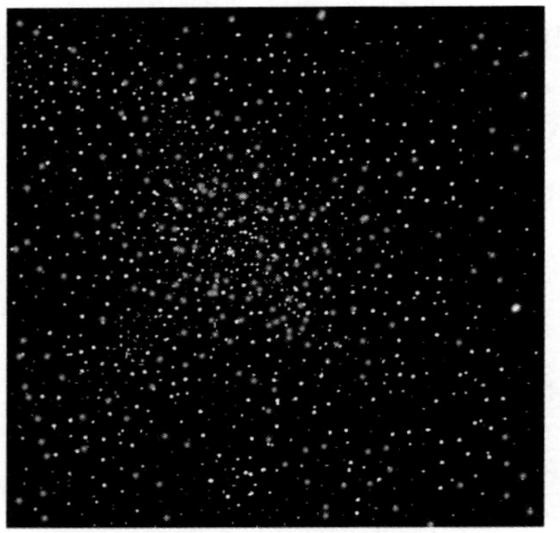
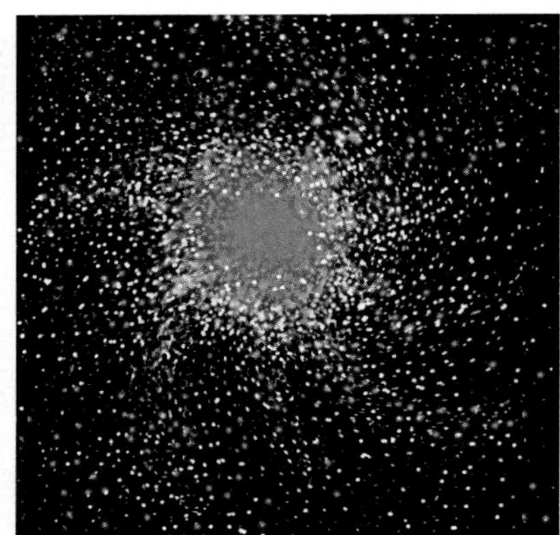

Figure 20: The formation of a star
Note: As gravity pulls a cloud of dust and gas together (left), the compression creates great heat and pressure and the hot cloud begins to glow (center). Eventually the temperature and pressure are great enough to cause fusion to begin in the new star (right).

move randomly at first, but over time they drift within range of one another's gravitational pull. Once their gravitational forces lock on to each other, the loose particles drift slowly together.

Collecting Dust

As this matter comes together, the dust and gas become tightly packed, with more and more particles pushing inward. A dense center forms, and incoming material begins to swirl around this core. The core also starts to warm up because molecules are colliding with one another and releasing heat energy. At first the heat is too weak to detect, but things gradually begin to change.

Over millions of years, the growing center of the mass becomes extremely dense. The denser and more massive it becomes, the more strongly its gravity pulls in the material at the surface. As more gas and dust are pulled in, heat and pressure build up in the core. The whole mass becomes so hot that it begins to glow. The cloud of dust and gas has become a star (see Figure 20).

Many space clouds are too small to build up enough energy to become stars. Although these clouds may collapse and form objects with extremely hot centers, they remain cool on the surface and do not produce light. The planet Jupiter may be such an object—a star that never formed. Jupiter is too small to become a star. It does not have enough gravitational force to develop the heat and pressure necessary to form a star. However, while Jupiter does not emit light, it does give off bursts of radio waves. In this respect, Jupiter is like a star.

Star Power

The high temperature and pressure that exist in the center of a star force atoms to merge. In this process, **fusion**, the gravitational pressure overwhelms the force that normally keeps atoms separated from one another. When atoms fuse together, they release energy (see Figure 21). Fusion is the source of a star's tremendous power.

Most of the atoms that fuse in a star are hydrogen atoms. When two hydrogen atoms merge, they form a helium atom, which has

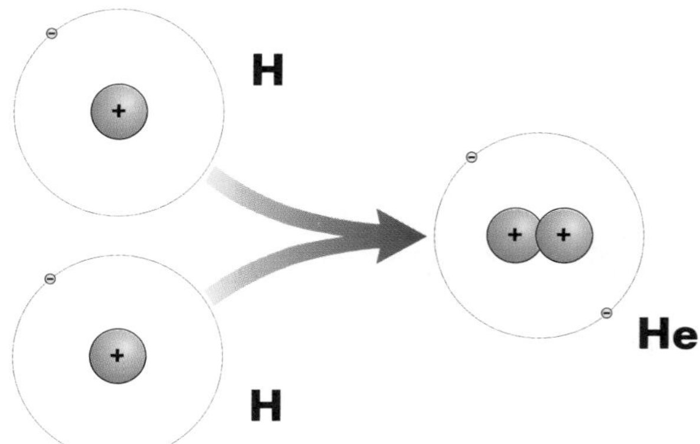

Figure 21: Fusion of hydrogen into helium
Note: The intense pressure and heat in stars force hydrogen atoms to merge, creating helium atoms. During this process, a tiny part of the mass of the hydrogen atoms is converted to an enormous amount of energy.

slightly less mass than two hydrogen atoms. A small amount of matter from the hydrogen atoms is converted to energy. The star emits part of this energy, and part of it drives more atoms to fuse. The star keeps itself running.

Stars radiate huge amounts of heat and light energy. For 90% of a star's lifetime, it produces energy by fusing hydrogen atoms to make helium atoms. If the star is hot enough, some of the helium atoms fuse to make heavier elements as well. Eventually, however, all stars run out of hydrogen fuel. For stars the size of the Sun, this process takes about 10 billion years.

What a Way to Go

When the fuel in some stars runs low, the helium and heavier elements form an extremely dense core. Fusion continues near the surface of this type of star, but fusion in the core ends when iron forms. Without fusion, the core no longer produces enough energy to support the star's huge mass. The iron atoms in the core collapse, releasing a huge, explosive burst of energy that blows off the surface of the star, flinging it millions of kilometers into space. An exploding star such as this is a **supernova**.

A supernova may be bright enough for people to see it in broad daylight. Historical records show that people on Earth have seen a supernova every few hundred years, without telescopes. Supernovas that were recorded in the past became small, dim stars surrounded by nebulas. A **nebula** is a cloud of dust and gas (see Figure 22). These remnants of supernovas remain visible today through telescopes.

Red Giants and White Dwarfs

A star may go through several periods of contraction and expansion, cooling and heating, during its lifetime. At the stage where a star expands to enormous size but

Figure 22: Nebula NGC 604
Note: As shown in this Hubble Space Telescope image, Nebula NGC 604 is located in the neighboring spiral galaxy M33. New stars are being born in this vast cloud of dust and gas, which is a remnant of a supernova explosion.

Little Equation, Big Idea

Part of being a good scientist is knowing how to make good guesses. One of Albert Einstein's good guesses led to his famous equation $E = mc^2$.

You have probably seen this equation, but you may not know what the letters stand for. "E" stands for energy; "m" is mass; and "c" is the speed of light. Einstein's intuition led him to make a good guess about that last item, "c."

When Einstein published his ideas in 1905, scientists thought that the speed of light was variable. Einstein disagreed. He was only 16 when he began thinking about this problem, and at 26 he published his special theory of relativity. Here he presented the idea that light is made of photons and that its speed is constant. In his next paper, he published the equation $E = mc^2$, which shows that matter and energy are equivalent: The energy of a quantity of matter equals its mass multiplied by the square of the speed of light. The speed of light is a very large number. Squaring it makes a tremendously larger number. This shows that a small amount of matter can be transformed to a huge quantity of energy.

Although Einstein's equation eventually led to a revolution in physical science, it could not be tested and verified until years after he had "guessed" at it. He probably didn't mind. After all, it took him 10 years to formulate the equation.

cools down in temperature, it is called a **red giant**. This type of star has used up much of its fuel. It cools still more as its huge surface radiates greater amounts of light and heat energy than it did before it swelled in size.

A red giant can again become so dense that gravity takes over and makes it collapse. As its atoms of heavy elements fuse together, the red giant becomes a **neutron star**. A neutron star is denser and more compressed than the original star, and it produces more energy. Only in the tremendous power of a neutron star can many of the heaviest elements form. Just as a hydrogen star makes the heavier element helium, so also a neutron star builds heavier and heavier elements from hydrogen and helium. A neutron star that begins with very heavy elements produces a great amount of energy but burns out quickly.

Throughout its lifetime, a star changes size and color, generally becoming smaller as it uses up fuel and redder as it cools down. A star's original mass determines how long it remains at each stage. Once a star has become so small that it can no longer cycle through explosions and steady fusion, its light slowly fades. Every star, even a supernova, eventually burns out, becoming smaller and dimmer—a **white dwarf** (see Figure 23).

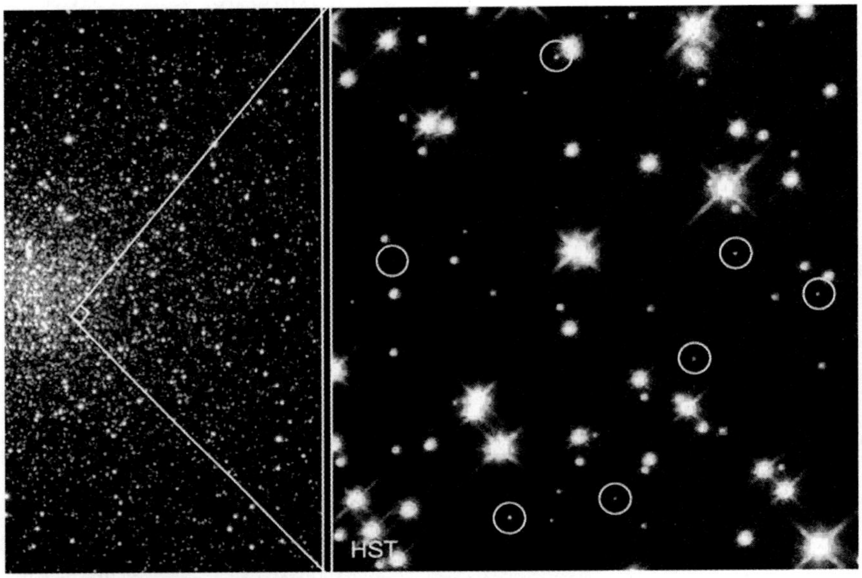

Figure 23: White dwarf stars in the star cluster M4

Note: Many red giant stars are visible in cluster M4 (left), but the Hubble Space Telescope reveals that it also contains white dwarf stars, marked here with circles (right).

A star's changing size and color are clues to its age and fuel supply. For example, the Sun is yellow and contains a large amount of hydrogen, indicating that it is still fairly young. The star Sirius B is very small and white-hot from the compression of its remaining matter in a dying burst of light. Stars of all ages and types exist. Some are just now being formed, while others are almost as old as the universe, which is about 15 billion years old.

On Your Own

Answer the following questions based on "The Life of a Star."

1 Suppose you located a star that burns hydrogen for fuel and has far more hydrogen than helium. Would it be an old star or a young star? Explain.

2 How can you tell whether a cloud of dust and gas is in the early stages of forming a star or in the final stages of a supernova explosion? Explain your thinking.

3 As a star's temperature and size change, which of its other properties change?

4 Because light from the stars takes a long time to reach Earth, space distances are measured in light-years. (A **light-year** is the distance that light travels in one year.) Most stars are thousands or millions of light-years away. Based on these facts, what could you say about a supernova that you saw in the sky?

Which is hotter, an orange fire or a blue one? What does the color of the flames have to do with their temperature? Watch closely as your teacher shows you a video segment that will help you answer these questions. As you watch, consider what you have learned about stars and their colors and see if you can make a connection with fire colors. Then discuss the video segment with the other students in your class. After the discussion, read "Cosmic Colors."

READ ALL ABOUT IT!

Cosmic Colors

COLORS can tell you a lot. When you carried out Investigation 5, the colored lines in a spectrum told you the chemical elements in a solution. The color of the metal rod in the video segment revealed its temperature. Just as each element has its own color spectrum, objects also glow in colors that depend on their temperatures.

Think of what happened in the video as the thin wire heated up. When the dull metal glowed red, you knew it was hot. Did it surprise you that the rod then turned yellow? Did it surprise you to see that yellow is hotter than red? Heating the rod meant giving it more and more heat energy. It glowed red when it reached a certain temperature—energy level—above normal. It glowed yellow and white when it reached even higher temperature and energy levels.

HOT COLORS

As more and more heat entered the metal, it radiated more and more energy. Its color changes showed you this. When the rod turned blue, it was even hotter, emitting more energy than when it was red, yellow, or white. All heated matter follows this same sequence, changing in color from the red end of the spectrum to the blue. This occurs because of the connection between energy and color.

Every color of light carries a different amount of energy. Red light has the lowest amount. Yellow light carries slightly more energy. Green has still more, and violet has the most of all. Hot objects glow with different colors, depending on how much energy they emit. (All objects, including ones that are not hot enough to glow, produce invisible **infrared** rays, which have even less energy than red light.) If you heat an object for a long time, it will absorb more and more energy—and it will give off more and more energy. As the metal rod absorbed and released greater amounts of energy, its color changed from red to yellow to white.

Stars have different colors too: red, orange, yellow, green, and so on. Stars also vary in brightness. If two stars are emitting the same amount of energy but one of them is smaller than the other, the smaller star will look brighter because its glow is spread over a smaller surface area. A star's color and brightness depend on both its size and its temperature.

Colors and Temperatures of Stars

Color	Typical temperature (Kelvin)
Red	3,000
Orange	4,500
Yellow	5,500
White	7,000
Blue	15,000

Figure 24: A table of star colors and temperatures
Note: On the Kelvin temperature scale, one K is the same as one Celsius degree. However, 0°C (Celsius) is the temperature at which water freezes at atmospheric pressure, while 0 K (Kelvin) is "absolute zero," the lowest temperature that anything can possibly be.

Charting the Lives of the Stars

When a star's color and brightness change, this indicates that it has entered a new stage of its life. For example, if a star becomes brighter but then dims and turns red, it has expanded into a red giant. It turned red because it cooled down. When a star becomes a white dwarf, it has thrown off all of its outer matter and exposed its intensely hot core. Though it gives off a huge amount of energy, it has already used up its fuel. As it cools, this dying star slowly turns from white to red, brown, and black. Eventually it becomes invisible, emitting only infrared "colors." By looking at the colors of the stars, it is possible to chart their lives (see Figure 24).

Not all the colors that a star emits show up in its spectrum. Some colors are absorbed by atoms in the star's atmosphere. As you learned earlier, every element has colors that it emits as it heats up. Similarly, every element has colors that it absorbs. In a star's spectrum, these colors show up as dark **absorption lines** (see Figure 25). Absorption lines provide additional clues about which elements a star contains.

A spectrum reveals a great deal of important information about a star's temperature and composition. The task of interpreting all that information is a complex process.

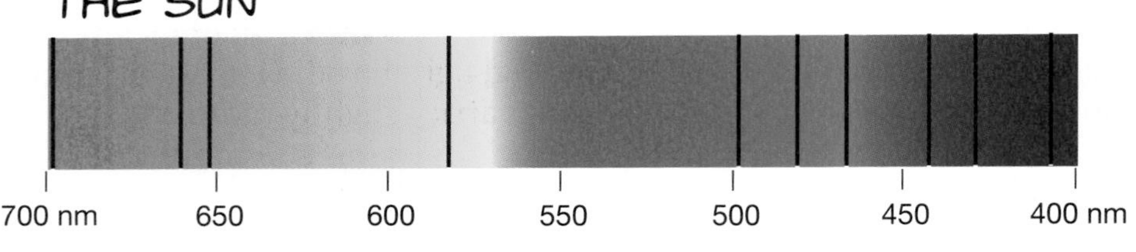

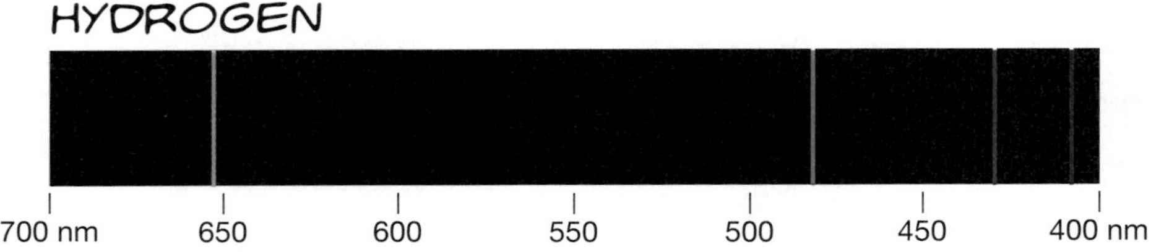

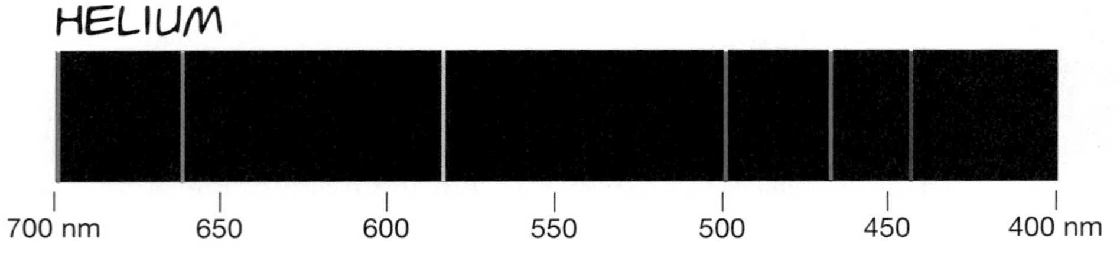

Figure 25: Absorption lines
Note: In a star's spectrum, black absorption lines that match the bright lines in the spectrums of hydrogen, helium, and other elements provide clues to the composition of the star.

On Your Own

Answer the following questions based on "Cosmic Colors."

1 The metal rod in the video segment changed colors because it was being constantly heated. What causes a star's temperature and color to change?

2 A campfire often has flames that are orange and yellow on the edges and blue inside. What does this reveal about which parts of the flames are the hottest? How about when the flames are gone and the coals glow red?

3 The planet Jupiter is sometimes called a "brown dwarf" and classified as a type of star. What does this name indicate about Jupiter?

INVESTIGATION 7

Finding the Pattern

Ever Wonder?

Some stars in the night sky are thousands of light-years away from Earth. How bright must they be in order to be visible over such a vast distance? Are most stars bright enough to be seen from very far away? How does the Sun compare with other stars in brightness and temperature? Is the Sun a very large star? Are most stars yellow, like the Sun? If you knew a star was yellow, could you tell anything about its age? In this investigation, you will explore some patterns among the different kinds of stars in the Milky Way galaxy and the rest of the universe.

Materials List

- Blank diagram of star types
- Star Data Table
- Colored pencils

Step-by-Step

1 Examine your group's Star Data Table. Compare the stars on that list to see if it includes a set of very similar stars.

2 If your group decides that some or all of the stars are similar, describe this set of stars in your logbook. If your group does not see any similarities in the stars, record that fact.

3. Listen carefully as your teacher explains the diagram of star types.
4. On your blank diagram, plot the stars listed in your Star Data Table. Use colored pencils so that each plotted point is the same color as the star it represents. (Use a black pencil for white stars.)
5. Based on the information that you have plotted on your diagram, make a prediction about some other set of stars. For example, if you have plotted a set of blue stars on your diagram, you might try to predict the average temperature and brightness of red stars. Record your ideas in your logbook. Be sure to include the reasons behind your prediction.
6. Give your data table to some other group, and obtain a data table from a different group.
7. Using your new Star Data Table, repeat the procedure you followed in Steps 1–6, but plot the new data on the same diagram.
8. Continue exchanging data tables and repeating the procedure until you have studied all four tables and all information is plotted on your diagram.
9. With your group, examine your diagram of star types. Identify any clusters or bands of stars on the diagram. In your logbook, describe the stars in each cluster or band of points on the diagram.

TALK IT OVER

Work with the other members of your group to answer the following questions.

1. How well did your predictions match the general patterns of the stars? Where did most of the stars fall on the graph?
2. Are most of the red stars located in one area of the diagram? How would you explain the way they are distributed?
3. Where do you think the oldest stars are on the diagram? (Hint: Recall what you have learned about the stages of a star's life.) Give your reason.
4. Do blue stars differ very much in brightness? What feature of blue stars causes them to differ or not differ very much? Explain.
5. Suppose you discovered a new yellow star. How hot do you think its surface would be? What would affect its brightness? Explain your thinking.

SHOCKED BY THE UNIVERSE

"If you aren't shocked by the universe, you haven't understood it."

—Attributed to Niels Bohr, Danish physicist

SPREAD THE WORD

Work with the others in your group to share your findings with the rest of the class. Construct a large, colored diagram of star types. This will make it easier for your audience to understand what you have learned. Point out those areas in the diagram where most stars tend to cluster. Explain any relationships that you have discovered between a star's color, temperature, and brightness. Choose a few stars from your diagram or from one of the data tables, and list two of their three properties (temperature, brightness, and color). Have the class try to identify the third property. Tell how they could use this information to learn about newly discovered stars.

List several professional persons and some everyday situations in which it is important to know about the relationships between color, temperature, and brightness.

Read All about It!

Starrybooks

Looking at the stars is like reading the history of the universe. The light that comes from a distant star began its journey hundreds, thousands, or perhaps billions of years ago. When you look into the sky at night, some of the stars that you see may not even exist anymore. If a star that was 500 light-years from Earth exploded 300 years ago, it will take another 200 years for light from that explosion to reach Earth.

Despite how far away the stars are—Proxima Centauri, the nearest star, is 4.3 light-years from Earth—you can learn a great deal about them. By looking at a star through a telescope and a spectroscope, you can tell how old it is. By studying the properties of a star, you can compare it with other stars to see how it is likely to change over its lifetime. As you filled out your diagram of star types in Investigation 7, you were plotting the color and other properties of stars as a way to reveal their life stories.

Star Charters

A diagram of star types is called an **HR diagram**. It shows the color, brightness, and temperature of various stars. (The letters HR stand for Hertzsprung and Russell, the astronomers who invented this kind of diagram.)

No Escaping This

"Captain! We're being sucked into a black hole!"

You may have heard a panicky cry like this in a science-fiction movie. What would happen to a spaceship that was sucked into a black hole? Would it pass through the hole to another dimension? Would it travel back in time? What happens in the movies is probably not what would happen in the real universe.

Black holes may be the collapsed matter that remains after the death of enormous stars. Such objects may be even denser than neutron stars. Black holes may also exist at the center of galaxies. One theory is that when a galaxy forms, the region near its center contains too much matter to form regular stars, and so some of this matter forms black holes instead.

The extreme density of a black hole creates a gravitational field so strong that nothing can escape from it, including light. And if light cannot travel away from it, the black hole cannot be seen. Anything that enters this region of space will disappear, as if falling into a dark hole. But the black hole is not really a hole. It is an object that is so dense that it captures and crushes whatever comes near it.

Because black holes are invisible, they cannot be directly observed. The possibility that they exist is based on indirect evidence. For example, in the late 1960s astronomers discovered that some galaxies were emitting great quantities of X rays. Black holes attract gases from neighboring stars, compressing and heating the gases so much that these gases emit vast quantities of X rays. More recently the Hubble Space Telescope has found gases moving at tremendous speed near some stars. Such high-speed motion may be caused by the overwhelming pull of a black hole.

More important, an HR diagram shows special patterns among these properties. In graphing data for various stars, Hertzsprung and Russell observed these patterns and realized that plotting a star on this kind of graph was like charting the course of the star's life.

As you discovered, the stars on your HR diagram did not cover the graph randomly. Instead, they fell into a few clumps, leaving the rest of the graph empty. Most stars fell along a diagonal line that ran from the upper left to the lower right of the diagram. This grouping is called the **main sequence**. All stars in the main sequence use hydrogen for fuel. As a result, they all display the same relationship between temperature and brightness. About 90% of all stars are in the main sequence.

The main sequence spans the entire range of both temperature and brightness (see Figure 26). Cold, dim stars appear at one end of the sequence, while hot, bright stars appear at the other end. More massive stars have more fusion reactions occurring, and so they are hotter. The cold, dim stars tend to be smaller and to have fewer fusion reactions. Their small size makes them less bright, and their slower rate of fusion makes them cooler. The hot, bright stars tend to be larger and to have more fusion reactions. Their large size makes them brighter, and their faster rate of fusion makes them hotter.

GET THIS . . .

An **HR diagram** shows the color, brightness, and temperature of stars, as well as the patterns among these properties.

ON-LINE AND OFF

Stars change over time, becoming hotter or cooler, brighter or dimmer. For example, once a star has used up most of its hydrogen, it might explode, becoming brighter—but cooler—as it expands. When a star's temperature or brightness changes, its position on the diagram also changes. If a star becomes cooler, it moves to the right of the chart, off the main sequence. Aging stars become cooler as they use up fuel; therefore,

CAREER LINKS

IBM

METALLURGICAL ENGINEER

Metallurgical engineers develop and supply metals for producing goods. They specialize in three general areas: mineral processing, metal extraction, and materials engineering. The job of a mineral processor is to concentrate minerals and recycle metallic ores. From these, the extractive metallurgist produces pure, high-quality metals. Materials engineers use the metals produced to make finished items from jewelry to medical supplies to spacecraft. Metallurgical engineers also test metals for various qualities, such as strength, resistance to corrosion, thermal conductivity, hardness, and flexibility. To pursue a career in this field, you will need at least a bachelor's degree. For more information, write:

Minerals, Metals & Materials Society
420 Commonwealth Drive
Warrendale, PA 15086
http://www.tms.org

Related occupations: materials scientist, product engineer, miner, geologist, mineralogist

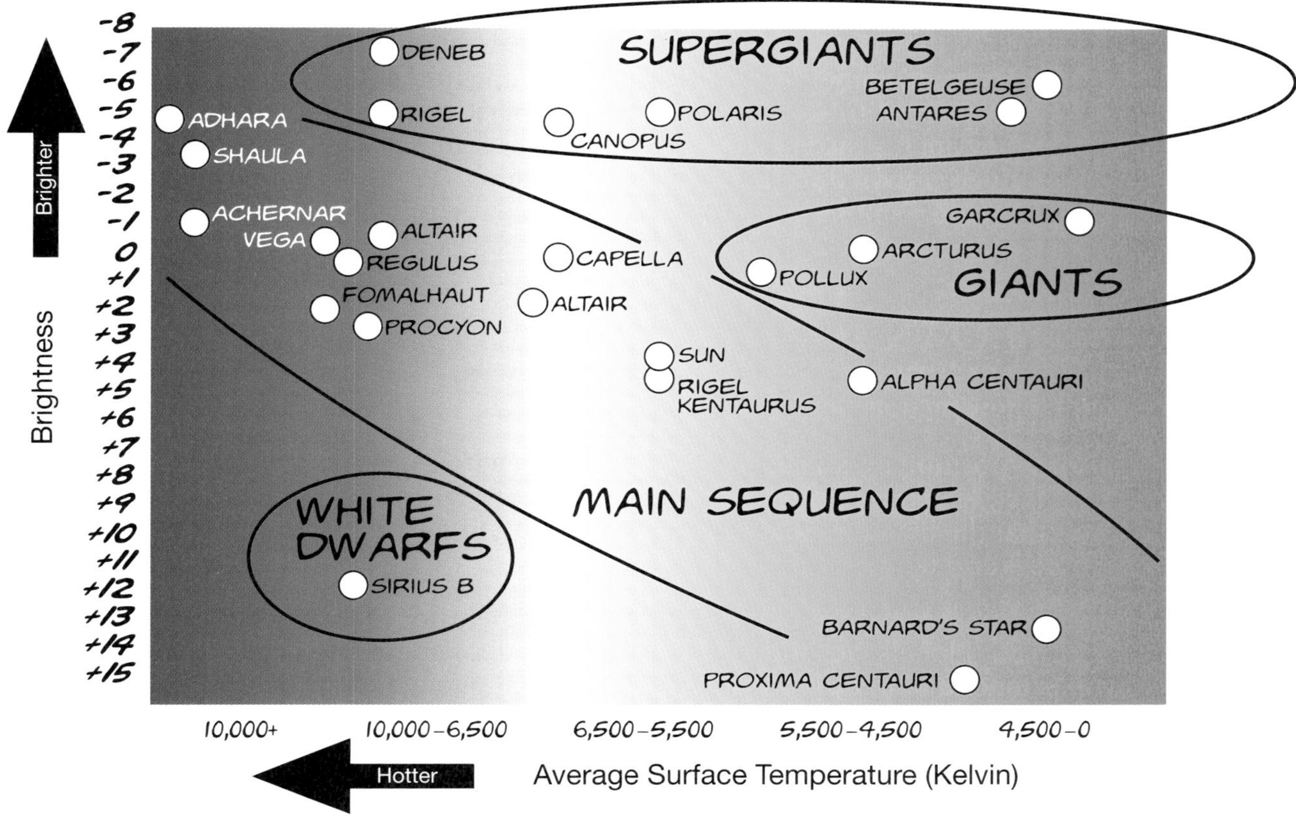

Figure 26: HR diagram

Note: Stars spend about 90% of their lifetimes as hydrogen-fueled stars in the main sequence. Other major groups of stars include small, hot, white dwarfs that consume their fuel quickly, producing brilliant light. The direct relationship between brightness and temperature found in main-sequence stars does not apply to white dwarfs, giants, and supergiants.

they too move to the right in the diagram. Later, an older star may begin fusion again and move back to the left as it becomes hotter.

Every star begins its life outside the main sequence. Most young stars first appear in the lower right-hand part of the diagram to the left of the sequence. Most older stars appear to the right of the sequence. For example, Proxima Centauri is a red dwarf, an old star with low energy. Even though it is the Sun's closest neighbor, it is barely visible. Its dimness and color are sure signs of old age.

Stars spend most of their lives along the main sequence. How long a star stays there depends mainly on its mass. A large star, such as SN1987A, which is 15 times more massive than the Sun, will spend only about 10 million years on the main sequence—that's a short time, astronomically speaking. The reason for this is that large stars are under such great gravitational pressure that they fuse their hydrogen quickly and run out of fuel. In comparison, the Sun has already been on the main sequence 500 times longer than SN1987A, and it will probably stay there another five billion years. Smaller stars stay on the main sequence even longer. These stars have the least gravitational energy pressing their atoms together, and so they take a very long time to use up their hydrogen.

On the Blink

Most stars have fairly constant brightness and temperature throughout their lives. However, some stars change brightness on a regular basis—they "blink." These stars are called **Cepheid variables**. Some Cepheid variables vary in brightness because their surface radiates different amounts of light in different places. As they rotate, they sometimes show a dim spot, sometimes a bright spot. Others vary in brightness because of the elements they are fusing. For example, those that produce carbon during fusion expel dark clouds, like smoke around a fire. This "smoke" hovers around the star, blocking its light. When the star contracts and uses up another layer of matter, its surface explodes, pushing away this smoky layer and becoming bright again. Cycles of brightness among Cepheid variables run from days to millions of years.

On Your Own

Answer the following questions based on "Starrybooks."

1. Not every position on an HR diagram is filled in with a point representing a star. In fact, whole regions on the graph are empty. What do you think is the reason that the diagram does not show stars with many other combinations of brightness and temperature?
2. As with stars, the cores of planets become extremely hot as gravity forces them to contract. (Planets lack the mass needed to get hot enough to begin fusion.) If you extended both axes of your HR diagram far enough, do you think Earth could appear on it? Explain your reasoning.
3. Suppose the spectrum of a star revealed the presence of calcium and magnesium, elements that are much heavier than helium. Where would you expect this star to appear on the HR diagram? Explain.

INVESTIGATION 8

Light from Far, Far, Far, Far, Far, Far Away

Ever Wonder?

The stars that you see in the sky at night are incredibly far away. How can you measure their distance from Earth? If you look out the window of a moving car or bus, distant trees and buildings do not seem to change position much but closer objects do. For example, a billboard may seem far away one minute but very close the next. Did you ever think about using the way things seem to change position to measure how far away they are?

In this investigation you will compare the positions of "stars" as you see them from different places to discover how to measure their distances.

Materials List

- Pencil
- 2 paper stars
- String
- Scissors
- Key
- Masking tape
- Meter stick
- Calculator (optional)
- 15- or 30-cm ruler (optional)

Step-by-Step (Part 1)

1. In your logbook, draw a right triangle. (**Math tip:** A right triangle contains a 90° angle, which looks like the corner of a square. The longest side of this kind of triangle is called the hypotenuse. It faces the right angle.) Make the sides of your triangle 6 cm, 8 cm, and 10 cm. The 6-cm side should be at the bottom; the 8-cm side should be perpendicular to it at the left end (forming the right angle); and the 10-cm side should be the hypotenuse.

2. Measure 2 cm along the bottom of your triangle from the end where it meets the hypotenuse. Mark this point. Draw a vertical line straight up from the mark to the hypotenuse so that it forms a right angle with the bottom of the triangle (see Figure 27).

3. Notice that the large and small triangles are similar. This means their sides have the same proportions and their angles are identical. You can use this fact to find out how long the vertical side of the small triangle is. In your logbook, set up a fraction that shows you are dividing the length of the large triangle's vertical side by the length of its horizontal side. This gives you the ratio of the perpendicular sides of the large triangle.

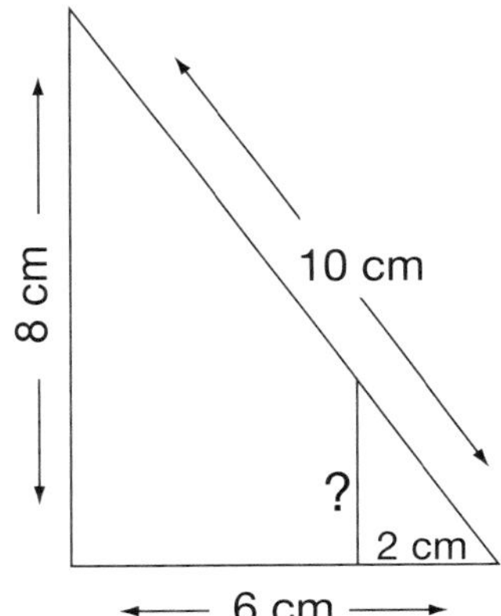

Figure 27: Right triangle for Investigation 8, Part 1
Note: This sample triangle is not actual size.

4. Set up the same kind of division problem for the small triangle:

$$\frac{\text{length of vertical side}}{\text{length of horizontal side}}$$

Use "X" to represent the unknown length of the vertical side.

5. Because the two triangles have the same proportions, the ratio of the lengths of the two sides of the large triangle (Step 3) is equal to the ratio of the lengths of the corresponding sides of the small triangle (Step 4). In your logbook, write an equation that shows these two quantities are equal.

6. Solve your equation by multiplying both sides by 2. Your solution will be the value of X, the unknown length of the vertical side of the smaller triangle. Record this number in your logbook.

7. Use a ruler to measure the length of X. Make sure that this result agrees with your calculation in Step 6. If the numbers are not the same or if your partner has a different answer, check your work and try again.

STEP-BY-STEP (PART 2)

1. Tape a star on the wall at your eye level. See Figure 28 on page 10.69 for an example.

2. Tie one end of the string to a key.

3. With your arm stretched out straight in front of you, hold the string so that the key hangs down. Cut the string so that it is long enough to hang just above the floor when you hold it this way.

4. (Either you or your partner should carry out this step while the other partner does Step 5.) Stand against the wall opposite the star, facing it directly so that the line between you and the star is perpendicular to the wall. Hold the other star in your hand straight out in front of you so that the two stars line up in your vision when you close one eye. Do not move until your partner marks the floor.

5. Mark the floor with masking tape where your partner is standing. Use short tape strips to make an "A" where his or her feet are.

6. If you performed Step 4: With your back to the wall that is facing the star, move several meters to your right. If you performed Step 5: Mark "E" in masking tape at the point where your partner has moved.

7. Use a meter stick to measure the distance between "A" and "E." Record this distance in your logbook.

8. (Either you or your partner should carry out this step while the other partner does Step 9.) Stand on the "E" and face the star on the opposite wall. Hold a star and the string in one hand straight out in front of you so that the two stars line up when you close one eye. The key should hang just above the floor. Do not move until your partner has marked the floor below the key.

9. Mark the floor below the key with a "v." Then mark the floor with a "w" at the point that lies between "A" and "E" directly opposite the "v" (see Figure 28).

10. Measure the distance between "v" and "w." Record this number in your logbook.

11. Measure the distance between "E" and "w."

12. In your logbook, draw a diagram of the triangle formed by "E," "v," and "w" inside the larger triangle formed by "E," "A," and the star on the wall. Label all the distances you have measured. Also label as "X" the distance between "A" and the star on the wall. (This is the unknown distance to the star.)

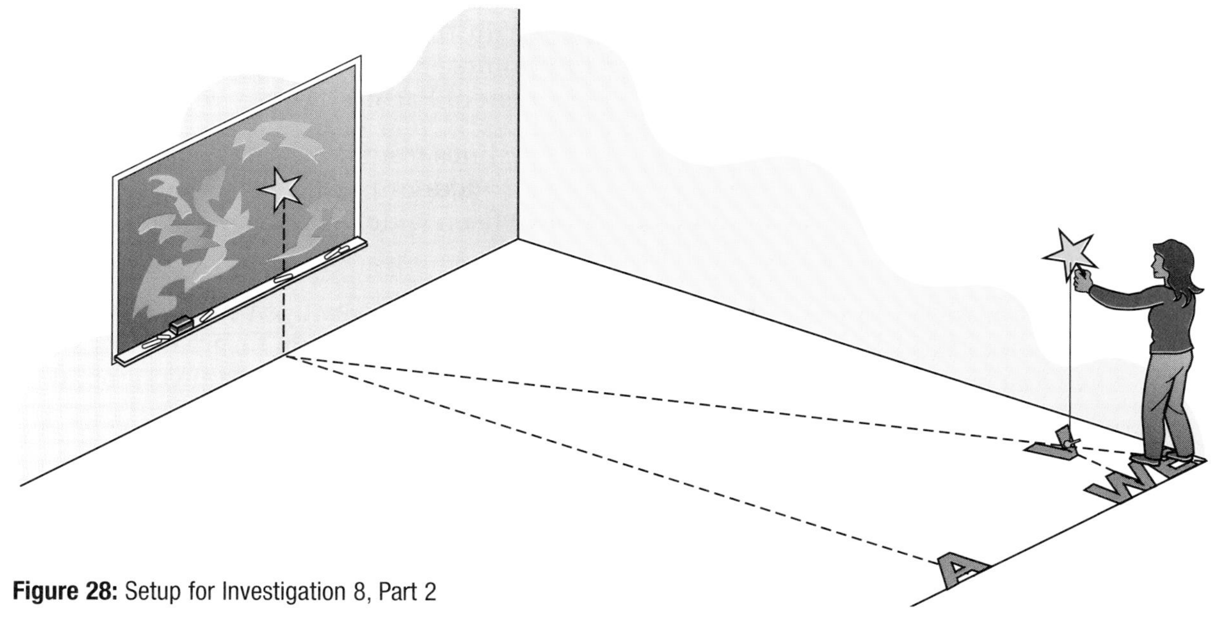

Figure 28: Setup for Investigation 8, Part 2

13 As you did in Step 4 of Part 1, find the ratio of the lengths of the perpendicular sides of the small triangle: Divide the distance from "w" to "v" by the distance from "w" to "E." Write your calculations in your logbook.

14 In your logbook, set up the same kind of division problem for the large triangle: Use "X" to represent the unknown distance from "A" to the star on the opposite wall. Divide "X" by the distance from "A" to "E."

15 Write an equation in your logbook that shows that your results for Steps 13 and 14 are equal.

16 Find the value of "X" by multiplying both sides of your equation by the distance from "A" to "E." Record the result in your logbook.

17 Measure the distance between "A" and the star on the wall. Compare this number with your result from Step 16. If they differ greatly, repeat your measurements and calculations.

18 Remove the star from the wall, and return all supplies to your teacher.

Talk It Over

Work with your partner to answer the following questions.

1 How was the procedure that you followed in Part 1 of the investigation similar to the procedure you followed in Part 2? Explain.

2 If you were using this method to measure the distance from Earth to a star, could you observe the star from two points a few meters apart, as you did from points "A" and "E" in Part 2, and then calculate the distance as you did in the investigation? Explain your reasoning.

3 If you were using this method to measure the distance to a star from Earth, how could you arrange for your two viewing points ("A" and "E") to be as far apart as possible? (Hint: Think about the movement of Earth.)

4 Notice the angle formed at the star by the lines from the two viewing locations ("A" and "E"). Would that angle have been wider or narrower if "A" and "E" had been farther apart? Would the angle have been wider or narrower if the star on the wall had been farther away?

5 Suppose you were observing some real stars in this way from two different points. Would the angle described in the previous question be greater for stars that are closer to Earth or for those that are farther away? Explain your answer.

RESULTS Spread the Word

Work with your partner to give a presentation to the rest of the class about what you have learned in this investigation. Start by preparing a large diagram of your triangles. Label all the sides and corners, and include the distances you measured. Go over your calculations, and explain how you were able to use your measurements to determine a distance without measuring it directly. Discuss several applications of this method in workplaces or in daily life. List a few professions in which this technique would be a useful measuring tool.

Read All about It!

How Far Is That Star?

How can you measure the distance to a star? You can't measure it directly by traveling there—the stars are too far away to visit, at least with today's spacecraft. So how do astronomers know how far away they are?

An important method for estimating the distance to a star is called **triangulation**. In Investigation 8 you used triangulation to estimate the distance to a paper star. Instead of using a meter stick to measure the distance directly, you set up a triangle with the unknown distance as one side and a known distance as another side. Then all you had to do was set up a smaller, similar triangle whose three sides *could* be measured directly. A simple equation gave you the length of the unknown side of the larger triangle (see Figure 29).

Astronomers use a form of triangulation to calculate the distances to stars. They view a star twice, six months apart. The distance between the positions of the Earth at these two times is the diameter of Earth's orbit, which is known. The star and the two points from which it was observed form the three corners of a triangle (see Figure 30).

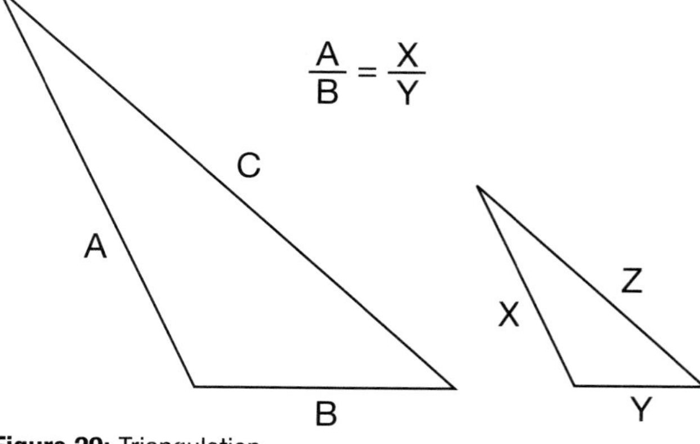

Figure 29: Triangulation

IBM

LAND SURVEYOR

Land surveyors measure and map surface areas. They write descriptions of the sites they survey, research legal documents about land areas, and establish official boundaries. Surveyors use instruments to measure distances, establish directions, and calculate horizontal and vertical angles. Those who measure very large areas may use the Global Positioning System, which sends out signals from satellites. Some of the fields in which surveyors work are engineering, architecture, construction, and government. To pursue this type of career, you will need a four-year degree or accreditation from a technical or vocational school. For more information, write:

American Congress on Surveying and Mapping
5410 Grosvenor Lane, Suite 100
Bethesda, MD 20814-2144
http://www.landsurveyor.com/acsm

Related occupations: marine surveyor, cartographer, urban planner, architect, civil engineer

Imagine looking at the star from those two points. Each time you would have to turn your head at a different angle to see the star. The angle between the two lines of sight is called the **parallax angle**. The farther away a star is, the smaller its parallax angle will be (see Figure 30). Astronomers can use the parallax angle and their knowledge of the diameter of Earth's orbit to calculate the distance to some stars.

Only about 1,000 stars are close enough for their distances to be estimated with the parallax method. Billions of others are so far away that their parallax angles are too small to be measured accurately. Another method is used to calculate their distances.

The key is to locate a Cepheid variable. As you learned earlier, a Cepheid variable is a type of star whose brightness varies in a regular cycle. In 1912 Henrietta Leavitt, an astronomer, discovered that these stars all have the same relationship between brightness and the length of their cycles: the longer the cycle,

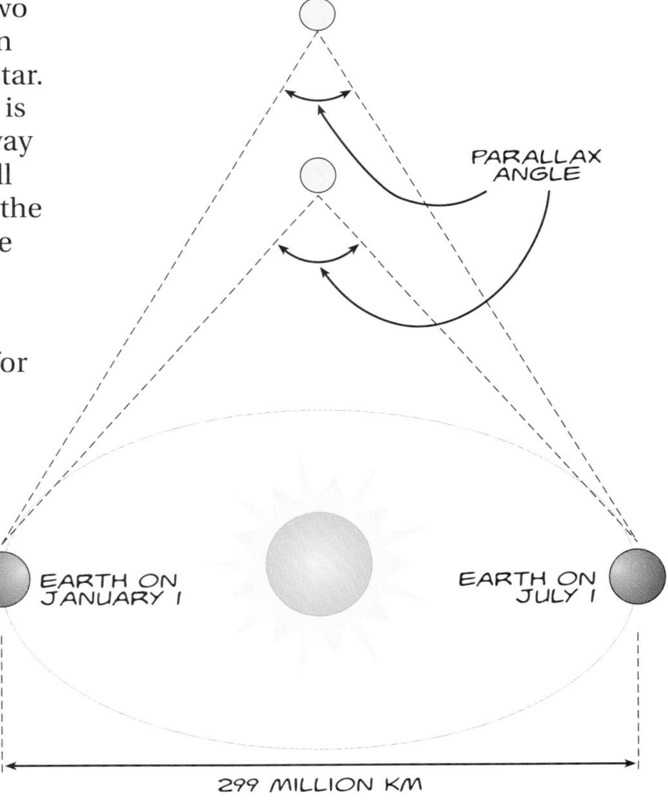

Figure 30: Using parallax to estimate distance to a star
Note: The farther away a star is, the smaller its parallax angle will be. Most stars are too far away for parallax measurements.

the brighter the star. If you observe a Cepheid variable for a period of time, you can measure the length of its cycle. This allows you to estimate the actual brightness of the star. By comparing this brightness with how bright the star appears as seen from Earth, you can calculate how far away it is. Astronomers use a simple equation to do this. Once you know the distance to the Cepheid variable, you can also determine how far away neighboring stars are.

Figure 31: The Crab nebula

One of the first uses of the brightness method was to calculate the distance to the Crab nebula (see Figure 31). This nebula is one of the larger and more colorful clouds of dust and stars in the sky. It contains an aging Cepheid star that became a supernova. (The Chinese observed the supernova explosion in 1054, but the star had exploded 5,000 years earlier. The Crab nebula is 5,000 light-years from Earth, and so it took 5,000 years for light from the explosion to reach Earth.) The nebula's distance can also be used to estimate how far the debris from a supernova travels through space.

On Your Own

Answer the following questions based on "How Far Is That Star?"

1 Suppose you measured the distance to a star and found that it was much farther away than previously thought. How would this affect its position on an HR diagram? What else would this new data tell you about the star? Explain.

2 What reasons are there to trust estimates of the distances to stars based on triangulation or brightness?

3 How can you use a Cepheid variable to learn about other stars that are near it?

Do you ever think about "big questions" like these: When did the universe begin? Is the universe still changing? Will it all come to an end? As you take part in the next demonstration, think about the types of observations you could make to determine how the universe is changing. Then discuss your ideas with the rest of the class. After your discussion, read "The Red Shift."

Read All about It!

The Red Shift

As you listened to the ringing alarm clock in the last demonstration, you could tell from the pitch whether the clock was getting closer or moving away. The pitch rose as the clock approached you, and it fell as the clock moved away. Without seeing the clock, you could tell whether it was coming or going simply by listening to the sound.

Stars are also in motion. The light they emit behaves like the sound that the alarm clock emitted. Both light and sound are forms of wave energy, like ripples caused by a stone tossed into a pond. You can tell whether a star is approaching you or moving away from you by the way its motion affects its light.

When a source of sound or light moves, the sound or light waves that it produces squeeze together in front of the moving source, and they spread out behind it (see Figure 32). For example, if an ambulance approaches with its siren wailing, you hear the bunching up of sound waves as a higher pitch. But as the ambulance moves away, the sound waves spread out and you hear these longer waves behind it as a lower pitch. This effect of motion on waves is called the **Doppler effect**.

The Doppler effect causes a slight change in the color of starlight. The color of light depends on its **wavelength**—how far apart the peaks of the light waves are. Short, closely spaced waves appear as blue or purple light. Long light waves appear red. If a star is approaching Earth, its light waves will squeeze together and appear bluer. If a star is moving away from Earth, its light waves will spread out and appear redder.

Figure 32: The Doppler effect
Note: Sound waves (top) and light waves (bottom) are squeezed together in front of a moving source, producing higher-pitched sounds and bluer light. They spread out behind the source, reducing pitch and reddening light.

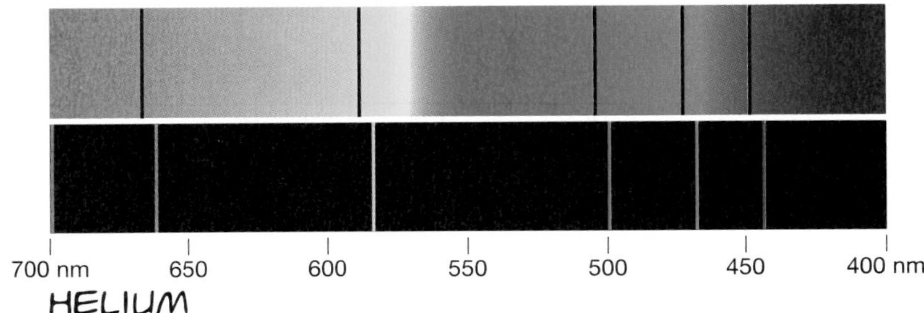

Figure 33: Helium absorption in a star's red-shifted spectrum
Note: The absorption lines in this star's spectrum (top) have been shifted toward the red end, indicating that the star is moving away from the observer.

Working the Light Shift

You may be wondering how anyone could know that a star's light is being distorted by its movement. After all, you cannot stop the star to see how it looks when it is not moving. To detect the change in wavelength, you must examine the star's spectrum. For example, if you compare a star's spectrum with the spectrum of a sample of hydrogen gas, you will find many of the same lines in both. This indicates that the star contains hydrogen. But in the spectrums of many stars, the lines that reveal the presence of hydrogen and other elements are all shifted toward the red end of the spectrum. Such a spectrum is said to have a **red shift** (see Figure 33).

The faster a star is moving away from Earth, the more red shift its spectrum will show. Most stars in the universe are moving away from the Milky Way galaxy, which contains Earth. In addition, the more distant a star is, the faster it is moving away from Earth. What could be the reason that most of the universe is moving rapidly outward? You will discover the answer to this question in the next demonstration.

On Your Own

Answer the following questions based on "The Red Shift."

1 If you measured the red shift of several stars in another galaxy and obtained similar data for all of them, what could this tell you about that galaxy?

2 Imagine that you observe a comet made mostly of methane ice. The spectrum lines of the methane are shifted to the blue. What would you conclude about the motion of the comet?

3 Suppose you observe two stars that are very close together. Their positions seem to move back and forth in a regular pattern. At the same time, their spectrums change back and forth from red-shifted to blue-shifted. How could you explain these observations?

The Search for Extraterrestrial Intelligence

Television programs and movies give you the idea that the universe is crawling with intelligent beings. In reality, no life has yet been discovered outside Earth. How many intelligent species—ones with the ability to make themselves known across space—*might* be out there?

Dr. Frank Drake made the first radio-telescope search for extraterrestrial technology in 1960. He came up with a formula to estimate the number of civilizations in the Milky Way that could transmit signals into space. Drake and Dr. Carl Sagan concluded that the Milky Way is likely to have one such civilization for every 100,000 to one million stars. (The Drake Equation is shown at right.)

Researchers who specialize in SETI—the search for extraterrestrial intelligence—use radio telescopes. They hope to find radio signals that differ from those produced by stars and other natural objects and by transmitters on Earth. Such a difference might mean that the signals are coming from intelligent life on other planets. Some SETI researchers focus on regions that seem most likely to support life. Others use what is called an all-sky survey. Their goal is to coordinate 5,000 radio telescopes around the world to search all areas of the sky.

The Drake Equation

$$N = R_* \cdot f_p \cdot n_e \cdot f_l \cdot f_i \cdot f_c \cdot L$$

N — The number of communicative civilizations (civilizations in the Milky Way galaxy whose radio emmisions are detectable)

R_* — The rate of formation of *suitable* stars (stars with a large enough "habitable zone" and a long enough lifetime to be suitable for the development of intelligent life)

f_p — The fraction of those stars with planets

n_e — The number of "earths" (planets in a star's habitable zone) per planetary system

f_l — The fraction of those planets where life develops

f_i — The fraction of life sites where intelligence develops

f_c — The fraction of those planets with intelligent life where technology develops

L — The "lifetime" of communicating civilizations (the length of time such civilizations release detectable signals into space)

Have you ever heard someone say the whole universe is expanding? Is this true? If the universe is getting larger, what lies beyond the universe? In other words, what is the universe expanding into? When did the universe begin, and how did it look before it began to expand? Will it keep expanding forever? As your teacher presents the next demonstration, consider how it can help you understand the idea of a universe that is growing larger and larger. Discuss your ideas with the rest of your class, and then read "Expanding Forever?"

Read All about It!

Expanding Forever?

How could nearly all the stars in the universe be moving away from the Milky Way galaxy, where Earth is? Does that mean we are at the center of the universe? If a star moves away from one neighbor, wouldn't it come closer to another one? The balloon in the demonstration can help you answer these questions. If an ant were standing on the balloon as it was being inflated, what would it see? It would see all the other dots moving away, with the farthest dots moving the fastest. If the ant were able to think the way a person thinks, it might decide that it was at the center of the balloon's surface and all the dots were moving out from this center. Another ant on a different dot might reach the same conclusion.

From your point of view—beyond the balloon—it seems obvious that each part of the balloon moved away from every other part. Like the dots on the balloon, the stars beyond Earth's galaxy are moving away from it. Every part of the universe seems to be moving away from every other part, just like an expanding balloon. No matter where you would be in the universe, almost all the stars would be moving away from you.

In the Beginning

If the universe is expanding, it must once have been much smaller and denser. Using estimates of how fast stars are moving (as based on red-shift observations), scientists developed the **big bang theory** that the whole universe exploded from a single, intense concentration of energy about 15 billion years ago. Before the big bang, even the dust and gases that would later form stars did not exist. The universe contained no matter of any kind. There was only pure energy. When the big bang occurred, this energy exploded and formed the first particles of matter, which became the dust, gases, stars, and galaxies that make up today's universe.

Most scientists accept the big bang theory for three reasons. First, it explains the fact that the stars seem to be moving away from one another. Second, in every direction of space you can detect **background radiation**—energy that may be the remains of a giant explosion that occurred long ago. Third, it accounts for the way elements are distributed in the universe. Remember that the heavier elements are formed by the intense heat and pressure of supernovas. Based on the rate that supernovas seem to occur, it would take about 15 billion years for the universe to build up its present supply of heavy elements.

Big Crunch?

If the big bang theory is correct, then what will happen in the future? That depends on how much matter is in the universe. If enough mass exists in the universe, the gravitational force of this mass will eventually stop the expansion and cause the universe to collapse in a "big crunch." Present knowledge indicates that the universe does not contain enough mass to make this happen. Unless a great deal of undiscovered matter exists, the universe will keep expanding forever.

Not all scientists accept the big bang theory. Some argue that the idea of a universe where nothing but pure energy existed makes no sense. Space, time, and the laws of nature would not exist in such a universe. And what would have made that energy explode? A more concrete problem has to do with the amount of matter in the universe. If the big bang theory is correct, the universe should contain more matter than it now appears to have. This conclusion is based on the fact that the amount of known matter in the universe is not great enough for the expansion to have slowed as much as it has.

The **steady state theory** is an alternative to the big bang. It suggests that the universe is always expanding or contracting somewhat, but overall it remains the same. Stars and planets form and eventually break down. After star explosions, dust and gases drift off to meet other matter and form new objects.

The steady state theory offers its own explanations of the background radiation and the distribution of elements in the universe. However, this theory has some problems. If the universe is in a steady state, stars of various ages should be evenly distributed throughout all regions of space. But there seems to be a limit on the age of stars, and all the oldest objects seem to be farthest away—at the outer edges of the universe.

A Window on the Past

Other theories have been proposed more recently. All contain some part that either cannot be tested or does not make sense. As astronomers learn more about the distant universe, they will develop better and more complete theories. Light from distant stars not only provides a window on the past—it also opens a door to the future.

THE DARK SIDE

With modern telescopes you can see an amazing number of stars. But even the best telescopes show only a tiny portion of the matter in the universe. The "missing" matter is called dark matter.

Dark matter does not emit enough radiation for current technology to detect it, but other evidence suggests its existence. By observing the speed and motion of galaxies, scientists have determined that the universe must contain far more matter than they have found.

To produce enough gravity to keep the galaxies from flying apart, the universe must contain at least twice the matter that has been observed. The exact amount that exists will probably determine whether the universe continues to expand or eventually collapses on itself in a "big crunch."

One popular theory is that much dark matter consists of red dwarf stars. But it is now known that there are far too few of them to account for the majority of dark matter. Another theory is that very dense objects, such as black holes and white dwarf, brown dwarf, and neutron stars, may contain much of the dark matter. Astronomers also look for dark matter in galactic halos—the light around the edges of galaxies.

Some scientists think most dark matter may be composed of subatomic "exotic" particles, which have such high energy that they can pass through ordinary matter.

ON YOUR OWN

Respond to the following items based on "Expanding Forever?"

1 Suppose you discovered a star that was 20 billion years old. The star would be older than the universe, according to the big bang theory. Would this mean the big bang theory is wrong? Explain your thinking.

2 What kinds of observations or data would show that the universe is collapsing?

3 Describe at least two ways in which the expansion of the universe is not exactly like baking raisin bread.

SECTION WRAP-UP

Light from the Past

How did the universe begin? If you traveled back through time to observe the beginning of the universe 15 billion years ago, what would you see? You would see nothing.

If the big bang theory is correct, the universe began as a small, dense concentration of energy. You would not be able to observe that energy because to do so you would have to be outside your own universe. (That could be even more difficult than traveling back through time.) In addition, if you went back to the very beginning of the universe, your body would not even exist—except as energy. And then—*kaboom!*— you're in the big bang.

It is hard to imagine that space and time—and all the stars and other objects that exist in space and time—were once compressed into a dense "bundle" of energy. It is also hard to imagine how that concentration of energy suddenly exploded, blasting outward in all directions. But though you can't travel back in time to observe how the universe formed, you can get some idea of how it looked billions of years ago by studying the light of very old stars.

It Takes Time

The light of the farthest stars travels for billions of years before it gets to Earth. When that ancient light reaches your eyes, you see a star as it was at the time it emitted the light. Starlight is like a page in the history of the universe. Every star's light can show you a different period of time.

Valuable data about stars come from their colors and spectrums. The red Eagle nebula, the yellow Andromeda galaxy, and the blue spiral arms of the Milky Way provide clues to the temperature and age of these objects.

Like anything else that radiates heat, a star emits light whose color indicates its temperature. If you heat a metal rod, its glow passes through several colors of the spectrum, first red, then yellow, and finally blue-white at its hottest. You can tell by the brilliant white of the star Vega that its surface temperature must be tens of thousands of degrees.

The colors in a star's light also provide clues to its composition and source of energy. For example, if you examine the Sun's light with a spectroscope, you can see lines indicating the presence of hydrogen and helium. The fusion of hydrogen into helium fuels the Sun's production of light. Shifts in the positions of these spectral lines indicate that most stars are moving away from Earth. Their light waves spread out behind them, shifting their colors toward the red end of the spectrum.

Not only a star's spectrum but also its brightness and position reveal important information. A star's true brightness—how much light it produces—and its distance from Earth determine how bright it appears. Some stars seem bright because they are close, while others appear bright because they are large. If you can measure two of these features (true brightness, apparent brightness, and distance), you can calculate the third. One way to figure the distance to a star is to use the diameter of Earth's orbit as the base of a triangle for parallax measurements. The large base of this triangle allows you to use parallax to estimate the distances to about 1,000 stars.

Bright Idea

If a star is too far away for the parallax method to work, you can estimate its distance if a nearby star is a Cepheid variable. The length of the Cepheid star's cycle tells you how bright the Cepheid actually is. By comparing the Cepheid's true brightness with its apparent brightness (how it looks from Earth), you can estimate its distance.

You can summarize this information about the brightness, color, and temperature of stars on an HR diagram. If you extended the lower right-hand quarter of an HR diagram, you could plot the positions of clouds of dust and gas that are collapsing to form a new star. As these dense clouds heat up and begin to glow a dull red, they move upward and to the left on the diagram, approaching the main sequence. New stars are often small, hot, and bright blue or white when they join the upper left end of the main sequence. You can see stars forming in the bright Orion nebula. This bright cloud swirls and contracts, turning gravitational energy into heat and pressure.

For most of a star's life, it falls along the main sequence. The brightness of main-sequence stars increases with their temperature in the same way because they all produce energy the same way: They fuse hydrogen. Older, larger stars that have converted much of their fuel to heavier elements, such as iron, move off the main sequence. Such stars may explode as supernovas.

Superstars

Every few hundred years, people have seen a star explode in a blazing supernova. Material produced in the heat of dying stars may be recycled in new stars. Spectral lines of iron, magnesium, and aluminum in light from the Orion nebula indicate that such recycling is occurring there.

With the information you collect from starlight, you can get a good idea of how the universe has changed over time. The fact that most stars appear to be moving away from the Milky Way suggests that the universe is expanding in all directions. This means that the universe was once much smaller, perhaps an extremely dense concentration of energy that exploded with a big bang. The universe may continue to expand forever. Or there may be enough matter in the universe to exert enough gravitational force to stop the expansion and pull everything together in a big crunch.

Starlight is like a page in the history of the universe. Every star's light can show you a different period of time.

A Universe of Possibilities

On the other hand, perhaps there was no big bang. Perhaps the universe has always been about the same. Maybe the universe is much older than astronomers think it is. Or perhaps it formed in some other way. And maybe it is not the only universe. Who knows how many there might be?

That may sound more like science fiction than scientific fact, but when you are trying to answer questions about how the universe formed and where it might be going, it helps to use your imagination.

On Your Own

Answer the following questions based on "Light from the Past."

1. Could a star be moving rapidly yet not have a detectable red or blue shift? (Hint: Think about the directions in which things can move in the universe.)
2. How would the history of the universe outlined in this reading have to be changed in order to conform to the steady state theory?
3. Some galaxies discovered in the 1980s and 1990s are much dimmer than previously known galaxies. They are very blue, and they have much less hydrogen than brighter galaxies. Some of them are also very large in comparison with the known, brighter ones. Based on this information, how old would you say these galaxies might be, compared with others? Explain your answer.
4. Suppose you observe two stars, Star Close and Star Far. Star Close is nearer to you and has a strong red shift. Star Far is 50 light-years farther away and has a strong blue shift. If you could observe these same stars in a few hundred years, would they look different? Explain your answer.

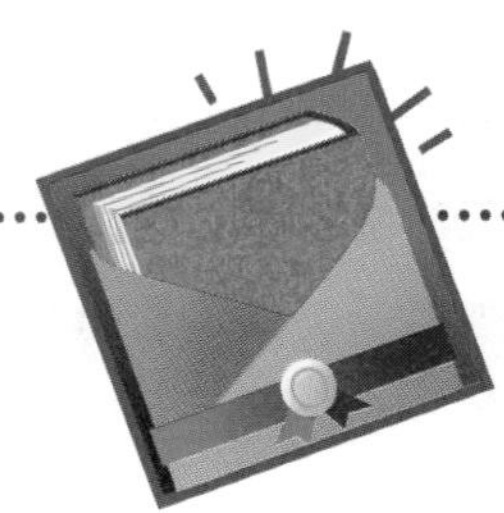

Module Wrap-up

Turn Left at Alpha Centauri—A Study of Space and the Universe

No planets, no stars, no galaxies, no space, no time—but enough energy to make a universe. Fifteen billion years ago the entire universe may have been packed into a tiny, dense concentration of energy. The forces of heat and pressure were so great that even the smallest particles of matter could not exist. This energy exploded in a big bang that began the expanding universe in which you live.

100,000,000,000 K

As soon as the explosion occurred, the universe began to cool, but it was still about 100 billion Kelvin after the first hundredth of a second. Three minutes later the universe had cooled to roughly one billion K. That was cool enough for small atoms, such as hydrogen, to form.

For the next few billion years, an increasing amount of matter formed as colliding particles drove the universe to expand. Red-shift measurements show that this expansion still continues. The denser concentrations of mass pulled in more material through gravitational attraction. Clouds of matter swirling around these massive centers became the first galaxies.

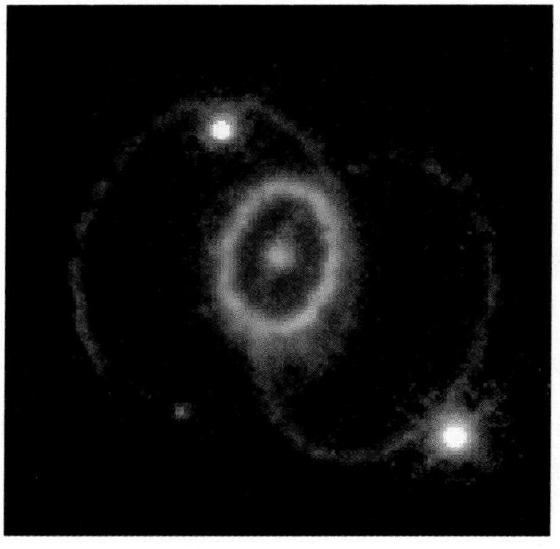

Those huge early galaxies produced enormous, bright, hydrogen-fusing stars. The first stars blazed for only a few million years before forming the first heavy elements, such as carbon, oxygen, and silicon, and exploding as supernovas. Debris from the explosions was recycled in new stars. Continual cycles of star birth and death sent new elements into space. Continued expansion spread out the star-forming material more thinly, producing smaller stars and galaxies. These stars consumed their fuel more slowly, and so they were dimmer and lasted longer. Light from some of these stars on the distant edges of the universe can still be observed today, billions of years later.

Hello, Sun

The Milky Way galaxy formed more than 10 billion years ago. Some of the central stars collapsed and became supernovas. Some of their remains drifted out toward the edge of the Milky Way, where new stars were forming. One of these new stars was the Sun.

Most of the cloud that formed this new star became the Sun itself, but some material remained. This material became the planets and moons of the solar system. Those pieces with the right combination of speed and inertia went into stable orbits around the Sun. Others may have broken up, forming the asteroids. Some of the smaller bodies were captured by the gravity of the new planets and became moons.

As it does in stars, gravitational compression heated the cores of the planets, though not enough to produce fusion. Over time, the planets have cooled slowly and become solid. The core of Jupiter, the largest planet, is still hot enough to produce bursts of radio waves, but Jupiter does not have enough mass to begin fusion and become a star. Like steam that rises from a hot pie, gases inside the planets escaped as they cooled. Gravity is strong enough on the largest and densest planets to keep these gases from drifting off into space. These planets have atmospheres.

Meteors constantly bombarded the planets during the first few billion years of their existence.

A planet with an atmosphere has some protection against the large number of meteoroids that wander around the solar system. Meteoroids pulled in by gravity streak through the sky as meteors. The friction of air resistance causes most meteors to burn up in the atmosphere as they fall. Larger meteors, as well as those that fall on planets or moons without an atmosphere, may remain intact until they hit the surface. These impacts can produce huge craters. On small bodies they can scatter debris great distances and form rays, such as those around some of the craters on the Moon.

Meteors constantly bombarded the planets during the first few billion years of their existence. Such impacts on Saturn may have helped to create that planet's spectacular rings of tiny ice and dust particles.

Bad Day for Dinosaurs

A meteor impact probably contributed to the extinction of the dinosaurs and other species. The collision of a large meteor with Earth would have sent huge amounts of dust into the atmosphere, blocking out sunlight for many months. The size of the crater it formed and the distance to which it scattered debris provide evidence of its size and speed. The composition of a meteor can be determined by analyzing the spectrum of its fragments. Every element that it contains displays unique spectral lines when heated.

Secrets of the Spectrum

Elements that appear in a star's spectrum reveal its age and its source of fusion power. By combining this information with a measurement of a star's brightness, you can learn quite a bit about the star. You can then use Cepheid variables or parallax measurements to obtain data about the star's neighbors. At that point, you are well on your way to understanding how the universe developed in that region of space.

Starlight is like a window to the past. By analyzing starlight emitted in the distant past, you can learn about earlier conditions in the universe and how the universe is changing today. Will the universe go on expanding forever? No one can say for sure, but as more information becomes available, it may someday be possible to answer that question.

On Your Own

Respond to the following items based on the Module Wrap-up.

1 Estimates of the age of the universe are based on data from the oldest stars. Looking at the light from these stars is like looking into the past. Could you "see" all the way back to the very beginning of the universe in this way? Explain.

2 Describe how the spectrum of a galaxy would look different from the spectrum of a star. Explain your answer.

3 Suppose you discovered a large number of galaxies that showed a blue shift. How might this alter current ideas about how the universe developed?

4 Two factors that helped life develop on Earth are its temperature and its composition. If a deep-space probe with powerful telescopes observed a planet in another solar system, what kind of evidence could the probe collect to help you decide if that planet were likely to have life on it?

How to Use Your Logbook

All through ***Science Links*** you will use a logbook to keep records of your work. A logbook is an important tool in scientific investigation. It provides a place to take notes, collect data, enter observations and conclusions, and jot down questions and ideas. Most scientists keep a log like this one.

In science it is essential to keep accurate records. The information that you collect is valuable—you must work to get it! So write down your ideas before you forget them.

Your logbook will also help you share your ideas with other students. In most of your investigations, you will work as a member of a group. In any situation where people must work together, whether it's flying a jetliner or leading cheers at a basketball game, teamwork is critical. One of the most important aspects of teamwork is communication. No team can succeed unless its members communicate effectively with one another.

Good Writing Is Clear and Simple

Effective communication means writing and speaking in ways that other people will understand. Your logbook can help you develop a good writing style. Whenever you make an entry, try to express your thoughts as clearly and simply as possible. When you finish writing, step back and look at the words as though you are reading them for the first time. If someone else had made this entry, would you be able to understand it? Is the writing clear? Does it cover all the points it was supposed to? You know what you meant to say, but did you succeed in saying it? If you have any doubts, go back to work on the entry.

Writing makes you more aware of your thinking process. This is useful in science because sometimes you don't even realize that you do not understand a concept until you try to express it. Communicating scientific ideas through writing and discussion helps you understand what you are doing. And in ***Science Links*** the emphasis is on doing science.

Your logbook gives you an opportunity to show your teacher what you have learned. It will reveal how you and the other members of your group are collaborating. The notes you take during presentations by other groups will show if you are receiving useful information from them.

Organizing Your Logbook

Your logbook should be organized chronologically. Every time you make a new entry, put the date in the upper left-hand corner of the page. Next, in the upper right-hand corner, write a few words that tell what the entry is about. Then write the entry itself. (A sample entry appears on the next page.)

Various types of entries are possible. Here are some of them:

- notes based on what occurs during procedures (**Step-by-Step**)
- summaries of group or class discussions (**Talk It Over**)
- outlines for presentations by your group (**Spread the Word**)
- notes and questions about presentations by other groups
- data collected through research
- ideas for projects or reports
- personal views concerning ***Science Links*** activities

Use your logbook regularly. It will help you keep track of and understand the science you are doing in ***Science Links***.

September 30, 1998

Module 2, Investigation 4
Calculations and Observations

Step-by-Step

Step 4	baking soda & paper	5.46 g
	paper	–3.46
	baking soda	2.00 g
Step 9	beaker & contents	123.76 g
Step 12	beaker & contents after reaction	–122.31
	weight lost	1.45 g

After Kim poured the vinegar in the beaker, it foamed up. Giselle said it smelled sour.

Step 14	baking soda & paper	4.83 g
	paper	–2.83
	baking soda	2.00 g
Step 21	bottle & contents	90.50 g
Step 23	beaker & contents after reaction	–90.30
	weight lost	0.20 g

After I poured the vinegar out, it foamed up.

Talk It Over

#1–4. Everybody agreed that the beaker lost more weight than the bottle. Kim said this was because something turned into a gas and it went out of the beaker but couldn't get out of the bottle.

Module Glossary

absorption lines—dark lines in a star's spectrum that indicate that specific substances are absorbing particular wavelengths of light (60)

acceleration—any change in speed or direction of movement (30)

artificial gravity—a force, such as centripetal force, that is applied to a spacecraft to replace gravity (17)

asteroid—an orbiting rocky object that is smaller than a planet or moon and larger than a meteoroid; many asteroids orbit the Sun between Mars and Jupiter (37)

background radiation—radiation that travels through the universe in all directions; many scientists believe that background radiation is left over from the big bang (76)

big bang theory—the idea that the universe began as an explosion of a tiny center of compressed energy and has been expanding ever since (75)

biosphere—the system composed of all living things and their environment (5)

centripetal—toward the center; all circular motion, including the orbits of planets and moons, depends on centripetal force (28)

Cepheid variable—a star that varies in brightness in a regular cycle (65)

comet—an object that is made mostly of ice and that produces a long, glowing tail as it orbits the Sun on an elliptical path (36)

Doppler effect—a change in the length of waves produced by a moving object; the wavelength shortens in front of the moving source and lengthens behind it (73)

escape speed—the minimum speed needed to escape from a planet's gravity (16)

fusion—the merging of atoms to produce larger atoms; fusion releases tremendous quantities of energy (56)

galaxy—a large group of stars held together by gravity (28)

gravity—the force that attracts all matter together; the amount of force depends on the masses of the objects involved and on their proximity to one another (14)

HR diagram—a graph that shows stars according to temperature and brightness (63)

inertia—the tendency of an object either to remain at rest or to continue moving in a straight line at the same speed until a force acts on it (16)

inertial balance—a device used to measure mass without depending on gravity (16)

infrared—a type of invisible radiation that carries less energy and has a longer wavelength than visible light; infrared radiation carries heat energy (59)

ion—an atom or molecule that has become electrically charged by gaining or losing one or more electrons (8)

legume—a group of plants that includes peas, beans, peanuts, clovers, and locust and acacia trees; their roots often contain bacteria that convert atmospheric nitrogen to forms that plants can use (8)

light-year—the distance that light travels in one year, 9.461 trillion kilometers (58)

main sequence—the part of the HR diagram that contains most stars; within the main sequence, brightness depends on temperature (64)

mass—quantity of matter; an object's mass does not depend on gravity (15)

meteor—a small space rock glowing brightly as it falls through the atmosphere of a planet or moon (37)

meteorite—a piece of space rock that has hit the surface of a planet or moon (37)

meteoroid—a rock that is smaller than an asteroid and is moving through space (36)

nebula—a cloud of dust and gas in space (57)

neutron star—an extremely dense star whose atoms have collapsed to form neutrons; neutron stars form as the debris from a supernova collapses (58)

Newton's First Law of Motion—the principle that moving objects tend to continue moving in a straight line at the same speed and that objects at rest tend to remain at rest, until a force acts on them (16)

Newton's Second Law of Motion—the principle that a force causes an object to accelerate at a rate directly proportional to the size of the force and inversely proportional to the object's mass: $A = F/M$ (30)

parallax angle—the angle by which an object's apparent position changes when it is viewed from two different points (71)

rays—lines of rock or other debris surrounding a crater (37)

red giant—a large red star that is brighter than main-sequence stars of the same temperature and color (58)

red shift—the movement of absorption lines in a star's spectrum toward the red end; the shift is caused by the movement of the star away from the observer (73)

spectroscope—a device for observing spectrums (45)

spectrum—a rainbowlike band of light created when a prism or diffraction grating spreads out light according to wavelength (43)

steady state theory—the idea that the universe has always been approximately its present size (76)

supernova—the explosion of a very large star (57)

triangulation—a way of estimating how far away an object is by viewing it from two points that are a known distance apart (70)

wavelength—the distance from one wave peak to the next (73)

weight—the force of gravity on an object (14)

white dwarf—a small, hot white star that is less bright than main-sequence stars of the same color and temperature (58)

For Further Study . . .

Books and Articles

Couper, H., and N. Henbest. 1994. *How the Universe Works.* Pleasantville, NY: Reader's Digest.

Ferguson, K. 1996. *Prisons of Light—Black Holes.* New York: Cambridge University Press.

Henbest, N. 1991. *Universe: A Computer-Generated Voyage through Time and Space.* New York: Macmillan.

Martin, J. 1997. Interactive astronomy. *Science Teacher* 54 (March): 50–52.

McKay, D., and Smith, B. 1986. *Space Science Projects for Young Scientists.* New York: Franklin Watts.

Ronan, C. 1991. *The Natural History of the Universe.* New York: Macmillan.

Internet

Agency for Instructional Technology (AIT):

- World Wide Web—http://www.ait.net
- *Technos,* a journal for education and technology—technos@ait.net
- Sales and marketing—ait@ait.net

South-Western Science:

- World Wide Web—http://www.thomson.com
- Gopher—gopher://gopher.thomson.com
- FTP—itp.thomson.com (log in as Anonymous)
- Science Discussion List—To join, contact majordomo@list.thomson.com and in the body of the message include "south-western-science" followed by "[your first name]_[your last name]" (for example, "south-western science Jane_Smith").

Audio/Video

Cosmos. In this 13-hour series, Carl Sagan explores such topics as astronomy, the origins of life, the stars, black holes, and Einstein. Contact Wellspring Media, 65 Bleecker Street, 5th Floor, New York, NY 10012; e-mail, mail@wellmedia.com.

The following 15-minute videotapes are available from Agency for Instructional Technology, Box A, Bloomington, IN 47402.

Gravity. This program describes the function of gravity in mechanical operations and in its role of providing balance in the universe. From *Physics: What Matters, What Moves,* part of the Science Source series.

The Solar System. Exploring Earth's "local" environment, this video probes the solar system's planets, origins, and probable future. From *Earth, the Environment, and Beyond,* part of the Science Source series.

What Are Stars? This video describes the various types of stars, their origins and locations, and the basic characteristics of the Sun. From *Earth, the Environment, and Beyond,* part of the Science Source series.

Software

Astronomy Village: Investigating the Universe. This CD-ROM has 10 investigations. It includes an image browser, a program for accessing the World Wide Web, and simulation programs. It also provides digitized video clips, documents, and images from the Hubble Space Telescope. Compatible with Macintosh. Contact NASA Classroom of the Future, Wheeling Jesuit College, 316 Washington Ave., Wheeling, WV 26003; e-mail, astrov@cotf.edu.

A

B

C

D

E

F

G

H

I

J

L

M

Illustrations and Photos

Illustration Credits—Mike Cagle, 11, 16, 18, 26, 28, 29, 45, 56, 65, 69, 71, 73 (top); Brenda Grannan, icons; Jay Hagenow, 44, 46, 60, 67, 70, 73 (bottom); Vance Lawry, 9, 50

Photo Credits—Corel Corporation, 7, 30, 59, 76; Goddard Space Flight Center/The University of Iowa, 34; Meteor Crater, Northern Arizona, USA, 38 (bottom); C. Allan Morgan/Biosphere 2 Center, Inc., 6; NASA, viii–1, 10, 17, 19, 20, 21, 23, 35, 36, 39, 42, 47, 48, 49, 52, 53, 57, 58, 72, 75, 80; NASA/Corel Corporation, viii (inset), 3, 14, 16, 22, 24, 37, 38 (top), 78

module 10

Safety Symbols

TAKE appropriate precautions whenever these safety symbols appear at the beginning of the Step-by-Step instructions. All safety icons that apply to a particular investigation appear at the beginning of that investigation. In addition, a step number that is printed in red indicates the first time a certain kind of safety hazard exists in an investigation.

Disposal Hazard

- Dispose of this chemical only as directed.

Fire Hazard

- Tie back hair and loose clothing.
- Do not use a burner or flame near flammable materials.

Eye Hazard

- Always wear safety goggles.

Poison Hazard

- Do not chew gum, drink, or eat in the lab.
- Keep your hands and all chemicals away from your face.

Inhalation Hazard

- Avoid inhaling the substance.

Thermal-Burn Hazard

- Wear gloves and do not touch hot equipment.

Breakage Hazard

- Do not use chipped or cracked glassware.
- Do not heat the bottom of a test tube.

Corrosive-Substance Hazard

- Wear safety goggles and a lab apron.
- Do not touch any chemical.

IN CASE OF EMERGENCY . . .

Immediately report any accident, injury, or spill to your teacher. Know where to find the nearest fire blanket, fire extinguisher, eyewash, sink, and shower.

Here's what to do:

Fire—Turn off all gas outlets and unplug all appliances. Use a fire blanket or fire extinguisher to smother the flames. When using a fire blanket or extinguisher to smother flames, take care not to cut off or impede the victim's air supply.

Burn—Flush the affected part with cold water.

Poisoning—Take note of the substance involved and call the teacher immediately.

Eye Injury—Flush eyes with running water; remove contact lenses. Do not allow injured persons to rub their eyes if a foreign substance is present.

Fainting—Open a window or provide fresh air as best you can. Position the person so the head is lower than the rest of the body. If breathing stops, use artificial respiration.

Spill on Skin—Flush with water.

Minor Cut—Allow to bleed briefly and then wash with soap and water. If necessary, apply a bandage.

Remember to call your teacher right away in any emergency!

You will perform most of your investigations as a member of a small group. After your group completes its work, you and your teammates will have an opportunity to present your findings to the other students in your class. In the real world—the world of work—many jobs are based on teamwork, men and women working together to solve problems and share information.

In a few years you will be joining the adult workforce. ***Science Links*** can help prepare you for that important step in your life.

To give you a broad introduction to science, ***Science Links*** blends biology, chemistry, physics, and earth/space science into a single course. You will learn how various scientific concepts are used in the everyday world, both at home and in the workplace.

This book and the related video segments will also show you how science is used in dozens of careers, from food science to auto mechanics, from welding to respiratory therapy. Check out these careers. Maybe one of them is right for you.

When you picked up this book, you picked up a golden key. Use it now. Open the ***Science Links*** door, and step right in to the amazing world of science.

Log It!

As you perform the investigations in ***Science Links***, you will record various kinds of information in a logbook. Use your logbook to take notes, to collect data, and to enter your observations and conclusions about the experiments you perform. The logbook is also a great place to jot down any questions and ideas that occur to you, either inside or outside the classroom. Put them on paper before you forget them!

If you get in the habit of using your logbook, it will help you learn to express your thoughts simply and clearly—that's good writing. The logbook will also give you a permanent record of your work—that's good science.

For more suggestions on using your logbook, see Appendix A (pages 82–83). The appendix also contains a sample logbook page.

Science Links . . . Where You and Your Future Connect

YOU can't see them, but there are thousands of doorways in front of you . . . doors to your left, doors to your right . . . big doors, little doors, revolving doors, trapdoors...doors stretching into the distance as far as you can see. . . . Each of these doorways is a possibility, an opportunity for a successful and prosperous life. But most of the doors are locked. You need the right keys to open them. How many doors will you be able to open?

The more you learn in school, the more keys you will have . . . the more choices . . . the more control over your own life.

Science Links is one key to your future. In the world of tomorrow—the world of computers, robotics, the World Wide Web, gene therapy, space travel—your knowledge of science can help you keep up with the latest developments in technology. More important, it can help you find a good job and pursue a great career.

Many students consider science a difficult subject, but as you will see in this course, science can be fascinating. In *Science Links* you will learn science by doing many laboratory investigations. (Investigations that are too dangerous for the classroom will be demonstrated in video segments.) These experiments will help you understand scientific principles.

YOUR LINK TO SCIENCE

Science is an attempt to make logical sense out of the natural world. It generally involves observations, experiments, data collection, analyses, and logical conclusions. ***Science Links*** will let you experience science, and the experience will be informative, interesting, and fun. You will be doing many laboratory investigations that will demonstrate the importance of science in your life, both now and in your future career. Following one or more investigations, a brief reading will explain the scientific principles further.

This course gives you a great opportunity to learn about science, but the learning is up to you. Learning science can be challenging, but if you work at it, you can master the contents and processes of this fascinating field. Put your full effort into this course and you will gain the satisfaction of learning many useful things about science. More important, you will advance to the next level of your education with greater confidence, a better self-image, and a strong motivation to learn even more.

So work hard, and enjoy your ***Science Links*** experiences.

—Professor Marvin Druger, Past President
National Science Teachers Association

Professor Druger teaches biology at Syracuse University, where he is also chairperson of the Department of Science Teaching.

CONTENTS

SCIENCE LINKS STAFF

PROJECT DESIGN

Chief Consultant
Marvin Druger, Ph.D.
Department of Science Teaching
and Department of Biology
Syracuse University

Instructional Designer
Diana W. Lee, Ph.D.
Agency for Instructional Technology

Project Developer
Jonathan Greenberg, Ph.D.
Agency for Instructional Technology

PROJECT MANAGEMENT

AGENCY FOR INSTRUCTIONAL TECHNOLOGY

Director of Projects and New Products
Frank J. Batavick

Project Management Specialist
Sharon K. Masters

Formative Evaluation
Rockman et al.

Administrative Assistant
Connie Williamson

SOUTH-WESTERN

Publisher
Thomas A. Emrick, Ph.D.

Project Manager
Karen Roberts

Editor
Marianne Miller

Marketing Manager
Susan Denney

Marketing Assistant
Kris M. White

SCIENCE LINKS REVIEWERS

Gary Abbas, West High School, Davenport, Iowa; **Robert Allen**, Victor Valley Community College, Victorville, California; **Millicent Anderson**, Los Angeles, California; **Carol Bedford**, Smart Intermediate School, Davenport, Iowa; **Jennifer Braught**, Shakamak High School, Jasonville, Indiana; **Matt Braught**, Linton-Stockton High School, Linton, Indiana; **Glenda Burrus**, Pinetown High School, Pinetown, North Carolina; **Sergio Cartas**, Miami Coral Park Senior High School, Miami, Florida; **Michael A. D'Agostino**, Kings High School, Kings Mills, Ohio; **Ron Endris**, Floyd Central High School, Floyds Knobs, Indiana; **Sheila Engel**, Smart Intermediate School, Davenport, Iowa; **Tom Ervin**, North High School, Davenport, Iowa; **Marcy Gaston**, Pike High School, Indianapolis, Indiana; **Laine Gurley-Dilger**, Rolling Meadows High School, Rolling Meadows, Illinois; **George Hague**, St. Mark's School of Texas, Dallas, Texas; **Mary Halsall**, Hughes Center, Cincinnati, Ohio; **David Kukla**, North Hollywood High School, Los Angeles, California; **Priscilla Lee**, Los Angeles, California; **Craig Leonard**, Abraham Lincoln High School, San Francisco, California; **Ann Lumsden**, Florida State University, Tallahassee, Florida; **Jim Oberdorf**, Lincoln High School, San Francisco, California; **Jan Pierson**, Bloomington North High School, Bloomington, Indiana; **Eva M. Rambo**, Bloomington South High School, Bloomington, Indiana; **Willa Ramsay**, Madison High School, San Diego, California; **Kathleen Schuehler**, Liverpool High School, Liverpool, New York; **Len Sharp**, Liverpool High School, Liverpool, New York; **Dwight Sieggreen**, Cooke Middle School, Northville, Michigan; **Gerald Skoog**, Texas Tech University, Lubbock, Texas; **Ernestine B. Smith**, Tarboro High School, Tarboro, North Carolina; **Charlotte St. Romain**, Carenco High School, Lafayette, Louisiana; **Denise Tompkins**, Southwest Edgecomb High School, Pine Tops, North Carolina; **Kevin Tsui**, Woodside High School, Woodside, California; **Rick Wells**, Central High School, Davenport, Iowa; **Eric Worch**, Indiana University, Bloomington, Indiana

VIDEO AND PRINT DEVELOPMENT

VIDEO

Executive Producer
David Gudaitis, Ph.D.

Associate Producer
Brad Bloom

Video Editors
Amy Crowell
John MacGibbon

PRINT

Senior Editor
John Pesta

Features Writer/Editor
Lisa Williams

Safety Editor
Doug Mandt

Science Writers
Sara S. Brudnoy, Ph.D.
Jonathan Greenberg, Ph.D.
Judy E. Hammett
Nancy V. Ridenour
Michael Svec, Ph.D.
Polly Carter Weissman

Assessment Writers
Jennifer L. Chidsey
Laura Henriques
Margaret A. Jorgensen, Ph.D.
James A. Shymansky, Ph.D.

Layout Designer/Compositor
David Strange

Cover and Page Designer
Brenda Grannan

Print and Art Coordinator
Jay Hagenow

ISBN: 0-538-66887-3

1 2 3 4 5 6 7 8 PR 02 01 00 99 98 97

Printed in the United States of America

International Thomson Publishing

South-Western Educational Publishing is a division of International Thomson Publishing, Inc.

This book is printed on recycled, acid-free paper that meets Environmental Protection Agency standards.

TURN LEFT AT ALPHA CENTAURI

A Study of Space and the Universe

Developed by
The Agency for Instructional Technology

JOIN US ON THE INTERNET
WWW: http://www.thomson.com
EMAIL: findit@kiosk.thomson.com
A service of I(T)P®

South-Western Educational Publishing
an International Thomson Publishing company I(T)P®

Cincinnati • Albany, NY • Belmont, CA • Bonn • Boston • Detroit • Johannesburg • London • Madrid
Melbourne • Mexico City • New York • Paris • Singapore • Tokyo • Toronto • Washington